Bertrand Russell

Fortune's Hostages
Sidney Bernstein: A biography
Freya Stark: A biography
Beyond the Rim of the World: the Letters of Freya Stark (Ed.)
Troublesome People
Betrayed: Children in Today's World (Ed.)

BERTRAND RUSSELL

A Life

CAROLINE MOOREHEAD

VIKING

VIKING
Published by the Penguin Group
Penguin Books USA Inc., 375 Hudson Street,
New York, New York 10014, U.S.A.
Penguin Books Ltd, 27 Wrights Lane,
London W8 5TZ, England
Penguin Books Australia Ltd, Ringwood,
Victoria, Australia
Penguin Books Canada Ltd, 10 Alcorn Avenue,
Toronto, Ontario, Canada M4V 3B2
Penguin Books (N.Z.) Ltd, 182–190 Wairau Road,
Auckland 10, New Zealand

Penguin Books Ltd, Registered Offices:
Harmondsworth, Middlesex, England

First American edition
Published in 1993 by Viking Penguin,
a division of Penguin Books USA Inc.

1   3   5   7   9   10   8   6   4   2

Acknowledgments for permission to use copyrighted material appear on
pages 4 and 5.

LIBRARY OF CONGRESS CATALOGING-IN-PUBLICATION DATA
Moorehead, Caroline.
Bertrand Russell: a life / Caroline Moorehead.
p.   cm.
Includes bibliographical references and index.
ISBN 0-670-85008-X
1. Russell, Bertrand, 1872–1970.   2. Philosophers—England—
Biography.   I. Title.
B1649.R94M66   1993
192—dc20   93-4207
[B]

Printed in the United States of America

For Jeremy

Contents

When will people learn the robustness of truth? I do not know who my biographer may be, but I should like him to report 'with what flourish his nature will' something like this: 'I was not a solemn stained glass saint, existing only for the purpose of edification; I existed from my own centre, many things that I did were regrettable, I did not respect respectable people, and when I pretended to do so it was humbug. I lied and practised hypocrisy, because if I had not I should not have been allowed to do my work; but there is no need to continue the hypocrisy after my death. I hated hypocrisy and lies: I loved life and real people, and wished to get rid of the shams that prevent us from loving real people as they really are. I believed in laughter and spontaneity, and trusted to nature to bring out the genuine good in people, if once genuineness could come to be tolerated'.

Bertrand Russell to Lady Ottoline Morrell,
27 August 1918

Preface

'I wanted certainty,' wrote Bertrand Russell on his eightieth birthday, 'in the kind of way in which people want religious faith.' He found neither certainty nor faith, but if his long life was characterised by any one virtue, it was curiosity. He never stopped asking questions: about mathematics and philosophy, about politics, words, sex, religion, war, education, fear. What was singularly attractive was that he asked – and answered them – in a way that ordinary men and women felt they could understand. It was exciting and it made people feel clever.

For the first half of the twentieth century Russell was seen as one of the three philosophers, with G. E. Moore and Ludwig Wittgenstein, who dominated British philosophy. In the 1940s and 1950s he lost some of his standing, paradoxically because the clarity of his style obscured rather than illuminated the complicated issues of his mathematics, philosophy and logic. He also changed his mind constantly, and moved at speed from one topic to another, making him one of the most challenging philosophers of our times.

This book is about Russell's character and ideas, about his friends and the women he loved, about the causes he fought for and the sense of wonder and eloquence he brought to everything he touched. His friend and collaborator, Alfred Whitehead, said Russell was a Platonic dialogue in himself.

Russell, the godson of John Stuart Mill, was born halfway through the reign of Queen Victoria. He died almost a century later, at the age of ninety-seven, leading demonstrations against nuclear weapons which he saw as the final threat to civilisation, and chiding the world for its apathy and shortsightedness. He was profoundly of the twentieth century in his political and social concerns while remaining the last of the great eighteenth- and nineteenth-century philosophers, both for the range of his interests and his desire to be understood. At a time when people sought reassurance, Russell preached a stark message that, in the end, nothing is absolutely certain. But he also showed that the unbeliever and the sceptic can live without fear. He was perhaps the last public sage.

The search for knowledge, unbearable pity for suffering, and a longing for love were, he wrote, the three passions that had governed his life: 'I have found it worth living,' was his conclusion, 'and would gladly live it again if the chance were offered me.'

Towards the end of his life Russell sold his archives to McMaster University in Canada. The library has continued to acquire and buy ever since, making it one of the most remarkable collections of papers, books, letters and manuscripts ever assembled around a single person. In the past ten years, through the deaths of Russell's friends and colleagues, more material has come to light. Dora, Russell's second wife, died in 1987; her papers have gone to the International Institute for Social History in Amsterdam and to the Bertrand Russell Archives at McMaster; they became available for consultation in 1991. The letters of Colette O'Niel, Russell's lifelong friend, are now also available at McMaster, and there are new letters and diaries in the Goodman collection which were the property of Lady Ottoline Morrell. The correspondence between Alys, his first wife, and Russell, and a number of her private diaries have been purchased by Camellia Investments in London – though some of the originals are at McMaster – as have the papers concerning Russell's fifty-year relationship with his publisher, Sir Stanley Unwin. Very little of this has been published. The descendants of several of Russell's friends and colleagues have provided me with further unpublished material, and many of those who knew him, particularly in the last twenty years of his life, have kindly talked to me.

The copyright in most of the letters and documents quoted is owned by McMaster University. Whether in the original or as photocopies, they are mostly to be found in the Russell Archives. Those not remaining in private hands can be seen in the following places: G. E. Moore, Margaret Llewelyn Davies and Gilbert Murray in the Bodleian Library, Oxford; Margaret Llewelyn Davies, University of Hull; Lady Ottoline Morrell in the Harry Ransom Humanities Research Center, University of Texas, Austin; Helen Thomas/ Flexner in the Flexner papers of the American Philosophical Society; Beatrice Webb, at the London School of Economics; Ivy Pretious, in the private collection of her son Hallam Tennyson; papers relating to the pacifists of the First World War, in the Liddle Collection, Leeds; Catherine Marshall's papers, in the Cumbria Record Department; J. M. Keynes, in King's College Library, Cambridge; John Dewey, Southern Illinois University at Carbondale; Bernard Berenson and the Pearsall Smith family in Harvard University Center for Italian Renaissance Studies, Florence. Naomi Bentwich's papers are in her son's private collection; further material on the pacifists of the First World War is in Cumbria Record Department; the papers and letters of Isaac Deutscher and Emma Goodman are at the International Institute for Social History, Amsterdam, and correspondence relating to the schooling of the Russell children is in the Dartington School Archives. The papers of Ronald W. Clark are with the National Library of Scotland. I would like to thank the librarians, archivists and owners of the private collections for their assistance.

A number of people have given me a great deal of help in the preparation of this book, have read it and have offered corrections and suggestions. First of all, I want to thank the members and staff of the Bertrand Russell Archives and Editorial Project – in particular Kenneth Blackwell and Sheila Turcon, Richard Rempel and Louis Greenspan. It could not have been written without them. I would also like to thank Professor Bernard Williams; Professor Mark Sainsbury; Christopher Farley; Teddy Hodgkin;. my publisher and editor, Christopher Sinclair-Stevenson, who gave me the idea for the book; Kathy van Praag, who did the picture research; my agent, Anthony Sheil; Jeremy Bennett and Elizabeth Clark.

Bertrand Russell's surviving family – Katherine Tait, Sarah

Russell, the late John Russell, and Conrad Russell – were kind enough to talk to me and provided family memories.

I would like to thank others who were generous with their time and help: Polly Allen, Luke Alvarez, David Astor, David Bacon, Michael Barratt Brown, Sir Isaiah Berlin, Ben Birnberg, Theodore Birnberg, Robin Blackburn, Mrs Bride, Michael Burn, Hugh and Mirabel Cecil, Ken Coates, Diana Collins, Father Frederick Coplestone, Lawrence Daly, Tamara Deutscher, Michael Duane, Anton Felton, the late Lord Fenner Brockway, the Honourable Michael Foot, Henrietta Garnett, Richard Garnett, Adrian Goodman, Phillip Goodman, Harman Grisewood, Jon Halliday, David Harley, Kenneth Harris, Royden Harrison, Jacquetta Hawkes, Joy Hill, Michael Holroyd, Diana Hopkinson, Lady Juliette Huxley, Christopher Ironside, Dai and Sylvia Jones, Jonah Jones, Mervyn Jones, Dr Sheila Jones, Monsignor Bruce Kent, Doris Lessing, C. W. Kilmister, Peter Liddle, John Lloyd, Leo Matarasso, Olive Markham, Leonard Miall, Professor R. Milliband, James Murphy, Kate Newman, M. B. Nicholson, Sybil Oldfield, Frances Partridge, Lyndal Passerini Hopkinson, Professor David Pears, Pat Pottle, Dr J. C. Pritchard, Michael Randle, Jasia Reichardt, Adam Roberts, Ernest Rodker, Deborah Rogers, Frances Ronald, Professor Joseph Rotblat, Pierre Salinger, Professor Laurent Schwartz, Miranda Seymour, Professor John Slater, Dr Frederick Spotts, Barbara Strachey, Ann Synge, Hallam Tennyson, Jon Tinker, the late Julian Trevelyan, Mary Trevelyan, Rayner Unwin, Phyllis Urch, Daphne Uribe, J. O. Urmson, Henry Usborne, the late Julian Vinogradoff, Nick Walters, Harriet Ward, Sir Michael Osmond Williams, Pamela Wood.

I am grateful to the following for permission to use copyright material: The Bertrand Russell Archives Permissions Committee for Russell's letters and papers; Unwin Hyman for Russell's *Autobiography*, *Portraits from Memory* and *My Philosophical Development*; Barbara Strachey for *Remarkable Relations*; Laurence Pollinger Ltd and the Estate of Frieda Lawrence Ravagli for selections from the letters of D. H. Lawrence; The London School of Economics and Virago for extracts from Beatrice Webb's diaries; Constable for the poems of

Arthur Waley and extracts from *The Longest Journey*, by E. M. Forster; Michael Holroyd for extracts from *Lytton Strachey* and *Bernard Shaw*; Frances Partridge for extracts from *Julia*; Blackwell for the letters of Wittgenstein; Mrs Valerie Eliot for the letters of T. S. Eliot; Random Century Group for extracts from *Remembering my good friends* by Mary Agnes Hamilton, for extracts from the Diaries and Letters of Virginia Woolf, and for extracts from the Autobiography of Leonard Woolf; Mrs Laura Huxley and Random Century Group for extracts from *Crome Yellow* by Aldous Huxley; the Society of Authors for the letters of Katherine Mansfield; T. Birnberg for the letters of Naomi Bentwich (Birnberg); Katherine Tait for extracts from *Bertrand Russell my Father*.

I am grateful to the following for permission to reproduce photographs: 6, 7: the Principal and Fellows of Newnham College, Cambridge; 19, 21: Adrian and Philip Goodman and Michael Joseph, publishers of *Lady Ottoline's Album* (in U.S. edition, Alfred A. Knopf); 14: Little, Brown & Company; 15, 16: the Society of Authors on behalf of the Estate of Bernard Shaw; 36: Philip Jones Griffiths/Magnum; 27: the Press Association; 17: the Alfred North Whitehead Collection, MS 282, Special Collections, Milton S. Eisenhower Library, the Johns Hopkins University; 30, 33, 37, 38: the Hulton-Deutsch Collection; 22: *Objection Overruled* by David Boulton, MacGibbon & Kee, 1967; 9, 10, 23: the Master and Fellows of Trinity College, Cambridge; 11, 12: Barbara Strachey; 40: Snowdon; 20: Lady Ann Hill; 28, 29, 31: Katharine Tait; 1, 2, 3, 4, 5, 8, 13, 18, 24, 25, 32, 34, 35, 39: © McMaster University. Every effort has been made to trace copyright holders.

One

Pembroke Lodge
and the 'Deadly Nightshade'

On Saturday, 18 May 1872, Lord Amberley, heir to Earl Russell, twice prime minister under Queen Victoria, recorded in his diary the birth of his second son. The weather was cold, the thermometer having registered forty-two degrees at 8 a.m. The baby arrived at 5.30 in the afternoon, weighing 8lb 11½ ounces and measuring 21 inches long. The doctor remarked that 'not one child in thirty was as big and fat'. His mother, Kate, agreed, writing to her mother, Lady Stanley, that she found him 'very fat and ugly . . . blue eyes far apart and not much chin', and that he kicked and trembled with rage when not fed quickly enough.

Within hours, a restrained family row broke out over what the new baby should be called. Lady Russell, Amberley's mother, favoured the name of Galahad, but she feared the child might be laughed at, so what did they feel about Basil, Ambrose, Godfrey, Leo or Lionel? Lady Stanley was indignant. She wrote hastily to Kate, 'Pray do not inflict such a punishment on your child as to call it Galahad.' Lord John Russell proposed William, in memory of an ancestor executed in 1683 for his part in the Rye House Plot, then changed his mind to Edward, victor of The Hague, for 'thanks to The Hague, the Moyne and Blenheim we are a free nation.' The baby's parents appear to have paid little attention. Their third child was given the names Bertrand Arthur; as an afterthought was added William in deference to the beheaded hero. His two 'godless' godparents were John Stuart Mill, the empirical philosopher, and Mill's stepdaughter, Helen Taylor, one of the earliest suffragettes.

'I hope', wrote Amberley to the godparents, who were abroad at the time, 'he will turn out mentally not unworthy of your regard.' The Amberleys did not, however, go so far as to christen him: that had to wait until he was eleven.

The choice of godparents, two of the most advanced rationalist radicals of their time, was not unexpected, nor was the decision to ask Elizabeth Garrett Anderson, the pioneer women's doctor, to act as midwife. Both Amberley and Kate lived on the margins of radical liberal politics and were regarded as somewhat shocking by the more conservative Whig aristocratic families among whom they had grown up, though the Russells had a long and honourable tradition as morally courageous defenders of liberal values. John Russell, founder of the family and a courtier and favourite of Henry VIII, had been rewarded for his loyalty with the gift of Woburn Abbey and had died one of the richest men in the kingdom, with large estates in nine counties. Throughout the eighteenth and nineteenth centuries, there had been Russell diplomats, soldiers, bishops, cabinet ministers and local government officers, men who governed from habit as well as duty, and who had culminated in the brilliant Lord John. Born in the year the Tuileries were stormed, the third son of the sixth duke and author of the Parliamentary Reform Act of 1832, Lord John Russell was a lifelong servant to Queen Victoria, serving as foreign minister as well as prime minister, and receiving an earldom in 1861. His first wife was Lady Ribblesdale, who brought with her four children by a first marriage; she was to die giving birth to her second daughter by Lord John. His second marriage was to Bertrand Russell's grandmother, Frances Anna Maria Elliot, daughter of the Earl of Minto, then aged twenty-four. They had four children: Viscount Amberley, William, Rollo and Agatha.

Kate, Amberley's wife, was descended from the second Lord Stanley of Alderley and a noble family of Irish Jacobites, and was the seventh child in a family of 'exceptional vigour, healthy, boisterous, argumentative'.

Neither the Russells nor the Stanleys, however, found the young couple's opinions or behaviour altogether easy.

Amberley's unorthodox views had started early. As a small child he had been a frequent visitor to Buckingham Palace, and had been painted by Landseer, but by the time he reached Harrow at fourteen he was already beginning to abandon his early religious fervour for agnosticism, or rather for a form of theism: he was prepared to accept the existence of an 'unknowable'. His schoolboy diaries are full of religious self-examination; they reveal excruciating shyness and a longing to be liked, though he reports, with admirable honesty, that his schoolfellows objected to his 'biting wit'.

At Edinburgh University, the 'modern Athens' of the day, Amberley took rooms with Professor Alexander Campbell Fraser, professor of logic and metaphysic and editor to Locke and Berkeley; he soon abandoned classics and mathematics for moral science and philosophy. At Trinity College, Cambridge, where he spent the next eighteen months, he completed his political metamorphosis by becoming a democrat and a freethinker, and making a close friend of J. J. Sanderson, who later married a daughter of the Victorian radical Richard Cobden, taking her name, and became a celebrated bookbinder and printer as Cobden-Sanderson. By now, Amberley had grown into a less self-obsessed young man, while remaining highly conscious of being 'lonely and unsocial'. In a revealing self-portrait written at the time, he noted that his mother had accused him of dogmatism, of being too positive in stating his own opinions and supercilious in discussing the errors of others. He complained that he found it irksome to comply endlessly with other people.

In June 1863, when he was twenty, Amberley met Kate at a ball given by Lady Westminster and fell in love with her. She was older than him by a year, and her diaries reveal her to have been a lively, humorous and observant girl, fond of balls though possibly fonder of the more serious pursuits of life. At the age of eighteen, she remarked that she had finished a volume of Macaulay's speeches, and wished there were a second. A fortnight after their first meeting, Amberley was describing her as 'wonderfully intellectual'.

Neither family favoured an early marriage, and the Stanleys feared contact with a young man of such provocative views. It was decided that they should spend six months apart. Amberley spent the time travelling, writing long letters to Lady Stanley in which he suggested books for Kate to read and enquiring anxiously about her health. As soon as the six months came to an end, they became engaged.

Something of Amberley's interests, to reappear with such similarity in his second son, can be seen in a letter he wrote to his future wife in October: 'For, though I think too that the universe will never cease to be a mystery, I can ... see that the great thinkers of the world, who have never discovered the absolutely true, *have* been able to break down superstition and to diminish the intolerance of mankind.'

They were married on 8 November, and were lent Woburn by the Duke of Bedford for their honeymoon. In miniatures of the couple, they appear young and curiously innocent, like two children. Amberley is short, with black hair; he looks much as Bertrand was to look at the same age. When her brothers came down to Woburn to pay them a visit, there was much joking and fooling around. One night, over dinner, the party discussed the kind of sons they would like to have. Kate announced that she would like genius 'and did not mind eccentricity'.

Soon after the marriage Amberley was befriended by John Stuart Mill, then emerging from a long period as a recluse after the death of his wife. They talked about religion and doctrinal differences, about the franchise, slavery and the iniquities of treating women as machines for bearing children, as well as war, about which Amberley felt passionately. When the Amberleys told him that they were planning to give up London and society and retire to the country to read and study, Mill approved. Solitude was necessary, he said, and it was right 'not to be always in the world'. Once away from balls and friends, the young couple talked at length about the issues of the day, and read aloud to each other from Gibbon and Montaigne. They had also become friends with Trollope, Herbert Spencer, Thackeray and T. H. Huxley, with whom Kate discussed children and the dangers of bringing them up 'in a different way from those around them, in the fear of making them pariahs, or making them think themselves superior to others'.

In 1865, Amberley decided that he would follow his father into politics. He stood for Leeds and lost, but the following year he won Nottingham for the Liberals, as the political heirs to the Whig reformers called themselves. He gave his maiden speech in the House of Commons under a Conservative government, his voice having been trained for the occasion by the actor-manager Horace Wigan, who remarked that his manner was atrocious, lacking in gesture and intonation, and that what he needed was gymnastics to improve his physique. The assumption throughout Amberley's childhood had always been that he would enter politics; when, shortly afterwards, he lost Nottingham, it was natural that he would stand again for the Liberals, this time in South Devon. But by now he had become somewhat tainted by his unorthodox views, and when he refused to tell the selection committee whether he was or was not a Christian they decided not to have him. His peculiar theism was not the only thing that stood against him. Earlier that year, as a convinced Malthusian, he had addressed the London Dialectical Society, of which he was vice-president, on the need to discover medical means for limiting the size of families. This had led to an outburst from the medical profession, who protested that birth control was purely a matter of morality and political economy. 'We cannot find words', wrote a furious doctor in the *Medical Times*, 'sufficiently strong to express our utter abhorrence and condemnation . . .' In South Devon, the voters attacked 'Vice-count' Amberley, a 'filthy foul-mouthed rake', for advocating 'unnatural crimes'. The Roman Catholic bishop of Liverpool preached a sermon accusing him of favouring infanticide.

Amberley never stood for Parliament again. Victorian morality made it impossible to discuss openly what he might, or might not, have said about birth control, but some vague air of scandal, fanned by the Tories, had settled around his head. He turned to literature, writing a long and prescient article on the avoidance of war, in which he made a plea for the creation of a 'League' which would make violence less likely, and would 'often suffice to prevent war, until at last men would grow so used to peace as no longer to admit the alternative of war into their calculations'. War, he concluded, was never justified except in self-defence.

It was now Kate's turn to take up unpopular causes. She was, in many ways, a rather more radical figure than her husband. Encouraged by Helen Taylor, and taking it as an obvious and natural right that women should have the vote, she lectured on emancipation, equality and education, not so absurd a notion since a Women's

Suffrage Act was being widely debated. Even so, after she discussed the Married Women's Property Bill, *The Times* commented that she was proposing to 'unsex' British women. One family story, repeated ever after, was that the Duchess of Cambridge received her one day with the words: 'I know you, you are the daughter-in-law, but now I hear you only like dirty people and dirty Americans. All London is full of it, all the clubs are talking of it. I must look at your petticoats to see if they are dirty.' Kate, it appears, laughed and replied that she had not been aware until then that dirt was her 'speciality'. But it was not only London society that found her views extreme: apart from Helen Taylor, almost all her friends and acquaintances found her outspokenness disconcerting.

In 1865, just nine months after her marriage, Kate gave birth to a boy called John Francis, but soon known as Frank. Two years later, after a long trip to America to study education, she produced premature twins. One was born dead; the other she named Rachel. By now, the family had moved from Gloucestershire to Ravenscroft, in the Wye valley, three miles from Tintern Abbey, to a fine white mansion with ornate timbers and huge chimney stacks set in forty acres of wood and parkland, with a large walled garden and views across wild and open countryside. There were stables, a kitchen garden and beehives. It was here that Bertrand Russell was born, into a family whose diaries show them to have been warm, energetic and, despite their curious views, sociable. There is much talk of otter hunts and croquet parties, cottage flower shows and the picking of bilberries, to be eaten in the fields. At the age of about three days, the new baby, by now called Bertie, was lifting his head and looking about 'in a very energetic way'. His questions, as soon as he began to speak, were noted as being remarkably 'penetrating'.

It was a good moment to be born. Europe was at peace. Queen Victoria was halfway through her reign, and Disraeli her prime minister; William I was Emperor of Germany, and Pope Pius IX enthroned in the Vatican. Tennyson was poet laureate. In London, work on an underground railway had started, to supplement the horse-drawn trams. The Suez Canal was open. Throughout France, Germany and Italy, opera was flourishing. Darwin had just published his *Descent of Man*. Dynamite and antiseptics had recently been invented. Jules Verne, Turgenev, Thomas Hardy and Samuel Butler were the fashionable authors of the day, and Eleonora Duse was celebrating her début. That same year, 1872, saw the birth of Giuseppe Mazzini, Diaghilev, Calvin Coolidge, Léon Blum and Max Beerbohm.

The Amberleys were unorthodox not only in their political and social views; they shared what was, in the 1870s, a decidedly unusual approach to daily life for an aristocratic Whig family. The children were allowed to sleep in cots at the foot of their parents' bed. Parents and children spent an unusual amount of time together, without nannies or governesses, going for walks, reading or taking holidays together. Frank was permitted to run about barefoot and rode his pony without a saddle. Something of Kate's free yet precise ideas about children comes across in a letter to a woman whom she was planning to employ: 'I like them to be much alone and unwatched . . . I care for them to learn to be *useful and independent* as much as anything else.' The children were to make their own beds and fold their own clothes; work was to be seen as both 'necessary and desirable'.

Frank was turning out to be wilful and very wild, prone to climb on to the roof and hide if anything displeased him, but clever and forward for his age. The Amberleys ascribed his unruliness to an 'attack of brain from overwork' and recommended to the new governess that he be 'kept back' but not contradicted, which may explain his later obstinacy. Not that his childhood was without challenge: some time before his fifth birthday he had been taken by his father to see a butcher slice open a sheep 'to improve his knowledge of physiology'.

In 1873 Amberley had what was diagnosed as an epileptic fit; and at much the same time his close friend and mentor John Stuart Mill died, after catching a cold when on a botanical walk. An air of gloom settled over Ravenscroft. A new tutor was engaged for the children, an able Darwinian scientist, called Douglas Spalding, who was studying the instincts of birds. Spalding rapidly turned the drawing room and library into a barnyard, allowing his experimental chickens to wander at will and insisting on keeping a hive of bees indoors. His presence only added to the Amberleys' reputation for eccentricity. He was a consumptive, in an advanced state of the illness, with sunken cheeks and a little wooden pipe to help him breathe, and both Kate and Amberley agreed that it was hardly fair that he should be condemned to absolute celibacy. It became known that from time to time Spalding shared her bed. Amberley was now at work on an 'analysis of religious belief'. His health was still bad and his doctor suggested that he should take a complete rest. They decided to spend a winter in Rome and early in 1874 they left for the continent taking Spalding and Frank, but not the two younger children, who were sent to stay with their Russell grandparents.

They arrived home in May, with Frank complaining of a very sore throat. Diphtheria was diagnosed, and he was immediately put into isolation under Dr Garrett Anderson, and nursed by Kate and her sister Maude. When he was considered no longer infectious, the family returned to Ravenscroft. What they had not done, however, was to take into account the long incubation period of the diphtheria bacillus. Within a few days, Rachel came down with the disease, and then Kate. Bertie was hastily removed to a nearby farm, with a maid to look after him. On 27 June 1874 Amberley wrote to his mother-in-law Lady Stanley to tell her that Kate's throat had closed and that she was growing increasingly weak. The doctor was trying to inject food, and giving her port to drink. The next day, Amberley wrote again: 'You will know . . . that all is over. It ended this morning early. I am too wretched to write more.' Five days later, Rachel died. To his mother, Amberley wrote that the two 'greatest treasures in this world' were gone.

Kate had left a note in her journal about her last wishes. 'If I die,' she had written in April 1872, not long before Bertie's birth, 'I wish to be buried here in the wood . . . I should like a long narrow approach to it through cypress trees and all the herbs and flowers . . . my wish would be to be ever present with them all, a household word of living presence and not a skeleton in the cupboard . . . One word only will I write on the past – ever since I have known my own one, life has been perfect, blissful, and full of meaning, joy and purpose . . . were there more marriages such as ours life would indeed be bright.'

Amberley stayed on at Ravenscroft, writing his book and keeping his diary; the entries became terse, recording only what he had read or written. He complained that he felt too miserable to write well and that his book had become flat and dull. By November 1875 it was finished and he added a sad dedication to Kate. The last pages, on what man suffers, suggest that he no longer cared greatly what became of him. 'For myself,' he wrote to his mother, 'no anxiety or even shrinking . . .' He did not live to see his book published; the task of editing it fell to Lady Russell, who must have recoiled at some of its more freethinking passages. Early on the morning of 13 January 1876, suffering from what was diagnosed as acute bronchitis and in a scene worthy of the highest Victorian drama, he called for his children. Frank cried bitterly and clung on to his hand, while Bertie was held up to be kissed. 'Goodbye my little dears, for ever.' At 9.30 he died. 'Father died in the morning,' wrote Frank in his diary. 'Went sliding in the afternoon.' Family and friends gathered and Amberley was buried in the garden at Ravenscroft between the house and the rockery, next to his wife and daughter.

Later, Bertrand Russell would say that he had no memory at all of his mother, though he did just recall his father once giving him a leaflet printed in red letters, and that the red letters had pleased him. But he did tell Edith, his fourth wife, that he suspected his parents of being excessively domineering, and that he often wondered how he would have managed not to quarrel with them. What he could remember, all his life, was a moment that occurred very soon after his father's death, when he saw the big glass roof at Paddington station before arriving at Pembroke Lodge, the house of his grandparents in Richmond Park. 'I trust', Queen Victoria had written to Lady Russell in her letter of condolence, 'that your grandsons will grow up all that you could wish.'

This comfort, observed Bertrand Russell many years later, 'was denied her'.

Frank and Bertie settled down in February 1876 at Pembroke Lodge, gift of Queen Victoria to Lord John to use in his lifetime. They were aged ten and three. There had been some acrimony over their future: the Amberleys had appointed Douglas Spalding and another agnostic, Cobden-Sanderson, as guardians, but this had been overruled by Chancery, and the two boys had been confided to their grandmother, who quickly destroyed some of the more damaging family papers. They reached the house in time for tea in the servants' hall, a large, bare room with an immense table and a high stool, on which Bertie was placed and closely scrutinised by the assembled staff. A photograph taken of him at about this time shows a fair-haired, round-faced child, in the inevitable frocklike garment of the day, wearing a quizzical, hopeful look.

Several people have left accounts of Pembroke Lodge, but none more glowing than that of Rollo, Lord John's third son. The house had been altered many times in its history, having started life as a molecatcher's cottage, in which the gamekeeper let rooms to visitors from London. From a mound in the garden, Henry VIII was said to have watched for the signal announcing the execution of Anne Boleyn, while the house was described by Kinglake, historian of the Crimean War, as the place where the Cabinet met (and some of its members dropped off to sleep) while the war was decided on. By the time the two boys went to live there, it was a long, two-storey, architecturally undistinguished house, surrounded by thickly wooded grounds and open vistas through which could be seen the Thames Valley and Windsor Castle one way and Epsom Downs and Crystal Palace the other. 'I grew accustomed to wide horizons,' Bertrand Russell was to write many years later, 'and to an unimpeded view of the sunset. And I have never since been able to live happily without both.' Later, a good view was to be one of the first requirements in any future home.

The house was approached by a drive between oak trees, some of them well over 700 years old, limes and two immense poplars, and entered through a porch covered in wisteria. In front of it stretched a lawn with a raised flowerbed, an herbaceous border and a bowling green, which later became a tennis court, surrounded by lilacs and holly bushes. Everywhere, there were exotic trees and shrubs, many of them presents to Lord John from grateful foreign princes, as well as patches of wild garden with hawthorn, laurel and rhododendron, between which had been cut shaded walks where wild hyacinths grew. The walls of the house were covered in laburnum and white climbing roses. In winter, Lady Russell, wrapped in shawls, would sit on the verandah that lined one side of the house with a basket of books and a plate of bread and scraps of meat to toss to the birds.

In the spring of 1876, Lord John was eighty-three and very frail, spending his time reading Hansard in his room or being wheeled around the garden in a wicker bath-chair. Born in the eighteenth century, a fortnight after the birth of Shelley and at the start of the French revolution, he had been a friend to Garibaldi, whose exploits were now recounted to the children. A cold and forbidding man in public, he was kindly and tolerant at home; he was fond of speaking French, Italian and Spanish and of rereading *Don Quixote*, which made him laugh aloud. Even so, the air at Pembroke Lodge was formal, a little like a museum, with medallions, busts, trophies, porcelains and portraits – all of them inviting but forbidden to a small child – which gave the feeling of a splendid past and an immutable present. The length of Lord John's time in Parliament, as well as his successes as a reformer – fifty years devoted to the elimination of religious disabilities, parliamentary reform, free trade and the extension of empire across the world – had made him one of the most esteemed political figures of the Victorian age. If few political activities remained, there were still letters from Queen Victoria to answer and occasional deputations of foreign visitors to receive. One of Bertrand Russell's earliest memories was of watching as a crowd on the lawn cheered Lord John on an anniversary of his first great achievement, the repeal of the Test and Corporation Acts, which had excluded non-conformists from office and Parliament.

Soon after Christmas 1877, Lord John took to his bed. As his health grew worse, so visitors came out from London to pay their respects. One of his last callers was Gladstone, who arrived at five o'clock on Easter Sunday, and spent half an hour discussing world matters. Rollo noted in his diary: 'He was as usual full of interest and conversation . . . Speaking of liberty, he saw it was never safe, never safe enough to allow us to cease being watchful.' Lord John died on 28 May. Bertie, just five, would remember little of his grandfather beyond his affability, but his liberal cast of mind obviously left its trace. Nothing in his daily routine altered, as the lodge remained Lady Russell's to use for her lifetime, and, other than cutting down on the number of servants, she continued to live much as she had always done.

Lady Russell was a very different figure from her husband, and arguably the greatest influence on Bertrand Russell's childhood. She had been very young and very shy when she married Lord John, so much so that when the poet Samuel Rogers came to breakfast he is said to have remarked with some malice, 'Have a little tongue. You need it, my dear.' By the time she entered Bertie's life, she had long since lost her meekness, becoming in the process both radical, in a fairly narrow way, and extremely authoritarian. Known as the 'Deadly Nightshade' by Lord John's Cabinet colleagues, she shocked conventional London by becoming a Unitarian at the age of seventy, supporting Irish Home Rule and opposing British imperialist wars. The least self-indulgent of women, she had endured several tragedies by the time Bertie and Frank came to live at Pembroke Lodge; and more were soon to come. Her eldest son was dead; William was insane; Rollo had to give up his career in the Foreign Office due to failing eyesight, and was to lose his wife giving birth to their son. Agatha, not the most stable of characters, was soon to break off an engagement after suffering delusions. Portraits of Lady Russell show her as having rather a long face with a wide mouth and a slightly chilly expression; her grey hair is drawn tightly back and she wears spectacles.

By birth a Scottish Presbyterian and by temperament a puritan, she was indifferent to money, personal comfort or food, and regarded tobacco and wine as sinful. What she wanted for her children – and now for her two grandsons – was for them to live useful and good lives, with little regard for worldly success and none at all for what was then described as a 'good marriage'. She was also cultivated, speaking accurate French, Italian and German, and well read in English history, poetry and the European classics. Her blind spot was Turgenev, whose books she refused to read, even after he had personally presented one to her, but she loved Byron, saying that he was merely the unhappy victim of unrequited love, and was fond of quoting 'Childe Harold' to her grandsons: 'I have not loved the world, nor the world me; / I have not flatter'd its rank breath, nor bow'd / To its idolatries a patient knee.'

It was not surprising, then, that she should not only impose a spartan regime on herself, eating little and then mainly vegetables, and refusing to sit in a comfortable chair until after tea, but that she laid down an even more austere rule for her grandsons. Meals were serious and frugal. The boys were allowed no sugar and no fruit, which was considered bad for them; if apple pie and rice pudding appeared, they were given only the rice. Cold baths were taken every day and piano practice lasted from seven-thirty to eight each morning in an unheated room, to be followed by prayers. When a niece of Talleyrand came to tea one day bringing a box of chocolates, they were allowed one each, but only on Sundays. Later, Bertrand Russell would remember that he suffered acutely from being always rather oddly dressed. It was all very different from the comfortable confusions of Ravenscroft.

Pembroke Lodge had two other occupants, apart from the many servants, who were kept in place by a severe and elderly housekeeper called Mrs Cox, and a butler, MacAlpine, who read the boys accounts of railway accidents from the newspapers. There was Uncle Rollo, who was small and shy and was to do a serious study of the Krakatoa volcanic explosion of 1883, and who now wrote modern psalms, using biblical measures, but bringing in references to modern scientific discoveries – particularly ether – 'which bearest messages from matter through all creation'. He was interested in meteorology and the effects of climate on health, producing a well received treatise on 'strength and diet'. And there was his unmarried sister Agatha, only nineteen years older than Bertrand, a thin, somewhat sorrowful girl with a long pointed nose who dressed in white shawls and black velvet slippers. Agatha never married and was to become miserly and eccentric, leading Bertrand Russell to comment in later years that she was a 'victim of my grandmother's virtue. If she had not been taught that sex was wicked, she might have been happy, successful and able.' The person who was missing was their eldest brother Willy, a lieutenant in the 9th Lancers, who was admitted to an asylum for knifing two men in a workhouse not long after the boys reached Pembroke Lodge. Like all the Russells, Willy was short, but unlike the others he was muscular and had a 'nervous temperament'. He had long suffered from fits of depression

and paranoia which, fellow officers complained, were highly disconcerting. He spent the rest of his life in a mental hospital.

It was Frank, rather than Bertie, who suffered most from Lady
Russell's austerity. He longed to be loved, but could be cruel when
thwarted; he felt trapped, rebelling against the soft voices and
constant overseeing. When his wilfulness – he had again taken to
hiding on the roof when displeased and was prone to steal money
and try to run away – proved too disruptive to the calm ways of the
house he was sent off to Cheam preparatory school, leaving Bertie
to be educated at home.

Life at Pembroke Lodge was not all solemn, as most accounts of
Russell's life make out, and as he himself liked to suggest. 'In
solitude I used to wander about the garden ... meditating on the
flight of time,' he would say. His memory was excellent, and he
developed early on a habit of weighing things up in his mind and
relating them backwards and forwards across his life, but the light
he chose to cast was often pessimistic. As an adult, he described the
'day of continual sunshine' he had once experienced at Pembroke
Lodge, which came to an abrupt end when a visitor, perhaps in true
Victorian style disapproving of the boy's ebullience, told him gravely
that the human capacity for enjoyment decreases with the years and
that never again would he enjoy a summer's day as much. Bertie
wept. In his autobiography, he speaks of an increasing sense of
loneliness and 'of despair of ever meeting anyone with whom I could
talk'. How slanted are these memories?

It is true that Bertie spent much time in the eleven acres of
gardens, wandering in a distant wooded corner where adults rarely
went, conjuring up in his mind the glories of his grandfather's
achievements and hunting for birds' eggs, but he also played tricks
on visiting coachmen, tied cans full of rattling stones to the tail of
Rollo's donkey, terrified the grown-ups by hanging upside down in
the trees, and raced along the paths in his grandfather's bath-chair
until reprimanded by Lady Russell. Yet she was plainly very fond of
him: she read him 'Jack and the Beanstalk' and later Scott and
Shakespeare, played Scottish songs to him on the piano and talked
to him of the past, while Agatha challenged him to draughts and
chess and invented plays in which they both acted. She also took him

to the seaside where, according to family history, he once asked whether limpets could think. 'I don't know,' Agatha is supposed to have replied. 'Then', said the young Bertie impertinently, 'you must learn.' Agatha kept a scrapbook full of pictures and postcards and cuttings, with several references to 'King Rollo the Weatherman'. And Rollo did indeed spend considerable time with his inquisitive nephew, telling him of the scientific discoveries of the day and showing him glass slides of such things as snow crystals. If Bertie missed the company of Frank, he also felt freer without the older boy's overpowering and sometimes bullying personality. In his own memoirs, Frank recalled the atmosphere as 'timid, shrinking, that of a snail withdrawing into its shell . . . sex, birth, swearing, trade, money, passion were subjects I never heard mentioned.'

In summer, Bertie played cricket or croquet with the servants on fine evenings on the lawn, and he was allowed to gallop his pony around the grounds. He fished for carp, roach and perch, and in winter went skating on Richmond ponds. A room near the servants' hall was cleared of boxes and turned into a playroom for him. A letter from Bertie to Frank, dated 5 July 1885 and written with a leaking pen in a somewhat messy hand, is that of a very ordinary small boy, telling his brother that he is learning how to swim and that he plays tennis every day. Another describes, with considerable enthusiasm, the arrival of a new tutor, and goes on: 'Have you seen any more adders? Or found any larks' nests?' These letters are easy and affectionate, full of references to 'Auntie', the weather, nature, birds, excursions and conversations about Home Rule. They are neither sad nor dutiful. Even if there were relatively few companions of his own age – one child who did visit Pembroke Lodge has left an account of him as a solemn child in a blue velvet suit in a household of adults who all 'drifted in and out of the rooms like ghosts and no one ever seemed to be hungry' – there were constant older visitors, and Lady Russell went to great lengths to find him friends to play tennis or go boating. Relations with young children were frequently invited to tea.

It is clear, too, that both his aunt and uncle were very attached to him. A letter to Rollo, who had been appointed one of the boys' guardians, written in April 1890 and pondering piously on the lessons of life he would like to impart to his nephew before he died, shows how attached he had become to the boy. 'Work well and steadily at great subjects, and be moderate in everything . . . Take life calmly and resolutely . . . The age is soft, luxurious and easily led away by specious argument. Do you love simplicity. Now good-bye . . . I wish I could have said much more . . .'

When Bertie was seven, Lady Russell took a house in London and the boys were able to see something of their mother's family, even though a certain rivalry had developed between the two households. Their grandfather, Lord Stanley, a successful Liberal politician known affectionately to friends as Sir Benjamin Backbite, after Sheridan's scandalmonger, was dead, but his wife presided forcefully over her eight remaining children. Lady Stanley had grown up in Florence, after her father, Lord Dillon, fled to Italy as a Jacobite, and her outlook was pronounced to be 'continental'. Photographs show her to have been a round, somewhat stout woman, with beady eyes and the cheerful face of a hamster. She was forthright, talkative, impatient of superstition and humbug, and a great supporter of women's education; she became a founder of Girton College, Cambridge. 'Fools are so fatiguin',' she would say after receiving distinguished literary visitors like Matthew Arnold at the house in Dover Street. At the age of eighty she still regularly attended lectures at the Royal Institution, and was not above making remarks like: 'I have left my brain to the Royal College of Surgeons, because it will be so interesting for them to have a clever woman's brain to cut up.'

Frank, liberated from the disapproval of Pembroke Lodge, whose 'mournful Christian humility' he had come to loathe, greatly enjoyed the outings to the Stanleys, where he could speak and not be snubbed, but Bertie sometimes found his grandmother and her household intimidating. Two flunkeys, in full livery and silk stock-ings, would open the doors to an immense square hall; visitors then climbed the red-carpeted stairs to a vast gallery running the length of the first floor, with parquet floors and sofas lining the wall. The food was delicious, but he dreaded remarks about his precocity and pedantic ways. Sunday lunch, an important event at Dover Street, could be overpowering and very noisy, since it was attended by as many of the eight children and their husbands or wives as could be cajoled into coming. Talk was good tempered but extremely boisterous and argumentative, with Henry, the eldest son, who was very deaf and described himself as a 'Mohammedan', calling out constantly for explanations, and Algernon, the youngest son and an Anglican clergyman, who was fat, witty and jovial like his mother, shouting back replies. Lyulph, a keen supporter of Free Trade and later a good friend to Bertrand Russell during his pacifist days of the First World War, had been Kate's favourite brother; but as a child Bertie felt closer to Maude, who gave him marrons glacés and had a parrot which talked. He called her 'a perfect aunt'. He felt keenly the difference between the Stanleys and the Russells. When he was able to look back on these occasions more sanguinely, he complained that it was the large doses of 'artificial mildness' he had endured at Pembroke Lodge which had made him oversensitive, while what 'vigour, good health and good spirits' he developed he owed entirely to the Stanleys. Frank agreed. In his memoirs, he wrote that he had inherited from the Russells 'bad eyes ... coupled with a certain ineffectiveness and hesitation which prevent my being good at games ...', while Bertie, he said, had been left with 'a touch of the Russell instability'.

'My childhood', Bertrand Russell would write many years later, contradicting some of his more gloomy memories, 'was, on the whole, happy and straightforward.' There is little evidence of the misery many people have ascribed to his early days. That was to come soon.

Lady Russell did not believe in school for her younger grandson. She disapproved of public schools – except in the case of the recalcitrant Frank, now at Winchester and happy and excelling at mathematics – suspecting them of being 'conventional', something she abhorred. And she wanted to protect the 'angel child' from the vices and irreligion of the day, and to keep him 'pure' and 'affection-ate'. A succession of governesses and tutors arrived, to some of whom Bertie became extremely attached. There was Wilhelmina, or Mina, who was German, and then Dora Buhler, a lively nineteen-year-old Swiss girl. When she left, Bertie, then aged eleven, was inconsolable. 'I hear the most fearful wailing going on next door from Bertie and Miss B at their approaching separation,' Frank

noted scornfully in his diary on 20 September 1883. Then came
Louis-Lucien Rochat, a pastor from Geneva, who had written four
tracts on the misuse of alcohol. The boys were taught German and
French.

One way out of the sadness of these constantly changing companions was reading, retreating into a distant and increasingly
abstract world, and Bertie would read late into the night, by a single
candle, listening out for his grandmother's footsteps on the stairs.
Although the books available were only those of his grandfather's
library – Machiavelli, Gibbon, Swift – he also came upon some
volumes of poetry and, quickly rejecting Tennyson and Byron, settled
on Shelley who 'remained for many years the man I loved most
among great men of the past'. Once he could read fluently, without
stumbling, he also read aloud to his grandmother, though she was
quick to censor anything she thought unsuitable. During one particularly scandalous divorce case, she had the newspapers burnt – but
not before Bertie had read them between the park gates, where he
went to collect them, and the drawing room. 'Alas! indeed, for the
coarseness!' complained Lady Russell to her sister, on 27 January
1887, on the subject of Shakespeare's histories, which they were
currently reading together: 'I never can understand the objections to
Bowdlerism. It seems to me so right and natural to prune away what
can do nobody good . . .'

When he was eleven, Bertie discovered Euclid. During a school
holiday, Frank offered to teach him some mathematics, and at the
end of their first lesson, the older boy noted, in his diary, 'Bertie did
very well indeed, and we got half-way through the Definition.' What
he could not know was that the occasion had been, for Bertie, a
revelation but also something of a disappointment. Frank had told
him that Euclid proved things, but when the axioms had been written
down, Bertie asked his brother to explain why he should simply
accept them. Frank grew impatient: axioms, he said, had to be
accepted just like that, without proof, and if Bertie went on making
difficulties, the lesson would have to stop. 'When I got over my
disappointment,' noted Bertrand Russell later, '. . . I found great
delight in [Euclid] . . . This interest was complex: partly mere
pleasure in discovering that I possessed a certain kind of skill, partly

delight in the power of deductive reasoning, partly the restfulness of mathematical certainty; but more than any of these . . . the belief that nature operates according to mathematical laws, and that human actions, like planetary motions, could be calculated if we had sufficient skill.' This insight gave him a first, enchanting glimpse that he might, after all, be intelligent. 'This was', he wrote in his autobiography, 'one of the great events of my life, as dazzling as first love. I had not imagined that there was anything so delicious in the world.'

Not all his enquiries were as easy or as pleasurable. When he was fourteen his grandmother sent him to bed one day on bread and water after hearing that he had had 'doubtful' conversations about sex with one of the pageboys; and a tutor to whom he had grown very close and who had listened to his questions without dismissing them as dangerous or absurd, was unexpectedly fired. Bertie later suspected that this might have been caused by the tutor discussing Marx. It is more likely, however, given Lady Russell's open-mindedness about politics, that the tutor owed his dismissal to something she would have found far more disturbing: any questioning of the Christian faith. His gradual loss of faith during his formative years, and with it a rejection of much that the Russells stood for, was to become one of the determining events of Bertrand Russell's childhood.

Religion, at Pembroke Lodge, was the foundation and structure of everyday life, though it did not take the form either of sectarian obedience or theological constancy. Since her conversion from Presbyterianism to Unitarianism, Lady Russell's religious views had become eclectic. Bertie was taken on alternate Sundays to the parish church and to the Presbyterian chapel. Conscience, seen as the voice of God, was to act as infallible guide, rather than the teachings of any one church. If no cards were played on Sundays, it was more out of a feeling that the servants would be shocked than religious piety. 'Thou shalt not follow a multitude to do evil', Lady Russell wrote on the fly-leaf of his bible on his twelfth birthday. It meant little to him at the time, but it was this emphasis, Russell was to write, that 'led me in later life not to be afraid of belonging to a small minority'.

There was almost no moment of his childhood when he did not question what he saw around him. As soon as he was of age to reflect, he cast a sceptical eye on the unquestioning faith in God which hung over Pembroke Lodge. As his doubts took shape, and as he began to meditate not only on the patchwork of creeds he was offered but on the nature of religion itself, he began to feel more isolated and more lonely. Once he ceased to believe altogether, he began to think he would be doomed to perpetual unhappiness, yet he felt he had no alternative to exploring the ideas that were filling his mind.

Belief in free will, the first subject he tackled, was also the first credo to be rejected. 'I became convinced that the motions of matter, whether living or dead, proceeded entirely in accordance with the laws of dynamics, and therefore the will can have no influence upon the body.' After this came doubts about immortality, and then the very existence of God. It was an unnerving and lonely business.

Bertie was only fourteen. Not unnaturally, he turned for help to his tutors and to his grandmother. The tutors were firmly discouraged from indulging the boy's more challenging lines of thought. As for Lady Russell, she adopted the tone she considered most likely to dampen these dangerous ideas: mockery. When he tried to engage her in debate about one of his new beliefs – that, for instance, the fundamental principle of ethics should be the promotion of human happiness, a view he reached independently long before he had had a chance to study John Stuart Mill – Lady Russell would subject him to a burst of ridicule. 'What is mind? No matter. What is matter? Never mind', was the ditty that accompanied his first searches in philosophy. She even composed a poem, accompanying herself on the piano: 'O science metaphysical And very very quizzical You only make this maze of life the mazier . . .', and so on, for four stanzas.

At this time, Russell was to write later, 'my interests were divided between sex, religion and mathematics.' Sex had entered his life at twelve, when a friend called Ernest Logan tried to explain to him the 'nature of copulation'. This remained a mystery, however, until he talked to the garrulous pageboy, after which he turned to a medical dictionary for enlightenment. He continued to feel acute guilt when erections interrupted his work and he stopped to masturbate – which he went on doing, 'in moderation', until the age of twenty, when he fell in love. During his adolescence, the closest contact he had with girls, apart from trying to glimpse the maids dressing, was when he persuaded an obliging housemaid to kiss him.

He began to feel that there was no one to whom he could confide what was going on in his head, and he was increasingly apprehensive about what would happen if anyone guessed what he was thinking. So he took to writing down his thoughts in Greek characters, though he already rather despised the learning of dead languages. These coded entries were set down, mostly in pencil, in a black exercise book, which was kept hidden. There are twenty-two entries, all but one written in 1888, when he was sixteen. They deal with prayer, the existence of God, immortality and his fears for himself as the holder of such strange views; they touch on melancholia, suicide and madness. What he seems to have been doing was struggling to reconcile the code of beliefs of the inhabitants of Pembroke Lodge with the new moral codes he was encountering in his reading, as well as squaring religion with the scientific principles which now occupied his mind.

April 2 . . . I now come to the subject which personally interests us poor mortals more perhaps than any other. I mean the question of immortality. This is the one in which I have been most disappointed and pained by thought . . .
April 9 . . . I do wish I believed in the life eternal. For it makes me quite miserable to think man is merely a kind of machine endowed unhappily for himself with consciousness . . .
April 18 . . . Now my idea is that our conscience is in the first place due to evolution, which would of course form instincts of self preservation, and in the second place, to civilization and education . . .
April 20 . . . My rule of life, which I guide my conduct by and a departure from which I consider as a sin, is to act in the manner which I believe to be most likely to produce the greatest happiness . . .
June 3 . . . The search for truth has shattered most of my old beliefs.

Years later, looking through his Greek Exercises, Bertrand Russell added in the margins: 'Prig . . . Prig'.

Lady Russell had long since abandoned any ambitions for Frank, but about Bertie she had few doubts: he was to follow his grandfather's Liberal path and go, like his father before him, into politics. For this he needed a more serious education than could be provided by tutors, and it was decided that he should attend a crammer to obtain the qualifications necessary for a place at Trinity, his father's old Cambridge college.

Oppressed by never being able to mention any subject that was preoccupying him, except perhaps for politics, deeply self-absorbed and convinced of his inherent wickedness, Bertie welcomed the decision, hoping it would dispel some of his moroseness and melancholia. The crammer chosen was B. A. Green's University and Army Tutors in Southgate, London, and he spent eighteen months there as a boarder. When he went there at the age of sixteen, he was younger than most of the other boys, but well up to their standards, as his serious and reflective essays on evolution, state socialism and anarchism show. At first, he found the place 'pleasant', and made friends with the son of a rich Canadian called Fitz or Edward Fitzgerald, whose soft voice and melancholic posture matched his own, and for whose sister Caroline he conceived a 'romantic attachment'. But he soon came to deplore the boorishness of his other companions, most of whom were destined for the army, complaining that they had 'no mind, no independent thought, no love of good books, nor of the higher refinements of morality . . .' and congratulated himself on his own 'calmer, thoughtfuller, poeti-caller' nature. He was appalled to find, when Robert Browning died, that none of the boys had ever heard of him. In July, when he went home for the holidays, he recorded in his Greek Exercises that although he had told everyone he was enjoying it, he hated the 'disturbance', the mockery of the other boys, and 'being made to sing, to climb on chairs, to get up for a sponging in the middle of the night' . . . 'I am always kept up', he wrote, with more than a touch of self-righteousness, 'by a feeling of contempt, erroneous though it may be, for all who "despitefully use me and persecute me".' He took refuge in essays, many on the themes that were to occupy so much of his later years: 'Evolution as affecting modern Political Science', 'State socialism' and 'Contentment, its good and bad points'.

His friendship with Fitz, whose sophistication he had so much admired, cooled and he experienced bitter disappointment when he saw his new friend's finer feelings coarsen in the unintellectual atmosphere of the crammer; he decided to break with him altogether after he saw Fitz being rude to his mother. Later, he recalled an occasion when, needled beyond endurance by Fitz's taunts, he tried to strangle his former friend.

Not that he wasted many lines of his Greek Exercises on Southgate. He preferred to continue his unhappy and high-minded reflections on free will and immortality, very reminiscent of his father's diary entries at much the same age. In any case, the holidays contained pleasures: Uncle Rollo had moved to Hindhead and into a farmhouse called Dunrozel – named after Rozel in Normandy, supposedly the original home of the Russells. Hindhead was sandy, and it had become fashionable among people with a taste for open air and high ideals. Local inhabitants included John Tyndall, the physicist and mountaineer, T. H. Huxley, Mrs Humphry Ward and Tennyson. Bertie went to spend some weeks with Rollo, starting a tradition that was to continue for some years; they explored the surrounding countryside and discussed the scientific discoveries of the day, and he was taken to call on Tyndall, who made him think that he, too, might become a physicist. With his uncle, he talked easily: about poetry, sermons and reason.

Just before Christmas 1889, he won a place at Trinity, coming first in both parts of the 'Little Go' and in an additional paper on mechanics, and winning a minor scholarship in mathematics. A newspaper cutting, probably from a Richmond paper, reported him as saying complacently that he never worked for more than six hours a day. He spent the next ten months living at Pembroke Lodge, working three times a week with a tutor called Henry Cumming Robson at Wren's Coaching Establishment in Notting Hill, reading Mill's *Autobiography* and finding in it the refutation of the First Cause argument for the existence of God: that 'Who made me?' cannot be answered because it necessarily suggests the further question 'Who made God?' which he had for so long been seeking. He was also teaching himself Italian in order to read Dante and Machiavelli in the original. He settled into a routine of work during the day, broken perhaps for a game of tennis with his friend Fitz,

with whom he was on better terms now that they had tacitly agreed
to avoid serious conversations, then either dining nearby with friends
or spending the evening reading with his grandmother. One night he
was taken by Rollo to the Duke of Bedford's box at Covent Garden
to hear his first opera, Gounod's *Romeo and Juliet*, with the Australian
soprano Nellie Melba. On another occasion, as the only man in the
house, he was left alone with Gladstone after dinner, and 'wished
the earth would swallow me up' when Gladstone asked why he had
been given port in a claret glass. It was the only remark Gladstone
addressed to him. 'Since then', he wrote later, 'I have never again
felt the full agony of terror.'

He revelled in having at last left Southgate. On Sunday, 18 May,
he noted in his new diary: 'My birthday. One of the pleasantest that
I have ever spent. A beautiful day ... My hopes for the coming
year are that I shall become less introspective, less shy, more
genial, less cynical, more firm and steadfast of purpose. My fears are
that I shall become more conceited, more argumentative, more
conventional ...'

He was due at Trinity for the autumn term. When the day came
for the final break with Pembroke Lodge, he was just eighteen, a
small, slender boy who looked younger than his age, 'shy, childish,
awkward, well-behaved and good natured' as he described himself
in his autobiography, and 'unusually prone to a sense of sin'. He was
also somewhat arrogant, with a prim and precocious manner,
believing himself uniquely unhappy because he had lost his faith,
and still highly confused about the larger issues of life, despite
considering himself an atheist, a Darwinian and a Cartesian – though
he had not, as yet, read Descartes. There was little of the humour
and wit that were to come. His writing style was mature, economical
and clear, which he later explained by saying that reading aloud to
his grandmother had forced him into the habit of turning a sentence
over and over again in his mind, until it had the right 'combination
of brevity, clarity and rhythm'; and his choice of words was poetic
now that he had taken to contemplating nature and admiring Shelley,
'whose self-pity and ... atheism alike consoled me'.

Apart from a few happy months with the tutor who had been
dismissed, it was many years since he had felt able to discuss his

religious doubts, and he had great difficulty believing that he would ever again find anyone with whom he could really talk. As for his studies, these worried him least: he left for Trinity determined to pursue his conviction, however disturbing the path down which it led him, that the mathematical model was the solution to everything. 'I thought', he explained, many years later, 'that it should be possible to clear away muddles, and that everybody would be happy in a world where machines would do the work and justice would regulate distribution. I hoped sooner or later to arrive at a perfected mathematics which should leave no room for doubts, and bit by bit to extend the sphere of certainty from mathematics to other sciences.'

He left Pembroke Lodge, and his adolescence, with few regrets. If his childhood had been on the whole contented, his boyhood, by contrast, had been 'very lonely and very unhappy'.

Two

Angels and embryos

Russell arrived in Cambridge at the beginning of October, 1890. Trinity had been the obvious choice: not simply was it his father's old college but it was also the leading college in the country for mathematics and natural science. The alternative would have been King's, then enjoying enormous prestige and attracting excellent teachers, like Nathaniel Wedd, who wore bright red ties, or J. E. Nixon, who collected umbrellas, or the classicist Goldsworthy Lowes Dickinson, but King's was by tradition a college for classicists, and mathematicians had little say there.

As the holder of a scholarship – Trinity offered six entrance scholarships a year, each tenable for three years, and they were advisable for anyone who planned to apply later for a Fellowship – Russell was entitled to rooms in college. He was allocated a second-floor bedroom in Whewell's Court, across the street from Trinity, an undistinguished Victorian quad of yellowish stone and double gothic windows, named after a former master of the college. G5, Russell's room, had a coal fire, a jug and a porcelain basin, a hard narrow bed and a view of a monklike gargoyle on a facing wall, as well as a glimpse of Trinity itself. It was rather dark, and the bathrooms were three floors down, in the basement. A manservant or 'gyp' delivered coal and water to his room every day. It was up to Russell to buy whatever furniture he needed, and to acquire the distinctive blue Trinity gown, which, together with a mortar-board, students had to wear whenever they left their rooms on an academic pursuit, on Sundays or after dark. Trinity was by far the largest college in

Cambridge, with a student population several times that of any other college except for St John's.

At the beginning of the 1890s, Cambridge was a pleasant, small town of about 35,000 inhabitants, with open patches of common land, rows of private gardens and extensive college grounds. The streets were lined with trees, and in summer the gardens were full of roses. Trams ran along the main roads, each drawn by a single horse, so slowly that children raced them with ease. A few undergraduates had tandems or tricycles, but the bicycle revolution was not to begin until the end of the decade. Pillar boxes were painted green, the colour chosen by Trollope while he was the Post Office surveyor, while the shops were still family-run businesses. It was all very peaceful.

It was just eight years since Cambridge Fellows had been allowed to marry, and dinner parties, the standards set by the heads of the various colleges, were frequent and elaborate occasions. The dons' lives were leisurely, and not overburdened with teaching or administrative duties. Cambridge had long aspired to high ideals of truth and free speech, and to this credo the outstanding young don at King's, Lowes Dickinson, had now added a new view about the relationship between Fellows and undergraduates. 'Boys and young men', he observed, 'were no longer to be snubbed and put down by their elders: they were to be taken up, encouraged and befriended.'

For all the conviviality and pleasant surroundings, Russell did not take instantly to Trinity life. At just eighteen, he was younger than many of the men in college, as well as shy and awkward; he was also highly indignant to find that, like the boys at Southgate, many behaved with a complete lack of intellectual seriousness. On 20 November, he noted tetchily in his diary: 'The people I have hitherto met here are every one of them unsatisfactory . . . The dons are sad specimens of wasted power . . . In fact flippancy strikes me as *the* besetting sin of the whole place.' He had the grace to continue: '. . . perhaps the friend I look for may appear in time; perhaps the fault lies in me.' His teachers in particular he despised, finding their lectures dull and pointless and swearing that he would do better himself were he ever to teach. Dons, he concluded, were a 'wholly unnecessary part of the university'.

By Christmas, his feelings about Cambridge had altered dramatically. During the autumn term Russell had discovered what it was like to work among equals, among people as curious as he about the limits of knowledge, and Trinity, with its large quota of prize-winning mathematicians, now struck him as the ideal place to pursue his quest for certainty in mathematical propositions. Cambridge, he wrote many years later, fitted him like a glove. 'To find myself in a world where intelligence was valued and clear thinking was thought to be a good thing caused me an intoxicating delight.' He was also beginning to read more widely, not just in mathematics and philosophy, but novels, plays, histories and biographies. Lady Stanley had presented him with a small notebook, bound in black morocco, to record his reading, and he was soon filling it with Thackeray's *Virginians* ('excellent'), Dowden's *Life of Shelley* ('moderately good'), Byron's *The Deformed Transformed* ('Caesar excellent; otherwise feeble'), and the anonymous *Amaryllis* ('very silly').

Most importantly perhaps, he was at last meeting people who 'neither stared at me as if I were a lunatic nor denounced me as if I were a criminal', who were interested in poetry, philosophy, ethics and the 'whole world of mental adventure'. After the restrictions and piety of Pembroke Lodge, it was heady stuff. By the last evening of his first term, Russell was writing in his diary that Cambridge had turned out far more successfully than he had expected, and that he had now found a set of most agreeable friends.

Among these was Goldie Lowes Dickinson, a gentle, modest man nine years Russell's senior, who shared not just his love for Shelley, calling him a 'visionary about life', but his quest for an 'ideal'. Goldie, whose manner was the very opposite of dogmatic, inspired great fondness in his pupils, and Russell soon noted with some surprise that whenever he made a 'brutal statement' or produced 'unpleasant truths' Lowes Dickinson seemed to recoil with pain. He determined to check his 'stark realism' in his company.

Also at King's, though never very close to Russell, was Oscar Browning, for twenty years the most energetic and snobbish of dons, who founded numerous societies, including the Swimming Club, whose members he led running, totally naked, across the meadows. 'Browning', wrote Lowes Dickinson, who had an affair with him, was 'Falstaffian, shameless, affectionate, egoistic, generous, snobbish, democratic, witty, lazy, dull, worldly, academic . . .' For many years Browning's rooms were considered some of the most entertaining and stimulating in Cambridge.

A. N. Whitehead, the mathematician who had examined Russell for his entrance examination, had evidently been greatly struck by the young man's intellectual abilities. He was a kindly man of just twenty-nine, and he now endeared himself by turning to Russell during a class one day and remarking that there was no need for him to study a certain text as he clearly knew it well already – a fact he remembered from the examination ten months earlier. About this time Russell discovered that another man had obtained more marks than he during the examination, but that Whitehead, sensing Russell to be the abler of the two, had chosen to burn the record of his rival's marks. Too senior at that time to become a real friend, Whitehead agreed with Lowes Dickinson's vision of dons as catalysts and mentors,.and went out of his way to introduce Russell to possible younger friends.

One of these was Charles Sanger, an extremely likeable young man, and a fine linguist and economist. He was very short in stature with 'bright, sceptical eyes', whose round head, likened by one friend to a cannon ball 'to symbolise the ballistic and shattering quality of his arguments', made him look somewhat like a gnome. Russell and Sanger studied mathematics together, and were to remain very close until Sanger's death in 1930. Russell was to call him one of the 'kindest men that ever lived'. Comparing the two, Lowes Dickinson remarked that while Sanger was 'very small, face all alert, bright complexion, eager movements', Russell looked like a French abbé of the eighteenth century 'crossed with an English aristocrat'. Another introduction was to the Llewelyn Davies boys, the younger sons of a vicar from Kirkby Lonsdale: Crompton, funny, given to passionate likes and dislikes, whose recital on the staircase at Trinity of 'Tyger, Tyger, burning bright' so dazzled Russell that he felt dizzy and had to lean against the wall; and Theodore, a young man much beloved by everyone, who worked extremely hard and possessed enormous charm. Russell considered Crompton his closest friend, 'at the University and ever after'.

Then there were the Trevelyan brothers, whom Russell had first met at dinner with the Master of the college when he came up for his entrance examination. Charles was already at Trinity, reading history; Robert, known as Bob or Trevy, came up at the same time as Russell, and a third, George, later the well-known historian, was due to arrive the following year. Robert had already attracted Russell's attention by fainting at dinner with the Master when the conversation turned to surgery and wounds. A mutual friend said of him that he 'made one think of a charming young woolly bear, all the more charming for not having been too thoroughly licked'. Of the three brothers, Robert was to become closest to Russell, who called him a 'scholarly poet' and greatly enjoyed his 'delicious whimsical humour' and his passionate appetite for walking. The group was soon joined by Edward Marsh, a lanky young man with a square head covered in thick fair hair brushed hard back; he had been christened 'cold white shape' by Bob after he had appeared at breakfast looking frozen and miserable.

Finally, there was the philosopher Ellis McTaggart, who was older than the others by five or six years and was about to become a Fellow of the college; he was so shy that when he first called on Russell in his rooms neither was able to speak, and so awkward that he sidled round like a crab. He was prone to stop abruptly when seized by an idea, and talk aloud to himself. Local children called him 'loonie'. A thin young man with expressive eyes and a large head, McTaggart was so precise in his habits that he noted down the exact number of pages he had read each day. He rode an ancient tricycle around Cambridge, went rowing on the Thames, and gave memorable Sunday morning breakfasts, for which he often forgot to buy any food, so that his visitors took to bringing their own eggs. McTaggart loved everything about university life, from its ceremonies and feasts to its committees and debates. There is a charming account of a visit to McTaggart by a woman friend which gives some idea of how easy the people who knew him well found this physically gauche man. 'What did we talk about? Well, ourselves, cats, Alice-in-Wonderland, immortality, the newest stories from Trinity high table ... God, novels, neighbours, plans for meeting in the holidays, vestments, dreams, ourselves ...' McTaggart introduced Russell to a friend from his schooldays at Clifton, Roger Fry, later to become the most influential art critic since Ruskin, and who first introduced the English to French Impressionism.

These, then, were the men who had transformed Russell's life by the end of his first term. With them, he studied and ate and pondered whether to join one of the many clubs which played such an important part in undergraduate life, like the Epicureans or the Political Society, or the Musical Club, or the Moral Sciences Club, which discussed philosophy and invited Sanger and Russell to become members soon after their arrival. Over the next twenty years, Russell was to use this club as an audience before which to try out his ideas.

Persistent and extremely demanding work left the undergraduates with little time or energy for the 'more strenuous kinds of amusements', though Russell did play tennis occasionally – he was said to be so bad at it that he could beat only the ungainly McTaggart. He also swam and walked, beginning a tradition of walking parties that was to continue for many years, covering fifteen to twenty miles easily in a day, while Russell, as his friends sometimes complained, never stopped talking philosophy for a single minute.

Accounts of him at this time describe a neatly dressed young man, in a white starched collar so high that his neck seemed to disappear into it, and which he insisted on changing every night even while on walking tours. He was considered something of a fop, with his lavender gloves, gold-headed cane and knife-edge creases in his trousers; he wore dark suits in town and tweeds in the country, ordered from the Eton tailor called Tom Brown whom he was to use all his life. His manners were formal, courteous and old-fashioned, even by the standards of the Victorian age, and they were to remain so all his life. When introduced to someone he did not know, he bowed from the waist, objecting when teased that he did not know where else to bow from. He was invariably punctual, regarding lack of punctuality as the worst of bad manners, and a sign of thoughtless misjudgement. Even at the age of twenty, he liked everything to be in its place and resented change as a waste of time, using valuable concentration which could better go on intellectual pursuits. It is noticeable how the picture he painted of his Cambridge life, whether at this time or later, contains no references to its architecture or beauty, to the routine of his days, to what he ate or what he studied. He was bored, as he was to be all his life, by the trivia of everyday life, preferring to dwell instead on work, specific amusements like chess or walking and ideas of all kinds.

Above all, of course, what he enjoyed most about his new life was talking – late into the night, pacing up and down the cloisters of Nevile's Court, or during long Sunday walks – about all the ideas he had for so long repressed. The tone of these conversations was optimistic and enquiring, with none of the cynical superiority which was soon to descend on the university. The world seemed to Russell and his friends a hopeful and solid place, where the progress made during the nineteenth century was bound to continue, and to which each agreed that he had something real to contribute. Darwinism, they said to one another, had proved that the laws of society tended inescapably towards material progress, and the 'scientific method' was now to be brought to bear on the social problems of the day like unemployment and poverty. War seemed to them a very remote possibility, and politics were safely in the hands of able men. Everything could and would be solved, given the right education and sufficient intelligence. 'The world in those days', Russell was to remark later, 'permitted more happiness to the young than it does now. It was possible to be passionate, and yet cheerful, public-spirited and yet happy, intelligent and yet optimistic.'

'For a long time,' Russell wrote, 'I supposed that somewhere in the university there were really clever people, whom I had not yet met, and whom I should at once recognise as my intellectual superiors . . . but I discovered that I already knew all the cleverest people in the university.' What was more, he was happy at last, as he somewhat reluctantly admitted in his diary, so happy that to assuage any lingering puritanism he vowed to do at least one unpleasant task each day, though he was unable to prevent himself from adding that happiness was probably bad for both moral and intellectual health.

No sooner had Russell reached Trinity than Whitehead suggested to the Conversazione Society, the most prestigious of Cambridge societies, that they keep an eye on him and on Charles Sanger as potential recruits. Since the essence of the society was total secrecy, the two young men knew nothing of the scrutiny they were subjected to over the following months. Both, in the event, proved worthy. In February 1892, towards the end of their fifth term, Sanger was elected member number 223, Russell number 224.

The Apostles, as the society was better known, was not merely Cambridge's most desirable intellectual club. It also had – and had always had – an immense importance for its members, far greater than other clubs, affecting not only their intellectual development and the nature of their friendships but their future lives. The Apostles had been founded in St John's in 1820 as a small, unremarkable debating club, by a future Bishop of Gibraltar, George Tomlinson, who felt that the university was not doing enough to explore philosophical issues. The early members were, even by the clerical spirit of the time, destined to an unusual extent for the Church: of the first twelve, nine took holy orders.

After the first few years, the society fell into the hands of two undergraduates from the more fashionable Trinity College: Frederick Maurice, later an outstanding Anglican theologian, and John Sterling, best known as the subject of one of Carlyle's biographies. They gave it a second birth, made it a secret society and invented formal rules, such as the holding of regular Saturday-night meetings, always behind closed doors. They were Apostles, they would say, in opposition to the Philistines, whom they referred to as 'Stumpfs'.

Arthur Hallam was an early member (number 68) soon followed by Tennyson, who devoted a canto of *In Memoriam* to the society, though its significance was largely incomprehensible to all but initiates.

> . . . Where once we held debate, a band
> Of youthful friends, on mind and art,
> And labour, and the changing mart,
> And all the framework of the land . . .

But it was Dean Merrivale, rather than Tennyson, who best described the society's ethos as it was until Russell's day and beyond. 'Our common bond', he wrote, 'has been a common intellectual taste, common studies, common literary aspirations, and we have all felt, I suppose, the support of mutual regard and perhaps some mutual flattery . . . We began to think that we had a mission to enlighten the world upon things intellectual and spiritual . . .' Three decades later, Henry Sidgwick, the moral philosopher considered by many the perfect Apostle, if not the greatest of them all, for his rare dedication to the quest for philosophical knowledge, was thinking along much the same lines: 'Absolute candour was the only duty that the tradition of the Society enforced . . . truth as we saw it then and there was what we had to embrace and maintain, and there were no propositions so well established that an Apostle had not the right to deny or question, if he did so sincerely and not from mere love of paradox.'

If the society was understandably cautious in its choice of members, it was not always predictable: men who were later to excel in their fields did not always find their way into its magic circle. Neither Kinglake nor Thackeray, for instance, was ever elected. Likely candidates were seldom in their first year at Cambridge, and were usually aged about twenty. Most were Etonians or Harrovians, and nearly every member belonged to King's or Trinity. By the time of Russell's election there had been Apostle classical scholars, theologians, poets, historians and statesmen, but no natural scientist, the sciences having as yet little place in the curriculum. Charles Darwin was never asked to become a member.

By the spring of 1892, Russell was 'less and less solemn', extremely 'sociable' and no longer a 'shy prig'. He was delighted to be elected, all the more so when he discovered that membership was confined to twelve current Apostles, among them several of his closest friends, like McTaggart, Lowes Dickinson, Crompton and Theodore Llewelyn Davies, Roger Fry and A. N. Whitehead. He took considerable pleasure in its rituals. Every Saturday night during term time – no member might miss a meeting – the Apostles gathered just before ten o'clock, as Trinity's gates were closing, in the room of the member (or moderator) chosen at the previous meeting to play host for the evening and to give the paper. The topics covered tended to be philosophical: 'Is one life enough?' but very occasionally someone would take up an issue in politics or social economics.

The moderator's paper lasted about twenty minutes, and set out the proposition together with the writer's opinions. When he had finished reading it aloud, he would call on the other Apostles in turn, selected by drawing lots, to stand on the hearthrug, face the 'brothers' and say what he thought. Nothing was to be held back. Truth was what mattered, and the promotion of good causes, even at the price of relevance and regardless of what the others thought. At the end of the evening, a vote was taken, members declaring themselves for or against the moderator's proposition, and the next moderator was then appointed. 'The soul of the thing,' wrote Lowes Dickinson in his autobiography, 'as I felt it, is incommunicable. When young men are growing in mind and soul, when speculation is a passion, when discussion is made profound by love, there happens something incredible . . .'

The Apostles enjoyed themselves. They felt, and indeed were, part of a charmed group, conscious of their intellectual superiority, but not disposed to take themselves too seriously. Meetings were at once profound and humorous, with proceedings conducted in the special language which is often a hallmark of secret societies. In lieu of the sacrament, 'whales' were consumed, in the form of sardines on toast, washed down with coffee. Taking the vocabulary of the German metaphysicians, and making something of a joke of their ideas, the society called itself the 'world of reality', or 'noumenal', arguing that since the metaphysicians held that space and time were unreal, they would declare themselves free of such bondage. Potential members were 'embryos', true members 'apostles' and outsiders 'phenomena'; the induction ceremony was known as 'birth', and sponsors took the name of 'father'. When a member left Cambridge, he 'took wings' and became an 'angel'. Not that a member ever really left. Election was for life. As an angel, a member was entitled to attend the Saturday-night gatherings if he was in Cambridge, as well as the annual dinner in London, and many did so throughout their lives. It was also not unusual for a previous Apostle to help a younger member, once he left university, to find a job, especially in the worlds of politics, the law, education and literature, though there was no obligation to do so. It was a question of loyalty to a group of congenial and like-minded friends. When E. M. Forster, elected to the society in 1901, published his biography of Lowes Dickinson, no one was surprised, though many were presumably mystified, when he decided to dedicate it to 'Fratrum Societati'.

Apostolic talk, which clearly possessed considerable charm for the inner sanctum, could sound pompous and silly to an outsider. 'I am most awfully glad', McTaggart wrote to Russell in May 1892, soon after his election. 'I hope you have been told of our brother Whitehead's penetration, who detected the apostolic nature of yourself and Sanger . . .' Other friends sent similar greetings, of a less precious sort. 'Hurrah', wrote Crompton Llewelyn Davies from India, where he was travelling. 'You will of course get your own impression, but it was certainly a true new life for me, and a revelation of what Cambridge really was.' His words might well have been written by Henry Sidgwick, the 'perfect Apostle', who wrote in his autobiography that his election had 'more effect on my intellectual development than any one thing that happened to me afterwards'. Both men were echoed by Russell himself, who was coming to regard his association with the Apostles as the 'greatest happiness of my life at Cambridge'. To his uncle Rollo, that December, he wrote that 'instead of finding the terms grow less pleasant as time goes on, they seem to get more and more so to me.' He was also becoming more interested in politics, and particularly socialism, which he was looking forward to discussing with Rollo in the holidays.

Like other shy and lonely undergraduates before him, Russell was now finding Cambridge and his Apostolic friends all he had dreamt of. Accustomed to walking by himself in the grounds of an enormous and deserted park, thinking about the past and agonising over his personal failings, with often only the company of pious women to look forward to in the evenings, he now delighted in dropping into the rooms of friends, whom he would find deep in the very conversations he most wanted to have. His friends noticed how, all through his second year, Russell was blossoming in the atmosphere of 'daily Platonic dialogue', as Whitehead described it, puffing away on his pipe and infecting his listeners with some of his own excitement about philosophy, even if some were becoming wary of his intellectual sharpness, Charles Trevelyan remarking that he felt that Russell was a 'great man who would see through me'.

There were, of course, no women Apostles, and no true women undergraduates either. By the early 1880s, Girton and Newnham had women students, but though granted the right to be examined and classed in the Tripos examinations women did not formally become full members of the university until 1947. Within the Apostles, there was some talk of women's right to an education, and both Sidgwick and McTaggart took prominent parts in pushing for some kind of equality. Russell was never to become a leading feminist, even if he was to devote considerable time to the matter, but given that his grandmother, Lady Stanley, was a founder of Girton, and that his godfather John Stuart Mill was the author of *The Subjection of Women*, which he had read and admired as an adolescent, and went on regarding with 'complete agreement', it was hardly surprising to find him advocating their cause while an undergraduate. In March 1894, he read a paper to the Apostles, taking his title of 'Lovborg or Hedda' from Ibsen's *Hedda Gabler*, in which he argued that women should be admitted to the society itself. There were, he conceded, dangers, such as 'degenerating into sentimentality' or love affairs between members, but since, in his view, the society was about friendship as much as intellectual sparring, would they not be a valuable addition? All but Lowes Dickinson voted in favour, but it was almost eighty years before a woman was elected.

There is little mention of women in the memoirs and diaries of these Apostles; their bantering intellectual exchanges have a distinctly male flavour. Russell did, however, make a few women friends during his four years as an undergraduate, two of whom were to play important roles in some of his later activities. The Llewelyn Davies brothers had an elder sister called Margaret, who became a considerable figure in the suffrage movement. Russell met her one day in their rooms and was much struck by her beauty and idealism; he was to work closely with her for many years on matters of public interest. There was also Mary Sheepshanks, a tall, domineering young woman in a pince-nez, with the trenchant, no-nonsense and highly articulate style which appealed greatly to the Apostolic mind.

About sex or his emotional life Russell said very little, beyond describing in his autobiography how on moonlit nights, 'I used to career round the country in a state of temporary lunacy . . . The reason, of course, was sexual desire, though at the time I did not know this.' He was never drawn towards the suppressed (or not so suppressed) homosexuality of Oscar Browning's entourage, or the particular intimacy of some Apostolic gatherings, though there is one peculiar entry in the 'locked diary' which he had begun on his eighteenth birthday. 'Dec. 5 1892. 1 a. m. O God forgive me; I have sinned grievously. What the others did, that I did also for fear lest I should seem to set myself above them, for fear lest I should seem a prig. How ought I to glory in that name, could I indeed deserve it! . . .', and so on, for many lines. Just what befell Russell that evening no one knows.

At about this time, there was worrying news of Frank. In 1883, he had gone up to Balliol College, Oxford, to read mathematics, which he abandoned in his second year for classics. He had become a keen club member, and an active sportsman – bicyclist, sculler and oarsman – and had carried out experiments in telegraphy. He was at last 'absolutely happy', while remaining deeply conscious that happiness was not considered a desirable state of mind by his grandmother, who was decidedly 'sniffy'. His happiness, however, was not to last. Some of the truculence and wilfulness of his early years re-emerged to plague him. As his second year was drawing to a close, he was suddenly accused of writing a series of scandalous letters. The truth about these letters is still not clear, and Frank appears to have been innocent, but they led to his being sent down from Balliol for a month. He refused to leave, and his rustication was increased to a year. Infuriated by such injustice, he announced that he was leaving for good.

He was nineteen and a half at the time, and still a ward of Chancery, but with a yearly income of £400 he was determined not to return to live at Pembroke Lodge. He rented a house at Hampton, hired a tutor, and dabbled for a while in vegetarianism and Buddhism. When he became twenty-one, he bought a house at Teddington and ran a steamboat, before travelling around America, where he met Walt Whitman and the philosopher, George Santayana. His life might now have gone well, for there was something sturdy and fundamentally generous about Frank when he was not in the throes of rancour and hostility, had he not chosen this moment to take an unfortunate step.

In 1890, the year that Russell went to Trinity, Frank became engaged to a young woman called Mabel Edith Scott, whose mother, Lady Scott, was a notorious adventuress of her time and whom Lady Russell absolutely refused to receive at Pembroke Lodge. Russell evidently thought little of his future sister-in-law, writing pompously in his diary: 'Poor Mabel. She seems very nice by nature, but from education utterly without firmness or moral courage.' The marriage lasted barely a few months, and Bertrand Russell soon heard from his grandmother that Frank was to be sued for judicial separation on the grounds of cruelty. 'I was', wrote Frank long afterwards, with a rare show of honesty, 'prickly all over with principles,' with a 'violent reforming zeal . . . and I was very tidy and faddy about little things'. Though he was acquitted on the charge of cruelty, the affair made the headlines, and large posters, deeply embarrassing to the inhabitants of Pembroke Lodge, appeared in the streets. This was the beginning of a series of sordid lawsuits in which Frank was accused by Mabel and her mother of having had an affair with a teacher called H. A. Roberts, an apparently remarkable and able man. In the end, the courts found the accusation false, and in 1897 Lady Scott was sent to jail for eight months for criminal libel, Lord Halsbury declaring that her attacks amounted to 'legal cruelty', and the newspapers branding her 'a hate crazed Society lady'. However, teachers could not afford scandals in those days, particularly of a homosexual nature, and Roberts's life would have been ruined had it not been for Cambridge friends like McTaggart and Dickinson, as well as his teaching colleagues, who supported him financially and provided him with excellent testimonials. When his name was eventually vindicated, he settled in Cambridge and became senior tutor of Caius. Frank retired to his riverside house, where he set about installing electricity and building an engine house.

It was through his Apostle friends that Russell, on his return to Trinity for his third year in the autumn of 1892, met G. E. Moore.

The meeting has been described as a landmark in the development of modern ethical philosophy. For a while at least the two became close friends, Russell having decided that the younger man was a 'genius' after hearing him read a paper which began, 'In the beginning was matter, and matter begat the devil, and the devil begat God . . .' 'Although he was two years my junior,' Russell wrote later, 'I was quickly attracted by the clarity and passion of his thinking, and by a kind of flame-like sincerity which roused in me deep admiration.'

George Moore was the son of a doctor from Dulwich, and the brother of the poet T. Sturge Moore. He was nineteen when he went up to Trinity – slim, with soft brown hair parted in the middle and already receding from a wide, domed forehead; he had delicate features, a charming, gentle smile and an air of acute shyness. His contemporaries considered him extremely beautiful. Russell noted that he had a 'kind of exquisite purity'. Though neither as witty as Russell nor as sharp and quick as some of their friends, he was set apart from the others by what has been called a 'kind of magic'. His nature was modest and almost childlike, and he had a simple, apparently naïve way of tackling questions which was quite new to the Cambridge set he now joined. Arguments, in his opinion, had to be pursued patiently and painstakingly, point by point, wherever they led, and however long it took to follow them to their ends. Edward Marsh described the effect Moore's arrival had on them: he 'whipped us up with an egg-whisk', and had the 'most discovering face I ever saw, with sharp little bespectacled eyes that lit up the lowest bottom of the Erebus, and a nose that looked ready to cut plutonium.'

Like the others, Russell was charmed. He was struck by Moore's intellectual fearlessness and impressed to discover that they shared a common interest not just in philosophy, but in poetry and religion. The admiration was mutual. Many years later, Moore was to say that of all the philosophers he had known Russell had the greatest influence on him. Like Russell two years earlier, he was delighted with Cambridge and his new circle of friends, declaring that he had never realised how exciting life could be. His letters home describe, in admiring terms, dancing classes, games of fives, playing the piano and going for long walks. The endless talk, far into the night, always such a crucial ingredient in Russell's enjoyment of the place, now found new directions under Moore's persistent questioning, while much amusement was afforded by the way the young man would strike a match, intending to light his pipe, but then become so completely absorbed in an argument that it would burn out, only to be replaced by another, and so on until the box of matches was empty and the pipe remained cold. 'Do you *really* think that?' he would ask, shaking his head in vigorous disbelief, as the match went out yet again.

Moore was a natural Apostle. Early in 1893, Russell arranged for him to meet the man who counted most when it came to selecting new members: McTaggart. He invited the two of them to tea in his rooms, and the conversation quickly turned to the question of time, which McTaggart maintained was unreal. Though easily intimidated and very conscious of being eight years younger than McTaggart, who was now a Fellow of the college, Moore held his own, declaring that he thought this a perfectly monstrous proposition. Evidently the baptism was successful, for a year later, in February 1894, Moore was elected to the Apostles, nominated by Russell. The subject of his first meeting was 'What ought Cambridge to give?' When Moore rose to speak, he did so with no sign of nervousness but looked, as Russell observed, 'like Newton and Satan rolled into one, each at the supreme moment of his life'. Russell propounded the idea that so intense was the scepticism instilled by Cambridge that none of its graduates was equipped to lead a practical life. Moore, when he had stopped laughing, replied that in his view their duty was to spread scepticism 'until at last everybody knows that he can know absolutely nothing'.

'We all felt electrified by him,' wrote Russell in a letter, 'and as if we had all slumbered hitherto and never realised what fearless intellect pure and unadulterated really means. If he does not die or go mad I cannot doubt that he will somehow mark himself out as a man of stupendous genius.' He was enchanted by his new friend.

At the beginning of that year Russell had left Whewell Court and moved to some of the most prized rooms in Trinity. He was given Q3, on the far left-hand corner of Great Court. Its sitting room had three vaulted windows overlooking the chapel and clock tower, and was conveniently close to the dining hall. With it went a small separate bedroom, with room for little other than a bed and a side table, and a view over Trinity Lane and the back of King's.

With the first part of his tripos only six months away, he was working extremely hard. Taking stock of himself, he wrote in a letter to Rollo, 'I think I am less morbidly introspective than I used to be; I have my time so much busier and more occupied than I used to that I feel my thoughts are perhaps too much taken up with the work or pleasure of the moment; but I still try to know myself as well as I can, both for the sake of my own improvement and because I think it leads to a better understanding and a readier sympathy with other people.' Photographs show a serious young man, with a great intensity of expression and a thin, sensual mouth.

Although aware that he had covered a certain amount of mathematical ground, he was still uncertain as to his likely place in the final exams, especially as he had fallen ill for a while and found it extremely hard to work. Not knowing of his illness, his tutor, James Ward, summoned him and sternly urged him to concentrate harder on his mathematics, presumably sensing that Russell's interests were rapidly turning towards philosophy, which he was soon to describe as a 'No Man's Land . . . intermediate between theology and science . . .' and exposed to attack from both. It was hardly surprising. Despite its national reputation the mathematical tripos in the 1890s was, as Russell complained, an exercise in 'artful dodges and ingenious devices and altogether too much like a crossword puzzle', in which marks were awarded not for mathematical intuition but for the efficient solving of problems. Lasting six days, this exam was based largely on rote learning and often achieved only after intensive coaching. It had changed little since its inception shortly after Newton's death, and was bitterly resented by many of the candidates. Only those who came in the first of the three divisions, the wranglers, were allowed to move on to the concluding part of the tripos, in which they would have to write on more advanced problems. If Russell wanted a career in mathematics, and if he intended to apply for a Trinity Fellowship, he needed to come in the first division, preferably among the first dozen wranglers.

During the summer, he learned that he had been placed seventh wrangler, but having decided that mathematics was 'disgusting', that his tutors had not succeeded in producing any argument to convince him that calculus was 'anything but a tissue of fallacies', he sold his textbooks and resolved never again to open a mathematics book. He still hoped to find a reason for supposing that mathematics represented the truth, but the search would have to wait.

With part one of the tripos behind him, Russell was able to turn his mind fully to the subject that had been drawing him most powerfully in the past few years: the 'fantastic world of philosophy'. Before coming up to Trinity, his only real philosophical mentor had been his godfather John Stuart Mill, whose attempts to combine moral and social philosophy under a unifying principle of utility had seemed to him most satisfactory. At Trinity he continued to read Mill, as well as Hume and Plato. He also consulted Harold Joachim, an Oxford philosopher who was now Rollo Russell's neighbour at Hindhead, about what other philosophers to read. Joachim suggested more Plato, the early Greeks, Descartes, Leibniz, Spinoza, Hume, Bacon, Kant, Bradley ('first rate but very hard') and Bosanquet ('good but still harder'). Since there is only one volume of philosophy among the list of books recorded in his black notebook for January to June 1893, it seems that Russell waited before following his advice, especially after being cautioned by James Ward that he was falling behind in mathematics.

Throughout the eighteenth and most of the nineteenth century, philosophy in Oxford and Cambridge had been dominated by the British empiricists – Locke, Berkeley and Hume – who held that knowledge, apart perhaps from mathematics and logic, is derived from experience. By the time Russell reached Cambridge, however, their ideas were rapidly being supplanted by those of the German idealists like Kant and Hegel, with their emphasis on the perfectibility of man and society and the spiritual nature of ultimate reality, which was more in tune with Victorian thinking and its reaction against the perils of agnosticism and materialism.

Russell's tutors, in his fourth and philosophical year, were James Ward, G. F. Stout and Henry Sidgwick, the dedicated Apostle, each of whom expounded a slightly different version of Hegel or Kant and taught their pupils in very different styles. Sidgwick, whom the undergraduates called 'Old Sidg', was certainly the most distinguished. A member of Trinity in one capacity or another since the 1850s, he was a true adherent to utilitarianism and the author of at least one important book, *Methods of Ethics*; but he was an essentially dull teacher, with a stammer and an agonising habit of lingering for hours over every detail. Of the three, Russell found him the least impressive, remembering him as a man who included one, but only one, joke in every lecture, after which the students' attention would invariably wander. In private, Sidgwick could be witty and shrewd; it was only with students that he seemed pedantic. In later years, Russell went out of his way to praise him for his intellectual honesty and the time and attention he gave to correcting essays.

James Ward, Russell's main tutor, lectured in metaphysics – the whole of philosophy other than moral philosophy – and saw the universe as a plurality of minds. He was a relaxed and engaging talker, conducting his classes seated around a table with his students and taking enormous pains to make himself understood. Melancholy and puritanical by nature, with an early interest in psychology, Ward tried to make his students see what he saw as the magic of the philosophy of mathematics, showering Russell with titles of relevant books, which for the moment Russell scorned. Stout shared Ward's gift of making philosophy exciting – in his case the history of modern philosophy – which he did by seizing on the points he considered most important and putting them across as directly and conversationally as he could.

In Hegel's philosophy, only the mind is real, by which he meant not that only the mind exists and not material things, but that 'mind' is a system of individuals actively developing their potentials by embodying them in increasingly complex forms. Freedom is a fundamental feature of mind, and nothing that is finite or partial can ever be wholly free. Mind – the only reality – is therefore infinite. Philosophy, said Hegel, as Spinoza and Pythagoras had said before him, is an activity which frees and purifies the mind, and the philosopher's task is to make men conscious of art, politics and religion, so that the mind can exert itself to the utmost, and thus become absolute. The most comprehensive and influential of the absolute idealists, Hegel was famous for his dialectical method, and the way he set out his writings in dialectical triads, consisting of thesis, antithesis and synthesis. Hegel, the patriotic Prussian, Russell was to say later, was the hardest to understand of the great philosophers.

In 1893, the most important idealist philosopher in Cambridge was Russell's fellow Apostle, McTaggart, who impressed Moore greatly with his clarity, and with the way he kept asking: 'What does this mean?' 'Woolliness' in McTaggart's vocabulary meant the philosophical obscurantism he most mistrusted. Though Russell was not his pupil, the two men exchanged letters – McTaggart's are all about philosophy, boyish, Apostolic letters written in black ink in minute characters – and spent much time in talk, with McTaggart pacing up and down his room, where everything had its precise place, replying to questions in short, rapid sentences, insisting he could prove by logic that the world was good and the soul immortal. McTaggart, a writer of clarity and grace, was much liked by his students, who became used to his terse speaking style and seemingly unfriendly manner, and were overwhelmed by the excitement conjured by his ideas. If he was exacting, he was also kind and convivial, eager to open the door to his ideas even to non-philosophers, and prone to remark that undergraduates should get drunk at least once a week to prove they were not teetotallers.

For a while, Russell held out against the Hegelians. He was not convinced by their arguments, and was deeply sceptical of McTaggart's attempts to provide religious consolation as part of his Hegelian doctrine. He complained that this was 'hopelessly mystical'. But in the summer of 1894, while walking up Trinity Lane to buy a tin of tobacco, he suddenly understood the meaning of Hegel's ontological argument: a proof of the existence of God, by seeing God as neither grander nor more powerful than the natural world, and yet fundamentally like it, and not something beyond the world that must remain forever inaccessible to man. He threw his tobacco into the air and exclaimed, 'as I caught it: Great God in boots, the ontological argument is sound.' As a result of this newfound conviction, he began to read avidly F. H. Bradley, Joachim's 'first rate' philosopher, who represented the school of absolute idealism. Bradley's intention was to establish important conclusions about the universe as a whole and about reality, and to show that reality is to be found only in the 'absolute' or 'whole', in which all distinctions vanish. He wanted to arrive at 'ultimate truths', and thought it was up to philosophers to debate them. Absolute idealism was an ambitious approach to philosophy, since its exponents believed that while 'understanding' was the method of thought used by ordinary people, 'reason' was higher thinking, proper for philosophers. Later, Russell was to remember wondering 'as an almost unattainable ideal, whether I should ever do work as good as McTaggart's'. At that moment, however, the 'absolute' seemed to offer precisely what Russell was looking for – some kind of harmony between emotion and intellect. Moore, who, like Russell, had long held out against the idealists, now accompanied him into their fold. Neither was to remain there long.

In *Portraits from Memory*, written in the 1950s, Russell said that he had been led to study philosophy by two motives. One was a wish to find knowledge 'that could be accepted as certainly true'. The other was a 'desire to find some satisfaction for religious impulses' and some system of belief which would allow him to see life as whole and steady.

By now, as his Greek Exercises reveal, he had been worrying about religion for nearly ten years, trying to reconcile religious belief with scientific knowledge. His grandmother had not been against scientific enquiry – Rollo, after all, was an exponent of Darwinism – but Russell had found it almost impossible to reconcile 'reverence for Christ as Perfect Man' with the supremacy of individual conscience. The mystical longings of his adolescence, which had made him search among the orthodox teachings of the various churches he attended, while grappling with the implications of Darwin's evolutionary theories, had led him early on to look for solace in Wordsworth. 'As I grew fonder of nature,' he recorded in his diary, 'and came more in harmony with her spirit . . . a new aspect of God burst upon me . . . God became part of my life.' Like his father, Russell found Wordsworth's philosophy of natural beauty soothing.

Such feelings of comfort had not lasted long. As his mind veered back towards scepticism and analysis, he had rejected Wordsworth and his arguments for immortality as being of a 'vague, poetic nature'. From Wordsworth he had moved on to Shelley, recalling many years later that Shelley's charms first became apparent to him one day when he was waiting for his Aunt Maude in Dover Street and happened to open a book of verse at *Alastor*. Shelley, it seemed, had found a way of combining religious veneration with a devotion to scientific truth by approaching eternity through human love. But even that had proved ephemeral, and it had been in a state of religious despondency and confusion, finding the idea of a godless world intolerable but not knowing what could replace it, that Russell had gone up to Cambridge.

He could not have come to a better place: progress, optimism, Darwinism and the scientific method were at the heart of the prevailing intellectual atmosphere. People were talking about how to extend education throughout the country, in keeping with the spirit of the 1870 Education Act, and a few were beginning to discuss Freud, whose teachings were just reaching London through a paper read to the Psychical Research Society. Gone were the clerical pieties of the nineteenth century: the 1860s, and not the 1890s, had been the decade when Cambridge men lost their faith, unable to find spiritual explanations in a world which could be explained entirely by natural mechanical laws. The current undergraduates, many of whom had been through similar crises of faith and soul-searching to Russell's, were now living easily with their lack of faith. Their calm impressed Russell, who by November was recording in his diary that he was becoming quite reconciled to being an agnostic.

His path was made easier by the Apostles, whose style of thought and speech was dominated by scepticism and integrity; most of them were already accepting agnostics – both Moore and McTaggart declared themselves as such, though McTaggart continued to believe in immortality and saw death as a passage to continued life. 'It was', Russell wrote in his autobiography, 'a principle in discussion that there were to be no *taboos*, no limitations, nothing considered shocking, no barriers to absolute freedom of speculation.' Speculation of the kind enjoyed by the Apostles did much to curb, at least for a while, Russell's yearning for worship, particularly as Cambridge Hegelianism did not reject religion altogether but saw it as one ingredient of truth. Although the whole question of how science could be fitted into a humanistic education, and the very nature of faith itself, were issues which continued to preoccupy him, it was as an agnostic that Russell finished his undergraduate years at Trinity in the summer of 1894. 'It was with a genuine sense of relief', he wrote later, 'that I discarded the last vestiges of theological orthodoxy.'

Four years at Cambridge had altered Russell profoundly. He was still searching for certainty – philosophical? mathematical? – 'in the kind of way in which people want religious faith'. But from a shy, precious young man, with an overdeveloped sense of his own sinfulness, he had turned into someone who felt at ease in the intellectual atmosphere of university life, and extremely content with the friends he had made there. He had, he noted, become 'gay and flippant'. For many years, he was to write, 'I felt that Cambridge was the only place on earth that I could regard as home.'

Three

Alys

One Sunday in the summer of 1889, when Russell was seventeen and spending his three-month summer holiday with Rollo in Hindhead, his uncle took him for a long walk. They had reached Friday's Hill, near Fernhurst, when Rollo suggested calling on an American family, the Pearsall Smiths, who had recently settled in the neighbourhood. Russell was appalled and begged his uncle at least to make the visit brief and not to stay for supper. In the event, the Pearsall Smiths proved too pressing to refuse; and Russell fell in love.

Hannah Whitall and Robert Pearsall Smith were 'birthright' Quakers from Philadelphia, both born into prosperous, pious and narrow-minded families. Their son Logan's description of them as a 'handsome, florid father and a beautiful straightforward Quaker mother' is somewhat fanciful. Hannah was an exuberant, domineering matriarch whom some found unbearably bossy; she had been a rebel since childhood, and had refused to wear the 'sugarscoop' bonnet of devout Quakers for her wedding. Robert was indeed a good-looking man, but he had become involved in his own form of evangelism which he called 'Betrothal with Christ', and which he was apt to take literally, sealing his baptisms of young women with an 'unholy kiss'; this eventually led to a scandal and caused him to have a nervous breakdown. Both husband and wife were excellent preachers, and had been immensely popular in London in the revivalist days of the 1870s, drawing crowds with their 'higher life' movement and appeal to simplicity, and with their fresh, energetic manner. Eighty thousand people came to hear them preach one year in Brighton.

By 1889, Robert had been forced to retire from active preaching, though Hannah continued to entertain London drawing rooms with racy talk about the conquest of sin, providing her own somewhat earthy interpretation of God's word – when challenged about the Trinity she would say it was just like a threepenny bit – and producing homely devotional bestsellers. She was also a moving force in the temperance movement. The family had a London house in Grosvenor Road, Pimlico, and a rented country house at Fernhurst. Thickly covered in ivy, Friday's Hill House was an ugly building, with a hideous central gable, but it was conveniently large, with fourteen bedrooms, a billiard room, a conservatory, and a studio, where guests were given paints and brushes and told to produce something. It had fine views south over the downs, a tennis court and two hundred acres of woodland. Hannah and Robert were snobbish, but they were also extremely hospitable.

One of their reasons for settling in England was to be close to their children: Logan, who was reading Greats at Balliol; Mary, a tall, good-looking girl with heavy black eyebrows and a determined chin, now married to an Irish Catholic barrister called Frank Costelloe; and Alys, the youngest, known as Lurella or Loo after a favourite family novel by William Dean Howells. By the summer of Russell's first visit, Friday's Hill House was already the centre for a large circle of Costelloe's Fabian friends, as well as Logan's Oxford ones. Gosse, Millais, Burne-Jones, Mrs Hodgson Burnett, author of *Little Lord Fauntleroy* and the mother of a childhood friend of Russell's named Maude, Leslie Stephen and the Webbs were all regular visitors summoned by Hannah by letter or telegram. The atmosphere was welcoming and cheerful.

That summer day of 1889 the whole family was present. Costelloe, a solemn, rather short young man with a beard and political ambitions as a radical, having beaten George Bernard Shaw as a candidate for Chelsea, held forth during dinner with a description of a dock strike and talk about trade unionism; but it was Alys who caught Russell's attention. A little over four years older than Russell, she was a very pretty girl with dark curly hair, blue eyes and a slightly placid manner, and was soon to be described in a newspaper as 'one of the most beautiful women it is possible to imagine and gifted with a soul of imperial stateliness . . .' She had recently graduated from Bryn Mawr and put the younger man at ease by asking him whether he had read a German book, *Ekkehard*. By chance, he had finished it that morning. 'I felt', he wrote many years later, 'this was a stroke of luck. She was kind, and made me not feel shy. I fell in love with her at first sight.'

At the time he said nothing, nor did he mention his feelings during subsequent summers when he returned to stay with Rollo and visited Friday's Hill as often as he decently could, walking the four miles from Hindhead every Sunday morning and hoping to be invited to stay to lunch and dinner. Each summer, he found himself still in love, attracted by Alys's lack of 'priggery and prejudice', admiring her as the most emancipated woman he had ever met and hoping that she would stay unmarried until he had time to grow up. He was also captivated by the freedom of Friday's Hill House, where critics, writers, painters and socialists talked far into the night, enthusiastic and uninhibited. It was worldly and exciting and a perfect complement to the high philosophical talk of Trinity.

One of the visitors to Friday's Hill was the Spanish-American philosopher George Santayana, who had befriended Frank in America in 1886 and was regarded by the Pearsall Smiths as a fellow expatriate and member of the American intelligentsia in Britain. Santayana was much taken with the young Russell, though he was later to say that he 'petered out' and failed to live up to his early promise. Russell was, he noted, 'small, dark, brisk, with a lively air and a hyena laugh. According to some people he was the ugliest man they had ever seen. But I didn't find him ugly, because his mask, though grotesque, was expressive and engaging. You saw that he was a monster, that if he spat fire, it was a *feu de joie*.' He added that the young man's laughter could be 'savage' and that there was something of a 'many-sided fanatic' about him. In a letter he observed that while Russell was 'mathematical', he was also satisfactorily 'human'.

During those first years, Alys did not appear to notice Russell's interest in her. She had embarked on a life of good works, obediently following her mother's path by espousing the temperance cause, for which she travelled around the country running youth meetings: she was to remain a teetotaller all her life. Russell took the pledge in the spring of 1893, though he had evidently given up drink the summer before. She had also begun working for children and women in the slums, and brought groups of factory girls to join the other visitors at Friday's Hill. For a while, she took a job in a factory herself, to be able to write and speak more authoritatively on women's rights. Her manner was a little earnest, and her conversation could be, at times, disconcertingly literal. For relaxation, she fenced.

In May 1893, Russell came of age. Under the terms of his father's will, he inherited £20,000, which brought him in £600 a year, a considerable sum for the time, and he felt in a position to press his case. In June, Alys and her cousin Madge Whitall, to whom she was devoted, paid a visit to Cambridge. Russell met them and the two discussed their feelings, though they managed to do so in an entirely theoretical way. A month later, Russell was recording in his diary: 'I think of A all day long.' Before long, she was back in Cambridge, and this time Russell took her boating on the river. They talked without pause, moving from social ethics to love, marriage and divorce but always cautious about speaking too frankly. Russell declared that he thought that love, in the shape of sympathy and friendship, was the greatest thing man could hope to attain; Alys said that she favoured independence and was a believer in free love. Though she still appeared not to understand Russell's overtures, she did agree to exchange occasional letters. 'The greatest day in my life hitherto', noted Russell in his diary.

Within two weeks, each had written two letters. Though their tone remained formal, Russell felt not only 'the keenness of my love, which has become a clear and certain fact to me', but that Alys was at last beginning to respond. By September, he was back at Friday's Hill for a successful visit, when they sat together in the Bô Tree House, named after Buddha's tree of enlightenment. This was a room built twenty-five feet up a tree by Robert, with windows, chairs and even a sofa, where guests could meditate. Next morning, they rose early and long before breakfast walked through the dawn mist to a nearby hill, covered in beech, which reminded Russell of a magnificent early gothic cathedral. For the first time, he spoke openly. To his proposal of marriage, Alys said neither yes nor no, but tried to hold him at bay, promising for the time being only friendship but agreeing to more frequent meetings.

For the rest of 1893, Russell and Alys continued to exchange letters and to meet, going on long walks through the woods or travelling around London on trams. They talked, earnestly and at great length, about the nature of love, religion, sexual relations, marriage, divorce and children, but steered away from their emotions about each other. When, in October, Alys announced that she was going to Chicago to attend a temperance conference, Russell felt betrayed. Alys, for her part, was confused, drawn ever closer to him, yet apprehensive about their differences, which now seemed to her very great. She worried about the difference in their ages, in their attitudes to religion (she had told him that she could not help believing in God), about Russell's superior intelligence, about her sociable nature and his more solitary one.

'You have such an abnormal capacity for suffering that it frightens me . . .' she wrote to him on 18 December 1893. 'I wish you did not care so much. And yet I do value your love more than I can say, and I cannot imagine my life without it now. Only you *must* be more critical, and never *never* say again that everything I do is right in your eyes . . . I have tried so hard to be more reserved (not with you!) ever since you once said I was too unreserved. Your nature improves and develops best under kindness and sympathy and love, but mine does not: I begin to deteriorate in a loving and sympathetic atmosphere.'

Few romances can have been so minutely dissected, but Alys was right to worry. Had she scrutinised her nature more closely, her tendency to evade and conciliate, to be pliant sometimes to the point of supineness, she would have realised just how unsuitable the match was. Even by the rigid morality of the day, Alys and Russell were, by temperament as well as upbringing, extraordinarily prudish. For all the outpourings on paper, it was not until January 1894, almost five years after their first meeting, that they kissed.

Russell had come from Pembroke Lodge to Grosvenor Road to see her. It was a very cold day and six inches of snow covered the London streets; something about the strange silence of the snowy city made the day particular. 'We spent the whole day, with the

exception of meal times, kissing,' Russell wrote exuberantly that
night in his diary, 'with hardly a word spoken from morning to night,
except for an interlude during which I read *Epipsychidion* aloud.'
That night, very late, he walked the mile and a half from the station
to Pembroke Lodge in a blizzard 'tired but exultant'. Apart from his
earlier experience with the housemaid, this was the first time he had
kissed a woman. The events of the snowy day, however, did strangely
little to alter the lofty character of their relations, though Alys had
now taken to addressing him with the intimate Quaker 'thee', which
he soon adopted. In July, he was 'happy, divinely happy'. Above all,
he announced, 'I can still say Thank God Lust has absolutely no
share in my passion.' Alys replied that she deplored sexual relations
between men and women 'who love each other for spiritual and
intellectual reasons'. Russell agreed: 'so lately as last May term I
remember a discussion in which I expressed the opinion that love
was degraded by sexual intercourse; but nobody seemed to agree
with me . . .' He was reading one of Victorian Britain's most popular
prophets of what was known as 'human fellowship', Edward Carpenter's three short pamphlets on sex and marriage, pressed on him by
Lowes Dickinson. Carpenter's message about personal redemption
through individual regeneration filled him with 'devout admiration',
just as his arguments about chastity in marriage, the 'mystical union
of souls' rather than any cruder 'physical union', appealed to his
inexperienced nature.

Alys had taken a long time to feel certain about Russell, but she
was now falling in love. She was later able to date the moment
exactly: on Friday 2 March 1894, her diary reads: 'I suddenly began
to love him today with an intensity I never felt before which is almost
painful.' She wrote to him: 'Every now and then when I am busy
with something else, the remembrance of thy love comes over me
with such a joyous rush that it seems too good to be true . . . I do
love thee, dear Bertie.' And later, 'Thee has all the qualities I would
wish thee to have; in my eyes thee is perfect . . .'

As early as the autumn of 1893, Russell and Alys, sensing the
opposition they were likely to encounter, decided that their best
course was to tell their families of their interest in each other. As

they had predicted, neither family was pleased. In the spring of his last year at Cambridge, Russell made a trip to Rome, returning via Paris to meet Alys, who was visiting Logan, then living on the Left Bank. The weather was wonderful; they went to Fontainebleau, took a boat on the Seine and lunched out of doors. On her return to London, Alys received a summons from Lady Russell. 'I knew', she noted despondently in the 'locked diary' she now shared with Russell, 'she would send for me.' The visit took place on a Sunday, ten days later, and Alys recorded it: 'Reached Pembroke Lodge at four o'clock and saw Lady Russell alone for half an hour. Then Lady Agatha came in, and finally the ex-governess and tea. I left at five, as the conversation was painful and very fruitless. They think I am behaving in a very dishonourable and indelicate manner in seeing so much of B. and writing twice a week.'

Lady Russell was indeed appalled, but there was little she could do until Russell, having taken his tripos, told her he would like to become engaged. Lady Russell looked pale and sad and deeply reproachful. In her eyes, Alys was a schemer and a dull one at that; what was more, she was a foreigner, and her parents were distinctly common. She told him that Alys was 'no lady, a baby-snatcher, a low-class adventuress, a person incapable of all finer feelings, a woman whose vulgarity would perpetually put me to shame'. Russell fought back. He reminded his grandmother that she had bitterly opposed his father's marriage, which had turned out very happily. He said that she had been unkind to Alys, at which she looked mortified and finally agreed to a meeting with Hannah. Russell's other grandmother, Lady Stanley, was more reasonable, but also disapproved, arguing that he was making a bad mistake in marrying an American and someone out of his class. Aunt Maude wrote to caution him against such a hasty step when he had seen so very little of the 'world of Young Women'. Even Rollo was made to call on Alys and beg her to change her mind.

Hannah was not pleased either. Though Mary was her favourite daughter, she had great fondness for Alys, whom she had described as a baby as 'the very personification of a fat, old, comfortable country Friend, with about an acre of face'; she was reluctant to part with her. Though always portrayed as ruthlessly snobbish, Hannah was in fact ambivalent in her attitude to the British and their aristocracy. She had been heard to make remarks like 'an earl was more like an archangel than a man, and to be an earl's daughter was almost akin to being a daughter of heaven,' but she had also written to Alys, some years before: 'I am glad thee doesn't like Englishmen. The more I see of them the less I like them. They have no manners for one thing, and they *are* arbitrary, say what you will.' Hannah proposed a six-month separation.

Then there was Logan to win over. Logan was fair, over six feet tall and heavily built, with a faint American accent, a light and ironic tone, a nervous disposition and a thin moustache. As photographs show, he invariably wore button boots and a wide peaked cap. He was homosexual, with a large circle of friends whom he enjoyed shocking with outrageous remarks, and took great pleasure in gossip. When tetchy, his voice rose to a disagreeable shriek. By nature he was a spectator, an essayist, a dabbler in fine literature, with none of the public-spiritedness of his mother or sisters, 'these vehement, powerful, Penthesilean females', as he once called them. However, his opinion counted.

He did not dislike Russell, with whom he had exchanged a long and precious correspondence about a new club, to be called 'the Order of Prigs', with 'arch prigs' and penances, but he was critical of his ignorance of the arts and the way in which Russell insisted on describing pictures as 'the useless works of dead men'. It was true that Russell had little interest in music and none in painting, and Logan saw it as his duty to educate him. In 1893 he was living just round the corner from Whistler in Paris, and during Russell's visit with Alys that spring he did his best to convey to him something of the beauty and wonder of the city and its art, taking him several times to the Impressionists in the Luxembourg, and telling him about Manet, Monet and Degas. Russell tried to understand, but felt detached. 'I think I can't talk Art any better than Sport', he conceded to Alys, but added that 'although I can't understand what they're doing, or why anybody paints, I feel the greatest sympathy with their aims and habits which I don't with the sporting man's.' Logan must have been reminded of his mother, who had once complained: 'Not one Madonna have I yet seen who seems to know her baby at all . . . I fairly ache sometimes to take him in my arms and give him one real good motherly hug.'

Logan was not against the match, even if he thought his potential brother-in-law rather young. Both men found it hard to drop their earlier cynicism and banter, and in answer to an anxious enquiry, Logan wrote: 'Yes, I *do* believe in you, Bertie, though the faculty for belief is not one of the most developed in me . . . Win your spurs, *mon cher* – let us see that you are good and sensible – as indeed we believe you are.' For his part, Russell felt somewhat awkward about talking to a close man friend, fearing, as he wrote to Alys, 'to acquire a habit of expressing myself to men: it would not increase their respect for me, and in most cases wd. be apt to destroy friendship', a remark which makes one wonder at the intimacy of his Cambridge friendships.

When it looked as if the engagement could not be postponed much longer, Lady Russell suddenly drew out her trump card. A marriage between Russell and a Pearsall Smith was out of the question: there was insanity on both sides of the family. To prove her case about the Russells, she sent her grandson to see the family doctor, a Scot with mutton-chop whiskers called Dr Anderson, who explained that his father's epilepsy was hereditary and reminded him about Uncle Willy, by now confined permanently to an insane asylum and prone to sudden attacks of violence, followed by loud shouting and singing and pulling strange faces. Agatha's engagement to a curate many years before had been broken off because of her 'insane delusions'. As for the Pearsall Smiths, their Uncle Horace was known to be depressive and Madge Whitall suffered from bouts of extreme melancholia, while Robert himself was thought by Lady Russell to be 'crazy or at any rate queer'.

Russell began to feel a sense of deep gloom, made worse by several nightmares about insanity. One night he dreamt that his mother was not dead at all but in an asylum, and that his family had lied to him. He searched out material on heredity, read Francis Galton, the influential Victorian eugenist, and reported later to Alys that his views on genius and 'natural inheritance', reached by means of statistics, were '*most*' beautiful. He also turned to Ibsen's *Ghosts*, noting forlornly in his diary: 'I feel as though darkness were my native element . . . I am haunted by the fear of the family ghost, which seems to seize on me with clammy invisible hands . . . PL is to me like a family vault haunted by the ghosts of maniacs', though he added that these thoughts were probably absurd, brought on by chocolate cake and staying up too late.

The question of what should now be done could not be long avoided. Lady Russell had undoubtedly hoped that this last blow would finally cause them to part; she was mistaken. After a despondent conversation, Alys convinced Russell that she did not want children: they should marry, but undertake to produce no offspring. Russell, who wanted children, finally agreed, possibly helped by Carpenter's words about self-control being preferable to the 'child-bearing function of sex'. The only horror that now remained was that of contraception, which Lady Russell considered almost as bad as the marriage itself, and which Dr Anderson hinted had probably been the cause of Lord Amberley's epilepsy in the first place. Alys was furious when she received a letter from Anderson saying that he considered what they were proposing 'so unhallowed and unnatural . . . very probably highly injurious to both of you, mentally, morally and physically', and she attacked Lady Russell to her grandson: 'thy grandmother is neither Fate nor Destiny, but only an old lady who leaves no stone unturned to get her own way.' Russell, disgusted and depressed by the whole subject, and haunted by the idea of insanity as he was to remain on and off all his life, with repeated dreams about being murdered by a lunatic, resolved to stay away from Pembroke Lodge, which was now filled with 'sighs, tears, groans and morbid horror'. Having come down from Cambridge with a first-class degree with distinction, he moved into Friday's Hill House, and settled down to work on his Fellowship dissertation on non-Euclidean geometry.

There was a truce. Lady Russell was persuaded that insanity was a very unlikely outcome for any children they produced, while Alys and Russell agreed to part for three months. After that, if they were still resolved on marriage, Lady Russell conceded that she would not stand in their way. Russell felt he had no choice. He accepted an offer to become an honorary attaché to the ambassador to Paris, Lord Dufferin, only to receive shortly after an invitation that 'would have been 1000 times more interesting', to become private secretary to Lord Morley, the Liberal statesman and biographer of Gladstone, who was then chief secretary for Ireland. Consoling himself with the thought that the Paris embassy might at least provide him with an intriguing glimpse of diplomatic life, he agreed to leave for Paris early in September – but for three months only. After his departure, Lady Russell took to her sick bed, saying mournfully that she was near death, leaving Agatha – nicknamed by Frank and Russell as 'HP' or 'human perfection' – to keep Russell informed of her health. Agatha seldom missed an opportunity to increase his sense of guilt: 'Granny is much less well again', she wrote on 30 October: 'Bad nights, pain and weakness ... I'm certain [she] will be medically ordered never to touch on painful subjects.'

Russell's job in Paris turned out to be extremely tedious. It consisted in copying out long dispatches about fish; when he complained that this involved persuading the French government that a lobster was not a fish, the French replied that it had been a fish at the time of the Treaty of Utrecht in 1713. After two weeks in an hotel, he was given two rooms, one with a washstand, a sofa that turned into a bed and a spirit lamp. It made him feel as if he were back at Cambridge, a sensation he encouraged by setting to work on a dissertation on ethics for the Apostles, whom he was greatly missing, and a paper on space. To Alys, he wrote one of his more self-satisfied and buttoned-up letters: 'Intellect is a great safeguard, because it makes one's passions more abstract and less ephemeral ... It is lucky for us that my mind is not more concrete and artistic and pictorial ... all my thoughts being about abstractions, my passions too are very abstract, and it is often surprising to me to find how my love for thee is reinforced by several highly abstract passions – the love of sanity, of health, of independence, in women especially . . .'

Away from the embassy, his life was not without pleasure. It was a time of military and civil splendour. If he was not invited to many diplomatic parties at the embassy, he enjoyed his occasional lunches with Lord and Lady Dufferin – he referred to the ambassador as a 'charming humbug' and reported that Lady Dufferin was '*atrociously* dressed in a sort of grey serge' – and rode his bicycle happily in the

Bois de Boulogne. He also met some remarkable people, including Mallarmé and Whistler, though he did not take to the French, explaining in a letter to Edward Marsh that this may have been because they were unchaste.

Early in November he was in touch with Mary, Alys's sister, now estranged from Frank Costelloe and involved in an affair in Paris with the art historian, Bernard Berenson. As his admiring letters home revealed, he was delighted with her company, describing at length how they talked metaphysics together, though some at least may have been written with the intention of making Alys jealous. 'She is so nice and emotional that she fits my present life to perfection,' he wrote to Alys on 8 November. 'But I shan't succeed in falling in love with her, because every now and again one hits a hard rock of strong selfishness beneath her silken exterior wh. gives one a bit of a shock.' Just the same, he and Mary exchanged kisses, of a scarcely fraternal kind, and shared a sitting room in the same hotel. Mary was not an altogether likeable figure, being exceedingly selfish and a meddler.

There is something revealing, and not entirely sympathetic, about Russell's letters to Alys from Paris. On some days he wrote twice. Gone were the tentative overtures, the openness to influence. Though often very loving, Russell was now the more forceful partner in their relationship. Advice, admonitions, gentle scoldings, exhortations for the future, sometimes phrased in critical and even pompous tones, poured into Grosvenor Road. Not all of them can have been easy to take. The first of these letters was written from Pembroke Lodge, after they had parted and shortly before he left for Paris; the others are from France:

Sep 3 1894: . . . I have a passion for experience, but if I am to make anything of the talents I have, I must eschew a vast deal of possible experience, shut myself up in my study . . . Casual experience of life is of very little use to a specialist, such as I aspire to be; good manners are *absolutely* useless . . .

Oct 7 1894: Kissing thy breasts (since thee has written it) was certainly physical, in the sense that the feeling was the direct consequence of a physical act – but of course the distinction of physical and mental is a purely popular and inaccurate one which eludes one as soon as one tries to make it precise . . . It is the only definitely sexual thing we have yet experienced . . . I believe a *purely* physical experience could give us no considerable pleasure . . .

Oct 8 1894: . . . Thee has a particularising mind, which cares nothing for principles . . . mine is the other way round.

Oct 16 1894: . . . I think my intellectual honesty is fairly trustworthy, though it is the very hardest thing in the world to acquire – but I have in great strength the intellectual passion . . . it is no temptation to avoid pain at its expense, because it is much stronger than the love of happiness.

Oct 15 1894: . . . Don't be afraid I'm going to try and make thee into an abstract thinker wh. thee isn't by nature – I was only thinking that thee probably knows thyself less than I know myself . . . and that if thee ever got a taste of the joy of thinking . . . thee might wish to have some hours every day for bookwork of a historical or economical kind.

Nov 22 1894: . . . I am glad thee has been thinking about religion . . . I cannot get over a sort of contempt for a Xtian in our generation, and it is annoying to feel that about thee.

Though complaining occasionally that his letters sounded like 'brains in the abstract', Alys was extraordinarily good-tempered, on paper at least, replying to his barbs about Mary that she was glad that her sister was making the time pass for him. 'I never mind *thy* criticism, dearest . . .' In private, she often felt desolate. 'I am so afraid I shall not be able to make B. happy,' she wrote in her diary on 9 November. 'I am so dull. Cried'; and three days later: 'Felt depressed and teary'. Many years later, under the heading 'Sense of Sin', she confided in her diary that she had always suffered from an 'overdeveloped sense of sin . . . If blamed, I at once think I must be wrong . . . even when I *know* I am right, I often *feel* I am wrong . . .'

For all his strictures, however, Russell clearly missed her, saying that she was the only person with whom he always felt safe from anything 'rasping'. When his grandmother managed to upset Alys with her coldness and criticisms, he wrote consolingly, adding however that he was certain what he was doing was right, and that had he not obeyed Lady Russell he would have felt remorse all his life. To give him his due, when many years later he looked back over these early letters, he marvelled that Alys had been able to endure his conceit.

Towards the middle of his stay, Frank appeared in Paris. Together they went to see Sarah Bernhardt, dined at Lapérouse, and discussed

women, morality and casuistry. 'I *shall* be glad when he goes', Russell
wrote to Alys, saying that Frank gave him a sense of perpetual
discomfort, like wearing a hairshirt. 'I hate him and half fear him –
he dominates me when he is with me because I dread his comments
if he should know me as I am.' But he did not prevent himself telling
her that he did not feel his brother had really taken to her, finding
her hard and not sensual, and passing on a remark of Frank's: 'He
says American women only love from the waist up.'

When the three months were up, he returned thankfully to
England, where he spent the remaining few days of separation in
Cambridge, delighting in being back with the Apostles; after which
Russell and Alys set about planning their wedding, though Alys had
already made most of the arrangements. Both, in fact, had much to
get away from: Russell from an intrusive family and an oppressive
adolescence, which continued to haunt him; Alys from her domineering mother and Mary, under whose judgemental hand she had
lived for so long and whose morals, in her affair with Berenson and
her behaviour towards her children, she deplored. In an unpublished
memoir, written in old age, she recorded how hopelessly inferior she
had always felt to Mary, with the result that 'I became a terrible prig,
and my unselfishness, rather ostensibly displayed, had always dogged
my actions.' At every turn it is hard not to feel sympathy for Alys.

Lady Russell still had one more shot to fire: that of causing as
much muddle as she could over the date of the wedding. Alys and
Russell had chosen 14 December, partly for the sentimental reason
that it marked the anniversary of his first proposal, and partly
because Alys had decided to run for office as a vestrywoman in
Westminster. The election fell on the fifteenth and to qualify she
needed British nationality, which she would automatically acquire on
marrying Russell. But Lady Russell decided the day was unsuitable
because it was also the anniversary of Prince Albert's death. With
some irritation, they agreed to the thirteenth. A dispute then broke
out over the wording of the 650 invitations, the Pearsall Smiths
objecting to the use of 'The Hon.', the Russells, in a series of chilly
letters, pointing out that it was more correct. Lady Russell's health
was made the excuse for having no reception. Finally, Frank
Costelloe said he would not allow his daughters, Ray and Karin, to

be bridesmaids, because their mother Mary, from whom he was now separated, was due to attend.

During the late autumn, presents poured into Grosvenor Road: 216 in all, from marmalade dishes to travelling clocks, from cushions to silver sugar tongs. Roger Fry sent one of his paintings, Frank Costelloe a desk, Lady Russell a silver teapot, cream jug and sugarbowl and a complete set of the Waverley novels.

Because the Pearsall Smiths were Quakers, the ceremony was to be in the Friends' Meeting House in St Martin's Lane. Alys apologised repeatedly to Russell for having a religious ceremony, but neither her family nor convention would have tolerated anything else, and the Quaker service was very easy on an agnostic like Russell, since there was no need for him to profess beliefs he no longer held. Even so, he wrote rather ungraciously to Alys on 23 November: 'Don't imagine I really *seriously* mind a religious ceremony – *any* ceremony is disgusting, and the mere fact of having to advertise the most intimate thing imaginable is loathsome to me.'

The night before the wedding Alys and Russell went out canvassing for her election, then met next morning at the Friends' Meeting House. Alys was wearing an engagement ring of a diamond and rubies which had been made from an old (and very ugly) bracelet of Lady Amberley's, a fawn velvet dress, trimmed with white silk and gold, designed for her by her temperance work patroness, Lady Henry Somerset – Lady Russell protested bitterly that she was not in white – and a white felt hat with ostrich feathers. She carried no flowers. Russell looked very young, with his hair parted to one side and rising to a quiff on the right, a shaggy moustache and bright eyes. A friend of Alys's described him as 'pretty ugly to begin with . . . but very, very nice, I think, and very, very clever, I suppose'. The Pearsall Smiths turned out in force; the Russells in rather smaller numbers, with Lady Russell, Agatha and Rollo all absent and Lady Stanley using the silent pauses in the Quaker ceremony to drop her stick and shawl. Frank was best man, and he and Robert Pearsall Smith acted as witnesses. When it was all over, Alys and Russell left for a honeymoon in Holland, where they planned to skate on the canals.

It was not altogether an easy start to a marriage. Russell was twenty-two, shy but extremely self-possessed; orderly, but also a bit priggish and mannered; a young man with an exceptionally clear idea about his intellectual future and the life he intended to pursue, and entirely satisfied that intellect and abstract thought governed his mind, rather than passion. Alys, at twenty-seven, was emotional, a bit humourless, conscientious and accustomed to a great deal of company, saying that her ideal home was a 'sort of hotel'. She was probably reaching the end of some kind of crisis of faith, for by now Russell had been working on her for some years to abandon her Quaker beliefs; he maintained that they represented a barrier to all social and intellectual progress, though he remained half hopeful of finding in pantheism a 'finer, a far more inspiring faith'. Although she was less able than he to live without certainties, preferring the clarity of a decision to the unease of constant questioning, Alys capitulated. 'Lost my religion when I married BR', she wrote in the margins of a profile of her in *Christian Age* in 1906.

Neither knew anything about sex, and each had professed disgust at the idea of it. Alys was convinced that women could enjoy making love only 'psychologically', while Russell continued to point out that the very slightest difference of opinion between them was enough to make him not even wish to kiss her. After the honeymoon, he complained that he had found Alys's heavy flannel nightdresses most unappealing. He added, however, that both of them had been able in the end to regard the whole experience not as embarrassing but as extremely comical.

It was not cold enough to skate in Holland, but after three weeks in the Twee Steden Hotel in The Hague, taking long walks in storms and gales along the beach at Scheveningen, they moved on to Berlin, to the Hotel Windsor, where they went skating on a sunny, frosty day. Berlin was full of new buildings. They walked everywhere, and went to the opera and concerts. Russell was still uncertain whether to pursue philosophy or the family career of politics, so he enrolled to read economics at Berlin University and settled down to work on his Cambridge Fellowship thesis. Alys, who had never found inactivity easy, decided to carry out an investigation into the status of women in the German Social Democratic Party, and she persuaded

Russell to accompany her to some of their gatherings. Both became intrigued with the idea of writing a book on the party, still more so since they found themselves ostracised by the British diplomatic community after Alys had revealed to the ambassador that she had been to a socialist meeting. Russell wrote to his grandmother that he could not stand the sight of a Prussian officer, because he felt such fury about Prussian militarism and Alsace Lorraine.

It was now that Russell had one of his momentous flashes of understanding, when his entire life appeared to open out before him. Walking one day in the Tiergarten, thinking about Hegel and about the future, he suddenly became convinced that he should devote his life to producing two strands of work, the first a series of books on the philosophy of the sciences, the second a parallel series on social questions. His idea, which he held to for most of his life, was that the two might eventually meet in a 'synthesis at once scientific and practical'. A young American writer and reporter, Hutchins Hapgood, a friend of Berenson's, was in Berlin at the same time as the Russells, and he described the impression Russell made on him: '. . . he gave me a feeling of intense mental life almost unrivalled in my experience. Ideas simply leaped from him; he bubbled with thick-coming fancies. He excited me like a strong drink or a beautiful woman.'

In March, the Russells moved on to stay with Mary, who was now living near Berenson outside Florence. Berenson was Jewish, of Lithuanian descent, and had grown up in Boston. Aged twenty-five, he was a year younger than her, and two or three inches shorter; but he was a good-looking man, with dark curly hair and grey eyes set wide apart. He talked about poetry, music and the Renaissance, which had so captivated him that he intended to settle in Italy. Mary had been overwhelmed and soon, leaving her children and quarrelling bitterly over their future with Costelloe, she had followed him to Florence, an ideal city for an illicit relationship, with its large expatriate community of eccentrics and amusing people passing through.

Russell had met Berenson at the embassy in Paris, when he had lent the runaway couple £100, and had professed himself charmed by the American. At the Villa Rosa in Fiesole their relationship was tested by the extreme difference in their tastes. The days were spent in excursions to art galleries, churches and private collections; in the evenings they read aloud to one another, or took parts in *Prometheus Unbound*, while Russell obediently read his way through Berenson's first book, *The Venetian Painters of the Renaissance*. He felt no more drawn to art, though he admitted that he was making progress in understanding aesthetics. Berenson, for his part, made little effort in Russell's direction, telling Mary that he considered philosophy a 'pursuit for pretentious muddle-headed fools: it leads nowhere, and it is a sheer waste of time.'

But the two men enjoyed each other's company, Berenson reporting to Bob Trevelyan that the Russells had left behind them 'a very sweet odour . . . I liked him better and better. His mind is exquisitely active. True it has as yet perhaps not gone beyond picking up one moss-grown stone after the other to see what is under it but that by itself is perfectly delightful . . . Mrs R improves on acquaintance. She has wit and good intentions . . .'

Alys and Russell were getting on extremely well, though Mary, who overheard their frequent laughter, could not refrain from recording maliciously in her diary: 'Poor Alys gets *so* bored and sleepy with all these talks and readings and keeps continually looking at her watch and tries to cheer herself up looking at other things.' From Florence the Russells travelled down the Adriatic coast, stopping at Pesaro, Urbino, Ravenna, Rimini and Ancona, bathing naked in the sea, and lying on the sand to dry. 'This remains', recalled Russell in his autobiography, 'one of the happiest moments in my life.'

They returned to England so that Russell could finish his Fellowship dissertation and went to live at Friday's Hill. It was here that Russell experienced one of his first moments of intellectual euphoria. Since what he was seeking – and was to go on seeking – was certainty, he was examining the foundations of geometry, and considering Kant's question: 'How is geometry possible?' 'I fully believed', he wrote later, 'that I had solved all philosophical questions connected with the foundation of geometry.' It gave him an extraordinary feeling of jubilation.

In August, his thesis was sent to Cambridge. Two months later,

Russell set off to hear the results. Since the dissertation was part philosophy, part mathematics, it had gone both to Whitehead and to his old tutor, James Ward. Before the verdict was announced, Whitehead suddenly informed Russell that he disagreed with many of the points he had made. Plunged into gloom, Russell became convinced that his work was worthless and his chances of winning the prize Fellowship negligible. 'Adieu to sweet dreams', he wrote to Alys.

Alys then went to Cambridge so that she could be with him to hear the results. She described the scene in a letter to a friend: 'It was announced today and we watched it all from Bertie's window. The Master and Examining Fellows wrangled about it for three hours and a quarter – then they marched across the court in the rain, old Sidgwick running after (he always runs, it's good for his liver) to the Chapel ... There the Holy Ghost revealed the names of the four Fellows, and these were announced to an expectant crowd waiting in the drizzling mist outside. Of course, we could only see the excitement, not hear anything, but Bertie's friends soon came rushing over to tell him.' Russell, unable to understand what had happened, went off to see Whitehead, who told him, smiling, that he had thought this the last chance anyone would have of finding real fault with his work.

During the first years of their marriage, the Russells were always on the move. With the Fellowship secure, they returned to Berlin, as they had decided to study the Social Democrats in some depth. Russell was particularly drawn to them after reading Engels's claim that its supporters were the true descendants of the German classical philosophers. Like similar parties in other European countries, its members were basically Marxist. For six weeks, they spent their time almost entirely with the Social Democrats, whom Russell called 'fiery revolutionaries', going to meetings – about trade unionism, transport, hospitals and even the city lighting – in vast, crowded halls, with mounted police outside and much singing of the 'Marseillaise'. As a woman, Alys sometimes found herself excluded, but as general secretary of a branch of the women's temperance movement she addressed some meetings herself, telling her audience that she was bringing greetings from English working women.

It was an extraordinary time to be in Germany, and Alys kept a diary of their stay; like Russell's earlier notebooks, it is all about politics and work, with no mention of friends, food, art or culture. The autumn was marked by growing hostility between socialists and the government, with repressive measures constantly being passed against the socialists. Towards the end of November, the Berlin chief of police closed down eleven Social Democratic clubs. Through friends the Russells met August Bebel, the socialist member in the Reichstag, and Wilhelm Liebknecht, the friend of Marx, Engels and Lassalle. They were still there when Liebknecht was sent to jail for 'lèse-majesté', after giving a rousing speech which the government considered critical of the emperor. The kaiser, for his part, said that the socialists were a 'traitorous rabble unworthy to bear the name of Germans'. Having collected their material, and agreeing that Russell would write the bulk of the book and Alys would do a concluding chapter on women, they set off back to London, spending Christmas at The Hague on the way.

The result of their two months in Germany, followed by extensive reading on their return to London, was a series of six lectures at the London School of Economics and Political Science, which had recently been founded by Beatrice and Sidney Webb, each lecture forming one chapter of the book as well as a talk to the Fabian Society in Clifford's Inn. Russell was a nervous speaker, and had to be coached by a friend on replying to questions.

It was a good moment to be writing and talking about Germany, which was attracting much curiosity and interest. The Russells' book, *German Social Democracy*, described the intellectual origins of the socialists, analysed Marx and Lassalle, and urged both socialists and the German government to adopt a moderate, constitutional path. The *Communist Manifesto*, Russell declared, was one of the best pieces of political literature ever written 'for terse eloquence, for biting wit, and for historical insight'. But he disagreed with Marx's theory on the concentration of capital, saying that the state should take over industries not simultaneously and at a single blow but one by one as they reached the monopoly stage. Where the German socialists had gone wrong was in losing all 'sense of what was practicable from moment to moment'.

The book was widely reviewed and most of the notices were flattering, *The Times* saying that it had 'insight and judgement', and adding that Alys's chapter, on German women, was 'sensible'. One of the few sour notes came from William Dawson, an expert on German affairs, who complained in the *Economic Journal* that Russell had shown bad taste in branding the emperor a 'puppet of the police'.

German Social Democracy is among Russell's least known and least read books: years later, he dismissed it as something written when 'I was too young to realise what they would be like when they acquired power.' But it did provide evidence of a fluent, readable prose style, employed on a wide canvas and full of the prophetic warnings that were to become a hallmark of his later popular books, and it did say something about his early political beliefs. Russell considered himself a socialist, of a liberal sort, and his interest lay in working out how a social reform movement could adjust its means to achieve its ends.

By the time it appeared, Russell and Alys were in America, so that he could meet more of her family. It was the first of nine visits Russell was to make over more than fifty years, and the beginning of a passionate but ambivalent attitude towards its inhabitants, which had its roots in adolescent admiration for Jefferson and Paine. It was to end in a hatred so intense that in his last years Russell came to compare the Americans to the Nazis.

In 1896, however, Russell set out for the New World full of hope. He liked the Americans he had met at Friday's Hill, finding them refreshingly free of prejudice, and he wanted an opportunity to lecture further on the foundations of geometry. He had excellent references from H. Montagu Butler, the Master of Trinity, James Ward and Henry Sidgwick, and Alys had written to her first cousin, Dr Carey Thomas, the president of Bryn Mawr, the women's college in Pennsylvania, and to her uncle, who had connections with Johns Hopkins, the men's university in Baltimore. There were no difficulties with Bryn Mawr, Carey Thomas being a forceful and autocratic woman, but it took some time to secure an invitation from Johns Hopkins, where the board complained that they had never heard of Russell, and Thomas Craig, the editor of the *American Journal of*

Economics, dismissed the suggestion as a 'sort of dilettante affair at best'. His contempt shows how little known Russell was beyond his immediate British circle.

The Russells started their trip in New Jersey, with a visit to Walt Whitman's house. Whitman, now dead, had been a close family friend of the Pearsall Smiths; he had once said of Alys that she was the 'handsomest, healthiest, best balanced young woman in the world known to me'. From there, they moved on to stay with a cousin, Bond Thomas, manager of a glass factory in a small manufacturing town called Millville, where Thomas's wife Edith carried a revolver and took Russell for drives in a buggy. They reached Bryn Mawr, where Russell found himself less intimidated than anyone else by Carey Thomas – he referred to her as 'Zeus' – largely because he found her so easy to shock; he complained that her dinner parties were like committee meetings.

He delivered his lectures on non-Euclidean geometry, and on socialism and the ways in which state action could increase individual liberty. To the gratification of his hosts, he pronounced Bryn Mawr greatly superior to Newnham and Girton, in that it gave its students considerable freedom. Alys, meanwhile, gave talks on temperance, women's suffrage and free love. These caused acute embarrassment, which failed to bother her: though shy in private, she was unexpectedly intrepid when it came to public appearances, and the Russells' unconventional attitudes and tendency to speak out boldly on any subject provoked Carey Thomas a great deal.

Russell renewed his friendship with Helen Thomas, Carey Thomas's younger sister, whom he had met in Paris when he was at the embassy and she had been visiting France with a friend, Lucy Donnelly. Both women were to play important parts in his life, but it was Helen, struggling to make a career of teaching in the face of repeated ear infections which threatened deafness, who now attracted him. She had not greatly taken to Russell in Paris, finding him conceited and prone to generalise, but in America she liked him better; he was captivated by her gentle manner and splendid red hair. Helen was soon reporting to a friend: 'Bertie I find full of queer contradictions, and it grieves me to say so, of monstrous unexpected prejudices ... But at bottom he is really charming, I think, and I suspect that there is a bit of modesty hidden away in his nature, though awfully hidden!' Alys, she added, was distinctly in Russell's shadow: 'To outsiders she seems really to be a slave. It's quite tragic, I think. I keep wondering whether Bertie is worth it, and how long it will last . . .'

The trip ended in Boston, with a visit to William James, whose *Principles of Psychology* Russell had recently read and admired, noting in the margins of his copy, next to James's description of a 'non-visualiser', 'This would do for a description of my own case, except in the case of childish memories, and a few others of strong emotional interest.' What he thought of James's new book, *The Will to Believe*, which emphasised religion as a cure for the 'moral sea-sickness' of the age, is not known. In Boston Russell also met another young woman who appealed to him, a very beautiful girl called Sally Fairchild, from one of Boston's old families.

He left America intrigued by what he had seen. He had found the people curiously innocent – several asked him what Oscar Wilde had done – and lacking in political maturity and courage, but he had come to admire their intelligence and their great regard for education. What was more, his travels around American academia had challenged his insularity and made him realise that Cambridge was not, after all, the only seat of true learning in the world. Much that was important was going on elsewhere.

Earlier that year, the Russells had moved into a workman's cottage in Fernhurst, a mile and a half from Friday's Hill, called the Millhangar, to which they had added a sitting room and two bedrooms. Water came from a well in the garden, and had to be carried in and heated for the tin hip-bath; the earth closet was at the end of the garden. Cambridge University Press was about to bring out his rewritten dissertation as a book, under the title *An Essay on the Foundations of Geometry*. Russell was later to dismiss this too, saying that it was much too Kantian and 'somewhat foolish', but *Science* praised the author's 'mathematical equipment' as 'refreshingly sound' and his metaphysics as 'delightfully suggestive.' The book prompted an admiring letter from the French philosopher of mathematics and later Leibniz scholar, Louis Couturat, who told him that since he knew no English he had been forced to work his way through 'armé d'un dictionnaire'. His letter marked the start of a long correspondence in French, for Russell's written French was excellent, which lasted until Couturat was killed by a lorry during the mobilisation of 1914.

The success of his Fellowship dissertation had convinced Russell that his future lay unquestionably in mathematics and philosophy, and not in politics. He was now prepared to settle down in The Millhangar, for what was to prove a happy stretch of his life, and to start work on what was to become *The Principles of Mathematics*. Happy, that is, at the time; later, Russell said it had been the wrong kind of happiness, 'associated with hardness and conceit and limitation', and that the real value of this peacefulness lay only in the fact that it had been a 'rest to nerves'.

In January 1898 Lady Russell died. Both Agatha and Rollo were too ill with flu to be with her, but she had a nurse and the housekeeper at her side. Her coffin was covered, in the tradition of her family, by red cloth, and she was cremated in the Duke of Bedford's private crematorium. Her ashes were taken to the Bedford vault in Buckinghamshire.

Looking back on his childhood, Russell judged that he owed much to her fearlessness, public spirit and contempt for convention. He had also been fond of her, and was relieved that he had fallen in with her wish that he and Alys separate for three months before their marriage even though the whole episode had caused so much anguish. After their marriage, Lady Russell tried to be pleasant to Alys, but, since she prided herself on her scrupulous honesty, she was prone to make disconcerting remarks. Praising a photograph of her grandson in a letter to Alys, she had remarked of a similar portrait of Alys: 'As for you, we don't like you, and I hope Bertie doesn't, neither pose, nor dusky face, nor white humpy tippet . . .'

In April, Robert Pearsall Smith also died, and the Russells spent some months at Friday's Hill. Russell was finding Hannah harder and harder to bear. He had been shocked, while Robert was still alive, to hear Hannah discuss her husband's love affairs openly with her daughters, picking snippets of letters out of the wastepaper basket to read aloud, and he now began to see her not just as cruel and dishonest but as a profoundly bad influence on Alys. When

Oscar Wilde went on trial, she advocated castration as the 'only effectual remedy I know'.

Logan, too, was beginning to try him. Russell blamed Hannah for making her son malicious and frivolous, a process he considered had begun when Logan was three and had done something bad, and Hannah had whipped him until he was black and blue, without being able to make him repent. 'He has a passion to be first rate and says other people's good work makes him miserable,' Russell wrote, himself descending to a touch of malice, 'It is unfortunate for him, as he will obviously not get it satisfied.' For his part, Logan complained that he found Russell and Aly's love-making 'rather mildly disgusting'. Yet Russell was still impressed by Logan's knowledge of the arts, and agreed to contribute to a journal privately printed by Logan under the title *The Golden Urn*.

Using the name Orlando, Russell was asked to reply to some questions about his 'own sensations', and what things in life 'came to him most vividly and appealingly'. There is something revealing in his answers however light his tone. 'I am quite indifferent to the mass of human creatures,' he wrote, 'though I wish, as a purely intellectual problem, to discover some way in which they might all be happy . . . I live most for myself . . . I often wish to give pain, and when I do, I find it pleasant for the moment. I feel superior to most people . . . I wish for fame among the expert few, but my chief desire . . . is a purely self-centred desire for intellectual satisfaction about things that puzzle me.'

It was true that at this stage Russell and Alys were still close. An excellent portrait of them at the time is to be found in Beatrice Webb's diaries. 'The Russells are the most attractive married couple I know,' she wrote after spending a day with them. 'Young and virtuous, they combine in the pair personal charm, unique intelligence, the woman having one, the man the other, in superlative degree . . . She is charming to look at – tall, graceful, with regular features, clear skin, bright blue eyes and soft curly nut-brown hair, always smiling, often laughing, warm hearted and sympathetically intelligent . . . She has no art of flirtation . . . She has no moods . . . She seems always happy and grateful for happiness and yet perpetually thinking how to make others happier . . . If she has a defect it is a certain colourlessness of intellect and a certain lack of "temperament" . . .

'Bertrand is a slight, dark-haired man, with prominent forehead, bright eyes, strong features except for a retreating chin, nervous hands and alert quick movements . . . in speech he has an almost affectedly clear enunciation of words and precisiveness of expression. In morals he is a puritan . . . But intellectually he is audacious – an iconoclast, detesting religious or social convention . . . He indulges in the wildest paradox and in the broadest jokes, the latter always too abstrusely intellectual in their form to be vulgarly coarse. He is a delightful talker . . . fastidious with regard to friends and acquaintances. He dislikes bores and hates any kind of self-seeking selfishness or coarse-grainedness. He looks at the world from a pinnacle of detachment, dissects persons and demolishes causes . . . What he lacks is sympathy and tolerance for other people's emotions, and, if you regard it as an emotion, Christian humility . . . He is a good hater.

'. . . He is intolerant of blemishes and faults in himself and others, he dreams of Perfection in man. He almost loathes lapses from men's own standards . . . I have no "sense of sin" and no desire to see it punished. Bertrand, on the other hand, is almost cruel in his desire to see cruelty revenged.' A vivid portrait, and not exactly flattering: it is all there, the intolerance and cruelty, the detachment and lack of humility, the brilliant intellect and the yearning for perfection; even the love of 'broad jokes', though these qualities and failings would not manifest themselves to others clearly for some years to come. Beatrice Webb was always one of Russell's shrewdest critics.

At The Millhangar, Alys did all she could to provide him with the tranquillity he needed for his work, and in the evenings they read aloud to each other from Shelley's *Epipsychidion*, in memory of earlier days, as well as from Gibbon and Shakespeare, Schmöle and Maeterlinck. Visits to doctors had convinced them that fear of insanity in their children was nonsense. Russell had considerable misgivings, but they were of a different nature than before. 'I have been realising that I don't do enough for Alys,' he wrote in his diary of 8 March. 'But the thought of doing more is unbearable almost.

There is only one thing more that I can do, and that is children . . . that is what I must do.'

Alys was often away lecturing on temperance or suffrage with her mother or Lady Somerset, and Russell in Cambridge talking philosophy with his Apostolic friends, but when they were apart they continued to exchange fond letters. 'I agree with thee,' wrote Russell on one of these occasions, 'it is much worse being separated now than it was a year ago. I think at bottom we get fonder of each other – I do of thee, I know.' Russell's diaries and letters of the time are frequently at variance with each other, the diaries expressing an often intense dissatisfaction with himself, his work and his life in a way he was careful to keep out of his letters.

Alys had learned to bicycle, wearing what she called 'rational dress', consisting of loose Turkish trousers, a Zouave jacket and a broad sash tied around her waist. Visiting Italy to see Mary, she accompanied Russell on bicycle trips, taking with her a wraparound skirt for going through towns. Alys's legs were not her best feature, but she laughed when she overheard a man say 'Certe colonne di gambe!' (what columns of legs!) Russell loved these journeys, writing to Moore that Italy was 'the most perfect country ever invented' and that Venice was 'like Heaven, too good for morality. One has only to float lazily through the warm days and nights, and allow every sense to be perpetually steeped in the best things the world can offer it . . .' A strong vein of sensuality was coming to life; already it was beginning to lead to a serious crack in the wall of reason and intellect.

Now came the first signs of marital trouble. Sally Fairchild, the aristocratic girl from Boston, turned up at Friday's Hill, and Russell abandoned his reading to take long walks with her late at night. When, one day, Russell said, in front of Mary and Alys, that he had resigned himself to being *always bored* after the age of thirty, Alys foolishly asked: 'At home, too?'

'Especially at home,' replied Russell.

Four

Aristoteles Secundus

After just over three years of married life, much of it spent travelling, the Russells returned for part of their time to rented rooms in Cambridge. For Alys, this meant facing up to people in whose company she often felt insecure, with none of Friday's Hill's 'hotel' atmosphere and its casual crowd of political and artistic people. For Russell, it meant more regular contact with the Apostles, in an intellectual atmosphere which he still considered, for all his American discoveries, ideal for scholarly work.

To the long-standing habit of spending every Saturday evening talking together, and much of Sunday walking and talking, was now added a new Apostolic pleasure: reading parties. Largely Moore's idea, they took place during the Easter holidays, and Moore chose cottages in remote and rugged parts of the countryside where the fireplaces smoked but the walking and the views were superb. Women were seldom included: when they were, they seem to have been largely ignored. The Apostles were energetic walkers, but Bob Trevelyan was the most enthusiastic of them all, covering forty miles a day, with ease, at a great pace. In the evenings, when not reading to one another or talking, they played beggar-my-neighbour. These reading parties, remembered with great pleasure by all involved, were to last until the outbreak of the First World War. To be invited to take part was an honour, a proof of membership of the magic inner circle of the Apostles, and they provided another sign of Moore's emerging pre-eminence in the group.

Russell had first gone walking with Moore in May 1894, when

they were waiting for the start of their tripos. On a road in Norfolk one day they fell in with another traveller, who seemed keen to discuss Petronius, and in particular his bawdier tales. Russell egged him on. When they parted, Moore was at first silent, then burst out saying that the man had been one of the vilest people he had ever met. Russell, who in other circumstances might have been as repelled as Moore – though later in his life he was to acquire a taste for risqué jokes – reported to Alys smugly that Moore was too innocent and needed shaking up. Whatever the truth, it was clearly a setback to their friendship, and Russell cannot have been unaware of it. A letter to Alys includes a telling note of anxiety: 'Moore and I have arguments occasionally, but they are very amicable, and I have elicited from Moore that he laughs not at me, but with me, wh. is a great comfort.' But there was more of a rift than he suspected.

Of far greater importance to both of them was a shared change in philosophical direction. They put on one side whatever personal differences they felt and spent much time in discussion together. The first public sign that the two young philosophers were rebelling against idealism came in a paper written by Moore for *Mind*, called 'The Nature of Judgement', though some of his new thinking could already be seen in his dissertation on Kant. For Russell, the visible revolution occurred in a paper he read to the Apostles just before Christmas 1897 under the title 'Seems, madam? Nay, it is'. A second paper, 'The Constitution of Matter', read to the Moral Science Club, spoke of space as the ultimate nature of matter. What both were doing was breaking with the German idealism still dominant among Cambridge philosophers.

The idealists, who fell roughly into three groups, following Berkeley, Kant or Hegel, had in common the view that what would ordinarily be called the 'external world' is somehow created in the mind. Mind and spiritual values are thus fundamental in the world as a whole, and idealism is seen as the opposite of naturalism – that is to say, the view that both mind and spiritual values have emerged from material things and processes. The word comes from the Greek *idéa*, meaning something seen, or the look of something. Most of the nineteenth-century idealist philosophers in fashion in Cambridge agreed that utilitarians and individualists had a false view of what

constitutes an 'individual' person. Since individuals are formed by
their relations with one another, the notion of society as an association of independently existing individuals was perceived as absurd.
There was more to freedom, they claimed, than simply being left
alone by the government: insofar as government is concerned with
the common aim of individuals, it is not simply a constraint on them
but a manifestation of their most rational purposes.

Moore and Russell now agreed that this idealism, though capable
of splendid rhetoric, was in fact highly unsatisfactory. Both saw
idealism as being in conflict with something they believed to be more
certain than philosophy, Moore because he was a classical scholar
trained in the precise meaning of words, and because he was interested
in common sense, Russell because, as a mathematician schooled in
the exactness of reasoning, he was finding that their views made any
precise philosophy of mathematics impossible. Both agreed that there
is a real, objective world of which it is possible to have exact
knowledge, and that philosophy *could* give a new picture of the world
as a rational unity. Neither was opposed to metaphysics, but Russell
wanted to replace absolute idealism with a different system of
metaphysics, while Moore was more concerned with trying to establish
the meaning for the many surprising things said by other philosophers.
Philosophy, argued Russell, returning to the theme which had long
concerned him, should be more rigorously 'scientific' than even the
physical sciences. The idealists, with their loose and obscure propositions, could have no part in this. Nor could McTaggart, author of
the most rigorous metaphysical system of any British philosopher,
who concluded that reality was a society of immortal souls related by
love, that time and matter were unreal, and who held that wishes and
needs could influence philosophical enquiry. Both Moore and Russell,
however, found it easy to go along with McTaggart's pronounced
hatred of what he called 'woolliness', if not with his defence of
metaphysics for the emotional comfort it could yield.

Moore may not have been as fast and sharp as the others, but it
was his particular character, which was at once mild and unusually
strong, that made people listen to him, particularly when what he
was saying was so beguiling. When statements appeared to have no
meaning, Moore questioned them. He took propositions, one at a

time, and chewed them over again and again. The idealists were not accustomed to being asked why ordinary opinions and ordinary ways of speaking were defective. Moore's bafflement, his suspicion about theories and his claim not to be quite certain about the precise task of a philosopher, were, for many people, not only radical but liberating. Unlike Russell, Moore felt intuitively that philosophy could never be regarded as an aspect of science.

Chance took a hand by carrying McTaggart off to New Zealand to visit relations, leaving Russell to give McTaggart's lectures on Leibniz in his place. In the course of studying Leibniz, the seventeenth-century German who suggested that the basic task of the philosopher was to break down complex ideas into simple ones, and went on to seek a method of ultimately revealing the structure of the universe, Russell settled on 'absolute realism', which provided him with precisely the kind of structure and support he needed for the philosophy of mathematics he was moving towards. Taking from Leibniz the idea that there is a deep structure of syntax of grammar below that of the spoken or written language, he hoped that by reducing complex notions to their simple constituents he would lay knowledge of the world before his audience like a map. But he continued to differ from Leibniz in his belief that knowledge comes not from innate notions but from experience. Russell's flight from what he called 'the bath of German idealism' filled him with elation. He felt, he wrote later, 'a great liberation, as if I had escaped from a hot-house on to a wind-swept headland. I hated the stuffiness involved in supposing that space and time were only in my mind.' In rejecting Hegel, Russell felt the universe 'grow full'. Once again, it could contain not just tables and chairs, green grass, the sun and the stars, but the freedom to return to mathematics.

His method as a philosopher was now taking shape. While Moore's starting point was common sense, Russell's was instinct. As he put it later to Bradley: 'I don't know how other people philosophise, but what happens with me is, first, a logical instinct that the truth must lie in a certain region; and then an attempt to find its exact whereabouts in that region. I trust the instinct absolutely, though it is blind and dumb . . .' Rejecting idealism meant a new beginning in the search for truth. Unlike Moore, who was essentially conservative,

Russell was at his happiest as an iconoclast, destroying common sense and common beliefs.

For all their shared beliefs – a not inconsiderable bond, given that most of the other philosophers remained wedded to idealism – Moore and Russell now began to grow steadily further apart, with Moore becoming clearer in his views about the here and now and Russell keener to reject the Hegelian status quo and moving towards the day when he would say that 'common sense' was nothing but the 'metaphysics of the stone age'. Moore seems to have felt a combination of unease and irritation in his company, but there is no evidence that Russell had yet shed his vision of Moore as a genius. The fault for their growing estrangement may have been largely Russell's. Since returning to Cambridge, he had spent many Saturdays among the Apostles, giving his papers and commenting in a lively and forceful way on the papers of others, both those more frivolous in nature: 'Is it virtuous to wash?' and those which laid down a marker in the speaker's intellectual development. In these gatherings, there is no doubt that Russell, the quicker and wittier of the two, provoked the more painstaking and gentler Moore by his teasing, just as he irked Moore when he appeared to miss completely what he was trying to say. That year, 1899, the annual Easter reading party went to Gunnerside in Yorkshire. Desmond MacCarthy was there, as were Sanger and Bob Trevelyan; Russell was not.

In the autumn, when the Russells were back at The Millhangar, the Boer War broke out. Russell, who believed in the Empire but wanted it tempered by liberal values, was made so anxious by the possibility of British defeats that he walked four miles every evening after he had stopped work to buy the paper at the station. So strong was his sense of patriotism, at the time, he was later to observe, that he had felt as 'if someone were seducing a woman' he was in love with. Writing to his friend Couturat in France, with the sense of gloom and despair which was later to accompany all his pronouncements on war and conflict, he complained that he could no longer concentrate on his work. 'La philosophie ne me semble plus qu'un jeu d'enfant en comparaison des événements contemporains.'

*

It was only after his marriage that Russell really began to see A. N. Whitehead, who was twelve years his senior, as a friend rather than teacher, though he continued all his life to admire him for the care he took of his pupils, trying to bring out the best points from them and never resorting to sarcasm. Something of that earlier relationship was to persist even after they became collaborators, for it was in Russell's nature to need reassurance and encouragement, and in Whitehead's to give it. It was Whitehead, furthermore, who had given Russell a new perspective during his death throes with Hegelianism, showing him 'how to apply the technique of mathematical logic to this higgledy piggledy world'.

The son of a schoolmaster and clergyman from Kent, Whitehead had come up to Trinity in 1880 as a scholar. Four years later he was invited to join the Apostles, and that same year he won a prize Fellowship in the field of mathematics. He stayed on at Trinity, first as ordinary college tutor, then as full lecturer. What interested him was carrying out a detailed investigation into the systems of symbolic reasoning allied to ordinary geometry. *A Treatise on Universal Algebra*, a comparative study of the main algebraic systems, including symbolic logic, appeared in 1888.

When he was thirty, a bachelor deeply immersed in his teaching and research, contemplating a move from the Anglicanism of his childhood to Roman Catholicism, he met and married the daughter of a family of Irish landed gentry. Her name was Evelyn Wade, and she was a handsome woman, slightly taller than he and five years younger, with a strong face and almost black eyes. Where Whitehead was quiet, unassuming and the most modest of men – he was nicknamed the 'Cherub' at Cambridge – Evelyn was outgoing and volatile, and cared a great deal about the appearance of things. She had style. However, she considered mathematics unintelligible, and science of little interest; what she liked were people – her highest word of praise was 'gallant' – and beautiful things.

By the end of the 1890s, the Whiteheads had three children and had moved to Grantchester, three miles south of Cambridge, to a charming seventeenth-century white, two-storey farmhouse with a tiled roof, flowering creepers and a garden with yew trees. The surrounding country was flat and watery, but in May the meadows shone the colour of gold from the marsh marigolds. The Mill House stood on the edge of a pool, immediately below the mill itself. 'In the spring', wrote Whitehead many years later, 'nightingales kept us awake, and kingfishers haunted the river.' Grantchester was the perfect village for the Whiteheads, close enough to Cambridge for Whitehead to bicycle to Trinity and for Evelyn to conduct an energetic social life. When they went out together, she travelled in a basket trailer attached to his bicycle. The Mill House became something of a salon for the Apostles and clever dons from the university. Among the many visitors was Russell, whom Evelyn had first befriended when she defended him at the time of his Fellowship dissertation, scolding her husband for his churlish behaviour towards the young philosopher. Russell impressed the Whiteheads by his evident ease with children and the pleasure he took in bathing in nearby pools in the Cam, or riding tandem on Whitehead's bicycle with Jessie, his daughter, squashed between them.

By the spring of 1898 Russell had decided that he wanted to write a book on the foundations of mathematics. The subject had lost none of its charm for him: it provided not just intellectual fascination, but a way of seeing the world which he found comforting. Mathematics, as he explained later, 'rightly viewed, possesses not only truth, but supreme beauty, a beauty cold and austere, like that of sculpture, without any appeal to any part of our weaker nature, without the gorgeous trappings of painting or music, yet sublimely pure . . . The true spirit of delight, the exaltation, the sense of being more than man, which is the touchstone of the highest excellence, is to be found in mathematics as surely as in poetry . . . Real life is, to most men, a long second-best, a perpetual compromise between the ideal and the possible; but the world of pure reason knows no compromise, no practical limitations.' At Millhangar he started work, inspired by his rebellion against idealism and its negation of mathematics.

In the summer of 1900, with *A Critical Exposition of the Philosophy of Leibniz* about to appear – it was later praised as the best work ever written by one philosopher about another – and a growing reputation for his work on the axioms of geometry, Russell joined Alys and the Whiteheads on a trip to Paris to attend the First International

Congress of Philosophy. Both he and Alys were to give papers – he on space and time, she on the education of women and 'against family life' as Mary put it in a letter to Berenson – and this was followed by the Second International Congress of Mathematicians. The occasion was the intellectual turning point of his life.

He had gone to Paris in a state of irresolution about his mathematical book, satisfied with the philosophy that underpinned it but lacking an appropriate technique to reach the foundations of mathematics themselves. Among those attending the congress was Giuseppe Peano, professor of mathematics at Turin university, and the author of an important contribution to arithmetic, a set of axioms for the natural numbers. More importantly, Peano had just composed a new symbolism, which, extending that of existing algebra, provided a way of representing these foundations. Both Russell and Whitehead knew of Peano's work, and his journal, the *Rivista di Matematica*, but according to Russell they had not gone so far as to master his symbolism. Noting appreciatively how much quicker and more precise Peano was than any other speaker, Russell approached him and asked for copies of his works. When the congress was over, the Italian returned to Turin, where he turned his attentions to linguistics, while Russell hastened back to Millhangar and spent August reading all Peano's writings, an immense undertaking in itself, and September applying Peano's notation to the logic of relations in a paper which appeared in the *Rivista di Matematica*. Many years later, Russell was to say that Peano's method had 'extended the region of mathematical precision backwards towards regions which had been given over to philosophical disagreement'.

The two men corresponded in French, for Peano knew no English and Russell only a little literary and traveller's Italian. It was a time of extreme mental excitement. He was later to remember each day as warm and sunny, and his mind as agile and lucid as he went over every word written by Peano and his disciples. The Whiteheads came to stay and Russell explained his new ideas; the two men talked of how Peano's work seemed to mark a transition from the old algebra of logic to something new. 'Every evening the discussion ended with some difficulty,' he wrote in his autobiography, 'and every morning I found that the difficulty of the previous evening had solved itself while I slept. . . . My sensations resembled those one has after climbing a mountain in a mist, when, on reaching the summit, the mist suddenly clears, and the country becomes visible for forty miles in every direction.'

That autumn, while Whitehead went back to Trinity to teach, Russell wrote the bulk of the first draft of *The Principles of Mathematics*, producing ten pages a day; by the end of December he had written 200,000 words. His intention was to reject the fasionable view that mathematics was distinct from logic and to advance 'logicism' instead to prove that mathematics was part of logic and derivable from a number of fundamental principles which were themselves logical. A second volume was planned, giving a strictly mathematical exposition of his ideas, while the first laid down his philosophical foundations. Russell had come to the conclusion that there was a difference between seeing mathematics as a body of certain, objective knowledge and seeing it as a fundamentally subjective construction of the human mind. In a preface, he thanked Whitehead, who, as the author of *Universal Algebra*, was equally interested in the foundations of mathematics, for his suggestions and help. What *The Principles of Mathematics* had done was to provide a commentary and introduction to Russell's logicism written in ordinary English; what it had not done was to set out a formal argument worked out in symbols, and this was to be the second volume.

If these days of intense and dazzling work had been intellectually the happiest of his life, such as he was never to experience again, those which followed were correspondingly unsettling. It was not simply that the heady flight of creativity had come to an end for the time being; emotionally, he was about to plunge into confusion.

In the Lent term of 1901, the Russells and the Whiteheads had moved together into a house vacated by a professor from Downing who had gone abroad. They were all much concerned with Evelyn's health, for she was rapidly turning from an exuberant and lively woman into an invalid with chronic heart trouble.

Russell's cousin, Lady Mary Howard, had married Gilbert Murray, who was to become England's best-known and most popular Hellenist; a gentle, old-fashioned liberal, he had been given the chair of Greek at Glasgow University at the age of twenty-three. Murray saw it as his task in life to make the Greek poets and playwrights come alive for modern listeners and readers, and had begun retranslating some of the classics. By 1901, he was lecturing on Greek drama, and giving readings from some of his translations. That February, he came to Cambridge, to read his new version of *Hippolytus*. Alys and Russell attended the reading, and Russell wrote to Murray immediately afterwards to tell him how keenly he had felt the power of what he called a 'new masterpiece'. 'Your tragedy fulfils perfectly – so it seems to me – the purpose of bringing out whatever is noble and beautiful in sorrow; and to those of us who are without a religion, this is the only consolation of which the spectacle of the world cannot deprive us.' Murray was delighted. Russell's praise, he replied, 'made a sort of epoch in my life and in my way of regarding my work'.

These exchanges marked the beginnings of a friendship which would grow very close in the following years. More immediately, the reading of the *Hippolytus* was a crucial event in Russell's life, in that it provided a trigger, probably one of several, in an episode which has become known as Russell's 'conversion'.

After the Murray reading, the Russells went back to Downing to find that Evelyn had had what was assumed to be a heart attack; she was in such agony that she appeared to be completely cut off from the world. Taken together with the emotions he had experienced during *Hippolytus*, the sight of her suffering brought on some kind of mystical trance in Russell, which he described in one of the most famous and frequently quoted passages of his autobiography:

> . . . the sense of solitude of each human soul suddenly overwhelmed me. Ever since my marriage, my emotional life had been calm and superficial. I had forgotten the deeper issues, and had been content with flippant cleverness. Suddenly the ground seemed to give way beneath me . . . Within five minutes I went through some such reflections as the following: the loneliness of the human soul is unendurable; nothing can penetrate it except the highest intensity of the sort of love that religious teachers have preached; whatever does not spring from this motive is harmful, or at best useless; it follows that war is wrong, that a public school education is abominable, that the use of force is to be deprecated, and that in human relations one should penetrate to the core of loneliness in each person and speak to that.

Evelyn's younger son, Eric, who was three, much the same age as Russell when he lost his own mother, was with her when this seizure took place, and was clearly very upset. Russell led him away. It is impossible to say whether his own memory of loss and the trauma that followed were significant, as analyists have suggested, but it is clear that Russell himself believed that he emerged from the scene altered. He felt, he recorded later, suddenly far closer to his friends and far more understanding of their frailties; from having been a keen supporter of Empire, he turned into a pacifist; and having all his life thought chiefly about mathematics and the intellect, he now felt his whole nature drawn towards beauty, and the need to discover a new philosophy of life. 'A strange excitement possessed me,' he recalled later, 'containing intense pain but also some element of triumph through the fact that I would dominate pain, and make it, as I thought, a gateway to wisdom.' The question of pain, the role it played in man's life, was one that interested Russell all his life. His theory that evil, in the form of pain, was an ineradicable feature of the universe was to alternate with a feeling that there was already too much sorrow in life to require any more of it, and that self-control must be summoned to conquer it.

What, precisely, was this 'conversion'? From his adolescence at Pembroke Lodge, Russell had retained a heightened sense of his own solitude, while what he called his 'vain search for God' had led him in the direction, if not of Christian mysticism, at least towards a mystical vision which owed much to nostalgia for the past and to aesthetic feelings about poetry and nature. These in turn fed his sense of absolute isolation. The mystical crisis sparked by Evelyn's attack was too unusual and dramatic to last long and Russell was soon back in the fold of mathematical analysis, where he inevitably found comfort. However, something of the spiritual excitement of those new feelings entered his being and set what he was to call a 'new emotional tone'. Its first signs took the form of a resolve to bring some good into Evelyn's life and, as Whitehead's biographer Victor Lowe suggests, a gradual falling in love with her.

Russell believed he had seen a human being on the edge of death, in agony and condemned to ultimate loneliness and the imminent annihilation of the soul. In this he was wrong, for Evelyn's heart trouble, though undoubtedly painful, was not critical, and continued for the next sixty years. An assistant pathologist at St George's Hospital, who lived with the Whiteheads in the early 1920s and was present during one of her attacks, came to the conclusion that they were not cardiac in origin but hysterical. They were, of course, very real to Evelyn. She was lonely, or believed herself to be, for Whitehead, though clearly attached to her, was not a demonstrative man; worse, he preferred to spend every waking moment contemplating mathematics.

Lowe portrays Evelyn as a strong but not dislikeable woman, who resented her husband for condemning her to a grey academic existence rather than providing her with a colourful artistic one. She was also given to self-dramatisation. Perhaps unconsciously trying to build on the traumatic effect she knew her crisis had had on Russell, she told him that Whitehead was on the edge of insanity, spending his days in total silence or muttering in a way that frightened both her and the servants. Russell was sympathetic, particularly when he learned that one of Whitehead's obsessions was lack of money, and that he was perversely making matters worse by running up bills with Cambridge tradesmen.

One way in which Russell could be of assistance, in a secret 'alliance with her to keep him sane' as he later wrote, was to provide Evelyn with some money to keep the family solvent, leaving Whitehead to continue with his mathematical research. In an early draft of his autobiography, he claimed to have provided £8000, part of it capital, part of it money he was forced to borrow; but this figure was subsequently deleted, perhaps because Russell could not remember and had no way of checking, or because it seemed improbably large – though there was a new bedroom at Mill House to show for it. But there was no evidence for Whitehead's profligacy other than Russell's word, based on what Evelyn had told him. There remains something baffling about the whole episode, particularly since it was Evelyn, and not Whitehead, who ran Mill House and dealt with tradesmen. If he appeared extravagant when it came to books, it may simply have been that, having sold a valuable collection of religious books to a Cambridge bookseller, Whitehead was obliged to collect the money not in cash but books. It should be remembered too that it was Evelyn, not Whitehead, who enjoyed fine furniture and silver and dinner parties, though there were some complaints that while the table looked superb, there was seldom enough food on it, and the style of life she delighted in was not one readily managed on Whitehead's Cambridge salary. It is unlikely that anything more will come to light about the episode: Whitehead was a determined destroyer of papers and what he did not get rid of was thrown away by Evelyn, on his instructions, on his death in 1947. She also threw away Russell's letters to her.

After her collapse, the routine at Mill House, where they were again living, revolved almost entirely around her desires. The three children, Jessie, North and Eric, had a nanny, who spent some of her time looking after the invalid, so Alys took over some of her duties. That summer of 1901 Evelyn at last felt well enough to travel, and the Whiteheads and the Russells took a train to Venice in August, then boarded a steamer that stopped at every port down the Adriatic and up the Mediterranean to Genoa, before visiting the northern Italian cities. Before going on shore, Whitehead would study his Baedeker and read aloud information on the towns they were about to visit. Evelyn's headaches abated as she began to enjoy herself more. Beyond a few cards from Alys, no record exists of this trip, but it seems likely that Alys, with her sturdy literal-mindedness, was a decidedly less amusing companion than the frail and witty Evelyn.

However, there is no evidence that whatever there was between Evelyn and Russell ever turned into a love affair: any passion on his part would have been tempered by the fact that her husband was his former teacher and friend, and it was not in Evelyn's nature to be unfaithful beyond a light flirtation. Whenever it seemed that the two might find themselves alone together, Evelyn took a child along.

Russell never mentioned Evelyn by name as a woman he had loved. But much later, in a poem composed for Ottoline Morrell, he wrote 'Thrice have I loved . . .' The first was clearly Alys, and the third Ottoline, but the second stanza reads:

> Again I loved. Piercing the prison of flame,
> Where one stern soul in lonely anguish burned,

> Forgetting earth once more with love I came
> Into that hell whence no light hopes returned.

In a letter, also addressed to Ottoline Morrell, he was slightly more explicit, but still gave no name. In it he spoke of his love for a certain woman dying a 'gradual death for want of nourishment'. (Edith, Russell's last wife, believed that this 'second' love was not Evelyn at all, but Margaret Llewelyn Davies; but she seems to have been alone in thinking so.) For her part, as a few remaining letters indicate, Evelyn continued to think of Russell as a friend for the rest of her life.

Whether it was Russell or Whitehead who first proposed collaboration is not absolutely clear. In an article written for *Mind* in 1948, the year after Whitehead's death, Russell announced that since he was the only living witness to their agreement he wanted to put the record right. After their meeting in Paris with Peano, he said, 'I saw that methods analogous to his would clarify the logic of relations, and I was led to the definitions of cardinal, ordinal, rational and real numbers . . . Very soon Whitehead became interested. The prospect of deducing mathematics from logic appealed to him, and to my great joy he agreed to collaborate. I knew that my mathematical capacity was not equal to accomplishing this task unaided.' In this, he was correct: Whitehead was regarded by many as his intellectual superior when it came to ordinary mathematics, and was considered more adept at inventing logical notations.

Later, in *My Philosophical Development*, Russell returned to the question of their partnership, saying that Whitehead had invented most of the notation, apart from what they took from Peano, leaving the philosophical side to him. It was never altogether clear when Russell became aware that the main thrust of their endeavour had been anticipated by the German mathematician Gottlob Frege, perhaps the greatest figure in the history of mathematics, a genius but also a racist, and a surprisingly mild and genial man for all his self-importance, with a whiskery moustache and beard. In 1893, Frege had produced a much neglected work, the *Grundgesetze der Arithmetik*, which dealt with the very challenge Russell and Whitehead were now facing. Russell may in fact have been the first to appreciate Frege's importance.

According to Victor Lowe, the discussions about a possible joint venture between Russell and Whitehead started around September 1900, after which they began to see how they could merge their two streams of work: Russell's plan to provide a formal symbolism, a conceptual advance on *The Principles of Mathematics*, combined with what was to have been the second volume of Whitehead's *Universal Algebra*.

Whitehead estimated that *Principia Mathematica*, as their joint work came to be called, would take them 'a short period of one year'. He was totally wrong; it was to occupy them for much of the first decade of the century. They had set themselves an immense task, comprising, as they were to explain later when applying for a grant to the Royal Society, 'a complete investigation of the foundation of every branch of mathematical thought'. In their new mathematical logic, a number of different logical forms were to be distinguished, while certain relations between propositions, not expressible in Aristotelian logic, were to find expression. None of this could be done in haste.

Traditional logic, which had descended from Aristotle via the Scholastics and dealing with the individual rules of valid inference, was still central to the study of logic in British departments of philosophy. Throughout the nineteenth century, logicians had made some attempt to set these rules down in mathematical form, but what Whitehead and Russell proposed to do – as Frege had done – was to formulate a mathematically rigorous system with a new notation. Their intention was to devise the notation in such a way that it became possible to state not just the whole of logic but the whole of mathematics: it was to be more comprehensive than all that had gone before. Russell's brilliance as a logician lay not just in the way that he showed that there were many more forms of inference than Aristotle had found, but in demonstrating how little logic can do. 'As logic improves,' he said, 'less and less can be proved.' Furthermore, he insisted that all the knowledge provided by mathematics and logic is only hypothetical: it merely tells us that if something is true, then something else is true.

In the first months of their discussions, Russell was still at work on *The Principles of Mathematics*. The intellectual honeymoon had come to an abrupt close when Russell stumbled over a 'paradox'. Initially it seemed a fairly trivial point of logic, and less challenging than others he had worked on, but it threw him totally off balance, in that it invalidated not only his own work but that of his predecessors. Russell found that if you follow a certain path in reasoning you reach a contradiction. The paradox had to do with the notion of 'class', which Frege had defined as the extension of a concept. Russell's paradox, in simple terms, went like this: Take the class of all classes that do not belong to themselves. Does it belong to itself? Whether you answer 'yes' or 'no', you encounter a contradiction. This led him to conclude that in that case no such class exists, but the difficulty was to provide a satisfying and systematic account of the nature of classes which would ensure this result. Battling with his paradox, he was often in a state of extraordinary mental exaltation, writing to Alys, 'I have been so long without real work, that I have come back to it with a kind of fever: *everything* else seems unreal and shadowy to me just now and I work as if I were possessed . . .', 'formal Logic fills the crannies of my mind.'

It was not until the autumn of 1902, almost two years after their first discussions, that work on the joint project began in earnest, Russell perceiving it at least partly as a way of finding some resolution to the infuriating paradox. Whitehead was still fully occupied teaching at Cambridge, so much of the early work, the writing out of proofs, fell to Russell. Some of this had already been done by Frege, who had also set out to show that mathematics belongs to logic, but it was some time before Whitehead and Russell realised this, and time was wasted in re-inventing his work. In the meantime, Russell sat down to formulate for himself the premises of symbolic logic. The relationship between the two men remained at least partly that of teacher and student, with Whitehead spurring Russell on with support and encouragement, often in the form of telegrams. 'HEARTIEST CONGRATULATIONS ARISTOTELES SECUNDUS', he cabled, after one apparent breakthrough. But he could also be critical. 'Everything, even the object of the book,' he wrote sternly after an early draft on the logic of propositions, 'has been sacrificed to making proofs look short and neat. It is essential, especially in the early parts, that the proofs be written out fully.' Underneath the existing letter, Russell has written: 'Whitehead was quite right.' He sat down to amplify his draft.

In his article for *Mind*, written almost half a century later, Russell recalled that their relationship, during their entire collaboration, was 'completely harmonious', but in his autobiography he contradicts this, saying that throughout the writing of *Principia Mathematica*, 'my relations with the Whiteheads were difficult and complex.' For much of the time, he was trying to help sort out Whitehead's financial problems and act as his wife's confidant; Whitehead himself had to cope with Evelyn's occasional crises. But the working partnership between the two men seems to have been largely enjoyable. 'We had a great day of work, morning, afternoon and evening,' Russell wrote to Alys. 'Even after lunch we still worked. Much of the time we spent discussing whether the present King of France is bald . . . We finally decided that he isn't altho' he has no hair of his own. Experienced people will infer that he wears a wig, but this would be a mistake.'

As the book got under way, they shared out topics, each producing a first draft of his assignment before sending it to the other for revision, after which the original author would do further revision and editing. Many of their exchanges took place by letter. The 102 letters of Whitehead still in existence consist almost entirely of detailed mathematical analysis, while Russell's are more philosophical, dealing with such principles as Occam's Razor ('entities are not to be multiplied beyond necessity'), the paring away of ideas not ultimately necessary, never assuming this or that hypothetical entity if everything can be interpreted without it, and using it to lessen the number of undefined terms and unproved propositions required in any given body of knowledge. Occam's razor, he was to say, gave him a more 'clean-shaven picture of reality'. (It is known today to American philosophy students as Occam's 'eraser'.) But the two men also met on family holidays, at Trinity, in Mill House or at Fernhurst, where the Whiteheads at one point rented a cottage. The two couples often lived as paying guests in each other's houses. Of the two men, Whitehead was the more accurate and painstaking, saving Russell from hasty and even superficial solutions, while

Russell found ways of simplifying and clarifying Whitehead's denser passages.

The story of *Principia Mathematica* is probably best completed here. For most of the first six years, Russell continued the struggle to find a complete solution to the paradox which had plagued him in *The Principles of Mathematics* and which now continued to haunt him, in that any system he devised seemed to entail a contradiction. No other intellectual problem ever caused him such anguish. At times he thought he had found a solution, and sent euphoric telegrams to Whitehead; at others, he knew that the answer remained buried and he despaired that by trying to reduce mathematics to logic all that he was discovering were unresolved contradictions in logic itself. Whitehead continued to encourage him. On 23 April 1905, he began a letter with the words: 'Dear Bertie, Your work is admirable. I think you are in sight of land,' followed by ten pages of detailed comments. As the work progressed, the subject seemed always to expand, growing well beyond its earlier scope. Just how much Russell suffered during this interminable labour is clear from the letters he exchanged with a mathematician called Philip Jourdain, five years his junior, whom he got to know in the winter of 1901. Jourdain, who became editor of the *Monist*, was deeply interested in the history of mathematics, and asked Russell fundamental questions about his own understanding of the earlier mathematicians and the progress of his personal patterns of thought.

Day after day of mathematics made Russell even more critical of Cambridge undergraduate teaching, with its emphasis on manipulative skills rather than logical reasoning and insight. He continued to find mathematics 'capable of a stern perfection such as only the greatest art can show', as he wrote in *The Study of Mathematics*.

In the year 1905 Russell discovered his Theory of Descriptions, the first step in overcoming the difficulties of the paradox that had been plaguing him for so long. It was set out in a paper called *On Denoting*, which Russell submitted to the leading philosophical journal, *Mind*. In time, and certainly by the 1920s, it was recognised not only as one of Russell's most important contributions to logic – perhaps even the most important – but as one of the essential essays of twentieth-century philosophy. His theory was a doctrine about the relations between words and objects, and it arose partly as a reply to the Austrian philosopher Alexius von Meinong who had debated at length on the status of things which do not exist. Meinong had concluded that even if things like round squares did not exist, they must have some kind of being. Russell suggested that instead of saying 'the round square does not exist' one could say 'there is no entity which is both round and square'. Thus the phrase 'the round square' was removed from the sentence, and with it any cause for believing that it denotes something which has some kind of being. Russell distinguished between what is known directly by 'acquaintance', and what is known at second hand by 'description'. Where the Theory of Descriptions represented a fundamental advance was in Russell's idea that there might be many ways in which we could be misled by words and the form of sentences. If, at first, it appeared to some as simply a knack of saying the same things in different words, it soon became apparent that the Theory of Descriptions could provide a starting point for an entire new view of the universe.

On publication, Russell's new theory perplexed nearly everyone: it was extremely obscure, and entirely original. Moore was to say that he understood it only when Russell rephrased it later in the introduction to *Principia Mathematica*. When he did understand it, he called it Russell's 'paradigm of philosophy'.

This was Russell's first major advance in overcoming the difficulties of his paradox. The following year, 1906, he went on to the Theory of Types, in which he tackled the problem of self-reference, producing two versions, a simple and a 'ramified' one. He had at last found his solution: it lay in saying that self-determining statements are meaningless, and that we have to think of sets as constructed from the ground up. He found to his delight that, once it was seen that any statement referring to other statements must be of a higher order than the statements it is about, his paradox disappeared. Thus the class of all first order classes, which are not members of themselves, is a second order class – and it becomes nonsense to say of a class that it is, or is not, a member of itself. 'After this,' he wrote, 'it only remained to write the book out.'

It was not until 1907 that Russell started a final draft of *Principia Mathematica*, keeping the manuscript in a long row of box files.

Whitehead was once again teaching, so it fell to Russell to spend up to ten hours a day, for months on end, covering page after page with symbols. Most of the time he sat on a low pouffe, with the papers in a circle about him on the floor. 'I work 9 or 10 hours most days,' he wrote to a friend on Christmas Day, 'so that the rest of the day I am in a mere lethargy. Today, in honour of our Saviour, I have only done 7½ hours . . .'; by March 1908 he had completed 2400 pages. He was still working ten hours a day, but he was also correcting the proofs of the French translation of his book on Leibniz and becoming increasingly involved with women's suffrage.

A year later, he was at last nearing the end. 'Every time I went out for a walk,' he wrote in his autobiography, 'I used to be afraid that the house would catch fire and the manuscript get burnt up.' He later told G. H. Hardy, the mathematician, that he had a nightmare in which he was working in the Cambridge Library, in about AD 2100. A library assistant was walking around with an enormous bucket, collecting books to be destroyed. When he reached the only copy of *Principia Mathematica* in existence, 'he took down one of the volumes, turned over a few pages, seemed puzzled for a moment . . . closed the volume, balanced it in his hand and hesitated . . .' Russell woke up.

On 19 October 1909, the book was finished: it was over 4000 pages long, about the same length as Newton's work of precisely the same title, so bulky that its authors had to hire a four-wheeler to carry the manuscript to the University Press. When the cost of publishing 750 copies was calculated, however, it was found to be 'alarming'. Rather than cut the manuscript, which would have been impossible, Russell and Whitehead agreed to seek a grant from the Royal Society to defray half of the £600 costs, together making up the remainder. Early the following year, the society replied that it would pay a subsidy of £200 in two annual instalments. As Russell remarked later, 'We thus earned minus £50 each by ten years' work.' To Lucy Donnelly he reported that he felt 'more or less as people feel at the death of an ill-tempered invalid whom they have nursed and hated for years'. (Once finished, Russell hated going through his books, complaining to Dickinson that he wished books could be published 'without one's having to see any more of them – it is really disgusting returning to one's own vomit'.)

Printing was slow, since there was only one compositor at the Cambridge University Press able to deal with the special symbols. Volume I of *Principia Mathematica* appeared in December 1910; Volume II in 1912; Volume III in 1913. The reviews were flattering. The *Spectator* observed that it marked 'an epoch in the history of speculative thought', in that it had sought to put mathematics on a basis more solid than the universe itself, capable of remaining true if the universe itself were swept away. An ordinary reader, the *Spectator* reviewer remarked, would be able to follow it, provided they persevered, 'without any overwhelming strain upon the mind', which says much about *Spectator* readers of the time, since most of *Principia Mathematica* consists of symbols.

Its reception by the academic world, however, was disappointingly muted. By the end of 1911, only 320 copies of the first volume had been sold. The greatest single contribution to logic since Aristotle, a notation able to distinguish certain relations between propositions in a way that could not be expressed in Aristotelian terms, and capable of acting as the basis of all modern symbolic logic, it was greeted with awe, as a monument to the fortitude of its authors, but not always by the right people. It was read by logicians, and by philosophers curious about mathematics, but many of these found it too technical to comprehend fully. Mathematicians, on the other hand, were frequently overwhelmed by it. Daunted by its cumbrous techniques, they ignored many of its findings. In any case, later mathematicians, particularly in the 1930s, found that mathematics had developed so far that there was no longer any need to go through such intense labour.

What, then, did *Principia Mathematica* achieve? It formulated a new propositional and predicate calculus or method of calculation, more rigorous than Peano and, unlike Frege, taking note of the contradiction. It made the foundations of mathematics, if not simple, less mysterious. These landmarks were acknowledged; but perhaps not as they might have been.

In Cambridge, part of its quiet reception stemmed from the fact that its mathematicians, though more highly trained than those in any other British university, were still trapped in nineteenth-century mental habits. In Europe, the other great centres of mathematical learning were similarly unreceptive to the pure mathematical and logical exercise Whitehead and Russell had produced. In any case, there was very little time for concentrated appraisal: the First World War was about to break. 'I used to know of only six people who had read the later parts of the book', Russell wrote in his autobiography. 'Three of these were Poles, subsequently (I believe) liquidated by Hitler. The other three were Texans, subsequently successfully assimilated.'

Whitehead's reputation was not greatly altered by *Principia Mathematica*, but Russell's was. In Cambridge, it became fashionable among more dismissive academics to say that Whitehead had merely done the leg-work for Russell – ignoring the fact that Whitehead had created a great deal of the mathematics and invented the method of theoretical construction. Russell felt that he had, in large measure, achieved what he had set out to do: give mathematics a logical foundation while showing that previous mathematicians had both over-estimated and under-estimated the ability of logic to provide knowledge about the nature of the universe. From the age of eleven, when he first discovered that Euclid gave no proof of his axioms, he had wanted to find out whether, by pushing the deductive system back far enough, he could find something certain. If *Principia Mathematica* had not succeeded in doing that, at least a symbolic technique for dealing with 'structure' had been found and Russell's instinct for dissection rather than contemplation had paid off. His thesis that all mathematics could be reduced to logic was accepted by later mathematicians, provided logic was clearly understood to contain the theory of sets. They did, however, come to believe that there was much more to their field than had been indicated by reducing mathematics to logic and set theory, and that any true understanding of mathematics had to involve an explanation of which set-theory notion had 'mathematical content'. And this was not a question reducible to a problem of logic. Only in the 1930s did Gödel disprove the theory that all mathematical truth was provable by logic.

These labours, Russell was to say ever afterwards, had exhausted him, and from now on he was more often to write on subjects which came more easily to him. He was, after all, almost forty. Never again, would he say later, was he able to achieve a similar intellectal feat.

Principia Mathematica, the result of ten gruelling years of mental labour, probably the longest collaborative stint of such intensity ever made by two mathematicians, was also the end of Russell's and Whitehead's collaboration. They had been united in their views on mathematics, but they diverged fundamentally on questions of philosophy, and the way in which each saw the world – an estrangement that was to grow more bitter in the coming war. By 1910, the two men were ready to go their own ways: Whitehead in the direction of the principles of the natural world, and the geometry that was to have been the seventh part of the *Principia*, Russell to new concepts in philosophy. 'Neither of us alone', Russell would conclude, 'could have written the book; even together, and with the alleviation brought by mutual discussion, the effort was so severe that at the end we both turned away from mathematical logic with a kind of nausea.'

If Russell spent the early 1900s working with astonishing intensity, it was at least in part to escape from what was fast becoming an insupportable marriage. Alys's final capitulation to him in 1893 had been a sincere prelude to a lifetime's commitment; his early infatuation had not. Not much more than a boy when he married, he had become by the turn of the century a respected philosopher and mathematician, with marked views and a considerable sense of his place in the world. Alys, by contrast, had more or less lost hers. In the six years of their marriage, Russell had grown up. Alys, grown up already, had not altered with him. Worse, she had become craven for his affection.

During the years of *The Principles of Mathematics* and the start of Russell's collaboration with Whitehead, they were constantly on the move – abroad, to Cambridge, at Fernhurst or staying with the Whiteheads. The life they led was largely dictated by Russell. It was a frugal life, since he had no appetite for luxury and had in any case given money to Alys's family and to Evelyn. When on their own, they breakfasted in the study at 9 a.m., worked until 12.30 p.m., spent three-quarters of an hour reading aloud, then strolled in the garden for fifteen minutes before lunch. At 4.30 p.m. Russell returned to his mathematics. After dinner at 8 p.m. they read aloud to each other for an hour, almost invariably from serious works of literature or history. In October 1901, for example, they read three books by Jowett, Berenson's *Italian Art*, Murray's *Greek Literature*, and a volume of historical essays. Beatrice Webb, whose life was just as regular, came away from a visit applauding the modest nature of their daily routine. The Russells kept just one servant and did not drink. A letter to Gilbert Murray, written while on a visit to I Tatti, Berenson's house near Florence, is revealing of Russell's austerity at that time. 'The house has been furnished by Berenson with exquisite taste; it has some very good pictures, and a most absorbing library. But the business of existing beautifully, except when it is hereditary, always slightly shocks my Puritan soul . . . I think one makes great demands on the mental furniture where the outside is so elaborate, and one is shocked at lapses that one would otherwise tolerate.' In an essay written at about this time, he noted: 'All greatness of soul is rooted in renunciation – not only of actual and particular goods, but still more of the greed for personal goods of some kind.'

While Russell was engaged on his mathematical notations, Alys tried to keep up with her temperance duties, though she worried ceaselessly that she ought to be finding work of a kind that would interest her husband more. During the autumn of 1900, her diary reveals, she addressed fifty-nine meetings. These separations tended to cause a renewal of affection, even passion, in Russell.

'I am longing to see thee,' he wrote to her on 29 June 1900. 'My spirits gradually sink when thee is gone, and only rise again when thee comes back . . .' And on 6 November the following year: 'Dearest, thee does give me more happiness than I can say – all the happiness I have in fact . . . It is alarming to be absolutely dependent, but so it is . . . Separations grow more and more unendurable. I feel as tho' I could spend my life making love to thee, and never work any more.'

Alys's family, however, were causing Russell ever greater irritation. He found them vulgar, mendacious and a thoroughly bad influence on Alys. Hannah now repelled him to such an extent that he wanted to abandon Fernhurst. Even Berenson, whom Russell had formerly admired, he now regarded with some suspicion, though the feelings he expressed about him seem to say more about Russell than about Berenson. 'If only', he wrote petulantly to Alys, 'he would not permit himself the physical liberties which Jews indulge in of touching one and putting their hands on one's shoulder and so on.'

Had Russell been happy, it is arguable that none of these feelings would have mattered. But he was not. Alys too was beginning to get on his nerves. It was not just her lack of wit or lightness of touch, but her very character that he now began to scrutinise and find distasteful. He read insincerity into her attempts to be virtuous, malice into her stories about other people, lies into her evasions. He found her trivial; he complained that she made people quarrel; he criticised her lack of self-control: 'thee with thy damnably friendly manner cannot help ingratiating thyself with them all!' By contrast, he saw other women as being more splendid and desirable: Evelyn Whitehead, with her quick wit and sense of style, the handsome Sally Fairchild from Boston, with whom he had walked late at night around the countryside, and even Helen Thomas, Carey Thomas's red-haired younger sister who came to pay the Russells a visit and with whom, he admitted later, he had tried to exchange a kiss or two.

Helen was a lively observer of people. 'Personally,' she wrote to a friend, 'I cannot understand the life they lead . . . Rush, rush, rush; talk, talk, talk, with hundreds of people always around . . . Bertie I like immensely, but he is really not much better than a spoiled baby. He scolds his partners at croquet and whist, so that everyone hates to play with him, and he has to be arranged for and pampered every hour of the day . . .'

It was at about this time, anguished no doubt by what she saw was happening, and perhaps sharing the family disposition towards depression, that Alys began to fall to pieces. She found Mill House and the ailing Evelyn difficult to handle and often broke down in tears. In the spring of 1902, she finally accepted that she was suffering from a 'nerve collapse' and agreed to spend six weeks in Brighton in a clinic run by a woman doctor friend of hers. She counted every day she spent apart from Russell; she dreaded them all. From the clinic, she wrote on 10 May 1902: 'It is funny how my depression suddenly appears and disappears for no reason at all. If I

had been at home, I should probably have fancied it was all my fault
. . . I was growing very near to developing the ridiculous delusion
that thee no longer cared for me.'

It was, alas, no delusion. At her request, they met briefly in early
June. She wept all the time he was with her, and the letters he wrote
to her after that visit were cool. The most distant, explaining that he
was now practising self-control, was signed, not 'thine devotedly,
Bertie,' but 'Most affly Bertrand Russell', though later he apologised.

The truth was that in her absence Russell had had another of his
celebrated flashes of intuition. The words he used to describe what
happened are among the best known in the autobiography. 'I went
out bicycling one afternoon,' he wrote thirty years after the event,
'and suddenly realised that I no longer loved Alys. I had had no idea
until that moment that my love for her was even lessening.' The
words are a little disingenuous. Russell had been picking fault with
her for months. What had changed now was that, unlike many other
people in similar quandaries, his instinct was to be blunt. He
believed, he would say, in telling the truth. When Alys returned
home from the clinic, he told her he no longer loved her. 'And then
in the bedroom,' he noted in one of the more detached passages of
his private journal, 'her loud heart rending sobs, while I worked next
door . . . How she was crushed and broken! How I nearly relented
and said it had all been lies!. And how my soul hardened from
moment to moment because I left her to sob! In the middle of the
night she came to my door to say she was calmer now, and would
hope – poor, poor woman.'

Alys begged him not to leave her; he agreed. Terrible years
followed for them both. The more Alys tried to please him, the more
faults he found; the harsher he became, the more guilty he felt and
the more he vowed to try to be more tolerant. Florence, wife of Elie
Halévy, the French historian, first met Russell at about this time.
She found him 'small and thin, ugly, but with beautiful eyes' and a
'sarcastic and paradoxical' way of talking – but very charming.
Frequently suicidally depressed, Alys struggled not to blame him for
what had happened, though at times she found his censorious tone
more than she could bear. From Trinity, that September, Russell
wrote: 'I am sure thee would be better off if thee could believe that

by deliberate courage it is possible to be happy . . . But this is a hard doctrine, of which I have only very lately learned the truth; perhaps thee will find it too hard. What it requires is resignation . . . To me, this feeling has become part of my habitual consciousness, I hope it may in time become part of thine . . .' Next day, Alys replied, 'I quite agree with thee about resignation, and I have already had two hard fights with it and conquered – first to accept my illness and the separation from thee, second to face a life without love.' But the hardest fight, she wrote, had been to realise that for eight years she had been wrong, and that she had given up much of her work in the hope of caring for him only to find that she had harmed him. 'But no doubt I shall accept this fact, too, in time, but thee must leave me to carry on the fight in my own way. Thee could help me with tender sympathy, but as that is impossible, thee must not upset me with strenuous advice.'

Never had the conflicting strains in Russell's nature been so much at war, with the austere philosopher battling it out with the passions of a man who was undoubtedly capable of warmth and humanity, but who had learned to give voice to them in the guise of flashes of wit or outpourings of romantic despair. 'Tender sympathy' was not in Russell's nature, except perhaps when he was in love. They now settled down to a chilly truce, Alys doing her best to control her incessant crying, keeping the truth from everyone, and so efficiently fooling the world that even Mary, long sceptical about their relationship, could write in her diary, 'Bertie is grown much older with the responsibility of Alys's illness, and has become very charming and interesting.' A few weeks later, Mary wrote to her mother: 'He is certainly the most brilliant man of our acquaintance and he is worth all the "humouring" that he might desire. I say *might*, because I think, as a matter of fact, he is very reasonable and easy to get on with.' Alys confided in no one, not even her diary; her entries stop in July 1902, and the next is six years later. The enforced silence can only have added to her sense of loss and isolation.

Soon afterwards, she spent three weeks in Switzerland with Beatrice Webb, who had taken pity on her depression but remained somewhat mystified by the unhappiness she witnessed in the Russell house. Before setting out, she noted in her diary: 'It is the wantonness of this unhappiness which appals me, saddens and irritates both of us. Bertrand Russell's nature is pathetic in its subtle absoluteness: faith in an absolute logic, absolute ethic, absolute beauty, and all of the most refined and rarefied type ... the uncompromising way in which he applies these frightens me for his future and the future of those who love him or whom he loves. Compromise, mitigation, mixed motive, phases of health of body and mind, qualified statements, uncertain feelings, all seem unknown to him.' Though fond of him, Beatrice Webb was never uncritical. Better than anyone, she had detected the conflicting forces in his nature and the intense difficulty he had in keeping his intellect and his passions harnessed together, something that only his diaries, which did not appear until well after his death, would confirm.

The two women travelled to Monte Generosa for a week, and then on to Sils in the Engadine. Alys would remember their holiday as another chapter in her unhappiness. Beatrice Webb, enjoying the leisure, curing herself of drinking coffee which she believed was poisoning her, and concentrating on getting rid of some lingering eczema in one ear, had a better time. She found Alys, whom she had always liked, a pleasant companion and willing 'attendant', and congratulated herself on having done her some good. 'I have given her back a sane perspective of her own and Bertrand's life,' she noted in her diary. 'She is a warm-hearted, intelligent and attractive woman, and deserves to be happy and useful.' Happy she could not be; useful perhaps. Alys returned to her philanthropy, distancing even her nieces with her hectoring manner, odd remarks and bouts of uncontrollable depression. Russell, too, was miserable and took to walking alone around the fields near Grantchester, once even contemplating suicide under a train. He told Beatrice Webb that he was not in a mood for Trinity's parties: 'I sit in Fellows' Gardens, watching the fading twilight through the willows.'

That autumn the Russells moved to a rented house in Cheyne Walk where, escaping each other's company, they took to seeing more people. The practice of reading aloud, begun nearly nine years before, seems to have stopped abruptly in the late spring of 1902, presumably while Alys was in the clinic. It was never resumed. One visitor to Cheyne Walk was Lucy Donnelly, the Bryn Mawr lecturer who had become a friend during their visit to America in 1896. She wrote to Helen Thomas that she found their flat 'cheerless' and 'uncared for', Alys increasingly hard, bitter and remote and Russell swinging suddenly from gaiety to 'dumb hatred', when he grew restless, irritable and impatient. Whether Lucy ever fell in love with him is not known, but it is clear that she greatly enjoyed his company and relished their long talks in his study and walks along the Embankment. He told her how hard he found it to get on with uneducated people, how he concealed his feelings by haughtiness and superiority, and how he minded being so bad at observing and understanding ordinary people. Lucy was much in awe of him, storing away his conversations to ponder over back in Boston. 'Bertie's the most brilliant living man . . .' she wrote to Helen on 1 November. 'Heavens at what pace does he not carry one on – the strain is often terrible as it is exciting. And the high rarefied atmosphere in which he lives and into which he takes you makes you find the other air heavy and unvivifying.'

After Lucy's return to America, he wrote her an oblique letter about his marriage. 'It is ghastly to watch, in most marriages, the competition as to which is to be torturer, which tortured; a few years, at most, settle it, and after it is settled, one has happiness and the other virtue. And the torturer smirks, and speaks of matrimonial bliss; and the victim, for fear of worse, smiles a ghastly assent. Marriage, all such close relations, have quite infinite possibilities of pain; nevertheless, I believe it is good to be brought into close contact with people . . .' The torturer, presumably, was Alys, though it is unlikely that she felt like smirking. Russell complained to Lucy that she and Helen seemed so far away that he felt as if he was 'writing to dead people whom I have read about in books.'

After the celebrated bicycle ride, Russell had told Alys that he no longer wished to share a bedroom with her – a further blow, as it was the one time when they discussed the day's events. Alys said very little about her feelings at the time, so almost all that is known of their life together comes from Russell. In his autobiography, he wrote: 'So long as I lived in the same house with Alys she would every now and then come down to me in her dressing gown after she had gone to bed, and beseech me to spend the night with her.' Many years later, he told a distant relation that Alys would climb on top of him and try to force him to make love. 'About twice a year,' he was to write, 'I would attempt sex relations with her, in the hope of alleviating her misery, but she no longer attracted me, and the attempt was futile.'

One reason for these painful attempts was that sometime in 1903, Russell came to the conclusion, after consulting a doctor, that he ought to try to make Alys pregnant – 'the last sacrifice', as he put it. 'Dr Savage', he noted in his journal, 'said it was my duty to run the risk of conception, the fear of heredity being grossly exaggerated. He says 50 per cent of insane have alcoholic parentage, only 15 per cent insane parentage.' Hardly surprisingly, he failed, noting in his diary that 'in return I am to have three weeks liberty.' The next occasion 'was not adequately carried out, and failed totally.' Alys's dignity and the efforts she made not to plead with him won her back some measure of his respect, though never his love. Having promised her that he would stay – he claims that she threatened suicide to prevent him going – he did so, but the toll he exacted can seldom have been easy to bear.

Five

A secret worship of
the same goals

Once away from Friday's Hill, Fernhurst, and the Pearsall Smiths, who now repelled him to such an extent that he forced Alys to give up Millhangar, Russell began to find life 'more bearable', though he complained of the city and the difficulties of modern life.

'London is a weary place,' he wrote mournfully to Gilbert Murray, 'where it is quite impossible to think or feel anything worthy of a human being – I feel horribly lost here. Only the river and the gulls are my friends; they are not making money or acquiring power.' From his study, he could see Orion rise and Saturn set, and watch the barges on the river 'float dimly through the brightness like dream-memories of childhood'. A tolerant man with a keen sense of the ridiculous, a brilliant raconteur, vegetarian and teetotaller, Murray was fast becoming one of his closest friends – Russell defining friendship at this stage as the 'discovery of an isolation like our own, a secret worship of the same goals' – and it was to him that he poured out the loneliness and misery provoked by the failure of his marriage to Alys. 'I have been merely oppressed by the weariness and tedium and vanity of things lately: nothing stirs me, nothing seems worth doing or worth having done: the only thing that I strongly *feel* worth while would be to murder as many people as possible so as to diminish the amount of consciousness in the world.' To Lucy Donnelly in America, he said: 'Two things are to be cultivated: loftiness of feeling, and control of feeling and everything else by the will.'

With the Boer War over, England was enjoying a period of

exceptional calm and prosperity, with plenty of money around and taxation and the cost of living low. Queen Victoria, 'the giant paperweight that for half a century sat upon men's minds', as H. G. Wells described her, was dead. There were new discoveries in the air – the first motor taxis, wireless telegraphy – and music, theatre and the arts were all prospering. Pinero, Ibsen and Shaw were the playwrights of the hour. London had nineteen morning and ten evening papers. What came to be known as 'gas and water socialism', municipal enterprise, was bringing public transport, libraries, parks, gas and electricity supplies and schools to the capital. Yet from all this Russell remained curiously detached, seldom remarking on anything topical or trivial in his letters, which he preferred to confine to ideas, solace and *angst*.

These were strange years for Russell. Nothing was going quite right for him. He settled into a kind of resigned and humourless melancholia, which found expression in his writings and letters in a way that friends must at times have found tiresome. His work, for all its engrossing demands, was not altogether able to keep the world at bay, and Russell was uneasy about himself, about people, and about his emotions and beliefs. Though he was approaching middle age, there was something youthful, even immature, in his character, and this tendency to grow and change would last until his death over half a century later. He was the least fixed of men. Just as his philosophical work altered over the years, so his views of the world, his friends and colleagues and himself changed, so that, more than most people, he seemed to become a different person. Ten years of often unsatisfactory marriage had made him more aware of the value of friends and yet more solitary, more appreciative of what friends had to offer, yet more demanding. The new Russell could sometimes appear, both to old friends and to new acquaintances, a touch too judgemental and austere. They recoiled from a certain chilliness with which he disguised the confusion within.

And yet if Russell complained that he found it hard to deal with ordinary people and their ordinary emotions, and others found him unpredictable, he was proving he could be an excellent friend to those in trouble. Both Murray and Lucy Donnelly were going through unhappy times, Murray because he was in the throes of doubts about his work and often ill, and Lucy because her particular friend at Bryn Mawr, to whom she was more attached than to anyone, Helen Dudley, the red-haired girl whom Russell had tried to kiss, had suddenly announced that she was getting married. To Lucy, Russell sent long letters urging the sort of resignation he imposed upon himself, and these intimate and fond letters were the start of a regular correspondence, which lasted until her death in 1948.

As for Murray, he tried to think of something that might distract him, and arranged for him to visit Berenson at I Tatti in Fiesole. 'I am grieved', he wrote, 'that you should be suffering from depression – it is a strange curse that seems to afflict all who try to live a life of the mind.' From Italy, Murray wrote ecstatically to say that he both liked and admired his host, even if he sometimes found that Berenson's frailty, sensitivity and cleverness made him feel like a robust cow, and that he occasionally longed for plain air and to escape from the exoticism and intellectual exclusivity of the household. Berenson declared that he liked Murray so much that he felt 'school-girlish' about him. Their one disagreement, whether Milton or Shakespeare was the better poet, was hurriedly glossed over.

Now that they had left Fernhurst, the Russells rented a house for the summer in Churt, on the Surrey-Hampshire border, to be near the Murrays. They were even thinking of settling somewhere in the neighbourhood. Walking alone late at night on the common, once again reflecting on the misery of the human condition, Russell congratulated himself bleakly on having at least learned to recognise the three different calls made by night-jars. 'The world seems to me quite dreadful,' he wrote to Dickinson, 'the unhappiness of most people is very great, and I often wonder how they endure it all. To know people well is to know their tragedy.'

By day, there were many visits to Barfurd Court, the Murray house, where Russell's cousin, Lady Mary, was a hospitable hostess, if somewhat erratic and high minded. When the two families were apart, Russell and Murray continued their conversations by letter, discussing morality, ethics and the philosophy of resignation much as if they had been sitting talking together. To Lady Mary, the mother of three children, Russell spoke about parenthood, a subject which was beginning to preoccupy him greatly. 'It seems to me that children, in spite of all the anxieties and labour they cause, are the greatest tie to life that one can have . . . And they provide a transition out of one's Ego which seems easier and more natural than any other.' Russell observed that he liked his cousin 'better than she deserves'. In his journal he painstakingly drew up a list of her faults – jealousy, anxiety over trivial things, bad temper, lack of self-control – somewhat longer than that of her virtues, which he named as public-spiritedness and a desire to do good work and behave kindly.

During the months that followed the celebrated bicycle ride, Alys, who had never ceased to love Russell, had little to sustain her. Russell, who was often just as wretched, had his work, the Apostles and a growing number of commitments. When these proved not enough, he explored the unhappiness that gripped him in a spirit of what he called 'pure contemplation', and made a fresh attempt, in the wake of his 'conversion', to find a set of beliefs that would provide him with the religious certainty he still craved. 'For my part', he wrote to Lucy, 'I am constructing a mental cloister, in which my inner soul is to dwell in peace, while an outer simulacrum goes forth to meet the world.' His earnestness could be overpowering.

Between March 1902 and the end of the year, Russell carried his melancholia over to a new dimension: he wrote twenty-one short essays, 'disjointed reflections' on religious topics, on gentleness and forgiveness, many of them sentimental and even cloying, in the form of an introspective, allegorical journey. They were composed during his walks around the countryside. 'Sadness', the 'spectres' of the past, the 'wintry' world crop up repeatedly. 'I have learnt at last the old Stoic secret,' he reported to Helen Thomas, 'hope nothing, fear nothing, desire nothing . . .' What he was trying to do was concoct a 'religion of sorrow', to bring a sense of the spiritual to those who, like himself, found it impossible to believe in God or immortality. Having come to mistrust the 'real' world, he now sought refuge in a timeless one, 'without change or decay or the will-o'-the-wisp of progress'. In one essay, 'The Atonement', he wrote: 'To each of us the choice is open, whether to add to the burden of humanity or to bear it, whether to crucify or be crucified.' Given his trust in the purity of mathematics, he was in a somewhat awkward position, a dilemma he summed up in his journal on 12 November: 'Nature is my inspiration, and mathematics my purifyer.' *The Pilgrimage of Life*, the name given to this collection of essays, was not published until long after his death.

By the end of 1902, he was at work on a more astringent essay, which effectively cleared his mind and laid down the fundamental credo he had been looking for. *The Free Man's Worship*, Russell's most quoted, most translated and most reprinted essay, is a paean to the vulnerability and solitude of mankind. He began writing it in Florence, on a visit to the Berensons, while wandering alone on the hills above Fiesole among the olives and cypresses. The language is majestic; the message ultimately one of hope, if of a bleak kind.

> To abandon the struggle for private happiness, to expel all eagerness of temporary desire, to burn with passion for eternal things – this is emancipation, and this is the free man's worship . . . The life of Man is a long march through the night, surrounded by invisible foes, tortured by weariness and pain, towards a goal that few can hope to reach, and where none may tarry long. One by one, as they march, our comrades vanish from our sight, seized by the silent orders of omnipotent Death.

Worship, for the man who is truly free, Russell concluded, can be based only on fact. Science has shown that the universe is unfathomable and hostile; man has no choice but to accept that he owes his existence to a random scatter of atoms. This is not a world, clearly, which can be worshipped; what can, on the other hand, is something created within the imagination of a brave man who burns 'with passion for eternal things'. It is a good deal crisper than the *Pilgrimage*.

The essay was finished at the end of January 1903 and Russell gave it to George Trevelyan, who pronounced it the best thing he had ever read. Not all his friends were as enthusiastic and some, clearly, were baffled by this new vision of an almost adolescent, romantic Russell, just as they were confused by his unpredictability. Theodore Llewellyn Davies complained that it would be far better to say 'Damn, and go on'; Murray confessed himself puzzled by some of its implications; and Dickinson, who respected religious certainty and was himself writing a series of articles on religion, remarked that though his attitude was possibly ultimately the 'only great one', and that Russell had 'drunk deeper of the cup than I have', he personally could not stomach the belief that a scientific view of the universe was the only true one. The *Independent Review*, a highbrow magazine founded that autumn, with George Trevelyan and Dickinson on its council, agreed to publish the essay in their December issue.

The public, presented with this first evidence of Russell as a popular essayist, greeted *The Free Man's Worship* with pleasure, seeing in it yet another expression of cosmic pessimism, along with Conrad's and Hardy's novels and Ibsen's plays. It soon became known as the 'sceptics' manifesto'. Russell, who believed it to be not just an essay about belief but a reaffirmation of liberal values at a time of ideological confusions, noted wryly in his journal that part of it had in fact been written as an exhortation to himself to treat Alys better.

Russell was not altogether pleased with his literary efforts of the autumn and winter, suspecting rightly that his intellect interfered with his imagination, though he considered *The Free Man's Worship* greatly superior to the *Pilgrimage* and his best attempt so far at a baroque style in the manner of Milton. Later he changed his mind, saying that he found the style 'florid and rhetorical', but he remained faithful to its message about the cosmos and the nature of faith. He was also much upset, Lucy Donnelly observed, by a feeling that his friends were 'sneering and laughing at his intimate feelings', a suspicion that was at least partly justified, in that Beatrice Webb told Logan Pearsall Smith that she had at last understood Russell perfectly: 'What he wanted was unhappiness, he enjoyed the luxury of it and Alys need no longer trouble abt. him.' In her diary, she added: 'Tragedy is a pose with him, and both the facts of the universe and the facts of matrimony must live up to it.'

The essay left Russell feeling not better but depressed. 'The fire and inspiration I had has left me,' he noted in his diary, in a fresh bout of self-pity, 'and I cannot believe I shall do any more useful things to make the long path worthwhile.'

*

Now that Russell was working closely with Whitehead, Alys could not understand why they did not move to Cambridge, rather than staying on in London. She pressed Russell repeatedly for an answer. At last, unable to prevaricate any longer, he told her that it was because she got on his nerves when she was with his Cambridge friends. Alys was mortified. What he did not tell her was that he was also increasingly annoyed by the way she seemed to be estranging him from Beatrice Webb and the Murrays by making him appear ridiculous in their eyes, and by taking them into her confidence about the real state of their marriage. Given Alys's discretion, and the lengths she went to keep their problems secret, whereas he appears to have shared them with both Gilbert Murray and Lucy Donnelly, his criticism seems unnecessarily harsh.

So they stayed on in Cheyne Walk, where Alys spent more time on her temperance and factory work, leaving Russell to pay frequent visits to Cambridge on his own. He usually stayed in Trinity, where, when able to stop revelling in melancholy, he greatly enjoyed the company of other men – 'the absence of women gave me a moment of real delight,' he noted in his diary on 8 March 1903 – and the philosophical talk. But to Dickinson, during one of the long Cambridge holidays, when there were few of his friends about, he complained that pretending to renew the joys of youth was rather like trying to eat cold bacon.

It was the Apostles, however, who continued to provide him with his most pleasurable moments, even though both its members and its atmosphere were becoming very different. Of his former Apostle friends, who had by now taken 'wings', there were the resident Cambridge dons: McTaggart, the eccentric Hegelian with a memorable capacity for periods of total, unfathomable silence; Lowes Dickinson, the bachelor misogynist, who once remarked that he was unable to tell his women students one from the other since they all looked like cows, and Oscar Browning, now in his middle sixties, the flamboyant mentor of the young at King's College, whose enormous yellow bald pate was still crowned by a ring of black curls – and of course Whitehead. Then there was Charles Sanger, by now a successful barrister in London; Bob Trevelyan, the untidy and benign poet; and Moore, who said that he revisited the Apostles to sing and play the piano rather than talk.

Other visiting Apostolic 'wings' were E. M. Forster, known to his friends as the 'elusive colt of a dark horse' and the journalist and critic Desmond MacCarthy, later to become literary editor of the *New Statesman*. MacCarthy was the Apostles' raconteur, a sociable and much liked man who entertained the 'phenomena' with excellent stories, and whom V. S. Pritchett later described as 'soft, warm, idling'. There was also Roger Fry, the tall, stooping, silky-haired art critic, once described by a friend as a 'highly sagacious rocking-horse'.

In 1902, Whitehead was forty-one, Russell thirty and Moore twenty-nine. The society was smaller than it had been in their day, but it was about to be taken over by a new and powerful group of friends, who would cast a wholly new light over its deliberations. The first of these was Lytton Strachey, a pale, lanky figure with spidery arms and legs, long horsy teeth and a manner which could be both ribald and priggish. Prone to uttering falsetto squeaks, Strachey enjoyed shocking the people of Cambridge by roaming the streets shouting out 'Damn God' and waiting for the heavens to strike him. His mannerisms and sheer strength of character made a great impact on his fellow Apostles, not least because he was even cleverer and more articulate than most of them, and one of the very few newcomers capable of holding his own with Russell.

After him came Leonard Woolf, soon to depart for the Colonial Service; Clive Bell, a stout, boyish figure with ginger hair and the dark, shiny eyes of a small woodland animal, and Maynard Keynes, Apostle number 243, an ungainly young man with thick lips and blue eyes under heavy black eyebrows, who was said by his friends to look just like a gorilla except when he smiled, when his expression was extraordinarily sweet. Russell, who had learned syllogistic logic from his father's book, took a liking to the 'admirable youth' ten years his junior, writing to Alys that from all he heard Keynes was a 'person I ought to know and talk to . . .' These new Apostles went in for nicknames. Keynes was 'Pozzo', apparently after a Corsican diplomat called Pozzo di Borgo; Moore was 'the Yen' for being so wise and inscrutable, and Forster 'the taupe', because his modesty and civility, combined with his pale complexion and pale clothes, reminded them of a mole.

The routine of Apostolic life was largely unchanged from the 1890s, and for Russell, now a respected elder of the group, it was as enjoyable as ever. Members met every Saturday evening to eat their 'whales', discuss the 'phenomena' and greet visiting 'angels'. They shared in-jokes, a private language and a sense of superiority. They continued to venerate aesthetics, unworldliness, cleverness and philosophical talk of a tough-minded intellectual kind. However, a new note was creeping in: that of considering people and their feelings – and not only their opinions – as important. They read Tolstoy, Dostoyevsky, Ibsen and Flaubert, declaimed Swinburne, and quoted Henry James. Something of this new spirit was described by MacCarthy. 'It seems that we take everything more *personally* than our predecessors . . . The last generation were much less sceptical . . . They did not think less *of* their friends; but they thought less about them, not less of friendship, but less of intimacy.' Many years later, Leonard Woolf wrote that, 'We were intellectuals, intellectuals with three genuine, and, I think, profound passions: a passion for friendship, a passion for literature and music . . . a passion for what we called the truth.'

In the opening lines of *The Longest Journey*, E. M. Forster has left an account of an Apostolic Saturday meeting. It was published in 1907, but the picture it gives seems reminiscent not so much of the new Apostles as of their predecessors in Russell's day, when Moore fascinated those around him by his endless lighting of matches:

> 'The cow is there,' said Ansell, lighting a match and holding it over the carpet. No one spoke. He waited till the end of the match fell off. Then he said again, 'She is there, the cow. There, now.'
>
> 'You have not proved it,' said a voice.
>
> 'I have proved it to myself.'
>
> 'I have proved it to myself that she isn't,' said the voice. 'The cow is *not* there.' Ansell frowned and lit another match . . .
>
> It was philosophy. They were discussing the existences of objects. Do they exist only when there is someone to look at them? or have they a real existence on their own? It is all very interesting, but at the same time it is difficult. Hence the cow.

The Victorian age was over. One topic, discussed only in the abstract before but now brought repeatedly into the open, was that of homosexual love. Oscar Browning, Dickinson, and E. M. Forster were all homosexuals, but their affairs with men remained largely secret. With Keynes and Lytton Strachey this changed, but only after the old guard, in the form of George Trevelyan, had fought a losing battle with Strachey over how far such relationships should be made public. The actual homosexuality of some of the Apostles remained a secret for many years, like that of Keynes, which though openly discussed in his extensive correspondence with Strachey, was not even mentioned by Roy Harrod in his biography.

Married now for almost a decade, and with a decided interest in women, Russell had little but contempt for homosexuality. He found it distasteful, and this mild sense of disgust found its way into his relationship with the new Apostles. Strachey, he was to write to Ottoline Morrell many years later, 'is diseased and unnatural' and 'only a very high degree of civilisation enables a healthy person to stand him'.

1903 was a remarkable year for British philosophy. Russell had published his well-acclaimed *Principles of Mathematics* and was now at work with Whitehead on what would become one of the most important mathematical documents of the twentieth century. It was also the year when G. E. Moore published his *Principia Ethica*. The extent of this book's influence has been much debated but there is no doubt that its appearance was a landmark for its Apostolic readers.

The members of the Conversazione Society had long been interested in ethics. Papers and letters show that in the 1890s, when Russell arrived at Trinity, Apostles were already deeply immersed in questions of 'good', 'truth', 'happiness' and 'passion'. As early as 1893, Russell wrote a paper for Sidgwick entitled 'The relation of what ought to be to what is, has been or will be'. In 1902, his regular correspondence with Murray included many ethical debates. 'Circumstances', he wrote, 'are apt to generate perfectly concrete moral convictions . . . we see goodness or badness in things as we see their colours and shapes . . . I should . . . regard the true method of Ethics as inference from empirically ascertained facts, to be obtained in that moral laboratory which life offers to those whose eyes are open to it.' But it was Moore, not Russell, who was to provide the Apostles with their ethical bible.

Moore began work on *Principia Ethica* in the late spring of 1902. Just over a year later, the book reached proof stage and was published that October. The press was not altogether impressed: the reviewer in the *Scotsman* observed that the style was 'somewhat pedestrian and unillumined', while the *Oxford Magazine* accused Moore of immoral tendencies. The Apostles, on the other hand, were dazzled. A few days after publication, Strachey wrote to say: 'I think your book has not only wrecked and shattered all writers on Ethics from Aristotle and Christ to Herbert Spencer and Mr Bradley . . . not only left all modern philosophy *bafoué* . . . but henceforth who will be able to tell lies one thousand times as easily as before? . . . I date from October 1903 the beginning of the Age of Reason.' Russell spoke of it as 'beyond praise'.

In 1903, German idealism, with its metaphors, was still the preferred language in which most philosophers laid down the relations between man and society, and Moore's and Russell's rejection of idealism had not yet been widely followed. In *Principia Ethica* Moore changed all this, by pointing to a linguistic fact that had long been overlooked: the word 'good' cannot be defined in terms of any natural characteristics, because whatever natural characteristics you choose, you will always have to ask whether anything possessing these characteristics is 'good'. Neither utilitarianism nor any other existing moral theory could thus be founded on an analysis of the meaning of words: for that a non-verbal affirmation was headed. Moore claimed not only that the word 'good' is indefinable, but that 'goodness' is a non-natural, simple quality, which we apprehend in some way directly, much as we apprehend shapes and colours, by some kind of intuition.

Certain things, said Moore, are intrinsically 'good'. 'By far the most valuable things which we can know or imagine are certain shades of consciousness which may roughly be described as the pleasures of human intercourse and the enjoyment of beautiful objects. No one, probably, who has ever asked himself the question has ever doubted that personal affection and the appreciation of what is beautiful in Art or Nature, are good in themselves.' To hope for a correct answer, Moore said, you have to ask the right question. He began by asking two: what things are good in themselves? and what kind of action ought we to perform? What interested him, now as in all his philosophy, was the common-sense answer: what, in this case, was the 'common-sense' meaning of good? These formed the basis not just of *Principia Ethica* itself, but of Moore's most valuable contributions to philosophy.

Most of Moore's friends at Cambridge regarded him with affection and a slight sense of awe. Though never a particularly witty man, and certainly not as intellectually agile as Russell – Leonard Woolf saw them as the tortoise and the hare – there was something in his nature which had provoked admiration in this new generation of Apostles even before *Principia Ethica* turned him into their guru. Few bothered to analyse the early chapters, which are a complicated philosophical credo, but turned instead to the last two, which laid down Moore's personal thinking on moral conduct, defined as an obligation to select the action which will achieve more good than any other. Each saw in Moore's words something he had been looking for, whether a rejection of Hegelian pomposity, or a means of shedding the 'fog and fetters' of Victorian morality, or, in Strachey's case, a tacit endorsement of his homosexuality. For Leonard Woolf, this clear pursuit of truth 'with the tenacity of a bulldog and the integrity of a saint' was another proof of Moore's greatness; he was 'the only great man whom I have ever met or known in the world of ordinary, real life'.

Woolf, possibly the best commentator on the Apostles, recorded the impact of *Principia Ethica* in *Sowing*, the first volume of his autobiography. Moore's book, he wrote, 'suddenly removed from our eyes all obscuring accumulation of scales, cobwebs, and curtains, revealing for the first time to us, so it seemed, the nature of truth and reality, of good and evil and character and conduct, substituting for the religious and philosophical nightmares, delusions, hallucinations, in which Jehovah, Christ, and St Paul, Plato, Kant, and Hegel had entangled us, the fresh air and pure light of plain common sense.'

No longer, the Apostles agreed, were they going to be bound to any one religious or philosophical creed: rather, before each and every statement, they were to ask themselves: what, precisely, does it mean? Moore's genius, they said, lay in seeing what was important and what was irrelevant. Strachey remarked later to Russell that when he died he wanted his tombstone to be engraved only with the words: 'He knew Moore and Russell'.

For many of these younger Apostles – Woolf, Strachey, Saxon Sydney-Turner, Clive Bell – 1903 was their last year at Cambridge. They passed it in a kind of idolatry of Moore, dominated by him both intellectually and emotionally, plunging from extremes of happiness to depths of misery, confident that they were now all embarked on lives of immense promise, even if unsure of the course they would take. They preferred to regard what they had learned from Moore as a 'science' and not a 'religion', though 'religion' was how Keynes was to describe it, in a famous half-mocking, half-sincere memoir, *My Early Beliefs*, which he read aloud to the Memoir Club, a gathering of the Bloomsbury group, one afternoon in 1938. 'The appropriate subjects of passionate contemplation and communion were a beloved person, beauty or truth, and one's prime objects in life were love, the creation and enjoyment of aesthetic experience and the pursuit of knowledge.' None of this, he added, had prevented them from laughing most of the time, or from feeling supremely self-confident, and superior to and contemptuous of the rest of the 'unconverted' world.

The disciples regarded themselves as sceptics in search of the truth, a band of serious young men conscious that they were living through a period of dramatic social change, who were fascinated by questions of right and wrong, by what they ought or ought not to do. To the rest of the university they must have appeared maddeningly arrogant, conceited and mannered – Strachey's squeak alone was deeply curious – to themselves they seemed to have a unique understanding of the 'truth'. They had Moore's stamp of approval for believing that their duty lay in challenging the stifling Victorian codes of conduct and establishing themselves as champions of free speech, reason and common sense. They were not, of course, alone in their perception of a changing world, but they saw themselves as discussing the undiscussable and freeing ethics from religion.

This veneration of Moore must have been irritating to Russell, who could be forgiven if he felt somewhat jealous of the shy, gentle, slightly absurd Moore and at the way he himself had been eclipsed. If anything, it served to emphasise how different he was from them. Many years later, in one of his *Portraits from Memory*, he was to make a sly dig at the way in which the Apostles had venerated Moore. 'The generation of Keynes and Lytton . . .', he wrote, 'aimed at a life of retirement among fine shades and nice feelings, and conceived of the good as consisting in the passionate mutual admiration of a clique of the élite . . . those who considered themselves his disciples . . . degraded his ethics into advocacy of a stuffy girls'-school sentimentalising.' This in turn infuriated Forster, who complained that Russell had been singularly ungenerous, and that he had completely misunderstood the essence of Strachey's enigmatic character. Though capable of being romantic almost to the point of becoming maudlin, Russell greatly disliked intellectual flabbiness or lack of rigour in others.

Moore's immediate influence on Russell can be seen in Russell's repeated references to his work in the books and papers he published in the early years of the century; after which he seems to have had no serious effect on him at all, and Russell soon came to disagree with him. But both men were generous about each other in their writings. In *Principles of Mathematics* Russell wrote that many of his fundamental questions of philosophy were derived from Moore; while Moore insisted many years later that all Russell owed him were mistakes, and that he had spent more time studying Russell than any other single philosopher.

In the wider world, Moore's influence re-emerged some ten years later, when he became one of the sages of the 'Bloomsberries' (as Russell's cousin Mary Murray was to christen them), a 'group of lifelong, like-minded friends who happened to differ in outlook from their contemporaries'. They accepted his religion and discarded his morals, as Keynes put it, and drew from the *Principia Ethica* those doctrines which suited them, making them an intellectual underpinning for their own pursuits and shared views about common sense, candour, friendship and the need to reject Victorian hypocrisy. If it is true, as Leonard Woolf maintains, that the real Bloomsbury came into being only in 1912, it is also true that the movement was born among a group of friends who had been contemporaries, or near contemporaries, at Trinity and King's in the late 1890s, when the Apostles elected Leonard Woolf, Lytton Strachey and Saxon Sydney-Turner as members, who listened to the 'extraordinary outburst of philosophical brilliance' of McTaggart, Whitehead, Russell and Moore, swept away religion in favour of ethical assertions, challenged traditional obedience, imperialism, clericalism and militarism, and adopted a new code of honesty in personal relations. Only three of its ten founders were not Apostles; all were influenced by Moore's 'ethics of liberation', just as they were to read and admire, during the decade between *Principia Ethica* and the birth of Bloomsbury, Russell's work on logic and analysis. Maynard Keynes, in his paper written for the Memoir Club, was to say that it was a 'purer, sweeter air by far than Freud cum Marx . . . This religion of ours was a very good one to grow up under. It remains nearer the truth than any other than I know, with less irrelevant extraneous matter and nothing to be ashamed of . . .'

In the spring of 1904, six months after the publication of Moore's book, came an astonishing testimonial to his influence on the young Apostles. Sydney Waterlow, a former classical scholar from Trinity, though not an Apostle, together with several of those involved in the *Independent Review*, tried to organise a tribute to its author in the form of a series of essays, a manifesto on practical ethics aimed at the ordinary reader and written by some of the Apostolic luminaries. Moore was asked to 'do' either Truth or God, and opted for Truth. Russell was to interpret Moore for the plain man – an experiment that failed when Moore evidently did not care for what Russell had written. The project eventually foundered; but the very fact that it was suggested in the first place gives some idea of the esteem in which Moore was held.

Unlike Moore, whose absurdities made him human and lovable, Russell was regarded as a somewhat chilly figure with a manner which could be trenchant and dismissive. His passion lay, not in the 'finer shades' of friendships, nor in the intimacies of frivolity and gossip, but in ideas. They all accepted that he was brilliant – probably the most brilliant of them all – but he was not cosy, and they did not always feel at ease in his rather formal company. They saw in his clever rejoinders a desire to exalt himself, to prove himself their intellectual superior, and sometimes found him immature, even sentimental. Moore had carried them along a path which was fundamentally alien to Russell's nature, and from which he felt himself often excluded.

'He has not much body of character', Virginia Woolf was later to write in her diary. 'This luminous vigorous mind seems to be attached to a flimsy little car, like that of a large glinting balloon . . . And he has no chin, and he is dapper. Nevertheless, I should like the run of his headpiece.' Both the Apostles and the Bloomsberries were captivated by that headpiece, but not always by the man who owned it.

Who, then, were Russell's real friends in the early 1900s? And how important was friendship to him? There was Charles Sanger, whom he continued to meet in London, the Murrays, Lucy Donnelly in America, Goldie Lowes Dickinson, with whom he exchanged letters about religion, and Philip Jourdain, the young historian of mathematics with whom Russell had remained in touch, and who was now suffering from a wasting disease. When he could, Russell went to see him, recording one day in his journal: 'He is very ill . . . and at first sight almost half-witted. But when he begins to talk of mathematics, his face shines, his eyes sparkle, he speaks with fire and ability, one forgets he is ill, or remembers only in passionate admiration of the triumph of the mind.'

There was also Desmond MacCarthy, with whom Russell became close when the two men took to confiding in each other their emotional problems. MacCarthy always urged Russell to act more impulsively; while Russell acted as a sounding-board and a giver of advice. Then there was Bob Trevelyan, 'Trevy', who by the turn of the century had married and was living with his wife Elizabeth, or Bessie, in a house called The Shiffolds in the woods of Leith Hill, near Dorking in Surrey, where they invited their Apostolic friends to stay for weekends. Russell increasingly regretted the lack of children of his own. To Bessie, congratulating her on a new baby, he wrote, 'I feel as if those who have no children had really a very small share in the life of mankind . . .' Trevy, who always believed himself to be less intelligent than the others, was an eccentric, awkward, endearing man in baggy knickerbockers and huge walking boots, tall, big-boned, with a large humorous mouth. His friends, one of whom described his mind as a 'junk shop of wisdom and learning', used to laugh affectionately at the way he jumbled his words and flailed his arms around searching for the right one. He was more than willing to play jester for the others. Russell, who liked him, despite recoiling from his 'utter' egoism, spent many enjoyable weekends at The Shiffolds, where the talk went on all day and far into the night as it had during their Cambridge days, stopping only in the evenings for music or reading aloud. Many years later Trevy's son Julian, the painter, described his father shaving in the drawing room while his mother read aloud from Boswell. Books, he said 'were chewed over until there seemed to be no more to get out of them'. One of Russell's contributions to these gatherings was his prodigious memory: he could quote from books and poetry flawlessly and at great length, which must have pleased Trevy enormously, as he believed his role in life was that of a poet, though he was never a good or successful one. A letter Russell wrote to Lucy Donnelly is revealing of his feelings about his friends. 'One comes to feel strangely a spectator and not an actor. I watch people year after year, I know their faults and virtues, their pleasures and pains, and yet I say nothing and they say nothing, and I remain a casual outsider.'

There was E. M. Forster, who one day gravely thanked Alys for her hospitality with the words, 'I enjoyed my visit so much: it was very kind of you to ask me. I hope the cat is well: ours would send some kind enquiry, but has just been smacked for eating a beetroot.' And even Keynes, though ten years younger than Russell, became enough of a friend to feel able to ask whether he might come to stay for a 'restful weekend'. Russell replied that he could promise him total tranquillity. When the weekend came, however, it transpired that the two men had very different notions of tranquillity. Within five minutes of Keynes's arrival, a vice chancellor appeared to discuss university business, and every meal saw the arrival of other unexpected guests, including six for breakfast on Sunday. By Monday morning, when Keynes left, there had been twenty-six additional guests.

Walking was still a passion shared by nearly all of them, and Russell frequently went off on holidays with Sanger, Trevy, or George Trevelyan, or Desmond MacCarthy. He enjoyed Mac-Carthy's 'kindly humour, which makes the world seem gay', more than George Trevelyan's 'air of settled gloom, by comparison with which my jokes against optimism seem full of the joys of life!' One particularly successful walk with Trevy gives an idea of the vast distances covered: from Taunton, along the Quantock Hills, to Glastonbury and Wells, ending up in Oxford. Another year, he walked with Theodore Llewelyn Davies in Brittany; the apples were ripe and their smell reminded Russell of Devon or Cornwall. The rain poured down, but it did not prevent them from covering twenty-five miles a day. Sometimes he walked on his own, using the solitude to think through seemingly insoluble problems, and to 'lay up a store of peace of mind to last through the agitations and fatigues of ordinary life'. In the evenings, staying at an inn, he observed in minute detail the idiosyncrasies of his fellow guests, but it was not as much fun as being with the others, talking late into the night, while MacCarthy told his stories and Moore shook with paroxysms of laughter, or protested, his eyes wide and his tongue stuck out of the corner of his mouth, 'I *simply* don't understand *what* he means!'

The main organiser of the famous Apostolic walking parties was, of course, Moore. He and Russell had papered over their differences to the extent that they would discuss philosophy, but Moore in particular continued not to care very much for Russell, and even less as he became aware of Russell's real feelings towards Alys. During discussions about one forthcoming reading party, Moore observed to MacCarthy that Russell's presence 'was a great damper on me . . . I think Russell has seen that I want to avoid him.' One day Russell asked him directly: 'You don't like me, do you?' Moore pondered, then replied: 'No'.

Russell's sometimes uneasy relations with the reading parties reached a climax in the spring of 1903. Over lunch with MacCarthy, Russell mentioned that he would like to join a group of Apostles

who were planning to spend Easter vacation at the Lizard in
Cornwall. MacCarthy, who liked Russell, went along with the idea,
saying that since Fry and Lowes Dickinson were likely to be among
their number, the outing would be pleasant. Russell then wrote to
Moore asking if he might join them. Moore was furious: 'Since you
ask me to say if your coming would make any difficulty, I think I had
better tell you that it would.' What particularly displeased him was
that Russell was proposing to join them for the entire fortnight. To
MacCarthy, Moore quickly wrote: 'Of course, I can't be sure that he
would spoil it for anyone but me . . . And then I do think that the
effect he would have on me would also indirectly make it much more
unpleasant for the rest of you: I can't be at my ease, while he is
there, and I don't know how miserable I might not get . . .' Three
days later, he wrote again, saying that MacCarthy's liking Russell so
much made him think he ought to like him – but he couldn't.

    Russell was extremely upset. He told MacCarthy that though he
had been aware of Moore's reservations about him, he had never
realised how intense they were. He went walking for a week with
George Trevelyan in Devonshire instead, and said nothing more
about it. It was not in his nature to bear lasting grudges. 'I think',
MacCarthy wrote to Moore, 'he has taken it very well.' Moore's curt
note was, however, a final breach in what had passed as a friendship
of sorts, and the relations between the two now remained cool, with
Moore avoiding Russell whenever he could. 'Russell bores me,' he
remarked on one occasion, and he 'behaves badly, I think' on
another. In public, however, he remained loyal, and when Trinity
College tried to strip Russell of his lectureship Moore was one of
the few people who supported him. It was left to Russell, fourteen
years later, to write the epitaph to their friendship: 'What has stood
between Moore and me is . . . jealousy on both sides.'

    1904 and 1905, Russell was to say were singularly unhappy years.
He was troubled about friends and constantly redefining his position.
His relations with Alys were virtually unbearable. 'I wonder how
another twenty-four hours of such utter misery can be endured,' he
noted, in his diary, 'but there is every reason to expect forty years of
just such torture . . . She is always bumping into furniture, treading
on one's toes, and upsetting lamps; and mentally she does just the

same sort of thing.' In the summer of 1905, he suffered a further blow.

After Cambridge Theodore Llewelyn Davies, a distinguished classical scholar and a fine-looking man with cropped, curly hair, a square open face and heavy eyebrows, shared a house in London with his elder brother Crompton. He became private secretary to a succession of chancellors of the exchequer, worked extremely hard, and was much loved by his friends, who looked up to him rather as they did to Moore. All agreed he was an exceptionally charming man. In the summer of 1905, when he was thirty-four, he was found dead in a pool near his parents' house in Kirkby Lonsdale, having hit his head on a rock while taking a dip on the way to catch a train. Russell heard the news from Crompton. The Apostles were soon exchanging appalled letters: 'He was extraordinary to all of us', Fry wrote to Dickinson, 'the most wonderful affection, that was his genius, I think, in his human relations. And I feel so much poorer for all the rest of life.' 'He was the best of all of us,' remarked George Trevelyan.

Charactistically, Russell turned instantly to help the family and particularly Crompton, who had been devoted to Theodore and seemed completely destroyed by his death. Russell went to London to be close to him, writing to Lucy Donnelly: 'Crompton's sorrow is crushing, and I hardly know how to bear it.' Planning to take Crompton abroad as soon as he could, he found himself prey to memories of 'buried griefs' which 'burst their tombs, and wailed in the desert spaces of one's mind, from which philosophy offered no comfort whatsoever'. In August, he went with Crompton to Normandy to stay with Roger Fry, and the two friends spent their days walking along the shore and reading on the sandy beach. Mary Sheepshanks, one of Russell's women friends from Cambridge, had been much in love with Theodore, and she too turned to Russell for solace. 'I can't hear about him from anyone else,' she wrote despairingly to him in September. Something important in Russell, whose sense of friendship could seem inadequate at ordinary moments, responded well to deep unhappiness in others – Philip Jourdain, Evelyn Whitehead and Gilbert Murray among them.

'The loss of Theodore seems still a mere phantasy and the strange mixture of dream and waking thoughts and recollections . . . leave me in bewilderment . . .' Crompton wrote to Russell that autumn. 'I cling to you with all my heart and bless you for loving and helping me.'

Six

A razor to chop wood: the philosopher in politics

In the spring of 1904 the Russells began to look for land somewhere near Oxford on which to build a house. They had been almost constantly on the move for most of their married life. Alys, who visited the city in March, reported to Russell that 'Oxford people are much flattered by thy wanting to come here, and the philosophers, while disagreeing, are prepared to be very friendly.' They found an ideal setting in Bagley Wood, three miles south of the city centre; it was thickly wooded, very green, with open meadows across which could be seen the river and the spires of Oxford. The architect Henry Martineau Fletcher, a Trinity man and a cousin of the Llewelyn Daviesses, was asked to draw up plans for a house in a clearing in the woods, a little back from the road. The place is much the same today, wooded and rural, though the cars from a main road can now be heard, and a line of detached houses runs along the side of the road. The neighbours have long since forgotten the Russells.

Lower Copse House is a white, undistinguished building with Italianate shutters and brick work. It is remarkable inside chiefly because it is almost without corridors, one room leading straight out of the next. It is light, the architect having angled the windows so as to bring in as much daylight as possible from the surrounding woods, and the Russells filled it with Delft tiling. It was ready in the spring of 1905.

Russell's mood, as they moved in, had improved, despite his chilly marriage, not least because he was becoming increasingly involved in the political issues of the day. Given his upbringing, and his earlier ambivalence about a career, it was inevitable that at some stage the political arena would come to look attractive.

He was glad to leave London and seems not to have minded the procession of feminists and college women who came to call on Alys – though there was nowhere for him to escape to inside the house – just as he seems to have welcomed the unmarried mothers whom Alys chose to employ in the kitchen. Among the first visitors was one who was to play a crucial part in their lives: Lady Ottoline Morrell, the wife of the politician Philip Morrell, who struck Alys as a 'wonderful vision of spotted muslin and pearls'. To the Halévys, who also came to call, Alys seemed like a large child: very blonde, very upright and very simple. They found Russell 'sarcastic and paradoxical'. Russell wrote to Lucy Donnelly to say that at last he was hard at work, and that 'work restores me to a belief that it is better I should exist than not exist.'

With his work on *Principia* flowing ahead quietly, and various philosophical papers unfolding in his mind, Russell was now drawn into politics. His grandmother had never really imagined that he would do anything but follow in Lord John's footsteps, though when the excellent results of his Fellowship exams convinced him that his future lay not on a platform but in a study, she had accepted it with good grace. Now, at the age of thirty-three, with an extraordinary piece of work behind him, and increasingly taken by Liberal ideas, he became convinced that the future of society lay in reshaping its contours, so that evil people and institutions were replaced by virtuous ones. Russell's view of human nature, though often bleak, was not altogether despairing. He believed man to be capable of altruism, though he sensed that the strongest motive governing human behaviour was the appetite for power – a belief he would play with all his life, just as he would go on struggling to balance a life of action with one of scholasticism. The moment had come to stop avoiding the political world, and to test it out.

In this he was encouraged by his friends, who had perceived his talent when it came to a public platform. 'It was all very clear and intellectual and even witty', wrote Logan Pearsall Smith to his mother Hannah, describing a talk given by Russell. 'It seems like using a razor to chop wood, but such people are necessary to the

State . . . He is not as yet a party politician, so I don't think that he will stand for Parliament. But he is conscientious, public spirited and likes excitement, so I suppose he will always be popping out of his cloister into the world.'

It was hardly surprising, given the social reforms which interested him, that Russell should be drawn into the net of Beatrice and Sidney Webb. Neither of the Webbs was much interested in friends, seeing people primarily as 'instruments' for advancing their cause, and ruthlessly rejecting those they labelled 'time wasters', though Beatrice did occasionally feel twinges of unease about the readiness with which they manipulated acquaintances. There were a few people whom she liked and considered friends, and Russell was one of them. She appreciated his puritan ways, his intellectual audacity and his delightful conversation, even if she found him lacking in sympathy and humility; for his part, Russell admired her integrity, warmth and hard work, but disagreed with her over religion and complained that she lacked imagination.

Russell had first met the newly-married Webbs while staying with the Pearsall Smiths in 1892. Over lunch he had observed somewhat maliciously that Sidney peered around uncertain which knife and fork to use for the various courses, but in that he may have been influenced by a conversation with his grandmother. Sidney Webb, she had declared, was 'not quite'. 'Not quite what?' asked Russell. 'Not quite a gentleman in mind or manners', Lady Russell replied.

Though Lowes Dickinson had invited the Webbs and Shaw to lecture in Cambridge the following year, it was not until 1897 that Russell joined the Fabian Society, the socialist group founded in 1884 to promote the spirit of public duty and the notion of man's accountability to society, of which the Webbs were the guiding spirits. From then on, particularly after Russell had given his lectures on German social democracy at Webb's newly founded London School of Economics and donated his fellowship money to it for research studentships, the Webbs and Russells met frequently, either over dinner or on holidays together.

By 1903, the Webbs were becoming an influence in British socialist circles. Beatrice was soon to be appointed to the Royal

Commission on the Poor Law. A review of earlier poor laws was direly needed by the turn of the century, and as an instinctive reformer, she was to make it her life's work, following naturally from her earlier work on poverty in London and from the Webbs' seminal history of the trade-union movement.

Beatrice was the eighth of nine daughters of a wealthy Gloucestershire railway promoter called Potter – 'the Potter sisterhood' of social butterflies was how Russell's mother once described them. Considered beautiful by many people with a pale skin, clear features, dark silvery hair and bright brown eyes, Beatrice was far from being a social butterfly; Desmond MacCarthy once compared her to a 'benevolent hawk'. Nor was there anything frivolous about Sidney. He was a short man with small hands and feet, a high-domed forehead, thick dark hair, a goatee beard and a lisp, but he could seem a little absurd at times, when he insisted on referring to himself and Beatrice as 'we' and telling people 'our age this year will be 157'.

The Webbs were living at 41 Grosvenor Road in Pimlico, three doors from the Pearsall Smiths, in a tall, narrow terrace house in what was still virtually a slum despite the Tate Gallery nearby, close to a disreputable pub, several derelict houses and a factory, and with a view across the river to the ugly tower of Poulton's Pottery Works. But the view the other way, over Vauxhall Bridge, was pleasant, and since the house was agreeably quiet, it was perfectly suited to the rigid Webb routine and their prodigious output of material on economic history. They rose at 6.30 a.m., took cold baths, breakfasted at 8 a.m., and worked together on the dining-room table until lunch, after which Sidney left for his job with London County Council.

Both were intensely social, in a purposeful sort of way; they had turned their house into a political and literary salon and kept the drawing room bare, with plain matting on the floor and long alcove seats but no sofa, so as to pack in the maximum number of guests. They were not so much stingy as frugal, declaring that fasting produced exquisite visions, and offering their guests modest helpings of profoundly unappetising food. Both Webbs ate at great speed, leaving the table the minute the meal was over. They shared a revulsion against idleness, a conviction that they and their friends should train themselves to be instruments of social progress, and a belief that they needed to keep their bodies in a state of healthy efficiency – a desire Beatrice thought she recognised in Russell's asceticism and attention to health. (Their frugality paid off: Beatrice lived to the age of eighty five; Sidney to eighty-eight.)

Neither was much interested in individuals or their misfortunes, preferring the larger canvas, the relations between the different classes and central government. In later life, Beatrice would jokingly describe herself and her followers as the 'B's' of this world, 'bourgeois, bureaucratic and benevolent', as opposed to the 'A's', people like Russell, who were 'aristocratic, anarchic and artistic'. Russell considered them the most 'completely married couple' that he knew: Sidney produced a phenomenal amount of work and took a more public role, while Beatrice was better at ideas, and remained more private. Not all their friends were as uncritical. Crompton Llewelyn Davies, in particular, complained that, having taken up the cause of defenceless paupers, they practised their beliefs at home by employing a pauper with a peg-leg to dig holes for potatoes.

To keep their bodies in shape, the Webbs cycled, often taking the Russells with them. This was their great outdoor pleasure, just as work in all its forms was their main indoor activity, though even when cycling they were perfectly capable of continuing to talk about work. By the 1890s, after Dunlop had invented the pneumatic tyre, the bicycle boom had come to England, and the Fabians, with their bicycles, tricycles and tandems, were greatly excited by their new toys. (The hero of Wells's *The Wheels of Chance*, a draper called Hoopdriver, provides an excellent picture of the Victorian and early Edwardian delight in bicycles: 'He did not ride fast, he did not ride straight, an exacting critic might say he did not ride well – but he rode generously, opulently, using the whole road and even nibbling at the footpath.') When the Webbs took holidays, and they found time for a surprising number, they spent the mornings at their desks and the afternoons on their bicycles. Bernard Shaw, who spent practically every holiday with them until his marriage, once wrote to Ellen Terry complaining of the number of female bicycle tyres he was forced to mend: 'I wonder what you would think of our life – our eternal political shop; our mornings of dogged writing, all in our separate rooms; our ravenous plain meals; our bicycling; the Webbs' incorrigible spooning over their individual and political science . . .'

Russell, who had met Shaw as an undergraduate, came to know him better through the Webbs. He always remembered a bicycle accident during a holiday at Tintern Abbey, when Shaw, still a novice cyclist, hurtled into his machine with such force that he was thrown twenty feet on to his back. Shaw's bicycle was undamaged, but Russell's was mangled. During the slow train ride back to where they were staying, Shaw, who had climbed back on to his bicycle, appeared at every stop, put his head into the carriage and jeered. Shaw described the episode to a friend: 'If you hear rumours of my death, contradict them. I have had a most awful bicycle smash – the quintessence of ten railway collisions – brother of Earl Russell of conjugal fame dashed into at full speed flying downhill – £3. 10s damage to machine – Russell bereft of knickerbockers but otherwise unhurt.' Russell did not wholly take to Shaw. 'I think Shaw, on the whole, is more bounder than genius,' he wrote to Lucy Donnelly, '. . . he hates self-control, and makes up theories with a view to proving that self-control is pernicious . . . I couldn't get on with *Man and Superman*, it disgusted me. I don't think he is a soul in Hell dancing on red-hot iron. I think his Hell is merely diseased vanity and a morbid fear of being laughed at.'

Nor did he greatly take to H. G. Wells, whom he met at a talking and dining club called the Coefficients, which had been started in 1902 by Sidney Webb – the idea being that each member would be jointly 'efficient'. Wells was then in the early days of his popularity and had been earmarked by Beatrice as a 'good instrument for popularising ideas', though she thought his personality unattractive and dismissed his wife as a 'pretty little person with a strong will, mediocre intelligence and somewhat small nature'. For his part Russell remarked dismissively to Halévy that he considered Wells 'first rate in the second rate category'.

The club met once a month at a restaurant in Westminster to discuss the future of what Wells described as 'this perplexing, promising and frustrating world of ours'. Its twelve members included H. J. Mackinder, the authority on German 'geo-politics', whom Russell considered 'the head Beast of the School of Economics'; Sir Edward Grey, a prominent Liberal imperialist, and a number of politicians and businessmen. Shaw, who despised meals of this kind, and found conversation about such things pointless, refused to join. The talk was all about the Empire, whether it might yet be a 'free-trading, free-speaking, liberating flux for mankind', and about Germany and militarism. Of the members, only Wells and Russell were more interested in issues than in party politics, and it was not long before acrimonious discussions broke out, with the rest of the gathering speaking up in favour of armaments and defensive alliances while Wells and Russell insisted on discussing education and branding great wars as madness. Russell did not last long as a member. One day Sir Edward Grey spoke in favour of a policy of entente with France and Russia, which Russell considered likely to lead straight to a world war. He left the room and resigned. 'I have left the Coefficients,' he noted in his journal, 'because the Empire has come to seem to me not worth preserving.'

He had come a long way since he had tramped four miles to the station in an ecstasy of patriotism at the height of the Boer War. Russell, these days, was in a mood for resignation. His 'conversion' during Evelyn's seizure had left him deeply opposed to authoritarianism and he now moved away from the Fabians and the Webbs, and their support for imperialism. In any event, Russell was never a true Fabian by temperament. He may have shared the Webbs' moral conscience, and been attracted by their austere style, but he was not driven by social guilt in the way they were, and he disagreed with them profoundly over their faith in the state, their fundamental credo. Nor did he share their certainty about the means to achieve social reform. As with the Apostles and Bloomsbury, Russell remained on the fringes, for a while engaging in some of their discussions, but not central to their deliberations: he was never as isolated or élitist, nor did he share their suspicions of democracy. He had also become somewhat disenchanted personally with the Webbs, explaining in a letter to Gilbert Murray, after a bicycling holiday in Normandy: 'I minded them worse than usual. They have a competent way of sizing up a cathedral, and pronouncing on it with an air of authority, and an evident feeling that the LCC could have done it better. They take all the colour out of life, and make everything one cares for turn to dust and ashes.'

Not for nothing was Russell the godson of John Stuart Mill, who had sought to liberate the individual from external coercion and proposed the taxation of the unearned increase in land values; or the grandson of Lord John, who had carried the Reform Bill through Parliament in 1832. Born a Whig, of radical aristocratic parents, he was a Liberal until the outbreak of the First World War. Liberal perhaps, but not deeply involved, at least not before the middle of the first decade of the new century.

The great political controversies of Edwardian England – British foreign policy, Ireland, the armaments race, the grim conditions of the working classes – are barely mentioned in his letters and papers. What stirred Russell to active politics was an issue which he felt lay at the very heart of the democratic process and internationalism: free trade. It brought out in him a new political voice, an eloquent and rousing note which was to run through the rest of his life; and it gave him a temporary release from logic, mathematics and his mournful religious longings. Still stamped by his utilitarian tradition, Russell was concerned with the value of individual judgement, the role of government and the necessity of forging a link between equality and liberty. But it was more a case of seeing politics, not in the new 'positive' liberalism of men like Hobson or Hobhouse, but as the need to settle unfinished nineteenth-century business; and Russell was always happier on the high ground of theory, writing, than down among the foot soldiers, knocking on doors.

The issue which drew him now into the political field was free trade versus tariff reform. On 15 May 1903, Joseph Chamberlain, colonial secretary in Arthur Balfour's Unionist government, who had been warning for years that Britain's economy was being eroded by competition from abroad, announced that he intended to campaign for a policy combining imperial preference with domestic protection. Preference, said Chamberlain, would be a first step towards imperial federation; protection would help British industry and provide money for social reform. Since both Whigs and Tories had championed free trade from the early 1850s, after Sir Robert Peel's repeal of the

Corn Laws, what he was proposing was little short of an attack on all that Victorian politics had stood for. So intensely did Chamberlain feel the need to advocate these proposals, however, that when the Cabinet would not accept them, he resigned as colonial secretary and set off on a speaking tour of Britain, unleashing one of the major political crises since the Irish Home Rule battles of 1886.

The Liberals and most Tories believed that free trade led to prosperity, peace and class harmony; they feared that tariffs would set the country on the path to class conflicts, international tension, corruption in Parliament and a trade war. For Russell, following Cobden, the free trade issue – an implicit credo of his liberal heritage – provoked a sudden and unprecedented sense of urgency about politics, strengthened by his 'conversion', which had convinced him that imperialism led to war and suffering, and free trade to peace and compassion – no tariff wars, and cheap food. For him, it was a question of morality more than one of economics. 'We are all wildly excited about Free Trade,' he wrote to Lucy Donnelly on 29 July 1903, 'it is to me the last piece of sane internationalism left, and if it went I should feel inclined to cut my throat.'

Characteristically, Russell proposed to point out what he saw to be the logical inconsistencies of the tariff reformers, and hoped by doing so he would demolish their case. Retaliation, preference and protection were the three tenets at stake, and Russell challenged each in a series of public talks delivered from the spring of 1904 at the New Reform Club, as well as in various town halls around London, and in the newspapers. The *Daily News*, referring to his lectures, called him 'probably the deepest thinker at present standing next-door to a peerage'. What was possibly his finest declaration on the subject, containing, as he explained to Halévy early that spring, all he thought and had to say on the subject, appeared in a review of various pamphlets and parliamentary papers entitled 'The Tariff Controversy'. He wrote anonymously for the *Edinburgh Review*, a Whiggish quarterly, edited by Arthur Elliot, a first cousin of Lord Amberley's.

The piece is long, detailed and persuasive, and ends on a bracing note: 'The ideal of a great empire inspired by higher purposes, preserving liberty and justice, pacific in its dealings with foreign powers, fulfilling its trust towards subject races – this is an ideal which has inspired many of the best in our nation, and the hope of its realization has formed a part of daily happiness. . . . England has been in the past, and is still, pre-eminent in liberty; freedom in government, in religion, and in trade are English contributions to political practice. Nothing but a steadfast adherence to the ideal of freedom can preserve our Empire . . .' Something of the exhilaration felt by Russell during this campaign was to mark his political style for ever.

Russell believed that the forces lined up against Chamberlain were so formidable that he was unlikely to succeed in his campaign. 'The idiocy and blackguard cowardice of the Liberal leaders does often nearly drive me mad,' he wrote to Halévy, 'and if I really thought Chamberlain had a chance, I don't know what I should do. As it is, I feel no serious doubts of his being badly beaten.' Russell was partly right; tariff reform, in the shape proposed by Chamberlain, did not win through.

He had enjoyed his fight. The energy he brought to it – at least thirteen lectures in just over two months – had been pleasurable and distracting. 'I was less unsuccessful as a speaker than I had expected to be,' he noted in his journal, 'but what I liked was the cooperation with such a large part of the nation in an object which I believed to be very important.' What was more, it had brought him into contact with the secretary of the Free Trade Union, a young woman called Ivy Pretious. Their relations were almost certainly platonic, but while they lasted they did much to console Russell for his persistent failure with Alys.

Ivy Pretious was just twenty-four when Russell first met her, probably with George and Janet Trevelyan. She had large, luminous eyes, and an ivory complexion which made her look vaguely oriental; her exquisite cursive handwriting was said by Margot Asquith to be the most beautiful she had ever seen. The illegitimate daughter of a man who had disappeared when she was two, and granddaughter of the builder of the first ship to ply the Danube, her education had stopped altogether at the age of thirteen, when her mother also ran away, abandoning her and her brother, possibly after embezzling some funds. She put her hair up, bought a long skirt and, pretending to be fifteen, found a job with a music publisher. By 1905, she was secretary of the Free Trade Union, with a flat of her own off the Kings Road and a living-in maid. For Russell, Ivy was the epitome of the independent new woman.

According to her son Hallam, Ivy was probably in love with Russell and may even have pursued him. Russell was certainly flattered. 'It will be very jolly, and I shall enjoy seeing you,' he wrote, just before a meeting with her. 'I feel as tho' I shall be in a rollicking mood, and talking nonsense all the time.' He soon took her into his confidence about Alys, telling her of a possibility of 'emancipation from my bondage' before too long. Many of his letters were written on the train between London and Oxford. 'You have a very special place in my thoughts,' he wrote on 15 October 1905, 'from which you are seldom long absent . . . I have never before or since made friends so quickly, or wished to, with anyone as with you.' He warned her not to write to Bagley Wood, since Alys was liable to steam open his letters.

Before long their friendship was causing gossip. George Trevelyan's wife, Janet, summoned Russell and warned him to take care, as Ivy was plainly falling in love with him. Many years later, he scribbled a note at the bottom of his letters, saying that he had been 'scolded as a philanderer'. Whatever he felt, he acted on her advice and in July wrote from Bagley Wood to say that it would be better if they ceased to meet, as Alys seemed happier now that she was living away from London, and that he was loath to give her 'so much pain unless it is for some very important and definite purpose' – which this apparently was not. Ivy must have been pressing, because he wrote several times more in the same vein, promising friendship but nothing more. They stopped meeting. 'I saw you one day in a bus in Victoria Street as I was walking there,' Russell wrote to her sometime later, 'but I had no time to see more than that you looked sad and had a nice hat.'

They continued to write to each other, Russell's letters decidedly avuncular, full of sympathy and concern; when she met the MP and future Cabinet minister R. M. McKenna, whom Russell mistrusted, he wrote feverishly to Lucy Donnelly that he feared Ivy was 'in the greatest danger'. Later, Ivy met Charles Tennyson, a brilliant but shy barrister, who proposed to her, and Russell agreed to come to dinner to meet him. After that, with Russell's interest in the free trade movement at an end, they never met again. But in the 1950s, Hallam Tennyson, her son, met Russell. 'Tell Ivy', Russell said, 'that I think of her.' He paused, in search of the right span of time: 'Every week'.

'At present, men and women seldom have any real companionship, or any real understanding of each other's best: brought together by a temporary attraction, they remain strangers, and as a rule hamper each other's development', Russell declared in a paper called *The Status of Women*. 'To teach men and women to love equality and liberty is the beginning of all reform in personal relations.' The essay had been written for Ivy Pretious, as an introduction to the subject of suffrage, but it says much about the way Russell felt about women in general and his relationship to Alys in particular. What was more, it signalled the start of a second political campaign which, now that his work on free trade was finished, was beginning to interest him.

For many people like Russell, the 1906 Liberal triumph under Sir Henry Campbell-Bannerman – the biggest landslide in British history since the Whig victory of 1832 – opened the way to a rethinking of Liberal theories and policies, and to a belief that the broadening of the franchise was a necessary condition for any true progress in politics or society. That women had no vote at all was, for Russell and others like him, a disgrace. Most Liberal MPs were by now in favour of some kind of female suffrage, and many of them had been committed to full male suffrage – current restrictions meant that no more than 60 per cent of adult men had the vote either – since well before the turn of the century. Russell was a fervent believer in equal rights for women, both by upbringing – through his godfather J. S. Mill, and his maternal grandmother, Lady Stanley, a founder of Girton College – and by temperament, for he hated conventionality, authoritarianism and anti-intellectualism, and any opposition to the female franchise seemed seemed redolent of everything he most loathed about Victorian values. Equality, truthfulness and above all liberty between the sexes, as he explained to Ivy Pretious, lay at the heart of all true companionship; a decent relationship between a man and a woman was not possible without them. It was not surprising that Russell had joined the governing body of Newnham College, Cambridge, in 1902. What makes Russell's entry into suffrage politics the more interesting is the way his words anticipate so much of his later thinking on marriage, children and divorce.

The suffrage cause was by no means perfectly straightforward. However loudly they proclaimed their support, few Liberal MPs were fundamentally committed to female suffrage, being more concerned with social reform and defence. Between 1906 and 1909, private members' bills on suffrage were either defeated or talked out. Two private bills, in particular, kept appearing and kept being defeated: the first gave women the vote on the same basis as men (which Liberals feared would only strengthen their Unionist middle-class women opponents), and the second advocated adult suffrage.

By 1906, the year in which Russell probably composed his essay for Ivy Pretious, there were two, vastly different bodies campaigning for female suffrage: the National Union of Women's Suffrage Societies (NUWSS), composed of Millicent Fawcett's 'suffragists', and the more militant 'suffragettes' of the Pankhursts' Women's Social and Political Union. Russell, though not altogether in favour of either, since he advocated full adult suffrage, suspected that the NUWSS, with their pledge to give the vote to women on the same rather limited terms as men, were more likely to get women the vote. He joined its council in 1906 and was elected to its executive committee in 1907. He wrote to his friend Margaret Llewelyn Davies, 'I detest the general assumption of women's inferiority, which seems to me degrading to both men and women.' Margaret, who had come to regard Russell as a possible successor to J. S. Mill as popular theorist for the movement, was urging him to hurry up with 'The Book' (*Principia Mathematica*) so that he could turn his attention to a new classic on suffrage. 'You see what faith I have in you', she wrote, 'as an unprejudiced, logical and right-feelinged person.' Russell was not so much unconvinced as curiously modest. 'I have at times made attempts', he replied, 'and they have been so lamentable that I came to the conclusion I was incapable of that sort of writing.'

Early in 1907, the seat for Wimbledon fell vacant on the resignation of its MP. It was a safe Tory seat – possibly the safest in the country – and the Liberals decided not to contest it. The NUWSS announced that they would make it their first election campaign, and approached Russell. 'It is a howling joke,' Russell reported to Ivy Pretious, 'and amuses me almost as much as it annoys me.' But he agreed to stand. Russell's opponent was an old-fashioned parliamentary warhorse named Henry Chaplin, a corpulent, genial Tory who had sat for the same rural Lincolnshire constituency for thirty-eight years until he was thrown out in the Liberal landslide of 1906. Friends called him 'Squire', and he was, as he complacently admitted, 'an old offender upon the question of female suffrage'. George Trevelyan observed in a letter to Russell that there could not have been a 'pair of more oddly contrasted candidates . . . What a sporting cove you are!'

The 'Squire' told the *Westminster Gazette* that he was confident of a 'walk-over'. But he had not reckoned with the determination of the suffrage brigade. Hundreds of women, bold, hard-working, serious and wearing enormous hats, poured into the constituency and got down to work. Newspaper photographs of the time show a row of formidable women towering above a small, heavily moustached Russell, who wears a wry smile. Around the constituency were life-sized cardboard cutouts of women, with the words VOTE FOR RUSSELL written on their aprons. Since some of Russell's campaign slogans were so close to their own, the Liberals, though refusing to support him openly, agreed to allow their speakers to go to Wimbledon and lobby for him. George Trevelyan was one, Philip Morrell another. Somewhat disconcerted by all this activity, Chaplin drafted in battalions of supporters of his own. The newpapers, suddenly alerted to the possibilites for comedy in this contest, sent down droves of reporters. Russell remarked wearily to Alys one day that he had given fifty interviews.

The Russells – Alys no less than Russell himself – fought a hard battle. Alys, dressed in a silk suit, lace blouse and borrowed blue feather hat, looked handsome and imposing though she worried about her outfit 'getting be-egged'. They talked – in a single week, Russell spoke at nineteen meetings and Alys at sixteen – they canvassed, they visited railway stations in the morning and the evening to distribute leaflets to commuters. Because female suffrage was still regarded by many as a fundamentally frivolous topic, meetings were sometimes broken up by practical jokes. One day in May when Beatrice Webb, Ethel Snowden and Alys were all on the platform, rats were let loose in the audience and cayenne pepper shaken around the hall, so that the audience was soon sneezing and in a state of hysteria, while men standing at the back shouted: 'Someone has been farting in here!' and 'We don't want a petticoat government.' Three days later, Alys was hit between the eyes by an egg. Both Russells earned much praise for the calm way in which they handled these outbursts, and Chaplin wrote to apologise for the manners of his supporters. 'Politics', Russell told his listeners, 'is a question of babies. Women do not want to lose their children, or to have 120,000 babies dying yearly because they have no proper homes and nourishment.' The *Daily Mail* remarked: 'Mr Russell (suitably for a feminist candidate) is a student, a mathematician, something of a philosopher. He reads Leibniz . . .' *The World* was less flattering: 'The sight of these violent, manly women would make me move heaven and ·earth to defeat Mr B. R. Mr R, under the best circumstances, is not a person of great charm or persuasion . . .' The *Daily Express* insisted on calling his supporters 'lady window-break- ers', while the *Daily Mail* published a poem:

> Since first the unequal strife began,
> The end indeed, was plain to see –
> The downfall of the ladies' man
> And all his petty-coterie!

Polling took place on 14 May, in the middle of a tropical downpour, which drove away all but forty of Russell's promised one thousand women supporters, and kept the Liberal voters at home. Chaplin won his walk-over with 10,263 votes to 3299. Russell described the experience as 'arduous', but he never regretted it.

Just over a year later, Asquith, who had taken over the prime ministership after Campbell-Bannerman's death in 1908, offered an amendment to the proposed Electoral Reform Bill which promised some measure of votes for women. There had been heavy rain and Bagley Wood was flooded. 'I wonder', wrote Russell to Margaret, 'if God is going to send another flood to drown the suffragettes, and if so whether Asquith and Mrs Asquith will be the new Noah and Mrs Noah.' Russell urged supporters of the NUWSS to be conciliatory, sensing that endless hostility to Liberal offers would be counter-productive. By now he took the view that the battle could be won only in stages, and that only limited bills had any chance of becoming law. The ladies of the NUWSS were not in a conciliatory mood; Russell's position within the organisation became untenable, and he resigned from the executive committee. In any case, Liberal suc-cesses were on the wane, and in the House of Lords the Unionist coalition was able to sink many of the proposed government bills.

For a while longer, Russell, watching from the sidelines, was able to persuade himself that the NUWSS was becoming more politically reasonable, particularly when contrasted with the suffragettes, whose courage he admired, but whose heckling he deplored, saying that he never judged law-breaking 'by any other test than whether it paid', and that this time it was not paying. He was later to add that he believed violent tactics had effectively 'put off women's suffrage for twenty years', but later still to say that their stand had carried the day. The whole question of political violence, and under what circumstances it achieved its goals, was to exercise him for the rest of his life. But in 1909 he took a tough stand when there was public outrage about the force-feeding of suffragettes. 'It has been con-stantly resorted to for ordinary criminals without anybody objecting to it,' he wrote to Lucy Donnelly. 'The women to whom it has been applied have committed serious acts of violence . . . If the Govern-ment lets them out when they starve, all criminals will adopt the hunger strike, and the criminal law is at an end.'

When he eventually concluded that the NUWSS was committed only to subordinating all other public issues to the question of female franchise, Russell withdrew his support, complaining to Helen Thomas: 'I wonder whether your suffragists are as trying as ours. Ours have the bigotry of a small religious sect, and the suspiciousness of Parisians in the war of 1870.' In any case, Margaret Llewelyn Davies was beginning to draw him in the direction of her own campaign, the People's Suffrage Federation, of which she was one of the two honorary chairmen. The PSF goal was suffrage for all adults, women as well as men, on a 'short residential qualification'.

This fitted in far better with Russell's views on equality. The only reason he had not gone over earlier, he now confessed to Margaret, was that he had felt that he was 'not being quite a true friend to women'. To Lucy Donnelly, he explained, 'It is not women as women that I want enfranchised, but women as human beings. And even *poor* women are human beings.'

By January 1910, Russell was on the PSF executive. He was toying with the idea of standing for Parliament as a Liberal candidate, for he had become increasingly involved in other Liberal causes such as the taxation of land values, social reform and the need for restraints on the House of Lords, by then widely regarded as an enemy to the most important pieces of proposed Liberal legislation. 'All the brains and all the oratory are on our side,' Russell remarked scathingly to Lucy Donnelly. 'All the money is on theirs.'

An offer of a possible Oxford seat came his way. He turned it down, but agreed to go for selection at Bedford, a traditional Liberal stronghold, which had been lost as a result of internal wrangles. Bedford had a strong Anglican tradition. Russell was summoned to address the electors on the evening of 26 April, but before he could do so he was led to a small room behind the hall. 'Are we to understand that you are an agnostic?' 'Yes,' Russell replied. 'Would you be willing to attend church occasionally?' 'No, I should not.' That was the end of his candidature, just as it had been the end of his father's in South Devon in 1868. He was never again to stand so close to the British political party process. In any case in the early summer of 1910, he heard from Whitehead that Trinity was considering offering him a five-year lectureship in logic and the principles of mathematics, for which he would receive £200 a year, a room in college and free dinners, in return for twenty-four lectures each term.

Until 1913, he continued to support the PSF with public talks and fund-raising, but he was deeply relieved when C. K. Ogden agreed to take over the secretaryship of the Cambridge branch. He was, he admitted, 'bored to extinction' by the whole subject. When, in 1916, he was asked for £31 to wind up the PSF he expressed surprise. He thought it had 'had its funeral long ago'.

*

Russell's own relations with women at this time were somewhat more complicated. The closing years of the decade saw the final erosion of his marriage to Alys. It was not simply that he no longer loved her: he did not even like her any more. His journal bears witness to endless bouts of guilt for not treating her better, but it is also coldly analytical. Every fault, every clumsiness is recorded, as with a difficult child. Alys is jealous; she spreads slanders; she lies; she is clumsy; she tries too hard to be liked; she is malicious; and, above all, she is stupid. So as not to feel overpoweringly irritated, Russell decided to stop looking at her. How long, he wondered, would he be able to endure this growing animosity? 'I foresee that continence will become increasingly difficult,' he noted coolly in his journal, 'and that I shall be tempted to get into more or less flirtatious relations with women I don't respect . . .'

For the moment, serious desires were kept at bay by self-control and passing unimportant flirtations. Ivy Pretious had been one; Helen Thomas another. A third was Mildred Minturn, a young graduate from Bryn Mawr, whom Russell had met in America. She was a friend of Lucy Donnelly's, and had paid several visits to England in the early years of the century. Mildred was amusing and flirtatious, but she cannot have been very perceptive. 'I know of no couple', she wrote fulsomely to her future husband, after a visit to the Russells, 'that combine so much, and no home that I like better to go to.' Russell was both physically drawn to her and a little repelled, complaining that she was shallow and frivolous and lacked a 'nice sense of honour', while confessing that she 'flirts very charmingly – I enjoyed her operations, tho' no doubt I ought not to have . . .'

All three young women were possibly more than a little in love with him; considerably older than any of them, Russell appears to have felt no more than a passing infatuation. He was far more concerned with the exhausting demands of his work and what he saw as a long-term strategy for freeing himself from Alys. 'My impression', he noted in his diary, '[is that] she will get tired of living with me, and will take to paying longer and longer visits to her people. They are her only real friends: everyone else who knows her well dislikes her . . . I have now definitely given up the hope of any serious improvement in her, and I look forward to a gradually increasing separation . . .'

To distract himself, he took walking or cycling holidays in England with the Whiteheads' eldest son, North, a delicate, clever boy whom Russell greatly liked, or with the Murrays, Desmond MacCarthy or George Trevelyan, with whom he visited Sicily, after attending a mathematical congress in Rome. The occasion, he reported to Alys, was a 'grand affair', with parties, special coaches and the king himself opening the conference in the Palazzo Corsini; the German delegates were 'polite but cliquey', Peano very cordial, and the French unfriendly. Russell was charmed by Sicily, where the asphodels and wild flowers were out, and he found Segesta 'unimaginably beautiful', but the sight of walkers was so unusual that horses shied from them on the roads, and he took against the 'natives of Calatafini', saying, in one of his more fastidious moods, that they were a 'revelation of human degradation and bestiality'. One summer, he spent a month in the Tyrol with Charles Sanger, walking from Innsbruck to Lake Garda, starting out early each morning and spending the heat of the day bathing or lying by a stream or lake. Sanger hated heights, so Russell scaled the peaks of the Dolomites on his own. On another occasion he spent two months by himself in Bideford working hard in the mornings and wandering in the afternoons through the woods which sloped down to the sea, across valleys filled with fern, moss and wild flowers, relishing his contented solitude. 'I do not now care greatly what other people think of my work,' he observed to Lucy Donnelly. 'I did care, until I had enough confidence that it was worth doing to be independent of praise . . . I feel better able than anyone else to judge what my work is worth.'

When in London or Oxford, he pursued an agreeable social life with old friends as well as new ones, though he complained to Lucy that since Theodore Llewelyn Davies's death he felt he was no longer capable of being the good friend he had once been. 'I feel increasingly helpless before misfortune; I used to be able to speak encouraging words, but now I feel too weary, and have too little faith in any remedy except endurance.' This did not prevent him from being extremely concerned when another brother of Margaret Llewelyn Davies, Arthur, got cancer and died, shortly followed by his wife.

Their children were eventually taken in by J. M. Barrie, and one of them provided the original for Peter Pan.

Alys for her part was confused, lonely and often depressed. When Russell seemed particularly remote she took to writing letters to him from upstairs, while he sat in his study below. In them, she poured out her feelings of guilt about making him unhappy, and interfering with his work. On his thirty-second birthday, she had written to tell him 'again how very much I love thee, and how very glad I am of thy existence'. Having cut herself off from her friends, she threw herself into hard work; she left the temperance cause because she felt it had become too pious, and took to the suffrage movement instead, in which at least she could be of some use to Russell and feel some sense of pride when she accompanied him on his election tours.

Hannah Pearsall Smith had turned seventy in 1902. After the Russells had built Lower Copse in Bagley Wood, Friday's Hill was given up, and she moved with Logan to Court Place, a pleasant house with a magnificent garden on the banks of the Thames not far away. Russell saw as little of her as he could. 'We are to have the great honour of having Bertie to a New Year's dinner tomorrow,' Hannah wrote to her daughter Mary: 'I daresay he hates coming, but I thought he ought to come *once* a year.' At Court Place Alys became a focus for the family, looking after Hannah, who was now confined to a wheelchair by arthritis, and acting as a chaperone for her nieces, Ray and Karin. Both girls often found her tedious, and did their best to escape her kindly overtures, but Ray conceded that she had a 'sort of audacious wit that seems to belong to her subconscious self, and she is simply made of kindness'. One can only guess at Alys's unhappiness.

In 1906, she had developed what she thought and hoped was breast cancer. When she discovered that the lump was not malignant, she was annoyed. She returned to the diary she had abandoned almost exactly six years before. 'Little duties keep me going from day to day. But they don't satisfy the awful craving hunger for Bertie's love. It is always there, the volcano, & at first it used to burst out very often in the most unpleasant scenes ... Now I can control its expression & I have only made one scene this winter, and only kissed him once since February. At first I couldn't live without kissing him every night and morning . . . If only I could die – it's such a simple solution. And yet when I dream of it, the agony of parting from Bertie is too great . . . My wound is healed up very nearly outside, & only grows deeper and stronger within. I have no way to express my love now, except by trying to arrange what he wishes . . . it is my despair that I had to lose his beautiful feeling of love for me because I was not worthy . . .'

The next entry was two years later. The lump was still with her, and it was growing. Once again, she was cast down to learn that it was not malignant: 'Time drags, drags . . . But things will seem different, I am sure, when I am old . . . It is equally painful to wake from a dream in which he is my lover as from a dream in which he is scolding me – more painful, because more difficult to readjust myself to. But this is all the Me, Me, the sickening me which he hates and I do too.'

Public honours were now coming Russell's way. In 1908, nine Fellows of the Royal Society, including Whitehead, voted to make him a member for his contribution to logic and mathematics. It was a considerable tribute. The following spring, he was elected to the Athenaeum Club. Though very agreeable to him, these honours touched only a part of his life. 'I have made a mess of my private life,' he wrote mournfully to Lucy, towards the end of 1909. 'I have not lived up to my ideals, & I have failed to get or give happiness. And as a natural result, I have tended to grow cynical about private reactions and personal happiness . . . therefore year by year work has become a more essential outlet to my rage for perfection.' All this was now about to change.

Seven

Russell in love

With the free trade battles behind him, and feeling that he had done what he could on the suffrage issue, Russell decided he still wished to do something further for the Liberals. Campaigning on behalf of an MP seemed the obvious activity, but he did not greatly approve of the Bagley Wood MP, so he offered his help to Philip Morrell, who held the constituency across the river. Russell had known Morrell's wife, Lady Ottoline, very slightly since childhood but had not much liked her, saying that she offended his puritan instincts by wearing too much scent and face powder. Ottoline was rather taken by Russell: 'I don't think I have ever met anyone more attractive but very charming, so quick and clearsighted and supremely intellectual,' she wrote in her diary. 'His notice flattered me very much – but still I trembled at it feeling that in half an hour he would see how silly one was and despise me.'

Working for Morrell, who was running for re-election as a Liberal for South Oxfordshire, Russell addressed meetings nearly every evening and canvassed by day. He grew to like Ottoline somewhat better, admiring how kind she seemed to everyone she met. It was not particularly surprising, therefore, that when he was invited to give three lectures in Paris in the spring of 1911, he should ask the Morrells if they could have him to stay in London for the night before he caught his train.

He reached their house at 44 Bedford Square on the evening of 19 March, to find Philip unexpectedly called away. Ottoline, nervous at the thought of entertaining Russell alone, had asked two friends to dine. She had been reading Colette and noted in her diary: 'But we women can love – and love passionately apart from the physical . . . or that at the end only – as a sacrament . . . I believe most women really think it brutal.' The word 'bestial' has been crossed out.

They talked about politics. 'The atmosphere . . .' Russell wrote later, 'fed something in me that had been starved . . . I felt rested from the rasping difficulties of the outer world.' After dinner, the others left and Russell and Ottoline sat by the fire. The conversation became more intimate. Ottoline's drawing room was magnificent, with heavy yellow curtains against grey walls covered in contemporary paintings, and richly scented with bowls of pot-pourri and jugs of flowers. Russell, tense, his hands clenched, attempted a few timid overtures. Ottoline encouraged him. He grew insistent. They talked and kissed well into the night, finally agreeing that they would become lovers as soon as possible. By the time he got on to his train the next day, Russell was in love. 'The nine years of self-denial had come to an end,' he later wrote. He left London almost frantic with impatience to clarify matters to everyone, particularly Philip and Alys.

Ottoline was a strange figure. When Russell dined with her she was thirty-seven, just over a year younger than he – a tall, stately, exotic woman with marmalade-coloured hair, a long thin face which Russell unflatteringly referred to as horse-like, a straight, pointed nose, and a jutting chin. Apparently indifferent to public opinion, she dressed in startlingly bright clothes, with many shawls, feathers, swirling silks, tassels, pearls and immense hats, heavily made up and towering over both men and women in her high-heeled shoes. Occasionally she would appear as a shepherdess, her Pekinese dogs attached to her crook by ribbons. She enjoyed slapstick comedy and music halls and vulgarity, and never objected to a little dirt or dust; she could be regal, spiritual or almost childishly gleeful. Virginia Woolf, who first met her in 1909, could never decide whether she was innocent or calculating. 'Her appearance', she wrote, 'made one think that she was vicious, devious and complicated to a degree. For she was as decorative and outlandish as an Austrian baroque church . . . she had a certain grace, a certain majesty of address which was at once intimidating and seductive.'

The daughter of Lieutenant-General Arthur Cavendish Bentinck, and a half-sister of the Duke of Portland, she had grown up in the family seat of Welbeck, where an eccentric former duke had built an underground ballroom, and a railway to carry food along the passages beneath the house. She had never cared for the life of a Victorian debutante, and to escape the tedium had dabbled with evangelical prayer meetings, which embarrassed the footmen. She then travelled with a companion to Italy, where she fell in love with the light, and then with Dr Axel Munthe, the society doctor specialising in nervous ailments in Rome; after which she tried her luck at St Andrews university and then at Oxford. By the time she met Russell, she had been married for eight years to Philip Morrell, the good-looking son of an old Oxford brewing family, and a partner with Logan Pearsall Smith in an antique shop, with whom she shared a taste for art – they went to museums and concerts and travelled abroad together – and an interest in Liberal politics which her family found shocking. A photograph of them together on the Lido in Venice shows two tall figures strolling on the sand, Philip long and elegant, with a thin face and a white panama hat, Ottoline in a billowing pale dress. It was evidently very windy, for the chiffon scarf which tethered her immense hat was flowing out behind her like an enormous butterfly. They had one child, a girl called Julian. Ottoline became intensely social, filling 44 Bedford Square with artists and writers – the very people denied her during her lonely youth – and sat for her portrait to Charles Conder and Augustus John. Her parties were regarded as amusing. She kept a store of oriental clothes, and guests danced to Philip's rendering of music-hall songs on the pianola. Duncan Grant leapt about like a Russian ballet dancer, while Lytton Strachey danced a delicate minuet.

Many people have written about Ottoline Morrell, not all of them kindly. Lytton Strachey, who accepted her generosity and hospitality for years, once observed that her tête-à-têtes were 'exactly timed – like a dentist', and described her as 'thickly encrusted with pearls and diamonds, crocheting a pseudo-omega quilt and murmuring on buggery'; Aldous Huxley, a regular visitor, put her into his novel

Crome Yellow as the booming Priscilla Wimbush, with her 'massive projecting nose and little greenish eyes'; D. H. Lawrence, whom she believed to be a good friend, made her Hermione in *Women in Love*, the tortured, colourful, middle-aged woman 'impressive, in her lovely pale-yellow and brownish-rose, yet macabre, something repulsive . . . She always felt vulnerable, vulnerable . . . It was a lack of robust self, she had no natural sufficiency, there was a terrible void, a lack, a deficiency of being within her.' What seems to have obsessed them all was not so much her mannered ways, nor her distinctive barking voice – Leonard Woolf called it nasal and neighing, Virginia Woolf as something between the cooing of a dove and the roaring of a lion – nor even her remarkable appearance, but the way she gathered people up and almost suffocated them with her concern and hospitality. Regarded by most people who knew her as forceful and demanding, she felt herself to be, on the contrary, uncertain and nervous, often unhappy and always worried about what others thought of her. Her diary is that of a troubled, wistful woman. There is something dated about her, as if she belonged to an earlier time.

'My dearest – My heart is so full that I hardly know where to begin', wrote Russell from his train to Paris on the morning he left her. 'It is altogether extraordinary that you should love me – I feel myself so rugged & ruthless, & so removed from the whole aesthetic side of life – a sort of logic machine warranted to destroy any ideal that is not very robust.' Paris, where he was lecturing to three highly demanding academic audiences, passed in a dream. Ottoline was due to go to Studland in Dorset, and he planned to join Alys for the weekend in Cambridge and then meet her there.

On the way back through London, suffering from toothache, he visited his dentist, who abruptly informed him that he was suffering from cancer, and needed to see a specialist – but that the right man was away for the next three weeks. Russell, reflecting that this was the kind of news most likely to intensify his feelings for Ottoline, decided to say nothing about his mouth. Instead, he told Alys that he had fallen in love. They had an appalling row. Alys, beside herself, her worst terrors now confirmed, told him that if he left her she would divorce him, and cite Ottoline; he replied that if she did so he would commit suicide. Alys stormed and raged. Russell's famous bicycle made a second appearance. He coolly gave Karin Costelloe, Alys's niece, who was about to take her tripos, a lesson on Locke's philosophy, then climbed on to his bicycle and rode away. 'And with that', he noted in his autobiography, 'my first marriage came to an end.'

His meeting with Ottoline was, in some sense, the second stage in his 'conversion'. In her company he became all the things that he had hitherto only spoken of: tender, open, alive. Much of this was to express itself in the letters he now poured out to her, three, even four times a day.

Nineteenth-century educated people were letter-writers: not simply because they had no telephone, but because that was what they had been brought up to do. Russell was in any case a natural letter-writer, but his affair with Ottoline unleashed an extraordinary talent for putting his thoughts down on paper. He was never a good poet, or a good writer of fiction, though he tried his hand at both. It was autobiography, self-revelation, reflections on the state of the world, on friends, on politics, on emotions he excelled at, and nowhere is this more vivid than in his letters to Ottoline. Written in a small, neat hand, fluent and with singularly few corrections, they are funny, revealing, evocative and invariably elegant. To Ottoline, he found and exposed an apparently undiscovered soul, ardent and full of excitement, which had lain concealed behind moroseness and self-indulgence. In love, he suddenly wanted to lay bare his entire character, every nuance of it, every memory repressed since childhood, and as he began to explore it, so he discovered new facets. Between March 1913 and January 1914 he wrote her nearly a thousand letters. They offer a truly remarkable, perhaps even unique, view of a man's nature.

Russell must have guessed at the passion and curiosity seething within himself, below the rational exterior he chose to expose to the world. But he cannot have known how explosive, once released, it would be. One can only wonder what would have happened to his life had he never met Ottoline. During the first days of their love affair, Russell's letters came almost hourly; they chronicle his growing involvement.

How can you ask if your love can be anything to me? It can be everything to me. You can give me happiness, & what I want even more – peace. All my life, except a short time after my marriage, I have been driven on by restless inward furies, flogging me on to activity & never letting me rest . . . You could give me inward joy & expel the demons . . .

Life is like a mountain top in a mist, at most times cold and blank, with aimless hurry – then suddenly the world opens out, and gives visions of unbelievable beauty . . .

So long as you can bear with me, I shall give you absolute devotion & tenderness & reverence. But if in the end you find me not good enough, I shall feel it was only to be expected.

O my heart I ache for you. I feel as if I could hardly live through the joy of your kiss tomorrow. I have never imagined your love.

Wherever I go & whatever I am doing you are always with me like remembered music . . . everywhere the radiance of your love lights the world for me.

Russell in love could be demanding, and Ottoline, who was fond of Philip, and of the life she had carved out for herself, was a little apprehensive. Though at first overwhelmed – 'You are the most wonderful gift that any woman ever had, because I feel no woman ever had the love of anyone so much in accord with her as you are with me' – she was put off by his bad breath, his tooth trouble having turned out not to be cancer, but pyorrhoea which he was not aware of for a long time, and apprehensive lest at any moment he might find her silly. His reassurances on this score sound like the old Russell: 'You seem to think I want you to be clever, but I have never thought you that, if that is any comfort to you' . . . 'it is not the thing I really want. No woman's intellect is really good enough to give me pleasure as intellect . . .'

They spent three days in Studland. Julian was with them and they walked on the beach while she collected shells. The days, Russell was to write, 'remain in my memory as among the few moments when life seemed all that it might be but hardly ever is'. The day they parted, he wrote her five letters.

After Studland, the magic was shattered by Alys's scenes, Logan's outrage, Philip's demands, and a sense of disapproval from the few friends who knew what was happening. The Whiteheads urged

Russell not to press for a divorce: it would damage his career, Philip's political future and Ottoline's reputation. Russell wanted Ottoline to leave home instantly. She was more hesitant and, after Logan had paid Philip a terse visit, it was agreed that while Russell and Ottoline would be allowed to meet, they were never to spend a night together; he begged her at least not to let Philip share her room. Russell had no choice but to accept. Logan, who had once admired Ottoline as a 'noble, great-winged, grave-eyed bird', could now hardly bring himself to speak to her. Ottoline dreaded these discussions, particularly when told by visitors that she was killing Alys. In her journal she wrote how strange she found it that so many people whom she had considered cynical and libertine were turning out to be puritans. There is something disingenuous about the surprise she and Russell expressed about the fuss. Lingering Victorian morality still frowned on liaisons of this nature, in public if not in private.

That summer, when Ottoline went to stay at the Morrells' small house at Peppard, near Henley-on-Thames, Russell moved into lodgings at Ipsden, six miles away, and bicycled over every morning, along the escarpment, up hills and down into valleys, through beautiful and empty countryside, taking perhaps an hour each way, on gravel tracks. It was an exceptionally fine July. They took picnics into the beech woods on the Chilterns, looking out across the fields. One day, they bathed in the river, and she gave him a lock of her hair. When she had to leave for London before he did he sat in the woods, writing letters to her, sometimes riding as much as fifty miles in a day, backwards and forwards to the post office, to see if there had been an answer.

Back in London it was not so easy. They met furtively, at the British Museum, on buses, walking on Putney Heath, and even occasionally at the Whiteheads in Carlyle Square, where Evelyn had given them permission to see each other but not too often, because she did not want her son or the servants to know. That autumn, Russell rented a small flat in Bury Street near the British Museum, and Ottoline helped him to decorate it. When they were apart, he continued to deluge her with letters about his new-found soul. But these had broadened out to include fragments about his work, his ambitions and his friends, whom he had recently come to view with a more critical eye, as if his passion for Ottoline had further sharpened his feelings about other people.

Crompton, since Theodore's death, had 'imperceptibly . . . hardened & closed up'; Lowes Dickinson, of whom he had once been so fond, 'has the uneasy jauntiness of a man seeking pleasure in ways his conscience disapproves, and the things he says seem to me to show an occasional coarsening that disgusts me'; Roger Fry's 'intellect is not as clear cut as it might be . . . I think really what one minds is that his feelings seem blurred as well as his thoughts'; and Trevy, his old walking companion, had become a bit of a bore, with 'an odd, placid existence with his books – no temptations or storms or upsets – only the half-faced knowledge that he is no good'. Freedom had brought a touch of cruelty. 'The just men usually bore me', he remarked, 'because they are usually very limited . . .'

About his own plans and his future, however, he was full of hope and a new sense of excitement. '1. I want to keep you & I want not to ruin your life . . . 2. I want to accomplish, during my life, a good deal more work in philosophy . . . 3. I want to write general things of religion & morals & popular philosophy . . . 4. I like teaching, but that is incidental . . . I believe seriously that the spring of life would be broken in me if we parted now . . .'

Ottoline was not only distinctly less in love than Russell, she was on the rebound from an unsatisfactory relationship with the artist Henry Lamb, with whom Lytton Strachey was also in love. Her letters speak of her and Russell as being 'twin souls' who had been wandering about the world and had just found each other, of sharing a 'communion of souls – that is as great and as vivid an ecstasy as any physical sensation' and of their relationship being as 'good as one can get on earth'. Her diaries tell another story. She is 'overwhelmed' by the 'upheavals', and by the 'frenzy of Bertie's meteor coming flashing into my life', upsetting 'all those meaner stars'. But she is also anxious and uncertain, afraid of being possessed and constantly self-critical about her role: 'How old and how little I have done', she notes. 'What do I accomplish? Nothing. Read; learn; hold to God.' Philip, evidently, behaved with dignity and restraint, and as the affair went on, she repeated several times how much she really loved him. Ottoline was never a letter-writer in the way that Russell was, or as skilled at autobiographical self-knowledge; her sentences were staccato, her sentiments often fulsome and her handwriting almost impossible to decipher. The feelings that come across from these early days of their affair are, however, very clear: they are tentative and vacillating, with none of Russell's passionate conviction. 'He was like a Savanarola,' she wrote in her journal, 'exacting from me my life, my time, and my whole devotion, and I cried out "Oh, to be free!"'

That their affair was so minutely documented is due not only to the hundreds of letters they exchanged, but to Ottoline's private diaries. The early ones contain photographs and cuttings, of herself and Philip and Julian, sitting in gardens or wandering on beaches. When, towards the end of her life, Ottoline decided to publish her memoirs, she, and then, Philip did some careful editing. In Philip's hands, Russell became 'Herbert' and Alys, 'Lucy'. There had not been a great deal about Russell in the original – the entries covering her meetings with him are often no more than a few sentences – but what little there was was further pruned, leading to a slight shift in emphasis. Talking about the Peppard summer, for instance, her published memoirs are brief. 'The beauty of his mind, the pure fire of his soul, began to affect me and almost attract me.' But in the diary the sequence continues: 'and magnetise me with an attraction almost physical, carrying me into such ecstasy as Donne expresses; his unattractive body seemed to disappear, his spirits and mine united in one flame. . . .'

On another occasion, recorded in the diaries but not reproduced for publication, Russell broke down and 'sobbed and sobbed' and she longed to 'bound away, wild and free from his self-analysis . . . He is too insistent, so tidy and neat, too unfantastic and lacking in grace; his movements are painful to me.' She found 'his hands . . . the hands of a bear. They have no expression in them, only force.' Ottoline hated it when Russell seemed to sit waiting 'with a long, melancholy face for me to give him stimulus and praise'.

Their affair lasted, with a number of short breaks, until 1916; and they remained friends and correspondents until her death in 1938. The pattern, after the first few confused months, seldon varied. They met when and where they could, and stole nights together despite the interdictions; they walked, and talked, and read aloud to each other from Plato and Spinoza, Vaughan and Carlyle and Dostoyevsky whose characters Russell found 'medieval', and from Russell's old love, Shelley. He taught her philosophy; she taught him to take some pleasure in the arts. They even talked of having children. 'I have been slow to achieve inner harmony, & but for you I might never have achieved it . . .', he said to her, 'and out of this inner harmony I feel the power to give a great gift to the world – our child.' To please her, he agreed to shave off his over-large moustache, reporting that he was going to cremate it in the fireplace, and that he now looked older, thin-lipped and rather cynical. Ottoline remarked that without it he stopped looking like a don, and turned into a combination of Voltaire and an actor, becoming, in the process, more 'bold' and 'reckless'.

From the first, it was Russell who was always demanding more, more commitment, more love, more intensity and frequently accusing her of indifference; Ottoline who vacillated, terrified that he would leave her, but overwhelmed by the strength of his demands. Repeatedly, after scenes and recriminations, they parted; repeatedly, they came together again. For her, it was undoubtedly an immensely important event; for him, it was perhaps the single most dramatic thing that had happened to him and he would never be the same again. 'She laughed at me when I behaved like a don or a prig,' he wrote in his autobiography. 'She gradually cured me of the belief that I was seething with appalling wickedness which could only be kept under by an iron self-control. She made me less self-centred, and less self-righteous . . . She made me less of a Puritan.'

When Russell returned to Trinity to take up his lectureship, the house at Bagley Wood was sold and a lease taken on a cottage at Fernhurst called Van Bridge. Here, Alys spent most of her time when not caring for her mother, brooding and lonely, filling her days with good works. In the late spring of 1911, after a short illness, Hannah died, aged seventy-nine. Russell, by now settled in London and entirely engrossed with Ottoline Morrell, offered to come down for the funeral. Alys, not least because she remembered how much he had despised Hannah, was very angry. Hannah, for all her eccentricities, had been much loved, especially by Alys, Logan and her two grand-daughters, Karin and Ray, who had grown up happily in her house after their father's death in 1899. At one point there had been talk of Alys and Russell becoming their guardians, but they were turned down on the grounds of their 'rather rampant irreligiousness' and the fact that Alys had spoken on 'free love' while in America in 1896.

Alys, who still nurtured some hope of winning Russell back, was appallingly unhappy, though she pretended not to be, which irritated those around her. Even Mary Berenson, never a loving or charitable sister, now felt concern: 'Alys'[s] situation is much worse,' she wrote to Berenson during a visit to England, 'she seems to grow sadder and sadder as the days go by.' Determined that no one should hear of their separation from gossip, Alys herself wrote to tell their mutual friends. Bertie, she explained in a letter to Mary, had simply 'married very young, and probably estimates freedom of that kind too high'. Like Ottoline, it was in her diary that her grief found real expression: 'It is just six months since I have seen Bertie,' she wrote on 23 November 1911, 'and what I suffered in those nine years was as nothing to the misery I have endured since . . . I am but dead & my life & spirit are fled with him. Never to see him again, never to hear his voice or his laugh, never to know what he is thinking or doing . . .'

Mary, who was calculating as well as censorious, having been brought up by her doting mother to regard her own pleasure and desires as paramount, wrote to Russell, assuring him of her own and Berenson's 'continued friendliness'. Others were not so forgiving. Both the Murrays and the Whiteheads felt that Russell had behaved badly, and the Halévys declared that if they ever did meet him, it would be not in their own home but on neutral ground.

Over the Webbs, Alys was generous, telling Beatrice she would be grateful if they would continue to view Russell as a friend. 'Caring is not always enough, I know, and we are very different. He wants constant change and new friends, whereas I love my old friends the best and cling to old habits.' She was capable of considerable insight when it came to Russell's character: 'I can tell a lie from cowardice and other motives, but I always know it is a lie and regret it, whereas Bertie has to persuade himself first that it's true.' Russell was less charitable: 'If Alys had to choose between regaining my love and knowing all my movements, she would choose the latter.' Only later would he learn about real jealousy.

In the autumn of 1911, the Webbs were in China and India, where they complained that sodomy was destroying the vigour of the population, leading Russell to comment that they would be the last people he would trust to know. When they returned, Beatrice wrote a stern but friendly note to him. She had, she told him, always felt his 'peculiar charm', but had often had doubts about his character. It was natural, she added, that they should feel 'sore' about him: what would he feel if Sidney had done the same? Russell wrote crossly back that he had not believed that they were the sort of people to apportion blame, and in any case it was wiser to be charitable if one was ignorant of the facts. The break between them was not final, and the Webbs had other problems to worry about. Both Shaw and Wells were trying to dislodge them from their hold over the Fabians, Wells saying that they were overly self-satisfied, and caricaturing them in his novels. The Webbs took it all surprisingly well. 'I'm in this one too', Beatrice is reported by Desmond MacCarthy to have said. 'I'm the woman whose voice is described as a strangulated contralto, but you're not in it, Sidney.' 'Oh yes, I am,' said Webb. 'I'm the man who is described as one of those supplementary males often found among the lower crustacea.'

Alys and Logan now moved together into a Tudor farmhouse on the Solent called Chilling. It had magnificent gardens, and Logan filled the house with blue tiles, Morris wallpaper and *toile de Gênes*, and bought a yacht. On fine evenings they sat outside in deckchairs and read aloud. Alys became his devoted housekeeper, pampering him and dealing with his 'ups' which he insisted on calling 'happies' though they were less happy for those around him, as he would insist on playing endless practical jokes. The entire Pearsall Smith family suffered from swings of moods, as Russell had most feared when talking to doctors before his marriage. For Alys, domesticity with Logan was peace of a kind, after a decade of torment. From Mary, she received a letter urging resignation. She did her best, but her innocent, round, pretty face, with its heavy eyebrows and thick hair, never really looked happy again.

Over the years, Alys had become very attached to her two nieces, Ray and Karin, and if they considered her tiresome, they also appreciated her efforts to find them partners and chaperone them when asked. Karin, of whom Russell was particularly fond, continued to go to him for coaching, as she was sitting for her tripos finals at Newnham. To his delight, she was not only awarded a first but a 'star', thereby becoming the first woman philosopher in Cambridge with a distinction.

Ray, Alys's favourite, now married Oliver Strachey, Lytton's brother, who had a daughter, Julia, by an earlier marriage. When Ray became pregnant and was ill, Alys offered to take the child, who was then eleven. The record Julia left of Alys may not always have been perfectly accurate, but the picture is vivid: her great-aunt Alys, Julia was later to write, was parsimonious, wearing the jumble sent over by American well-wishers for the London poor, including voluminous skirts and jackets with huge flapping sleeves. Over these, she put tippets of fur, tucked into a cape, and underneath a broderie anglaise shirt, which, she told Julia, had started life as Russell's christening robe. She was chaotic, untidy, and flapped about like a wild goose 'that had been too long confined and crushed into some tiny canary's quarters, had burst open its cage door at last and shot honking away . . .' Her friends were 'bosomy hens with spreading hips and feet, tending to be ginger colour all over'. Alys would tell the girl to keep her mouth turned up, so as not to look glum; even as a child Julia found nothing admirable in what she recognised as a 'truly soul-freezing artificially cheering mask', which did nothing to hide a 'most pitiable, barren desolation'.

Alys was a more interesting woman than she was given credit for. She had campaigned ably for temperance and suffrage, lectured widely on all sorts of subjects, written a chapter of a book on German politics, and taken a job in a factory to study the conditions of working girls. She could be both irritating and possessive, but it was Russell who effectively destroyed her. She was thirty-nine when he left her; eighty-eight when she died. The rest of her long life was devoted to Logan, good causes, bouts of depression and forced jollity. When the 1914 war broke out, she moved with Logan to a tall, elegant house in Chelsea, painted white and filled with chinoiserie, so as to work more effectively for the Belgian refugees. She wore a large whistle round her neck, to summon help if she were buried in a bombing raid.

Once again teaching in Trinity, Russell was trying to form an idea of his new students. He did not find them particularly lively, reporting to Lucy Donnelly that he had invited them to his regular Thursday evenings, and asked them to drop in to see him whenever they wanted, 'to try to get them accustomed to civilised talk, but it is hard work, and sometimes even sinks to very trivial topics'. What he preferred were Platonic dialogues. His friend G. H. Hardy, a shy, self-effacing and kindly mathematician, teased him by saying he had informed one potential pupil of Russell's that he was frighteningly profound, and another that he was full of jokes. Personally, Russell rather despaired of this new batch, suspecting they would never go far in the world of philosophy. Teaching, too, he found hard. 'It is like Max Beerhohm's Walt, "exhorting the bird of freedom to fly",' he told Lucy. 'And the bird so seldom does – never unless he is a foreigner & seldom unless he is a Jew ... I try to make them feel that thinking is delightful, & that it is not impossible to build up the cosmos from the very beginning. ... Revolution tempered by reverence – do you like that as a watchword?'

Russell had been given two attic rooms in Nevile's Court, overlooking the Master's garden, St John's and the Cam, and conviently close to the Wren Library. He filled them with books and busts of Spinoza and Leibniz, and described them as 'rather severe'. He settled down to an austere regime: two boiled eggs for breakfast, bread and marmalade for lunch, cold lamb for supper, which was far from unenjoyable after Bagley Wood, with the daily pleasure of long talks with old friends. He went bicycling, rowed on the river with Whitehead, discussed Plato and Aristotle with Sydney Waterlow, dined with Moore, McTaggart, Keynes and Rupert Brooke (whom he dismissed as a 'self-deceiver ... too soft and flabby'), and talked of seeing as many people as possible, to create the impression that he was in Cambridge all the time and to scotch rumours that he was in London with a married woman.

He was immensely busy. 'I feel like Napoleon playing 6 games of

chess, and dictating to 7 secretaries all at the same time', he wrote
to Ottoline. His floor was littered with books, 'which makes me
uncomfortable. I can't bear a piggery . . .'. There were not only his
never-ending *Principia Mathematica*, his classes and the remains of
his suffrage work, but he was once again involved in political issues,
including the wave of strikes breaking out across Britain, of which
the coal strike was the worst, sparked off by complaints about wages.
Russell was increasingly critical of Asquith's high-handed methods,
and considered the Liberals lacking in sympathy for the workers.
His later interest in guild socialism possibly dates from this period,
and he was asked by a publisher whether he would write a book on
syndicalism. 'I wish life was long enough', he wrote to Ottoline, 'I
should *love* doing it, and I should love the excuse for getting to know
all sorts of "revolutionaries". Everyone keeps saying it is the enemy
. . . This makes me like it – if only I knew what it is.'

   Principia Mathematica had entered its closing phase, and Russell
was putting together a collection of essays, on ethics, pragmatism
and truth, including *The Free Man's Worship*, intended for people
interested in questions of philosophy, but with no formal training in
the subject. When it was published, a reviewer spoke of it as an
'event in the philosophical world', though the *Tablet* complained that
the 'naked nescience of a personal God chills and repels us. A
truncated theism, even in the guise of an aesthetic appreciation of
Tragedy, does not appeal to the human heart.'

   After so many years of pure mathematical research, Russell was
mentally exhausted; his intellect, he was to say, never quite recovered
from the strain. The easier task of popular writing was understandably seductive, and when Gilbert Murray wrote to ask whether he
would turn his hand to a volume for his new Home University
Library, a 'message to the shop-assistants about philosophy', he was
tempted. 'See if there is anything you want to say to 75,000 people',
Murray urged. Russell hesitated; Murray was insistent: 'Tell me of
another philosopher who is 1. completely alive and original. 2.
democratic . . . 3. sharp-edged and not wobbly or sloppy in thought.
And then I will cease to persecute you.' To Bernard Shaw, Murray
described his library. 'I hope to make it the vulgarest and most
successful thing ever seen in the publishing trade.'

Russell's contribution, *The Problems of Philosophy*, was published in January 1912. He was delighted at its reception, believing he had managed to produce a book of real worth: for the first time he had made philosophy simple. 'I feel', he wrote to Lucy Donnelly, 'as if I had just discovered what philosophy is and how it ought to be studied.' Had he been writing technically, there is no doubt that he would have explored further points at greater depth; as it was, he felt he had succeeded in including all the 'essentials' – the means by which man can discover what the physical world actually is. Since abandoning idealism, Russell had held to the belief that knowledge basically comes to us through the senses. Given the recent scientific discoveries – ranging from the atom to radioactivity – the senses were turning out to be less reliable than they had seemed.

In *The Problems of Philosophy*, which opens with one of his most famous phrases – 'Is there any knowledge in the world which is so certain that no reasonable man could doubt it?' – Russell adopted the position that he would cut out anything he could do without, and then chop up everything that remained into small pieces. He would then be able to see precisely what was left. What he came down to were what he called 'sense-data', something rather like perception of different patches of colour. This was the most certain empirical knowledge possible, and he named it 'hard data'. The question was how, by starting with this sense-data, you could arrive at the existence of the physical world. Talking at length about tables, which can appear as oblong, brown and shiny, and feel smooth, cold and hard, yet seem different as the person perceiving them moves around, Russell concluded that the table that he was considering was *really* there. *The Problems of Philosophy*, as an introduction to the subject, has never been altogether replaced and continues to be set for undergraduates in many universities throughout the world.

Whitehead, to whom Russell sent what quickly became known as his 'shilling shocker', was, as in the past, both flattering and critical. The original thought was excellent; the received ideas less satisfactory: Russell should learn to place greater faith in his own ideas. Many pages of detailed comments arrived by post.

Murray's instincts had been right: *The Problems of Philosophy* was a great success with the reading public, going into its ninth edition by 1924; it has remained in print ever since. When, in 1966, at the age of ninety-four, Russell was consulted about a jacket for yet another edition, he replied: 'The most suitable cover, for this volume, in my opinion would be a picture of a monkey tumbling over a precipice and exclaiming: "Oh dear, I wish I hadn't read Einstein . . ." P. S. On no account should the monkey look like me.'

It was at this moment, with Russell in a state of heightened awareness, his interests broadening all the time, that chance brought another challenge. On 18 October 1911, Ludwig von Wittgenstein entered his life. For both of them, it was a meeting of utmost importance. Having concluded that the best of his technical work was done, Russell was casting gently around for a disciple, someone with the brilliance, youth and energy to take over where he had left off. Wittgenstein was to be that one. He 'began as my pupil', Russell wrote forty years later, 'and ended as my supplanter at both Oxford and Cambridge.'

Wittgenstein was born in Vienna, in 1889, the eighth and youngest child of an Austrian family of Jewish descent. His family, whose wealth came from the iron and steel industry, tended to be musical and depressive – three of his brothers were to commit suicide. Ray Monk, Wittgenstein's recent biographer, records that as a boy of eight or nine, Wittgenstein was already asking his first philosophical question: 'Why should one tell the truth, if it's to one's advantage to tell a lie?'

Until the age of fourteen, he was educated at home, but after studying engineering in Berlin he registered as a research student at the University of Manchester, with the intention of designing a jet-reaction engine for aircraft. In the process, his interest began to shift from engineering to mathematics, and from pure mathematics to its philosophical foundations. By the summer of 1911, his work on the propeller was sufficiently advanced for him to be elected a research student and to have a patent accepted. His aeronautical days, however, were fast coming to a close. The question was: what should he do next? He went to the University of Jena to consult Frege. Frege advised him to get in touch with Russell.

In the autumn of 1911, Russell was thirty-nine and Wittgenstein was twenty-two. An exceptionally good-looking, slender man of medium height, with curly brown hair and an aquiline profile, he was commanding in manner, and could be disagreeably imperial. He was, all his life, to stand on his own, both as man and philosopher, disregarding fashion or established schools of philosophy and retaining a sort of ethical purity. He shunned publicity and wrote very little, yet the issues he raised and developed are considered among the most important contributions to twentieth-century philosophy. 'I think I summed up my attitude to philosophy,' he once wrote, 'when I said: philosophy ought really to be written only as a poetic compositon.'

When Wittgenstein appeared in his rooms, unannounced and insisting on speaking rather bad English, Russell was having tea with C. K. Ogden, later to become the translator of Wittgenstein's *Tractatus Logico-Philosophicus*. He was intrigued by his curious visitor, reporting to Ottoline that 'I am much interested in my German & shall hope to see a lot of him.' A lot soon became too much. Wittgenstein haunted his rooms, arguing, debating, contradicting, appearing at midnight and then walking up and down Russell's small attic room like a tiger in a cage. Later, Russell was to say how impressed he had been by his 'fire and penetration and intellectual purity': it must indeed have been a relief from some of his more pedestrian students. At the time he grumbled about Wittgenstein's relentless arguing: 'he is armour-plated against all assaults of reasoning', and joked that he was unable to convince his new disciple of anything. 'I wanted him to consider the proposition "There is no hippopotamus in this room at present." When he refused to believe this, I looked under all the desks without finding one; but he remained unconvinced.' For Wittgenstein, it was all a question not of empirical but of metaphysical knowledge. 'The world', he would say in the famous first line of the *Tractatus*, 'is the totality of facts, not of things.'

At first, Russell was hesitant about his pupil's fundamental ability, and made attempts to mould his style. 'I told him', he wrote to Ottoline, 'he ought not simply to *state* what he thinks true, but to give arguments for it, but he said arguments spoil its beauty, and that he would feel as if he was dirtying a flower with muddy hands.'

But when in January 1912 Wittgenstein appeared with a manuscript he had written during the Christmas holidays, Russell was quickly convinced of his extraordinary talent. His pupil asked him for advice: should he abandon engineering for ever and pursue mathematical logic? Russell did not hesitate. 'Wittgenstein', he wrote to Ottoline, 'has been a great event in my life ... I think he has *genius*. In discussion with him I put out *all* my force and only just equal his ... I love him & feel he will solve the problems I am too old to solve – all kinds of problems that are raised by my work, but want a fresh mind and the vigour of youth. He is *the* young man one hopes for.' What was more, in Russell's eyes, Wittgenstein possessed the kind of mind ideal for a philosopher: energetic, ironical, devoted to truth and fascinated by analysis. On 1 February 1912, Wittgenstein was made a member of Trinity College, with Russell as his supervisor, and an eminent logician called W. E. Johnson to give him the extra coaching in logic Russell considered he needed. He moved into Moore's old rooms at the top of a tower in Whewell's, with views over Trinity. Later, he was to tell a friend that it was Russell's support that had saved him, and brought to a close nine miserable and lonely years. He furnished his rooms austerely, complaining that he could never find furniture plain enough to suit him. In keeping with his views on aesthetics, there were no comfortable chairs, no reading lamp, no ornaments, paintings or photographs.

Wittgenstein was never an easy man. He was uncompromising, highly volatile and domineering. He could also be excessively argumentative. Johnson was soon fed up with him, and even Russell, captivated as he was by the realisation that he and his pupil were alike when it came to passion, vehemence, jokes and the conviction that one 'must understand or die', was often annoyed by his persistence: 'He has more passion about philosophy than I have; his avalanches make mine seem mere snowballs.' The avalanches were not without their dangers: Wittgenstein went through periods of obsessive, neurotic self-analysis, convinced that his work lacked brilliance and that no one liked him; at such times he would threaten suicide, until Russell was reduced to telling him he thought too much about himself.

By the beginning of the summer term, their relationship was

beginning to fray. Wittgenstein had gained greatly in confidence and felt able to criticise Russell's work. He admired the *Principia* enormously, but objected violently to *The Free Man's Worship* and to the way Russell had chosen to write popular philosophy for the masses in his *Problems of Philosophy*. One effect of this was that Russell became anxious to secure Wittgenstein's approval for his work. That summer, he finished a paper *On Matter*, in which he sought to reach the very heart of philosophy 'with the cold steel in the hand of passion'. Wittgenstein dismissed it as trivial, which must have pained Russell enormously. At the same time, Wittgenstein was beginning to feel that Russell did not always understand him, that he could not really grasp his notion of personal integrity, and treated it as a joke. Earlier that year, they had begun discussing ethical matters, and their discussions were proving curiously unrewarding. When Russell declared of Wittgenstein that his 'outlook is very free; principles and such things seem to him nonsense, because his impulses are strong and never shameful,' it was somehow to miss the point.

It was inevitable that Russell should introduce Wittgenstein to his Apostolic friends, among them Keynes and Strachey, who soon considered the young Austrian a promising 'embryo'. The only question was whether Wittgenstein would find the society interesting, particularly as he was known to despise the various undergraduate brothers and no one more so than a man called Bliss, who was to be elected with him, and whom even Russell considered odious and conceited. Russell was worried that Wittgenstein might object to the current Apostolic mood of homosexuality, and the way the brothers were all in love with one another. Strachey, hearing of Russell's hesitations, dismissed them as jealousy. 'The poor man', he wrote to a friend, 'is in a sad state. He looks about 96 – with long snow-white hair and an infinitely haggard countenance ... Bertie is really a tragic figure, and I am very sorry for him; but he is most deluded too.' To Keynes, he wrote, 'Have you heard about our shocking pangs and subsequent torments? And what a beast Bertie has been making of himself? And how our new brother's only objection to the Society is that it doesn't happen to be Apostolic? and what an amazing character he is?'

Strachey was being unfair. What Russell feared was that Wittgenstein's election would lead to 'some kind of disaster'; he would have
been more than happy to have others share the load of his intensity.
In the event, there was no explosion, but by the end of the autumn
term, Wittgenstein had indeed left. It was, it seems, boredom not
disgust which drove him away: he was already involved with a
Cambridge undergraduate called David Pinsent. Russell himself
complained that what he minded about the current Apostles was
their 'conceit and feebleness ... they care about some imaginary
tone of mind, or taste, or delicacy of feeling, rather than about
getting things done.'

By 1913, the two philosophers were working on very different
things. Russell was developing his 'new science', a combination of
physics, mathematical logic and psychology, reading widely, speaking
of a big work to come, the idea of which excited him 'like great
music'. It was no surprise, he told Ottoline, that art was now
languishing: science was at a moment of incredible brilliance. 'It is a
grand thing to be one of those who bring light into the outer darkness
– I have done some part of this and I long to do more.' While Russell
dreamed of starting a school of mathematically trained philosophers,
Wittgenstein was fully caught up in the analysis of logic, Russell
having, it appeared, bequeathed him the task. Wittgenstein was at a
peak of exhilaration, turning out new ideas about the fundamentals
of logic and finding what he believed to be errors in *Principia
Mathematica*. There were, for the first time, signs of more serious
friction between them, with Wittgenstein pouring scorn on Russell's
work on suffrage, while Russell accused him of being in danger of
becoming 'narrow and uncivilised'. Yet Russell continued to feel
strangely bound to him, sensitive to every twist in his moods, much
as he was to Ottoline's; though it sometimes embarrassed him to
realise that Wittgenstein cared for him more than he was able to
reciprocate. When they now talked, it was to discuss Wittgenstein's
work, not Russell's. Russell was again worried about him, as he
seemed gloomy and restless, and he urged him to take up tennis and
boating on the Cam, and eat better meals, and keep biscuits by his
bed for when he lay awake. Wittgenstein went on being difficult and
troubled. When Russell took him to watch North Whitehead racing

on the river, Wittgenstein was disgusted by the whole thing, and said so loudly, explaining that he had found the entire afternoon vile, and that nothing in life was worth anything except producing great works of art or enjoying those of others. Russell commented that it all made him feel like a 'bleating lambkin'.

Russell was now engaged on a new project, a book on the *Theory of Knowledge*, and even before he read it Wittgenstein professed himself full of forebodings. Russell declared him to be a tyrant, though he also went on insisting that Wittgenstein was more creative, more passionate and clearer in mind than he (though he reserved for himself greater sympathy and sanity). This was only the beginning. After weeks of intense labour, Russell completed the first six chapters; he was convinced that what he was producing was at the very least a 'good book'. Wittgenstein's first assessment was muted; he simply pointed to an error that was easily overcome. Then, abruptly, came a second verdict: Russell's fundamental thinking on the matter was totally wrong.

Russell was appalled. He felt, he told Ottoline, ready for suicide, with poison spreading rapidly through his system; only her love and gentleness, he told her, gave him back a 'purity of heart'. 'My impulse was shattered,' he wrote later, 'like a wave dashed to pieces against a breakwater.' *Theory of Knowledge*, which in fact marked an interesting next step in his development of logical atomism and theories of judgement, was abandoned, and disappeared from view until the 1960s, when Russell sent his archives to be catalogued. He told Ottoline later that he had come to see Wittgenstein as 'right, and I saw that I could not hope ever again to do fundamental work in philosophy'. What he really minded was the sudden knowledge that he was no longer capable of producing first-rate philosophy and that he should leave such work to the younger generation – in particular, Wittgenstein. It was characteristic that he seems to have felt little bitterness towards the younger man, only pleasure when he heard that his work was going well. They even discussed whether Wittgenstein might rewrite the first eleven chapters of *Principia Mathematica*.

Wittgenstein began to talk of going off to Norway for two years, to live on his own. Russell considered the suggestion extremely foolish, though he remarked somewhat callously to Ottoline that 'I expect he will commit suicide towards the end of the winter, but it can't be helped. He has done admirable work.' Admirable perhaps; but very little of it was on paper. Before he left, Wittgenstein wanted to see some of his ideas put down but hated the thought of committing anything imperfect to paper, so Russell agreed to talk to him about it, extracting it 'with pincers, however he may scream with pain'. The two men sat down, with a shorthand typist transcribing Wittgenstein's remarks, for what was to become the Austrian philosopher's first major work. *Notes on Logic* contained the seeds of his credo: there are no deductions in philosophy, which is purely descriptive, gives no pictures of reality, consists of logic and metaphysics and is based on logic. This credo was to remain basically unaltered for the rest of his life. That autumn, he left England. 'My day passes between logic, whistling, going for walks, and being depressed,' he wrote to Russell. The war was to separate the two philosophers for six years.

There was, however, more friction to come. Russell, still in Cambridge, was doing his best to absorb and understand Wittgenstein's ideas, but in the Austrian's eyes he was failing to do so. 'I beg you to think about these matters for yourself,' Wittgenstein wrote to him tetchily from Norway. 'It is INTOLERABLE for me, to repeat a written explanation which even the first time I gave only with the utmost repugnance.' Whatever offence he might have given was tempered by a tone of despair, and his saying that he thought he might be going mad. He was, he wrote, absolutely incapable of doing any work at all.

Whether Wittgenstein was suffering from an acute depressive breakdown or not, he now decided to destroy, one by one, all that he considered to be the 'sordid' compromises of his life. Russell was the first to come under attack. Wittgenstein wrote to say that they should never have anything to do with each other again: they were fundamentally incompatible. It was not just a question of their philosophies, but of their very natures. The best thing was to make a clean break, and Wittgenstein would start by never writing to him again. If Russell was appalled, he chose not to take offence. He wrote back in conciliatory fashion. Wittgenstein weakened, but only to the extent of agreeing to remain friends with Russell on a personal, not on a working basis. There was to be nothing further between them on 'music, morals and a host of things besides logic'.

More hurtfully, perhaps, Wittgenstein turned to Moore, who had once praised Wittgenstein for being the only man to look puzzled in his lectures, and begged him to come to Norway to work further on his notes. Reluctantly, Moore went to Bergen, but he was no more able to understand or placate Wittgenstein, who was furious when he learned that despite all his labour, he was still not eligible for a bachelor's degree under the strict requirements governing the university. Wittgenstein's next letter to Moore turned out to be so disparaging that even the mild and accommodating Moore resolved to have nothing more to do with him. The two did not meet again until they happened to find themselves on the same train in 1919.

Wittgenstein was not the only fresh voice in Russell's philosophical world during these years. In the autumn of 1913 another brilliant mathematician arrived in Cambridge. Like Wittgenstein, he was foreign – of German parentage but now American – and Jewish. Norbert Wiener had been a child prodigy, having graduated from college at fourteen, then gone on to Harvard to do his PhD on algebra, and particularly on the work of Whitehead and Russell. Now, at the age of eighteen, he had been awarded a year's travelling scholarship, and he wished to spend it at Trinity studying under Russell. A letter from his father, professor of Slavic languages at Harvard, assured Russell of his son's eminent suitability: Norbert was physically strong and healthy, perfectly balanced morally and mentally, and well trained in Greek, Latin, modern languages, mathematics and philosophy. The round face, straight brown hair and confident gaze of the boy philosopher who reached Trinity were soon supplemented by glasses and a tufted moustache.

Norbert Wiener's first encounter with Russell was not propitious. He reported to his father that the British philosopher had been insolent, conceited, rude about his mathematical abilities and utterly indifferent to his research successes. Wiener was both precocious and maddeningly over-confident. To Ottoline, Russell complained that the youth considered himself God Almighty and that there was already a contest over who was teaching whom. Coming so soon after Wittgenstein's attacks, it cannot have been easy for Russell to be told that Volume Two of *Principia Mathematica* was 'quite easy sailing', that his ideas on sense-data were all wrong, and that his courses were ones Wiener had done many times before. By the end of his first month, Wiener was telling his father that he detested Russell, that he was an iceberg and that his mind was a 'keen, cold, logical machine that cuts the universe into neat little baskets'. Russell had apparently informed him that his ideas were a 'horrible fog' and that he was much too 'cocksure'.

Wiener was less bumptious than his words suggest, and he found Cambridge a lonely and intimidating place. As he began to settle in, he made a few friends and came to appreciate G. H. Hardy, under whom he was sent to study mathematics. When he finally produced a piece of work that impressed Russell, the older man was not only generous with his praise, and spoke of incorporating it with some of his own work, but even seemed to apologise to Wiener for the way he had treated him earlier. Wiener was invited to Russell's Thursday evening 'squashes', where he was much impressed by the distinguished company.

As a stranger to Trinity, in the last few years before the First World War, Wiener's picture of Cambridge's philosophical circles and the life of the university is revealing. His landlady, he observed, was bad-tempered, stingy, snobbish and a terrible cook; the undergraduates were 'young sports of the aristocracy', leading lives almost identical to those of privileged schoolboys. The dons, however, and particularly the younger ones, he found tolerant, kindly and receptive.

What he found most noticeable, however, was the style and eccentricity of the three most eminent philosophy dons: Russell, McTaggart and Moore. These three, declared Wiener, could be likened only to the Mad Hatter's Tea Party. McTaggart, with his pudgy hands, innocent sleepy air and sideways shuffle, was obviously the Dormouse; Moore, his gown covered in chalk, his cap in tatters, his hair unkempt, through which he constantly raked his hands, and with his habit of turning up for classes at a run in bedroom slippers and wrinkled white socks, was the March Hare. Russell could never be anything but a distinguished, autocratic Mad Hatter.

Eight

Imprisoned voices

In the space of just a few years, Ottoline had coaxed out of Russell needs and emotions he had not imagined existed; while Wittgenstein had challenged his basic philosophical and intellectual abilities. In terms of people, and the excitement of a life filled with new possibilities, the last years before the First World War were an extraordinary time for him. A third figure, who was to exercise an influence as strong and as lasting, but altogether different, the Polish expatriate novelist Joseph Conrad, was about to appear in his life. With him Russell was to forge what he described as a 'bond of extreme strength'. It was a surprising friendship, and one never perfectly understood by Russell or anyone else.

Before this meeting, however, the spiritual search he had embarked on many years earlier in *The Pilgrimage of Life* was reawakened by Ottoline's Christianity. The spiritual adventure he set off on in her company was based on scepticism, doubt and a longing for reassurance. It did not survive long, but while it lasted it was a consuming interest, and led him to a completely different kind of writing.

After his meeting with Ottoline in the spring of 1911, mathematics had come to seem cold and unresponsive. 'You have released in me imprisoned voices that sing the beauty of the world,' he wrote to Ottoline within days of their first dinner. 'All the poetry that grows dumb in the years of sorrow has begun to speak to me again.' Up to that point, Ottoline had been perfectly clear about her religion: it was a comforting, lofty but not intrusive part of her everyday life. It was Russell who was not so clear. He suggested, but stopped short of saying, that anyone with a real passion for the truth could not really believe in God; and yet at the same time he accepted that part of what he most liked about her, her large-heartedness, came precisely from her faith. He felt, he said, 'healed' by her. They read Spinoza together and Russell was struck by a different understanding of the Dutch philosopher and his assertion that once man is able to go beyond his passions, and understand the causes of strife, he will be able to rise from a state of 'less perfection' to the 'intellectual love of God', freeing himself from the bondage of the self and becoming a willing part of the whole. A quality of inner harmony, Russell began to think, might indeed be compatible with a respect for reason.

Through the autumn of 1911 and the early spring of 1912, Russell worried away at the question of faith. If he and Ottoline were truly to become as one, she was going to have to abandon her dependence on her God, or at least come to question Him, or he was going to have to find some compromise acceptable to them both. Always, he came back to questions of reason and truth: they were the main tenets of his life, and he refused to give them up. 'I cannot keep away from the search,' he wrote to his father's friend Cobden-Sanderson, 'though my inmost conviction is that there is nothing to be found – except courage and a certain indifference to fate.' Almost every day, he poured out to Ottoline his thoughts and anxieties on the matter, which were sometimes obsessive and sometimes contradictory.

> Oct. 16 1911. I think, like most believers, you greatly overestimate what your belief in God does for you . . . If I could make you feel that unbelief is nobler I should begin to have hope.
> Dec. 27 1911. Turbulent, restless, inwardly raging – I shall always be – hungry for your God & blaspheming him – I could pour forth a flood of worship – the longing for religion is at times almost unbearably strong.
> Dec. 29 1911. What you call God is very much what I call infinity. I do find something in common with all the great things . . . But truth is the one I have mainly served, and truth is the only one I always feel the divinity of.
> Dec. 30 1911. I don't think God *exists* ready made. I think he is an ideal we can conceive and do something to create . . . I cannot pray or lean on God. What strength I need I must get from myself or those whom I admire . . .

Jan. 1 1912. Religion makes you feel the world great and full of mystery and sadness, & human beings strangely errant . . . I care for it more than anything else in the world. Without it the whole world would be dross. With it there are strange possibilities, glimpses that blot out complacency, & leave one in almost prostrate wonder . . .

Early in 1903, Russell had written in his journal of the 'prison' of his unhappy relations with Alys. He now used the word again, in a book that was to show how the 'religion of contemplation' could become the means of escape from the prison of human life. He had in mind not so much an actual belief in God as a kind of mystical union with the universe, in which man becomes at one with infinity.

'What is [a] prison?' Russell asked in his outline. 'Self-interest, subjectivity, insistence. Why a prison? Because [it] shuts out the love, the knowledge, and the attainment of goods otherwise possible'. 'Prisons' was to encompass the whole range of his religious experiences and establish common ground between Ottoline's faith and his agnosticism. 'Now there is no prison for me', he wrote to her. 'I reach out to the stars, & through the ages, & everywhere the radiance of your love lights the world for me.' 'Prisons' was going to be their 'child'.

By the late spring of 1912 one section was finished, and Russell showed it to the Whiteheads. Their verdict was disappointing. Whitehead said that anything ethical bored him; Evelyn that it was dull and did not come across as true. Russell was beginning to wonder if it did not all sound rather tendentious and accepted the criticisms. With surprising ease, and apparently few regrets, he abandoned the idea of making it into a book, and used parts of it instead in an essay called 'The Essence of Religion', in which he argued that, given the widespread decay of traditional beliefs, the most valuable elements of Christianity – those of worship and love – should be freed from dogma. The essence of religion should be that spirit which allows man to stand alone with his ideals and 'conquer, inwardly, the world's indifference'. 'Every demand', he concluded, 'is a prison; and reason is only free when it asks nothing.'

Before leaving for Norway, Wittgenstein told Russell that he detested this essay, that Russell was a traitor to the gospels of exactness, and that in any case themes of this kind were too intimate to put into writing. Russell minded Wittgenstein's criticisms all the more because he half agreed with him.

Ottoline's influence was not confined to religion. Whereas both Berenson and Logan Pearsall Smith had failed to interest Russell in the visual arts, Ottoline was gratified to find that she did somewhat better when it came to religion and music. 'I have been ascetic and starved of beauty,' Russell had told her. Together, they listened to Beethoven, who appealed to Russell as 'tumultuous, wild, despairing and triumphant', and to Tchaikovsky, whom he found feeble, self-pitying and moralistic; and they looked at Chinese pictures, which Russell noted were the only ones he enjoyed, apart from those of Giorgione. They gave him, he said, anticipating some of the pleasure he would later get from living in China, a 'sense of wonder combined with exquisiteness which moves me very much indeed'. Something of these various new strands – religion and the arts – now led Russell in the direction of fiction. In a novel or a short story, he thought, it might be easier to convey the need to reconcile religion with scientific knowledge. ' "Prisons" was wrong . . . because it was expository,' he wrote to Ottoline. 'One must have a more artistic form'.

The Perplexities of John Forstice, written closely with Ottoline, and representing a fusion of their natures at the pinnacle of their affair, was completed in the summer of 1912. It is Russell's only work of fiction before the short stories he wrote in his eighties. 'All great literature requires the rare and all but impossible combination of fiery emotion with an intellect capable of viewing it impersonally . . . 'It is, I am quite sure, a mistake to suppose that without an intensity of feeling which would crush an ordinary mortal it is impossible to produce Shakespeare, Milton or Carlyle. But when the feeling has been got, it is necessary to have the strength of a giant, so as to turn it into literature instead of mere lamentation,' he had written to Helen Thomas ten years earlier. In the event, even with Ottoline's developed sensibilities, Russell was not able to live up to these hopes. *Forstice* was a failure, a dry, stilted and rather precious piece of writing about a spiritual awakening.

Its form is that of a Platonic dialogue between a passionate young man and a set of characters introduced to express various ideas and themes. Part of the last section was written by Ottoline, who based it on a relationship she had had with a nun when she was a child. Forstice is a scientist. He goes to a garden party where he meets a bored financier and a socialist who tells him that all of life will soon be run with the 'order and regularity of the post office'. He goes home to find that his wife is dying of cancer. Suddenly filled with universal love, he sets out to seek a rational explanation for these emotions. He attends a meeting in Florence, where a poet, a mathematician, a novelist, a civil servant and a nun all give him their views. 'I don't really desire a God or a future life,' says Forstice; 'I want a world where there is always something to be done – a virgin forest in which to hew one's way – a night to illuminate by beacon fires – an infinite chaos with a core of cosmos gradually growing. That's what I *really* want – that's why I don't like a God who planned it all. I want man to have courage in the face of an alien universe . . . I must have something to *fight*. My inmost soul is wild & raging, full of storm & infinite conflict . . .'

Forstice did not appear until after Russell's death. Almost as soon as it was finished, Russell decided it was too sentimental. Before he died, he was to say, somewhat unkindly, that it had been unduly influenced by Ottoline.

His failure to find a 'fused whole', whether in essays or in fiction, left him less depressed than one might have expected. In 1913, in words which foreshadow many of his interests of the 1920s, Russell wrote an essay on science in education, in which he said that the cultivation of a scientific outlook made the harmonious development of a personality easier: the union of the self and the not-self were the ultimate goals, not just of religion and philosophy but of education.

By 1914, coached by Ottoline, he had finally found a spiritual code which was to remain more or less unchanged for the rest of his life. He ceased to advocate worship, and proposed in its place impartiality and an acceptance of the universe. Although apparently free of the narrow religious credos of his grandmother and Pembroke Lodge, he remained all his life a puritan. He had discovered 'intellectual love'; but he had not found God. As he was to write despondently in his autobiography: 'I have loved a ghost, and in loving a ghost my inmost self has itself become spectral. I have therefore buried it deeper and deeper beneath layers of cheerfulness, affection and joy of life. But my most profound feelings have remained always solitary and have found in human things no companionship. The sea, the stars, the night wind in waste places, mean more to me than even the human beings I love best, and I am conscious that human affection is to me at bottom an attempt to escape from the vain search for God.' Like so often in his writings on these subjects, he is at his most eloquent and his most bleak.

Into all this came Conrad. In 1913, Ottoline, always on the lookout for new guests for her Thursday evenings at Bedford Square, decided that she would like to meet the successful writer, then living at Capel, a village near Ashford in Kent. She asked Henry James, a neighbour and friend of Conrad's, to introduce them, and an invitation to Capel followed. Ottoline consulted Desmond Mac-Carthy about what to wear, and was told something 'smart and rather elaborate'. She arrived at Hamstreet Station and was met by Conrad's son Borys. Conrad was waiting at the door of his house. When Ottoline returned to London, she had been captivated by his 'tragic and worn and suffering' eyes. 'How odd it is in life to desire to hook one's personality on to others and to get in touch with them,' she wrote, adding that she thought it to be 'the most poignant desire I have in life'. She wanted to share her new friend with Russell.

That year, Conrad, who had two sons, and a wife called Jessye – Ottoline described her as a 'comfortable fat body' – was fifty-five, fourteen years older than Russell. Polish by birth, a Catholic, the orphaned son of landed gentry, he had started life as a merchant seaman, risen to the position of master mariner in the British merchant navy and become captain of a Congo river boat, before settling in England to write. By the time Russell met him, Conrad was one of the most highly regarded writers in English literature, together with James and Hardy. He was dark-haired, short and round-shouldered, with nervous gestures, a questioning expression, and a heavily lined face. A picture of him, cut from a newspaper and pasted into one of Ottoline's diaries, shows an exceptionally wide forehead and almond-shaped eyes; she had written beside it: 'very foreign . . . and slightly artificial in manner'. Edward Garnett, the reader for Fisher Unwin who first advised the firm to take him on, said after his introduction to Conrad that 'I had never seen before a man so masculinely keen yet so femininely sensitive.'

On 10 September 1913, Russell caught the train to Conrad's local station. He had offered to bring his bicycle, but Conrad insisted that Borys would meet him in their 'ancient puffer'. Conrad was one of the few people to own a private car at this time. Their meeting was delightful. Russell came away in a state bordering on hero-worship, having undergone an experience of friendship of quite a new order. He had read and admired many of Conrad's books, none more so than *Heart of Darkness*, the story of a man driven insane by loneliness and the horror of the tropical forest. In it, Russell had detected a view of life which perfectly matched his own, 'as a dangerous walk on a thin crust of barely cooled lava which at any moment might break through and let the unwary sink into fiery depths'. As he talked to Conrad about writing, about authors, about his childhood in Poland, he noted that both of them were preoccupied with the same themes of loneliness and the fear of being alien, and that Conrad was also fascinated by characters who fought inner battles against good and bad passions which invariably led them towards destruction.

Russell was overcome: 'I *loved* him, & I think he liked me,' he wrote to Ottoline on the train home; 'when we were out walking his reserve vanished and he spoke his inmost thoughts. It is impossible to say how much I loved him.' Years later, in *Portraits from Memory*, he described in lyrical words what happened: 'We seemed to sink through layer after layer of what was superficial, till gradually both reached the central fire. It was an experience unlike any other that I have known. We looked into each other's eyes, half appalled and half intoxicated to find ourselves together in such a region. The emotion was as intense as passionate love, and at the same time all-embracing. I came away bewildered, and hardly able to find my way among ordinary affairs.'

Three days later, Russell received a letter from Conrad. 'It seems to me that I talked all the time with fatuous egotism. Yet somewhere at the back of my brain I had the conviction that you would understand . . . Your personality drew me out. My instinct told me I would not be misread.' Only eleven letters from Conrad to Russell survive; and one from Russell. They are not enough to explain the rapturous nature of their friendship, and Russell, usually so lucid at explaining every facet of each thought and action, was never fully able to describe it. The nearest he got was in a letter replying to a Mr Watts, who must have questioned him about Conrad: 'As for the strange sympathy between Conrad and myself, I cannot pretend that I have ever quite understood it. I think I have always felt that there were two levels, one that of science and common sense, and another, terrifying, subterranean and periodic, which in some sense held more truth than the everyday view . . . I suppose that the feeling I had for Conrad depended upon his combination of passion and pessimism . . . You ask whether my feeling for Conrad was based upon a common sense of loneliness. I think that may have been the case, but the experience, while it lasted, was too intense for analysis.'

Only after Conrad had praised *The Free Man's Worship* as a 'gift from the gods' did Russell feel bold enough to show him *Forstice*. Conrad was anxious not to hurt Russell's feelings, but it was plain that he felt Russell would do better to stick to his philosophical essays than venture into the world of fiction. Russell's departure from serious work had been, in his eyes, a mistake. 'I rebelled,' Russell wrote to Ottoline, 'but he was inexorable'

Both he and Ottoline developed something very close to adulation of Conrad, at times becoming almost comic in their efforts to make certain every encounter had a perfect, magical quality. To make the most of every minute, they decided to visit him on their own, and at times they sound like rival suitors, courting a loved one. Russell maintained that what he had found was something he had first seen in Ottoline – and, so far, only in Ottoline: an identical way of viewing the 'ultimate sadness of the world – the deep tragedy of life'. Yet the words are not so very different from the phrase he had used about Wittgenstein and their shared commitment to the idea that one must 'understand or die'. Certainly, Russell's encounter with Conrad came at a most fortuitous moment, when his love affair with Ottoline had made him receptive to emotion, while his struggles with *Forstice* had alerted him to the difficulties of writing good fiction. At a different moment in his life, their meeting might have passed unremarkably.

There was something else that was unusual about his friendship with Conrad. Unlike most of Russell's other close relationships, it never had a chance to wither: the two men met only rarely before the war, not again until 1921, and then only briefly. Conrad died in 1924. With many other close friends and lovers, Russell's feelings tended to follow a similar and somewhat sad pattern: great intensity, considerable enjoyment and a conviction that the friend was somehow unique, followed after a while by slow disillusion. Trevy, Lowes Dickinson, Mary Sheepshanks, were all to suffer from this, and many, like Clifford Allen later, were to feel betrayed.

The ruthlessness with which Russell was able to sever the past – as he had with Alys – goes some way towards an explanation. As he once wrote perceptively to Ottoline: 'When people have touched one's imagination, and then for some reason no longer do so, it is hard to begin again.' With some, he did not bother a second time, and if this gave him regrets, they were not such as to alter his behaviour. The Webbs, the early Apostles, the Bloomsbury set and later the war resisters all fell into this pattern, so it is hardly surprising how seldom Russell appears in their autobiographies. His rejection of them was understandably reciprocated. They, too, came to feel that he was marginal to their lives.

Russell's affair with Ottoline was neither altogether happy nor altogether easy. Though they were in some ways alike and looking for the same things, the fundamental differences in their characters were so great that it is surprising that their relationship lasted as long as it did. Though no longer 'all brain in the abstract', as Alys had complained, Russell was still self-contained, rational and critical; Ottoline was romantic, taking pleasure in running through the grass barefoot at dawn, self-doubting and worldly. During the height of their affair, Russell learned not only about real love but about jealousy and possessiveness – something he had never been able to understand or accept in Alys. There is no doubt that Ottoline was flattered by his need for her and at times believed herself deeply in love with him; equally there is no doubting that Russell was in love, and minded dreadfully whenever she seemed to reject him. Ottoline's health was never good; she suffered from neuralgia and appalling headaches, and spent weeks having painful treatments under a Dr Combe in Lausanne. Later there was more helpful treatment by a psychotherapist called Dr Roger Vittoz, who, before Freud's views became widely accepted, had already been trying to give his patients insights into the causes of their suffering.

After a while, their exchanges fell into a routine: sudden swings between ecstatic love and hurt misunderstandings, most often brought about when Ottoline drew back, overwhelmed by him. When this happened, when she did not want to sleep with him – which Russell later blamed on his bad breath, of which he was not then aware – he became frantic. His reproaches grew wild and he could be cold and cruel. Several times he threatened never to see her again, as it was clear to him that she no longer loved him. Each time she relented, the crisis passed, and they were entranced by each other again.

Russell's letters at the start of their affair, once he had given up trying to persuade her to leave Philip, are tender and full of gratitude. 'I don't think you know at all how *deep* is your hold on me,' he wrote to her. Soon after came, 'I have grown quite amazingly in this last year. There was a kind of weakness and self-pity & sentimentality about me, which made it hard for me to deal with anything human', though he warned her, 'I have a perfectly cold intellect . . . it will sometimes hurt you . . . you won't like it but it belongs with my work . . .'

In July 1911, they had shared a mystical experience while lying together on the hillside above Peppard. 'Something passed from you to me . . .', he wrote. 'I thought I had lost you, and then suddenly found the key – not by seeking it but by the same thoughts growing up in me.' But before long he was again accusing her of not loving him enough; her judgement about sex, he said, had become 'morbid and *maladif*'. All year, they swung between passionate closeness and terrible recriminations. By the spring of 1913 he was in a state of almost permanent frenzy. 'It is your gradual and inexorable with-drawal – like the ebbing tide – that keeps me over and over again at the very last point of agony. You flatter yourself in thinking you can imagine passionate love; as far as I have observed, you can't imagine it a bit.' But then a week later: 'I always bring great misery to anyone who has anything to do with me; I can't help communicating the inward misery which I carry about like the plague . . .' And, 'Forgive me dearest – I will try to love you with more moderation . . . it is like a child crying because its parents have left it in the dark all alone . . .'

There are several coy but understanding references to her 'lady', Ottoline's name for periods. Russell could also be very bossy: 'Learn not to be ruthless & overbearing . . . Practise gentleness . . . Do not mistake passion for virtue . . . Companionship is unnecessary: you know what you are in the world; do it . . .' One day, he dreamt that she had been transformed into a cat, 'a very nice cat, very affectionate, purring and rubbing soft fur against me – & for some time I didn't much mind. It was only gradually I began to regret that you had lost the power of speech.' Ottoline took this as criticism.

She wrote letters of great affection, but seldom of deep analysis. It was in her diaries that she recorded her real view of the affair, as well as her endless insecurities about life, about her appearance, about whether people liked her. These diaries confirm that she and Russell went through wonderful patches – in Lausanne, where he followed her several times, clamouring for more love and eventually feeling it returned, or during the writing of *Forstice* when she found him 'softer', more imaginative, 'less definite' and 'more open to spiritual things'. Looking back on 1913, she considered that her relationship with Russell had been on the whole good and 'courageous'; that two years of great doubts had left her feeling much older; and that while her 'passionate' love was reserved, in the end, for Philip, she had within her a 'sea of love . . . to be poured out to others'. The trouble was, Russell did not want simply a share in a sea; he wanted it all. He could not tolerate sharing Ottoline with Morrell, though it is possible that he never knew the extent of her continuing affection for her husband. On 23 February 1913, Ottoline wrote: 'It was pure madness of me to be intimate with Bertie or anyone – for I can give them so little. P. takes all I have . . . I would give my right hand to be free from B. – but how can I now as he depends on me? . . . I feel how wonderful his intellect is – and then this awful shrivelling comes over me.' Philip, while behaving with great restraint over their relationship, was also having affairs. A good month together was followed by further uncertainty. 'I think', she recorded on 7 March, 'he is *incapable* of giving . . . His brain is absent . . . His terrible *intellectual* understanding. *It chills me.*'

The good days were as wonderful as the bad times were terrible; bit by bit, the swings were becoming intolerable to both of them. At the end of August 1913 they decided to try to part. After two and a half years of intensity, with little let-up, they were exhausted. Russell was now permanently reproachful, Ottoline guilty. Russell had been complaining that she kept his nerves so stretched that he could no longer work. 'When you spoke the other day, the bitterness of all the pain and hunger I have suffered became just too much and I couldn't bear it any more . . . I must break with you, or I shall be broken . . .You think I no longer love you, & that that is why I break. That is an *absolute mistake* . . . I break only to save the spring of life & energy I need. . . .'

'Bertie has gone', wrote Ottoline one day. 'He has written to me saying his love for me – is cold – is gone . . . He is extremely self-centred poor man – and says that I was selfish because I did not sacrifice myself more to him. I feel his letter tonight is final – and that most probably I shall never see him again . . . Yes, I feel the poorer a great deal. But I don't think he loved me – only desired me.'

She was wrong in thinking herself free. This crisis, like the others, passed. Ottoline and Russell were soon talking of the 'great happiness' that awaited them in the future.

After Russell had moved out of Pembroke Lodge, and when his grandmother had died, he had distanced himself from his relations and from the past. He kept in touch with Agatha only by letter, and he seldom saw Frank, but when he escaped the emotional aridity of his life with Alys, and learned about being in love, he found Frank a more agreeable companion. The two brothers were very different in appearance and character. Russell was slight, dark-haired, and brisk, with a laugh friends likened to that of a hyena. Frank, who had taken his seat in the House of Lords in 1887, at the age of twenty-two, was a big burly man with a florid complexion and clear steel-blue eyes, who moved slowly and carefully. He could be contemptuous,

outspoken, possessive and quarrelsome. What the two men discovered they had in common was that neither found relationships
with women smooth, Russell because he alternated between passion
and detachment, Frank because of his petty tyrannies and his
tendency to blame them if they tried to get away from these. Yet
there was affection between the two brothers. 'He is good natured,'
Russell observed to Ottoline, 'full of jollity and life and with much
good in him; but he is coarse in texture, he would sully anything one
cared about.'

After Frank had successfully sued for libel his first mother-in-law,
Lady Scott, and sent her to jail, he spent much of his time abroad,
sailing his yacht, *Royal*. Through local politics, he had met a widow
working for the London County Council, Mollie Somerville, who
was a supporter of women's suffrage: a 'fat, florid, coarse Irishwoman
of forty . . . with black curls, friendly manner and emotional opinions', as Santayana described her. She was eager to remarry and
though Frank failed to win a divorce in England from Mabel Edith
– Lady Scott took care to see he had no grounds – the couple went
to live in Nevada for the statutory six months and returned with an
American certificate of marriage. They were badly advised; British
courts recognised the marriage, but not the divorce. In 1901, Frank
was arrested for bigamy, tried by his peers in the House of Lords
and sentenced to six months in jail. After giving an excellent speech
in his defence, he settled down in his cell to write a book of secular
sermons.

When he emerged from prison, he returned to Mollie, who
placated the servants when he was rude to them, wore loose tea-
gowns to cover her girth and surrounded herself with a pack of white
lapdogs. Frank became a county councillor, gave card parties and
motored around in his car. Its number was A1, because he had been
the first to apply for a licence.

By the time of Russell's affair with Ottoline, Frank had fallen in
love again. 'How queer everybody is,' Russell remarked, 'almost as
queer as oneself. Poor man, he is full of unsatisfied domesticity. He
used to say he wanted a wife and a cat – he got both in one.' Frank's
new friend was Elizabeth, Countess von Arnim, author of the best-
selling *Elizabeth and her German Garden* and the youthful-looking

and well-dressed mother of three girls and a son at Eton. Small, energetic and extremely attractive, with tiny features and an innocent mouth, Elizabeth was full of amusing anecdotes about her life in Germany, though her cousin, Katherine Mansfield, described her as a 'bundle of artificialities'. Frank had bought and done up Telegraph House near Petersfield, a white pavilion with a flagstaff, which had once belonged to the man in charge of the semaphore between London and Plymouth. It stood high on the downs and was reached by a steep track, surrounded by bare rolling country, from which on clear days it was possible to see as far as the Isle of Wight. Frank had originally bought Telegraph House as a retreat, but by 1913 it had been enlarged, with a second storey, a library in one wing and a tower. It was to play an important part in both Russell's and Frank's lives.

In these last few years before the First World War, Russell combined his busy life at Trinity and his affair with Ottoline with his usual walking holidays. Some of them were taken in England; he made a long trip to the Scillies. Others were spent abroad, whenever possible meeting up with Ottoline during her many stays in the clinic in Lausanne. In the summer of 1913, Russell and Charles Sanger caught a train to Fontainebleau and travelled south to walk over the Mont Cenis pass into Italy, along what they believed to be Hannibal's route. Sanger wore a blue coat and waistcoat given to him by Alys from her box for the deserving poor, Russell a broad-brimmed light grey hat. He felt fit and vigorous, and practised his Italian, teasing Sanger about his fear of dogs and motorcycles. From Verona he wrote to Ottoline about the 'depth and passionateness of my desire for children'. He went to hear *Aida* in the Roman amphitheatre and read D'Annunzio, but complained to Ottoline that he was frequently beset by moods he had no power to banish: 'It is the same psychological process that makes people think themselves poached eggs or Isaiah . . . That is, I compare it to madness.' On the whole, though, he felt at peace. He and Sanger sat drinking tea on the hillsides under the cypress trees; they swam and discussed Shelley.

It was on this trip that Russell met a young German divorcee called Liese von Hattenberg, the mother of two small children, and discovered that he was, after all, capable of giving 'an affection worth having' to someone other than Ottoline. His earlier attachment to Helen Thomas had counted for very little, though he had continued to write to her when she returned to America. They met again in 1912, by which time she was married to Simon Flexner, director of the Rockefeller Institute for Medical Research. To Ottoline, he commented unkindly, 'It seems to me very common with women that marriage is a sort of death. She has become rather disapproving and puritanical with a tendency to a rather niggly morality. Her mouth has often a pathetic droop, indicating much pain with much self-pity – rather weak and defeated.' His brief attachment to Mildred Minturn, a student of Lucy Donnelly's at Bryn Mawr, and whom he had met in America in 1896, was also rather sharply dealt with. When she visited him in England, at the height of his affair with Ottoline, Russell was for once honest: 'I cannot be certain of continuing anything that goes beyond the strict limits of friendship,' he told her . . . 'and I cannot promise to tell you of relations I may have with other women.'

By the beginning of December 1913, Ottoline was back in Lausanne. Russell, longing to get away from the 'mere intellect' of Cambridge and 'into poetry and nature and walking . . . and . . . away from dryness', planned to meet her at the Hotel Minerva in Rome. When he arrived, he found Philip Morrell already installed, so he turned his attention back to Liese von Hattenberg and went walking with her around the lake at Nemi. Probably out of a desire to provoke Ottoline, Russell wrote to her of the encounter, adding that he had not, of course, fallen in love 'because I feel I can see all around her'. It was merely what he referred to as an '*éclairissement*', for he had found Liese funny, cheerful, courageous and truthful. Turning to his increasingly platonic relationship with Ottoline, he could not prevent himself from adding that it was 'against nature, & instinct revenges itself in all sorts of ways when one tries to ignore it'. Holidays were, he added smugly, very difficult: 'I realize that you are quite right to sacrifice me to P., only the result is that I *am* sacrificed to him.' When he told Liese von Hattenberg about Ottoline, she was much taken aback, and he never saw her again.

These were intense and busy years for Russell. Apart from Ottoline and his friendships with Conrad and Wittgenstein, and contributions to various publications, including the Webbs' *New Statesman*, he had hit upon a strain of thought which excited him as he had seldom been excited before. He was still at work on his perennial question, 'Can human beings *know* anything, and if so, what and how? The question is really the most philosophical of all questions.' In all his recent writing, he had accepted matter as it appeared in physics – but this had left what he called an 'uncomfortable' gap between mind and matter. Helped by Whitehead's method of constructing points of classes of events, and seeing the two as fundamentally entwined, he now settled down to work on both mind and matter. Matter, he told Ottoline, would be a 'model of cold passionate analysis, setting forth the most painful conclusions with utter disregard for human beings'.

Russell's letters to Ottoline give some idea of the excitement of his new work, and are revealing of the way that philosophical enquiry continued to engross him. 'It is like getting hold of the right end of a tangled skein,' he told her. 'I perceive dimly a whole new science to be created . . .' Then, 'one can never get on with only just knowledge that is strictly relevant, one has to know a good deal all around, to get atmosphere and depth . . . I feel I can only read things with such profit when they are in the very centre of my interest for the moment . . . my mind is like a search light, very bright in one direction but dark everywhere else.' He was both exhilarated and exhausted by everything he felt he wanted to do: found his school of mathematical philosophy, get on with the question of matter, discover the truth about causality, and much more. It was a time of great mental fertility. 'To see clearly after being puzzled', he said, 'is one of the God-like things in my life.' He was again being attracted by the clarity of science. 'A life devoted to science is . . . a happy life,' he wrote, 'and its happiness is derived from the very best sources that are open to dwellers on this troubled and passionate planet.'

By late 1913 the shape of his work had fallen into some kind of order. He planned to start with a theory of knowledge, then go on to matter. He had been writing ten pages a day and his concentration was excellent; then he increased it to twenty. He put it down to being happy again. 'My mind is intoxicatingly clear and full of power,' he told Ottoline. He was profoundly excited by what he was doing, and talked of achieving a triumph in mathematical logic. 'The excitement of philosophical construction is coming over me – When it comes, the whole great structure shoots up before one's vision with the swiftness of an Aurora Borealis ... great shafts of sudden light piercing the darkness. I suppose people who are not philosophers don't mind so much when things are puzzling – to me it is intolerable until I understand.'

Russell's philosophical work had been attracting admirers in the United States, particularly among the members of the 'neo-realist' school. In 1911, Professor Ralph Barton Perry, a founder of the 'neo-realists', had invited him to give a year's lectures at Harvard, which could be combined with the prestigious Lowell Institute lectures. Santayana, who had recently retired from Harvard, urged Russell to accept, even though the two men had become frankly critical of each other. Russell complained that Santayana was 'aloof, contemptuous and complacent', that he took himself for granted in the way a cat did, and that he was at heart a policeman, compelling others to live as he believed they should. Santayana had decided that Russell was untrustworthy as a thinker, and said later that while he could have been a political leader or philosophical genius, he was a failure, having squandered his time and energy on unworthy topics. At this stage, however, for all his reservations, Santayana's concern was that Russell would find America too depressing and Harvard a disappointment.

Russell hesitated over the invitation; he was greatly absorbed by his work at Trinity, by Ottoline and by his students. But when he received a letter from one of America's most important philosophers, Josiah Royce, pressing him to come, he agreed. He wanted to renew his contacts at Bryn Mawr, though since his estrangement from Alys, Carey Thomas had become cooler towards him. What had finally persuaded him, he said, was a 'princely' offer of £600 from Harvard, for he was short of funds. He did, however, say to Ottoline: 'I only wish the Americans had more brain and were less superficial' and slightly regretted turning down an offer from Göttingen, where he felt he would have found students more adept at logic.

Russell was planning to spend March, April and May in Harvard, giving six lectures a week. He had spent some time deciding what subject to take for the Lowell lectures, since the president had asked him to avoid too 'distinctly religious' a topic. On 1 January 1914, he summoned a shorthand-typist. 'As she entered the room,' he wrote in his autobiography, 'my ideas fell into place, and I dictated in a completely orderly sequence from that moment until the work was finished.' This was something Russell excelled at; to a friend, he boasted that he had put down 11,000 words in three days. He tried them out on his Trinity students, who were enthusiastic.

Before leaving for the New World, he gave a paper on 'Mysticism and Logic' which included a statement about his inner struggle with religion, as well as an account of how the greatest philosophers had felt 'the need both of science and mysticism' and the importance of harmony between the two. It was to be given as a public lecture in America, and appeared in the *Hibbert Journal* that July.

Early in March, Russell boarded the *Mauretania* for New York. The weather was perfect, the luxury 'insidious'. Russell shared a table with Francis Younghusband, the former soldier and famous traveller in Tibet, who had been to school with McTaggart, and who found Russell charming, in the best of spirits, and eager to talk about socialism and the labouring classes. 'A greater natural individualist I never came across,' Younghusband remarked in a volume of memoirs. 'He was *born* to stand by himself.'

Russell reached New York on 14 March 1914, and was met by Lucy Donnelly and Helen Flexner. It was his first visit to America in eighteen years. He was forty-two and possibly the most influential and best-known philosopher in the English-speaking world. The *New York Times* greeted his arrival with respect, and after a few hours he caught the train to Boston.

Intent on saving money, he had asked to be housed very simply. His arrival in Harvard was inauspicious, and he took instantly against the suburbs with their wooden houses and endless muddy streets with trams screeching down the middle, so unlike his elegant surroundings at Trinity. His rooms in the Colonial Club, he declared, were dirty and shabby, with windows that would not open, and spittoons in all the public rooms. In a letter giving his first impressions to Ottoline, he said that, by contrast, he found the 'coloured people friendly and nice – they seem to have something of a dog's liking for the white man – the same kind of trust & ungrudging sense of inferiority.' Happily he was soon rescued from the 'hard, efficient un-meditative men coming and going, talking in horrible American voices' by another visiting Trinity don, H. A. Hollond, who invited him to share his flat in Craigie Hall. The two shared enjoyable breakfasts criticising the American academic world. Their objections were not original. Henry Adams, an early student, said of Harvard that it was a social desert that would have starved a polar bear. From the turn of the century, academics from England had visited the New World and come away disillusioned. When Lowes Dickinson was in America in 1901, he described the country to Roger Fry as 'barbarous ... From one point of view it seems to be sheer decadence ... atrophy of the intellect and imagination and feelings; and then again it seems to be just rawness and untamed vigour ... One effect it has on me, is to make me realise that "culture" is really the most precious thing in the world.' It was to have much the same effect on Russell.

When he had settled down in Harvard, he embarked immediately on his Lowell lectures, which he had called *Our Knowledge of the External World as a Field for Scientific Method in Philosophy*. In these, for the first time, Russell publicly used the term 'logical atomism', and it marked a new stage in his philosophy, in which philosophical scepticism became the concern. Russell again returned to his sense-data, and to his tables. By now, however, his ideas had undergone a distinct change. Questioning whether or not it was possible after all to assume a table with 'substance' lying behind its appearance, Russell concluded that a table, as a 'logical construction', was actually impossible to discover from hard-data alone. More was needed, and he introduced the concept of 'soft-data'. As well as sense-data, 'sensibilia' had to be admitted – that is, the appearance of a table from points where no one is looking at it. 'The old logic', said Russell, 'put thought in fetters, while the new logic gives it wings.'

He was totally unused to public lectures on this scale – 500 people in the audience – and was overcome by stage-fright. With time, his

style improved, and when he had relaxed sufficiently he was able to
note that his audience paid far more attention to being punctual than
to listening to what he had to say. Reactions to him as a lecturer
were mixed. The Boston *Evening Transcript* praised him for 'cogency
. . . certitude . . . consistency', but the popular philosopher Will
Durant, after attending one of the lectures, noted that Russell looked
like 'his subject, which was epistemology – thin, pale and moribund;
one expected to see him die at any minute . . . cold blooded, as a
temporarily animated obstruction, a formula with legs'. Given that
Russell was again suffering from toothache – an American dentist
finally cured his bad breath – that he was homesick for friends,
Ottoline and talk, that he considered the Americans 'fat, stupid and
complacent' and America ugly and squalid, Durant's words may
have been a little harsh.

After a week, Russell sent his first impressions to Lucy Donnelly.
Professor Lowell's 'hard-slaving efficiency' he found loathsome, his
colleagues were disconcertingly alert and businesslike, 'but I miss in
the professors the atmosphere of meditation and absent mindedness
which one associates with thought'. Although the Harvard philosophy faculty had been, in Russell's own words, the 'best in the world'
between 1880 and 1910, the retirement of George Santayana, the
death of William James and the illness of Josiah Royce had robbed it
of much of its former distinction. Part of Harvard's desire to bring
Russell over to lecture in 1914 was a hope that they might persuade
him to stay on in America as their 'chief professor'. To this end they
fêted him ceaselessly, with invitations to dinner with grand Bostonian
families, sightseeing expeditions and lunches and teas. Russell
remained sceptical. He quite liked the old Bostonians, though he
found them 'musty and atrophied'. To Margaret Llewelyn Davies,
in London, he described them as 'against Wilson, against labour,
rich, over-eating, selfish feeble pigs . . .'

As for the academics he encountered, he found most of them
'virtuous – but none have any quality'. America, he concluded,
'produces a type of bore more virulent, I think, than the bore of any
other country – they all give exactly the same information, slowly,
inexorably, undeterred by all one's efforts to stop them.' He listed
among these the psychologist Hugo Munsterberg, 'not the sort of

man I could ever like because of the touch of Jew vulgarity' (Russell was not immune to the casual antisemitism of the day), while the young department chairman, Ralph Barton Perry, was 'quite without intellectual force'. The two exceptions were the law professor Roscoe Pound, and the psychologist John Dewey, also on a visit to Harvard. 'He has a large slow-moving mind', he wrote to Ottoline about Dewey, 'very empirical and candid, with something of the impassivity and impartiality of a natural force.' Apart from approving of these two, Russell had little good to say. 'Americans are *terribly* machine-made. They are only really nice when they are quite untouched by culture and retain the roughness of the people – and then they are generally so *terribly* tough they are like porcupines.'

He did not, however, extend his dislike to his pupils, to whom he tried to introduce the vigorous but relaxed atmosphere of Trinity. To shake up what he called the 'window-dressing' habit of young Americans, he told them they must interrupt his lectures with questions, and that no topic was exempt from scrutiny. He invited them to tea in his rooms on their own, and to evening discussions in groups. Within days of instituting this regime, he was enjoying himself, finding most of the young men, who were a 'motley crew' of Greek, Indian, German and Jewish, receptive, 'vigorous, intelligent Barbarians'. At least three were exceptionally promising: an unshaven Greek called Demos, who was paying his way by working in a restaurant in the evenings; a German-Danish physicist, Victor Lenzen, later professor at the University of California, and a well-dressed, extremely polished young man called T. S. Eliot who, Russell wrote to Ottoline, 'is ultra-civilized – knows his classics very well, is familiar with all French literature from Villon to Vildrach, and is altogether impeccable in his taste, but has no vigour or life or enthusiasm'. Eliot was a graduate student and had already written 'Prufrock' and 'Portrait of a Lady', and he too was somewhat disenchanted with the pomposity of his peers. He intrigued Russell by announcing that Heraclitus always reminded him of Villon, an affinity between a poet of passion and a philosopher of fire which Russell found interesting. Soon, Eliot wrote a caricature of Russell among the Bostonians:

When Mr Apollinax visited the United States
His laughter tinkled among the teacups.
I thought of Fragilion, that shy figure among the birch-trees,
And of Priapus in the shrubbery
Gaping at the lady in the swing.
In the palace of Mrs Phlaccus, at Professor Channing-Cheetah's
He laughed like an irresponsible foetus.
His laughter was submarine and profound
Like the old man of the sea's
Hidden under coral islands
Where worried bodies of drowned men drift down in the green silence,
Dropping from fingers of surf.
I looked for the head of Mr Apollinax rolling under a chair
Or grinning over a screen
With seaweed in its hair.
I heard the beat of the centaur's hoofs over the hard turf
As his dry and passionate talk devoured the afternoon.
'He is a charming man' – 'But after all what did he mean?' –
'His pointed ears. . . . He must be unbalanced,'
'There was something he said that I might have challenged.'
Of Dowager Mrs Phlaccus and Professor and Mrs Cheetah
I remember a slice of lemon and a bitten macaroon.

Russell later wrote to a friend asking whether he knew Eliot's poem about him. 'He seems', he observed, 'to have noticed the madness.'

In the middle of April, Russell went to Bryn Mawr, where Lucy Donnelly had been able to arrange only an informal talk, to be given in her own rooms. Bryn Mawr was not like Harvard. His success, she told him later, had lit up the university. 'You were like a wizard weaving your subtle wonderful spells . . . William James and Santayana had nothing like your magic or intellectual potency with their audience.' The young philosophers of Bryn Mawr now decided to use Russell as a basis for a future course of discussions. The only dissenting voice, protesting against Russell's presence, was that of Carey Thomas, Alys's cousin.

Towards the end of May, his appointment at Harvard over, Russell left for a lecture tour. His final verdict on the university was harsh. Apart from Royce, he said, 'nobody here broods or is absent-minded, or has time to hear whispers from another world.' He blamed neither the American characteristic of shallowness nor the peculiar tone of self-satisfaction he encountered everywhere, as much as the calibre of the men who taught there. Too much time was spent in teaching; too little in thought. For this, he attacked the 'deadly bore' President Lowell, and his apparent conviction that there was something unbusinesslike, and hence rather feeble, about men of learning. The other universities around the country where he spoke were little better. Princeton he found to be 'full of new Gothic . . . [and] as like Oxford as monkeys can make it'; Yale a 'one horse place'; Wellesley 'goody goody', while Brown and Columbia were completely unmemorable. He complained that the lecturers were fools. 'The mental atmosphere is foetid with putrefying puritanism, which survives in contempt for all beauties and sense, and in insincerity and in the substitution of pedantry for impulse . . .'

Russell then went on a short tour of Chicago and the Midwest. He had been invited to stay with an eminent local gynaecologist named Emelius Clark Dudley, the father of four daughters and a son, who kept open house for the most interesting people in the city 'of no matter what race, including Indian, Negro, Oriental'. Russell had met one of the daughters, Helen, in Oxford, and had been invited to stay with them while in America. On arriving at the station he was met by Helen; and was charmed. He felt more at home, he said, than he had with anyone during his entire stay away from England. Helen wrote poetry, knew about literature, and was 'passionate, poetic and strange'. Russell spent the night with her, while her sisters kept guard outside. By the time he left Chicago, Helen was saying that she intended to follow him to England, and they agreed that if Russell could get a divorce they might even marry.

Early in June, Russell boarded the *Megantic*, delighted with the £750 he had earned, but fundamentally disenchanted. 'I wonder whether I shall ever come back,' he wrote to Lucy Donnelly. 'America has treated me very kindly, but I do not think its output in philosophy will be very important for some time to come – the conditions, financially and mentally, are too adverse.' From the deck, he watched icebergs float by. He wrote a letter to Ottoline, telling her of his 'adventure', assuring her that he did not for a minute feel the same 'intensity or passion' for Helen that he did for her, and saying that it would make no difference at all to their relations. He took two pages to describe Helen. '28 – not good-looking – her mouth, and still worse her nose, very ugly'. She was, however, sincere and creative and 'withering, like a flower in drought, for want of love'. He ended, with customary disingenuousness: 'I do most intensely mind giving you pain, I do indeed. I long to be with you and to make you *feel* that my love is absolutely undiminshed.' On his arrival he found a letter from Ottoline telling him that she wished their relationship henceforth to be platonic.

Russell was to return to America many times, but his irritation and disappointment in finding that it was not after all 'a romantic land of freedom' coloured what was to come. Never again would he view the New World with the excitement of his first visit in 1896. 'Altogether the country is curiously Byzantine', he concluded in a letter to Ottoline. 'It lives on in a past which was more civilised than the present, it has the same kind of feebleness and same inroads of Barbarians.' Like Lowes Dickinson, he was always to dwell on the contrast between the energy and enthusiasm of the people and their lack of all real desire to think or dream. To the end of his life Russell retained a picture of a country which threw away its talents and vigour on corruption, petty snobberies, moral lethargy and philistinism.

Ottoline, Conrad and Wittgenstein had all, in their own ways, changed Russell. The clash between him and Ottoline – religion against agnosticism, mysticism against reason, instinct against logic, the world of society against that of the intellect – had produced a messy novel, but it had also given him a taste for culture, art and intimacy. It had given Ottoline far greater pleasure in analysis and reasoning. Their relationship could never have lasted. Victorian morality was still too powerful, and they were in any event too different in character. It was possibly Conrad, the master of both reason and passion, who effectively turned Russell back towards the road which suited him best. But Ottoline's influence was to last. It had made him open and vulnerable in a way that would be tested in the years immediately ahead.

Nine

Beetles and brothers

Just as the years between 1901 and 1914 had been a time of academic and emotional excitement for Russell, when he had produced a work of mathematical philosophy which had become an essential basis for much modern philosophy, had sought religious understanding and been in love, so the war was going to give him a wholly new sense of direction. Since 1908, he had been a Fellow of the Royal Society and, during 1911 and 1912, the President of the Aristotelian Society. Despite his incursions into practical politics with suffrage and free trade, and the discovery that he was good at putting complicated ideas into words ordinary people could understand, Russell was fundamentally a scholar, interested in the pursuit of pure knowledge and pure reason. His mental home lay not with the wider public, but among the academics. Without the war, despite Ottoline's influence, it is possible that he might have remained for ever an eminent philosopher, dabbling from time to time in the political causes of the moment. 'My life before 1910 and my life after 1914 were as sharply separated as Faust's before and after he met Mephistopheles,' he wrote in his autobiography.

The war brought him a new and quite different circle of friends and colleagues. Four years and three months of it drove him out of an academic world which had honoured but was now to reject him, and into a life of controversy, never out of the public eye. Before the war, he had looked on politics almost with detachment, preferring to observe rather than to take part in the Liberal causes he supported. The war turned him into a lifelong political being, brought him into campaigning organisations – the Union of Democratic Control and the No-Conscription Fellowship – and gave him a taste for heated discussions on social justice and violence and for political debate. It also deprived him of his Fellowship at Trinity, and cut him off for ever from a small number of former friends. The war, Russell would say, shook him out of his prejudices, and made him active once again, while rescuing him from the staleness he was beginning to feel over mathematics. 'I underwent a period of rejuvenation', he wrote later. It was to be a time of mental and emotional ferment involving several passionate love affairs, of new and disturbing friendships – an entire life recast. His 'conversion' at the time of Evelyn's crisis had opened his mind to pacifism: the war turned him into a vehement opponent of armed conflict and the most eloquent moral spokesman of his day. For a scholar dedicated to reason, the sheer magnitude of his outrage was impressive. Nothing had provoked such fire in him before.

Russell arrived back in London from America in the middle of June 1914, happy to be back in the 'complexities and diversifications' of old Europe, and joking that he might have become infected with Bostonian 'prosiness'. He met Ottoline and they went down to Burnham Beeches for the day, agreeing that they would meet every possible Tuesday. Despite their last exchanges of letters, their fondness for each other had been diminished neither by their months apart nor by Russell's affair with Helen Dudley, about whom Ottoline continued to be generous, even if she wrote in her diary: 'Why *should* one mind? But one does!' Within days of their reunion, she was able to write: 'Yes indeed, nothing has ever been quite as wonderful as these moments. We are *absolutely* one. *All* the hindrances and barriers gone . . .'

Soon afterwards, Russell returned to Cambridge. It was unusually hot. He found the fellows deep in acrimonious talk about the coming war. On 28 June came the news that the Archduke Franz-Ferdinand, heir apparent to the. throne of Austria and Hungary, had been murdered by a Serbian nationalist in Sarajevo. 'I am fixing some things in my mind', he wrote to Ottoline, 'which I forgot during the Boer War: not to hate anyone, not to apportion praise and blame, not to let instinct dominate. The force that in the long run makes for peace and all other good things is Reason . . .' He hurried around Cambridge collecting signatures from over sixty professors and Fellows to a statement that Britain should remain neutral, and sent it off to the *Manchester Guardian.*

He was to remember every day that followed with great clarity. On the Sunday, 2 August, he was crossing Trinity Great Court when he met Keynes hastening off to borrow a motorcycle to get to London. He told Russell that he had been summoned by the government. Realising just how imminent war now was, Russell went up to London himself and lunched on the Monday with the Morrells: they discussed Philip's plan to make a pacifist speech in the House of Commons. Russell then set off to hear Sir Edward Grey's speech, but found the House completely packed. Instead, he wandered around the streets, listening to what people were saying, horrified and disbelieving that everyone seemed delighted by the prospect of fighting.

On 4 August, at the very moment when the declaration of war was being announced to a House of Commons full of cheering Members, he and Ottoline walked up and down the roads behind the British Museum, gloomily discussing the future. Later in the day, he came across George Trevelyan in the Strand, and the two men quarrelled violently about the coming war. George's fault, he was to say later, was that he was a historian: 'I think history has a very bad effect on people's political morals, because it makes them content if we live up to the standards of the past.'

When Russell returned to Trinity, he was appalled to find how fast the war spirit had seized hold of the university. 'Most people like it', he wrote to Lucy Donnelly, 'because it is exciting and makes them feel brave and proud . . . You cannot conceive the loneliness and the moral upheaval that this has brought to me . . .' In a passage voicing his despair about the young men he had been teaching, soon to be sent off to die, and feeling 'responsible for every death', he wrote: 'We, the old, we have sinned; we have sent these young men to the battlefield for our evil passions, for our spiritual death, for our failure to live generously . . .' The Fellows were busy drilling; the students lining up to volunteer. Two thousand troops arrived to be stationed in Cambridge, and their officers were sent to dine in hall.

Nevile's Court was taken over by the War Office as a hospital, and Russell was put out of his rooms. There was even talk of turning the entire college into a hospital.

Russell felt disoriented, uncertain what to do, except perhaps write some kind of book on the psychology of war. He managed to persuade the *Nation* to print a letter: 'I protest against our share in the destruction of Germany. A month ago ... if an Englishman killed a German, he was hanged ... Now ... he is a patriot ... reason and mercy are swept away in one great flood of hatred ...' In quite a new voice, using a new vocabulary, he went on to attack 'official gentlemen, living luxurious lives, mostly stupid', the drifting diplomats, and the 'vast forces of national greed and national hatred'. It was strong stuff. Henry Massingham, a famous editor of the time, printed it only reluctantly and thereafter many papers were closed to Russell. It was not until late in 1916, when people were becoming alarmed by what they saw as a loss of civil liberties, that he again found it easy to be published. He very much wanted to reply to H. G. Wells's much publicised suggestion that a massive war might herald a better society – and to his famous slogan 'the war that will end all war', which had quickly seized the public imagination. In the end, the *Labour Leader* gave him space. 'All wars are thought to be righteous ...' he countered. 'But no war hitherto has put an end to war. If this war is to end differently, it must produce a different spirit, and above all it must make us forget, in the claims of humanity, our fiery conviction of the enemy's wickedness.'

'It is impossible to convey to you anything of the horror of these past weeks,' Russell wrote to Lucy Donnelly. 'Events of a month ago seem to belong to a previous experience. All our hopes and faiths and foolish confidences are gone flaming down into hell ... Hardly anyone seems to remember common humanity – that war is mad horror, and that deliberately to cause the deaths of thousands of men like ourselves is so ghastly that hardly anything can justify it.'

One of the most painful aspects of Russell's violent anti-war position was that the passion he felt was now beginning to cut him off from many of his friends. 'I don't understand people being really *miserable* about the war,' Moore wrote to Desmond MacCarthy, 'though rather admire people who are. . . . I believe, really and truly, it gives me much more pleasure than pain, simply because I am so interested in it. . . . But so far as I can gather, Russell does really feel miserable . . . but I think most people are much more like me . . .' He was right; most people did not share Russell's outrage. Bob Trevelyan refused to become involved; the Whiteheads, whose elder son North had volunteered, not surprisingly felt distanced from Russell, causing him to write miserably to Ottoline that 'it is so hard not to think one *must* be wrong when everyone is against one,' and, after he had been invited by Evelyn to go and stay: 'I find myself utterly remote from them . . . I fear sooner or later they will attack me, and I don't know what I shall do then. I want to escape.' Gilbert Murray supported Sir Edward Grey, causing Russell to comment that he was a 'snivelling sentimental ass' and 'squashy as a slug'.

From Dora, Charles Sanger's wife, in Bristol, came one of the few friendly notes: 'Even here among Quakers and Socialists, Charlie and I are alone too in thinking as you do.' Another came from Bernard Shaw. 'Our job is to make people serious about the war. It is the monstrous triviality of the damned thing and the vulgar frivolity of what we imagine to be patriotism that gets at my temper.' On this at least the two men were united, Shaw producing an odd, but impassioned autobiographical anti-war manifesto called 'Common Sense about the War', modelled on Tom Paine's *The Rights of Man*. When it appeared, librarians removed his books from their shelves and newspaper editors advised their readers to boycott his plays and published a cartoon of him wearing an Iron Cross, while the former President, Theodore Roosevelt, referred to him as a 'blue-rumped ape', one of the 'venomous' breed of socialists, all of whom were 'physically timid creatures'. The opposition to the war was beginning to provoke considerable verbal violence: because they appeared so isolated, so out of step with the men and women who applauded the war, it took little to brand the pacifists as cowards. The stand taken by Russell and others like him was already a brave one.

One of his problems was that while deploring the war, he felt isolated and 'tortured by patriotism'. He despaired at the thought of the men who were about to be slaughtered, felt murderous towards Grey and Asquith and the statesmen of Europe, and was troubled at having to rethink his previous views on human nature. Lecturing on logic to his few remaining students at Trinity, he began to see his work as futile, particularly as the days went by and his colleagues began crossing the quads to avoid him. 'I feel my inmost soul torn to shreds by the conflict,' he wrote to Ottoline. 'It is so dreadful to be parted from England at such a time.'

His private life was not helping. Helen Dudley had persuaded her father, who knew nothing of their affair, to bring her to Europe. She arrived in London to find Russell completely engrossed in the war, and his affections, if anywhere, back with Ottoline. Dismayed at the thought of a private scandal which would prejudice the public further against him and all he wished to say about the war, and realising that he had acted foolishly, Russell explained the impossibility of any serious relationship, though he did agree to 'relations with her from time to time'. To Ottoline he wrote, 'I do so want to get away from this horrible personal tangle, which seems so degrading at this time.'

Helen began to press him, and he took to refusing to let her into his flat at all, despite her poundings on the door, except once when she begged for a glass of water and he gave it to her on condition that she did not enter. Ottoline, who took her in at Russell's request, left a vivid but harsh picture of Helen. 'So lethargic and feline . . . She is really only a vampire of ideas and sentences. Meanwhile her body is laced and anaemic. What she really needs is blood, not ideas and words.' Helen was to have a most unhappy life. For a while she lived with Ottoline, where she filled her room with garish clothes, and paced up and down 'like a beaten, caged animal', or bored her hostess for hours, puffing smoke from innumerable cigarettes. She was tenacious, but neither tough nor a bearer of grudges. She returned to America amid fears that she might commit suicide. Later she developed a dreadful illness, becoming paralysed and then insane. 'I broke her heart,' Russell observed laconically in his autobiography.

In September, a Bostonian writer and lecturer on religion, Elizabeth Perkins, came to England on a visit. She had friends in the Wilson administration and had been following Russell's anti-war views from America, where his reputation continued high. She thought this might be the right time for another lecture tour of America, during which he could be introduced to President Wilson and put to him his views on neutrality and the possibility of Wilson playing the role of arbitrator. She got in touch with an official in the State Department, who, though not unfriendly to the idea, pointed out that Russell would have to be presented to the president by the British ambassador in Washington, and that the mood in Britain would not tolerate this intervention. However, Elizabeth Perkins also had friends among American publishers, and Russell was soon committing his views to paper for Ellery Sedgwick at the *Atlantic Monthly*. His first article, 'Is a Permanent Peace Possible?' appeared in the issue of March 1915. Russell spelt out the causes of militarism in Europe and called on America to take a firm position against the 'warring governments'. Many articles followed calling for an inter-national authority to bring about a just settlement between disputing nations, and for 'passive resistance' on the part of the British, which he suggested might be a 'better defense than war' – both causes he was to champion for the rest of his life. To find such a platform for his views possibly assuaged some of the pain of his isolation at home.

Russell now asked to have his academic duties at Cambridge suspended for two terms, and explored the possibility of returning to America to teach. In the end he decided against it, writing to Professor Perry that he did not feel that he could leave Britain while there was a war on: 'Just now it is dreary. The young men are gone, the old men are bloodthirsty, the streets are dark, and one sees nothing but soldiers, wounded and unwounded . . .' Professor Perry, in public, took a critical view of Russell, attacking him in the *International Journal of Ethics* for his philosophical and ethical stand against the war. Privately, he wrote to say how he wished they could discuss it all face to face, for the Americans were not really in a position to be able to judge, as they 'do not feel the hot breath of fierceness'.

Before 1914, Russell had been, by birth and inclination, a natural member of the Liberal Party, which he saw as standing for tolerance, a belief in progress and the need to convince people by reason. The war brought him – together with many other intellectuals like Charles Trevelyan and Lowes Dickinson – into the Labour Party, which had come out against the war and declared its duty to be 'securing the peace'. 'You were right about the Liberals,' he wrote to Margaret Llewelyn Davies, 'I have done with them. I never believed anything so frightful could happen.'

The ideal of political liberty was immensely important to Russell, and he would return to it in his writings and speeches again and again for the rest of his life, as he would to his belief in world government. 'It is bad that others should exert their will to induce a man, voluntarily but against his own judgement, to act as they think right,' he had written in *The Democratic Ideal* in 1906. Like his godfather J. S. Mill, he believed in the value of individual judgement and held that it was wrong for the state to use its power to achieve ends incompatible with the principle of liberty – a belief that was to be tested increasingly as the war went on. One of the most unacceptable steps, for those who opposed the war, was the passing of DORA, the Defence of the Realm Act, dealing with censorship and restrictions, which brought in its wake informers and spies and fostered a spirit of anti-German hysteria, including even the putting-down of dachshunds. As the mood of the war grew more bitter, DORA came to represent all that was most oppressive.

Russell always stood clearly among those who did not accept that Prussian militarism alone was to blame for the war. What the war demonstrated for him was what he called 'unthinkingness' or 'unreason'. War could, occasionally, be justified, but not this war, which he attributed partly to the secrecy and scheming of diplomats and politicians. Neither then nor later would he think all war wrong, stating in one of his most important contributions on the subject, 'The Ethics of War' published in the *International Journal of Ethics* in January 1915, that wars of self-defence – when an invasion needed repelling – were justified. The other causes of war – colonialism, principle and prestige – were justified only under very particular circumstances. 'But I think the judgement as to its justification', he wrote to Ottoline, 'ought to be in the hands of neutrals, whose interests and passions are not involved.'

In time, Russell came to blame the First World War for most of the evils which followed – Russian communism, Italian fascism, German nazism, and the creation of a chaotic and unstable world. Had Britain remained neutral, he wrote in the 1950s, the war would have been short, Germany would have won, America would not have been dragged in, and Britain would have remained strong and prosperous. In an interview with Royden Harrison not long before his death in 1970, Russell repeated that he had never been an absolute pacifist: 'My approach has always been utilitarian: a matter of balancing up the costs of war or surrender.' At the time, replying to an American called Chester Reed, who had seen the letter he had written to the *Nation* reprinted in the New York *Sunday Sun*, he wrote: 'Now that war exists, I consider the victory of the Allies of great importance to mankind: the defeat of democracy and the triumph of Bismarckian tradition would, I believe, postpone for a long time the political progress of civilisation . . .'

Many of Russell's pronouncements, then and later, had a prescient quality. He foresaw several possible futures for the world, including Britain drifting into mediocrity. More immediately, he foresaw the eclipse of the Liberal Party. The announcement by Asquith on 26 May 1915 of a coalition of Liberals and Unionists was, effectively, the end of Liberal government: by 1924, the Liberal Party would be reduced to the status of third and minor party. He believed that the Allies were bound to win the war, but became increasingly anxious about all forms of loss of liberty. Throughout the war, despite his fears about Germany, he remained strenuously opposed to Britain's participation. Having always maintained that men and women were the same when it came to political attitudes and abilities, he came to appreciate the particular work of women in the peace movement, saying after a rousing speech by the suffragist Helena Swannick, 'I almost began to think perhaps women had something of value to contribute to politics – some element of compassion in which men are different.'

During the summer of 1914, most people considered it right and sensible to go to war. In the previous war between two major European powers – France and Prussia – the hostilities had lasted only a few months and there had not been very many casualties. The general feeling was that however terrible war might be while it lasted, it would not last long. In military and political circles there was much reassuring talk about a 'short war'.

Before 1914, peace societies had existed in most European countries, but they held widely different views about how to bring about or keep the peace, and very few had formulated clear ideas about what sort of machinery of arbitration might be needed. The shooting of Jean Jaurès, the French socialist leader, in the wake of an enormous rally in Paris to protest at the war, had come as a severe blow to those who believed Jaurès was the one hope for a strong and united European peace party. After his death, most of the European peace groups simply melted away. In Britain, Philip Morrell, who was doing all he could to drum up anti-war feeling in the House of Commons, at tremendous cost to his popularity, now found himself at the centre of a new British peace party. It consisted of some forty Members of Parliament, with five International Labour Party members led by Ramsay MacDonald, twenty-five Liberals and a few Labour members. The Morrell house in Bedford Square became a rallying point for these anti-war parliamentarians, as well as for people like the founder of the Neutrality League, Norman Angell, the journalist E. D. Morel, Arthur Ponsonby, chairman of the Liberal Party's Foreign Affairs Group, and Russell.

It was here, in September 1914, that Charles Trevelyan, who had resigned as Parliamentary Secretary at the Board of Education on the outbreak of war, proposed a new group: the Union for Democratic Control. The idea behind it was not precisely pacifist: rather, it was intended to combat the 'secret diplomacy' of Sir Edward Grey which had taken Britain into the war, to call for a negotiated peace, to press for the founding of an international peace forum, to reduce the power of the arms manufacturers, and to fight what they saw as growing 'Prussianism' in Britain. The British people, they argued, were far more pacifist than their government, and should be given the chance to express their views. The UDC was born with Trevelyan's proposal that it should 'assist in securing peace at the earliest moment'. It became a sort of shadow Foreign Office, an unofficial, non-aligned, non-party group disgusted at the prevailing atmosphere in which it was regarded as treasonable to speak the truth about what was happening at the front. Working privately at first, they came into the open after the Northcliffe press began labelling them 'pro-German'.

The UDC continued to meet in Bedford Square, where, according to one regular member, Mary Agnes Hamilton, the 'dominating mind was Bertie Russell's'. He looked like Voltaire, she noted, and 'his devastating wit played like lightning against the dramatic background of the war . . . No resisting the force of his ruthless dissection of motive; no reply possible to the caustic comments he would emit in his high squeaky voice, and follow up with a cackle of curiously mirthless laughter, while his brilliant eyes, like high-power headlights, bored right into your head.' Though dazzled, Mary Hamilton was not altogether approving. 'He had a dynamo within that was too powerful for his own comfort and far too powerful for that of others: inevitably, he first swallowed admirers and then, with what they felt a heartless cruelty, spewed them out.'

By November, the UDC had seven branches, under a general committee of eighteen members. In February 1915, a branch in Cambridge held its founding meeting in Lowes Dickinson's rooms in King's. Soon the focus for intellectual dissent within the university, it was heavily influenced by Lowes Dickinson, whose reaction to the war had been one of horror, and who was now campaigning for an international league; by Leonard Woolf, who wrote a paper about setting up a high court of war arbitration, and by Lytton Strachey, who took over the *Cambridge Review* and made it a platform for dissenters. What all these men had in common was a feeling that the war was fundamentally wrong and absurd: they were determined to remain 'sane'. Russell seemed the most despairing of all, particularly when he saw his former students in uniform. 'We are far from the worst yet,' he wrote gloomily to Lucy Donnelly, 'Germany will grow more cruel and desperate as time goes on, and I fear in the end the brute will be dominant in us too . . . There lurks deep down in us a beast as cruel as any Prussian Junker . . . If the [Germans] succeed, all that has been good in English civilisation will be swept away.'

In these early months, Russell was much involved with shaping the UDC's policies, becoming president of the Cambridge branch and lecturing to more than thirty groups during its first year. In the summer of 1915, he spoke to a 'Pacifist Philosophy of Life' conference held in Caxton Hall in London, but reported irritably to Ottoline that the pacifists were 'an awful crew. Pacifists really are no good. What is wrong with mere opposition to war is that it is negative. One must try to find other outlets for people's wildness . . .' During the summer of 1915 he took part in a meeting with the Quakers, to discuss a common programme for peace. Like several other Labour and Liberal supporters, he remained wary of harnessing the future of the UDC too closely to the Independent Labour Party, who were out-and-out opponents of the war, and he baulked at joining its ranks. 'I have been for some time in two minds as to joining the ILP,' he wrote to its London secretary Herbert Bryan in July 1915. 'I agree most warmly with the attitude the ILP has taken up about the war, and that makes me anxious to support the ILP in every possible way. But I am not a socialist, though I think I might call myself a syndicalist.'

As UDC membership continued to grow, Russell turned his pen to articles on its behalf, for any paper that would still publish him. His favourite theme was that this war (and he would say it again, in later wars) was going to destroy civilisation. 'I hope somewhere among the men who hold power,' he wrote, 'there is at least one who will remember, at this late date, that we are the guardians not only of the nation, but of the common heritage of thought and art and a humane way of life into which we were born, but which our children may find wasted by our blind violence and hate.' Not surprisingly, this sort of language led him into frequent skirmishes with supporters of the war. After the Zurich-based *International Review* had published his 'Justice in Wartime', a tough statement against intellectuals who had abandoned internationalism in favour of militaristic nationalism, the professor of moral philosophy at the University of St Andrews, A. E. Taylor, wrote to *The Times* to ask 'Why does the British Post Office . . . lend its services to the enemy by distributing this pestiferous and mendacious stuff?' and why was Russell allowed to get away with statements which would send other, lesser-known people to jail? Russell, he went on to say, had clearly not read or cared about the Bryce Report, a recently published description, by a committee of lawyers, of German atrocities against the Belgians. Russell *had* read the report, and been much disturbed by it, but he was annoyed that English newspapers never subjected their own country to similar investigations. Next day, *The Times* carried a

Lady John Russell, the 'deadly
nightshade'

Lord John Russell, Bertrand
Russell's grandfather

Lord Amberley, Russell's father

Kate Amberley, Russell's mother

Rollo, Russell's uncle, as a boy

Aunt Agatha

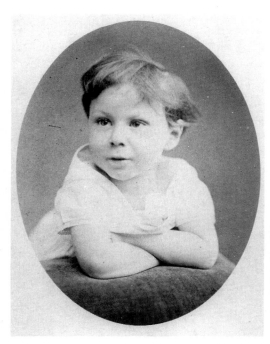

Bertie Russell, soon after the death
of his parents

Pembroke Lodge

G. E. Moore

Russell, seated on ground (centre), as cox of the First Trinity First Lent boat, 1891

Alys Pearsall Smith

Mary, Hannah and Alys
'these vehement females'

Russell's brother Frank with
Elizabeth von Arnim

Lucy Donnelly

Beatrice and Sidney Webb at the
turn of the century

George Bernard Shaw

Alfred and Evelyn
Whitehead, c. 1901

ADDITIONAL ERRATA TO VOLUME I. *210.1475012*

p. 5, line 20, *delete* " π ."

p. 34, line 20, *for* " yRx " *read* " xRy ."

p. 36, line 7 and line 10, *for* " $Q \mid R$ " *read* " $R \mid P$."

p. 44, line 17, *for* " $(p) \cdot p$. is false " *read* " $(p) \cdot p$ is false."

p. 103, in *2·06, in place of last " $p \supset q$ " read " $p \supset r$."

p. 112, in *2·52, *in place of* " $p \supset \sim q$ " *read* " $\sim p \supset \sim q$."

p. 129, in *5·11, *in place of reference to* " *2·51 " *read reference to* " *2·5."

p. 129, in *5·12, *in place of reference to* " *2·52 " *read reference to* " *2·51."

p. 144, *10·23 *should be* " $\vdash :. (x) . \phi x \supset p . \equiv : (\exists x) . \phi x . \supset . p$."

p. 157, line 12, *for* " *10 " *read* " *9.

p. 184, last line of *Dem.* of *14·111, *for second* " $x = c$ " *read* " $x = b$."

p. 228, in *23·81, *for* " $\doteq R \mathbf{G} \doteq S$ " *read* " $\doteq S \mathbf{G} \doteq R$."

p. 242, in *25·37, *for* " zRw " *read* " zSw ."

p. 2∠, in *25·412, *for* " R " *read* " S ."

p. 253, 2nd and 4th lines of *Dem.* of *31·16, *for* " *21·35 " *read* " *23·35."

p. 259, in note to *32·35, *for* " *32·2 " *read* " *32·3."

p. 263, in *33·16, 4th line of *Dem., *for* " *20·34 " *read* " *22·34."

p. 265, in *33·26, 2nd line of *Dem., *for* " *21·34 " *read* " *23·34."

p. 275, in *34·6, 4th line of *Dem., *for first* " S " *read* " R ."

p. 289, 1st line, *for* " $= \beta \uparrow \gamma$ " *read* " $= \alpha \uparrow \gamma$."

p. 322, in *40·18, enunciation, *for* " $\equiv$ " *read* " $=$."

p. 329, in *40·69, *Dem., *for* " $\overrightarrow{P}$ " *read* " $\overleftarrow{P}$ " (3 *times*).

p. 387, in *55·224, 1st line of *Dem., *for* " $\uparrow$ " *read* " $\downarrow$ " (*twice*).

p. 388, in *55·281, *for third* " $=$ " *read* " $\equiv$."

p. 410, in *60·53, last line of *Dem., *for* " γ " *read* " β ."

p. 453, in *71·25, *Dem., 1st line, *for* "$xRy . xRz$" *read* "$ySx . zSx$."

"   "   2nd line, *for* "$xRy . ySu . xRz . zSv . \supset . y = z . ySu . zSv$" *read* "$uRy . ySx . vRz . zSx . \supset . y = z . uRy . vRz$."

"   "   3rd line, *for* "$ySu . ySv$" *read* "$uRy . vRy$."

"   "   6th line, *for* "$xRy . ySu$" *read* "$uRy . ySx$" *and for* "$xRz . zSv$" *read* "$vRz . zSx$."

"   "   7th line, *for* "$x (R \mid S) u . x (R \mid S) v$" *read* "$u (R \mid S) x . v (R \mid S) x$."

p. 465, in *72·16, *Dem., 1st line, *for last* " κ " *read* " x ."

p. 483, in *73·44, *Dem., 1st line, *for second* " y " *read* " x ."

p. 485, in *73·511, *for* " β " *read* " α ."

p. 487, line 19, for " *95 " read " *94."

p. 522, in *81·23, enunciation and 2nd line of *Dem., *for* " $\overrightarrow{R}$ " *read* " R ."

p. 592, in *91·33, *Dem., 1st line, *for* " P " *read* " R ."

p. 614, in *93·36, *Dem., *for* " R " *read* " P " *throughout.*

p. 628, in *95·21, *Dem., line 6, *for* " Q " *read* " T ."

A page from *Principia Mathematica*

Lady Ottoline Morrell

Lady Ottoline in the garden at
Garsington

Lady Ottoline and T. S. Eliot
at Garsington

Catherine Marshall with the national committee of the No-Conscription Fellowship

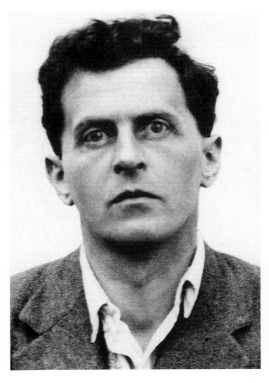

Ludwig Wittgenstein

Clifford Allen

second dig, by the Balkan expert B. R. Seton-Watson: 'A man who can write this is hardly qualified to act as guide in clear philosophical thinking to the youth of England.'

One of Russell's most painful confrontations was with his old friend Gilbert Murray. When war was declared, Murray was one of those who signed a letter of protest. But Sir Edward Grey's speech, which he heard from the distinguished strangers' gallery of the House of Commons on 3 August, had made an impression of 'goodness and simplicity' on him. Although he told Mary that he felt 'utterly abased and crushed by the war' he added: 'But mostly I do feel strung up and exalted by a feeling of the tremendous issue and the absolute duty that lies upon us to save Europe and humanity. We did not know, until the war revealed it, what the German system meant. Once it is revealed, I do feel we must strike it down or die.' This war, he felt, was just; to remain neutral would have been a 'failure in public duty'.

By the middle of September 1915, he had written a pamphlet for the Clarendon Press called *The Foreign Policy of Sir Edward Grey*, which was soon regarded as the orthodox defence of the foreign secretary. In it, he singled out for attack two UDC pamphlets; one had been written by the journalist H. N. Brailsford, the other by Russell. He accused them both of being 'not at present in a state of mind which enables them to see or even to seek the truth', of being pro-German and of 'trying to turn Grey into the "central enemy of the human race"'. Grey's principles, Murray argued, were 'triumphantly right', and such that any decent Liberal should find acceptable: no extension of British territories, the removal of frictions and the establishment of cordial relations with neighbours. Russell was quick to counter-attack. In a pamphlet called *The Foreign Policy of the Entente* he accused Murray of intellectual treachery. 'I felt ashamed of having ever liked him,' he wrote to Ottoline. In private, however, the two men were too good and too old friends to quarrel for long. Murray wrote a pacifying personal letter, mourning the thought that 'our friendship, which mattered so much to me, was for the time being broken,' to which Russell replied that he too was sorry and that 'I feel our friendship still lives in the eternal world, whatever may happen to it here and now.'

To help Russell with his foreign policy pamphlet, Ottoline introduced him to Irene Cooper Willis, a research assistant working for another UDC member, the writer Vernon Lee, and she offered to gather and check newspaper articles for him. Irene was in her early thirties, and Enid Bagnold, who met her with Russell in the Morrell house, has left a good description of her. 'She was beautiful, severe and Spanish looking . . . Her while collar and cascading linen gave her a Portia-like air . . . with indignant gravity, shy but rigid of the right . . . Her gravity drove men in and out of love with her. I don't think she was ever in love with any man. She loved and liked women . . .' Desmond MacCarthy was one of the intellectuals who believed himself in love with her; Russell, albeit briefly, was another, 'buzzing round her like a wasp – trying to get her to talk, turning away in exasperation . . .'

One of the first of Russell's friends to learn of his new interest was naturally Ottoline, to whom he made one of his usual confessions: 'I think I may easily come to have a *very* great affection for Irene . . . not a very passionate feeling, but one which might give happiness and be free from passion. And I feel pretty sure she would respond.' He was wrong. Irene, a barrister by training and destined for a serious career in the law, was clear about her affections. 'I have realised', she wrote to him, 'ever since we talked about it on the river, that I do not care for you in the way that makes me come up to your expectations. I am very much to be blamed . . . I should have told you before had I known before . . . I want to see you but not if you do not want to see me.' For a while, they continued to work together, and there was much talk of how they would remain friends – with occasional suggestions of more. Irene was later to make him a character named Tom Wolfe in her novel, *The Green-eyed Monster*, a man who was not so much dislikeable as insensitive, and prone to be bitchy about his friends, describing 'Edward' (Desmond MacCarthy) as 'no more than a watering-cart making the road of life very pleasant for his friends to walk upon'. Russell, ever more dependent on Ottoline for an emotional haven from the horrors of war, remarked only about Irene: 'I have a real and great affection for her, but I do like people to be willing to shoot Niagara.'

*

As the older dons at Trinity became more agitated about the war and more exercised about all forms of war protest, Russell found himself shunned at high table whenever he visited Cambridge. To counter his growing despair, Ottoline suggested that he take part in a charitable committee looking into the circumstances of destitute Germans caught in Britain by the war. He was touched to discover, dotted around the country, people with a core of decency, like the landladies who not only took in Germans but did not make them pay rent, knowing that it was impossible for them to find work. The Germans were all soon interned.

One day in October 1914, walking down Oxford Street, Russell ran into his old Harvard pupil T. S. Eliot, on his way to take up a scholarship at Merton. Eliot was now twenty-six, with clean features, deep-set eyes – he looked, according to a friend, rather like a sleek cat – and an articulated drawl which made a sleepy, droning sound. There was something of the early Russell about him, a little priggish, puritanical, intellectually ascetic and shy. Russell asked what he thought about the war. 'I only know that I am not a pacifist,' replied Eliot. It is an indication of how very friendless Russell was feeling that he did not seem to mind Eliot's acceptance of the war. Over the following months they became friends, Eliot observing that Russell was one of the dozen people in England he liked 'exceedingly', and no doubt pleasing Russell by settling down to read *Principia Mathematica*. Even though he was in the process of abandoning the 'appearance' of a philosopher for the 'reality' of a poet, Eliot was one of the few people who could manage its symbols, and said that manipulating them gave him a curious sense of power.

The following July, Eliot took his bride of a few weeks, Vivienne Haigh-Wood, to lunch with Russell, who described the occasion to Ottoline: 'I expected her to be terrible, from his mysteriousness; but she was not so bad. She is light, a little vulgar, adventurous, full of life – an artist I think he said, but I should have thought her an actress. He is exquisite and listless; she says she married him to stimulate him, but finds she can't do it ... I think she will soon be tired of him ... He is ashamed of his marriage, and very grateful if one is kind to her.' The Eliots had married without telling their

families, and his parents had been cast down, having wanted him to
return to Harvard to continue his philosophical studies.

Russell was not being altogether honest. Vivienne was twenty-
seven when they met. By all accounts, she was witty, frail, excitable,
and something of a beauty, with light brown hair and pale shining
grey eyes. She loved bold colours and dramatic clothes, and was a
graceful dancer, having taken ballet lessons. Many men found her
extremely seductive, with a mixture of melancholy and sensitivity and
a sardonic, playful manner. She was fun. A friend once spoke of her
as 'shimmering with intelligence'. What neither Russell nor Eliot
knew at that stage was that Vivienne was emotionally very unstable.
Her diaries of the time show her to have been highly nervous and
easily depressed, with sudden swings of mood. As a child, she had
had tuberculosis in one hand, which had left her with headaches and
cramps.

Vivienne soon captivated Russell. She did not attract him physically, he hastened to reassure Ottoline, but he was beginning to think
of her as a 'permanent acquisition'. As the weeks went by, he found
himself drawn closer into the Eliot ménage, particularly after Eliot
had decided to obey his parents and return to America to explain his
marriage. After a bitter row with his father, he returned to London,
penniless. Russell, with characteristic financial generosity, offered
the Eliots a tiny corner of his small Bury Street flat, and lent them
£3000 in debentures from an engineering firm. In 1912, Russell had
written to Ottoline: 'I don't have any *principles* about money, but I
am always coming across people who obviously need it more than I
do . . . So I grow poorer . . . I have a feeling possessions are a crime
– they put one in bondage to matter.'

Sharing a cramped flat, the Eliots and Russell grew close; Vivienne
typed for Russell; Eliot looked for work, and eventually found a job
teaching at the grammar school in High Wycombe. Russell was
feeling increasingly paternal towards him, almost as if Eliot were the
son he had never had. He wrote to Ottoline: 'It is quite funny how I
have come to love him. He is becoming much more of a man. He
has a profound and quite unselfish devotion to his wife, and she is
really very fond of him; but has impulses of cruelty to him from time
to time . . . I am every day getting things more right between them,

but I can't let them alone at present . . . She is a person who lives on a knife edge, and will end as a criminal or a saint – I don't know which yet. She has a perfect capacity for both.' If Vivienne was lively, Eliot could be languid, listless and without energy. 'I believe I like her', Russell wrote to Ottoline, 'really because I can be useful to her, and so I get over the sense of being a failure and making people unhappy when I want to make them happy.'

Vivienne's health, however, was beginning to deteriorate. She had ever more frequent 'nervous collapses', when she took to her bed for days or even weeks, dulled by drugs first prescribed to her when she was sixteen and thought to have contained ether, a common sedative in those days. Letters suggest that some of her problems with Eliot were of a sexual nature, but she was also suffering from faintness and toothache. At the end of the year, while Eliot was teaching, Russell offered to take Vivienne down to Torquay for a holiday. After nine days, Eliot, as Russell put it, 'replaced' him. Eliot was grateful. 'I often wonder how things would have turned out but for you,' he wrote. 'I believe we shall owe her life to you, even.' It was all, Russell assured Ottoline, quite 'proper'. His affection for Vivienne was that for a daughter. But Russell's relationship with Vivienne remains unclear. In the Bodleian Library are to be found four of Vivienne's diaries – for 1914, 1919, 1934 and 1935. They touch on friends, family, health, rows, her husband and her despair. 'Glad this awful year is over', she wrote, on Wednesday 31 December 1919. 'Next probably worse'. But there is no mention of Russell. About all his affairs, Russell tended to be honest; but he was singularly uncommunicative about the Eliots. No one has ever been sure whether Russell, by this time something of a philanderer, actually slept with Vivienne. From the moment of his 'conversion' in 1901, he had been easily moved by suffering women. Much later he explained their relationship as platonic, writing to Robert Sencourt, a friend of Eliot's, that they had 'never had intimate sexual relations'. Even to Ottoline, ever the recipient, however reluctant, of his sexual confidences, he had written, 'I shall never have a physical relation with her, which in any case she would not at all want . . . The affection is not constant, but the sense of responsibility is.'

In this case evidence other than Russell's own seems more

persuasive. There is Evelyn Waugh's entry in his diary, noting that Graham Greene told him that Vivienne's later insanity 'sprang from her seduction and desertion by Russell'. There are his other letters to Ottoline, in which he says how confused he felt about Vivienne and how 'I had a sense of success with Mrs E. because I achieved what I meant to achieve (which was not so very difficult).' There is his letter to Lady Constance Malleson (Colette O'Niel), the young actress who was about to play an important part in his life, to whom he explained: 'I am not in love with her, and I do not care whether I have a physical relation with her or not. But I am happy talking with her and going about with her . . . I expect that she will be an essential part of my life for some time to come.' And there is the more forthright assertion, again to Colette, that when he made love to Vivienne, he had found it 'hellish and loathsome'.

Whatever the truth, Russell was deeply enmeshed with both Eliots for several years. Because Eliot was perpetually broke, trying to find the money for Vivienne's doctors and medicines, he paid for Vivienne's dancing lessons and introduced Eliot to his friend Philip Jourdain, the mathematician and editor of the *International Journal of Ethics* and *The Monist*, for whom Eliot wrote a number of reviews, and to the *New Statesman*, which invited him to contribute various pieces. He reassured Eliot's mother about her son's marriage, telling her that Vivienne had a 'good mind, and is able to be a real help in a literary career, besides having a rare strength and charm of character . . .' He listened to Eliot reading his poems, and encouraged him. There is some suggestion that one of Russell's images about how troops departing from Waterloo Station gave him a sensation of London being a 'place of unreality' made their way into Eliot's verse. 'Unreal City', Eliot wrote in *The Waste Land*, 'Under the brown fog of a winter dawn, / A crowd flowed over London Bridge, so many, / I had not thought death had undone so many . . .'

He also introduced Eliot to Clive Bell and Roger Fry, through whom he met Lytton Strachey and Leonard Woolf, who drew him into the circle of Ottoline Morrell's friends. They did not feel altogether easy with him, finding his manners prim and his learning ostentatious, but they quickly recognised his talents. They were often cruel about Vivienne, parodying her extravagant manner and clothes.

In her memoirs, Ottoline commented that Vivienne seemed to her 'of the "spoilt-kitten" type, very second-rate and ultra feminine, playful and naïve, anxious to show she "possessed" Bertie'. She called her a 'frivolous, silly little woman'. Aldous Huxley observed that he rather liked her, and that she was devoid of all snobbery, but Virginia Woolf was sharper. Vivienne, she noted, made her 'almost vomit, so scented, so powdered, so egotistic, so morbid, so weakly'.

Having decided to settle in England, where Eliot felt he was a 'much more important person' than in America, the couple moved into a small flat off Baker Street, but continued to share a cottage in Marlow with Russell for a while. Eliot was by now working for Lloyds Bank in Queen Victoria Street, writing poetry, but slowly, two or three poems a year, telling a friend that what mattered was that 'these should be perfect in their kind, so that each should be an event.'

As the war went on, Vivienne became more of an invalid and more than ever dependent on Eliot, particularly after the death of her father, to whom she was devoted. Whatever love Eliot had felt for her had by now been replaced by a resigned and bitter sense of responsibility. Eventually Vivienne wrote to Russell to say that she disliked fading intimacies, and that she wished to have no more to do with him. Russell – out of a sense of concern perhaps – went on writing to her. Whether Eliot knew of their closeness or not, he was convinced that Russell was upsetting his wife. He wrote to say that she was under the orders of her doctor and that he was to stop. For a while, relations cooled between Russell and the Eliots.

In May 1915, Ottoline and Philip Morrell moved into Garsington, an Elizabethan manor house of Cotswold stone set in 300 acres of land, not far from Oxford. The property cost £8000. It stood on the side of a hill, surrounded by yew hedges and ilex, with an ornamental garden falling away to a vast fish pool and a charming view across the Thames valley to the Berkshire downs. Garsington has become a legend. Philip, a keen gardener, had spent much of the preceding eighteen months making the place ready: planting a formal garden, with Irish yew trees growing up in pyramids, a series of herbaceous beds in a rectangle, each with different-coloured blooms and surrounded by a box hedge, putting statues, brought back from Italy, into niches round the pool, and placing a reclining Etruscan figure on an island in the middle. At the back of the house, above the garden and the pond, he built a loggia, with romanesque arches and eighteenth-century stone pineapples. The effect was exotic, a little garish, Italianate and absolutely spendid.

Ottoline was the main architect of the inside of the house, which was largely Jacobean. She transformed the large, low, panelled rooms into an oriental fantasy with bright shades of paint, some yellow, some peacock-blue. The drawing room, which had a scarlet cardinal bird in a lacquered cage hanging from a beam, was painted scarlet and gold (Russell, reluctantly, had painted some of the panels) and was filled with cushions, pouffes, bright silk curtains and Persian carpets, while every available space contained cabinets, china, coloured hangings and boxes of incense. The entire house smelt of cloves and pot-pourri. The walls were covered thickly with pictures: drawings by Augustus John, paintings by Mark Gertler and Duncan Grant, sketches by Charles Conder.

The Morrells had decided to move out of London because of their daughter Julian's poor health. Ottoline's idea was to carry her Bedford Square salon to the country, making of it a 'castle of the spirit', though she remarked in her diary how very difficult people were to manage. Weekends, in particular, were crowded out with visitors and, as the war went on, Garsington became a rallying place for the anti-war movement. Guests arrived at the tall iron gates on Friday evenings, some by motorcycle or bicycle, some by cab, some on their feet, and then went down to the fish pond to swim. Then they talked, stretched out on the sloping lawn, listening to Ottoline's peacocks screeching. What gave her most pleasure, she would say, was bringing people into contact with each other. Regular visitors included Duncan Grant, 'looking like a winged elf', Clive Bell, whom Ottoline described as a 'faithful hanger on . . . with the momentary charm of a flatterer . . . the sniper, the traitor'; Aldous Huxley, sitting silent and aloof; Charles Sanger, 'like a very clever, alert, shy, nervous bird, his thin body in a white waistcoat tilted forward, and his head looking up, pince-nez on nose attached with a black cord'; and Lytton Strachey, who was given the best bedroom and the only bathroom, and whom the villagers called variously 'Christ' or 'Judas' because of his long, wispy, reddish beard. Strachey was also given extra helpings of cream, butter and milk, though he frequently forgot to bring his ration coupons.

Many of the visitors were Bloomsberries. After they had left Cambridge, the nucleus had gathered around 46 Gordon Square, the home of Virginia, Vanessa and Adrian Stephen, where the women were on equal footing with the men, and the freedoms born in Cambridge continued to be explored. With the marriage of Vanessa to Clive Bell, the group had acquired a second salon in Fitzroy Square. Their famous Thursday evenings were held in alternate houses. Conversation, started at Cambridge, carried on, much of its tone derived from Moore's teachings, in which high seriousness was mixed with gaiety, the search for truth with intense pleasure in gossip, what Virginia Woolf was to call 'the rich yellow flame of rational intercourse'.

The Bloomsberries had produced very little until 1910. Lytton Strachey wrote for the *Spectator*, and Virginia Stephen for *The Times Literary Supplement*; Maynard Keynes and Saxon Sydney-Turner were at the Treasury; Leonard Woolf was a colonial civil servant. In 1910, Roger Fry put on the first Post-Impressionist exhibition, which included work by Bonnard, Manet, Picasso and Cézanne, at the Grafton Galleries, with Desmond MacCarthy acting as secretary. Though not every member of the set was certain how much they liked the new art, Bloomsbury turned francophile, and Fry founded the Omega workshops to help impoverished painters. Bloomsbury read Proust and James Joyce. When Leonard Woolf returned from Ceylon after a seven-year absence, and married Virginia Stephen in 1912, he found the mood much as he had left it, the 'truths and values of my youth' unbroken, with belief in reason still tempered by sensitivity and love of beauty. What was new, perhaps, was awareness of contemporary and social problems, and a candour in language, with a lot of talk about 'copulation' and 'buggery'.

Ottoline Morrell and Russell were not part of inner Bloomsbury, though Ottoline lived on its fringes and drew Russell with her for a while, but Garsington provided a country retreat for the group's members throughout the war years. As news from the front grew more harrowing, and there was no sign of the promised 'short war', the Bloomsberries began to work out their individual attitudes towards the hostilities. Some, once conscription was introduced, became conscientious objectors, and used Garsington as their base; others accepted limited forms of military service, and went off to serve with such things as the ambulance unit; others became total pacifists and went to prison. What united them was their attitude to the war itself: it was wrong, and they refused to turn it into a crusade. At Garsington they found a refuge, and the comfort of other people who felt as they did. They felt warm there, emotionally and physically; too warm perhaps, as Mary Agnes Hamilton suggested, and a little too self-satisfied, though Philip Morrell often returned to Garsington profoundly shaken by the hostility he endured in the House of Commons.

Garsington exercised a kind of fascination over its wartime visitors, most of whom were men. There was something about the hotchpotch decorations, the marvellous garden and the wailing peacocks, which drew them back again and again. 'Is the sunlight ever normal at Garsington?' Virginia Woolf is said to have asked. 'No, I think even the sky is done up in pale yellow silk, and certainly the cabbages are scented.' Since most of the visitors were writers or keepers of diaries, almost all left a description of their hostess. Few were kind. Writing letters to Ottoline, they were affectionate; writing about her, they were most often malicious. Leonard Woolf wrote about her walk: 'her hat, hair, and clothes flopped and flapped around her; she looked like an enormous bird whose brightly and badly dyed plumage was in complete disarray and no longer fitted the body.' Portraying her seemed to stir people to new flights of fantasy. Enid Bagnold, one of the many visitors who described her voice, said it was 'double . . . like the two halves of a wasp'; another observed that when Ottoline said the name 'Derain', it sounded like a cow mooing.

Life at Garsington was informal, chaotic and fun. Sexual freedom was regarded as civilised and homosexuality was accepted as a natural part of life; constancy, on the other hand, was thought a bit ridiculous. There was not always a great deal to drink other than sparkling cider, the peacocks kept everyone awake, and the fact that there was only one bathroom meant that all male guests (except

Lytton Strachey, who had convinced Ottoline that he was too frail) had to go behind the bushes in the garden. 'Altogether', Strachey observed one day to Keynes, 'it's been more like a campaign in Flanders than anything else. The peacocks, too, have never once relinquished their shrieking.'

But the food was excellent, the beds comfortable – Virginia Woolf described hers as 'layer upon layer of the most springy turf' – the garden 'almost melodramatically perfect' and the conversation bewitching. On summer evenings, visitors followed Ottoline, perched on a high bicycle and wearing an embroidered linen dress and a silk handkerchief on her head, in a flotilla of brightly coloured cycles down the lanes, between the hawthorn and the honeysuckle. When the weather was good, they sat around the garden on deckchairs and rugs, played croquet and slept out of doors on a flat roof between the gables. On winter evenings they played charades, read aloud in French or German – Russell spoke French with a perfect accent – while Ottoline sat smoking and sucking peppermints, doing some crochet or embroidering a counterpane from a pattern found in the Embroidery Museum in South Kensington, her pugs curled up at her feet. Occasionally they danced. Juliette Baillot, who came as a governess to Julian, and later married Julian Huxley, remembers dancing with Russell who 'hopped about and was as light as a thistle'. During harvest time, guests were expected to help, but this was the sort of work Russell most disliked and his face would grow long and bored. There was a good deal of laughing: Clive Bell would guffaw and Virginia Woolf make birdlike crowing sounds while her sister Vanessa produced reluctant little snorts.

And of course, they talked. Conversations started at breakfast, picking up the threads of the previous night, then go on all day – on walks, in the garden, at meals, by the pond, and around the fire. After a while, Philip would have had enough and would wander off, and occasionally Lytton fell into one of his well-known long silences, but Russell never seemed to tire of the talk. When, late at night, the company made their way to bed, they paused at the foot of the oak staircase, all grouped together, holding their silver candlesticks, and went on talking, while a few followed Ottoline into her bedroom and crouched down beside her fire for more conversation. In his unfinished *Dialogue between Statues*, modelled on Garsington, Lowes Dickinson wrote of how 'All day long there had been talk, talk, talk. Young men had come out from the university by car or cab or cycle, in relays, to lunch, to tea, to supper. One topic after another had risen like a wave only to fall again, till the voyaging mind had grown sick or weary and the tongues began to flag . . .'

Both Ottoline and Philip were pleased with what they had created, even if Ottoline sometimes felt her visitors were simply there to enjoy one another's company and ignoring her. She told a friend that she felt like the manageress of a hotel; tactlessly, he agreed. Another episode, leading to considerable hurt on her part, was when Roger Fry, a strange figure with very round eyes, and who could be both sweet and malicious, accused her of spreading rumours that he was in love with her. She was mortified and burst into tears. When she next met him, she noted that his face resembled that of 'an untrustworthy dog, who softly pads up to one, fawns on one and licks one's hand but who will nearly always turn and bite.' Relations deteriorated further when she heard that he had been gossiping about her affair with Russell.

Russell was among the more frequent visitors to Garsington, spending weeks at a time there, going on picnics with Julian and Juliette, teasing them in French, and making them laugh. He was fond of Julian, giving her presents and sending her cards from his trips, and making much of the fact that they shared their birthday. Julian, who felt neglected by her mother, was acute when it came to detecting those who liked the company of children. Russell felt able to wander in and out of Ottoline's room, just as she wandered in and out of his. Some sort of *modus vivendi* had been established with Philip, who presumably found it easier to accept since he had been having affairs of his own. Two sons were born to him, within one month of each other, in 1917: one was by his secretary, the other by Ottoline's maid; and there were other children. Virginia Woolf described him as a 'weak, amiable long-suffering man who seems generally to be making the best of things, and seeing the best of people whom by nature he dislikes'. Rather more unkindly, Aldous Huxley portrayed him in *Crome Yellow* as a 'grey bowler hat'.

It was Russell, perhaps, who most enjoyed the Garsington talk, though visitors were to describe the sometimes unnerving effect his brilliance had on the company. One sardonic observer of these fashionable weekends was the Honourable Dorothy Brett, daughter of Viscount Esher, who had chosen to be known simply by her surname after entering the Slade in 1910, and suffered from such extreme deafness that not even an ear trumpet allowed her to take part in conversations. She has left a description of one of her first visits: 'The most frightening to me was Bertrand Russell. I never seemed to be adequate enough for him. I would say something quite simple, *quite simple*, and he would turn on me and say: "Why did you say that?" He would get quite upset and angry if I got up and went to bed at the precise moment he would want to read out loud . . .' Not everyone, of course, was daunted by his brilliance. 'Bertie appeared for dinner', Lytton Strachey wrote to Keynes in September 1915, 'and was idiotic . . . He seems to have all the right opinions, and yet so little passion. Grrr!'.

Casual liaisons were part of the Bloomsbury style, but those who indulged in them risked rumour, ridicule and explosions of jealousy, particularly because no one chose to keep anything secret and much could be found out by steaming open envelopes. The Bloomsberries were also prone to trigger off a series of intrigues, inspired as much by boredom as curiosity. Russell, who was able to conduct several emotional entanglements at the same time, all on different planes of intimacy and intensity, now embarked on a brief dalliance with one of Garsington's newest arrivals.

He had first met Katherine Mansfield in July 1915, when he wrote to tell Ottoline that he had been to visit John Middleton Murry and Kotiliansky, the Russian designer, and found them with Katherine, 'smoking Russian cigarettes without a moment's intermission, idle and cycnical. I thought Murry *beastly* and the whole atmosphere of the three dead and putrefying.' Middleton Murry was an Oxford classical scholar, who had co-founded *Rhythm*, an avant-garde magazine on art and literature, in which he had published some stories by the young New Zealander Katherine Mansfield, who had recently arrived in England. The two were to be together, on and off, for nearly eleven years, but did not marry until 1918, by which time Katherine was ill and soon to die. Perhaps the best description of her when Russell met her was provided by Brett, who, with a painter's eye, saw the young woman in minuscule detail: 'small, her sleek hair brushed close to her head, her fringe sleeked down over her white forehead. The dark eyes glance about much like a bird's, the pale face is a quiet mask, full of hidden laughter, a bit suspicious, on her guard.' Katherine was just the kind of modern, intriguing and independent woman Russell most felt drawn to. She was introduced into Bloomsbury by Lytton Strachey, and was invited to Garsington for Christmas. It was a splendid Garsington occasion, with Russell, Strachey, Aldous Huxley, Clive Bell, and the painter, Dora Carrington. They played parlour games, and Katherine wrote a short Russian sketch for which Strachey wore a bright red beard. There was much laughter. By now, Katherine was seeing something of Russell in London; long before the Christmas holiday Russell had assured Ottoline that though Katherine did indeed interest him mentally (one of his favourite phrases) because of her 'boundless curiosity', little would follow. Ottoline complained that she was kept awake all night by Russell and Katherine talking.

Their brief entanglement continued. They met and talked in restaurants, at parties, in each other's houses – Katherine was by now sharing Keynes's house in Gower Street with Carrington and Brett. Katherine wrote of it being 'so great an adventure that it is difficult to remain calm'.

If Bloomsbury smiled on such intriguing romances, it enjoyed muddling them up. Before her meeting with Russell, Katherine had been increasingly friendly with Ottoline. Their friendship cooled, as the gossip Katherine so much deplored spread around the group, and as Ottoline began to wonder if she had not fallen in love with Murry – or, come to that, with Siegfried Sassoon, whom she referred to in her diary as a 'wild hunting hawk'. Russell, as adept as any when it came to analysing complicated relationships, told Ottoline that Katherine disliked her precisely because Murry liked her, and that Katherine disliked Sassoon because she, Ottoline, liked him; therefore Murry was obliged to dislike Sassoon as well. It was really all very simple.

Katherine herself was in a turmoil, moving from house to house and taking brief jobs to keep herself solvent while she wrote.

Carrington, another Bloomsbury observer, remarked rather maliciously that she struck her as 'very much of an adventuress and with the language of a fish-wife in Wapping'. Katherine remained entranced by Russell's conversation. One night, after dinner, she went home to write to him. 'Yes, it was a wonderful evening. The thrill of it stayed with me all night. Even after I had fallen asleep ... I dreamed that ... I could see long waves of green water gleaming and lifting without sound or break as though we were far out at sea.'

How important were they to each other? Russell was still emotionally caught up with Ottoline and had embarked on another important love affair. Katherine was going through a confused and unhappy time. She trusted him, and they discussed the thing that was closest to her heart, writing, but there is something almost distant and ethereal in her letters to him, which makes them unlike the letters she wrote to other people. She was fascinated by what Virginia had called 'his headpiece' and more than a little in awe of him. Within a few months, their friendship was over, not least because she had learned how shockingly cynical he could be. There does not seem to have been much pain on either side, though it is probable that Katherine missed the high-minded talk, with all its oddities, excitements and intimacies. Later, Russell said, 'when she spoke about people she was envious, dark and full of alarming penetration in discovering what they least wished known', and that in the end he had believed very little of the unkind things she had told him about Ottoline. In a short note, scribbled in 1949, Russell denied that they had had an affair, saying that, while he admired her passionately, he had been 'repelled by her dark hatreds'.

D. H. Lawrence came into Russell's life through Ottoline. On the last day of 1914 she wrote to him about *The Prussian Officer*: 'I am amazed how good it is – quite wonderful some of the stories – he has great passion – and is so alive to things outward and inward.' That August, Lawrence, a slight, arresting but somewhat sickly young man, had come to one of her Thursdays. Now, full of excitement, she wrote inviting him to pay them another visit. In January 1915, the Lawrences came to dine, with David Garnett and E. M. Forster. It was not an altogether successful evening. Lawrence felt he was being patronised by Forster and took against his mild, Fabian outlook. Ottoline, however, was greatly taken by him, and said that he possessed what Russell lacked, the 'natural . . . and the aesthetic', and that he looked like someone who had been undernourished in his youth, making his body fragile and his mind too active. Characteristically, she wanted to share her new friend with Russell, much as she had shared Conrad. After a first meeting between them, Lawrence wrote to Ottoline: 'Bertrand R. wrote to me. I feel a quickening of love for him.' Their friendship was to last barely a year. In its intensity, and its later disillusion and acrimony, there is something of Russell's relationship with Wittgenstein.

In 1915, Russell was forty-three, Lawrence twenty-six. In background the two men could hardly have been more different. Whereas Russell was a liberal aristocrat, Lawrence was the son of a miner from the midlands, winner of a scholarship and a graduate from University College, Nottingham. They were alike, however, in that both were contemptuous of public opinion, outspoken, radical rebels and passionately against the war. Both were in some state of confusion. Russell was wretched about the hostilities, uncertain what he should do, and worried that his long years of mathematics had made him a slave to reason. Lawrence, who saw in the war a 'waste and squandering of life', was tormented by the suppression of his latest book, *The Rainbow*, on grounds of obscenity (though in fact because of its anti-war stand), being completely broke and unable to earn money writing, and by the fact that his wife Frieda was a German and suffering from public hostility. In each other, Lawrence and Russell saw some vision of salvation: Lawrence because he thought discussions with Russell might restore him to a sense of wholeness, lost by the war, and to be found only by a total reappraisal of the relations between the state and the individual; Russell, because he hoped that Lawrence would provide him with a 'vivifying dose of unreason'. 'We have our faith,' Lawrence wrote to Russell, 'we must unite in our fight.' To Ottoline, Russell said he found their new friend amazing, in that he could 'see through and through one' and that he was like Ezekiel or some Old Testament prophet. When not feeling overawed or threatened, Lawrence could be a most agreeable guest. He told Ottoline that Garsington was his 'spiritual home'.

Many years later, Julian would remember how kind he was to her, how he helped her to paint and how, in the evenings, he would read Swinburne aloud, or tell stories in a Nottinghamshire dialect about his early life.

Soon, Russell invited Lawrence to Trinity to meet Keynes, Lowes Dickinson and G. E. Moore. Lawrence asked whether he should bring an evening suit: 'I don't want to be horribly impressed . . . but am afraid I may be. I only care about the revolution we shall have. But immediately I want us to be friends. But you are so shy and then I feel so clumsy, so clownish. Don't make me see too many people at once, or I lose my wits. I am afraid of . . . clans and societies and cliques – not so much of individuals. Truly I am rather afraid.' The evening was a disaster; Russell had not paid sufficient heed to Lawrence's plea. Lawrence sat next to Moore, in silence, for he could find nothing to say. After dinner, he relaxed enough to exchange a few words with G. H. Hardy – he later called him a 'real man' – but by breakfast time he was once again moody, irritable and completely silent, visibly appalled when Keynes appeared in his dressing gown to eat with them. Returning to his cottage at Greatham in Sussex, he wrote to Russell that Cambridge had made him feel black and down: 'I cannot bear its smell of rottenness, marsh-stagnancy.'

It was not long after this that one of Lawrence's first Bloomsbury friends, David Garnett, the son of the editor Edward Garnett, who had helped Lawrence with his books, took his friend Francis Birrell over to see him. The occasion was again tense. Lawrence brooded silently, watching the others talk. During the night, Birrell was found wandering along the corridor in great distress. Something had happened to his tongue, which had swollen out of all proportion and now filled his entire mouth and throat. The party discussed what to do and ended by pouring almost boiling water down his throat. By next morning, Birrell had completely recovered. Lawrence, however, was beginning to turn against them. He sent a furious letter to Garnett, describing his revulsion at 'men loving men'. 'It is so wrong, it is unbearable . . . this horrible sense of frowstiness, so repulsive, as if it came from a deep inward dirt – a sort of sewer . . . something like carrion – a vulture gives me the same feeling . . . It makes me dream of beetles . . . It was one of the crises of my life. It sent me mad with misery and hostility and rage.'

The disgust, and possible jealousy, which Lawrence felt towards the Cambridge intellectual set soon infected his feelings about Russell. If Russell found the younger man youthful, muddled, not quite honest and tending to 'mad exaggeration', Lawrence began to say that he had mistaken Russell's liberalism for radicalism, and that far more of a gulf in fact existed between them than he had first thought. Still, he was anxious to see in Russell a comrade, a fellow spirit able not only to diagnose the dreadful ailments besetting British society but also to come up with a solution. Together, he hoped they would forge a true intellectual alliance, then carry it into open political agitation. His evening among the Fellows at Trinity, either homosexuals themselves or tolerant towards them, had, however, profoundly sickened him. He also felt at a disadvantage: whereas he had to fight to achieve literary recognition and was always poor, they had attained their positions without struggle, in a world of privilege, and as a result lived in 'hard little shells' with no feelings and no reverence.

For a while, Lawrence suppressed his doubts and continued to defer to Russell, who was beginning to find Lawrence's ideas increasingly bizarre and unsympathetic, and his views on life incomprehensible. The two had planned to give a joint series of lectures in the autumn, and Lawrence pursued Russell to discuss their content. Since the war was likely to end in a conflict between capital and labour, it was essential, said Lawrence, that 'real leaders' be found to prevent either from seizing power. 'You must drop all your democracy,' Lawrence insisted, 'you must not believe in the "people". One class is no better than another . . .'

The idea was for Lawrence to speak about immortality, and Russell about political ideals and ethics. With his customary speed, Russell sat down and drafted a twenty-two-page outline, which he sent to Lawrence. To his surprise, Lawrence was dismissive, even rude, about what he had written. Russell's views, he announced, were 'social criticism' and nothing to do with the far more important issue of 'social reconstruction'. What was worse, they were neither profound nor philosophical. Russell's reaction was to grow ever more convinced that the two of them would do better to keep their lectures well apart. By mid-July, Lawrence's tirades had become strident: he ordered Russell to dream up a new state, not keep harping back to the old. Meanwhile, he wrote his own paper and sent it off for Ottoline to read. She too was becoming unhappy with the way Lawrence's ideas seemed to be progressing. 'It is tosh,' she wrote in her diary, 'a volcano of words – reiteration – perverted and self contradictory – the Gospel of Hate – I am miserable that he has filled himself with these windy dyspeptic ideas . . .'

Relations between the two men worsened. Lawrence began to complain to Russell that he was now 'terrified of what you are putting in your lectures. I don't want tyrants. But I don't believe in democratic control . . . That is the worst of all . . . there must be an elected autocracy.' He told Ottoline that Russell's ideas were no good, that he thought his synopsis 'pernicious', and that all Russell was after was keeping his 'own established ego . . . free from contact and correction'. Russell, confronted by these outbursts, complained that he felt like a 'worm, a useless creature', but he was also beginning to find Lawrence despotic. The final attack came in the late summer. Lawrence's letters to Russell took on an accusatory, even hysterical tone and were full of personal invective: 'You simply don't speak the truth, you simply are not sincere . . . You are really the super-war-spirit . . . You are simply full of repressed desires, which have become savage and anti-social. And they come out in this sheep's clothing of peace propaganda. You are too full of devilish repressions to be anything but hurtful and cruel. I would rather have the German soldiers with rapine cruelty than you with your words of goodness.' And he ended, much as Wittgenstein had, 'Let us become strangers again, I think it is better.'

It was too much for Russell. He was stunned, and said later that for twenty-four hours he had contemplated suicide (much as he had after Wittgenstein's attack). The friendship ended, though it did not prevent Lawrence writing a few times more to tell him about his new theory of 'blood-consciousness', to borrow money, or to seek help with the publication of an article. Russell declared the theory 'frankly rubbish'. To Lady Cynthia Asquith, Lawrence complained that Russell and Ottoline were 'traitors'. 'They are static, static, static . . .

they filch my life for a sensation . . . the result is for them a gratifying sensation, a tickling and for me a real bleeding.'

Lawrence had been wrong about Russell's lectures. When he eventually gave them, between 18 January and 7 March 1916, under the title 'Principles of Social Reconstruction', audiences flocked to Caxton Hall to hear him. There were, he told his listeners, two kinds of impulse, one possessive and one creative. Social reconstruction should aim at diminishing the possessive by attacking the roots of overdeveloped individualism. Syndicalism was the right future for socialism, just as world government would bring an end to the anarchy caused by wars. All the old cohesions – state, property and so on – were disintegrating and needed fundamental reappraisal. War was precisely the result of the need for something new and exciting. The 'new life', in which material goods would play a far less important part, could be achieved by setting new standards, then by 'unity in freedom through new political institutions'. 'Principles of Social Reconstruction', in its attempt to analyse what makes human beings act, why they so often behave in a destructive fashion, and how they could be persuaded to act more positively, is one of Russell's most important and lasting statements. It is not just about war but about the need for a better political theory to replace rationalist liberalism, and about how to find ways of giving people more control over their lives, in politics as in work. These were themes which were to reappear again and again, in different forms, in Russell's political writings over the next fifty years.

Russell had told Ogden of the *Cambridge Magazine*, who had helped to organise the lectures, that what he wanted was a *succès de scandale*. He was gratified by the response. While the spring wore on, and Europe sank ever deeper into an apparently unstoppable carnage, both Bloomsbury and the general public turned out to praise his analysis of the destructive properties of war, wealth, marriage, education and religion. 'Government, religions, laws, property, even good form itself – down they go like ninepins – it is a charming sight,' commented Strachey approvingly, while Forster called the lectures 'brave and splendid'. Stanley Unwin, managing editor of the new publishing firm of George Allen and Unwin, asked permission to publish the lectures as a book. It came out in 1916, and Russell was later to call it the 'least unsatisfactory' expression of his 'personal religion', though he complained that no one had been 'practically' affected by his words, for if they had been they would have had to stop supporting the war. One soldier, a man called Arthur Graeme West, did write from the Somme to say that such was his support for Russell's position that after the war he intended to do 'twice as much'. Three months later, West was killed.

In England, the *International Journal of Ethics* called it 'a great book' and predicted its effect would long survive the war; in America, where it appeared under the title of *Why Men Fight*, it was described as 'one of the most outstanding books of the war'. It was left to newspapers like the *Daily Express*, always hostile to Russell and the war resisters, to dismiss his words as 'the bloodless philosophy of the worm in all its naked beauty'.

Russell's epitaph on Lawrence came in February 1937 in one of the last letters he ever wrote to Ottoline. Having failed to mention Lawrence's name in the first draft of his autobiography, written the year after Lawrence died, Russell commented to Ottoline: 'Lawrence is one of a long line òf people, beginning with Heraclitus and ending with Hitler, whose ruling motive is hatred derived from megalomania, and I am sorry to see that I was once so far out in estimating him.' Much later, in *Portraits from Memory*, published in 1956, he would say that Lawrence's notion of 'blood-consciousness' led straight to Auschwitz.

These were dismissive and disagreeable words, and they were quickly attacked not only by Frieda but other supporters of Lawrence, but it has to be remembered that well within all their lifetimes, Lawrence himself had taken two insulting swipes at Russell and Ottoline. In *Women in Love*, Hermione Roddice, with her exotic, soiled and dirty clothes and strange sing-song voice, is a faintly disguised Ottoline, while Russell is Sir Joshua Malleson, 'an elderly sociologist . . . a learned dry baronet of fifty who was always making witticisms and laughing at them heartily in a harsh horse-laugh.' Bredalby, the house over which Hermione presides, is a 'snare and a prison'. Worse was to follow. In the short story 'The Blind Man' Russell is probably Bertie, a frigid, isolated lawyer, terrified by the warmth of human touch, 'of the intellectual type, quick, ironical, sentimental and on his knees before the women he adored but did not want to marry'. The Bertie in the book can see, but his sight is a sign of feebleness compared to the vigour and robustness of Perrin's blindness. By forcing contact on him, the blind man penetrates his 'insane reserve' and destroys him: 'He was like a mollusc whose shell is broken.'

How far had Lawrence perceived Russell's painful sense of isolation, or guessed at the words Russell had written to Ottoline shortly after the two men had first met, 'How passionately I long that one could break through the prison walls in one's own nature'?

Lawrence may have been particularly malicious, but he was not the only person to caricature Garsington, the Morrells or Russell. There was something about Philip's passivity, Ottoline's flamboyance and Russell's manner which made them ready targets, and Ottoline, who rightly felt herself to be generous towards her friends and acquaintances, was greatly hurt and humiliated by their jibes. Lawrence's mockery bruised, but Aldous Huxley's ill-concealed portrait of Garsington in *Crome Yellow* struck a more bitter blow: Huxley, young, silent and observing all, had been a protégé. In the novel, Priscilla Wimbush is the manly mistress of Crome, with a 'massive projecting nose and little greenish eyes', booming and swishing her way across a room, trailing her silks and spending her days reading horoscopes. It is Russell, however, who comes off worse. He appears as Scogan, a small, gaunt man with a beaked nose: 'But there was nothing soft or gracious or feathery about him. The skin of his wrinkled brown face had a dry and scaly look; his hands were the hands of a crocodile. His movements were marked by the lizard's disconcertingly abrupt clockwork speed; his speech was thin, fluty and dry.' In some passages, Huxley scarcely even bothered with a disguise. He has Scogan make a speech: 'Thus, while I may have a certain amount of intelligence, I have no aesthetic sense; while I possess the mathematical faculty, I am wholly without the religious emotion. . . . Life would be richer, warmer, brighter, altogether more amusing, if I could feel them . . . I must have gone on looking at pictures for ten years before I would honestly admit to myself that these merely bored me . . .' Among his fellow guests at Garsington,

Russell had not been able to conceal much. And what of his new sensitivities, born of his relations with Ottoline?

Neither Ottoline nor Russell was ever a true part of Bloomsbury. They lived much of the war on its edges and Ottoline, at least, provided the group with a generous setting. But it was not enough. Nothing she did was, in the end, sufficient to protect her from her guests' clever barbs. They were for the most part creative and aesthetic, cool and sceptical, and intellectuals. She was romantic, impetuous and 'lived for beauty'. But she set out to capture them, and out of sheer persistence did so, at any rate outwardly, not least because she was basically entertaining, warm and a great promoter of young people whose talents she recognised. She was also their jester. Her own misery, self-doubt and fears she kept for her diaries.

Russell's position was somewhat different, in that his concerns were ultimately not the same, and his political interests were more developed than theirs. He attended Bloomsbury gatherings – though noticeably never those at Asheham or Charleston, the Stephen sisters' married homes – and they were entertained by his wit and his brilliance. They had admired the extraordinary mental ability which had gone into *Principia Mathematica* even if few of them could understand what it said; and with *Principles of Social Reconstruction* they found a moral framework which appealed to them. Bloomsbury wrote, at length, to and about each other. But not about Russell. Keynes's papers in King's, Cambridge, contain hardly a single reference to him; nor do Roger Fry's or Lowes Dickinson's. They were held spellbound by the 'circular saw' of his mind, but they did not find him easy. Like Lawrence, Russell came to dislike and disapprove of homosexuality: 'Lawrence has the same feeling against sodomy as I have,' he wrote to Ottoline in 1915. 'You had nearly made me believe there is no great harm in it, but I have reverted; and all the examples I know confirm me in thinking it sterilizing.' The examples were Strachey and Keynes; and they knew it.

Russell was something of a puritan, and they were not. They could and did appreciate his wit and the quickness of his thought, but they could not follow him far down the intellectual path, just as he could not follow them down the artistic one. There is a revealing letter to Ottoline later in the war: 'Ouf! I have had all the

Bloomsbury crew with their sneers at anything that has live feeling in it . . . They put up with me because they know I can make anyone look ridiculous – if I had less brains and less satire, they would be all down on me – as it is, they whisper against me in corners, and flatter me to my face. They are a rotten crew.'

Bloomsbury loved Moore because they thought he was a saint, because he appeared to have no public ambition and because they saw him as pure. They did not love Russell. Not that he cared; he found many of their interests trivial, and had no desire to become like them. It was fun while it lasted, but they made little enduring impression on him. *Portraits from Memory*, written when he was in his eighties, includes short sketches of friends and people he had admired: it contains no memories of the Bloomsbury group. Something of their instinctive antagonism towards him, however, made its way into a review Leonard Woolf wrote long afterwards, in 1968, of the second volume of Russell's autobiography, which covered the First World War years. It is neither kind nor flattering. Though it is not clear why he felt quite so strongly, Woolf seems to have actively disliked, perhaps even hated, Russell. 'He has the tongue of a witty, acidulous and far from benignant adder', he wrote in the *Political Quarterly*. He was, Woolf went on, fundamentally negative, with a profound dislike of men, ideas and things. His emotions were formed by the 'most vulgar kind of prejudice'. And he was antisemitic. 'He obtains the best of all worlds,' concludes Woolf, 'dislike and hatred of Americans, Jews, and even his personal friends.'

'Thou shalt not follow a multitude to do evil', Lady John Russell had repeated to Russell frequently as a child. Sometimes, it seemed that Russell was condemned to pursue his pilgrim's progress on his own.

Ten

A still small voice

On 20 May 1915, when it was becoming clear that British casualties were mounting and that advances on the Western Front, across the mud and fields of Flanders, were going to be very slow and very expensive in terms of men, a coalition government was formed. Asquith remained prime minister; Arthur Henderson was brought into the Cabinet to represent Labour. The new Cabinet, for the first time, gave positions of power to men who favoured conscription, just at the very time when volunteers for the army were beginning to fade away.

Britain had long prided itself on its lack of conscription: war was the business of professional soldiers, not raw recruits. But the army was running out of men. At the outbreak of war, a soldier had to be 5 feet 8 inches to join the army. After the battle of the Marne, which saw several hundred thousand British casualties, he needed to reach only 5 feet 5 inches; but after the second battle of Ypres, in May 1915, when the Germans used poison gas for the first time, he could be as short as 5 feet 3 inches. Soldiers went on dying. By the summer of 1915, over two million men in Britain had volunteered, and some 250,000 had been wounded or were dead. And the recruits were drying up fast.

In the Commons the debate about conscription, the drafting of unwilling men into the army, was prolonged and intensely bitter, fuelled by pro- and anti- factions of the public and by the newspapers. When a census was carried out to determine just how many men had failed to volunteer, the figure of some two million single men of military age came back. The question was: how to recruit them?

Asquith, shying away from the final step of military conscription, and trying to convince his anti-conscription followers that he was doing all he could, called on the remaining men to volunteer. He asked Lord Derby, a bluff and well-liked man, to become director general of recruiting, to try to draw enough men into the war without coercion. At first, his plan looked as if it would work. Long queues of men, anxious to avoid the opprobrium of being seen to shirk the war, dreading the white feathers handed out so freely by patriotic women, and fired by Lord Kitchener's 'Your country needs you', lined up at the recruiting offices. Soon, over another million men had come forward, but the army was still desperate; casualties at the front were growing steadily. Meanwhile, in Britain, more than 600,000 men were known to be still unaccounted for. Conscription was becoming inevitable.

In the Commons there was pandemonium, with acrimonious debates about liberty, about shirkers, about Britain and its libertarian traditions. Amendments were introduced. 'Do you want us to win the war or not?' demanded an irritable Sir Arthur Griffith-Boscawen. 'It is no good whatever talking about our liberties, our freedom, our voluntary system, if you are going to be defeated by Germany.' The voices in favour of conscription grew louder; those against, more subdued. Asquith made pledges: to married men and, most importantly, to all those who, as he put it, had a 'conscientious objection to bearing arms'. There were shouts from the more belligerent members of the House about a 'shirkers' charter'. In the end, after all the furore, there was only one resignation, that of Sir John Simon, the Liberal home secretary. 'The real issue', he said, with considerable eloquence and, as it turned out, foresight, 'is whether we are to begin an immense change in the fundamental nature of our society. . . . Does anyone really suppose that once the principle of compulsion is conceded you are going to stop here?'

Asquith had always foreseen that there would be trouble over conscription. He knew that the ILP, many liberals, religious groups, pacifists and organised labour would resist it, and he was right. When the unions were canvassed, their message was clear: over two million railwaymen, transport workers, locomotive engineers, firemen and dockers protested against what they called 'servitude'. As Beatrice Webb wrote to a friend: 'I believe the conscriptionist lacks imagination . . . he is asking [the working man] to give up all that makes daily life endurable.' Philip Morrell called the proposed measure 'one of the most potent instruments of privilege and oppression'. Writing of the decision in the *Labour Leader*, one of the only papers open to him after his letter to the *Nation*, Russell declared: 'There is no more horrible crime against liberty than to compel men to kill each other when their conscience tells them to live in peace . . .'

It was not the trade unionists, in the event, but the political and religious pacifists who were going to make themselves heard, as they embarked on a struggle which was to rank with some of the toughest rebel movements in the history of Britain. For one thing, conscription was adopted far too quickly; for another, no one gave it much thought. In his haste to make it seem not a radical departure from the British liberal tradition but merely a minor extension of the Derby scheme, Asquith did not pause to contemplate the implications of how it would affect the country. No one took time to analyse or draft effective legal provisions for conscientious objectors. On 24 January 1916, on its third reading, the Military Service Act (2) passed through Parliament. It was to remain in force for the rest of the war.

Along with other peace groups, the Union of Democratic Control now settled down to what was a fairly mild programme of opposition to the war, confining itself chiefly to what would happen to Britain and Europe after hostilities ended. The UDC took a decision early on not to oppose conscription. Russell, who had spoken somewhat scathingly of its leaders as 'eight fleas talking of building a pyramid', had for some time been disenchanted with its passivity. When the UDC resolved not to fight conscription, he moved away from them, though he continued for a while to attend their meetings and did not cease to be a member until the end of the war. What irritated him mainly about the intellectuals who looked to the UDC for guidance was their failure to see how important it was to match theory to action. The war was not something which could be opposed simply in theory; one had to act. As he had written in 'The Ethics of War', to act could also mean to resist passively. This paper, intended primarily as a call to pacifism on utilitarian grounds – that the 'evil' of war was greater than the 'good' – was interesting because it was the first time Russell advocated passive resistance, which was to play such a crucial role in his thinking in the 1960s. Passive resistance, Russell had come to believe, might achieve more than armies or navies, without the carnage and brutality – though whether it was right for this war he doubted.

However, he remained convinced that resisters were bearing a personal witness, that they should be prepared to die if necessary, and that this kind of death was no smaller or greater a sacrifice than dying from a bullet. Their purity, combined with the stand against the war he hoped thousands of men would now take, thereby crippling the government, should underpin the entire pacifist movement.

More and more, after *Principles of Social Reconstruction*, Russell was coming to see himself as a mentor, a teacher who would join with others once the war was over to create a new political and social system. 'I have given up writing on the war because I have said my say and there is nothing new to say,' he told Lucy Donnelly. 'My ambitions are more vast and less immediate than my friends' ambitions for me ... I want actually to *change* people's thoughts. Power over people's minds is the main personal desire of my life, and this sort of power is not acquired by saying popular things.' He had come a long way from the beauty of pure mathematical reason.

There was one organisation at least which opposed conscription with the rigour Russell now perceived as essential, and that was the No-Conscription Fellowship (NCF). It was to provide him not just with a platform but with a programme of exhausting and exhilarating work and, for the duration of the war at least, with a new group of friends, as well as placing him firmly on the far left of the dissenters.

The NCF had been born in November 1914, when Archibald Fenner Brockway, the son of an Indian missionary, a fervent pacifist and the twenty-five-year-old editor of the official ILP paper, the *Labour Leader*, began looking for ways to unite the scattered war-resistance movement into an active body. His wife Lilla suggested that he write a letter to his own paper, proposing the setting up of an anti-conscription organisation, so as to be prepared if and when conscription became law. Within days of its publication, he had received 150 letters of support. By the time the Military Service Act came into force in 1916, the NCF had its headquarters in London, branches around the country, elected leaders, and over a thousand members. What was more, it was growing fast. At this early stage of the war at least, its message and purpose were absolutely clear: it was to be an organisation of men intent on refusing all summons to fight because they 'consider human life to be sacred and cannot, therefore, assume the responsibility of inflicting death'.

An early supporter of Brockway was the secretary and business manager of the official Labour party newspaper, the *Daily Citizen*, a member of the Fabian Society and an international socialist in his twenties called Reginald Clifford Allen. Allen was a fanatical opponent of conscription. Mary Agnes Hamilton, the UDC member and an early supporter of the NCF, described him as having 'a strikingly handsome head . . . its mass of wavy auburn hair above a high forehead, which topped his tall, willowy, attenuated figure'. He looked, she said, like a saint, of the militant Jesuit kind, with a will of iron concealed behind apparent fragility. Allen had enormous charm, and he was clever; rather like Moore, he exuded a sort of goodness, almost a kind of purity, which drew people to him. As its chairman, he soon dominated the NCF.

Russell had been watching the growth of the organisation with interest, waiting for the day when the NCF decided to accept men beyond military age and women as associate members. He started to work for it on 1 April 1916 and at the NCF emergency convention a week later was drawn firmly into its net. The rally took place in the Friends' House in Devonshire Road, in London, a large circular hall with a gallery, and the delegates, Russell among them, spent a night in an hotel, so as not to have to disperse. Two thousand people turned up. Beatrice Webb, sitting in the gallery, has left a description of the young men who gathered to meet other pacifists like themselves and learn how to oppose conscription. They were, she said, 'intellectual, pietist, slender in figure, delicate in feature and complexion, benevolent in expression . . .' but, she added, basically 'unpleasing' by being 'saliently conscious of their own righteousness'. They were not the kind of political activists Beatrice Webb ever really liked. The *Daily Mail* was considerably nastier, commenting that these were 'mild-faced creatures, mostly thinnish and large eyed, with rakish, untrimmed hair, no hats and in many cases thin apostolic beards'. Allen's voice, the *Mail* reporter added, 'touched a lachrymose tenor'.

Russell, on the other hand, was captivated, in an uncritical and almost adulatory way. 'It has been a *wonderful* two days,' he wrote to Ottoline, 'the most inspiring and happy thing that I have known since the war began – it gives one hope and faith again . . . The spirit of the young men was magnificent. They would not listen to even the faintest hint of compromise. They were keen, intelligent, elo-quent, full of life . . . not *seeking* martyrdom, but accepting it with great willingness . . . I can't describe to you how happy I am having these men to work with and for – it is *real* happiness all day long . . .' Without knowing it, he had put his finger on some of the major difficulties to come.

The spring of 1916 was a moment of elation for the pacifists. They genuinely believed that 'a conscience against bearing arms' was going to result in the wholesale exemptions the NCF was pressing for: men whose conscience forbade them to carry arms were simply going to be allowed, so they thought, to stay at home. Recruits to the organisation included the respected journalist and ILP member H. N. Brailsford, a distinguished Quaker in his sixties called Edward Grubb, who had excellent connections and was made treasurer, and Francis Meynell, the book designer and Lawrence's friend, who became chairman of the London branch and earned from Russell the curious but approving accolade: 'I like you, Meynell, because in spite of your spats there is much of the guttersnipe about you.' The office, at 6 St John Street, was superbly organised by a remarkable and much underrated woman called Catherine Marshall, who now came to the NCF from the Women's International League, bringing with her all the campaigning skills and subterfuges of the suffragists. She was a large, soft woman with fair hair, painstaking and hard working to the point of collapse; she was shrewd but could also be bossy. Though nine years his senior, she was very much in love with Allen.

Russell, who because of his age could not be called up, became an associate member and was known to the office as 'Mephy', short for Mephistopheles. He was concerned mainly with the Associates' Political Committee, which was to work to repeal the Military Service Act and stand ready to take over the national committee should its members be sent to jail. They were all full of hope. 'I really believe they will defeat the Government and wreck conscription when it is found they won't yield', Russell wrote to Ottoline. At this moment, he still believed that 10,000 men throughout the country would stand firm.

It had been decided that the Military Service Act would use the same tribunal system as the Derby scheme, rather than the independent judicial bodies the pacifists had been hoping for. Before long, 2,086 of these tribunals were at work across the country, with seventy higher appeal bodies. The government intended them to be fair; their members had been told to be sympathetic, particularly towards working-class men and the conscientious objectors. The trouble was that by virtue of class, age and instinct they were very different kinds of people. They were chaired by aldermen, mayors and councillors, and their nine or ten members were invariably professional men, tradesmen or landowners, and every tribunal had one military representative. There were virtually no women – and those who served won a reputation for unnecessary harshness – and no teachers or clergymen, precisely the people who might have understood what pacifism was all about. No one was under forty. The War Office paid the costs of the tribunals and Lieutenant General Sir Nevil Macready, the staff officer who had taken over from Derby as head of recruiting, briefed the chairmen that their duty was to 'protect the nation by obtaining as many men as possible for the army'. It thus became inevitable that the tribunals would favour conscription. What was more, very few of their members were able or willing to follow the convoluted intellectual subtleties of the pacifist arguments or the inarticulate confessions of the young men – some no more than teenage boys – who paraded before them.

It was true that some of the conscientious objectors were a strange lot. There were those, like doctors, who could immediately be given total exemption on grounds of essential war work. There were the Quakers, of whom the tribunals had at least heard, so they gave them an understanding hearing. After them came the Christadelphians, the Plymouth Brethren, Jehovah's Witnesses and Peculiar People, whose varieties of apocalyptic visions and sectarian withdrawal baffled and irritated the tribunals. By profession, too, they were a mixed bag, including clerks, bootmakers, architects, accountants, farmers and, above all, teachers. The gap between the tribunals and the petitioners was immense.

Unlike the Second World War, there were relatively few people who would not fight on political grounds, but even so the NCF soon had on its books 1191 'socialist' objectors who believed in the brotherhood of man and rejected war as a means of settling international disputes. 'Poisonous and pestilential trash', an M.P., called C. B. Stanton (after taking Merthyr Tydfil in a by-election, when Keir Hardie died broken-hearted over the failure of the Labour movement to stop the war), labelled the lot of them in the *Daily Express*. 'In no country in the world but England would this horde of Quakers, Cranks, Radicals, Little Englanders, violent pacifists, vocal pro-Germans, and slobbery IL peers be tolerated for an hour.' They should all be deported to Germany 'if we are too mealy-mouthed to hang them'. Stanton's words were a good indication of the contempt – though loathing is perhaps more accurate – many of the public felt about these men. Even Mary Berenson from Fiesole wrote a censorious letter to Alys asking why Bertie, such a clear thinker, was making such a fool of himself. With Muggletonians speaking about literal biblicism and socialists about restrictions to personal freedom, it was not surprising the tribunals felt confused.

Nor was it altogether clear what the government had to offer these men who now refused to fight. Faced by the few whom they believed to have a sincere and overpowering case, they could grant complete exemption – but few tribunals chose to do so. They could offer partial exemption, in the form of alternative service either within the army or under civilian orders (Christadelphians confused everyone by saying that they were prepared to do war work, provided it did not come under the military). But the real problem, of course, was the 'absolutists', those whose beliefs, whether religious or social, precluded their accepting military service of any kind. If, at their hearings they were unable to persuade the tribunals that they had 'bona fide' cases, they had no choice but to go home to await arrest, court-martial and prison.

It was not until the summer of 1916 that the War Office, still reeling from the speed with which all this had gone through, issued proper guidelines for the tribunals, with suggestions on how to conduct the hearings and how to attempt to meet the young protesters halfway. For most of the conscientious objectors they came too late. Many of the first batch of 5944 were already in military hands. One, whose case quickly became famous, was a poet and clerk to the education committee of the London County Council called Eric Chappelow. Chappelow was called up, refused to join the army, and was sent before a tribunal, who could see no reason to grant him exemption for his spiritual and political beliefs. He was arrested, taken to an army barracks and told to put on a uniform; when he refused, he was held down, stripped by the guards and forced into khaki. As soon as they let him go, he pulled the uniform off again. The guards seized a blanket, strapped it round him, manacled his hands and took him to the orderly room, where a sergeant, ridiculing his appearance, took a photograph of him which found its way into the *Daily Sketch*. In the House of Commons, Philip Morrell argued that Chappelow was being subjected to mental torture.

Chappelow was a brave man, but he was no hero by nature. He soon became miserable and frightened, writing to Charles Sanger: 'I feel I am going mad. The strain is too great . . . Do you think I shall come out of this alive? I have no will to live.' To keep his spirits up he sang songs in Wandsworth jail, so sweetly that even the guards stopped to listen. Russell wrote to ask Shaw to intervene in Chappelow's case, but Shaw replied sternly. Chappelow should either serve or go 'through with martyrdom. Martyrdom is a matter for the individual soul . . . you can't advise a man.'

Clifford Allen applied for exemption as a socialist and on the grounds that he was doing work of national importance. He told the tribunal that he would never accept the 'degraded slavery' of any task offered him. He was sent off to begin his first sentence at Wormwood Scrubs, to loud cheering from his supporters in the gallery and an observation from a member of the tribunal that he was the 'leader of the gang'. The *Daily Sketch* reporter observed that he would have liked to have had 'the drilling of Clifford Allen'.

Allen was one of the most intransigent of the pacifist prisoners, spending much of the war in various jails, endlessly released, endlessly rearrested, his frail body becoming frailer all the time, but still fired with the same passionate fury against the war. 'I believe in the inherent worth and sanctity of every human personality, irrespective of the nation to which a man belongs,' he told tribunal after tribunal. Months in the punishment block, usually for refusing to work, were followed by weeks in the prison hospital, when his headaches grew insupportable and a prison doctor diagnosed tuberculosis of the spine, aggravated by hours sitting on a backless prison stool. In one letter he wrote that he had spent 195 days stitching, and that each day consisted of twenty-three hours and fifty minutes of silence. 'Solitude is a terrible thing when enforced,' he wrote. 'I've become quieter, and, I think, stronger. My determination is, I think, now inflexible.' Catherine Marshall repeatedly warned the authorities that it was unlikely Allen would emerge alive. Allen's courage made him a hero and a model to other conscientious objector prisoners, and men who were interned with him spoke of walking with a 'lighter step'. Mary Agnes Hamilton observed that he had a 'scarifying realism, which had the tang of authentic power. He could have filled a revolutionary role, been a Saint Just who condemned backsliders and deviators to death from the loftiest motives.' Ottoline was rather less flattering. She conceded that Allen was good-looking in an 'ethereal, Shelley-like style' but complained that he was also 'rather suburban'. Once conscription was introduced Garsington became even more important. Not all visitors held identical views about the war, but the majority were against it, either on pacifist principles or because they thought it an improper war, a war about nothing, which would do no one any good, or because they found violence emotionally and morally repugnant. Together with the Woolfs' house at Asheham, and, later, the 1917 Club in Soho, founded by Ramsay MacDonald and others as a meeting place where they could talk freely without risk of being overheard by DORA spies, Garsington was where they went to give each other support, discuss the forthcoming tribunals of those young enough to be called up, and talk endlessly about war, morality and questions of coercion and liberty, as well as the work many of them were now doing in NCF offices. Lytton Strachey, Maynard Keynes, David Garnett, Clive Bell, Mark Gertler, Duncan Grant, and a poet called Frank Prevett all came and, from time to time, Russell, with 'his laugh like a crazy horse and his dominating ego', as Brett put it. They found Garsington beguiling, particularly as hostility built up towards them and they were accused of being left-wing pro-German intellectuals, of ducking armed service and of being moral and physical cowards.

Naomi Bentwich was a young Newnham graduate and member of the Moral Sciences Club, and she wrote to a friend describing a weekend at Garsington soon after the introduction of conscription. Eliot and Lytton Strachey were present, and the Bishop of Oxford came to tea. Russell was also there, and he seemed to hold the floor, talking hour after hour about NCF work, going through strategies and plans, reviewing documents, planning letters and articles, and then settling down to a long conversation about Plato with Strachey, who had just finished reading *The Republic*. 'There were long silences on both sides; none of us spoke; the men puffed away at their pipes, and then one of them would come out with something wonderful. They were both very wound up . . .' Russell struck her as formidable and high spirited, but she wondered whether he was perhaps over-susceptible to flattery and not very sensitive to 'les affaires du coeur'. She noted that, when speaking of Allen, he was somewhat dismissive, saying that 'he was so eaten up with his cause, that he thought there was no spark of humour left in him.'

It was not long before Garsington's visitors began to receive their own tribunal papers. For some, there were no problems. Maynard Keynes was fully occupied at the Treasury, and as such was exempt. Roger Fry was almost fifty, too old to serve, and was left to devote himself to his Omega workshops. Desmond MacCarthy enrolled with the Red Cross as an ambulance driver, and E. M. Forster was in Egypt working for the newly formed Wounded and Missing

Bureau of the Red Cross. For the others, it was not quite so easy. Leonard Woolf was medically examined and exempted on the grounds of an 'inherited nervous tremor'; he settled down to a study of 'international government'. Clive Bell, who railed against the war as the 'end of civilisation', was allowed to take alternative civilian service, as were David Garnett and Aldous Huxley.

The Morrells acted with characteristic generosity. They arranged a comfortable flat for Russell in the bailiff's house, and did up one of their farmhouses, Home Close, and a number of cottages for their young conscientious objector friends, who had won from the tribunals a concession to work on the land. Philip took them as farm labourers. The Morrells' generosity was not altogether rewarded. Few of them took to farm work with much enthusiasm, standing morosely around in heavy coats, peering gloomily at the surrounding countryside. 'The Bloomsburies' were observed by P. Wyndham Lewis 'down in some downy English county, under the wings of powerful pacifist friends; pruning trees, planting gooseberry bushes, and haymaking, doubtless in sunbonnets', while H. G. Wells called them 'genteel Whigs'.

The First World War is not remembered for its charitable attitude towards the men dubbed 'conchies', 'worms' and 'shirkers'. Those who failed to win alternative service were often treated with great cruelty. Their prison regime included total silence, inadequate food, backbreaking work sewing mailbags in poor light, and very little exercise. The 'cat-and-mouse' strategy invented for the suffragettes – being let out of jail only to be immediately rearrested – ensured that prisoners regarded by the authorities as particularly recalcitrant went through the remainder of the war on repeated sentences. Life became all but intolerable for men who fell into the hands of sadistic officers, or even simply rigid men infuriated by what they saw as stubbornness, who kept them on bread and water, gave them 'shot drill' (carrying a thirty-pound weight at arms' length till they dropped and were put in the punishment cell), tied them by their arms and legs to the beams of the guardroom, or put them down dungeon-like holes. A few chose to commit suicide rather than face what awaited them. Harold Brimley took poison in the Charing Cross Hotel; George Osborne of Stirling suffocated himself over a gas fire;

Charles Hale cut his throat in a barracks in Cardiff; and Alfred Bamford of Roath hanged himself.

One difficulty for the NCF was that its own position towards the exemptions was never entirely clear. Not all members agreed that conscription meant 'all or nothing'. How, after all, did one reconcile freedom of conscience, which lay at the very heart of NCF policy, with a single way of behaving? Russell, ever realistic about man's frailties, wrote to Catherine Marshall that 'total exemption cannot be got till a good many have suffered intensely.' Yet he also believed that a man who had been subjected to repeated solitary confinement and petty brutality was likely, in desperation, to accept some form of alternative work. As he explained to Gilbert Murray: 'We who believe that it is wrong to fight are bound not only to abstain from fighting ourselves, but to abstain from abetting others in fighting.' Inside the ranks of the NCF, the question of absolute refusal versus partial refusal was the topic of many heated debates, and was constantly rehearsed in the pages of the *Tribunal*, the organisation's paper, which appeared weekly for most of the remainder of the war, with Russell a frequent contributor and later its editorial writer. He had strong views about what the NCF should be doing, and they were not always those of his colleagues. He wanted it to do more than just help imprisoned conscientious objectors and oppose conscription. What he had in mind was leading an 'army' of COs to oppose the war and force the government not just to repeal conscription and release those imprisoned because of it, but to begin to sue for peace. When he saw that was not happening, and that only 1300 men, out of the 16,500 who had registered as COs, took the absolutist stand and went to prison again and again, he tried other strategies. He had never worked harder, and seldom had he been more cheerful. Lytton Strachey remarked rather sourly that he was 'at last perfectly happy – gloating over all the horrors and moral lessons of the situation'.

In May 1916 there occurred an event of considerable brutality which to some extent changed public attitudes towards the 'conchies', moving people in a way that stories of beating and sadism had not done. It was just the kind of episode that had most worried Russell: 'If the government chooses to shoot some 5000 people (which it has a legal right to do) it can crush the whole thing,' he had written to Ottoline; and again, '*the* important thing is to get them put under the civil authorities instead of the military.'

Walking one morning along a stretch of track leading to the South coast, a railway worker saw a scrap of paper lying on the ground. It contained a cry for help from a conscientious objector and had clearly been thrown from a passing train. He took the message to an NCF office. Investigations revealed that some fifty conscientious objectors had been rounded up and shipped to France in the middle of the night, where, it was assumed, they would refuse to fight. The commanding officer would then have the right to have them court-martialled and shot. A telegram with the news had also reached Gilbert Murray. He hurried off to see Asquith, as did Russell, Catherine Marshall, Philip Morrell and the Bishop of Oxford. After looking at the cable, Asquith is said to have muttered 'abominable', and immediately contacted the commander-in-chief in France to tell him that no death sentence was to be carried out on a conscientious objector without the consent of the Cabinet.

The order arrived in time to save the men's lives; but not to spare them the terror of being paraded before an entire regiment and hearing themselves sentenced to death. One by one, the men were called out and told they were to die – before being told that their sentences had been reduced to ten years' hard labour. 'Ignorant, lying, dishonourable fool', Russell said of H. J. Tennant, under-secretary to the War Office, adding that, after witnessing what the government and military were capable of, he felt 'like a lion refreshed – as if there were no limit to what I can do'.

Russell was now beginning to run into problems of his own, though they did little to dispel the feelings of euphoria which had overtaken him working for the NCF. On 10 April, a teacher and member of the Liverpool branch of the NCF, Ernest F. Everett, was court-martialled, and became the first man at home to be given two years' hard labour. Russell regarded Everett as something of a hero, and in any case he had been on the lookout for an issue on which he could make a personal stand. After six men were sentenced to prison for distributing an anonymous leaflet about Everett, Russell wrote a letter to *The Times*. Under the heading 'Adsum qui feci', he declared himself the author of the leaflet.

The authorities hesitated. Russell was, after all, an academic of some reputation, not only in Britain and Europe but in America, where he was widely viewed as the world's most important mathematician and philosopher. Minutes and circulars travelled around the Home and Foreign Offices. Lord Newton referred to Russell as 'one of the most mischievous cranks in the country'. Finally the military authorities decided to act. On 30 May two detectives appeared at his flat with a summons under the Defence of the Realm Act. The case of Rex versus Bertrand Russell came up on 5 June before the Lord Mayor, Sir Charles Wakefield, in the Mansion House Justice Room. Shaw had written to Russell, urging him to make a great scene and not allow himself to be shunted through like a mere pickpocket. Archibald Bodkin, for the prosecution, spoke of the way Russell had prejudiced the 'recruiting and discipline of His Majesty's forces'. London members of the NCF turned out in force, including Fenner Brockway, whom Russell described to Ottoline as a 'pink-cheeked boy, very handsome, with a gay smile', and two prominent Quakers, Barrett Brown and Leyton Richards. Lytton Strachey was heard to observe that the Lord Mayor looked like a 'stuck pig'.

Russell decided to conduct his own defence. He had a lot to say. He spoke about tradition and loyalty and truth, about honour and persecution. 'Other nations may excel us in some respects, but the tradition of liberty has been the supreme good that we in this country have cultivated. We have preserved, more than any other power, respect for the individual conscience. It is for that that I stand.' He would have said more had the Lord Mayor not interrupted him to say he was not prepared to listen to a political speech, and that he had been utterly unconvinced by what he had heard.

Russell was well pleased with his trial. He said it reinforced his belief in the basic helplessness of the state and its tribunals when confronted with resolute men. Waiting for the verdict, he told Ottoline: 'I can be just as useful in prison as out of it. I should rather enjoy the leisure to think things out in prison – and I should be immensely glad to have had the experience.' He was not to be given the chance. The authorities had as yet no intention of making a martyr of their most respected philosopher. Russell was fined £100, with £10 costs – or the option of sixty-one days in prison. He had no intention of paying the fine, but his belongings in Trinity were distrained, and a Chippendale sofa, various pieces of furniture and plate, and many books went on sale at the Corn Exchange in Cambridge at the end of July. The *Cambridge Daily News* reported that keen bidding was expected. Philip Morrell organised an appeal for funds, not so much to pay the fine as to buy back Russell's possessions for him; some twenty-five people subscribed. When Russell got his books back, he was delighted to find that an old bible of his had been stamped with the words, 'Impounded by the Cambridge Police'.

After the Everett case, authorities began to take a firmer line towards Russell. British officials began to discuss ways of preventing him from taking up a new offer to lecture in America. Professor James Woods, of the Harvard philosophy department, had written earlier in the year renewing his offer to Russell of three courses, one on formal logic, one on social psychology and ethics and the third on his political views on the war. 'I think you have an extraordinary opportunity,' Woods wrote, 'our thinking has been so hopelessly optimist and infantile.' Russell had cabled his acceptance in January 1916. However, anxious in case the trial had affected Russell's position, Harvard contacted Sir Cecil Spring Rice, the British ambassador in Washington. They were told that Russell was on their black list, and there would be no question of allowing him to visit America to make more mischief for the Allies. Grey, the foreign secretary, said that he personally was prepared to deny him a passport. On hearing the news, Russell was outraged. 'These are fierce times', he wrote in an angry and injured letter to Professor Woods. To Ottoline he spoke of the whole business as a 'piece of tyranny'. The letter and a report of Russell's trial were both stopped by the censor. They ended up in the Foreign Office files.

More and harsher methods followed almost immediately. Russell had won a Prize Fellowship to Trinity in 1895; been appointed lecturer in logic and the principles of mathematics in 1910, and, except for a brief spell in Harvard in 1914, had lectured in Cambridge right up until the start of the war, combining teaching and research. In February 1915, given the widespread feeling that a man of his distinction should be a Fellow of the college rather than a mere lecturer, Russell was asked whether he would accept the promotion. By then, he was much engaged in his war work, and it was mutually agreed that, for the time being, he would continue as a lecturer, which gave him more freedom. Unfortunately it also left the Trinity Council – most of whose members were already exercised by his anti-war pronouncements and his description of the belligerent states as 'dogs fighting in the streets' threatening 'the universal exhaustion of Europe' – with considerable powers over his future. 'If I were the Prince of Peace,' commented the poet A. E. Housman to a friend, 'I would choose a less provocative ambassador.' Russell was perfectly aware what the Fellows of Trinity felt about him. 'I am *intensely* disliked by the older dons,' he wrote to Ottoline, 'and still more by their wives, who think I should not mind if they were raped.'

Twelve days after his appeal in the Everett case, the Council met, in a mood of antagonism and determination. The Fellows – most of whom were in their early sixties – agreed that the university had already become an unsavoury nest of pacifists, given its well-attended UDC and NCF branches and Ogden's widely admired *Cambridge Magazine*, which treated the conscientious objectors with sympathy and the tribunals with derision. Their fear throughout the war was that it was being prosecuted not too vigorously but too weakly. The younger dons, who liked Russell and for the most part approved the passion of his stand, if not his actual views, were all away at the war. Led by McTaggart, the Master, Vice-Master and eight Fellows voted to expel Russell from his lectureship at Trinity.

There was uproar. Hilton Young, later Lord Kennet, wrote to Ogden's magazine: 'What brings us here? The desire that England should remain, and that Britain should become, a place in which the Russells whom fate grants us from time to time should be free to stimulate and annoy us unprosecuted ... That Trinity should gratuitously number itself among the persecutors, this is more discouraging than a German victory.' Twenty-two Fellows protested, led by Russell's old friend, the mathematician G. H. Hardy, who wanted to pass a vote of censure on the Council as soon as the war ended, leading to their resignation. Two former students of his course on mathematical logic signed the letter, C. D. Broad saying that he felt the college had disgraced itself, as did E. Neville, who called the Council's decision 'petty, impertinent and unpatriotic'. Evelyn Whitehead said she was furious about it, and Whitehead, confused but sympathetic, set about writing his own indictment, in which he rehearsed not only the Everett case but the entire question of conscientious objection as it applied to Cambridge: 'After the war, Reconstruction,' he wrote. 'Mr Russell has stood his trial ... We shall then stand our trial, not before the Mayor of London, but before more searching tribunals, our consciences, the nobler judgement of the world, and, as some hold, in that unknown future to which we all must pass ...'

But the deed had been done, not least because even among the younger dons serving at the front, there was a feeling that this should be sorted out later, when the war was over, and not in the middle of the fighting. They did not agree with Trinity; but they did not agree with Russell either. 'I find I should be rather sorry to be hounded out of this place', Russell had written to Ottoline before the outbreak of war. 'It is more nearly a home to me than any other place – I like the young men, or at least I like dealing with them. I believe I am really good for them, and a useful person ... If the place were closed to me, it would take away something which in the long run is important ...' The war was beginning to deprive him of the things he most cared about.

Instead, he went on talking about his future as a teacher 'for working-class men who are hungry for intellectual good'. 'I foresee', he wrote to Ottoline, 'a great and splendid life dealing with political ideas, but keeping out of politics.' What he had in mind was a movement of free education, to give those who were politically minded but uneducated 'a philosophy that will make their politics stable. History, economics, some psychology, a little ethics ... not ancient history, but very recent history ... Freedom, growth unimpeded, free play for people's best energies.' Slowly, Russell was sorting out his future.

The controversy over his dismissal was to last long after the war had ended, with G. H. Hardy leading several campaigns for his reinstatement, pointing out that Trinity's Council had behaved foolishly but not vindictively, and that their behaviour should be seen as a failure of imagination and common sense. Although Russell was punished in a more public manner than any other British academic, he was not alone. For many dons and intellectuals, the war had come as something of a relief, after years of uncertainty; 'peacefulness of being at war' as some people called it, when they could at last suspend their criticisms and doubts and unite against the German position. The philosophers in particular did so with real sadness, for academic relations between the two countries had always been exceptionally cordial, but after some 4000 German academics had signed a manifesto subordinating German scholarship to state policy they felt they had no choice.

Before the war, Cambridge had built up a long and honourable tradition of dissent, fostered by Norman Angell, who had argued about the unprofitability of war, and by Russell himself, with his call for 'a peaceful outlet for men's energies'. But with the outbreak of hostilities, and the emergence of 'nests of UDC supporters', a good many dons protested angrily about conscientious objectors, and against those with pacifist leanings who, like Lowes Dickinson, were now speaking out about post-war settlements and a league of nations. Lowes Dickinson, who wrote to Roger Fry on hearing of Russell's dismissal, 'There goes my last link with Cambridge. If I live, I shall have to clear out of there', endured the ostracism of his fellow dons by becoming a recluse, feeling, as he wrote to a friend, 'forlorn, indeed, worse than forlorn'. G. H. Hardy left for Oxford as soon as he was offered a place. Moore, a member of the UDC, put his head down and got on with editing *Mind*.

Besides Russell, perhaps the most persecuted was A. C. Pigou, a Fellow of King's and professor of political economy, who wrote in the *Nation* that he believed that Germany, like Britain, had entered the war reluctantly, and wondered whether the Allies were afraid to state their war aims lest the Germans accept them. The *Morning Post* led a witchhunt against him, accusing him of having favourable leanings towards the Germans. Efforts were made to oust him from his Chair. In the end, after four tribunal hearings – he was still of call-up age – the part-time work he was doing at the Board of Trade was deemed important enough to merit exemption from the services.

The whole affair, however, altered him profoundly. He entered the war a sociable, funny, Edwardian bachelor; he came out of it an eccentric recluse. As Russell had commented in his UDC pamphlet, *War, the Offspring of Fear*, Europe had indeed become a 'house on fire, where the inmates, instead of trying to extinguish the flames', were 'engaged in accusing each other of having caused the conflagration'. The mutual accusations left their mark both on the philosophers and on the whole academic world.

The grief Russell felt about Trinity was mitigated by one of his most memorable and enjoyable experiences of the war. Early in July, he set out on his first really important speaking tour, planning to give thirty-five talks in twenty-four days. It was planned as the first step in a nationwide stop-the-war campaign, and was one of his most public and provocative anti-war gestures to date. South Wales was chosen because of its number of anti-war miners and known sympathy for the ILP. Russell had never been a natural public speaker; his manner was too halting, his words too erudite. But his Welsh tour changed all that. He discovered a voice and an approach which were extremely appealing, a combination of common sense and extraordinary eloquence which seemed to hit a new and natural note. Everywhere he went he was cheered. On 6 July, to tumultuous applause, Russell spoke about security, liberty, democracy and the notion of evil, in a Quaker meeting house in Cardiff. The authorities, who had been following his progress with close attention, decided to act. Herbert Samuel, the home secretary, asked for a transcript of the shorthand notes taken by a reporter from the *Western Mail*. After declaring Russell's speech 'vehemently anti-British', he went to see Lloyd George, who was to take over as prime minister in December 1916, and urged him to ban Russell from the prohibited areas, which included most of the British sea coast and all 'sensitive' large cities, covering about one-third of the country. The banning order was too late to affect his Welsh tour, but it did prevent him from visiting Glasgow, Edinburgh and Newcastle during a second tour in October.

Before Russell set out, General Cockerill, director of special intelligence at the War Office, summoned him. He said he would drop these foolish banning orders if Russell agreed to abandon political propaganda and return to mathematics. Russell denied that he was involved in propaganda, while admitting that men 'with sufficient logical acumen' might well read certain messages into his words. But he would give no guarantees. Cockerill said he had no choice but to ban Russell from lecturing in the prohibited areas. The two men parted cordially, despite their opposed views. 'You and I', said Cockerill, 'probably regard conscience differently. I regard it as a still small voice, but when it becomes blatant and strident I suspect it no longer of being a conscience.'

Russell had given the title 'The World as It Can be Made' to the lectures he had written for his second tour. Since he was no longer allowed to travel wherever he wanted, the president of the Miners' Federation, Robert Smillie, read Russell's speech in Glasgow (a port and therefore prohibited), to an audience of well over a thousand people, many of them drawn by the publicity given to the ban, and when he stopped reading they rose and cheered. What made Russell's ban the more absurd was that the speech was published as an NCF pamphlet, freely available to anyone. In September, H. W. Massingham, editor of the *Nation*, wrote a letter to *The Times*, strongly condemning the government's edict: 'Mr Russell is not only the most distinguished bearer of one of the greatest names in English political history, but he is a man so upright in thought and deed that such action is . . . repugnant.'

By now Russell had become a serious nuisance to the authorities. Towards the end of October, Lloyd George remarked that it was Russell himself who had rejected the chance of a passport for America: had he been willing to give a simple undertaking that he would not use his lectures as a 'vehicle for propaganda', there would have been nothing to stop him from going. Russell was adamant: he would give no such undertaking. Therefore, said Lloyd George, it was perfectly plain that Russell intended to do all he could to promote 'weakness, inefficiency, and, if tolerated, [he] would hamper us in the prosecution of the war'. In the House of Commons, Sir Charles Trevelyan and Philip Morrell kept up a steady barrage of questioning. 'I shall endeavour to show', announced Morrell, 'that he has been persecuted and pursued with a malignity which recalls the methods of the Middle Ages.'

Russell's tours had provided him with further proof of his abilities, and he would never again find public speaking awkward. He was, however, exhausted. He was also depressed by the realisation that he had lost his base at Trinity, miserable about the thousands of men who had been slaughtered in the Somme offensive, and deeply worried about Lloyd George's statement that he had no sympathy at all with the conscientious objectors and intended to make their path as thorny as he could. Clifford Allen, momentarily out of prison but resolved to turn himself over to the military again as soon as he could, also posed Russell with a dilemma: should he now commit himself to working full-time for the NCF, and identify his views entirely with theirs, or continue to speak out independently?

On the day Clifford Allen first surrendered to the police, Russell noticed, sitting in the police station, a young girl; he thought her very beautiful. She was an actress called Colette O'Niel – her real name was Lady Constance Malleson – and she was married to the actor Miles Malleson. For her part, as she surveyed the court, she noted 'a small man, with a fine brow, aristocratic features, silver-grey hair and a passionate expression'. Russell was dressed in his usual dark suit and stiff high collar; he was sitting absolutely still, his hands on his knees, 'detached in mind and body – but all the furies of hell raged in his eyes'. They were introduced. She could find nothing to say and left the court to stand in the street, in tears over Allen.

Russell met her again at one of the regular dinners for the NCF workers. He was charmed; so, clearly, was she. He saw her again, sitting at the back of one of his public meetings. That evening they went home and became lovers. The next time they spent the night together they heard a 'shout of bestial triumph in the street'. Russell leapt out of bed. A Zeppelin was falling in flames. 'The thought of brave men dying in agony was what caused the triumph in the street,' Russell wrote somewhat sanctimoniously many years later. 'Colette's love was in that moment a refuge to me . . . from the agonising pain of realising that that is what men are . . .' He hurried back to bed.

In his autobiography, Russell wrote that at this point in the war he was seeking 'some other woman to relieve my unhappiness', and who could also comfort him for Ottoline's growing detachment. These words are slightly disingenuous. At that particular time, and in the months that followed, not only was he still meeting Ottoline, with bursts of affection followed by recriminations, but he was, at various times, and with various degrees of intensity, involved with both Vivienne Eliot and Katherine Mansfield. Did he ever really love Colette? He spoke of her as 'so much less of a personage, so much more capable of frivolous pleasures' than Ottoline, but he was certainly, from time to time, much infatuated with and very close to her; and there was something about her and her devotion to him, that would keep her part of his life until his death.

They were a curious couple. In 1916, Russell was forty-four. He was confident, successful, brilliant and tormented about the war, much caught up in himself and his own reactions. Colette was twenty, the daughter of an Irish peer serving as a lieutenant in the Scots Guards, whose brother had been killed in action in 1914. Her hair was black, with a widow's peak above a rather low forehead. She had a strong chin, haughty expression, a slightly coarse mouth which she kept carefully compressed, a gentle voice with a faint Irish lilt, and a 'suggestion of controlled tears'. When not on the stage, she wore flamboyant dresses, cut rather wider and longer than was then fashionable, leopard-skin coats, hats in the shape of turbans, and immensely high heels. On stage she played *femmes fatales* and comic roles; she could be witty, quizzical and tragic; audiences tended to remember her laugh, which came in sudden, spontaneous bursts.

Colette had come into the ranks of the NCF through Clifford Allen, whom she had met at Keir Hardie's memorial service. Miles Malleson, a short man with no chin and a toupée (which he insisted on wearing even when swimming), had been invalided out of the army in 1914 with a foot injury. He was a full member of the NCF and said, many years later, that his total opposition to the war had been the result of listening to Russell speak. Colette, being a woman, was an associate member. She addressed envelopes and kept an index of the names, addresses and sentences of all conscientious objectors. The Mallesons were passionate pacifists, but their relationship with each other was more like friends than a married couple. They were always broke, for the more they worked for the NCF the less they could find jobs on the stage, and they lived on 'tuppenny fishcakes from a shop up the back street' and 'best dried eggs'. They had taken Lawrence's old labourer's cottage at Chesham in Buckinghamshire, where neighbours still talked of Lawrence and Frieda chasing each other around the table with a carving knife. After their third meeting, Russell and Colette began to write to each other. Russell's letters are passionate, full of despair about the war, but they do not contain quite the depth or eloquence of his letters to Ottoline. Colette's are the more striking, with their gentle selfless-ness, rich images and tone of uncomplicated love. For a girl of twenty, they are curiously sophisticated. Her main fear – like Ottoline's – was that she would not prove 'worthy of him'. She likened herself to a 'sip of wretched after-dinner coffee' after the 'wonderful tapestry of his life'.

'I woke', wrote Colette, 'to the dim fog and hoarse shouting of the newsboy in the street below. Instantly my thoughts flew to you . . . You ask me what my thoughts were this morning on waking. I think they are just a brightly coloured hoard of pagan things.' Two days later, she wrote again: 'At this moment, everything brings me happiness because of you.' And the day after, 'I feel that you hold the shining keys to an endless peace. Teach me to go out into new and immense worlds: your worlds of thought and infinity.' Later, asking for a photograph of him with his 'heathery' hair: 'I'd like it looking robustuous, and revolutionary. Or do I mean rebellious?'

Russell was not only busy with the NCF and his pacifist articles, but was much caught up with his other emotional entanglements. He told Colette about Ottoline, and she took it well, saying that she too needed freedom, and accepted it as the most important thing between them. She was to return to this, in various ways, throughout her life; the need to be on her own, unusual in someone so young, was already clear in her mind. 'I think freedom', she told Russell again and again, 'is my fundamental credo.' For a while, he thought this splendid.

Before long, Russell had fallen in love with her. Several discursive and detached letters were suddenly followed by paeans of love. 'You can fill me with a greatness I have never known,' he told her, 'and I can give you love and more love and still more love – more and more always – the love of the passionate seeker, whose treasure is found at last.' It was to Colette that he wrote one of his most quoted letters about the war. A French friend and favourite pupil, Jean Nicod, had written to say that he was in the hands of the military and was about to go for a second medical examination, after which he could be shot for refusing military service. 'I hate the world and almost all the people in it,' Russell wrote bitterly; 'I hate the Labour Congress and the journalists who send men to be slaughtered, and the fathers who feel a smug pride when their sons are killed, and even the pacifists who keep saying human nature is essentially good, in spite of all the daily proofs to the contrary. I hate the planet and the human species – I am ashamed to belong to such a species.'

Colette and Russell settled down to a routine. During the week, they met whenever they could, usually in Colette's attic flat; on Sundays they walked in the country. They spent the afternoon of her twenty-first birthday together in Richmond Park, where they were caught in a shower. From time to time, they were able to seize two or three days in a country pub, when they would walk and she would look for plants, about which she knew a good deal. After these jaunts their letters reached new heights of emotion. 'Your love fills me with life and energy,' he wrote to her, nearly a year after their first meeting: 'It has smoothed out all the wrinkles in my instincts and brought light into the dark corners where terrifying pain lurked . . .' One day, he confessed to Ottoline that 'in a gay, boyish mood I got intimate with Constance Malleson, but she doesn't suit serious moods.' But not long afterwards, he wrote again to say, 'I think there *may* be more seriousness in it than I implied when we talked.' This, by now, was the pattern of Russell's affairs: a confession of what was going on, then its dismissal, followed sooner or later by a warning that it might be more important than he had first thought. Even to Colette, he was already adopting the same tone. While on a train to Manchester one day, he wrote her nine and a half quarto pages, analysing his feelings and discreetly referring to relations with a married woman – presumably in this case Vivienne Eliot. Then comes the telltale phrase: 'I shall make little of it.' Colette was a very different character to Ottoline. She approached her relationship with Russell in a straightforward manner. She told Miles what was happening, and when she learned from him that he too had found someone else, they agreed to keep things as they were. Colette congratulated herself that their marriage was not, in Blake's words, a 'hearse'.

Yet there was, in their relationship, something that doomed it to ultimate failure. The London stage reacted to the carnage at the front by putting on ever wittier, louder, more vulgar and more daring shows. Audiences flocked to musicals, and they came to laugh. Colette was part of the theatre world, and she was committed to becoming an actress. She knew that she had talent. As Bennitt Gardiner, a music and theatre critic, wrote about her presence on the stage: 'Each time the curtain rises, it is like a new dawn.' Young as she was, she was completely clear about her career. 'One has to stick to what one is *trained* to do,' she wrote to Russell. 'To lay hands on my own job and throw it out of my life would be like committing suicide.' Russell not only had very little interest in the theatre, but was irked by women who chose to take their professions as seriously as he took his. He also disliked the idea of her being an actress.

In *The Coming Back*, a novel Colette wrote many years later about their relationship, she describes how 'Deep in his heart, Gregory [Russell] deplored the importance Konradin [Colette] attached to her work. It was out of all proportion to the value of the work itself. She was so desperately engrossed in her own affairs. She had had the hard combativeness of extreme youth. She wanted, above everything, to make her mark on the world: to succeed. All that seemed a little futile to Gregory. He judged her; and in so doing, often forgot how great a part personal ambition had played in his own youth.'

This may have been one reason why Russell, infatuated at last with a woman without ties, did not propose marriage. Another seems to have been her attitude towards children. If Colette was clear about her career, she was also clear about not wanting children – though she later told a friend that she was frightened a child of hers might inherit the family strain of mental instability. Did Russell know this? Not long before she died, she wrote to Kenneth Blackwell at the Russell Archives in McMaster University, saying that she had, at about that time, had several abortions – whether she had been made pregnant by Russell is not known – and that Russell had visited her when she was recovering. Russell, on the other hand, had wanted children since the first days of his involvement with Alys, and was beginning to feel that, at forty-four, he did not have much time.

Early in December 1916, Russell informed Colette that his work and speaking engagements would prevent them from meeting 'for some considerable time' – the euphemism he used when contemplating breaking off relations altogether. Colette, more in love than ever, was remarkably understanding. Her letters, loving, touching, continued to come; she could be remarkably acute: 'I do sometimes think that you may very likely want to cut adrift and run off. . . . I've sometimes noticed that when you really want anything, you are quite simple about it.' At the end of February, she fell ill. She was having difficulties with Miles, and she was desperately worried about not being able to find work. On 6 March, she wrote to Russell again: 'I'm writing all this, but I don't know where you are, yr. address or when you'll be back. I daresay a certain misery will end when the war ends, but the war of life goes on, doesn't it?' Russell took her to the Swan Inn at Streatley-on-Thames and Colette was happy again. They walked while he recited Shakespeare's sonnets and Shelley's 'Ode to the West Wind'; and he talked, 'holding forth on everything under the sun', forgetting the direction they had been taking and adding many miles to their route.

By the autumn of 1917 the Mallesons had moved their London home again, from one attic to another, this time to one in Mecklenburgh Square. Colette, delighted with their new home, stippled the fireplace apple-green and surrounded it with indigo, painted the front two rooms in ice-blue paint, then covered them with a coat of white, and wrote to tell Russell that she could now sit watching the plane trees in the square swaying in the wind. At the end of June they had taken another holiday together, moving after the first night in Knighton because they feared that Russell had been recognised, and finishing up in rooms in a charming farmhouse among poplars on the fringes of a hamlet underneath the Clee Hills. They stayed there almost three weeks.

This was, perhaps, the last entirely happy time they had together. Miles was fretting about their relationship, saying that he too wanted to have children, and when at last she found a part in a film Russell

was overcome with jealousy of the director, assuming that he and
Colette were having an affair and hearing rumours that the man had
syphilis. There were scenes. Russell took the opportunity to compose
one of his customary – and singularly brutal – character analyses,
brought on, it seems, whenever he felt rejected. She lacked self-
control, religion and public-spiritedness, he informed her. She loved
cheap success and notoriety. She was acquisitive, envious, commer-
cially minded, competitive, crude, sexually vain, shoddy in her work
and selfish. Colette did not reply; what she felt is not recorded.
Contrite, Russell apologised, but too much had been said. Using his
suspicions about the film director, Russell wrote to break with her.
At first, Colette was calm. From her attic she wrote: 'If you leave
me, I'll not kill myself, I'll not give up my work, I'll not give up the
NCF; I'll still love you as I'm loving you now; but I shall not tell you
what is in my heart. I know that we belong together. If you don't
know it, there is nothing I can do.'

Russell kept silent. Colette wrote again, with considerable anguish.
'I cannot understand. I cannot even attempt to put into words the
immense desolation in my heart.' This time, Russell did reply. He
wished he could still care for her, but he could not. 'I hope to God
we never meet again,' replied Colette.

They did, of course, meet again. Their affair did not close with
the abrupt callousness of his marriage to Alys, but followed the
Ottoline path of breaks, reunions, more breaks, more tearful
reunions, full of mutual recriminations and forgiveness. Yet for
Russell, though not for Colette, there was something that seemed
final in this parting.

Shortly before Christmas 1916, feeling increasingly thwarted in his
attempts to make a public stand for peace at home, Russell turned
his attention to America. He had been delighted at Woodrow
Wilson's re-election as president, and now smuggled him an Open
Letter. The moment was well chosen. Pressures against American
neutrality were growing. On 23 December, the *New York Times*
reproduced Russell's letter in full, explaining that they had received
a copy via a 'confidential agent' of Russell's, who had walked into
the Astor Hotel when members of the American Neutral Conference

Committee were sitting. The conference organisers agreed to hand it over to the president.

'You have an opportunity of performing a signal service to mankind,' Russell had written to Wilson, 'surpassing even the service of Abraham Lincoln, great as that was. It is in your power to bring war to an end by a just peace. ... It is not yet too late to save European civilisation from destruction; but it may be too late if the war is allowed to continue ...' It was a long letter. It spoke of courage, of death, of treachery and victory and the longing of all men for peace. Only the United States, said Russell, had the power to become a guarantor of peace, a mediator between the combatants. 'In the name of Europe,' he concluded, 'I appeal to you to bring us peace.'

Russell's letter, and his eloquence, had sadly little effect. President Wilson addressed the Senate on 22 January; it was his most famous wartime speech and in it he redefined American policy. 'There must be', he declared, 'not a balance of power, but a community of power; not organised rivalries, but an organised common peace.' What Wilson seemed to have in mind was 'peace without victory'. In the *Tribunal*, Russell observed: 'The truth of what he says is evident to all who are not caught up in the madness of war.' *The Times*, however, was quick to refute Wilson's suggestion: 'the Allies', it said, 'can hear of no peace which is not a "victory peace".'

The Germans now embarked on unrestricted submarine warfare, and in March America broke off relations with Germany. On 6 April the United States declared war. Russell complained bitterly that this would probably prolong the hostilities, since without America 'universal exhaustion might have driven all nations to a compromise peace.' Even so, he continued to see the United States as the one country able to work for a negotiated peace, in that the mixture of its races and the 'comparative absence of a national tradition make America peculiarly suited to the fulfilment of the task'. In America, Russell was now regarded as Britain's 'most extreme pacifist'.

He was, above all, excessively busy. By early 1917 there were over a thousand absolutists in jail, refusing all compromise, many serving a second or even third term in the third division with hard labour, which meant solitude, no pencil or paper, no books, or newspapers, and no contact with other prisoners. Those who refused to work were put into 'close confinement' – in smaller cells, with nothing in them but a bible, a hymn book and the prison rules, on Diet Number One (bread and water), followed by Diet Number Two (bread, porridge, peas and gruel). A truculent parliamentary candidate called Albert Taylor spent sixty nights on a stone floor with no mattress. Looking out of the window was a punishable offence; it was cold, dirty and the perpetual silence strangely eerie. Prisoners complained of headaches, a feeling that they were going mad, mental confusion, loss of memory and a strange furtiveness. To understand some of the brutality inflicted on these men – most in their late teens and early twenties – one has to remember the extraordinary bitterness of the soldiers and their families towards the conscientious objectors, fanned by their apparent obstinacy, and by continual attacks in the newspapers, where stories about their intransigence were printed alongside pictures and stories about 'our patriotic families'.

There were, moreover, cases of excessive brutality on the part of warders and guards, about which some members of the public were beginning to protest. The government, which longed for the whole subject to disappear, now pushed through a series of more lenient alternatives, whereby committees were empowered to offer different work in civil employment, or civilian work under the army reserve. Hundreds of men, brought back before tribunals, were taken out of their cells to do quarrying, roadmaking and felling. When the numbers began to exceed the jobs available, men were sent to former prisons, which had been emptied of criminals and turned into work-camps.

Not all conscientious objectors found these offers acceptable. When cases were reviewed, it was discovered that there was still a substantial number of men who would accept no alternative and had decided to make their stand in jail. These men stayed in prison. Within the NCF, bitter squabbles arose about the 'absolutist' versus the 'alternativist' position, about whether the refusal to have any truck with the military was part of a larger movement, which would eventually overthrow the military system, or whether, as many had come to believe, it was simply not fair to ask very young men, confused by months of isolation, to take on the entire military machine seemingly on their own.

By now, with so many of the leaders in prison, Russell had become acting chairman of the NCF, which involved fighting off calls for its suppression as a treasonable organisation, as well as running the headquarters together with the forceful Catherine Marshall who, as the war continued and the work consumed ever more of her days and nights, was becoming increasingly fretful, exhausted and prickly. From his prison cell, Allen wrote to Russell: 'I plead with you to make Catherine Marshall successful by bearing with the things that anger you.'

Catherine was in her middle thirties, a liberal feminist for whom the war had meant the dashing of all hopes about solidarity across national and international boundaries, and who spoke of the 'mother-heart of womanhood' as a way of healing the spiritual wounds nations were inflicting upon each other. She was also an exceptional lobbyist and the *Labour Leader* had called her 'probably the ablest woman organiser in the land'. But as letters poured into the NCF offices about conscientious objectors being bullied and beaten up, forced by soldiers into uniforms or dragged on to parade grounds and mocked, she began to lose her sense of proportion about the war. Her position was further undermined by her love for Clifford Allen and she was tormented with fears for his health. She had recently been allowed to visit him, and had found him frail, agonisingly thin and losing his sight, though not his determination.

At first, relations between Catherine and Russell were cordial, and there is no doubt that, as a master of political strategy, she taught Russell a great deal. Each admired the other's strengths. The letters they exchanged were those of office friends. 'I find myself constantly taking refuge from the present in more humane and kindly times, such as that of Nero,' Russell wrote jocularly to her; 'I think we shall have peace in the autumn, after Lloyd George has drunk the blood of half a million young Englishmen in an offensive which he knows will effect nothing . . .' If Catherine could be impatient, she too liked jokes. She scrawled a note back: 'For goodness' sake busy yourself again quickly and get rid of the distorted vision of truth to which idleness – or plum pudding? – seem to have given rise.'

There was no way, however, that the two of them could have worked harmoniously for long. Russell was accustomed to being listened to, Catherine to running organisations. If she found him discursive, prone to ponder on the issues of the war at the expense of hard and often dreary office work, he found her increasingly bossy. 'My relations with Miss Marshall get worse and worse,' he wrote gloomily to Ottoline, 'she is very difficult, bullying everyone, dilatory, untruthful, hating to part with power.'

'I like you fleeing to your funk hole!' Catherine wrote furiously at the beginning of March, and went on to berate him for thoughtlessness towards others, before ending: 'I wish I could think of one nice thing to say, but there is not one I have in my mind at present, and I have not time to think.' Next morning, Russell wrote back: 'You really must not write me letters such as the one I got from you this morning . . . In general, it is not from laziness that I do not do more work. I do as much as I can without doing it badly or becoming ill.' He urged her to take a rest, but sheaves of peremptory, handwritten notes kept appearing on his desk. In June, he finally wrote her a long, harsh, exasperated letter, in which he told her, 'your manner of fault finding fills one with despair . . . After you have been criticising, I have to go round consoling . . . Your present way of treating us all is paralysing . . . It discourages initiative to know that anything one may attempt will only lead to destructive criticism from you.' Wisely, he never sent it.

By now Catherine's friends had grown increasingly alarmed by her caustic tone and irrational outbursts, and feared that she was heading for a nervous breakdown. She was persuaded to take a holiday, causing Russell to remark that, though this meant he would not get one, just having her out of the office was a holiday in itself. On her return, relations calmed down.

Early in 1917, a work-camp had opened at Princetown, in what had been Dartmoor prison, a circle of wheel-shaped buildings 1500 feet up overlooking the moors, built to house prisoners in the Napoleonic Wars. It was a treeless, desolate spot, in a bleak landscape of ravines and granite. Some 900 men – doctors, clerks, labourers, tradesmen, teachers, of all shades of political and religious persuasion, but all sharing a conviction that war was wrong – were sent there to work at quarrying and agriculture under former prison officers. Unnecessarily bad conditions – little food, and what there was disgusting, long hours of meaningless work with equipment so antiquated that every turnip produced cost ninepence and it took sixteen men an entire day to crush five bags of oats – were exacerbated by the hostility of Princetown's inhabitants, and a campaign of vilification in the press. Dartmoor's new inmates were labelled 'pampered pets', 'strikers', and 'coddled men', who were said to idle on the moors in the sunshine, eating delicacies sent from the Army and Navy Stores. They were also accused of trying to corrupt local children.

A letter to his future wife from a man called Aylmer Rose described his arrival in Princetown. 'We were boo-ed, yelled at. "Cowards! Cowards! I wish the Germans had you! You should be shot! Devils! Where are your petticoats? Huns! Traitors!"' Some soldiers threw stink bombs, while girls prodded them savagely with sticks. 'What struck me most about prison', Rose wrote, 'was its brutality . . . One was locked up like an animal, exercised, supplied and cleaned like an animal.'

The fracas grew worse. The bewildering assortment of conscientious objectors at Dartmoor split into those who were prepared to work and obey rules, and a 'go-slow' faction. A tougher penal regime was proposed. Russell travelled down to Princetown to talk to both groups of prisoners and to their guards, and returned to London to attack the penal and ridiculous nature of the work being demanded of these men, not simply on Dartmoor but in other work-camps around the country. He proposed that they should at least be given work that was socially useful, without the constant threat of being returned to a prison cell if they failed to conform. By this stage in the war, public sympathy had swung in some small measure towards the conscientious objectors, fuelled by the NCF's excellent publicity machine and perhaps by the reputation of Russell himself, who was now much in demand and constantly addressing packed public meetings. According to his cousin, Margaret Lloyd, people were beginning to 'regard Bertie as an oracle'.

Stephen Hobhouse was a nephew of Beatrice Webb and a conscientious objector. By the middle of 1917 his health, after 112 days of hard labour in jail, followed by a second jail sentence, was poor and he was declining rapidly. His mother, Margaret Hobhouse, was determined to save his life and to draw attention to the conditions for others like him. An outspoken and determined woman, she had decided that 'absolutists' like Stephen should either receive a King's Pardon or be released into civilian life. To this end she produced a persuasive document, 'I Appeal unto Caesar', outlining with considerable passion and eloquence the fate of the conscientious objectors in the hands of the military. Only later did it become known that its author was Russell, who, hemmed in by government hostility, forbidden access to most newspapers and unable to go to America, had seen this as a way of getting his views heard. Pamphlets were an effective outlet for Russell's views, and some of his most eloquently phrased appeals for liberty and democracy appeared in booklets.

Russell was also engaged in an acrimonious altercation with Robert Graves over their mutual friend, Siegfried Sassoon, whom Russell had met at Garsington. Ottoline, feeling estranged from Russell, believed herself in love with Sassoon. Entries in her diary suggest the love was not reciprocated. After the Somme offensive when he was shot through the throat, Sassoon returned to Britain in a state bordering madness, insisting that the troops were being monstrously treated. He had been awarded the Military Cross, and chose this moment to throw it publicly into the sea. He then issued a statement: 'I am convinced that the war is being deliberately prolonged by those who have the power to end it . . . on behalf of those who are suffering now I make this protest against the deception that is being practised on them . . .'

Russell, though worried about associating Sassoon's position too closely with the NCF, encouraged his stand, and helped prepare his statement, writing to Ottoline that they should all make absolutely certain there was no cover-up and that there '*is* a scandal and no hushing up'. Robert Graves, who had got to know Sassoon during a shared period of convalescence, and had visited Garsington at the same time, intervened furiously to declare that Russell was exploiting Sassoon in the interests of the pacifists and regardless of his traumatised condition. Russell continued to claim that 'there was nothing in the faintest degree hysterical or unbalanced in [Sassoon's] attitude.' In the end, Graves's view prevailed. He persuaded Sassoon to go before a medical board rather than press for a court-martial, and Sassoon was sent, not back to the front, but to a convalescent home in Scotland. Graves wrote an angry note to Russell: 'There is nothing further for you to do with him for your cause. I blame you most strongly for indiscretion . . . Now you can leave things alone until he's well enough again to think calmly about the war and how to end it.' To friends, Graves spoke damningly of the way Sassoon was being callously 'exploited' by pacifists like Russell.

It has been claimed that Graves saved Sassoon's sanity and that Russell would have used him unscrupulously to promote the pacifist cause. Sassoon's own reaction, later, was to blame Graves for cheating him of the martyr's role. Although Russell could be ruthless, he was also capable of considerable concern, and Graves was probably being unfair.

The summer of 1917 provided Russell with one of his most exhilarating moments of the war. In February, the patience of the Russian people broke under a combination of corruption, inefficiency, privations, over five million casualties in the war, and the recruitment of many more unwanted soldiers. Strikes and riots broke out in St Petersburg. Soon, the troops joined the rioters, a provisional government was formed under Prince Lvov, and the tsar was forced to abdicate. In Britain, these events were warmly welcomed by the pacifists, for whom an early end to the war now seemed possible. A telegram went off from the ILP congratulating the Russian people on their 'magnificent achievements'. Since the revolution was seen to presage the coming of peace, based not on militarism but on democracy, there was much talk of 'following Russia'. Disappointed that none of his stratagems for peace had worked, Russell saw in the February revolution a confirmation of his views on non-violent resistance. He even believed at this stage that Russia could teach Britain about civil liberties, and he and Catherine Marshall set about drafting a British Charter of Freedom, linking the ideals of workers to those of the pacifists. When, a few days later, the provisional government in Petrograd renounced all claims to 'annexation and indemnities', Russell was even more delighted.

The first meeting of support for the revolution took place in the Albert Hall in London on 31 March 1917. There was room for 12,000 people: 20,000 showed up. Other meetings were held throughout the country, and it was agreed that a convention should be held to 'hail the Russian revolution and to organise the British Democracy to follow Russia', and 'to do for their country what the Russian Revolution had accomplished in Russia'. Leeds was selected to host the gathering.

Local dignitaries were unnerved. There were efforts to persuade local hoteliers to cancel the delegations' bookings, and many had to spend the night in a stationary train. By noon on the day of the conference, however, 1150 delegates were in Leeds and many more were arriving every minute.

Colette and Russell had not yet parted. They spent an afternoon in Cambridge, boating on the river, then caught a train for Leeds with Ramsay MacDonald, who regaled them with endless Scottish stories. It was very hot. That evening they wandered the streets looking for a sympathetic hotelier and when they found a restaurant the waiter was rude. When they were walking to the Coliseum – the hall had to be switched at the last moment – children in the street hissed at them.

Ramsay MacDonald moved the first resolution: 'Hail! The Russian Revolution'. Colette, from the back of the gallery, watched as Russell received the longest and most enthusiastic applause. When he spoke of Clifford Allen, still in prison, the applause began again, lasting well over a minute. Leonard Woolf, one of the delegates, remembered the event as one of the most 'emotional' he had ever attended. Three more resolutions were passed amid tumultuous cheers: to work for peace, with neither annexations nor indemnities, to champion civil liberties, and to set up councils of workmen's and soldiers' delegates 'for initiating and co-ordinating working-class activity'. Woolf, watching Russell from across the hall, saw a frail figure, speaking, when the cheering let him, in a 'precise, clipped, aristocratic voice'. Next morning, Colette wrote to Russell of 'the wonder and the splendour that last night has left in my heart . . . I didn't know, before, that such strength and fire could exist in mortal man.' By now Russell was talking about setting up a 'People's Party' with socialist guilds.

Plans to set up these delegates' councils were offensive to much of the British public, who were reading of Ypres and Passchendaele, where 300,000 men perished that summer and autumn. Crowds jostled and jeered at those who turned up for the meetings. One of the more violent confrontations involved Russell himself. After a meeting organised in the Memorial Hall in Faringdon Street had been cancelled by its nervous owners, it was decided to move the gathering to the Brotherhood Church in Hackney. It was unfortunate that bombs fell on the spot on which leaflets announcing the meeting had been left, and there were suggestions that the delegates were signalling to the Germans. Just before the meeting was due to begin, 300 men, led by soldiers, entered the church, singing 'Rule Britannia'. A Canadian corporal climbed on top of the organ and called for a pro-war resolution. Fighting broke out. The attackers were evicted and the doors bolted. There were loud roars from outside. The crowd, using pieces of wood and iron bars as battering-rams, broke down the doors and began tearing up the pews. Russell described the scene to Ottoline: 'There were two bestial women with knotted clubs, who set to work to thwack all the women of our lot that they could get at . . . I realised how ghastly the spirit of violence is, how utterly I repudiate it, on whatever side it may be . . .' *The Times* next morning noted that many of the delegates had been 'bearded men of foreign cast'. The police arrived but stood watching, though they were moved to act when they heard that Russell was the brother of an earl. He escaped by climbing on to the side of a moving tram, while the crowd jeered and tried to pull him off. Russell observed to Catherine Marshall that all he had lost was a new hat. In the end the councils were shelved in the face of public hostility and growing indifference on the part of the workers.

In the late spring of 1917 Russell had finally joined the ILP, not simply because it was the one party to oppose the war openly but because it had undertaken that the peace which followed would be secured and honoured on a new basis. For peace to last, Russell believed, it would have to have the support of a satisfied and participating public. As the years of war went on his views had swung around: what he now supported was not so much conscience as integrity. There was, he claimed, nothing particularly individual about a conscientious objection: it stood for comradeship. If nothing else, Leeds had proved that economics and social reasons lay behind most men's desire to fight. It was not, as the Bloomsberries held, that the war was simply an expression of 'unreason': it was to do with social need. The socialist peace camp, with its solution to the war lying in the organisation of labour, now seemed attractive to him: unequal distribution of wealth and power were what made capitalism offensive and caused war.

Russell was once again hard at work, his mind filled with books he wished to write. One was about his guild socialism, which he thought of calling 'Roads to Freedom'. His idea was that each factory would elect its own managers; they would federate into a guild with other factories in the same industry, and together pay a tax to the state, which, in return, would supply the means of production, regulate wages and working conditions and arrange for the products to be marketed. A guild congress would act as the ultimate court of appeal. He wrote to Leonard Woolf that he was planning a book 'of some 50,000 words, on Anarchism, Socialism and Syndicalism' . . . 'solely for the sake of filthy lucre'. He went on: 'Do you know of any anarchist literature that you could recommend? For my part I have never read any. I suppose Bakunin must have written something, but to me he is a mere name . . .'

Russell's friendship with Ottoline was cooling, and she noted that Russell wanted to 'shake her off'. She was confused about her feelings, but relieved. 'My rapier is out – I have eluded him. Defend myself from him and will be free for flight.' But flight to where? She was haunted by longing for Sassoon, and, above all, she felt lonely. On 6 June she wrote in her diary: 'I cry out and long and long for an unknown something,' and later, 'I think I want to be loved – just loved and not criticised. No one has loved me – in my life – they all want help – support – out of me.' Finally, 'Bertie is like a dead stick now – without any leaves or flowers.'

For Russell, no parting was really possible without recriminations.

Sensing that this time the end might be near, he accused her of not being able to console him for his growing despair about the war and the desolation which now so frequently overcame him. 'Everything that I do and feel nowadays is the outcome of despair. Absolutely my whole being went into my love for you, but that turned to despair . . . I am so weary that I can't think sanely. I have no real hold on life. I simply don't know how to express the utter devastation inside me. I feel that I am rotting away inwardly . . . The sort of thing you and I had in common depended upon faith and hope, but now I have neither . . . I used to hope you could help me to overcome the fundamental despair, but gradually I found you couldn't . . . There is no cure for it except rest. But unfortunately I can't rest with you, because I can't be superficial with you . . . I long for death with the same kind of intensity with which I long for the end of the war – How is one to bear such a world? I feel an alien, a being from another planet. Each fresh horror strikes at the raw place, and makes it quiver worse than before.' On the bottom of this letter, Ottoline scrawled: 'He was busy with Constance Malleson at this time & I thought was very happy.' She was quite right. Two days later, Russell took off for an ecstatic three-week holiday with Colette.

But Ottoline did protest. 'You have battered upon me hard,' she wrote, 'for many months, indeed years now, and even the poor rag doll will turn someday. It is surely useless to go on with these discussions as to my demerits . . . I don't blame you or criticise you. I only want you to see that your grievances against me are mostly imaginary . . . Nothing can efface for me the living fact in my life of all that we have shared together. The best this life could give, but I have said this so often. You know what I feel about it.' Like Alys, and Colette, there was something very generous about the women whom Russell drew to him.

Emotionally, 1916 and 1917 had been strenuous years for him. During part of the time at least, he was not only placating Ottoline but toying with Katherine Mansfield and Vivienne Eliot, falling in love with Colette, and trying to detach himself from poor Helen Dudley, who had stayed on in England and moved into his flat after Russell and the Eliots left. Some of his more callous letters, breaking off relations with one woman, can presumably be attributed to the emotional demands of one or more of the others becoming too insistent so that he was unable to cope with them all. His autobiography is coy on the subject, but to give two examples: the summer of 1917 was the zenith of his affair with Colette, and the two of them spent remarkably happy holidays in the country together. Russell was also planning to share a country cottage with the Eliots – apparently the place where he may have made love, hating it, to Vivienne – for Russell was in one way or another involved in the Eliots' lives between the summer of 1915 and the spring of 1919. The second example is that Russell met Colette on 31 July 1916, and their affair began on 23 September. By November he thought he had fallen 'more or less in love' with Katherine Mansfield, yet went off to the Cat and Fiddle with Colette. The letters he wrote to each of them were sometimes interchangeable; moving from rapture to disillusion, from disillusion to accusation, from accusation to the revelation of another (but probably unimportant) love, which was going to necessitate a (probably brief) separation. What was so extraordinary was how forgiving the women were and how energetic Russell was: he was conducting these highly emotional affairs at the same time as working full-time for the NCF, lecturing, writing, planning future work, and writing dozens of letters, amorous and otherwise, every day. Nothing, certainly, would ever be as hectic again.

Russell was also growing extremely weary of the NCF. Three years of intensive bureaucratic and public work, speeches, confrontations and personal attacks had left him longing to return to the privacy of writing, to books, and to philosophy. He was forty-five and there was much he still wanted to say. 'The NCF', he wrote to Ottoline, 'no longer interests me – all the best people are in prison & there seems no way of getting them out. Those who remain are full of petty quarrels and sordidness.' Again: 'Something is gone wrong inside me. I find the human race hateful – affection seems dried up. It makes me very very unhappy and I don't know how to cure it, except by waiting . . . I should like six months solitude in the desert.' At the end of 1917 he resigned from the executive of the NCF. For him, the war, or so he thought, was over.

Eleven

Angular thoughts

Russell was to be disappointed: his war was far from over. In 1918 a totally new experience awaited him, and it was to be one of the least pleasant he had yet encountered. Though he had left the executive of the NCF, he was still contributing articles to its paper, the *Tribunal.* On 3 January, he submitted a piece entitled 'The German Peace Offer', which drew attention to the willingness of the Germans to make peace provided the Allies agreed to exclude all indemnities and annexations. To refuse such an offer, he argued, was insane: it would lead to one thing only.

> The American garrison, which will by that time be occupying England and France, whether or not they will prove efficient against the Germans, will no doubt be capable of intimidating strikers, an occupation to which the American army is accustomed when at home. I do not say that these thoughts are in the mind of the Government. All the evidence tends to show that there are no thoughts whatever in their mind, and that they live from hand to mouth, consoling themselves with ignorance and sentimental twaddle.

It was as if the authorities had been waiting for just such an opportunity. The Foreign Office already had its eye on *Principles of Social Reconstruction*, having labelled it 'pernicious' and a phoney 'literary firework', but liable to influence 'superficial thinkers'. Throughout the book, according to a note that was doing the rounds of government offices, 'there is a tone of intolerable superiority, which characterises the pacifist.' Under DORA, the government had the power to prevent the spread of material 'likely to cause disaffection'. Detectives arrived to interview Russell in his flat; he was charged, and a date set for his trial. Whereas in 1916 and 1917 he had half longed to go to prison, to join the other conscientious objectors in his own stand against the government, now he no longer had any desire to do so. As he wrote to Gilbert Murray, who had sent him a sympathetic peace-making note, he would have toned down his article had he realised the danger he was in; though he suspected that he had been arrested simply because the authorities knew that he was about to retire from the NCF – his brother Frank had informed them, hoping it would cause them to lift their ban on his talks in the prohibited areas. This was their last chance to punish him. To William Hepburn Buckler in America Russell wrote: 'I should wish to assure you, and all Americans . . . that I had not the faintest intention or desire to cause bad blood between this country and the United States . . . The one sentence on account of which I was summoned was taken out of its context.'

Early in February, Russell appeared before the magistrate at Bow Street, Sir John Dickinson. Sir John was not in an accommodating mood. Russell had decided to prepare his own defence, which he based on material extracted from a US Congress report on industrial relations. It dealt with the use of troops during industrial disputes, and described how American soldiers had helped to put down strikers in Colorado, Idaho and West Virginia. Sir John stopped him before he could begin. 'Mr Russell', he said, 'seems to have lost all sense of decency and fairness . . . the offence is a very despicable one'. He pronounced sentence: six months in prison, with no option of paying a fine, to be spent under the harsh regime of the second division.

Bloomsbury had turned out in force to support Russell, and it may be that their giggles and mockery induced the magistrate to pass a harsher sentence. Later, in a letter to Ottoline, Strachey declared that he had come away from the court room with his 'teeth chattering with fury'. Russell told Ottoline he had never felt anything equal to the 'concentrated venom of the magistrate . . . it was a blast of hatred, quite astonishing'. Colette was comforting, telling him that he was better equipped than most to survive the ordeal, and that the strain of it could be nothing compared with writing *Principia*

Mathematica. Clifford Allen urged him to make as much propaganda as he could out of his sentence, and added, generously, 'If ever I contribute anything of value to this world, it will be in great measure due to the fact that you were willing to help me understand my own mind without patronising yours.' In his diary, Allen noted: 'terrible to think of that graceful person in a revolting prison'.

The trial received considerable attention in the newspapers. The *Manchester Guardian* singled Russell out as a rare figure of intellectual distinction; a New York daily branded him a 'depraved liar'. His friends were on the whole sympathetic, with one or two odd exceptions. When John Middleton Murry wrote to Katherine Mansfield to tell her what had happened, she wrote back scornfully: 'When I read about Bertie being carried shoulder high I felt quite *sick*. For such a silly, incredibly stupid thing. How humiliated he ought to feel. It would be for me, like if I was a burglar and was caught having burgled the potato knife. I expect if he goes to prison he'll get immensely fat in there, in fact he's so blown already I shudder.' Lowes Dickinson was kinder: 'I am at your service, for whatever is possible. I don't know the ways of prison. But of course I should want to see you . . .' Messages of 'hommage' came from Wilfrid Scawen Blunt, the poet, who had spent some time in a prison himself, for agitating in support of Irish independence.

At first, Russell accepted the idea of prison with composure. But as he took in more clearly what the second division meant – sewing mailbags eight hours a day on a small backless stool, with no privacy, no conversation and nothing to write with – he worried what this might do to his health, and tried to get himself transferred to the more lenient first division. There, at least, he would be able to get on with the philosophical work he was planning. Nor can he have failed to be struck by what the second division had done to Allen, who had recently emerged from many months' incarceration. A tall man, Allen now weighed less than eight stone; his usually pale skin had turned a greyish white, his cheeks were sunken and emaciated, his face lined and his neck scraggy. He was twenty-eight, but looked like an old man. He no longer smiled, Russell remarked sadly to Ottoline, saying that his smile had once been so particularly lovable. Russell was also depressed to learn that the government was considering raising the military recruitment age to fifty, which would effectively ensure that he would remain in prison until the end of the war. To make matters worse, he had piles and a doctor attributed some of his depression to them.

Russell's appeal had been set for 12 April. No one expected his sentence to be overturned. The night before, a farewell party was given for him by some Bloomsbury friends. Dolly Ponsonby, Arthur Ponsonby's wife, recorded in her diary seeing Russell, E. D. Morel (who had just emerged from prison) and Ottoline having lunch that day in a London restaurant. 'I talked to funny little dry, reserved, courageous Bertie. Quite determined not to be pitied.' (Ottoline, she added, was looking peculiarly ugly: her underclothes kept bursting out from under her black velvet dress and she made little effort to put them back.)

Russell's friends with political clout, like Gilbert Murray, fought hard to persuade the authorities to switch Russell to the first division, and in the end Balfour, the foreign secretary and a fellow philosopher, intervened, on the grounds that Russell's philosophical work should not suffer by the confinement. When his appeal duly failed, Russell spent his last days of freedom finishing *Roads to Freedom*, drafting a synopsis for a new book, and taking a few days' holiday with Colette, to whom he had once again become very attached. They went down to the country, and walked, and Russell read her extracts from his book, declaring that never in his life had he been happier. Early on the morning of 1 May she watched from her attic window as he walked down the stairs on his way to Brixton jail.

The first division was not altogether unpleasant. Russell's early impression was that of being cooped up on an ocean liner, unable to get away from people except in one's stateroom, but in any case preferable to his boyhood crammer or to being an attaché at the British embassy in Paris. He was given a decent-sized cell, for which he paid 2s 6d a week, and employed a fellow prisoner to clean it for 6d a day. His brother Frank had been able to arrange with the governor for him to take in furniture, wear his own clothes, keep money to buy food, have access to unlimited books and receive *The Times* every day (possibly because the home secretary, Herbert Samuel, had been his fag at Winchester). Colette sent in a green

vase, some lilies and branches of beech. Ottoline supplied strawber-
ries, scented soap and toilet water, and regular bunches of the
brightest coloured and most sweet-smelling flowers Garsington
could provide. Naomi Bentwich produced peaches.

There were even jokes, so much so that Colette suggested the
prisoners should go not on a hunger strike but on a 'laughing strike',
after Russell had been heard laughing aloud over Lytton Strachey's
recently published *Eminent Victorians*. Desmond MacCarthy told the
prison governor that what Russell really wanted was a canary. 'No,'
said Russell, when asked about this. He was currently doing some
research for *The Analysis of Mind*. 'What I really want is an orang
outang,' explaining that it would 'throw light on Mind in its origin
and in the Cabinet'. And Arthur Waley sent him a copy of a Chinese
poem:

> Sent as a present from Annam
> A red cockatoo.
> Coloured like the peach-tree blossom,
> Speaking with the speech of men.
>
> And they did to it what is always done
> To the learned and eloquent.
> They took a cage with stout bars
> And shut it up inside.

Perhaps not surprisingly, Horatio Bottomley, the notorious German-
ophobe and scurrilous journalist, complained bitterly in the pages of
John Bull that it was a great pity that 'the man Russell is not treated
like the common criminal he is.'

Russell was allowed one letter and one visit a week, when two or
three people could come together and spend up to half an hour with
him, under the supervision of a warder. He was also permitted to
write one letter a week, on four narrow sides of prison paper, and
this had to go before the governor for approval. Given the complexity
of his emotional affairs, he had decided that the weekly letter should
generally be a communal one, going off to his brother, Colette and
Miss Gladys Rinder – the dutiful secretary at the NCF – to read in
its entirety, and leaving it to them to convey his news and requests to
other people. With Colette, he had made a private arrangement that

if anything important happened, she would insert a message in the personal columns of *The Times*, under the initials G.J.; and that he would write her letters in French from historical figures or imaginary characters, which he could send out as if they were part of his work.

He took enormous care to organise his visitors harmoniously, so that they were either friends already or became friends during the train journey out from Westminster to Brixton. Colette tended to come with Miss Rinder, Ottoline with Frank, Whitehead with another philosopher, and once with his solicitor, so that he could draw up the draft of a contract. In between visits, he wrote letters. The early ones were not unhappy. He complained to Frank that he missed his friends, but that the leisure and lack of all responsibility meant that he was able to spend four hours a day on philosophical writing, four hours on philosophical reading, and four on general reading. Prison, he said, had some of the advantages of the Catholic church. 'I am quite happy and my mind is very active,' he wrote to Frank on 3 June. 'I enjoy the sense that the time is fruitful – after giving out all these last years, reading almost nothing and writing very little . . . it is a real delight to get back to a civilised existence.' Prison life filled his mind with brilliant images of past pleasures: early mornings in the Alps, sunsets, a man in Paris selling 'artichauts verts et beaux' twenty-four years earlier.

To Ottoline, he wrote thoughtful, discursive letters, dwelling on the past and sometimes reverting to the reproaches which had afflicted their relationship in recent months. He accused her of being 'despotic', remarking one day: 'My mood is rather hard, because of the pain of the war: my thoughts are angular, and my feelings like a hedgehog's bristles.' Ottoline replied that she had decided to name her new pug (whose father was Socrates) after him. To Miss Rinder, in the communal letter, he wrote requests, instructions, orders, reminders. She was an obliging woman, but even she eventually complained to Ottoline that Russell did not trouble himself to think how much time it was taking her to cope with them. Ottoline considered the worthy Miss Rinder a terrible bore: 'She is so good,' she wrote dismissively, 'but so like a canary. Tweeting.'

His circular letters were all alike, uncomplaining except when fits of despair overtook him, descriptive, occasionally funny. Those to

Colette were different. They contained all the love and urgency of earlier times, long outpourings of dependency and need. 'My dear Heart,' he wrote in June, 'I miss you so dreadfully – you are the most wonderful lover that ever there was – I have been happy with you, happy beyond imagination.' And later: 'My Colette, my soul, I feel the breath of greatness inspiring me through our love.' '. . . It is through our love that I find it possible to keep hope alive.' Before long, he had found a way of smuggling letters out to her, 'dwarf handwriting on old scraps' slipped in between the pages of uncut books, some of them in French as they had planned. Sometimes she is Sophie and he Mirabeau; at others Mme Roland to his Buzot. 'Mon coeur est à toi complètement,' begins one of his early letters: 'Je baise ton portrait . . .' And a few days later: 'Oui, je vous aime, et je vous aime parce que vous savez aimer comme personne d'autre ne le sait . . .' They discussed what they would do together once the war was over: visit Spain to see the Velasquez paintings and Granada, from which Isabella and Ferdinand drove the Moors, and travel to Italy and Connemara. Russell was pressing her to make the break from Miles, saying that he had waited far too long to leave Alys, but added, 'if you disagree, I won't press it.' Colette wrote him sane and cheerful replies, called him her 'wild puss cat', and sent him messages via *The Times* personal column until the authorities got suspicious and sent a man from Special Branch to question her.

His friends sent warm letters of support. E. M. Forster, in Alexandria, heard the news of Russell's arrest and wrote at once to send his love. Brett, describing her deafness, told him that she suspected it must be quite like prison life, in which you see life 'revolving around you – see people talking and laughing, quite *meaninglessly* . . .' Russell replied kindly, saying that prison would indeed be worse in the long run, but that, since he was only to be there for a short time, her plight was infinitely more unpleasant. He urged her to 'practise the mental discipline of not thinking how great a misfortune it is.'

By August, after three months in prison, Russell was beginning to hanker for the outside world, not only because he was finding prison life disagreeable but because he needed to be free to pursue his philosophy with any seriousness. He observed to Frank that philosophic research was not, after all, like the 'work of a clerk or housemaid'. He was also beginning to have headaches, and dreamt of the countryside, of air, of libraries and of contact with friends. Prison was making him obsessive. 'I long for the SEA and wildness and wind', he wrote to Ottoline. 'I hate being all tidy like a book in a library where no one reads. Prison is horribly like that. Imagine if you knew you were a delicious book, and some Jew millionaire bought you and bound you uniform with a lot of others and stuck you up in a shelf behind glass where you merely illustrated the completeness of his system – and no anarchist was allowed to read you – that is what one feels like.' Jail had not altered Russell's prejudices.

Frank managed to arrange for him to keep his light on longer so as to be able to work later, to have decent writing paper for his letters, and even more fresh flowers. On one occasion he was allowed to talk to some German prisoners, who argued with him over a review that he had written on Kant. However, his appeal for early release was turned down. He contemplated going on hunger strike, like other conscientious objectors, and wrote to Colette for advice: 'Je souffrirais volontiers, mais je ne désire pas sacrifier mes travaux futurs sans rien accomplir.' She advised against it. Meanwhile, friends like Margaret Llewelyn Davies, the Webbs and George Lansbury signed a petition calling for his release, and saying that the whole affair gave rise to 'feelings of shame and indignation amongst all those who value liberty of opinion as one of our most precious national possessions.'

Russell found the remaining months very tough. He became fretful and jealous, chafing at the 'boredom, sense of impotence and impatience'. One friend urged him to knit. Much of the last weeks were spent planning the future, with growing excitement. 'I will do one big piece of technical philosophy,' he wrote to Colette, 'but I do not feel that will be my main work in future years. I want to teach and preach, and spread a view of life. My best work lies ahead of me – I owe that to you . . . Old fetters of tradition hampered me till very lately – but for the war, I should never have got free of them.' A week later, he added, 'Oh, I hope I shall live to be old – because I have such endless things I want to do.' He wanted, he said, to 'see a little more than others have seen, of the strange shapes of mystery that inhabit that unknown night ... I want to bring back into the world of men some little bit of new wisdom.'

One thing that did worry him was the question of how he was going to earn his living. He had given much of his money away and was left with £100 a year – not enough to live on. Ottoline was trying to arrange some sort of research fellowship for him, and eventually Charles Sanger and some of his other friends did secure a lecture-ship in philosophy for him in London.

By early September, having learned that he would soon be released, Russell began to plan his first hours of freedom. He was to be let out at 8.30 on the morning of 14 September and he told Colette that he would have a taxi waiting to take him home to collect some things and then to her. Should they, he asked, go out to an early lunch, then dine at home? Would she send the maid away early? 'I shall want to cling to you, & rock in your arms and laugh and cry ...' On 13 September she received his last letter from Brixton. 'Very soon now, dear love, this awful time will be over, and I shall hold you in my arms and kiss you – lips, eyes, hair, all of you – and I shall see the love in your eyes ... My dear love, my dear love, my dear love ...'

For all his plans and euphoria, Russell left Brixton in a prickly and unhappy mood. His reunion with Colette was spoiled by jumping to the conclusion – wrongly as it turned out – that she had been having an affair with an American colonel whom she had met over dinner. Colette promised she would not see the colonel again; but something of the magic had been lost. There were brief autumn meetings in London, and longer and happier ones in the countryside, when they returned to their old custom of staying in pubs or small hotels and walking, interspersed with Colette's jobs in the theatre and Russell's visits to other people. Between 19 September and 20 December, he wrote her forty-four letters; she sent him thirty-four. Hers are affectionate and calm; his a see-saw of jealousy, rejection, and love.

Clifford Allen was taking months to recover his strength, having lost half a lung while in prison, and he continued to suffer from incessant headaches. When his plan to share a flat with a friend in

Overstrand Mansions in Battersea fell through, Russell offered to move in with him, leaving Colette for the time being in Bury Street, where she felt happy, despite Ottoline's decorations and hangings. From her attic she brought with her a bearskin for the bedroom floor.

Allen was delighted with the arrangement, and wrote in his diary a perceptive entry about his new flat companion. 'He is very childlike in his engrossment with his own emotions, virtues, vices, and the effect he has on other people. The oddest mixture of candour and mystery, cruelty and affection, fearless concern for constructive philosophy and enormous personal interest in attitudes to himself of other philosophers.' In the flat, they talked about peace, Russell arguing that he would like to see an indecisive military ending to the war, believing that it would produce a better post-war spirit, yet admitting that he too longed for total victory soon. One day, not long after his release from Brixton, he sat by the fire, reciting from memory, for nearly an hour, Blake's poems and Shakespeare's sonnets. 'He was like a happy child,' Allen remarked later, 'and made me realise from his tenderness and brilliant mind why, with all his waywardness, I love him so devotedly.' They also talked about marriage; Allen was not yet thirty, but feared that given his poor health he might not have very long to live; he kept saying how he longed to find a wife. To judge by a letter Russell wrote to an American magazine which enquired what he ate, the two men lived simply. Their meals, replied Russell, took a quarter of an hour for lunch and dinner, and ten minutes for breakfast, and consisted mostly of toast, rice pudding, mutton chops and stewed fruit.

That Christmas, Allen, Russell and Colette went to Devonshire, where they stayed in a thatched house on the edge of a wood, 500 feet above the sea; they could hear the sound of the waves breaking on the rocks and the cry of the gulls as they circled above. There was snow on the moors. Back in London, Colette was again beginning to get small parts, and, through Lewis Casson, played Helen in a production of Gilbert Murray's translation of Euripides' *The Trojan Women*. Murray was pleased with her performance, saying she had got the 'psychology of the scene entirely right'. Colette, watching

Sybil Thorndike as Hecuba, realised how very little she really knew about acting, and she began to look for parts in the provinces.

Russell was restless. 'This letter', he wrote to Ottoline, 'is a cry of distress . . . I find it utterly impossible to work . . . I must find some way of enduring life, or else give it up . . . The truth is I am worn out . . . I need looking after.' He asked whether he might spend four days a week at Garsington. Ottoline immediately turned over to him one of her farm cottages, though he continued to take his meals with her in the manor house. While he was still in prison, Ottoline had learned from the unwitting Miss Rinder that Russell was still having a passionate affair with Colette. She was taken aback; nothing in his fond letters to her had made this plain. But when she thought about it, she was not altogether displeased, and wrote to tell him that they could now at last begin a new chapter in their long relationship, one 'fresh and clean and purged from all the old grievances and all the sharp pins that stuck out'. Russell was not quite ready to let her go. At Garsington, dwelling fretfully on Colette's possible infidelities, he again began to vacillate between emotional intimacy with Ottoline and cool distance, sometimes telling her that the happiest hours since leaving Brixton had been those spent with her, and then reproaching her for her character and her detachment. Ottoline, while fearing that he now found her 'dull and dead and stagnant', pitied him for his obvious misery, his sense of 'loathing the world and finding it disgusting'. Russell was entering another of his customary winter patches of gloom and self-obsession.

At Garsington, there was only Ottoline to take it out on. Their relationship, far from being the 'fresh' friendship she had hoped for, was reduced to what she called their 'sparring matches'. He accused her of depressing those around her with her incessant ill health. 'He has an inevitable way of hurting one,' she wrote resignedly in her diary. What was more, her uneasy relationship with her daughter Julian had grown worse. The child, thought Ottoline, was not simply selfish, but obstinate and unsympathetic. 'It is pure mockery', she noted, 'to think children are a pleasure to one. They may be a *duty* but no pleasure.' Philip was worrying about money; Ottoline about Julian, about her looks and about being a failure; Russell about what to do with his life. Garsington was not much fun. Recuperation and adjustment, after the strange confined life in prison, was not proving as easy as he had hoped. Soon, however, he was again hard at work, on a paper he called 'On Propositions' for the Aristotelian Society, and was consequently in better temper. He also had the philosophy lectures arranged by his friends to give; he had turned them into *The Analysis of Mind*, which he had started in prison. This work marked a significant moment in his philosophical development, for Russell had now reached the conclusion that any difference between mind and matter was illusory, that 'matter' is not so material and mind not so mental as commonly supposed . . . Both mind and matter seem to be composite, and the stuff of which they are compounded lies in a sense between the two, in a sense above them both, like a common ancestor.'

Other people had, of course, fared worse than Russell from the war. Alfred Whitehead had begun by being sharply critical of Russell's position, telling him that the conscientious objectors were 'contemptible', but as the war went on and the Whiteheads came to admire his courage and his single-minded stand, if not his views, Evelyn, in particular, tried to draw Russell back to them. In January 1917, she had written him a long letter, explaining that Whitehead was irritated with him not for his views but because he seemed to have deserted all those friends who were not pacifists. He was hurt, she had added, by the fact that Russell had made no effort at all to keep in touch, even though he knew that she was frequently on her own. 'Separation is a silly game,' she had written. 'Do come here and rest for a few days. You can stay in bed, or not, as you like, but you will be with old friends who love you; don't let us talk of the war, just come . . . I am having sheets put on your bed ready, just bring your valise, don't bother to write or wire . . .'

Russell had been devoted to the two Whitehead boys, North and Eric, as small children, taking them walking in the Lake District, and had been particularly close to North when he was a student at Cambridge. When North volunteered for the army, he kept in touch with Russell, writing him affectionate letters and making no mention of their opposing positions, and when he learned of Russell's prison sentence he wrote fondly to say that he often thought of him, and that he and Eric both remembered the happy times with him. 'You have such a unique gift of making children and young people really happy and interested at the same time,' he wrote. 'I hope that I may see you often when this nightmare of a war has ended.'

In the summer of 1917, Eric, who had become a pilot, was sent on a gunnery course. On 13 March 1918, he went out on patrol with five others, each flying a single-seater plane. His friends watched as Eric dived at a two-seater enemy machine and the wings of his plane began to break up. It was the last they saw of him. A week later, Evelyn wrote to Russell: 'You loved him and gave him much joy, there was no bitterness in his heart, he loved freedom. I ache for him – Alfred clings to the Hope that is no more than a cobweb.' Lowes Dickinson, who met Evelyn at this time, found her 'grey and almost speechless'. Since Russell's letters to the Whiteheads were destroyed, there is no record of his reply.

Another relationship changed, and in this case improved, by the war, was that with his brother Frank. Frank had been deeply sympathetic about Russell's dismissal from Trinity, even if in the style of older brothers, he had cautioned him about his future: 'Don't suppose the people you meet are as earnest, as deep or as sincere as you are . . . you see what I am trying to say is that you are wasting yourself.' When Russell was in Brixton, Frank went to remarkable lengths to improve his conditions, including getting a friend to rewrite his bold handwriting in small neat letters, so as to fit more on the page, for which Russell had been exceedingly grateful, remarking to Miss Rinder that no prisoner 'can ever have had such a helpful brother'.

Once again, Frank was in matrimonial difficulties. After falling passionately and possessively in love with Elizabeth von Arnim, telling Russell that she was the 'finest, most wonderful and most loving woman in the world', he had shed the plump and slovenly Mollie. Telegraph House had been finished, and he longed to install Elizabeth there. For a while, Elizabeth hesitated. She would rather have kept him as a lover, for Frank was no longer the slim, aristocratic figure she had once known, but a corpulent, middle-aged man, with a red face, longish white hair, a mouth which tended to pout, and blue eyes too sharp to be genial. (Colette described him as a 'huge blustering pink-cheeked schoolboy'.) As Russell wrote to

Ottoline, what was holding Elizabeth back, was that 'a) he sleeps with 7 dogs on his bed. She couldn't sleep a wink in such circumstances. b) he reads Kipling aloud. c) he loves Telegraph House, which is hideous.'

When Elizabeth joined Frank on the South Downs for Christmas one year, she was evidently taken with Telegraph House, for she described it later, in an otherwise ferociously accurate and unkind book, as a pleasant place: 'Grey sky, grey water, green fields – it was all grey and green except the house which was red brick, with handsome stone facings and made, in its position, unhidden by any trees, a great splotch of vivid red in the landscape.' Elizabeth decided that she too was in love, and the couple were married on 11 February 1916, in thick yellow fog; Russell was their witness.

Even before their honeymoon was over, Frank and Elizabeth had begun to fight. Frank was a bully, prone to childish tantrums, excessively possessive and not above adulterous affairs on the side. From time to time, Elizabeth, miserable, fled abroad. She was still very beguiling. Katherine Mansfield, her cousin, described her as wearing 'a frock like a spider web, a hat like a berry – and gloves that reminded me of thistles in seed'. During one of his many wartime moves around London, Russell went to live with them in their house in Gordon Square, on which someone had scrawled 'that fucking peace crank lives here.' Elizabeth was overjoyed, saying that at last the house contained an intelligence which had not been there before; while Russell always delighted in the company of a clever and handsome woman. Later, Elizabeth wrote that Russell reminded her very much of H. G. Wells, except for his eyes, which were brown, with orange centres. Ottoline, observing the new ménage, noted in her diary that Elizabeth was 'common and vulgar'. Russell began to spend a good deal of time at Telegraph House, making Frank so jealous that he accused his wife of having an affair with his brother. (There is no evidence of this.)

Frank became truculent and obsessive, and took to having more affairs; Elizabeth became furtive and planned revenge. She and Russell jokingly talked of writing a book together, in the form of an exchange of letters between a Mr Arbuthnot and a girl called Ellen Wemyss, whom he had met in a train and lent a book to. The project foundered when Russell rather insultingly declared Ellen to be an intolerably silly girl; Elizabeth planned to ask H. G. Wells to take over.

At this point, she decided she had taken all she could of Frank. Frightened of being confronted by an irate and even violent husband, she chose a moment when he was away to hire a removals firm to take away all her furniture from both Telegraph House and Gordon Square. Finding the houses half empty on his return, Frank flew into such a rage that, despite Russell's pleas, he could not be prevented from taking his wife to court, where Frank blustered, while Elizabeth sat childlike and composed. The verdict went against him. Elizabeth was not quite done. She sat down and wrote a novel called *Vera*, a thinly disguised account of their marriage. Rebecca West, saying that it was all about a 'comic character', reviewed it as a 'triumph'. Brett snubbed it by saying it was 'drivel in cold blood'. Either way, it received immense publicity, much increased by Frank's explosions of rage and threats of libel. Russell, appalled at the blatant portrait of his brother, did what he could to calm him down, while protesting that he was not cut out for the role of go-between.

Something of the old bitterness between the two brothers now flared again. 'Why do you just for temporary gratification make yourself so thick with Elizabeth?' Frank asked accusingly. 'You know that you have never been loyal to me in any crisis of my life. Do you not think it is time you began?'

On Armistice Day, Russell found himself in Tottenham Court Road. He watched as the streets filled with crowds, and shops and offices emptied as people came out into the streets to be together and to cheer. He saw buses being commandeered by laughing passers-by. He observed how relieved everyone looked, and how very happy. Russell walked along, wondering what he, and they, had learned in four and a half years of war. 'I felt strangely solitary amid the rejoicings, like a ghost dropped by accident from some other planet.' He reflected how he had always longed to belong to a crowd, to feel a 'oneness' with a group of people, but was obliged to conclude that he had never felt he really belonged, though he had managed to delude himself, at different moments, that he was a Liberal, then a socialist, and, most recently, a pacifist. These had all been fantasies. Even writing, the most intense activity of his life, had never allowed him to escape from the pain of solitude, in which his sceptical intellect refused to fall silent. Many of his friends were among the crowd, rejoicing; he avoided them all. A letter arrived from Lowes Dickinson: 'I cannot let the day end without writing to you, as my first thoughts were of you and England . . . It is unbelievably good to write in this new world.'

Russell shared little of this euphoria. The excitement for the future which he had felt after the fall of the tsar in Russia had died away, leaving him with the mournful feeling that there were very few hopes for a better world. 'When the war was over,' he wrote later, in a mood of profound pessimism, 'I saw that all I had done had been totally useless except to myself. I had not saved a single life or shortened the war by a minute.' What infuriated him most was that so many young men had died so pointlessly. Looking for culprits, Russell identified a number of writers who, in the immediate post-war months, began to celebrate their own deeds with sentimental humbug. One of his tirades was directed against his old Cambridge friend, Edward Marsh, who had written extravagant praise about the heroism of Rupert Brooke. Despite his dislike of Brooke, Russell fulminated to Ottoline against the trivia being spouted about the glorious dead. 'Marsh is the kind of obscene philosophic insect that ventures out from its crevice in the darkness provided by the war, crawling over defenceless corpses and polluting them . . . I try so hard not to hate, but I do hate respectable liars and oppressors and corrupters of youth – I hate them with all my soul, and the war has given them a new lease of power. The young were shaking them off, but they have secured themselves by setting the young to kill each other.'

Nor did Russell feel satisfied with his pacifist efforts or the work of the pacifist movement generally. At the height of its success, the NCF had numbered about 15,000 members. About 16,000 men either appeared before a tribunal or absolutely refused to join the war machine; 1350 'absolutists' had spent the war years on 'cat-and-mouse' charges, in and out of jail, until many had fallen ill with partial blindness, psychological problems and tuberculosis, from which they never recovered. Seventy-one of these conscientious objectors were dead. Long after the armistice, pacifists were still emerging in ones and twos from Wandsworth, Brixton and Winchester prisons.

The NCF, Russell concluded, had failed in each and every one of its declared goals. The pacifists never rose up, as he had hoped, in sufficient numbers to cripple the recruitment programme; the Military Service Act had been passed and retained; absolute exemption was won for exceedingly few people; and the endless debates of the pacifists never did produce the post-war socialist movement he had hoped for. The only thing that could confidently be said was that the pacifists had entered the war a vilified minority, and ended it having won some measure of respect. 'War', Russell wrote, 'develops in almost all a certain hysteria of destruction – self-destruction, among the more generous, but still destruction. We have to stand out against the hysteria, and realise that Life, not Death (however heroic), is the source of all good.' He commented gloomily to Ottoline: 'It is clear that all that pacifists have done has been wholly useless, except to show that it is possible to remain sane and courageous even in wartime.'

The peace movement had indeed entered the war full of hope and momentarily united. It finished it quite a different animal, with some sections strengthened and some weakened. It was inevitable that, with the war over at last, people should be anxious to turn to other thoughts. When Russell agreed to stand for election as Rector of Glasgow University against Gilbert Murray and Andrew Bonar Law, on an independent pacifist ticket, he lost ignominiously with 80 votes to Bonar Law's 1073 and Murray's 726.

In November 1919, the NCF held a final meeting in the same hall in Devonshire Road where the triumphant war resisters had gathered in the spring of 1916. Four hundred delegates rose to sing 'England Arise', and to agree that what they had stood for was not so much a protest against war as the defence of freedom and the dignity of human individuality. They then voted to dissolve, leaving just three small committees to keep an eye on conscription, on the future of a pacifist union, and on military training in schools. At a dinner for 1500 on the last night, Russell so far concealed his pessimism as to declare: 'The NCF has been completely victorious in its stand for freedom not to kill or take part in killings. . . . You have won a victory for the sense of human worth.' His view had not changed: some wars were justified, but this had not been one of them. Yet he continued to admire those who had not been shaken from their ideals: 'To stand out against a war, when it comes, a man must have within himself some passion so strong and so indestructible that mass hysteria cannot touch it.' The cheers that greeted Russell's speech say something of his influence among the pacifists. For over two years he had laboured on their behalf, and had even been to prison for his beliefs. Like Allen, he gave the conscientious objectors legitimacy, confidence and self-respect. These men, for the most part young, ill-educated, desperately insecure and without any kind of political voice, had been able to see themselves as valiant and as full of common sense as their formidable leaders.

Russell was prone to complain that all his war years had been given over to the pacifists. Yet his time in Brixton had been extraordinarily prolific, providing him with the time and peace not only to read a phenomenal number of books, but to work undisturbed on an impressive number of philosophical works. During his four hours each day of general reading, he finished, in under four months, forty-six books and articles. During the same period, he started work on his *Analysis of Mind*, wrote a 10,000-word review of Dewey's *Experimental Logic*, and a further 70,000 words of his *Introduction to Mathematical Philosophy*. This became a textbook for students trying to understand *Principia Mathematica*, though it is not in fact a direct account of it, but rather an introduction to logicism and the foundation of mathematics. Russell maintained that it was not beyond the capabilities of those with no previous knowledge, with no mathematics beyond what might be acquired 'at a primary school or even at Eton', but one sceptical reviewer noted that he considered it closed to all but higher mathematicians. In 1918 he also gave his lecture series, *Philosophy of Logical Atomism*, the next step in his work on logical analysis, which owed something to Wittgenstein. This was the theory of neutral monism, found earlier in the philosophy of William James, in which minds and bodies do not differ in their intrinsic nature: the difference lies in the way that a common 'neutral' material is arranged. This common material can consist of many entities – for instance, experiences – of the same fundamental kind. Later, Russell came to reject his theory on logical atomism, believing that it did not work as he had once believed it did, as a depiction of the structure of an 'ideally adequate language'.

Between 1905 and 1919, Russell had developed and changed his views over a wide range of philosophical subjects with great rapidity. He had strengthened the empiricism of John Stuart Mill and his disciples, by providing it with a theory of meaning which drew on the resources of his newly developed mathematical logic. That was not all. The war years had seen the production of other books, which were to shape much of Russell's post-war work. *Principles of Social Reconstruction* had been published in 1916 and had been greeted as 'a great book' by the *International Journal of Ethics. Political Ideals* was a compilation of five essays arguing for a logical approach to political issues; it had appeared only in America, though most of its essays had been given as lectures in Britain. In the Chicago *Dial*, a reviewer had compared it to Rousseau's *Social Contract*, and suggested that it should become a rallying point for a future generation. 'Russell', he wrote, 'keeps something of the noble intellectuality of Huxley and Mill, but with an added declassed revolutionary spirit.' *Political Ideals* contains one of his early and most optimistic appeals to the rational side of mankind. 'If a majority in every civilised country so desired, we could, within twenty years, abolish all direct poverty, quite half the illness of the world, the whole economic slavery which binds down nine tenths of our population; we could fill the world with beauty and joy, and secure the reign of universal peace.' Within twenty years, the world would again be at war; but for Russell, this appeal was to be a linchpin of much of his popular political writing in the years to come.

There was also, of course, *Justice in Wartime*, a collection of important essays, and *Roads to Freedom*, finished as Russell was preparing to go to prison, and as the war was approaching its climax: seen as anarchist by some people – Russell was in his most anarchistic phase – and profoundly dangerous to anyone of a militaristic or nationalist bent. In the *Dial*, Russell was accused of being over-simple, of having 'an air of jejune and ideological youth', though the reviewer also marked him down as one of the 'encouraging phenomena of this disintegrating age'.

Five books; many lectures and papers; plans for future work: hardly a poor output in nearly five years of war. The war had brought Russell a new and considerable following in America, where most of his income would now come from. On his release from Brixton, he had found a vast mailbag from across the Atlantic, including a letter from the sociologist Scott Nearing, who summarised much of what the New World now felt about Russell: 'I am writing . . . to tell you how much it means to us, here across the sea, to have a man in England stand up, as you have stood up, in these impossible heroic times, and face the music of time as you have faced it.'

With the end of the war, and the younger Fellows returning to Trinity, efforts were made to reinstate Russell at Cambridge. He was not enthusiastic. A letter from Lowes Dickinson described what he would be likely to find. 'The mind and soul of young England is still best expressed by the wild-beast-roaring that surrounds a football field.' Privately, to Keynes, Dickinson expressed his disbelief that Russell could even contemplate returning. 'I feel I would rather die if I were in his position. . . .' To Lucy Donnelly, Russell observed: 'I don't think I could stand the academic atmosphere now, having tasted freedom and the joys of a dangerous life.' He wrote to Ottoline, at greater length, '. . . the people I don't trust are the philosophers (including Whitehead). They are cautious and constitutionally timid: nine out of ten hate me personally (not without reason); they consider philosophical research a foolish pursuit, only excusable when there is money in it. Before the war, I fancied that quite a lot of them thought philosophy important; now I know that most of them resemble Professors Hanky and Panky in *Erewhon Revisited.*'

Within Trinity, twenty-two people had signed a statement saying that they were not satisfied with the Council's treatment of Russell, but for the most part both the men returning from the war and those who had remained in Cambridge were keen for conciliation on all sides. In 1919 a letter went to the Master, requesting that Russell be restored to his pre-war lectureship. Their reason, the authors of the letter explained, was twofold: they believed that Russell was now perfectly happy to put the past behind him, and they also felt that it would do much to promote the unity of the college, which had been fragmented by the whole episode. One of the signatories was Whitehead, who continued to be anguished by the affair, and wrote long and rather touching letters while he hesitated. (He eventually signed, when it was clear that Russell was going to be reinstated.) There were, none the less, a number of Fellows who felt far from forgiving. One of these was McTaggart, who went on voting against the reinstatement of conscientious objectors long after the war was over.

In the end, a decision was made to reinstate Russell, though the Fellows agreed that they would not as a body admit guilt for his dismissal. He was offered not a Fellowship but a return to his pre-war position: a lectureship, at a salary of 250 guineas a year. Russell did not go back to Cambridge. He gave as his reasons a series of long journeys he planned to make abroad; then, later, personal complications. Some of his old Cambridge supporters, like G. H. Hardy, who had campaigned so tenaciously on his behalf, begged him to come back, if only briefly, to lay to rest the ghost of Trinity's vindictiveness, and the quarrel which had done such damage to its reputation. He refused.

In 1919, the world was a very different place. Pre-war England, in which Russell had grown up comfortably, with its ruling class, privileges and comforts, had disappeared. A tougher, more egalitarian way of life had taken its place. Russell, too, had altered. The 'non-supernatural Faust for whom Mephistopheles was represented by the Great War' had become a changed man. The Liberal Party had been destroyed, but the Labour Party no longer seemed to him capable of exercising any decisive influence in the interests either of socialism or of peace. During the five years of war, Russell had acquired both a new philosophy and a new youth. 'I had got rid of the don and the Puritan. I had learned an understanding of instinctive processes which I had not possessed before, and I had acquired a certain poise from having stood so long alone.' He confessed to Ottoline, 'I used to be afraid of myself and the darker side of my instincts; now I am not. You began that, and the war completed it.'

Russell had started out the war as an academic, a philosopher who, more than any other, extolled the powers of reason, morality and truthfulness, with little regard for the frailties and prevarications of weaker people. Among the pacifists, he had met young men of a kind he had never come into contact with before, who touched him by their courage and suffering even when he did not agree with their views. A small, respectful and admiring audience of philosophers had been replaced, on both sides of the Atlantic, by a great new popular band of admirers. That they were ordinary men and women rather than brilliant students in ivory towers pleased him particularly, since he planned to help people understand what was wrong with the current political system, and make them demand improvements, by combining theory with practice, philosophy with politics.

Much is made of the fact that the First World War brought Russell into close contact with a new group of people. But was he closer to the pacifists than he had been to the Apostles, or to his Bloomsbury friends at Garsington? How close had he actually been to Fenner Brockway, or Grubb, or Catherine Marshall? Certainly, by the time the war ended, he was rapidly on the way to becoming, by his own choice as well as by circumstances, an outsider; and he was to remain one for the rest of his long life. Most of his pre-war friends had moved, or were now moving, in directions of their own: academics to new posts, Whitehead to London and then to America. Acquaintances like Shaw or Wells, with whom he had at moments of crisis united against the follies of the war and the philistine world, now drifted away. Apart from their stand, they had little in common. His affair with Ottoline, at last, was over; that with Colette in eclipse.

As for the Apostles, they had always preferred Moore, with his lack of personal ambition and vulgarity. Russell was neither as pure nor as nice. He was as clever, probably more so, but he was different from them, and he became more different after the war.

Bloomsbury, which according to Virginia Woolf had 'vanished like the morning mist' at the outbreak of war, was to come alive again, with the same, albeit somewhat changed members. There had been a break in time, 'between the acts', but that was all. Bloomsbury had shared Russell's stand against the war, his belief that the slaughter was senseless, and that one had to practise sanity and reason at a time of widespread hysteria, respect things of the spirit and remain convinced that the inner soul is more important than material possessions. But in other ways he was not one of their number. Most of them were against engaging themselves in the social and political issues of the day: for Russell, there was no other course. Nor did he ever really come to appreciate pictures or fine design. They felt uneasy because he had greater abilities than theirs, and they could not mock him. As his friendship with Ottoline waned, he saw less of them. For the members of Bloomsbury the twenties were good years: their views on the war came to be shared by many, and were celebrated in poetry and art; their tone of irreverence and irony was more widely accepted, and Victorian sexual morality, which they had seemed to transgress so blatantly, was on the wane.

Russell was not unaware of these changes in himself, particularly when his relationship with the good-natured Allen seemed to sour as a result of his irritable and dismissive manner. 'It seems', he said perceptively to Allen one day, apologising for his fractious behaviour, 'I can only be kind when I'm unhappy. If I'm well and happy, I'm boisterous and cruel.' He was nearly fifty, with no money, no wife and no children, and there was much that he still wanted to do. 'I cannot believe there is any goodness or beauty in the core of the world,' he wrote to Ottoline. 'I think whatever goodness or beauty there is *we* must put in . . . Hatred of some sort is quite necessary . . . I *will not* be turned aside from pursuing the things I think good . . . pride is the only unfailing prop . . . without some admixture of hate one becomes too soft and loses energy. . . . Ambition is oddly renewed in me . . . I feel only on the threshold of the work I want to do . . . vast schemes I have . . .'

By 1919, Russell was in too much of a hurry to look back on a past which was rapidly becoming remote.

Twelve

Two things in the world,
or three

In the summer of 1919, Russell and a mathematician called J. E. Littlewood rented a farmhouse at Lulworth, on the Dorset coast, and for Russell the next three months were very happy. Visitors came and went, while the party was looked after by the farmer's wife. On hot days, they swam, and Littlewood, a keen mountaineer, sought out cliffs along the shore to climb. In the mornings, the men worked; over meals they talked, about such matters as relativity, and speculated whether the distance from the farmhouse was the same as the distance back. They were never able to agree. Or they would discuss the differences between induction and deduction, and how one could never be certain that the sun would rise again the next day. In the afternoons, they walked; in the evenings, after dinner and more philosophical talk, they read aloud to each other from Chekhov. Allen, a frequent visitor, willingly took over the darning from any woman visitor while she took her turn to read. It was often very hot, and Russell, always delighted and soothed by a view, would remember all his life the wide, empty stretches of coastline he could see from the window.

One of the first visitors to Lulworth was Dora Black, a Girton graduate of twenty-four, with a first-class degree, and a close friend of Russell's pupil, the mathematician Dorothy Wrinch. She was the daughter of Sir Frederick Black, a prominent Liberal and civil servant working for the Admiralty, and a great friend of C. K. Ogden of the *Cambridge Magazine*. A young woman of considerable determination, she had not long before challenged H. G. Wells on his pro-war articles, and finally walked all the way from London to Dunmow in Essex to beard him in his home on a day when no trains were running. Russell had been introduced to Dora in 1916, when Dorothy had arranged a two-day walk over the downs near Guildford, staying the night with Bob and Elizabeth Trevelyan. Over lunch, up on the downs, Russell had set fire to the strawberry basket to prove that there is no such thing as a constant appearance of anything. Dora, like many of her generation an admirer of Russell's pacifist stand, noted, as Norbert Wiener once had, that he reminded her of the Mad Hatter, with his 'large sharp nose and small odd chin and prominent upper lip' and his impetuous energy.

In June 1919, they met again in London when Dora brought him a small folding table he had been wanting from Cambridge, and found him sitting in a silk dressing gown, nursing a broken collar bone, the result of tripping while running to catch a bus. This time, they discussed not philosophy but children. To his surprise, the emancipated Dora declared that she firmly intended to have children, and went on to say that they were the concern of mothers only. Russell laughed, protesting that he for one would never marry her.

In the three years since their first meeting, Dora had changed greatly. Gone were the boned corsets and black lacings to show off the small waist, the long skirts and large hats. Influenced by Roger Fry, the Omega Workshop and the Bloomsbury parties at which she was an occasional guest, Dora was now wearing cretonne peasant-style pinafore dresses in vivid colours over bright blouses. Like Russell, she had been jolted sharply to the left by the Russian revolution. She too was questioning the established moral order, and readily admitted to having lost her virginity to the captain of a merchant ship which had taken her and her father to America. She had accompanied him as his secretary on a mission to ask the United States government to reroute their tankers across the Atlantic, the British navy being low on oil. (She was later awarded an MBE for her journey to America at the height of the war.)

Dora was unlike the other women who had seriously attracted Russell: she was a suffragist and a feminist, highly educated and conscious of her own intelligence, and of the vast horizons opening up for women in the post-war world. She was argumentative, opinionated, full of curiosity about ideas and pretty rather than beautiful, a small woman with red hair pinned up in cartwheels over her ears. She and Russell, furthermore, had much in common: they had been incensed about the war, and were now fulminating about the brutality of capitalism; and they both viewed their own futures with energy. Russell invited Dora to Lulworth.

That summer, she was in the process of deciding whether to take up a Fellowship at Girton or to explore the real love of her life, theatre and singing. Either way, she had no immediate plans for anything other than a career. But she was rapidly captivated by Russell, laughing affectionately at the way his feet turned out when he walked and his grey hair stood up in the wind. If she was daunted, it was by his age – Russell was in his late forties – and she feared that if she became involved she might end up looking after him in his old age. After a series of funny, affectionate, pressing letters, many of them with amusing little sketches in the margins showing Russell becoming fat and lazy in the sun, and limericks about each other, she agreed to visit the farm.

Soon, they were walking alone together along the beach, sometimes taking out a boat and swimming naked; she pulled his hair, and said that he had the face of a goblin. 'Life is good here,' she wrote to C. K. Ogden, 'so happy that we fear the Gods and want to cast rings into the sea like that fellow Polycrates ... There is something grand about B., to which one responds, dropping all cheapness away. This place is rather like the Palace of Truth, when people come here, their real selves show and it's sad for them if they haven't any real selves ...' Into this pleasurable interlude dropped a telegram announcing Colette's arrival. Dora returned to London.

Russell's affair with Colette was not over. Kept alive not only by her elusiveness, which made him pursue her all the more, but also by a very real and lasting attachment, it continued to haunt and tempt him all through the summer and autumn months. When Colette was with him, he loved her; when she left, he wrote her anguished and passionate letters, as loving as any he had written to her before. There can be, he told her at the end of July, 'no parting short of death – life without you is become to me a thing unimaginable in its lonely terror.' After Dora's abrupt departure, in remembrance of their happy days together, he gave her a small diamond arrow. She gave him a gold coin to wear with his watch chain, on which she had engraved the words: 'Car, chaque jour, je t'aime davantage. Aujourd hui plus que hier, et bien moins que demain.' The trouble was that he now loved Dora too. As with other relationships, other revelations, he could not resist a casual allusion to 'Miss Black'. She was nice, he told Colette, but it was highly unlikely that he would ever have an affair with her; she lacked 'wildness'.

Russell's letters to Dora of the same period are missing. But her replies show how loving his letters must have been, and how insistent he felt about a continuing relationship.

> July 20 1919: I am numb with so much joy . . . I feel that my roots have gone down into you & that I really have a place in you.
> August 29 1919: You were the first man I met who drew that whole-hearted worship out of me.

At the end of the summer, Dora went off to Paris to do research into the origins of French free-thinking philosophy in the seventeenth and eighteenth centuries. To what must have been more passionate declarations of love from Russell, she replied cautiously, saying that her freedom was vital to her, 'I still have that queer savage pride that doesn't want you to have the whole of me, a sort of truculent socialism that hates to feel bad hurts can come from or through some one person.' She began to enjoy Paris, reading Proust while smoking a pipe in front of an open fire in her attic, and writing her letters to Russell seated on a bench in the Luxembourg gardens.

Russell, now back from Lulworth and in the Battersea flat he shared with Allen, was clearly in a growing state of confusion. In a memorandum to himself, written on 8 October, he set out his dilemma. It is a typical Russell document: lucid, perceptive, truthful and slightly chilling – all aspects of his mind and character that would allow him to remain both formidable and full of curiosity until his death. 'It is clear that unless, before very long, I decide between Dora and Colette, they will both find the strain intolerable and throw me over . . . For myself and my work . . . the best solution would be to abandon Dora and marry Colette. This would produce a life which would probably be happy, and without so much nervous strain as to make creative work difficult. . . . The fundamental fact remains that I love Colette too much to be able to face life without her. If I had finally broken with her, I might find absolutely everything dust and ashes and might be driven ultimately to suicide . . . By the end of the winter I shall know better what we all feel about it. At present I find it impossible to reach any decision.'

Russell wrote as if the decision were entirely his. He may well have been right, for both women were prepared to abandon if not their work, at least their freedom to him. By now, each knew about the other and, in the way of the times, kept up a pretence of being extremely generous, writing to Russell to say how clearly they understood his need for separate friends and for independence. However, Dora did remark: 'If Colette and I are still balanced in your heart, like the tea or the toast, you and I cannot build.' Their letters to other friends show a somewhat different picture, with both women apprehensive, jealous of each other, and fearful of what might happen. In later years, and particularly in his autobiography, Russell was prone to minimise the affection he felt for Colette at this time: his letters are proof of the contrary.

On 4 December, Russell left for The Hague, where he was to meet Wittgenstein, after six years' separation. During the last year of war, Wittgenstein, having miraculously survived a spell as lookout on the Russian front, before being made lieutenant in a mountain artillery regiment, had been taken prisoner, together with some 500,000 others, and sent to a camp at Monte Cassino, in southern Italy. He had been captured with a copy of a manuscript entitled *Logisch-Philosophische Abhandlung*, later translated as *Tractatus Logico-Philosophicus*, in his knapsack. He had managed to keep hold of it, and eventually send copies to Russell, Keynes and Frege. Finally, he believed, he had solved their philosophical problems; his only worry was that no one would understand him. On his release, he had given away the fortune his father had left him in his will. He now wrote to Russell: 'I suppose it would be impossible for you to come and see me here? Or perhaps you think it's a colossal cheek of me even to think such a thing. But if you were at the other end of the world and I *could* come to you I would do it.' Frege, in his seventies and with not long to live, had not, apparently, seen the point of his work; his one hope now lay in Russell, who had received it while at Garsington attempting to finish *The Analysis of Mind*.

As a former enemy alien, Wittgenstein was still not allowed to travel to England; he was also now almost destitute, so that Russell offered to buy his furniture and books, which had been stored with a Cambridge furniture dealer, and sent him £80 to enable him to come as far as The Hague. Before leaving for Holland, he read through Wittgenstein's manuscript twice. 'I am sure you are right in thinking the book of first class importance,' he wrote back. 'But in places it is obscure through brevity. I have a most intense desire to see you, to talk it over . . .' By late autumn, the various visas had been sorted out. The plan was for the two men to meet at the Hôtel des Deux Villes in The Hague (where Russell and Alys had spent their honeymoon), and spend a few days discussing Wittgenstein's work. Russell would then take it back to London and try to find a publisher. Russell took Dora with him, as he revealed casually in a letter to Colette.

The two men greeted one another with fondness, the pre-war unpleasantness forgotten. (Dora was overpowered by Wittgenstein, saying later that she fled from him 'like the devil from Holy Water, or else like one weak in faith from a severe temptation'.) Russell was shocked and touched to discover that, despite the winter cold, Wittgenstein had no coat, only a thin mackintosh. To Colette, he reported that he found the Austrian philosopher just the same as before the war, very affectionate and perhaps even a bit saner than he had been in 1913. 'He came before I was up, & hammered on my door till I woke. Since then he has talked logic without ceasing for four hours . . .'

By 16 December, they had been through every point in the book, an intensely complicated work concerned primarily with language as a 'representing medium', a means of conveying how things are in the world. To put it very simply, Wittgenstein had set down what *must* be true of the world and of language, in order to make such representation possible. The world is thus a totality of facts, states of affairs or the existence of certain situations. Facts can be more or less complex, but the theoretical, and in practice probably unattainable, limit of analysis would be 'atomic facts', which cannot be analysed into anything simpler, and which are virtually independent. All propositions, Wittgenstein went on to say, consist of what he called 'pictures'. He was so 'full of logic', Russell complained, 'that I can hardly get him to talk about anything personal.' Wittgenstein was to speak of the 'truth of the thoughts' set out in the *Tractatus*, as 'unassailable and definite', the 'final solution' to the problems of philosophy. The *Tractatus*, in its final form, was a distillation of all Wittgenstein's work since his arrival in Cambridge in 1911. The meaning of the book, Wittgenstein had written in his most famous last line, 'can be summed up as follows. What can be said at all can be said clearly, and whereof one cannot speak thereof one must be silent.' Central to it was Wittgenstein's abiding interest in the scope and limits of language, and the consequences for a philosopher of the fact that he is, inevitably, a user of this common language and thus bound by its limits.

In the years they had been apart, Russell's own philosophy had undergone profound changes, developing with extraordinary rapidity over a wide range of subjects, though much of his concern had been with the philosophy of logic and mind. *The Philosophy of Logical Atomism*, given in 1918 as a series of lectures, was a culmination of several years' work. Like Wittgenstein, Russell assumed a correspondence between the structure of the world and the structure of language. Facts were needed to give propositions, or sentences, something to reflect. Yet the two philosophers were basically very far apart, Russell maintaining that either philosophy could, or could not, solve problems, Wittgenstein believing that solutions were not the only way of coming to terms with the universe, and incorporating into his work 'mystic ardour' which Russell increasingly disliked.

Later, Wittgenstein was to speak of philosophers showing the 'fly the way out of the fly bottle'. Given the extreme complexity of his reasoning, which made him one of the most obscure and challenging of modern philosophers, it was not altogether surprising that there were those who declared that, far from showing anyone the way out of a bottle, Wittgenstein himself was trapped inside, unable to escape. It was in this spirit, of emotional goodwill but growing intellectual misunderstanding, that the two men talked. Wittgenstein, for his part, continued to have grave doubts about the meeting, having been disappointed by Russell's recent work and fearing that he was unlikely to understand the *Tractatus*, with which he had done, he believed, all that a philosopher could do. He was only partly mollified when Russell tried to reassure him: 'Don't be discouraged. You will be understood in the end.' It was only later that he came to see the *Tractatus*'s account of language as over-simplified.

One morning, Dora came in to find them sitting at a table and looking at a sheet of paper, on which were two or three heavy pencil lines. She asked if that was all they had to show for their entire morning's work? 'Ah,' they replied, 'we have been discussing whether there are two things in the world, or three.' 'He is glorious and wonderful,' reported Russell, 'with a passionate purity I have never seen equalled.' It was only later that all this closeness was to change, reducing their relationship once again to acrimony.

Before leaving, Russell offered to write an introduction to the *Tractatus,* to elucidate Wittgenstein's more difficult points. It was an offer Wittgenstein was pleased to accept, given that he was having trouble finding a publisher and that Russell was now a best-selling author. Even so, he was doubtful; it was not only that Russell seemed to refuse to accept what Wittgenstein considered the main thrust of the book, namely the doctrine that what cannot be *said* by propositions can be *shown*, but he remained uncertain about how much Russell actually understood him. In the event, he was right to be worried. When Russell's introduction arrived, Wittgenstein was horrified. He disagreed both with the nature of Russell's criticisms and with his rendering of the text. 'All the refinement of your English style', he complained bitterly in a letter, 'was, obviously, lost in the translation and what remained was superficiality and misunderstanding.'

With Dora, marriage was once again under discussion. She continued to hesitate, but decided to do nothing to stop getting pregnant. Russell 'is a terror', she complained to Ogden. 'Rages like a small boy in a temper when I refuse to marry him. Og, do you think I could bear country life and a domestic tyrant? . . . I don't want to give all my life to love, whether it's in affairs or marriage, it's indecent. If only we were certain of a child.' To Russell, she was more tender: 'I long to bear your child . . . Is all this clear to you? I *do* want you, o I *do* want you. I wish I could marry you tomorrow.' Evidently they had both come to think that a baby would settle their indecision, and that Providence – or 'Provy' – would lend a hand. When this did not happen at once, Dora wrote mournfully to Russell: 'Provy has certainly changed her mind, we let her see too soon how happy it would have made us . . . I am quite heart broken . . . It is too cruel . . .'

Russell, irked by Dora's resistance, went off to spend Christmas with Colette and Clifford Allen, leaving her to return alone to Paris. Colette was in an unhappy frame of mind, worrying about her failures as an actress, trying her hand at writing, with which Russell helped her, and often ill. Russell accused her of detachment. There were several references to her 'problems' which she would not let Russell share – possibly another abortion. Love letters from him to her now alternated with ones about Dora, in which he reproached Colette for refusing to have his child, but insisted that if she were prepared to leave him any room for hope, he would involve himself no deeper with Miss Black. In the weeks that followed, the emotional see-saw tipped up and down: as relations with 'Miss Black' went from bad to worse, because of her jealousy and her fury at being considered a promising secretary for him – 'I wanted a League of Nations, not warfare, or conqueror and conquered' – so those with Colette blossomed. 'For me,' she wrote, 'there's only one fixed star shining through the darkness of the world.' When Colette again withdrew, Russell swung back to Dora, who never made any secret of the fact that she found him physically attractive. Both women remained remarkably calm.

In the spring of 1920, on his way to give some lectures at the Catalan University of Barcelona, Russell stopped in Paris. He was thinking of joining a delegation to Russia, to see for himself what had happened since the revolution. Dora travelled on south with him: it was her first taste of the Mediterranean, and they took a brief holiday in Majorca. ('I don't know how to go on living,' Russell wrote to Colette, 'it all seems purposeless and futile without you'.) While there, according to Dora's memoirs, she and Russell discussed going to Russia together, and though she felt 'cautious', she agreed, and began to prepare for the trip, speculating about what clothes to wear, having some stout walking shoes made and taking lessons in Russian. Back in London, Russell learned that he had been invited to join a Labour delegation. Hearing that there was typhus in Russia, he insisted that he go alone; Dora, as determined by nature as Russell, argued that she should go, and complained that he had decided to leave her behind because he would have better opportunities to see the things he wanted with the delegation. 'I still think I was right,' Russell commented many years later, 'and she thinks she was right.' 'I knew', wrote Dora, in the first volume of her autobiography, *The Tamarisk Tree*, 'that this was the decisive moment in our relationship.' She was not blind to his drawbacks. But, more forceful and independent than either Colette or Ottoline, she fought back when he grew didactic and bossy. She told him that she would not be 'terrorised' into 'surrender', or become his secretary or 'nice placid stupid attentive and thoroughly obedient wife' or turn into his plaything or sofa-cushion. 'If I cannot be your comrade then it is no use loving you at all.'

Russell wrote to Colette at the end of February 1920: 'I have made it up with Miss Black. You give me so little now-a-days that I must find consolation . . . I am as fond of her as I can be of anyone while I care so deeply for you . . . Dora loves me, I love you, you love Casson, he loves his wife . . . Where is happiness to be found in all this chain? . . . My heart is yours, always and irrevocably.'

The knot was almost untied. Dora, trying hard to get pregnant, seemed to have accepted that, for the moment, she would exchange freedom for a degree of domesticity. Colette, her mind set against children, but not quite prepared to relinquish her career, received the news with sadness. 'I'm alone,' she wrote to him bleakly, 'existence is painful, and it takes considerable effort not to go under.' Russell spent his last night in England with her. During the day, they went walking, as they so often had, on the Sussex Downs. 'I suppose you wouldn't come to Russia?' Russell asked. Colette shook her head. 'I suppose you wouldn't chuck Russia and come on tour?' They stayed the night at the St Pancras station hotel.

*

Although both the February and the October revolutions in Russia had been greeted by the British political left with enthusiasm, there was still much confusion in people's minds about what, precisely, had been achieved. On 10 October 1919, at a specially convened meeting, the Trades Union Congress called on the British government to send an independent and impartial group of people to investigate the 'industrial, economic and political conditions of Russia'. The party was to consist of Mrs Snowden, wife of the pacifist Philip Snowden, Clifford Allen, several trade-union officials and a doctor called Haden Guest. Russell had applied to join the official delegation, in a personal capacity. They set sail from Newcastle on 27 April 1920. They were going to a country suffering the effects of civil war, with increasing famine and with the Red Army fighting the last pockets of the anti-Bolsheviks. The revolution of October 1917 had brought in a Council of People's Commissars as the executive body; Lenin had moved the capital from Petrograd to Moscow, and workers had been given control of factories. The treaty of Brest-Litovsk had brought an end to the war against the Germans, but many governments – including Britain – continued to withhold recognition of the Soviet regime.

The delegation was a curious and not altogether harmonious collection of people, and their expectations and reactions varied enormously. For Russell, the expedition was largely a voyage of personal enquiry, to satisfy his enthusiasm for the Russian Revolution. Disgusted by the war stance of the western leaders, Russell had approved of the Bolsheviks' decision to get out of the war as fast as they could and was prepared to overlook Lenin's autocratic measures. 'I know', he wrote to Colette not long before setting out, 'that no good thing is achieved without fighting, and without ruthlessness and organisation and discipline. I know that for collective action the individual must be turned into a machine.' Russell wanted to see the revolution at work.

The party reached Stockholm on 5 May, to find that Maxim Litvinov, the Soviet representative in Sweden, was still hesitating about issuing the British philosopher with a visa for Russia despite the fact that he and Russell had been fellow prisoners in Brixton. Once this had been settled, they travelled on to the frontier, where the delegates sang the 'Internationale'. They reached Petrograd at three o'clock in the morning, to be met by vast crowds, and were driven to a palace on the banks of the Neva, that had belonged to the mistress of a former tsarist minister, where they were welcomed by their trade-union hosts. Russell reported jocularly to Colette: 'I came prepared for physical hardship, discomfort, dust and hunger . . . Since crossing the frontier . . . I have had two feasts and a good breakfast, several first-class cigars, and a night in a sumptuous bedroom . . . Cynicism is called for, but I am strongly moved, and find cynicism difficult . . .'

At first, Petrograd seemed to Russell a very fine city, though he soon saw that it was actually in severe decline. Its former population of some two and a half million was down to less than a million. People in the streets looked hungry, dirty, and ill-dressed, and many of the women had their hair shaved to their skulls after the typhus epidemic. Dysentery, plague, malaria, scurvy, cholera and smallpox were rampant. Although the delegation had, by mutual agreement, brought only their oldest and shabbiest clothes, they none the less found themselves surrounded by envious crowds. They had been given to understand that they would be free to wander where they wished. This turned out to be perfectly true, except that wherever they went they were accompanied by officials in order, they were told, to have an interpreter on hand and to protect them from attack by counter-revolutionaries and Polish spies with bombs. They were never alone. All the same Russell, during these early days, was impressed: '. . . they are full of joy of life and a certain strange creative energy,' he wrote in his journal, 'unlike anything I have seen before.'

During the next few days, Russell went to the opera, attended a pageant re-enacting the fall of the tsar played on the steps of what had once been the stock exchange, talked to trade unionists and called on members of the Petrograd Mathematical Society. He discovered that these distinguished men were living in freezing houses, and were often hungry, but they said that the austerity was due simply to the war, and accepted the need for the rigid prevailing orthodoxy. They added, however, that possibilities for academic research had never been better, and that they were being allowed to teach things previously banned. Russell went to see Maxim Gorky, who was ill in bed and very miserable, in a cold flat full of magnificent Chinese porcelain and tapestries. Through incessant bouts of coughing, Gorky begged Russell to tell the world the extent to which the country had suffered. 'I felt him the most lovable and to me the most sympathetic of all the Russians I saw,' Russell wrote later.

Five days later, they set out for Moscow, where they were installed in an hotel with bedbugs, before being swept off to the imperial box at the Opera House for a performance of *Prince Igor*. During the first interval, they were told that Trotsky – then Commissar for National Defence – was waiting to see them in the ante-room. He was just back from visiting the Red Army at the front, and wore the uniform of a serving officer. He spoke little English, but excellent French. 'Very Napoleonic expression,' Russell wrote in his diary that night, 'bright eyes, military bearing, lightning intelligence, magnetic personality. Exceedingly good looking, which surprised me. Would be irresistible to women, and an agreeable lover while his passion lasted. I felt a vein of gay, good humour, so long as he was not crossed in any way. Ruthless, not cruel. Admirable wavy hair. Vanity even greater than love of power.' Trotsky followed the delegates back into their box, whereupon the audience rose and cheered, while he 'stood in Napoleonic attitude'. 'Conversation', concluded Russell, 'banal.'

When not meeting Bolshevik leaders, or being introduced to such figures as the anarchist Emma Goldman, Russell walked about the streets. For all its lesser beauty, he much preferred Moscow to Petrograd. He liked the churches, he enjoyed stopping and talking to passers-by, and he was impressed by the fact that there was no drunkenness and very little crime. Yet he also thought conditions hard for ordinary people who, he was told, frequently had to hold two jobs to earn enough money for their families to eat. Moscow, he decided, was neither as horrible as the Northcliffe newspapers claimed nor as delightful as the young socialists pretended, while the life of its inhabitants, compared to that of Londoners, was 'drab, monotonous and depressed'.

Whenever he could, he avoided the interminable entertainments, speeches and military reviews. One of the delegation later described him as having been somewhat aloof from the rest of the party, and unable to mix easily with the 'proletariat.' Russell, she wrote, took notes industriously but lacked the journalist's capacity for minute observation. But if he was not a very acute observer of place, Russell was a meticulous reporter of talk, noting down in his journal in great detail the conversations he had, down to exact words. He spoke to Kamenev, president of the Moscow soviet, with whom he discussed the Muslim population and speculated whether the Russian system of bringing members of the Muslim community to Moscow to study, and then sending them home to 'spread the light', might not be effective for India; to the Mensheviks; and to a group of Tolstoyans about the treatment of conscientious objectors in war, hearing that fifteen had been shot for pacifism not long before. All these conversations were carefully recorded in his journal. 'In order to understand what I was seeing,' he told Colette later, 'I emptied myself of my own personality and made myself merely receptive' – a mental knack he found useful all his life in achieving the objectivity he considered essential.

On the afternoon of 19 May, Russell was taken to see Lenin. Apart from Allen, he was the only delegate to see him alone. While they talked, Lenin went on sitting for his bust to a sculptor, and Russell noticed that every entrance to the room was guarded by a sentry. They spoke in English, which Lenin knew well. He struck Russell as small, with a fringe of reddish hair and a tiny red beard, a large mouth and thick lips. His eyes were red-brown and twinkled merrily. 'He is friendly and apparently simple, entirely without a trace of hauteur. . . . Nothing in his manner or bearing suggests the man who has power. He laughs a great deal; at first, his laugh seems merely friendly and jolly, but gradually one finds it grim. He is dictatorial, calm, incapable of fear, devoid of self-seeking, an embodied theory.' Russell asked the Russian leader what he knew of conditions in Britain, to which Lenin replied that there was little chance of a revolution. When Russell observed that even were there to be a revolution, it would certainly take place without bloodshed, Lenin waved the notion aside as fantastic. 'I got little impression', Russell remarked, 'of knowledge or psychological imagination.'

Lenin went on to discuss dictatorship and the differences between poor and rich peasants, and laughed about the exchange they were compelled to make 'of food for paper'. 'I think', concluded a disenchanted Russell, 'if I had met Lenin without knowing who he was I should not have guessed that he was a great man, but I should have thought of him as an opinionated professor . . . He has as little love of liberty as the men who suffered under Diocletian and retaliated (on heretical Xtians) when they acquired power.' Robert Bruce Lockhart had remarked not long before that Lenin made him think of a provincial grocer rather than a leader of men. It seems that Russell, before leaving, may have presented Lenin with a copy of *Principles of Social Reconstruction*, as it was later on his shelves, together with Shaw's *Back to Methuselah*; Stalin was later to devote an entire shelf in his study to Russell's works. Russell came away from the encounter reflecting that Lenin despised a great many people.

A six-day trip down the Volga had been planned by their hosts, starting by special train, then picking up their steamer, the SS *Bielinsky*, at Nijni-Novgorod. From its decks they watched barges floating slowly down the immense river, saw wild horses grazing on the shore and stared at the fierce-looking nomads camped at the water's edge. To Colette, Russell wrote a series of odd, almost mystical letters about the soul of Russia. One night, when the boat moored near a sandbank, he went on shore while the others slept, 'and found on the sand a strange assemblage of human beings . . . The flickering flames [of the fires] lighted up gnarled bearded faces of wild men, strong patient primitive women . . . Human beings they undoubtedly were, and yet it would have been far easier for me to grow intimate with a dog or a cat or a horse than with one of them.'

The British delegates were fascinated by what they saw, but they were not comfortable. The boat was infested with enormous black flies, so that by the end of every meal the tablecloth was a solid mass of wriggling black wings; the food was kept underneath the cloth and pulled out in sudden handfuls by the eaters before more flies settled.

Within twenty-four hours of reaching Saratov, a serious drama occurred. Clifford Allen, still sickly from his years in prison, came down with pleurisy and pneumonia, and for a while it looked as if he would die. At Saratov, where the delegates were to get off the boat and make their way back to Moscow by train, Allen was haemorrhaging and too ill to be moved, so he stayed on board to be nursed by Mrs Snowden and Haden Guest. Later, he was taken to a sanatorium in Reval in Estonia. He was by then past the worst, but very frail, and it was some weeks before he was able to travel.

The others made their way slowly back to Moscow, pausing at Astrakhan, which Russell found 'pure hell' with no drainage, stagnant water everywhere, black with mosquitoes, and mountains of excrement in the streets. After two more days in Moscow, they set off for home; they had been in Russia just over a month. On the way home they composed and sang a song:

> The people's flag is palest pink,
> It's not as red as you might think;
> We've been to see, and now we know
> They've been and changed its colour so.

Russell was delighted to leave. From Stockholm came his first real impressions of his visit, and they were extremely hostile. What he had seen had sickened him. The Bolshevik revolution had been neither pacifist nor socialist. The Bolsheviks themselves were, he told Ottoline, 'a close tyrannical bureaucracy, with a spy system more elaborate and terrible than the Tsars, and an aristocracy as insolent and unfeeling, composed of Americanised Jews'. He had found the entire visit as oppressive as a 'cope of lead'. To Colette he wrote: 'I loathed the Bolsheviks and their regime. I think there is less liberty in modern Russia than has ever existed anywhere before. I see their justification, and the way war has brought evil, but it is unspeakably horrible. I was utterly miserable there . . . I pray God I may never see any of them again. I felt too crushed and too afraid of the ubiquitous spies to write anything while I was there. I must begin now.' What Russell had come back with was a detailed appraisal of the political consequences of Bolshevism. He was to say little about the appalling conditions of everyday life, the collapsing economy, the growing famine, and the crucial shortages of medicines, anaesthetics and disinfectants. On 18 May, he had strolled around St Basil's in Moscow, hearing people complain about the cost of living. 'Just as in England,' he noted in his journal, 'discontent, but thoughtless and unpolitical'.

*

A not altogether welcome surprise awaited him in Stockholm. He found a letter from Dora, saying that she had decided after all to join him in Russia, intending to masquerade as his secretary – the very position which had seemed to outrage her at home. But she had missed him at every point in his journey. This did not stop her loving it all; she declared herself greatly impressed by Russia and its leaders. Privately, however, she was apprehensive about Russell's reactions to her escapade, confiding to her new friend 'Comrade' Reed, author of *Six Days that Shook the World*, 'I have got a very sick and panicky feeling about meeting R. again – I think everything is going to go wrong and I came here first of all in order that it might all go right. . . . If he were younger, I would feel more hopeful.'

Russell's virulent loathing of Russia was not shared by the rest of the delegation. Mrs Snowden returned to England praising the elasticity of the new government, and its readiness to turn from failure. She was convinced, she announced, that hope for the future lay in ending the Allies' blockade and promoting contacts with the outside world. 'The Russians are amongst the world's most tender dreamers,' she declared in her book, *Through Bolshevik Russia*, published later that year and hailed as a literary masterpiece. 'Humanity sorely needs their vision in this hour.' (Colette called it 'pitiful stuff: barley water laced with treacle'.) Even Allen, who while in Stockholm waiting for a boat home told a reporter from the *Morning Post* that he had hated the Bolsheviks, arrived at Liverpool station saying he believed the world had more to learn from the Russian experiment than from any other social achievement in history.

Russell was appalled. He accused Allen of indulging in self-deception, and reported to Colette: 'It is dreadful that I feel him quite a stranger to me and have no wish to be with him . . . I don't want to make people agree with me . . . I merely want to avoid those who disagree.' He was now to part company with the pro-Bolsheviks, just as he had parted from the pro-militarists during the war. 'I have returned', he told Gilbert Murray, 'more than ever a pacifist, as much against revolutionary war as against others . . . I think the future of the world depends enormously on peace with Russia – if that is got now, I believe the whole world will begin to mend, but if not, the evils of the last six years will be a trifle compared to the evils of the next six.' Allen took their breach wryly. They were, he reported to Frank's wife Elizabeth, 'like two cats fighting bitterly over Russia', especially after Russell announced that the Bolshevik leaders were dictators and disagreeably reminiscent of Cromwell's levellers. Not surprisingly, perhaps, Russell now briefly became friends with a thirty-nine-year-old Russian émigré, Vera Volkhovsky, who declared that his views were the most accurate she had heard, and fell in love with him. Russell did not return her affections, though for months she showered him with longing letters.

He retired to the comfort of Garsington, after deciding to write a book about his experiences. He told Colette, with all the bitterness of a man who realised his hopes had been proved false, that the Bolsheviks had destroyed all beauty, lacked human kindness, were completely indifferent to love or affection, and rejected free thought. Their propaganda, he said, had got on his nerves unendurably. Undaunted by a growing sense of isolation, not only from Allen and the other members of the delegation, but former friends like H. G. Wells, who refused to believe what he was saying, Russell now sat down to write. In an amazingly short space of time, *The Practice and Theory of Bolshevism* was finished.

It was a bitter attack on the methods used by the Bolsheviks to force through the transition from capitalism to socialism. Russell had always been an opponent of tsarist rule, but he now believed that what was happening under the Bolsheviks was worse. He was horrified that they did not seem to regret the loss of liberty their economic policies entailed but seemed, on the contrary, to be enjoying their power. 'I am compelled', he wrote, 'to reject Bolshevism for two reasons: first because I believe the price mankind must pay to achieve communism by Bolshevik means to be too terrible; and secondly because, even after paying the price, I do not believe the result would be what the Bolsheviks profess to desire.' He argued that the fundamental ideas of communism could still add significantly to the wellbeing of mankind, but not unless transition was handled very differently. The civilised world, he prophesied, would be bound to attempt a communist organisation of society within the next few centuries, but if it were foolish enough to use the Bolshevik model of transition, the world would relapse into the barbarism of the Dark Ages. Bolshevism could be defended as a discipline; but as an exercise in communism it was a failure. It was essential, therefore, to be honest, to tell the truth, to admit that it was all a disaster, and not, like Allen, pretend that it was all splendid.

Unlike the Webbs, who sincerely believed that what was happening in Russia was a vision of society as it should be, Russell regarded what he had seen with nothing but revulsion. Until his eighties, when first the death of Stalin, then the Cuban missile crisis and the war in Vietnam changed his views, he was to remain a ferocious critic of the Soviets, becoming ever more critical of their methods as time went by, and ever more disapproving of Lenin.

When others did not see the truth as he had, some of his friendships began to slip away. The first open and public break was, predictably, with the Webbs, who had become dedicated to what they considered to be the Soviet ideal and now attacked him in the *New Statesman*. They declared that Russell had been transformed from a revolutionary – if he ever had been one – into a 'reformer of the reformists'. His book was intellectually thin, good on journalistic descriptions but not properly thought out. He was also attacked in the Russian newspapers, which said that a little more than a month was hardly sufficient time to form such trenchant opinions, and that 'burdened down by prejudice', Russell had fumbled around the country, confusing the 'quiet speculations of the National Guildsmen in England with actual struggles of the Bolsheviks in Russia'. From the right in Britain came reproaches that his book was deeply disappointing, lacking all the rigour of his earlier works; from the left generally, a sense of betrayal. It was made worse by knowing that Dora, too, had formed very different views.

What was more, his friendship with Wittgenstein was again at a low ebb. He disliked Russell's introduction to the *Tractatus*, and talked again of suicide. 'The best for me, perhaps,' he wrote, 'would be if I could lie down one evening and not wake up again.'

With some of his friends now turning on him, and feeling uncomfortable in their company, Russell must have been delighted about the invitation he found waiting for him in London from the

Chinese Lecture Association, to lecture for a year in China. They needed an immediate decision. Russell, determined not to go without Dora, eventually tracked her down, and when she agreed cabled his acceptance. His next impulse was to get away into the country with Colette. They took a train to Rye and walked along the marshes from Appledore to Winchelsea, along a road built at the time of Napoleon.

Dora was still not back. Her letters from Russia reveal the anxiety she must have been feeling at leaving the field to Colette. 'Aristocracy is in your bones,' she wrote from Petrograd, 'and Colette is better at it.' From Russia, Russell had brought Colette a many-coloured coat, an icon and some painted boxes. They spent the little time that remained as much as possible together, managing to snatch twelve days at the fifteenth-century Mermaid Inn in Rye. The few days they were apart, they wrote loving letters to each other. They were as close as they had ever been, but both were aware that the coming separation would mark a momentous turn in their affair, particularly when Dora finally arrived back and, after arguing fiercely with Russell about the Bolsheviks, began to prepare for their departure to China.

During their days together, Russell and Colette decided to produce a book, made up of letters covering the early days of their love affair, Russell's trip to Russia and the coming year in China. (This plan came to nothing.) Before they parted, Colette, with remarkable generosity, agreed to a night of 'official adultery' in a West End hotel, so that Russell could file for a divorce from Alys.

Towards the middle of August 1920, Russell and Dora left London for Marseilles, to catch the *Portos*. Their ship was delayed by plague, so they stopped off in Paris and Dora passed the time selecting a trousseau of sorts. Just before the *Portos* sailed, Russell sent Colette a note. Having made up his disagreements with Dora over Russia, he told her, they had now become extremely close. It was very unlikely that they would ever part again.

One of the last letters to reach Russell as he waited for the *Portos* to sail was from Clifford Allen: 'Goodbye and the Lord bless you for the happiest eighteen months of my life.' It was a generous message, given their arguments about Russia; but it was a good note on which to leave.

The *Portos* was a French ship, carrying a number of Frenchmen to government appointments in the East. Whenever they could, Russell and Dora spent the night on shore, not least to escape the disapproval and pettiness of some of their fellow passengers. This became more spiteful after Russell had given a talk praising a few aspects of Bolshevik life, with the result that the British on board cabled ahead to Peking urging the consul-general to prevent a figure so dangerous from setting foot on Chinese soil. The British, Russell complained, were vulgar, the French superior, the Chinese learned, while the Dane who shared his cabin wanted to talk only about Einstein. One evening the captain held a fancy-dress party, and Russell dressed up as a Chinese philosopher of 2000 BC, Fu Ling Yu, wearing a pair of white silk women's pyjamas, a scarlet embroidered robe, a fan and Chinese slippers. On his head, he wore Dora's sewing basket, upside down; on his chin he glued a swatch of black hair, borrowed from the ship's barber. Dora, in peasant clothes, went as newly-born Bolshevik Russia, which infuriated the passengers even more. The Red Sea was almost unbearably hot: the cook died of the heat and two soldiers went mad. In Singapore, they lunched at Raffles Hotel, which reminded them powerfully of Conrad. From the Great White Horse Inn in Ipswich, Colette wrote him a sad note: 'I was twenty-five yesterday, the age when horses die.'

A few days later the *Portos* reached Saigon. It was their first real introduction to the East, to chopsticks, to the contrast between the natives and the Europeans, ferried about everywhere in rickshaws. Russell did not much care for what he saw. He found the city a 'nightmare', a mixture of Paris, with the European women superbly dressed, and Piccadilly, with its motor cars. The whites looked ill, cruel and half-mad. The place was surrounded by mosquito swamps. They stayed in Saigon four nights, and reached Hong Kong on 8 October. Here Russell was captivated; he thought the landscape the most beautiful he had ever seen, with its steep wooded hills and islands dotted around the water. It was windy and raining but deliciously cool.

When the boat docked in Shanghai three days later, there was no one to meet them. Russell and Dora stood at the rails, surrounded by a cloud of insects, laughing and wondering whether the whole thing had been a hoax. Then a crowd of officials poured up the gangway, bringing with them numerous requests for interviews and invitations to lecture. 'Professor Russell and the very intellectual Miss Black' were soon exhausted: Russell was fêted as a sage, and was assumed to have an immediate answer to every problem. He had told his Chinese hosts that he and Dora were not married, but would like to be treated as if they were. A message to that effect was published in the newspapers, and no further mention was made of their irregular relationship.

Their thoughtful hosts had planned for them to begin their Chinese stay with a holiday, and they were taken off to spend three nights at Hangchow, on the Western Lake, said to be the finest scenery in China, with densely wooded hills concealing temples and pagodas. One day, they were carried by sedan chair to a temple in a mountain of bamboo groves. 'Everywhere', Dora wrote, 'we are treated like an Emperor and Empress.' At Hangchow they were joined by Chao Yuen-ren, just back from ten years in America, who was working on a translation of *Alice in Wonderland*; he was to be Russell's interpreter for his lectures.

It was not all holiday. At Chang Sha, Russell was invited to take part in a conference on education, and gave a talk before an immense audience, while Dora spoke about art and education in Russia and about women's education. Russell's first impression was admiring: 'China makes the impression of what Europe would have become if the eighteenth century had gone till now without industrialism or the French revolution. People seem to be rational hedonists . . . They prefer enjoyment to power. People laugh a great deal in all classes, even the lowest.' To his sister-in-law Elizabeth, he wrote, in answer to her praise for his 'Bolshie' book, that it had pleased only people he hated, 'e.g. Winston & Lloyd George. I have no home on this planet. China comes nearer to one than any other place I know, because the people are not ferocious . . .'

Russell and Dora's arrival in Peking, in the autumn of 1920, coincided with the call, by a popular movement of students, the May

Fourth Movement, for a basic reform of politics, economics and society. For Chinese Marxists, the only successful model for communism lay in the Bolshevik revolution. Disillusioned with existing institutions in China, they were eager to consult westerners.

Russell had come to China at the invitation of Liang Ch'i-Ch'ao, the man responsible for the programme of foreign lecturers at the university, and of Chinputang, the Progressive Party, which was made up largely of bureaucrats and politicians. Capitalism, socialism and Marxism had all become important topics of debate, and guild socialism and syndicalism were widely discussed. Russell's political and economic views were well known in China through translations of *Roads to Freedom, The Problems of Philosophy* and *Principles of Social Reconstruction,* and Chinese liberals had long admired his view that institutions were good or bad according to how far they encouraged creativity, and that possessiveness was the 'ultimate source of war and the foundation of all ills from which the political world is suffering'. They were fast turning away from the idea that China's problems could be cured by nationalism; inner personal strength, not military strength, was the answer. Russell's rejection of syndicalism and state socialism, and his belief in guild socialism – 'autonomy within each politically important group, and a neutral authority for deciding questions involving relations between groups' – struck them as valuable, even though he had not been thinking of China when he advocated them.

Russell and Dora spent their first fortnight in Peking in an hotel, looking for somewhere to live. They were determined to find a Chinese lodging, not a flat among the expatriate community. 'Peking is beautiful,' Russell wrote to Colette, continuing their correspondence as if nothing had happened, 'with many wide spaces, trees, temples, gates and ancient walls. The weather is Indian summer, very delicious, crisp with bright sun,' though he complained that the country had at first depressed him by seeming so 'decayed and rotten, like the late Roman Empire'.

They soon found an empty house in the Chinese quarter, built around a series of courtyards, at No. 2 Sui An Po Hutung. It had a verandah and the roof was made of grey tiles. It was unfurnished, so they spent their afternoons bargaining for old Chinese cane furniture and silk for cushions in the junk shops outside the city walls, coming home one day with a dark brown redwood sofa, of a kind used by opium smokers. On the floor, they put straw matting, covered with hand-woven rugs. Among Dora's papers at the Institute for Social History in Amsterdam are many boxes of clippings, diaries, letters and accounts; poems, articles and translations, all from the year in China. On one scrap of paper is a bill for how much they spent on their matting in Peking: £7 11s for 55 yards – a considerable sum for the time. Dora filled the house with yellow jasmine, and put little fruit trees in pots in the courtyards. She had bought a camera in Shanghai and began to send photographs home to her family and friends. Before long, their interpreter Chao came to live in part of the house.

To their friends they both wrote saying how immensely happy they were. 'We live here in horrid and disgraceful luxury,' Dora wrote to Ogden. 'Four menservants and my maid for sewing and mending. Delicious rooms, warmed by sun and very efficient stoves . . . Sweet Og, I have an orange silk cloak lined with ermine. I look like a Queen in it . . .' Of her love for Russell at this time, she later wrote: 'He was lover, father-figure, teacher, a companion never at a loss for a witty rejoinder or a provoking bit of nonsense.' Russell coached her in history and on Einstein, and talked to her about his lectures, later to become *The Analysis of Matter*, and they continued to argue about Russia and industrialisation. In the evenings, they put on long Chinese robes and read aloud from books by early travellers to China.

Russell was extremely busy. The National University was in a ferment of new ideas, with its students eager for what they called the 'new learning'. They were avid for radical foreign publications, an appetite whetted by students returning from Japan and America, bringing new political theories. In Russell, they saw their mentor. Such was his renown that his picture was soon to be seen on advertisements for cigarettes, his hand held up in benediction. Unable to pronounce 'Russell', the students called him 'Luo-Su', the closest they could get, which loosely translated as 'simple oyster'. Dora remarked it perfectly conjured up his subtle and evasive way of dealing with all questions. As a further mark of reverence, a Society for the Study of Russell was founded, with a magazine called *Russell Monthly*.

Once a week, Russell lectured, following this up with a weekly seminar, held in English. Every two weeks, he took the class in Chinese, using Chao to translate. On Sundays, he ran a course in technical philosophy. He was also planning a series of lectures on social philosophy, and Dora helped him by giving lectures on political and economic theory. He also gave official lectures. The first was delivered to 1500 people, and he opened it with the words: 'I am a communist. I believe that communism, combined with developed industry, is capable of bringing to mankind more happiness and wellbeing . . .' These were later to become the basis of *The Prospects of Industrial Civilisation*. Though the original manuscript is entirely in Russell's hand, it was said to have been written jointly with Dora. The preface, also published in Chinese, shows how Russell was still trying to decide precisely where he stood politically. He took Mondays off, and he and Dora would make sandwiches and hard-boiled eggs, and take their picnic to the Temple of Heaven, together with a copy of Shakespeare and a game called Diabolo, which consisted of two sticks, string and a cotton-reel. To ward off the bitter cold of the Chinese winter, they wore heavy fur-lined coats, and Russell had a fur hat. They took exercise by skipping around their courtyards with a rope. In her free time, Dora wrote sentimental verse.

At first, Russell was not altogether impressed by his students, despite their enormous excitement about the future and their genuine desire for knowledge. He found them charming and fun to be with, and reflected wryly that they thought of him as an 'amiable old fogey, hopelessly behind the times'. But they were infuriatingly lazy, reluctant to read books, and wanted their teacher to make all the intellectual effort for them. 'Most of the students are stupid and timid,' he wrote to Colette, 'there is new intellectual life, but it is as yet very second rate. What they need is board-school teachers, not eminent professors, but all their actions are governed by swank.' Dora was more impressed. 'Young China', she wrote to her mother, 'is fresh, eager, intelligent, clear and undefiled as mountain streams.' She preferred the lower-class Chinese, claiming that the educated ones were 'soft and squashy in their minds'. The students were amazed by Dora's and Russell's unconventional attitude to marriage, and when a few of them did manage to persuade their parents to let them marry for love rather than by arrangement, they called it a 'Russell marriage'. When they got to know them better, Russell and Dora gave parties for their students, with fireworks in the main courtyard, which was heated by braziers and lit with Chinese lanterns, with singing, dancing, blindman's buff, and pinning the tail on a donkey. What the young Chinese made of all this is not known.

The foreign community irritated them both. Dora remarked that they were 'villainous or frivolous or both', and that the many missionaries, though undoubtedly good people, were also exceedingly boring. The foreigners in Peking in the early 1920s were a very mixed collection of people, from businessmen to those working for the various legations; there was also Mr Johnston, tutor to the young emperor. The Americans, though personally friendlier towards Dora and Russell than the English, were just as contemptuous of the Chinese. 'They are mostly vultures feeding on carrion,' Russell remarked, more than once. Dora observed that the Chinese got their own back by regarding the Europeans as court jesters, there merely to make them laugh. 'Europeans dash about in motor cars,' noted Russell, 'Chinese make a more stately progress in carriages with footmen standing behind, humble folk go in rickshaws.' He tended to walk everywhere for the exercise, but was invariably pursued by beggars, shivering figures in rags, shouting 'de la yen' (great old sire!). Twenty million peasants, it was said, were starving throughout the country as a result of prolonged drought, and they had taken to selling their daughters as slaves for three dollars each. When they could not get rid of them they buried them alive.

One of the few interesting foreigners was John Dewey, the American philosopher, and his wife, who were in China to reform the education system. The two men never really liked each other – Dewey was impassive, quiet, shy and not much of a conversationalist – and he was offended by the cavalier fashion in which Russell announced publicly that he was going to pay a visit to the missionaries with Dora, in order to broaden their cultural horizons. He thought Russell insensitive, with a streak of cruelty and an aristocratic disdain for other classes. To his children Dewey wrote about the gossip surrounding these 'travelling socialists'. Mrs Dewey was less censorious, and invited Russell and Dora to their house.

As time went by, Russell came to admire the openmindedness of his students, and was drawn increasingly into Chinese life, even if he remained somewhat perplexed by his own role in influencing its future. 'The Chinese community constantly remind me of Oscar Wilde in his first trial,' he wrote to Ottoline, 'when he thought wit would pull one through anything, and found himself in the grip of a great machine that cared nothing for human values . . . I would do anything to help the Chinese, but it is difficult. They are like a nation of artists, with all their good and bad points. Imagine Gertler [the painter, Mark] and John [Augustus] and Lytton set to govern the British Empire, and you will get some idea how China has been governed for 2000 years.' What he liked most about them was their understatement, their courtesy and wit, their obvious appreciation of beauty, and their gentle, contemplative natures. He was, he told Colette, 'full of beans', and reported to his sister-in-law Elizabeth that he had been 'happy for five months now, & grow more and more so'.

When he was invited to stay a further year, he hesitated. He told Colette that though he greatly enjoyed the calm and the 'time to possess one's soul and survey the world', he missed his friends, was homesick for the green countryside and the smell of rain, and feared that, like others who stayed too long in China, he would end up 'easy-going and lotus eating'. At the same time, he felt deeply uneasy about going home: 'The state of the world makes me very unhappy. Ever since I began to hate the Bolsheviks I have felt more than ever a stranger in this planet. . . . I feel civilisation is going under & one's work is futile,' an echo of the despair about the world he was to return to again and again for the rest of his life.

Early in March, Russell and Dora went with Chinese friends to a resort in the western hills above the city, to escape from the intense cold of the lecture rooms. They went swimming in a hot spring. When they returned to the hotel, Russell, who was already suffering from a mild bout of bronchitis, was shivering. Dora insisted on starting back immediately for Peking, but the car stalled and it was some time before it could be got to move again. When they reached the city, it was after sunset and the gates had been closed for the night. Chao was summoned and arrived by rickshaw to have them reopened. By now, Russell was feverish; he was taken straight to the German hospital and diagnosed as having double pneumonia.

This was long before the discovery of antibiotics; all that could be done was to wait for the crisis and hope he survived it. Towards the end of the month, despite a pneumococcus serum provided by the Rockefeller Institute, he appeared to be on the edge of death. On Easter Monday a doctor declared that there was no further hope. A deputation of students, in long black robes and caps, came to the hospital and stood bowing, with folded hands, begging to be allowed to hear the philosopher's last words. A report appeared in the *Japan Advertiser* saying that Russell was dead, and was quickly picked up by the English reporters. The news broke in London the day his divorce from Alys was supposed to come through, putting the lawyers into confusion: could a dead man be divorced? The *Sunday Express* took the occasion to publish a mocking and ranting article, in which James Douglas referred to Russell as a 'doctrinaire dreamer who spun Utopias in the vacuum of his brain', a man with 'a passion for dismal dialectics', a 'staggering view of marriage', a 'beautifully frozen mind' and 'exquisitely passionless intellectual frigidity'. Wartime hatreds remained strong. Among Colette's private papers, found after her death, was a pencilled note: 'That news broke me: a neat job, short, sharp and permanent . . . Only the mind in all its extreme agony (provided it remains intact) photographs what passes in front of it . . . Those things alone were real, more real than anything that had happened before, or has happened since: the sum total of life, photographed on your mind, cut into it, burnt into it in a moment of agony which lasts to the end of your days.'

Russell was not, however, dead. He was later to say that Dora's love and determination to keep him alive gave him the strength to struggle on. His temperature rose to 107 degrees, his heart missed beats and he was given oxygen. He coughed and coughed, and as he coughed he swore, leading his missionary nurse to assume he was calling on God for help, and to broadcast the joyful news that the atheist philosopher, in his final hours, had repented. Dora placed

violets, which he had always loved, against his nose, hoping he would
be able to smell them. Then the crisis came, and passed, and he
survived it. By April, despite a thrombosis, a kidney infection and
dysentery, he was well enough to receive gifts of cream and
champagne from the Russian delegation in Peking, and was sent
home to be nursed by Dora. He declared that he regretted not
having died in China, where he would have been buried with the
poets and emperors near the Western Lake at Hangchow.

While he was recovering, Dora discovered that she was pregnant.
The baby was due in November. To her mother, in a six-page letter
she wrote, 'We are perfectly crazy with delight and excitement.
Bertie had been, since the worry of the war, a little nervy and I
wasn't at all certain that he could have a child – also being of an old
family he thought he might have been sterile. His wife never wanted
children . . . But he of course has always longed passionately for a
child.' Poor Alys; how bitter she would have been had she known
Russell's version of their marriage. Dora urged her parents not to be
angry. 'With Bertie for a father it ought to be a very fine child
indeed. And how we shall bring it up!!' She reported that she was
feeling well, intelligent and looking 'more beautiful every day'. She
had developed a craving for olives. Russell told Allen that she was
indeed looking radiant 'like Sarah or some other old testament
woman'. For the moment, he said nothing to Colette, merely sending
her news of his recovery, written in pencil in a quavery and almost
unintelligible hand: 'When I come home, if you are willing, we can
still have times together as wonderful as the old times.' It was not
until the middle of June that he sent her word of the baby; Colette
was shrewd enough to calculate that he had known about it long
before his loving letter.

Russell took a long time to recover completely, and Dora nursed
him devotedly, winning grudging praise from the foreign community
for her dedication. As he got better, he was astonished to find how
pleased he was after all not to have died, and much touched when
he received a letter from Sanger: 'Until there was a false rumour of
your death I never really knew how *very* fond I am of you.' He also
greatly enjoyed reading his obituaries, not all of them admiring.

He had been intending to give a series of lectures in Japan on his way home, but now decided to give one only, staying in Japan for twelve days, and then heading rapidly for home. Before leaving China, Dora gave a rousing lecture of her own. Just as Russell had urged the Chinese to turn their backs on all things rotten and worthless, and insist on shaping their own future, she exhorted her audience: 'Down then, with tyranny and up with the banner of a new humanism, based on the findings of science!' Dora was learning to enjoy oratory.

Whenever the boat stopped at Japanese ports, journalists clambered on board to press for interviews. Dora was firm. 'Mr Bertrand Russell, having died according to the Japanese press, is unable to give interviews.' Russell was furious when photographers bustled forward to take their pictures, fearing for the health of the baby in the scrum. In Kobe, Russell went ashore, to visit the ancient town of Nara, and was taken to meet Kagawa, the Christian pacifist and socialist, currently leading a miners' strike. It was not a cheerful visit. Japan was tense, and there were police everywhere. Nor was the voyage itself that pleasant. Before they left China, the British legation had written to the ship's owners asking them to make certain that there would be no unpleasantness on board as a result of their not being married. Their words had no effect. Once the ship's doctor realised that Dora was pregnant, he told the rest of the passengers, who decided to shun them.

Russell was already thinking what he would write about his Chinese experience. He had admired a great deal in the Chinese character, but feared that, once they came into regular contact with the economic policies of the west, they would inevitably resort to the 'frantic militarism' of self-defence, as had happened in Japan. What he proposed, when he came to write *The Problem of China*, was that the country should try to follow an evolutionary model, and not the rapid Bolshevik one. Step by step, it should educate its citizens, industrialise, appoint a competent government and put through economic reforms, including nationalisation of the railways and mines. When it came to education, he was concerned that the Chinese should take pains to stay free of too much western influence, since, in his experience, it had made them too 'slavish'. He had also come to the conclusion that state socialism was more appropriate than guild socialism because it enabled the people to control the process of industrialisation. Above all, he urged the preservation of the admirable Chinese philosophy of life, the 'urbanity and courtesy, the candour and the pacific temper' of a nation who rightly still considered wisdom more precious than rubies. 'If Chinese reformers can have the moderation to stop when they have made China capable of self-defence,' he was to write, 'and to abstain from the further step of foreign conquest ... if they can turn aside from the materialistic activities imposed by the Powers, and devote their freedom to science and art and the inauguration of a better economic system – then China ... will have given to mankind as a whole new hope in its moment of greatest need.'

Russell's proposals for China never had much hope of success. The country was soon to embark on fifty years of violence, corruption and famine unequalled in this century; and Russia was to follow the same path. The countries Russell saw and wrote about in 1920 were soon to change beyond recognition.

By now, he had seen for himself the three places – America, Russia and China – whose interrelations were to preoccupy him for much of the rest of his life. America, Britain, France and Japan were already discussing the future of China at a conference in Washington. What worried him was that if the conference did not succeed in curbing Japanese interests, territorial aggression would lead to war and the destruction of Chinese civilisation 'not by war but by Americanisation ... America would feel they were conferring a boon in effecting this transformation, but no person with any receptivity or aesthetic sense would share their view.' Russell's views on the United States were becoming increasingly hostile. He foresaw a terrible day when China, leant on by Britain, France, Japan and America, would see its citizens turned into 'muscular Christians', and its countryside covered in YMCAs.

The Problem of China, which was published in 1921, looked well beyond Russell's experience of the country. It expressed his growing fears about industrial civilisation, which he emphasised would spoil the important things in life. 'At last I began to feel that all politics are inspired by a grinning devil, teaching the energetic and quick witted to torture submissive populations for the profit of pocket or power . . .' In the months that followed his return to Europe, Russell wrote a number of articles on this theme, mainly for American magazines, where they were seen as a challenge to those who still believed the white man was the highest product of civilisation.

Russell and Dora reached Liverpool at the end of August. It was raining hard. Lady Black came to meet them, and any awkwardness about Dora's pregnancy was dispelled by the time they got to London. Russell's divorce was coming through, largely due to Frank's insistence; once the rumours of his death had reached the solicitors they had been reluctant to pursue the matter. They went first to Clifford Allen's flat in Battersea; and then, as soon as they could, to a thatched cottage on the edge of the marshes at Winchelsea, lent to them by Dorothy Wrinch.

Thirteen

A watchman, telling of the night

Dora was often to say that she had been against getting married to Russell but that, realising how much it meant to him that any future earl be legitimate and how impossible it would be for either of them to return to the respectable academic world without marrying, she decided to capitulate. When they reached London, they discovered that the decree absolute was being hurried through so that the baby could be born in wedlock. On 27 September 1921, they were married, at Battersea registry office, with Frank and the historian Eileen Power as witnesses, after which they went off to have tea in a nearby café. Dora wore a vast, enveloping black cloak. They then set off back to Dorothy Wrinch's cottage in Winchelsea, taking Frank with them, and Dora remarked on the similarity of the two brothers' guffawing laugh. It was all very different from the chilly ceremony with Alys among the Quakers nearly twenty years before. Ottoline, who came to visit them, overheard them laughing together from very early in the morning, and concluded that they were indeed happy. 'Dora was enormous,' she wrote in her journal, 'she looks like a Swiss peasant – a healthy clear face with hard green yellow eyes but I like her and I'm sure she's Bertie's happiness.'

Rachel Brooks, a broad-minded missionary they had befriended in China, wrote to Dora telling her how she had betrayed all her vows not to marry, but Russell justified the marriage in a remarkably frank note to her, insisting that the 'fault' was his alone. Had they not married, he explained, the child might have grown up to hate them for the 'slur upon him'. What was more, given the prevailing morality, they would have had difficulty finding a house, a nanny, servants or a job. 'It is not unlikely that some peculiarly exasperating case of persecution would have driven me to murder . . . so don't let anyone be disappointed in her, *please*.'

They now needed a London home. Russell proposed taking over Clifford Allen's flat – Allen, too, was getting married – but the landlord refused to let it to him, apparently on the grounds of his wartime pacifism. Much annoyed, Russell searched for a house to buy and finally found what he wanted at 31 Sydney Street in Chelsea, though he complained to the agents that the house was filthy, full of fleas and that there were slates missing from the roof.

Within a short space of time, they moved into Sydney Street, furnishing it with the plain wooden furniture Russell had bought from Wittgenstein, who had designed it himself for his rooms in Trinity; they softened the austerity with books and with silks brought back from China. Russell took the front room, looking out over the street, as his study, placed his Voltaire bust on a strip of blue brocade on the mantelpiece, and hung what he called his ancestors, Leibniz and Spinoza, on the dining-room walls. From the street, he could be seen working at his desk.

Elizabeth, who went to call on them, found their 'snug and happy house' stuffed with 'tiny jackets and nighties and powder puffs and cradles', with Dora looking round and radiant and Russell 'perfectly blissful'. She suggested that they should ask the eminent gynaecologist, Sir Sydney Beauchamp, to deliver the baby; he took the surprising decision to induce it early, not so much for Dora's sake, apparently, as for Russell's, still frail from his illness and highly nervous. John was born on 16 November 1921 in Wittgenstein's wooden bed, to the sounds of bell practice from St Luke's Church. His jaw, dislocated by forceps, was quickly put right. As soon as Dora was well enough, Russell engaged a carriage and coachman to drive them in splendour around the streets and parks of London.

One of the first letters Russell had written on returning home had been to Colette. 'The spirit of our love is safe, but I do not know yet what to do about the body of it, and I shall not know until after the child.' This time, Colette was firm. Until then, lulled by Russell's loving letters from China, she had never quite been able to believe that he intended to make his life with Dora. When she rang in answer to his letter to fix a time for them to meet, he told her that he was not fully committed to his new wife. Two days later he received a letter from her. 'Let us now forget all that has happened,' she wrote. 'There's no new pain for me to learn . . . I shall not write again, you are not to write to me, I am your Colette.' To avoid a collapse, Colette threw herself into a series of stage parts, began writing books of her own, both novels and memoirs, published with some success, and spent as little time as she could in London, preferring the solitude of Somerset. She cut herself off from her former friends, including Clifford Allen and Elizabeth. It was four years before she heard from Russell again.

Russell was captivated by his small son. 'The little boy is lovely,' he wrote to Wittgenstein. 'At first he looked exactly like Kant, but now he looks more like a baby.' In October 1919, Joseph Conrad, whose royalties from films were at last bringing in some money, had bought a Georgian house near Canterbury. It was large, covered in creeper and surrounded by lawns. Russell asked him to be John's godfather, and proposed to give the baby a second name of Conrad. 'Of all the incredible things that come to pass, this – that there should be one day a Russell bearing mine for one of his names is surely the most marvellous,' Conrad replied, '. . . all I can say is that I am profoundly touched – more than I can express . . . I only hope that John Conrad has been born with a disposition towards indulgence which he will consistently exercise towards his parents . . .'

Conrad did not have very much longer to live. He sent Russell a number of amusing letters, giving his own views on China and challenging Russell's apparent optimism about socialism. 'I have never been able to find in any man's book or any man's talk anything convincing enough to stand up for a moment against my deep-seated sense of fatality governing this man-inhabited world,' he wrote, adding that although man had taken to flying, 'he doesn't fly like an eagle, he flies like a beetle. And you must have noticed how ugly, ridiculous and fatuous is the flight of the beetle.' Later, when Russell became more pessimistic about the world, he remarked how prescient Conrad had been. This was their last exchange. Russell caught a glimpse of Conrad in 1924, talking to a friend in a London street.

He did not want to interrupt, so walked on, saying nothing. When he heard, soon afterwards, that Conrad had died, he was mortified.

Russell now settled down to five unexpected years of happiness, based largely around his pleasure in children. Many of his earlier friends had moved away; Allen had settled in the country; the Webbs and H. G. Wells were alienated by their disapproval of his views, and the Apostles had dispersed. Wells was later to apologise saying that he had been 'rude and wicked', but that Russell 'was an entangler, and I have my cat for entanglements'. Even his friendship with Ottoline, if no less warm, was becoming more distant, and he seldom went to Garsington. Ottoline continued to hold Sunday court, but the guests were now Oxford dons and undergraduates. L. P. Hartley, Peter Quennell and Maurice Bowra had replaced Strachey, Keynes and Huxley. Ottoline was suffering from bouts of depression, insecure about these new friends, furious about Julian being so plain and difficult, and remarked in her diary, 'another year of sad travail . . .' Russell was no longer the recipient of her secrets. Nor had he kept up his once intense correspondence with Lucy Donnelly.

His friendship with Wittgenstein, too, seemed over. Through C. K. Ogden, Russell had finally found a publisher for the *Tractatus*, who was willing to run it in a series of monographs called 'The International Library of Psychology, Philosophy and Scientific Method'. Dorothy Wrinch, with whom he had left Wittgenstein's manuscript while he was in China, had also found a German publisher, who agreed to take it providing he could take Russell's introduction as well. Despite his initial pleasure at the news, Wittgenstein was furious when he saw the results, complaining bitterly that the German publishers had taken no trouble over the symbols. He and Russell met at Innsbruck, for what was to be their last encounter as friends. From the start, it was a disaster. There was nowhere to stay, and the Russells were obliged to share a small single room with Wittgenstein, who apologised miserably for his country. No one, later, could quite agree why the two men fell out. Dora claimed it was to do with philosophy, but Russell insisted that it was really about religion, and that Wittgenstein, currently in a state of religious fervour, was repelled by Russell's hostility to Christianity, as well as by his views on sexual behaviour. More importantly, perhaps, they had both been vitally changed by the war. Russell was now a socialist, and he had become more interested in finding ways of influencing governments and making the world into a safer place, while Wittgenstein had turned inwards, to ever greater introspection. They were barely to meet again. 'Wittgenstein was witty but a homosexual,' Russell told his friend Irina Strickland many years later. 'We were very close friends for a time.' That was all.

In the place of these old friends came new amusements. The Russells were living in a part of London he particularly liked, with the Sangers just around the corner in Oakley Street. There were dinner parties with friends like Arthur Waley or W. B. Yeats. Members of the 1917 Club – the Soho meeting place for liberals and members of the anti-war movement – and the Labour Party and the ILP were among visitors to the house, as were the Meynells, who ran the Nonesuch Press. Politics, sex, Freud and marriage were the favourite topics of conversation. Two memoirs of the time give enjoyable pictures of Russell in these post-war years. William Gerhardi, who met him with H. G. Wells, described his 'sensitive intelligence' shining 'in his large dark eyes. His mind was alert and ready to spot instantly some intellectual inaccuracy and put it right for you.' Only when Gerhardi, clearly intent on making trouble, mentioned Lawrence, did Russell's manner change. 'A note of intellectual fastidiousness crept into his voice, and he said: "Lawrence has no mind".' (When Gerhardi later bumped into Lawrence, he remarked provocatively on the 'lucidity, the suppleness and pliability of Russell's mind' and was amused to hear Lawrence sniff. 'Have you seen him in a bathing dress? Poor Bertie Russell! He is all Disembodied Mind.')

Virginia Woolf was more admiring. Meeting Russell at a dinner soon after the birth of John, she remarked, 'we struck out like swimmers who knew their waters. Bertie is an ... egoist, which helps matters. And then what a pleasure – this mind on springs. I got as much out of him as I could carry away.' At some point during the evening he said to her: 'If you had my brain, you would find the world a very thin, colourless place.'

Once again, Russell found himself used by a friend as an ill-disguised and not very nice character in a novel. In *Pugs and Peacocks*, Gilbert Cannan, another member of the 1917 Club, portrayed him as Melian Stokes, a famous but not greatly liked Cambridge mathematician. 'He was too disconcerting,' wrote Cannan about Melian-Russell. 'He was as abrupt in upsetting a discussion as his curiously blunt, square fingers, which he always held close together as he gesticulated. Oddly inhuman those gestures; they might have been made by an isosceles triangle.' What was there about Russell that drove so many contemporary writers – Huxley, Lawrence, Eliot, and now Cannan – to caricature him and take so few pains to disguise him?

In Dora, Russell had at last found a woman not easily intimidated by his eminence or his brillance. Recent biographers have tended to dismiss her role in Russell's life as negligible, as though she were there merely so that he could beget children. Their many letters to each other, and those to other people, as well as her private papers refute this. They bear witness to at least five years of mutual interest, respect and great affection. At first somewhat shy at the London gatherings of older, distinguished friends of her husband's, Dora quickly developed a voice of her own. It was that of a clever, thoughtful and hard-working woman, with intense interests of her own, which she was not willing to give up. What was more, at this stage in their lives, Russell and Dora were thinking very much alike: both sincerely believed that sex, love, marriage, fidelity and parenthood needed redefining to take in the vast changes wrought by the war, and both were interested not only in international politics but in the details of British political and social life. Though Russell was to say repeatedly that he did not believe women to be capable of the same heights of philosophy, he liked and admired clever women – like Alys's niece, Karin Costelloe, Dorothy Wrinch, Margaret Llewelyn Davies or Mary Sheepshanks – and maintained that they were equal to men in other things. While married to Dora, he went to considerable lengths to prove it.

Within a few months of John's birth it seemed that the baby was failing to thrive in the London air, so they decided to look for a house in the West Country where they could spend part of every year. Russell wanted somewhere open, where he could satisfy his love of views. Dora found what had been a boarding house called Sunny Bank, near Land's End, a plain brown stucco house painted dark red inside, with no electricity. They renamed it Carn Voel. 'It was a funny house,' Dora remarked later. 'From a distance it looked as if it would leap up into the air.' The views, however, were marvellous: to the south the sea, to the north a moorland hill, and to the west and east moors and open farmland. There were almost no trees. Within walking distance was a long white beach. The impression was one of barrenness and grandeur. To tame the gauntness, they made a terrace, planted a lawn and put up a porch with round pillars to remind them of China, though the plants barely survived the gusts of wind pounding in from the west and, when they did grow, lay bent over to one side. They talked of building a glass pavilion, to be called 'enjoying wind', like those they had seen in Hangchow called 'enjoying rain'.

Russell loved it. Visitors came from London, while other friends like J. E. Littlewood, who was slowly recovering from a nervous breakdown, bought themselves houses nearby. The neighbours were circumspect, though when Russell was spotted leaving the house one day in one brown and one black shoe, they became more than ever convinced of his eccentricity. In summer, the Russells crouched on the beach to escape the wind, often peering out to sea through a dense green mist, beyond which could be heard the mournful hooting of foghorns from passing ships. Whatever the weather, they walked for miles; as H. G. Wells remarked to Dora, 'those Whigs love striding over their barren moors.' It had been the fashion among Cambridge men to dress shabbily while on holiday. Russell, when walking, wore a loose flannel shirt, baggy grey trousers and a peaked cap pulled right down over his nose when the sun was bright.

There was, however, the question of work and an urgent need to earn money now that Russell was formally retired from Trinity. He had been working for some time on a pair of interlocking books of philosophy, influenced by current work in psychology and physics, having first begun to grapple with the idea of combining elements from both while in Brixton prison in 1918. In 1921, he returned again to the subject, and published *The Analysis of Mind*, begun in prison, then given as a series of lectures to his students in Peking. He had been reading the American behaviourists, who claimed that psychology could be studied with accuracy only by reducing it to what people do. 'Matter', said Russell, introducing his theory, 'is not so material and mind not so mental as is generally supposed.' Mind and matter, he now asserted, 'seem to be composite, and the stuff of which they are compounded lies in a sense between the two, in a sense above them both, like a common ancestor'. Ordinary speech, said Russell, lay at the heart of misunderstandings. When a table is said to be brown, what is assumed is that there must exist a table, of substance, while in fact all that is really known is that there is a sense-datum – that is to say a patch of colour. As he had put it three years earlier, in his lectures on logical atomism, a 'person is a certain series of experience'. Russell's intention now was to 'subject mind to the same kind of analysis as I applied to matter in *Our Knowledge of the External World*. Mind, he concluded, was a logical construction, based on 'sensations', and 'sensations' and 'sense-data' were the same.

When the book was ready, Russell jokingly suggested that it should be called 'Do men think?' or even 'I don't think', after the title 'Why men fight' given in America to his *Principles of Social Reconstruction*. Beatrice Webb, who was slowly getting over her indignation about his attacks on the Bolsheviks, declared *The Analysis of Mind* to be 'amazingly well written', but complained that Russell had an unfortunate tendency to toss provisional conclusions on to the 'scrapheap of *rejected opinions* whenever he found anything more to his taste'. Russell's willingness to rethink his position on all questions was something many of his other friends greatly admired.

Neither *The Analysis of Mind*, nor the new introduction to *Principia Mathematica* which he was working on, nor indeed any work of philosophy aimed at academics and intellectuals, was likely to bring in the kind of money Russell needed, now that he had Dora and John and two houses to support. On the other hand, *The Problems of Philosophy*, the 'shilling shocker' he had written for Gilbert Murray in 1912, and some of his wartime essays, had shown him that he had a definite talent for presenting complicated ideas simply, to appeal to a far larger public. He would try the recipe again. The 1920s and

1930s were to be filled by a remarkable stream of books and articles on happiness, marriage, education, science, freedom, and politics, his 'fugitive journalism' as he called it. (Not, however, on Confucius: when asked by a publisher to try his hand at Confucius, he replied that Confucius bored him.) Because he was such a distinguished figure, with a reputation as a thinker, he brought cachet to the progressive causes he took up. What with newspaper pieces, talks and books, there was almost no aspect of modern behaviour and modern ideas that he did not, at some time, touch upon, except, possibly, the arts, about which, despite Berenson and Alys's brother Logan, he had little to say. If the same themes tended to recur, again and again recycled from piece to piece, it should be remembered that Russell was worried about money, short of time, and much in demand by editors.

To some extent, articles and essays were Russell's natural genre, for he wrote nearly 2000 of them during his lifetime. He was a superb journalist. Their conscious brevity was ideally suited to what Santayana called the 'intensely concentrated searchlight' of his mind. Santayana was rapidly coming to despise Russell, saying that he no longer considered him a thinker, simply an amusing person: 'There is a strange mixture in him, as in his brother, of great ability and great disability; prodigious capacity and brilliance here – astonishing unconsciousness and want of perception there. They are like creatures of a species somewhat different from man.'

There could scarcely have been a better moment for Russell's particular vision. It was not only he and Dora who were seeking to alter the way they lived. People everywhere had emerged from four and a half years of war persuaded that the values which had seemed so important to the Edwardians were false, so false that they might actually have been responsible for the war. What they were looking for now was a new popular philosophy of life, leaning heavily on personal relations and creative instincts, which had echoes in Bloomsbury's rejection of conventional morality and in Moore's much repeated question: 'Is this true?' Patriotism was out, pacifism in, and with it Keynes's view that the war had been caused by the folly of politicians, while the peace was fast being lost by the ruinous terms imposed on the Germans at Versailles. A guide to the new age had to be clever, hostile to worldly success, amusing, intellectually outrageous and, above all, truthful. The future lay not in politics, but in education and psychoanalysis. What better sage than Russell?

Though other publishers were constantly trying to lure him away, and a number of his books were eventually written for other firms, it was Russell's collaboration with Stanley Unwin, who had published *Principles of Social Reconstruction*, which was largely responsible for the best-selling publications of the 1920s and 1930s. Unwin, once described as the 'most representative publisher of English books in the world', descended from a family of printers. He had started life in the shipping and insurance business, then gone to work for his step-uncle, T. Fisher Unwin, for whom he secured the Baedeker guides, before joining George Allen. His dealings with Russell were conducted almost entirely by letter. The two men seldom met. The only times they did so was when Russell had a manuscript ready, when he would call on Unwin in his office and the two men, addressing each other by their surnames, would drink a glass of sherry together. Stanley Unwin's son, Rayner, said that both men, the Victorian aristocrat and the tradesman, as Unwin insisted on labelling himself, had a precise perception of what their relationship should be.

As an author, Russell was pleasingly punctual, his manuscript startlingly clean. He also knew a great deal about advances, blurbs (he wrote most of his own), jackets, translation rights and percentages, and could be firm, even pernickety, when editors tampered with the way he laid out his paragraphs. It was to Unwin that he described the way he wrote, and why he was able to deliver such perfect manuscripts, with virtually no word crossed out. The clarity is awesome. 'My practice in writing a book is to compose it first completely in my head, in which re-writing is not difficult, and only begin the actual writing at a moment which enables me to finish it on the specified date by writing 2000 words a day. If I have to write any part of it sooner, the effect upon the whole is likely to be bad.'

In the mid-twenties, an American professor called Josephine Piercy asked him about his style, and the influences that had gone into forming it. Russell explained that he had spent his youth in a 'cultivated old-fashioned atmosphere' reading Shakespeare, Scott,

Cooper, Shelley and Keats, and picking his way through his grandfather's library. Later, at Cambridge, he had read Gibbon, Mill, Swift, Goethe, Heine, Racine, and Corneille. He had, he wrote, taught himself Italian to read Dante and Macchiavelli. His natural taste was the seventeenth century, and from the practice of reading aloud had come a sensitivity to prose rhythms.

The next passage is more revealing. Style, he wrote, like most other things, requires precision. 'From the age of about sixteen onwards, I formed the habit, in thought, of turning a sentence over and over in my mind, until I had a combination of brevity, clarity and rhythm. I could do this with every idea that came into my head. Brevity, especially, I always greatly desired. I wrote very carefully, with many corrections, until I had passed the year of thirty . . . After that I felt that my style was formed for good or evil . . . Style counts, fundamentally, not in ornament, but in following the reader's natural development – his breathing, as regards rhythm; his thoughts, as regards ideas. To ignore style is to make of life a succession of jolts and jars, a football scrummage instead of a dance.' Swift, said Russell, was admirable; the *Book of Common Prayer* perfect in its way; Shakespeare's prose was perfect. Really good things, he concluded, should always be learned by heart.

For *The Practice and Theory of Bolshevism* Russell was paid an advance of £75; it went rapidly into a second edition, selling over 4000 copies. *The Problem of China* was disappointing, selling only 650 copies in the first six weeks. Dewey criticised the book for failing to take into account China's 'ferment of reawakening'. Russell suggested to Unwin that the Japanese, usually avid collectors of his books, had possibly turned against it as a result of his having cancelled his lectures in Japan on his way home from China. 'They considered my refusal a sign of autocratic haughtiness, and I considered them a crew of inconsiderate bounders.'

During the 1920s, Russell published in rapid succession, aimed at much the same public who had admired and bought *The Problems of Philosophy*, several highly contentious volumes like *Free Thought and Official Propaganda*, based on a lecture in which Russell argued that he was a 'dissenter from all known religions, and I hope that every kind of religious belief will die out'. Later came *What I Believe*

('There is no short cut to the good life, whether individual or social. To build up the good life, we must build up intelligence, self-control and sympathy . . .') and *Why I am not a Christian*, in which he rehearsed the standard arguments for the existence of God and went on: 'One is often told that it is a very wrong thing to attack religion, because religion makes men virtuous. So I am told; I have not noticed it . . . It seems to me that the people who have held to it have been for the most part extremely wicked. . . . Religion is based, I think, primarily and mainly upon fear . . . of the mysterious, fear of defeat, fear of death.' Later still, in *Has Religion made useful contributions to Civilisation?* he repeated that it was, in his opinion, a 'disease born of fear and a source of untold misery to the human race'. He also attacked it for being morbid about sex. To Ogden, Russell wrote: 'I am *most* anxious not to be thought to have any truck with Xtianity however emasculated – I want religion to die out, in schools and everywhere. People misunderstand me. I dislike matter-of-factness and cocksureness, and I want the sort of spirit I often find among socialists, which has the earnestness of religion without its superstition. But I hate beliefs, optimisms, sentimentalisms and every kind of humbug . . . My whole bias is anti-Xtian.' Russell was fast becoming the most important freethinker of the day, his secular beliefs making him a hero to humanists and rationalists alike.

There was no issue in his writings of the 1920s which provoked greater fury among the Establishment and in the Church. Kenneth Ingram, the author and barrister, in *The unreasonableness of anti-Christianity*, took him to task for wild assertions, bigotry and sentimental intolerance, adding, 'if anyone is tempted on dark winter evenings to despair over the failures of professing Christians and to doubt if there can be a God, Mr Russell's pamphlet is a useful reminder that God must be very actively existent so to excite Mr Russell's violent indignation.'

Others took a tougher line. T. S. Eliot reviewed *Why I am not a Christian* for the *Criterion*, and compared Russell's so-called 'lucidity' to that of a mirror rather than of clear water. Then, one by one, he went on to demolish Russell's arguments, on philosophical and theological grounds. 'Just as Mr Russell's radicalism in politics is merely a variety of Whiggery, so his not-Christianity is merely a variety of Low Church sentiment. That is why his pamphlet is a curious, and a pathetic, document.'

Apart from religion there were books and pamphlets and essays on science, like *Icarus or the Future of Science*, in which Russell voiced his fear that science could be used to promote the power of dominant groups, rather than to make men happy: 'Icarus, having been taught to fly by his father Daedalus, was destroyed by his rashness. I fear that the same fate may overtake the populations whom modern men of science have taught to fly.' In *Icarus*, Russell made one of his prescient statements: 'The study of heredity', he prophesied, 'may in time make eugenics an exact science, and perhaps we shall at a later age be able to determine at will the sex of our children.' He went on to tackle a theme which was to preoccupy him for the rest of his life: 'the possibility of world-wide domination by one group . . . leading to the gradual formation of an orderly economic and political world-government'.

In 1923 he published the *ABC of Atoms*, which was praised for making intelligible one of the most abstract subjects in the world by explaining in non-technical language what was known about the structure of atoms. Science, Russell explained, requires that we re-examine what we believe to be 'solid' matter. 'It is, in fact, something much more like the Irishman's definition of a net, "a number of holes tied together with pieces of string". Only it would be necessary to imagine the strings cut away until only the knots were left.' The *ABC of Relativity* made Einstein approchable to the intelligent reader, and was greeted by reviewers as an excellent book for all but the intellectually lazy.

Russell's twenty-sixth book, *Sceptical Essays*, an enjoyable package on behaviourism, freedom, puritanism, scepticism and machines, came out in 1928. 'Will machines destroy emotions, or will emotions destroy machines?' he asked. It was a typical Russell question. Science is given a more flattering role, with Russell suggesting that the tendency in the future will be to turn from art and literature towards science so that every 'fairly educated person' will know a reasonable amount about mathematics, biology and 'how to make machines'. Education should be aimed at teaching people to do things rather than to think and feel. 'I think', Russell observed to

Unwin, 'the autumn would be a better time for publication than the month of June, for although statistics show that it is in the summer that people commit suicide, I do not think that it is then that they feel most sceptical.'

In Britain, these books sold well, and won the admiration of many of his friends. As Roger Fry put it in a letter: 'Just now I am reading Bertrand Russell's books. He is one of the men of genius in our time . . .' He wrote to Russell, 'You are of course a back number, unlike the advanced young thinkers you don't consider that cleverness deprives thought of all its value.' But not all his friends were as flattering. T. S. Eliot, with whom Russell was again in touch, sent him a proof of a critical review he wanted Russell to see before it appeared in print. It was not unlike his earlier attack. Protesting Russell's claim that science was the only subject of any distinction in the eighteenth century, he accused him of 'arrogance', 'a vulgar conception of culture' and 'sentimental brutality'. The words were severe, but they did not cause a fresh breach between the two friends. Not long afterwards, Russell received a miserable letter from Eliot about Vivienne, whom, he wrote, he continued to find 'perpetually baffling and deceptive . . .' 'She seems to me like a child of six with an immensely clever and precocious mind.' Russell never saw Vivienne again. She was moved into a nursing home from which she never re-emerged. In 1957 Eliot remarried.

Some of Russell's more apparently flippant remarks, designed, it sometimes seemed, only to provoke and outrage, were probably more a question of exhaustion than of a desire to play *l'enfant terrible*. The sheer amount of work he was now turning out, in his early and middle fifties, would have exhausted a far younger man. It was hardly surprising that not every performance shone, whether on paper or in person. Hutchins Hapgood, the young American who had revered Russell in Berlin in 1894, was deeply disappointed when he attended one of his lectures in London. 'The life seemed to have flown away from him . . . He seemed tired and spiritless; perhaps he had experimented too much individually with social problems which no egotistic individual can handle.' Though often driven by the need to make money, Russell did believe that what he was saying was important. Yet he seemed reluctant to use his philosophical training to make his articles more profound, so that he came to be judged by many of his peers as effective but shallow. Sir Isaiah Berlin, who got to know Russell only later, has said that he saw them as 'honourable exercises in moral philosophy, but lacking in life and flesh. It is as if he is talking about counters moving in certain directions, and not people at all.' Michael Foot was more complimentary. He remembered how impressed his generation of undergraduates were by the way Russell seemed to open up the world to them.

Russell had already made two journeys to America; in 1924, he made a third. This time, conscious of his growing popularity in the United States, he set off in the guise of both philosopher and political polemicist, to preach the new order, socialism and peace. He sailed on the *Celtic*; before docking in New York, then in the grip of prohibition, the passengers got very drunk. To secure as many lucrative lecture engagements as possible, he had been in touch with William Feakins, a 'transcontinental tour agent for lectures by Men of Fame', who asked exorbitant fees for his clients. Russell's topics were usually those of his books, and many extracts were picked up and published in American newspapers. By now, some of Russell's principal themes were in place and they grew more persuasive in the telling, as his thoughts were moulded by the reactions of his audiences. One of his favourite subjects was happiness, and how it was perfectly possible for man to be happy, provided he followed the right steps. Another was that the world was doomed, that it was hurtling towards a dark age and could not be saved unless men ceased indulging in insane political decisions. A third was that science, and possibly only science, was capable of providing the good life, by giving people self-control, knowledge and 'characters productive of harmony rather than strife'.

Russell's first speech was on 'Mechanism and Life' at Columbia University; his second to the New York Bankers' Club, on world peace; then came 'What is wrong with western civilisation?' to the League of Industrial Democracy, and later 'How to be free and happy', to the Rand School of Social Science in New York. His audiences laughed. In his first two days, Russell made £100; he was hoping to bring home at least £1000. He spoke at Columbia, Cornell, Northwestern, Brown and a number of other universities around the country, as well as giving at least fifty further talks to institutes and clubs in cities all the way from Pittsburgh to Milwaukee. 'Never in all my life have I been so busy,' he wrote to Lucy Donnelly. 'I preached leisure but had no chance to practise it myself.' As the days went by, he became increasingly irritated by the 'earnestness without truth, which the Yankees expect'. He compared himself to a 'species of mental male prostitute' and remarked to Dora that what he really hated most were the women's clubs. 'I doubt if the human race produces anything more repulsive than the American rich woman of middle age, very fat, very ugly, very expensively dressed . . .' But he was clearly in excellent shape, and the philosopher Will Durant, who had called him a 'moribund . . . formula with legs' during Russell's visit in 1914, was impressed to see him 'hale and jolly, and buoyant with a still rebellious energy'.

He also took part in several public debates, the best attended being a discussion with Scott Nearing, the American socialist, on the pros and cons of Bolshevism. To the embarrassment of his hosts, he frequently brought up the case of Sacco and Vanzetti, who had been in prison for four years and were soon to go to the electric chair, arguing that this was a miscarriage of justice and that their real crime for most Americans was their anarchism. Russell often adopted a tough line about America itself. To Eliot, he declared it to be a 'desert, though a wonderful source of dollars'. Its financiers, he warned, were set to rule the world, by a series of imperialist strategies. 'It will crush trade unionism, control education, encourage competition among the workers while avoiding it among the capitalists. It will make life everywhere ugly, uniform, laborious amd monotonous.' As a result, he was not always very popular. American audiences, who enjoyed his wit and his vision, as well as his increasingly fluent speaking style, did not greatly care to be told that 'oil and Morgan rule you', or that American universities were being manipulated by big business. Students enjoyed this; academics did not. All the same, given his eminence, it was remarkable that his entire tour, extremely popular with ordinary people, was largely ignored by Establishment America. 'A better measure', wrote an angry contributor to *Unity*, 'of the ignorance, cowardice and pharisaism of American academic life we have never seen.'

Russell returned to England satisfied. His audiences had been large, receptive and generous, while an eccentric publisher from Girard in Kansas, Haldeman-Julius, whose small-format 'Blue Books' were among the first mass-market paperbacks, was eager to introduce Russell's popular writings to the American public. Haldeman-Julius did not greatly care for philosophy, but he perceived in Russell a genuine populariser of those contemporary topics he most wanted for his series.

In *Impressions of America*, written for the English *New Leader*, Russell summed up his feelings about what he had seen. They were hostile. From the point of view of liberal politics, America was twenty years behind Britain. In the *Nation and the Athenaeum* he repeated that he believed American universities to be suffering from 'theological persecution', that American predatory power was on the increase, and that most citizens had no idea what was going on in their country. 'There is no opportunity for revolution in America . . . America is essentially a country of pious peasants.'

With his popular books now translated into many languages and selling briskly all over the world, Russell had effectively captured and charmed the spirit of the day. He had always, from boyhood, been a moralist, and his style had never been anything but concise and his arguments articulate and persuasive. None of these had needed adapting for his new audiences. What was new was his tone of urgency, his sense of indignation, and the way he used wit to ridicule accepted truths. When he wrote that something was good or evil, he sounded highly convincing, even if Beatrice Webb, who enjoyed putting people down, complained that though he had become more exciting company, he had aged and become mentally indolent. She wondered whether the 'strangely excited look in his eye' meant he was taking opium? Her views were decidedly patronising: 'He is not at peace either with himself or the world. His present role of fallen angel with Mephistophelian wit, and his brilliantly analytic and scoffing intellect, make him stimulating company. All the same, I look back on this vision of an old friend with sadness: he may be successful as a *littérateur*; I doubt whether he will be of value as a thinker.' Beatrice Webb was never anything but frank: 'When one remembers the Bertrand Russell of twenty years ago, with his intense concentration on abstract thought, his virile body and chivalrous ways, his comradeship and pleasant kindly humour . . . it is melancholy to look on this rather frowsty, unhealthy and cynical personage, prematurely old.'

The public did not agree with her. They found Russell's sentiments fresh, his words pleasingly easy to understand, his thoughts not only relevant to the day but prescient. And they were precisely what his audiences, weary of the sense of impotence caused by the war, wished to hear. By rejecting old taboos and superstitions, Russell was looking forward not only to a better age but to one in which man would take a hand in his own destiny, rather than being the pawn of policies he could not understand. He would thus become fearless and happy. Russell the philosopher had truly become the prophet of his age. As an American friend, H. M. Kallen, put it in a review of his *Selected Papers* in the *Dial*: 'To the intellectual masses, sick with doubt of old faiths and hungry for a new one, Russell is a watchman, telling of the night.'

In July 1903, Russell had written to his friend Halévy: 'I was brought up in the instinctive and unquestioned belief that politics was the only possible career . . . and since then, at intervals, especially at times of crisis, I have thought seriously of standing as a candidate.' Halévy always put Russell firmly 'among the individualists and libertarians', but when Russell's parliamentary moment came again in the early 1920s, and he contested a Tory seat in Chelsea as a Labour candidate, it would not have been easy to say precisely where on the political spectrum he stood. As he replied to a man who had written to ask him to define his politics, 'I do not fit it into any recognised orthodoxy, Conservative, Liberal, Labour or Communist . . .'

By birth, Russell was an aristocratic Whig, of radical descent; according to his own account, he remained an orthodox Liberal until 1914, when he turned against the Liberals and moved over to join the ILP. Shortly before being sent to prison in 1918, he finished *Roads to Freedom*, in which he examined the advantages of rival forms of socialism and came down firmly on the side of guild socialism. 'What our society needs is not a little tinkering', he wrote, 'but a fundamental reconstruction, a sweeping away of all the sources of oppression, a liberation of men's constructive energies, and a wholly new way of conceiving and regulating production and economic relations.'

Two questions, in particular, preoccupied him at this time: which form of socialism was best suited to the advanced countries of the west, and how far they could be prevented from resorting to war to acquire larger chunks of empire. The principles were what interested him, such as the need for an international authority which could impose disinterested rule on states, or the need for a complete change of emphasis, if socialism were to succeed. The details he preferred to leave to others. An old-fashioned liberal at heart, wedded to the virtues and language of his Whig childhood, he was never quite clear how socialism could accommodate them. Ambiguities and contradictions crop up throughout his political thinking.

As soon as the Russells were settled in Sydney Street, they began work on a joint book, which was to reflect their views on modern politics and economics. It is written as 'I', and Dora continued all her life to complain that, though it was based on her ideas, outlined on the decks of the *Porlos* as they crossed the Red Sea on their way to China, it was Russell, and not she, who got all the praise. How much of it was actually hers, no one knows; Russell wrote out all of *The Prospects of Industrial Civilisation*.

This is the book where Russell's socialism appears at its most unequivocal: he concluded that liberalism was obsolete and had no power to check the growth of capitalism. Business had been freed from the control of the state by 'liberalists', but they had to recognise that all they had achieved was to subject the 'State to the control of business'. Individual freedom, as conceived by liberalism, was no longer possible. The only way the community could avoid being 'enslaved to the capitalists' was by the collective ownership of capital by the community, 'as advocated by socialism'. America, as usual, came in for criticism. It was a country dominated by big business, an 'oligarchy of multimillionaires which controls an admirably efficient unified system of production'. This 'state capitalism' differed from socialism in that it was autocratic in design and run for private and not community benefit. It was in *Prospects* that Russell launched what was to become one of the crusades of his later years: the need for world government to enforce world peace. One reviewer, ignoring Dora, compared Russell to Rousseau, declaring that page after page was 'illuminated by an ironical and mordant wit'.

A serious move to the Labour Party now became inevitable. By the time *Prospects* came out in 1923 both the Russells were convinced that the Labour Party was the best political group available to them, and in the following months, while Labour was in as a minority government, Russell was surprisingly tolerant of all the things it was unable to do, such as nationalising industries, given its precarious electoral position. In October 1924, in an article in the *New Leader* entitled 'Why I Believe in Labour', Russell praised what he called 'a great work begun'. But he was not above sniping at politicians of whatever party, having lost his faith in all political leaders in the aftermath of Grey's secret diplomacy; he was heard to refer to some of them as 'mugwumps'.

In 1922, Russell had been asked by the Labour Party to stand for Chelsea. It was an old Tory seat, with an old Tory incumbent, Sir Samuel Hoare, but since Russell had no real intention of becoming a politician the fact that the seat was unwinnable did not bother him. Dora, still feeling somewhat insecure with many of Russell's eminent friends, braved herself to tackle canvassing; she soon discovered that as an incipient actress she was extremely good at delivering rousing talks from soap-boxes, even when heckled. Seeking supporters, Russell wrote to Shaw, asking whether he would speak on his behalf. He received a very Shaw-like reply. 'I must warn you . . . that, though, when I speak, the hall is generally full, and the meeting is apparently very successful, the people who run after and applaud me are just as likely to vote for the enemy . . . I addressed thirteen gorgeous meetings at the last election; but not one of my candidates got in.' In Chelsea, Shaw said, 'no Progressive has a dog's chance'.

On election day, 15 November, Russell did surprisingly well, increasing the Labour vote in Chelsea by almost 500. Across the country, Labour had doubled its votes, becoming the official opposition under Ramsay MacDonald's leadership. The personal outcome was precisely what Russell wanted: a modest success, but no further commitment. For Dora, it was something of a revelation. She had found that she had a definite talent for oratory, and was tempted to make a career in public speaking. She was therefore all the more chagrined to realise that she was pregnant again. In November 1923, Baldwin, who had become prime minister on Bonar Law's death, called an unexpected election for 6 December, three weeks before the baby was due. Russell agreed to stand again, and this time Labour increased its seats in the House of Commons from 142 to 192. He was not one of them.

Russell's political career, such as it was, was in abeyance once again, though he continued to write pro-Labour pieces, telling Upton Sinclair that he feared 'a strong movement to the right'. He went back to his writing, although there were always to be political concerns into which he could easily be drawn. When Emma Goldman, the Russo-American anarchist who had been deported to Moscow from the USA in 1919, declared that she was disillusioned with Bolshevism and wanted to come to London, Russell agreed to help. She came to tea in Sydney Street, but their friendship cooled when Russell refused to sign a letter to the Russian government, calling for a change in the leadership, because he said that 'the cruelties would be at least as great under any other party.' When she asked him to contribute to a book on the appalling conditions of political prisoners in the new Soviet labour camps, he sent her a distinctly barbed offering.

Dora gave birth to a daughter, Kate, in 1923. She had been drawn into the current birth-control campaign, where she rapidly became a considerable figure, with a sure, resounding voice. No longer affected by shyness in the presence of Russell's friends, she now appealed to people like H. G. Wells and Julian Huxley for funds for her campaign and began to lobby Parliament. 'Hooray!' H. G. Wells wrote to her, 'You *do* things . . . I just write about them. But Bertie *thinks*.' The basement dining room in Sydney Street was soon filled with earnest women holding meetings. As a new member of the Chelsea women's section of the Labour Party, she was put in charge of pushing through a resolution on birth control. From the rostrum, fielding such questions as 'Why should a woman go on bearing like a fruit tree forever?' she was at her best – eloquent, fearless and indignant. Her political education was in full swing. When the

Labour government fell in the autumn, Russell declined to stand again, and Dora took his place. It was a tough, nasty campaign but she was now skilled in the brief sarcastic reply. Labour lost.

When the Baldwin government, after the report of the Samuel Commission on the mining industry threatened the miners with a cut in wages and longer hours, the General Strike broke out on 4 May 1926. Baldwin recruited special constables, and used troops to maintain food supplies. Russell, in Cornwall with Dora, immediately offered to write a pamphlet on the coal crisis, to be distributed free to the public. Dora joined the Penzance strike committee and went off to address meetings, the only woman among them, dressed in a neat hat and coat. In the *New Leader*, on 28 May, Russell wrote a long piece which foreshadows one of the strongest commitments of his later years:

> . . . Those who proclaim that they will under no circumstances resort to force must always be defeated . . . It is possible to win personal immunity from persecution, as the Quakers did, by mere passive endurance; but it is not possible in this way to bring about a fundamental change in the structure of society, such as socialists desire. We must therefore be willing to use force at some stage, and the question must be: what is the most effective and least painful form in which the force can be applied?
>
> My own view . . . is that a General Strike is too tremendous a weapon to be used lightly, but that it has a definite place in socialist strategy. I believe its place to be resistance to Fascism after a socialist government has been democratically elected.

Russell's views on civil disobedience, on which the Committee of 100 was later to be based, took another step forward.

In 1924, the question of the China Boxer Indemnity was raised in Parliament, and it was decided that a new bill was needed. The Boxers were members of a Chinese secret society, traditionally possessed of supernatural powers. By the end of the nineteenth century, when poverty, drought, famine and political chaos had turned thousands of peasants into refugees, and disaffected former soldiers were roaming the countryside, a spirit of xenophobia gripped China. The situation worsened when the Boxers took control of the subsequent rebellion and declared that the foreign community was impinging on the prosperity and wellbeing of the Chinese. Foreign missionaries were branded 'primary devils', their Chinese converts 'secondary devils'. A number of Christians were attacked and killed. By January 1900, the four foreign powers – America, France, Britain and Germany – were demanding an end to the hostilities, but this was met by stronger calls for all westerners to be ousted. In June, the Boxers marched on Peking, where they murdered the German minister, and laid siege to the foreign legations. The siege was lifted by a hastily gathered international force, and the rebellion crushed. The Boxer Protocol of 1901 provided for a series of harsh punishments and indemnities.

After much talk between the powers, the indemnities to be paid by the Chinese were set at £67 million. Only the Americans objected that this sum was too crushing a burden for China to bear. In the spring of 1924, the incoming Labour Party in Britain decided to appoint a committee to look again at the indemnities, with the idea of finding a solution agreeable both to the British and to the Chinese. Russell and Lowes Dickinson – who had also travelled widely in China – were asked whether they would join the committee, under the chairmanship of Lord Phillimore. However, Lord Phillimore called at the Foreign Office to explain that he would be unable to chair the committee if Russell, 'a highly immoral character', was included. In the official minutes of 11 June, Sir Eyre Crowe, Permanent Under-Secretary at the Foreign Office, noted that Phillimore was earnest, puritanical and High Church and that Russell's 'rather unsavoury matrimonial adventures' alone would have put him off; but there was also the question of his 'avowed atheistical teaching and his known opposition to church and missionary schools'. In the event, Phillimore lost out. It was decided to look for another chairman, since Russell's qualifications were regarded by the Foreign Office as 'undoubted'.

None of this prevented Russell from continuing to air his views about what was right for China, in a series of increasingly outspoken and provocative articles on the subject. In September, the *New Leader* published an article on British imperialism in China, in which he accused the government of knowing nothing about China, praised Sun Yat-sen, whom they refused to support, for his efforts to curb the drug trade, and accused the British of hypocrisy, in that they were interested only in controlling the mines and railways.

In the Foreign Office, appalled minutes were circulated from department to department. 'I have known Mr R. for many years, at certain periods intimately,' wrote Sydney Waterlow, now a civil servant, 'and I greatly admire his genius. But he has always been a psychological trouble to me. How is it possible that a man with his scientifically trained mind should permit himself to write assertively and dogmatically on questions of fact of which he has only the most superficial knowledge? This peculiarity too often leads to mistakes and misstatements . . .' The wrangling went on. But by now the Labour government had fallen again, and Baldwin, the new prime minister, wrote to Russell and Lowes Dickinson to tell them that the invitations to serve were being withdrawn. The reason he gave was that 'two gentlemen with qualifications of a special kind' were needed. (In the minutes, these were referred to as 'two better members'.) It was just as Russell had suspected: 'business interests' were what counted. In the House of Commons, Arthur Ponsonby tried to challenge the decision, and in the Foreign Office, minutes continued to circulate. Russell and Lowes Dickinson were judged to have 'too pronounced views', and lacked 'practical experience'.

There the whole affair might have ended, had Russell not decided to keep sniping in a series of inflammatory articles, in which he accused the Foreign Office of chicanery, and of reneging on its earlier commitment to China on education. Even if their tone was designed to needle, there was nothing capricious in these attacks, for Russell wholeheartedly believed that the indemnity money should go on education, which would prove far more valuable in the long run; to do anything else with it was fundamentally corrupt, and put Britain in an embarrassing light *vis à vis* America, with its more generous intentions. Early in 1925, a Foreign Office civil servant noted, 'Like Tweedledum, Mr Russell, when he is angry, seems to hit at everything, whether he can see it or not . . .'

It was Russell, however, who had the final word. 'The British in China,' he wrote in the *Nation*, 'absorbed as they are in bridge and polo, have not noticed that China has become a political nation.'

This constant ridiculing of British foreign policy was not easily forgiven.

The political life of the 1920s made itself felt at every level of Russell's domestic life. When in London, Dora would often leave scribbled notes to Russell as she rushed out to meetings. There were instructions about the maid, about Harrod's bills to settle, about finding bulbs for the garden and a new range of paint colours for the walls. There were notes about the nanny and the two children. One day, there was one telling him how to warm John's bottle, when to take him out and how to be certain to get him to use his pot. Russell, in his early fifties, was being forced to practise the equality he had preached in his books and articles. What he felt about taking the children for walks and paying the Harrod's bills is not recorded, though Dora is known to have complained that Russell seemed incapable of shedding his aristocratic past, and went on treating servants as servants and not as people and being incapable of tying up his own parcels. Ottoline, who came to visit them one day, remarked in her diary that the house was sordid, dirty and untidy, and that both Russells were utterly absorbed in their work. She would have been still more disapproving had she come across Dora chain-smoking as she composed her articles, or smoking her pipe. She seemed quite another person from the smiling, round little woman Elizabeth Russell had so warmly admired.

Summers were spent in Cornwall, where the garden at Carn Voel was at last prospering in spite of dire local predictions of failure, with plants in the beds and tomatoes growing in the greenhouse. Dora took to wearing shorts, a radical sartorial step in the early 1920s, claiming that she was the first woman in England to do so. On sunny days there were long picnics on the sandy beaches, with both Russell and Dora working in the mornings, Dora in a black hut on the cliff-top to which she escaped to avoid household demands, mindful of Virginia Woolf's dictum that a woman should have a room of her own, if only as a symbol. Holidays were taken in the Valley of the Rocks Hotel at Lynton, Russell's village of earlier days, where friends like the Meynells and the Allens came to join them. For all their time apart, their separate concerns and the frenzy of their days, Russell and Dora seemed very attached to each other, and to the two children. If Elizabeth Russell could be malicious, she was also perceptive. After one visit to Sydney Street, she wrote to Katherine Mansfield: 'I am persuaded Dora is the very wife for him, and if one succeeds in heading her (& him) off politics, or indeed news of any sort she's a jolly, affectionate little dear. Last night she and I – can you picture it – danced a *pas de quatre*, to the joy of the others, so you see she has her moments . . .' Remarking on Dora's dimple, she added that such very bright eyes were surely a sign of great intelligence.

When apart, Russell and Dora's letters to each other were fond. 'Dear love,' wrote Dora on one of Russell's trips away, 'there is nobody like you for me in the whole world. Nothing and nobody could take your place. I believe nobody could ever take my place with you . . . we seem to be one person, that's all . . .' There are many references to the children: John is 'bright-eyed, sweet tempered, intelligent, glorying in life'; Kate 'too intelligent, that is part of the problem'.

At home, Russell had at last found a certain personal happiness; in his writings, he continued to pursue happiness as a major theme. On paper at least, he never underestimated the difficulties. 'There is no one key', he wrote in September 1927: 'politics, economics, psychology, education, all act and react, and no one of them can make any great or stable advance without the help of the others . . . It is necessary to embrace all life and all science – Europe, Asia, and America, physics, biology and psychology. The task is almost super-human. All that I can hope to do is to make men conscious of the problem, and of the kind of directions in which solutions are sought.'

Fourteen

A benign and dancing presence

'For some years', Russell wrote of his children in his autobiography, they 'filled my life with happiness and peace'. He was the most loving of fathers, and the most witty; but the standards he set, often unthinkingly, were ferocious.

He had long wanted children. From the earliest time with Alys, when he had been haunted by fears of hereditary madness, he had never ceased to think about them. The need cropped up again and again, in his letters to Ottoline, to Colette and to any woman friend who was about to give birth. When Helen Flexner produced her first son in the autumn of 1904, long before he and Alys formally parted, he wrote: 'Children are . . . one of the fundamental experiences, without which it is impossible to be fully a member of the human family . . . There is no healthy life except in the future; and to those who have no children, it is unavoidable that the past should gradually overburden the future.' In 1921, the year when John was born, Russell was forty-nine: there was not all that time in which to rescue the future from the past.

John's earliest memory was of the basement dining room in Sydney Street where the family had breakfast together. Around the time Kate was born, John was enrolled in a nursery school across Albert Bridge, Mrs Spencer's School. His second memory was of walking there with his father, over the river, on a foggy morning, with the mist rising from the water and the cab drivers shouting to their horses as they passed in the grey misty light. He would always remember the smell of the horses' warm dung. But it was in

Cornwall, at Carn Voel, that the Russell children formed their first real impressions of their parents, to be recorded many years later by Kate, in one of the most poignant books written about childhood, *My father, Bertrand Russell*.

From 1922 on, the Russells spent every spring and summer at Carn Voel. Memories of the journey there from London, by train, were largely happy ones. While travelling, Russell was at his most ebullient; like his father, he was fascinated by trains and timetables. At Paddington, he bought himself one or even two detective stories, to be discarded when read, and comics for the children. Settling down in an empty compartment, he would tell them to make faces if anyone approached and tried to join them. Russell was a neat, fastidious, polite traveller, making no fuss; he was always smartly turned out in dark grey suit and grey hat. John and Kate, on the other hand, were not prevented from racing up and down the corridor at will, and were never told to sit down or be quiet.

It is ten miles from Penzance to Carn Voel. The wind was too wild for trees, but by the middle of the 1920s Dora had succeeded in coaxing a sturdy hedge to surround the house, and had painted over the former boarding house's brown and green paint in blue, grey and white to blend, as she put it, with the sky, which seemed so immense on that flat and desolate promontory. She liked bright colours, Heal's furniture and Roger Fry designs. There was little she could do with the shape of the rooms, for the most part small and square, or the floors, which were stone downstairs and wood up, but she could and did paint every available surface in different colours, permutations of yellows and oranges, but no reds. The dining room was yellow. Upstairs, a rather larger sloping attic room was papered with a bold, bird footstep pattern, and the furniture picked out in orange and black. Apart from a few good pieces collected by Russell, there was not a great deal of furniture, and what curtains there were came highly decorated. The result was arresting, if not exactly stylish or cosy, neither Russell nor Dora having much interest in such things.

From the windows, across the wide view so necessary to Russell's wellbeing, could be seen on a distant hill by the sea three square houses in a row, and a fourth built at an angle to them. Russell christened these buildings Brown, Jones, Robinson and Ebenezer-Stick-in-the-mud, and for the children they came to symbolise, as Kate wrote later, 'respectability and oddity'. The sense of being different was encouraged. John, briefly at a Montessori school, was told by his father to use the equipment, not to make the conventional Montessori shapes but to build trains. Russell was delighted when the teachers complained that it showed a 'disordered imagination'. The Russells shunned local people and imported their own friends, like Colette Malleson who re-entered Russell's life after nearly five years of silence, when he wrote to say how much he would like her to know his children. Colette caught a train down to Cornwall and came back entranced. 'The children were the children of one's dreams,' she wrote in her autobiography, 'happy, fearless, free'. After this, she sent them boxes of crystallised fruit at Christmas, in generously large round trays with a small ivory fork in the middle. Kate and John, used to plainness, found them exotic.

Russell and Dora wanted, they repeatedly said, to protect their children from the crushing oppression of 'respectability'. The effect on Kate was to make her terrified of respectable people, so that she would creep past the neighbours' hedges, hoping not to be noticed. Later, both she and John became acutely aware of feeling superior, in the sense that they felt obliged to help those less fortunate than themselves. Being a Russell, Kate said, was not only a matter of pride, but greatly at odds with the other inescapable Russell properties of equality and fairness. At the same time, however contradictory this sounded, there was never any question that all were born equal in rights. And Dora made it plain that those who did not agree with her were usually fools.

It was Russell, and not Dora, for all her earlier assertions that 'all wisdom' and hence 'all power' flowed only from mothers, who captured the children's minds. He told them that Hungary had once been called 'Yumyum' and that it had been changed to Hungary to make it sound more dignified; and that the Duke of Wellington had a very small tail and had to have his saddles made especially for him. He teased the children, and played silly games with them, swinging his gold pocket watch on its chain when they were small and showing them how the mechanism worked when they grew older. When they went out in the car together, he told them to lean out of the window and shout 'Your grandfather was a monkey!' at passers-by to convince them of the correctness of Darwin's theory of evolution. He was, when not at work, funny, full of quirky jokes, and forever ridiculing pomposities; and he seldom lost his temper, saying it was a disgraceful thing to do.

These long summers at Carn Voel were also a time of visits from friends with other small children. On some days there were sixteen people in the house, packed into the nine small, square, brightly-painted bedrooms, buttering mounds of sandwiches for the beach picnic and sitting down to dinner at two long tables in the dining room. Several of those who were small children at the time can still remember the feeling of those summers, and the way Russell used to talk to them, not as children but as equals, fascinating them with his puns and the peculiar, un-adultlike way he talked about things. Frances Ronald, whose mother was a first cousin of Russell's, remembers the time she shared a room with John. He was three, she a year older. What impressed her was that when it grew dark he took her to the window and pointed out the stars to her, naming them one by one. For Polly Allen, Clifford Allen's daughter, the memories are of days on the beach and evenings listening to the adults talking below, noisily and far into the night. The Allens shared many of the Russells' opinions about childhood, and in particular the importance of turning out self-sufficient and brave individuals with little need for tenderness. Like Kate's, Polly's memories are not all happy ones; neither Russell nor Allen, she says, really knew how to be properly, unselfconsciously affectionate to small children, however much they believed they were.

Behind all this teasing lay a set of rules that became more pronounced as the children grew older, and as Russell started to formulate more clearly his ideas about education. Both he and Dora were convinced that what children needed was experience of the two activities most necessary to society: argriculture and industry. They wanted, as Dora put it, to produce a child who would 'understand the texture and habits of the world so completely that when exact science is added it will manipulate that world with all the sureness and grace of the artist or the dancer'. They believed that parents should at all times be fair and impartial, and that children should grow up tough and uncomplaining, able to get on with the business of enjoying life. 'Both children', Russell reported contentedly to his friend Lucy Silcox, 'prefer magic to religion.' One day, on the beach, John found a rock which he wanted to carry home for his room. The adults admired it. The walk home was three-quarters of a mile, and after a while the three-year-old began to fall behind. Eventually, he was obliged to give up his trophy. No one helped him. A lesson in self-reliance and resourcefulness had been imparted; but from it, according to Kate, John learned not independence but 'humiliation and despair'.

Not surprisingly, given his views on fear, Russell wished to make his children fearless; he thought the way to accomplish this was through 'love informed by modern knowledge'. The children perceived the knowledge, but not always the love. John was easily frightened. When he was two and a half he was terrified of the sea. The first summer at Carn Voel the Russells introduced him gently to the water. He cringed and wept. The following year they grew impatient with his terrors. They told him they were ashamed of him. For two weeks, despite his cries, they plunged him resolutely every day into water that was often choppy and always freezing. Eventually he gave up crying. (As a small boy, Russell had been held upside down in a fountain at Pembroke Lodge by a footman 'employed to make me not afraid of water'. For him, the treatment had worked.) On another occasion, he woke calling out during a violent gale. His parents gave him a night light. The next night he woke again and cried, and went on waking and crying every night. For a while, the Russells were comforting, then they left him to cry, Russell recording sententiously that after that the boy seldom wailed again. 'If we had been more indulgent,' he remarked, 'we should probably have made him sleep badly for a long time, perhaps for life.' It was all a little bleak. Fears, Kate was to write, 'grew and grew and grew, secretly, in John as in me, festering quietly and sapping our vitality'. Their father expected a lot, said John, when he was middle-aged, but 'he never gave enough'. He played at being a father, wrote Kate, 'but his heart was elsewhere and his combination of inner detachment and outer affection caused me much muddled suffering'.

The sad thing is that both Dora and Russell felt strongly that they were doing the right thing even if, in old age, Russell wondered whether this crude early conditioning had not been 'unduly harsh'. At the time, he had no doubts. He was, as he kept repeating, devoted to his children; he wanted to turn them into the kind of adults he most believed in: people who were both happy and productive. As he and Dora saw it, they were taking all the right steps, providing the children with countryside, fresh air, an open, empty beach on which to play, freedom from all inhibitions by being naked except for a hat against sunburn and shoes against lockjaw, together with adults who also swam naked – Kate would remember the way her father's red face and thick, windblown white hair reminded her of a cockatoo – and who listened to them and told them interesting things. When they were with them, that was, for Dora's determination not to be tied down by domesticity necessitated a considerable staff comprising a cook, a housemaid, a nanny and a man to garden and drive the car. Quite where these people fitted, in the square, windy house with its not very many small rooms, is impossible to work out.

Later, Russell was to remember that it 'was always sunny, and always warm after April' in Cornwall. Kate remembered chiefly the dark, stormy, furious voice that filled her head. Her mother was little more than 'one among a number of shadows in the bright light cast by my father'. It was not always a very kindly light.

There was much talk among the adults, over the picnics on the beach and during the long dinners at Carn Voel, about how to bring up children. Freud was greatly in vogue, and parents in England were beginning to worry about the dangers of children becoming too dependent. Far into the night, the Allens and the Russells and the Meynells would tell each other that parents really needed a vigorous course in hygiene and child psychology before they embarked on parenthood at all. Since the whole business was so tricky, should it not be entrusted to 'experts'? The Russells doubted that such experts existed. At two, Kate could already read; John, at four, was full of curiosity and very sociable. How best to nurture and bring out these talents?

The 1920s were a good time to be a child. True, a good many people were still wedded to the traditional virtues of obedience and respect, and wanted their children to grow up precisely as they had themselves, untouched by any of the social changes brought by the war. Such people went on sending their children to the schools they had been to themselves, and continued to resist all things eccentric, abstract, foreign, feminine or artistic. As the Reverend Edward Lyttelton, a former headmaster of Eton, wrote to the *Evening Standard* in 1925, 'Children go to school impressed with a belief that they have a right to be happy . . . This is the perversion of the true religion, self-denial and obedience.' Opposed to these parents, however, was a growing number who, like Russell and Dora, had emerged from the war unsettled but believing that what was needed was a different kind of childhood altogether, one not harsh or repressive or rigid, but which questioned everything and encouraged the freedom of thought that would produce adults capable of challenging governments and protesting against the folly of war. This new generation was to be outspoken, without taboos, self-reliant, full of scepticism and, above all, happy. Never before had there been so much attention to childhood, and so little desire to control it. As the post-war years witnessed a great extension in state education, and the building of both state and private schools, so the formerly narrow educational theory fanned out to include everything from total libertarianism – schools where children did what they pleased – to schools attempting to blend new patterns of thought with ancient practice.

If it was a fine time for children, it was equally an exciting time for people who wanted to educate them. Freud's *Introductory Lectures on Psycho-analysis*, first published in English in 1920, and W. H. Rivers's *Instinct and the Unconscious*, both warning of the terrible consequences of thwarting the libido, were enjoying brisk sales. Authority, to these new educators, was a dirty word. Euphemisms were discarded; frankness, particularly in matters of sex, was celebrated. As Vera Brittain put it in *Testament of Youth*: 'Where we had once spoken with polite evasion of a "certain condition" . . . we now unblushingly used the word "pregnancy". Amongst our friends, we discussed sodomy and lesbianism with as little hesitation as we compared the merits of different contraceptives.' In *Married Love*, Marie Stopes argued that women should be encouraged to enjoy sexual passion, and men to recognise that they did so. (The Catholic Women's Guild declared the book would lead to 'race suicide and moral degeneracy'.)

Into this state of flux was born the 'new schools' movement and the New Education Fellowship, which owed much to Pestalozzi, Montessori and Froebel, as well as to pioneering progressive schools like Abbotsholme and Bedales, where boys and girls were educated together in small communities and encouraged to express their natural feelings, and where all forms of punishment were banned. Docility was a virtue of the past. Knowledge was no longer to be handed down from above, but requested from below, by the children themselves, who, being happy and free, so the theory went, would also be inquisitive and eager for information. These educational pioneers were not popular with all parents: not every mother or father wished to be told that their child should go to boarding-school at the age of two, or that mothers were, without being conscious of it, turning out not happy adults but tortured and fearful emotional cripples.

The spirit behind these new schools could not but appeal to the Russells. Russell had been thinking about education for years, from both a social and a philosophical stand. Though his earliest real writing on the subject is *The Education of the Emotions*, which was written at the turn of the century and anticipated much of what he was later to say – the training of 'good impulses', the desirability of 'self-forgetfulness' and a 'broad, free adventurous spirit, a spirit of bold hope, of reckless daring, a spirit swept by a breath as uncontrollable as the Atlantic winds' – he had been discussing children and their upbringing for at least a decade before that. 'I wish', he had written to Alys from Paris, three months before they married, 'we were going to have children if only to give them a sensible education in the matters of sex – I should almost like to start a co-educational school for the purpose of applying my theories.' In 1901, while in the throes of his 'conversion' after Evelyn Whitehead's attack, he had declared that 'a public school education is abominable.'

Now that he had children of his own, it was clear to Russell that moral training should start at birth. With its first intake of breath should come a child's realisation that it had entered a moral world where 'it will always get its just deserts but must never ask for more.' In practice, as John and Kate knew from their own painful experiences, what this meant to him was leaving a newborn baby to cry, providing there was no immediate cause for its crying, otherwise it would turn into a tyrant. 'We should not give the child a sense of self-importance which later experience will mortify.' From birth, a baby had to realise that he or she was on its own.

Throughout the 1920s and early 1930s, Russell, who better than anyone understood that children should be prevented from repeating their parents' mistakes, turned his hand to a series of books and articles on education, expanding some of the more general views which had appeared much earlier in *Roads to Freedom* and *Principles of Social Reconstruction*, and moving up the ages as his own children grew older. *On Education: especially in early childhood* sold 'merrily'; it was praised by John Dewey as 'good sense illuminatingly uttered', and criticised by the *Manchester Guardian* as 'wrong headed' but not without charm. This was followed by *Education and the Social Order*, which was called *Education and the Modern World* in the USA, after the American publishers had objected to the words 'social order' on the grounds that no American would ever have heard of them, causing Russell to remark to Stanley Unwin, 'I suppose they only know what social disorder means.' Reviewers found the book lively, but baulked at the chapter on 'sex in education'. It 'reeks with unwholesomeness', declared the *Baptist Times*. 'Of course there must be sewers, but it is hardly necessary to compel people to stand over the open drain.' In 1917, Russell had spoken of the 'reverence' adults should have for the potential in every child; he now spelt out to teachers what steps they should take to bring this about. Like his pronouncements on religion, morality and the sciences, it formed part of Russell's role as modern tutor to the post-war generation. Aunt Agatha, with whom he exchanged sour letters about his treatment of Alys, did not care for this new Russell: '. . . to those who truly loved you, it is heart-breaking that you have not grown nobler, stronger, more loving . . . but in every way the reverse. You do not at all realise how much you have changed.'

Influenced in part by his conversations with Conrad, Russell had come to believe that impulse, not reason, was the primary moving force in human behaviour. After the war, he extended this to include 'herd instinct' as a powerful and potentially dangerous drive, with civilisation threatened by the new science and technology which would soon develop beyond man's control. Only by means of education, Russell came to think, would man triumph over these impulses and learn to steer the world towards a better, that is to say, more creative, form of society. The role of education was to enlarge the scope of these impulses, to increase their 'attendant thoughts' and reveal where 'personal satisfaction' lay.

By the end of the war, when he was looking forward to the new social order founded on socialism and syndicalism, yet was despondent about how little was being accomplished by the Labour Party, Russell began to embellish his earlier views on education. If society was to reach a 'good state' – one which contained much instinctive happiness, as well as the ability to create and enjoy beauty – and avoid a 'bad' state – filled with evil and hatred and lacking intellectual curiosity – it had to become more just, less utilitarian and more leisurely. All this was too important to be left to parents. Teachers had to be trained to turn out people capable of being 'good citizens' and 'good human beings'. Man, having rid himself of wars, armaments and commercial competitiveness, would find himself with many hours a day of leisure: he needed to be taught how to make best use of it.

The point of education, Russell claimed, was to form character and provide knowledge, in such a way as to banish the 'cruelty, oppression and war' of the past. Education should foster hope and imagination, and make children aware of what the world could be like. Discipline remained important, but it had to come from within, and not be imposed from without. The butterfly that was to emerge from this chrysalis was to be vital, sensitive and intelligent. The teacher had to be observant, patient and industrious. Punishment was to be used only when essential, and even then was never to be physical, only verbal. Cruelty, on the other hand, was to be curbed instantly, and sex treated always as perfectly natural.

Unlike some of the other exponents of the 'new schools' movement, however, Russell believed passionately in 'facts' and knowledge. These were to be introduced gradually, in a phased way, with nothing requiring serious mental effort before the age of seven. History and geography were to furnish food for the imagination, great literature to influence thought and style, plays and language to develop memory. At twelve should come science, mathematics and the classics; at fifteen a basic knowledge of Parliament and the democratic process. Russell's Rousseauesque ideal product, his 'free citizen of the universe', was a happy individual engaged in creative activities, with a purpose beyond simply his own satisfaction. All this was really addressed to younger children: as they grew older, his interest in their education began to wane (until they reached university age), partly because he was less concerned with secondary schools, beyond disliking any hint of militarism, and partly because he believed the important years to be over by the age of ten.

His ideas were somewhat different from those of other educational reformers, not least because they took the form of a series of separate views rather than a complete educational philosophy. Had he not had children of his own, it is possible that they would have remained simply one corner of his entire package of views on modern society and its future. If the details were worked out, it was because Russell could observe what his theories achieved by watching his own children. Now that John and Kate had reached school age, the Russells were faced with the problem of what to do with them. There was, of course, Bedales, or the newly founded Dartington Hall, or even The Malting House School or A. S. Neill's Summerhill, all of which shared a desire to produce the ideal society in miniature. The problem was that Russell found none of them quite right, while Dora, who had just published her own book on the subject, *The Right to be Happy*, felt no one she had talked to was capable of reforming the 'hideous nightmare' of the world or of dealing with the 'starvation and thwarting of sex-love'. She wanted to see men and women with the courage to 'build a human society in the image of human beings, vivid, warm and quick with animal life, intricate and lovely in thought and imagination'.

Neill's Summerhill was possibly the closest to their ideal, and he and the Russells were in close touch, but while Neill attached greater importance to the releasing of the emotions and blamed parents for failing to understand their children's unconscious wishes and needs, Russell had more regard for the 'humanising' power of knowledge. 'The aim of life', said Neill, 'is happiness. The evil of life is all that limits or destroys happiness. Happiness always means goodness; unhappiness at its extreme limits means Jew-baiting, minority torture and war.' It was revealing of the difference between them that while Russell had forced John to enter the sea even though he was terrified, Neill took no notice of two boys in his school who were frightened of the water, and told the other children to pay no attention to their fears. On the other hand, both men were convinced that all children had been inculcated by their parents with a 'diseased attitude to sexuality and bodily functions'.

'A child is nearer to God in masturbation than in repenting,' Neill was prone to remark, providing further ammunition for critics of his wickedness and degeneracy. Russell was equally forthright on the subject of sexual repression: 'I believe that no other evil in our society is so potent a source of human misery, since not only does it directly cause a long train of evils, but it inhibits that kindliness and human affection that might lead men to remedy the other remediable evils, economic, political and racial, by which humanity is tortured.'

Both the Elmhirsts at Dartington and Geoffrey Pike at The Malting House had started their schools to provide their own children with what they believed to be the right education. Russell and Dora considered themselves, if not the leading reformers of the day, at least as capable of rearing children. Why should they not do the same? If there were enough pupils for these other schools, there would surely be more around, and, given Russell's contacts in America, there were whole new areas to explore. As for a building, Frank, his various marriages in ruins, had now decided that he wanted to let Telegraph House, above Petersfield.

*

Beacon Hill School opened in September 1927. Its prospectus, sent to potential parents, friends and benefactors, does not seem radical today; then, it verged on the revolutionary. The school's intention, it said, was to turn out children equipped for the modern world, not 'listless intellectuals', but responsible and hopeful individuals 'conscious that there are great things to be done'. Pupils were to be allowed to run wild, much as in an 'old-fashioned large family'; they were to be kept interested by free discussions and inspired teaching, and watched carefully as to diet, health, moods and emotions. They were to attend lessons or not, as they wished, provided they disturbed no one else. Readers of Russell's book on education had little to learn from the prospectus, though it is surprising that parents were not more anxious about entrusting very young children, some not yet able to talk, to a teacher whose bleak vision of the world had led him to declare: 'those who are to begin the regeneration of the world must face loneliness, opposition, poverty, obloquy ...' Whereas Dora, who really ran the school, put her emphasis on producing children of balanced character, essentially at ease with themselves, Russell placed his on awakening a spirit of enquiry through development of the intellect. Beacon Hill School was to occupy most of the next five years of Russell's life.

Every pupil who arrived at the school would remember its position, high up on the downs, reached by a long winding drive of copper beeches planted by Frank, and tall hedges sheltering lawns and a tennis court from the wind. The house was an odd mixture of white paint, pebbledash, ivy, a formal entrance and a tower, but its views were exceptional. From every window could be seen sloping fields and forests of beech, ash, alder and chestnut dipping into other green valleys, a hundred acres of largely untamed wilderness. Some fifteen miles to the west were Portsmouth and the sea, and on fine days it was possible to see the Isle of Wight from the tower window. What struck the children as they wound their way between the mile of copper beeches, was the sense of silence, isolation and space. It was extraordinarily peaceful; it is easy to see why Russell believed children would blossom there.

The plan was for Beacon Hill to take thirty children, from the unusually young age of two up to about twelve. Telegraph House was ideally suitable: electric light and central heating had been installed by the mechanically minded Frank, and several huts and bungalows nearby – one of which had been built for Elizabeth to have her French lessons – provided extra classrooms. There was a science block; another for arts and crafts; a third held building equipment and ropes for rainy days. Dora's idea was to make the children see Telegraph House more as a home than a school and before moving in she ordered small-sized divan beds from a firm of blind bedmakers, various appropriate sizes of tables and chairs, and a quantity of matching cups and plates in bright blues, greens and oranges. She took on an excellent cook, to feed them well, and made a point of cuddling all those who seemed to be suffering from homesickness.

Russell's study was painted dark blue and cream to match the embroidered rugs they had brought back from China. Here, said Dora, far from the children, 'he would be above the battle, as and when he chooses', and able to write. She also bought a car, a dark brown Austin Twelve, and rented a comfortable house called Battine, in nearby East Marden, where parents could come and stay. It was here that Sylvia Pankhurst wrote a book, while her son Richard attended Beacon Hill as a day boy.

The first pupils reached the Russells before the move to Telegraph House, so Beacon Hill School can effectively be said to have started in Cornwall. Among the first parents were the Allens, who asked Russell to take Polly, then four, while her mother convalesced from a serious illness; an architect called Jack Pritchard, the modernist designer of the Lawn Road flats in Hampstead; Miles Malleson, by now remarried and father to three-year-old Nicolas; and various artists and writers, an astrologist and a 'real estate operator'. Several were American. Beacon Hill opened with five American and seven English children. 'Pioneers! O Pioneers!, as Whitman says,' wrote Elizabeth Russell, 'it's splendid of you both, and my love for you is only equalled by my respect.'

The first term went well, despite the usual childhood illnesses, and Dora finding a lump – which turned out not to be malignant – in her breast. Pupils were divided into 'smalls' – those still in prams

– 'middles' and 'bigs'. They went to classes when they chose to, swore as loudly as they liked, roamed the grounds, and set up a school council, at which everything except for matters of health was decided. One early motion passed was that 'sloshing as a method of settling an argument' was not a good thing. When the council voted to remove prunes from the menu, however, Dora was obdurate: prunes were health, and over health she was queen.

The knack of keen observation was developed by nature walks; science by the exploration of the properties of water and crystals; geology and ancient history – taught by Russell himself whenever he had the time – were thought to give the children a feeling of 'kinship with their own planet'. 'National' history was rejected, and the languages of the future introduced – Spanish, Chinese and Russian – though it was a while before they found teachers for them. The school secretary taught ballet. Goats, sheep, guinea-pigs and pigs were all kept at various times. One of Russell's more peculiar convictions was that water should not be drunk with meals because it diluted the stomach juices. After lunch, rows of thirsty children perched on the main staircase outside the kitchen waiting for mugs of tepid water.

Dora's papers about the school include menus – cereal and porridge for breakfast, mince, cauliflower and chocolate mould for lunch, raisins, watercress, bread and bananas for supper, lots of fruit and bread baked rock-hard to develop teeth – as well as letters to and from parents, newspaper cuttings, bills, receipts, ledgers, prospectuses, staff references, unfinished articles. They give a remarkable picture of the hard work that went into the school and which clearly took its toll of both Russell and Dora.

Because Dora was at Telegraph House most of the time, the bulk of the administration fell to her. Living with Dora, Russell came to say, was as relaxing 'as travelling on an express train bearing one to one's destination without effort on one's part'. More bitterly, in a letter he wrote but wisely did not post, he observed that, having frequently heard her complain that she did not want to do all the 'executive' work, he had come to the conclusion that she was right: 'It brings out the least desirable side of you: tyranny, rudeness, boasting and love of flattery. And you create around you an

Constance Malleson

Russell and Dora in Peking, 1921

Russell and Dora during the 1923 election

Russell with Kate and
John

A picnic in Cornwall

Russell at Beacon Hill School

Dora with John, Kate, Harriet and Roderick

Patricia Spence

Patricia, Conrad and Russell in Cambridge

Russell and Edith on their wedding day

Russell with his three granddaughters

Canon Collins
and Russell

Michael Randle,
Michael Scott
and Russell in
Trafalgar
Square

Russell outside the Ministry of Defence in Whitehall

Edith, Ralph Schoenman and
Russell in Wales

Russell at ninety-six

atmosphere of terror in which it is hard for others to work . . .' Her love of power, he warned, could easily cause her to mishandle the children as they grew older.

Still more revealing of the school and its workings are the five daily notebooks which record the first five years of Beacon Hill, filled in most often by Dora, with occasional contributions from Russell. They detail the weather, the psychological atmosphere of the school and a précis of all that happened, like the day when a group of children returned from a walk in the woods and reported that they had seen a fox. In the margin, Russell has written, 'I am sure this is so.' There are also the folders and notebooks kept by the staff for every child. Now faded and torn, they contained printed forms based on the Montessori method, giving the age of the child, its parents, brothers and sisters and even grandparents; there are sections for parents' occupations and characters; columns list the child's illnesses, details of his or her appearance and 'remarks'. Was the child breast-fed? What was his mother's character like? There is a separate sheet for bowel movements, considered so important that Russell himself would sit on the lavatory, his trousers round his ankles, surrounded by children on their pots. When these tipped over, as they often did, no fuss was made. The 'diary of psychological observations' recorded minor illnesses, medicines, and most importantly, behaviour.

Hywell Sims Williams, eight years old when he became a 'middle' at Beacon Hill, was a 'nervous, timid boy, but inquisitive and excitable'. His father was a surgeon; his mother, 'not musical, not studious, but shrewd', had died giving birth to twins. Hywell's brother David was 'pale . . . rather sedate, and has a vein of obstinacy'; the twins, who came to join their brothers, were 'small and possibly intellectually behind'. Terence Gordon's parents were 'unable to accept any supernatural religion'; David Boswell's maternal grandmother was 'definitely neurotic'.

Dora's notes give an excellent idea of the school's philosophy. 'At rest time', she wrote one day, 'Bob and Roger and Michael ran away – came back late – told they must rest ½ hour after dinner. Bob did. Roger and Michael ran away and played with pepper which was put into Sally and Sylvia's eyes. We put some into theirs, and put them alone for afternoon. They were very angry.'

Another day, there was a 'severe battle with big children at dinner time. Pudding was put into their plate instead of serving it . . . All insulted me cruelly . . . All seemed to regret the scene, but I offered no reproaches, merely explanation that my job was to look after their diet. Big children said: "Even John says he likes Mr R. better than you. We hate you, you are so stuck up." John: "I may have said that last term, Mummy, but I don't this." Revolutionary mood most interesting, and rather admirable.'

A few months later: 'Big ones dancing without clothes. Bob said he w'd not take his off. I said all right . . . Bob said he had peeped at Matron's breasts when she was bathing him. I said he c'd see me any day bathing if he wanted to know what grown-up women looked like. . . . John and Billy have drawn a man on their wall with a wee-wee tail stretching halfway across the room.'

Both Russells were determined to keep parents informed about their children's progress. Regular reports were written either by Dora or by the matron, but the troublemakers usually fell to Russell. What was remarkable was not just his courtesy but his patience. A boy called Jason, a nephew of Helen Dudley's, large in size and unusually bold for his age, was a menace to the other children from the day he arrived. Russell told his mother about his various misdemeanours, but without complaint. As the months went by, Jason became more rebellious and more of a hazard. He stole mole traps from a local farmer, threatened a small girl with a knife, and led the other children in an attempt to set a wood alight. Finally, Russell wrote to his mother in a polite and accommodating tone, saying that he felt that a school with more discipline might suit Jason better.

It was hardly surprising that Beacon Hill soon attracted the attention of the newspapers. Russell was already known as an adulterer with a string of provocative books and articles to his name. As soon as it became known that one of the tenets of the school was to promote free and open discussion on every subject, particularly sex, and to encourage nudity, telling children that it was right and not embarrassing to be aware of their own bodies, reporters came down to see what was going on. The *Daily Express* kept up a barrage of ridicule. The *Yorkshire Evening News* wrote about the 'so-called school' as the final proof that philosophers can easily turn into cranks. Even the *New Statesman* attacked it for being an 'artificial paradise', to which Russell replied that it was conventional education that was 'unreal' in that it led children to pretend to believe their teachers and parents were perfect, and their country always right. Such falsehoods, he remarked, led to cynicism. The *Weekly Illustrated* published a suggestive photograph of a woman teacher in shorts, with two girls naked to the waist, the beginnings of breasts clearly evident. The publicity made fund-raising difficult. As Russell explained in a letter to A. S. Neill, one reason why he could not get donations to the school was that he refused to forbid his teachers to have affairs with each other. Several did. 'Even people who think themselves quite advanced', Russell explained, 'believe that only the sexually starved can exert a wholesome moral influence.'

Abusive letters followed. 'Dear Dora,' wrote an anonymous correspondent from Redditch, 'I am going to send you some 60 boys and girls who would like to learn sodomy, as I have heard you and Bertrand are quite experts at this game of free-love. I propose to come myself and bring several other human stallions, who would like to get some good practice on you.' (Rather more flatteringly, Russell received the following letter: 'My wife and I thought that it would be nice if one of our children was fathered by the greatest genius alive. Naturally we picked you . . . She can be there in 24 hours.' They enclosed a photograph, drawing attention to the wife's beautiful red hair.)

Not every visitor was hostile. James Wedgewood Drawbell, a writer collecting material for a book on remarkable women, was full of admiration. When he encountered an eight-year-old boy in a red bathing suit, held up by a knotted bootlace, with a bright blue woollen cap on his head, he found nothing wrong in this eccentric turn-out. He was much taken with Dora, 'a firm, Red-Indian-like face . . . burned brown from the sun . . . a small clear-cut person in a loose-fitting flowered dress . . . Her brown legs are bare, except for short white ankle socks, and show innumerable insect bites. Her feet are encased in great square suede shoes.'

The attacks were disconcerting, but not very different from those received by other exponents of the new education. More interesting perhaps was the attitude of potential parents, who arrived to visit the school to find the children mostly naked or dressed in bizarre assortments of Wellington boots, dresses and trousers, setting forth, seemingly unsupervised, to explore the woods. One apocryphal story had it that a vicar arrived at the door, exclaimed 'Good God' and was sharply reprimanded by a small naked girl who informed him that there was no God. Bloomsbury, who came to stare, mocked. Other former friends were more supportive. H. G. Wells, who turned up unexpectedly with the Webbs one day when Russell was away, stated approvingly that 'all children should be tirelessly noisy, playful, grubby-handed except at mealtimes, soiling and tearing such clothes as they need to wear.'

Not all the staff, of whom there were at one stage twenty-two for the same number of pupils, found their jobs easy, particularly as Beacon Hill, like the other experimental schools, inevitably attracted more than its share of children with problems. They were expected to follow Dora's educational principles, and not mind when the children were rude to them, or sat at lunch flicking butter at the ceiling with their knives, or when the 'smalls' were allowed to throw their plastic bowls on to the floor with deafening clangs. When a boy stole thimbles and sewing things out of a teacher's room Dora said only that he was 'stealing love'. The Russells had kept faith with their earlier views on permissiveness and the lack of punishment, preferring to give a persistent wrongdoer a compulsory day in bed, not so much as chastisement as to give the other children a rest. Cruelty, however, was dealt with instantly, Russell saying later that it was the growth of nazism that made him realise one needed discipline to deal with bullies.

Mary Bailey, known to the school as 'Mouse', joined straight from college, on a salary of £90 a year plus full board and lodging, to teach painting, drawing, handiwork and the history of art and architecture. On the day she arrived, the pigs escaped from their pens and joined her class; not long after, she was told by Dora to dress up in false whiskers and cover her face in greasepaint and pretend to be an eminent visitor. Later, she remembered the comfort of the school, with early morning tea brought to her room, and sherry in the evenings; the day that the council voted to do away with adults, but soon felt at a loss without hot meals and a sense of order, however invisible; and how Dora went off to Paris, having heard that she would be able to find brightly-coloured chamberpots there.

Dora was a passionate believer in providing small children with experience of the theatre and the arts. She would dress up in a pair of Russell's trousers cut off at the knees, and lead a group of children on to the lawn, where she got them to wave and leap and kick their feet to the waltz from 'The Merry Widow', wheezing out on an old portable gramophone. Russell would sit the smaller children on his knee and thump out songs he made up himself on the pianola: 'Onery, twoery Tuckaby seven Allaby, crackaby, Ten or eleven . . .' But it was the plays that really counted. The children were told to decide on a topic and work out what parts they wanted to take; when the script was ready, they dictated it to a teacher. In theory, the plays were all the children's work; in practice, they had a strong Russell and Dora flavour. Any priest who appeared was a scoundrel and a fool. The most ambitious and longest remembered production was called *Thinking in Front of Yourself*, in which a hero, Youth, is faced with a choice between a worker, a 'modern' woman, and a factory owner and has to choose about Life. In *Poor and Rich*, Glaucus, a Roman boy, says to his companion: 'I believe that the rich care for nobody except themselves . . .' Just what the children themselves felt about these plays comes over in an account written by David Garnett's son, Richard, who remembered over-ambitious scenery, and a row of 'children gyrating their forearms like connecting-rods to simulate machinery', with John as the Youth, 'naked in a red cloak, performing very well despite having diarrhoea.'

The staff, most of whom were young and idealistic, and had answered advertisements in *The Times Educational Supplement*, knowing almost precisely what would be involved, soon adapted to Beacon Hill ways. Recruitment posed no problems: to one advertisement for a science master, the Russells received applications from chemists, metallurgists, engineers and geologists.

The reactions of the children to the freedom, and the hidden pressures, were mixed. Polly Allen – whose real name was Colette, after Constance Malleson – was nearly five when she went to Beacon Hill. She remembers Russell showing the children how to use a telescope, and how he never talked down to them. Equally, she remembers that neither Russell nor Dora thought to pick her up or comfort her physically. Richard Garnett, whose grandmother Constance, the translator, was excited at the thought of his being taught mathematics by Russell, recalls running around the lawn dressed in a sheet, acting a Roman. He says that science was taught by a series of extremely eccentric but very imaginative teachers, who made Guy Fawkes come alive by letting off little explosions, but he also remembers how acutely Dora embarrassed him by showing him off to visitors as if he were an exhibit in a zoo, and by saying things he knew to be untrue. Even so, he admits that Beacon Hill taught him the most important educational message: how to find things out for himself.

For Kate and John, the memories were sharper and often uncomfortable. From the day the school opened in Telegraph House, John felt despair. He was called 'teacher's pet' by the other children. In their anxiety not to show their own children any preference, Russell and Dora, he was to say later, effectively deprived him of parents. 'There was no special time for us,' Kate remembers, having in her mind a clear picture of standing alone in the front hall, a large L-shaped room with dark panelled walls and a parquet floor, 'not knowing which way to go or what to do, having no belonging place in all that vast building.' Barbara Hubbard, who was taken on to look after the 'smalls' and teach music, said that it was two months before she realised that John and Kate were the Russells' children.

Kate's verdict on the intellectual side of the school is good. For her, as for many of the other brighter children, Beacon Hill provided an exceptional grounding, so that ever after she felt not simply mentally free to question everything but full of the kind of knowledge that gave her a desire to know more. Emotionally, it was less of a success. 'It smashed my bright world of happiness,' she wrote in her autobiography, 'and left me to spend the rest of my life searching for a replacement.' Russell was to have doubts about what running a school had done to his own children. Many years later, by which time he had turned against almost everything Beacon Hill stood for, he was to write that the happiness he had enjoyed with his children was severed once they moved to Telegraph House, to be replaced by awkwardness and embarrassment. Dora never felt the same. For one thing, she was to go on running the school long after Russell gave it up. For another, she went on believing that it had provided freedom and curiosity about life to Kate and John as well as to all the other children.

'A school on a high hill was founded', she would sing, 'A school for you and for me, / With blue skies and green fields surrounded, / A school in which we are free.'

Free, perhaps, but at considerable cost. Neither Russell nor Dora was an efficient administrator, and what with the specially commissioned furniture, the generous number of staff, the wine served at staff meetings, and the fact that some parents were slow to pay the fees, Beacon Hill School fell rapidly into debt. By the end of the first year, 1927, Russell was forced to produce £1847 out of his other earnings, the £50 per term for day children and £150 for boarders being far too little to pay the bills. The following year the deficit rose to £2000.

To meet some of these costs, Russell wrote to ask friends whether they would help him to raise an extra £1000. The school, he told H. G. Wells, was successfully proving that 'stupidity is very largely the result of fear leading to mental inhibitions.' He added that his aim of 'training initiative without diminishing its strength' was already showing results, and that Beacon Hill was the only school in England to follow this ethos. Russell redoubled his efforts to turn out the popular books and lectures he now knew brought in money. During the second year of Beacon Hill, he wrote a book about relationships, taking in everything from early marriage contracts to eugenics, love, divorce and sex. Liveright, his American publisher, greeted the idea with enthusiasm and wanted to call the book *Sex Freedom*, but Russell refused, saying it was too 'propagandist'. 'At the moment I have no definite title in my head,' he wrote to Stanley Unwin, 'but I have certain moral principles in regard to sex, though not quite the conventional ones . . .'

Marriage and Morals was published in 1929, but not before the printers had suggested that Russell remove the sentence 'women are on average stupider than men,' on the grounds that any female reviewer would tear him apart. Russell replied that he did not care: 'The habit of flattering women does a lot of harm.'

The first British printing of 4300 copies sold out instantly, as did a second of 2000. In America, 13,000 copies were printed and they, too, sold out; requests for foreign translations poured in, including for Tagalog, the principal language of the Philippines. Russell, somewhat disingenuously, declared that he had never anticipated the outcry that followed its publication. Yet *Marriage and Morals* was remarkably outspoken for its time, not only on the subject of companionate marriage but on the desirability of sexual relations before marriage and the wisdom of allowing extra-marital affairs afterwards. Divorce, sin and taboos were all reviewed. Russell was more forthright and more provocative than he had ever been. 'Trial marriages' and 'mutual liberty' were not likely to go down well with the Church, or with the vast body of conservative opinion in Britain and America. Almost as if wishing to offend yet more people, he dwelt at some length on the much contested science of eugenics, suggesting it would be wise to encourage 'good stocks' by paying desirable people to become parents, and to sterilise 'feeble-minded women' whose offspring were more or less worthless to the country. It was controversial stuff, and there was something in it to offend just about everybody.

The British newspapers were surprisingly restrained, confining their reviews to summaries of the book and remarking that some of its opinions were long overdue. *Fabian News* called it an 'epoch-making book'. Attacks, on both sides of the Atlantic, came mainly from clergymen. The dean of St Paul's, W. R. Inge, while praising Russell for his mathematics, attacked him for being crude, rebellious and possessed of 'socialism run mad': 'No God. No country. No family. Refusal to serve in war. Free love. More play. Less work. No punishments. Go as you please. It is difficult to imagine any programme which, if it were carried out, would be more utterly ruinous to a country situated as Great Britain today . . .'

Russell's next book carried his message further. *The Conquest of*

Happiness was based on the assumption that most people are unhappy, and invited mankind to search for a new 'mood'. The secret of happiness, he said, was to let one's interests be as broad as possible, and one's reactions to people as far as possible friendly rather than hostile. He recommended 'zest', hard work, hobbies, no fretting, not thinking too much about oneself. Nothing very new, as Russell pointed out to Unwin, and perhaps even verging on the boring? But *The Conquest of Happiness*, published in October 1930, was reprinted twice before the end of the year. A reviewer noted that 'he sings like a doomed cricket on a dissolving iceberg'. Russell's call for self-forgetfulness, counter as it was to psychoanalytic views and seemingly completely at odds with his interest in the unconscious, was appealing to a generation baffled by its freedom. Once again, he appeared to provide the comforting belief that modern man was not a helpless victim, but a potent force for change; he was later to say that, of all his books, he felt this had done the most good.

Not everyone approved of Russell's talent for popular books. Wittgenstein loathed it, calling *The Conquest of Happiness* a 'vomitive'. The two men had met again, but with little of the warmth or mutual admiration of earlier days. In January 1929 Wittgenstein had returned to Cambridge, after years of teaching in Austria. He was welcomed back as a genius by the new generation of Apostles, now that the *Tractatus* was regarded by many as a brilliant piece of work. In May 1930, Braithwaite invited Russell to be one of Wittgenstein's examiners for his PhD, and Russell, with some reluctance, accepted, though once he had looked at Wittgenstein's new work he reported that it was 'novel, very original, and indubitably important . . . and may easily prove to constitute a whole new philosophy'. He did not, however, find it easy. 'I can only understand Wittgenstein', he complained, 'when I am in good health, which I am not at present.'

Wittgenstein's viva was held in June. The atmosphere was more like an Apostolic reunion than a formal examination, even if Russell did attack Wittgenstein for inconsistency, and Wittgenstein retorted that Russell was not capable of understanding his work. Moore, in his report, wrote that Wittgenstein was a genius. The PhD was awarded, as well as a grant to conduct research at Trinity. When a further grant became available nine months later Moore approached

Russell. This time Russell jibbed. 'I do not know anything more fatiguing than disagreeing with him in any argument.' A visit from Wittgenstein to the Russells passed off uneasily, after which an exhausted Russell begged to be allowed to submit a letter rather than an entire report, since 'reading Wittgenstein's stuff thoroughly is almost more than I can face'. At the end of 1930, Wittgenstein was awarded a five-year Fellowship at Trinity. The two men seldom met again, and when they did, Wittgenstein declared that his former tutor had left him with a 'bad impression', while Russell took refuge in contempt, saying that Wittgenstein's later work was no more than an 'abnegation' of his earlier talent, and that it was not by 'paradoxes that he wished to be known, but by a suave evasion of paradoxes'. In the late 1950s, he turned down a request by the BBC to speak on Wittgenstein, saying darkly that there were indeed things that he could say about him 'as a man, but I am not very anxious to say them'.

The Conquest of Happiness was written largely for the American market, which Russell had rightly identified as his real readers. When US sales overtook the British, Russell remarked to Unwin, 'I think they mostly share Al Capone's [the Chicago gangster] ideas of happiness, which are in a somewhat different vein from mine'. It was to America, however, that Russell turned when in need of real money. Between 1927, when the school opened and quickly began to show signs of financial difficulties, and 1932, when he ceased to be involved in it, he went on three long lecture tours, disliking each a little more than the last, but returning with considerable sums of money.

William Feakins, agent to the famous, was once again on hand when Russell docked in New York in the autumn of 1927. As always, Feakins had had no trouble arranging for him to move across the country, state by state, lecturing at least every other evening and sometimes even twice a day, on topics which ranged from social reform to war, though much the most interest was aroused by his views on marriage and divorce. This was probably inevitable, given the hostility to all moral reform sweeping America at that time. One of the public debates was with the philosopher, William Durant, Russell observing that he was a 'vain donkey, and did not afford very good sport'. He visited the Whiteheads (Alfred was now professor of philosophy at Harvard), and said sadly that he felt like a stranger with them, as both Alfred and Evelyn continued to behave like Victorians. Before leaving on his tour, he was taken to the fashionable Ebony Club, where, he wrote to Dora, he was expected to dance and flirt with black women. 'To my surprise, the mere idea was unspeakably revolting to me . . . I couldn't bear the jazz music or the futurist walls or the negro ladies got up like Americans . . . I just felt jungle poison invading all our souls. I believe you would have enjoyed it. I am too old.'

In terms of money, the trip was a triumph. Russell's fees were between $250 and $400 a lecture. He boarded the *Berengaria* shortly before Christmas, $9550 the richer, a remarkable sum for 1927, and arrived home in time to sing 'Tannenbaum' around the tree at the end of the festivities. Once again, his views on the United States were ambivalent, sometimes even mutually contradictory. He praised the country for being the least bellicose of all the great powers, for promoting the best work in contemporary philosophy and psychology, and for giving its citizens a belief that they were masters of their own fate. On the other hand, he attacked the mood of stern moral discipline, and lambasted its political leaders for allowing Sacco and Vanzetti to die.

He returned with some pleasure to Dora, but saw her only briefly, for she too was off on a two-month lecture tour of America, where *The Right to be Happy* was selling well. Her trip was a great success. An interviewer for *Equal Rights* said she was 'a little inconsistent, but very very genuine', while 2200 people jammed the auditorium at Dartmouth College, Hanover, to hear her speak, and laughed loudly when she declared that America had taught her a lot about hypocrisy. Dora was by now a commanding speaker, a master of inflection, with a penetrating voice, and she quickly made her listeners laugh. If not every college wanted her – Wisconsin cancelled her talk on the grounds that it was likely to be in 'very bad taste' – she drew headlines in the *Rocky Mountain News*: 'Wife of philosopher urges girls not to wait for Fairy Prince'.

A little over eighteen months later, Russell was off to America again, getting off the ss *Homeric* in New York to complain to Dora,

'I am getting old for these performances . . . This country seems to me like a young tiger, just growing up, learning to roar, and licking its lips in anticipation of the first meal of human flesh.' He was again in Feakins's hands. *Marriage and Morals* was selling well, so to his previous views on education Russell added fresh material on divorce and infidelity. With almost uncanny prescience, he remarked, 'those who advocate any ethical innovation are invariably accused, like Socrates, of being corrupters of youth.'

The press was, on the whole, friendly, but the Church decidedly less so, and where its influence prevailed invitations to speak were abruptly cancelled. To Rachel Brooks, his Chinese missionary friend, Russell wrote to say that he found relations between parents and children in America worrying. The American mothers of his Beacon Hill pupils whom he visited seemed to suffer from 'instinctive incompetence . . . The fount of affection seems to have dried up . . . The result of this physical aloofness is that the child grows up filled with hatred against the world and anxious to distinguish himself as a criminal . . .' This time, America depressed him. He was introduced to Otto Kahn, the famous educational philosopher, but found him uninterested in the Beacon Hill experiment. 'He is pure German, talking with a strong accent', he wrote to Dora, 'intelligent like a German, frightened like a Jew . . . If I ever want to come here again, please remind me not to: the people are horrible, and the beastliness of the country makes me miserable. It is getting worse.'

On this visit, he went to western Canada, where he remarked on the intelligence of his Vancouver audiences. *Marriage and Morals* went on enjoying steady sales, but he was forced to endure a discussion with John Watson, the behavioural psychologist, who got drunk on champagne, became rude and angry and then described to Russell his recent experiment with rats, in which he had curbed their adulterous behaviour by giving them electric shocks. Why couldn't one do the same to make man virtuous? 'All this time,' Russell told Dora, 'his eyes were sad, haunted, lonely, and frightened. He could be civilised but isn't, so won't admit there is civilisation and is wildly unhappy. He epitomises America.'

Russell sailed yet again for America in October 1931, this time on the *Bremen*. On his arrival in New York, the *Herald Tribune* described him as a 'ruddy little man with a gnomelike face under a thatch of white hair and a voice like a phonograph record'. To the *New York Times* reporter, on the other hand, he seemed 'a rather tall man' (he was 5 feet 9 inches tall). The difference, someone observed, surely lay in the fact that Russell radiated such a 'multicoloured glitter and dazzle and interplay of brightness that even his hard boiled observers . . . caught but one facet of his benign and dancing presence'. This time, reviewers surpassed themselves. 'He is a harbinger of Christmas,' wrote one. 'He is Christmas. He is better than Christmas.'

It was out of this third visit that a welcome contract came with the Hearst Press for a weekly article. Over the next four years, he was to send them 150 pieces, usually light-hearted and topical essays on everything from lipstick to the fierceness of vegetarians and whether socialists should smoke good cigars. One written on board ship sailing for England was surprisingly bleak. It was not often, in these years, that Russell allowed such pessimism to flow. 'Time, they say, makes a man mellow. I do not believe it. Time makes man afraid . . . I am thinking of the fear that enters the soul through experience of the major evils to which love is subject: the treachery of friends, the death of those whom we love, the discovery of the cruelty that lurks in average human nature . . . Christmas at sea . . . seems to symbolise the loneliness of the man who chooses to stand alone, using his own judgement rather than the judgement of the hero . . .'

Despite the Hearst contract, this final trip was a failure. The recession gripping America was eating into his book sales and lecture audiences, and although *The Conquest of Happiness* remained on the bestseller list, it was only selling a hundred copies a week. At home, financial pressures were mounting. Frank had died in March, and Russell had scattered his ashes, as requested, on the downs near Telegraph House. He described his feelings of shock in a letter to Ottoline; his brother had, he told her, died stoically, knowing he was about to die but joking about it, so that no one knew he was serious. 'It was a pity we quarrelled, as we were always fond of each other. . . . he evidently still bore me a grudge, as he left everything to a certain Miss Otter . . . I had to view the body for purposes of identification. It was very horrible as he had been dead rather a long time. He looked more than life size and terribly cruel, like some dark heathen deity to whom human sacrifices are offered. I wish that had not been my last impression of him.'

Russell was now an Earl, but Frank's final fling with Miss Otter had made him a poorer man, for he found that along with the title his brother had bequeathed him a debt, £400 a year to pay to his former wife, Mollie. True, Telegraph House now belonged to him, but Russell was beginning to have doubts about the school. What was more, the sexual infidelities which Russell and Dora had proclaimed wholesome in a marriage were about to tear theirs apart.

It was not just in their books and articles that Russell and Dora, by now secretary of the World League of Sexual Reform, had argued in favour of relationships which were free and 'companionate'. From the start of their relationship, both had declared themselves personally committed to the same ideal: sexual satisfaction for both; extramarital affairs, providing no one suffered; honesty at all times. By 1926, and possibly earlier, with John aged five and Kate three, Russell was once again embarking on emotional adventures. One of his earliest flirtations was reported laconically to Dora: 'I could not resist making love to Mademoiselle,' he wrote to her about the new governess at Carn Voel. 'You were right that one should be virtuous in the home, and I will be so henceforth.' Gilbert Murray is said to have remarked that Russell, having preached adultery, felt he should try it out.

His visits to America were consuming more and more of his time, and so he sought out new lovers during his speaking tours, some of them the mothers of children at Beacon Hill School, like Celeste Holden, whom he thanked for making the voyage 'a joy', or Barry Fox, who wanted him to father a child for her, and whose daughter Judith was an early pupil. Russell spent some enjoyable evenings with her in New York, though whether they actually made love is not clear, for as he wrote to her next morning, 'some underground remnant of puritanism is apt to make me queer about sex.'

There was Miriam Brudno in Cleveland, whose mother Mollie had sponsored his lectures. Miriam told her own daughter, many years later, that Russell had proposed to her, but that since he was older than her father her parents would not hear of it. They remained close friends. After a few nights in Cleveland, Russell wrote to her: 'Yesterday evening was an exquisite joy. I found myself thinking that I loved you more than anyone except my children.' Then there was Amber Blanco White, a witness at his next wedding (and a former mistress of H. G. Wells), to whom he proposed a meeting 'as occasion arises, and leaving things to the impulse of the moment'. In London, briefly, there was Antonia White, the novelist, though that relationship was mostly if not entirely platonic, if one believes a remark she made many years later to her daughter Lyndal. She had indeed considered sleeping with Russell, she said, one evening when they had had dinner together. But when Russell fell to his knees in the back of the taxi on the way home, 'bleating like a sheep, "Please, p-l-e-a-s-e"', she could bear the idea no longer. In a list of her lovers, written down in her diaries in the 1950s, there is no mention of him. On the other hand, there is a letter from Russell to her, highly romantic in tone, referring to his 'good fortune' and pressing her to stay the whole night the next time.

Russell is always portrayed as a womaniser, with some justification, for he pursued women, liked their company, and was capable of great heights of passion. All his major correspondents, and most of his closest friends, were women. He married four times, considerably more than was usual in a man born twenty-nine years before the end of Queen Victoria's reign. But he never really felt that women were his equal, not only because he knew himself to be exceptionally brilliant – he thought very few men his equal either – but because women, by definition, were less intelligent. As Dora wrote in *The Tamarisk Tree*, 'He did not much explore the inner workings of the female psyche, but would minister to a mind if it bore a resemblance to that of the superior male.' Russell did not wash his own socks, because he was a man and because, as Bertrand Russell, he did not think he should have to. True, he championed female suffrage; but that was because he felt it to be morally right, not because he was much interested in the domestic needs and social aspirations of ordinary women.

Nowhere were his feelings on this subject more clearly expressed, and more contradictory, than over education. Girls and boys, Russell declared, should be educated in precisely the same way. What happened when they became adults, and the girls wanted to work and to have children? His answer, though practical, is chilling. Women who wanted children must regard it as a profession. Those who wished to bring them up themselves should be trained and then paid to do so. The others should put their offspring into the hands of professionals, for nothing was more harmful to a child than a 'fussy and small minded mother'. Fathers, wrote Russell in *The Conquest of Happiness*, cannot 'be expected to do much for their children'. The idea of joint parenthood was not one that occurred to him.

There was now much more at stake than simple affairs. Not long after the birth of Kate, Russell seems to have become impotent with Dora. As the weeks went by, and the Russells spent more time apart on their various money-raising tours, so Russell wrote ever more dejected letters to her. 'I feel you despise me, and I feel sexually worn out . . . I have felt hurt for years, because you were either angry or patronising before I had come to the point . . . There is of course no hope unless I can satisfy you sexually . . . The chief thing, for me, is that you should be kind and gentle, not fierce and fault-finding. That terrifies me so that I become dumb. But oh my Heart, I ache for love of you.'

Dora was not as tough or secure as his words suggest. She, too, when Russell was in America, wrote loving and often anxious letters. 'I somehow keep feeling you don't love me as you did,' she wrote on one occasion; 'nobody else laughs as much as you and I have done,' on another. From Beacon Hill, taking in good part his 'safe escape from Circe', as he described an American entanglement, she wrote, 'O my darling, not all the Circes in the world would spoil our relation to one another.'

For a while, it was all a little like Valmont and the Marquise de Merteuil in *Les Liaisons Dangereuses*. The Russells became mutual confidants, describing their amorous encounters not in a spirit of guilt and confession but to make the other laugh. From time to time, among the witty scenes, are wistful remarks about their love for each other, and how soon they will give up other relationships and concentrate once again on their own. It was surely inevitable that this arrangement could not last. For both, the defeat of their ideals must have been bitter indeed.

Dora had been furious about Mademoiselle. It was not just that Russell was not playing fair by embarking on his sexual adventures so close to home, but the entire household became caught up in what had happened, with Dora's old and valued cook, Hannah, reporting on 'Master's' misdeeds with such venom that she had to be sacked for making trouble. Dora, meanwhile, had her own affairs, and for a while, she took up with a man called Randall. She told Russell all about him, as he told her about a girl who had written him a fan letter and with whom he decided to spend a weekend: 'I have often felt a desire to go with someone I scarcely knew.' A second letter followed rapidly, saying that he was 'bored to extinction'.

When she was in America in the spring of 1928, Dora was introduced to a freelance journalist, Griffin Barry. They talked at length about Russia, where both had been impressed by what they saw. According to a visitor to Beacon Hill, Griffin was an agreeable but somewhat mousy man. When he came to Europe, he and Dora met again in France. She says in her autobiography that once Russell realised he and Dora were not likely to produce another child together, he declared he would not object if she decided to have a baby by another man. In November 1929, when he was in America, she sent him a telegram to say that her period was two days late. What should she do? His reply, by letter, was generous: 'Since I cannot do my part, it is better someone else should . . . in any case there is no need to worry, you won't find me tiresome about it.' Another letter followed, containing a somewhat more cautious reaction: 'I do not feel the slightest anger . . . at the same time it increases the feeling that you do not belong to me; I feel aloof, though friendly. It causes a diminution of love, though not of goodwill. And it causes me to feel less willing to forgo my own pleasures . . . to please you.'

A warning had been sounded. Dora decided to ignore it. Believing Russell when he said that he was vehemently against an abortion, and would recognise the child legally if that was what she wanted, she went ahead with the pregnancy, but not before writing to tell him that she profoundly wished the baby had been his. She ended on a nervous note. 'I do hope no trouble will come out of this business. I feel worried about it, loving you so deeply as I do.'

Harriet was born in London, on 8 July 1930. Russell was at Carn Voel looking after John and Kate. Dora wrote to ask him whether it would be all right to call the baby Harriet Ruth Barry Russell? Russell, meanwhile, had found a new companion, a nineteen-year-old Oxford undergraduate, very pretty, red-haired, tall. Her name was Marjorie Spence, and she had been hired by Dora to help him look after the older children while she was having the baby. That summer, the Russell household reached a new pitch of emotional confusion. Griffin Barry, who was never very healthy, came down to Carn Voel, to be nursed by Dora for a duodenal ulcer. Marjorie Spence stayed on, but Dora suspected that before her arrival Russell had once again been consoling himself with Colette. It was perfectly true. That spring, walking the Mendips together, Russell had asked Colette to become his lover again. Colette visited Carn Voel, noting that Marjorie had freckles, that John looked just like his father and Kate had 'small button-boot eyes'. To her mother, she criticised the house as sordid, 'drab, *drab, drab*. Not one speck of imagination or taste', and Russell himself as 'gone to seed, poor lamb . . . His wry leanness is gone'. But, 'as for me, I care for him as much as ever.'

The following summer, the entire family – by now swollen to include, on a fairly regular basis, Griffin Barry, Marjorie Spence, who liked to be known as Peter, and one-year-old Harriet – rented a house in Hendaye, on the French-Spanish border, where they stayed for three months. Russell remarked how happy he was and how much he loved the view of the mountains behind the house. Before the holiday was over, Dora found herself pregnant once again. They returned to Telegraph House, but some months before the baby was due she left Russell in charge of the school and went to stay in Majorca with Barry. Russell wrote to her nearly every day, fond letters full of details about John and Kate and the school: 'I want to grow old with you about. . . . I do want you to know that I value you, and should feel maimed if I lost you.' Then Peter announced that she too was pregnant. It was Dora's turn to be generous. When Peter had a miscarriage Dora wrote to tell Russell she wished it had been her. On the matter of Peter, Russell was reassuring. She was very young and was bound to find someone her own age soon. The loving letters – about the school, the children, each other – continued.

Then on 20 March 1931, something gave. The news was communicated by letter to Dora, sitting in London awaiting the birth of her baby. Peter and he, Russell informed her, had decided they were so happy that they wanted to live together openly once Peter had completed her degree at Oxford. Two days later came Dora's hurt reply. 'It shows me clearly what I'd feared, that from you to me it is ended.' The next day, several weeks prematurely, Roderick was born. Dora, it seems, had still not quite taken in what Russell was saying. 'I do not think either that I will ever cease from mental companionship with you – the loss of your jokes and laughter and wit . . . My darling, I loved you first because you lived in the grand manner, and I learnt from you . . . I hope, too, that we will be able to meet and talk as friends and be with our children together.' But this time, it was different.

Fifteen

A nice clean sty

The next five years, Kate wrote later, were 'barren years . . . the unhappiest years of my life, a time of settled misery so deep and pervasive that I was barely conscious of it'. No one, during that period, managed to be happy, except perhaps Russell, who alone was capable, for short periods of time at least, of blotting out the matrimonial mayhem that surrounded him. The Russell divorce, between two adults committed to openmindedness and fair play, who had spent most of the ten years of their married lives telling each other and everyone else that adultery was perfectly manageable, was notable for its pettiness and vindictiveness. There was no real winner; only a family of losers, not one of whom would ever be quite capable of forgetting the nastiness and anguish that dragged on, month after month.

Between their first summer in Lulworth and their final parting in 1935, Russell and Dora wrote many hundreds of letters to each other. They give a unique picture of the slow destruction of a once happy love affair. In April 1932, when Dora returned to Beacon Hill with Roderick, she found that Russell and Peter had fled to Carn Voel, and that Peter had abandoned her plans to finish her Oxford studies. Once again, Russell had effectively climbed on to his bicycle and ridden away from a relationship he had decided was dead. To all Dora's appeals for meetings, he remained cold. The marriage was over: there was to be no going back, no meetings of any kind.

Dora's letters, some wistful and beseeching, others shrill and hostile, accusing him of wishing to disassociate himself from her because she had become too radical and he too aristocratic, received terse, evasive answers. By July she was complaining bitterly: 'I did at the onset want affectionate and friendly relations . . . But it will be very difficult if your attitude to me is that of a widower with two children only concerned about the cost of his wife's funeral.' Thinking back over Frank and his unhappy relationships with women, she wondered whether the coolness and detachment were not an unpleasant family trait and that if, like Russell, you 'spread your love over the human race', you don't have much left over for anyone else. In a letter to their friend Rachel Brooks, Dora recalled her original reluctance to marry Russell: 'I shall certainly never quite recover from the disgrace I had in marrying.'

Without the children, it is possible that Russell's second marriage, like his first, would have faded into his past, leaving few memories. But this time there were children, not just the two legitimate offspring of the marriage, but Dora's two by Griffin Barry, who were to be used, whenever it suited someone's purpose, as two extra pawns in the divorce proceedings. At the time of Harriet's birth, Dora and Russell had agreed, together, to put her surname down as Russell. This was used to complicate matters further. Who should divorce whom? and on what grounds? On the last day of 1932 a deed of separation was agreed on, but it contained a clause known as the Rose versus Rose clause, which provided that in any later proceedings no offence or misconduct committed *before* the deed be admitted in evidence. Former lovers and illegitimate children were thus to be forgotten.

Immediately Russell and Dora became locked in mutual recriminations about custody and control of John and Kate. 'Do try to divest your mind of the desire for revenge,' wrote Russell. 'So long as that exists, mere self-preservation requires me to keep my distance.' He argued that since Dora had her own two children, and the financial burden of the first two would fall on him, decisions regarding their upbringing and schooling should be his. Dora rejected this. Occasionally, she seemed to be on the verge of agreeing to divorce; more often, she simply ignored any papers sent to her. She wrote to him about money or about rude remarks that Peter made to her on the telephone, and announced that she blamed Peter alone for the break-up of an essentially happy marriage. She deluged him with letters about the children's teeth, their clothes and their progress at school. Russell replied that he would burn any letters which contained abusive attacks on Peter or on him. Soon, lawyers were drawn into their battles. The divorce papers alone – affidavits, memoranda, bills, accounts, depositions, letters and formal documents – fill five large boxes in McMaster's Russell Archives.

The divorce laws in the 1930s were not simple. They required proven adultery and a lengthy legal process. Both Russell and Dora wanted control of the children – Dora, sole custody; Russell joint – and were prepared to yield almost nothing; Dora equally wished for a decent financial settlement, so that she could continue with Beacon Hill School. Russell, who was prepared to negotiate over the money, dug his heels in about the children. To his old friend Crompton Llewelyn Davies, his solicitor and now reluctantly having to act for him, he wrote, 'I will never concede that the children shall be in Dora's physical care . . .'

Crompton was a charming man and a practised negotiator. All the same, his even temper became ragged as he embarked on years of mediation between two equally intransigent people. When the children went to stay with Russell, Dora pursued them with telephone calls, taking fierce exception to what she called Peter's 'snobbish' ways. 'I remain an unrepentant revolutionary,' she wrote sternly in the summer of 1933, 'and I do not like bourgeois values and elegances, for I think they stand in the way, especially at this time in history.' During one holiday, she rented a house a quarter of a mile from theirs and sat in her car at the gates, peering in to see what they were doing.

There were quarrels about clothes, about missing buttons, about combinations being too tight for John's testicles. When Russell returned the children to her, she looked through him. In return, Russell seized the children's passports, maintaining that she was about to whisk them off to America, and accused her of being an inadequate mother. 'Dora', he told Crompton, 'is slippery and very wicked; we must be careful.' As his patience began to give out, Crompton wrote to her: 'It is possible to admire, without emulating, your pugnacity, and we can take comfort in the pacifist's creed that the victor gets no real advantage over the vanquished . . . the chanting of Hymns of Hate only harm the hater, and if there are to be methods of frightfulness it is better to endure than to practise them.'

Sensible words, but little could distract Dora and, to a lesser extent, Russell, from descent into increasing spitefulness. He had the children made wards of Chancery, while Dora swore that any case would focus on her as the wronged wife, driven to desperation. No mention was made of Harriet and Roderick, which served to infuriate Russell further. In the spring of 1934, Russell began to write to her as 'Dear Madam' and sign himself, 'Yours faithfully, Bertrand Russell'. She continued to write to him as 'Bertie'. Squabbles and petty accounts filled pages and pages of letters.

Then the affidavits began and, in their wake, the evidence collected for Russell by a private detective. Dora was able to rely on the good testimonials of her staff; Russell, who was in a position to appeal to only a few of them, had to fall back on the report produced by a private detective, who spent a day interviewing innkeepers and bus drivers in the vicinity of the school, and hanging around the gardens of Telegraph House in wait for Griffin Barry, and taking cover in the wood whenever he caught sight of anyone. He lurked in the bushes until after ten at night, and was finally rewarded by the arrival of a smartly dressed man, '45ish', carrying a bag and wearing a trilby. This, he reported, was Barry.

Russell's witnesses included the former school driver and his wife, and a gardener, and the picture they gave of Dora was malicious. She was, they claimed, an irresponsible headmistress, a casual adultress and a heavy drinker. They had seen empty beer bottles outside the door of the cottage bedroom occupied by a certain Paul Gillard, a young friend of Barry's, who was 'tall, dark and Jew-like, with an effeminate appearance', and with whom Dora had fallen in love. They hinted that Dora had possibly become pregnant again, after Roderick, by Gillard, and had an abortion, because after Gillard died in mysterious circumstances following a fall, Dora had been observed in hysterics, screaming unashamedly in front of the entire school 'my lovely Paul'. There was also talk of her being a callous mother, in that she had not seemed greatly upset when Roderick fell out of an upper window.

Dora was not, however, without supporters. The staff at Beacon Hill were almost unanimously for her, and the local doctor came forward to say that the health of the children in her care had been excellent. Parents were canvassed, and Jack Pritchard, the modernist architect, was one of several fathers who came forward to swear that she had not slept with them. Lily Howell, the matron, gave evidence that the school was not, as had been suggested, filthy, that Gillard had not been a drunk, and that there had been no parties with 'excessive drinking' or 'loose relations'.

The wrangling went on. Francis Meynell, one of the children's trustees and an old friend of both Russells, now intervened, trying to persuade Russell to find a dignified way out of this 'impossibilist atmosphere'. Ottoline Morrell, canvassed by Dora, replied that she would not be drawn in: 'My own opinion is that the only possible way out of the difficulty is that there should be a divorce more or less by agreement, giving Bertie the custody of his two children, with some arrangement for you to see them from time to time.' Russell, meanwhile, had written to Julian and Juliette Huxley, friends from Garsington days, asking them to testify that he was a fit and proper father and saying that if all else failed he would rather not marry Peter than lose the children. He also approached Bob and Elizabeth Trevelyan, saying that if Dora succeeded in 'depriving me wholly of John and Kate, the whole of the rest of my life will be one of unbearable misery'. Curry, the headmaster of Dartington, provided another testimonial, but not before saying that the whole thing rather embarrassed him, as he considered himself a disciple of Russell's, and 'after all, curates do not write testimonies for the Archbishop of Canterbury.'

From a hotel in Wales, Deudraeth Castle in Penrhyndeudraeth, where he was sitting out the skirmish, Russell told Ottoline that leaving Dora for Peter was the wisest thing he had ever done. 'Two days ago we had a meeting of the children's trustees; Dora seemed much more insane than before. I hate the children having to associate with her. Perhaps in time she will be certified.' Finally, at the end of 1934, after almost three years of squabbles, an agreement of sorts was reached, and a decree nisi was awarded to Dora on the grounds of Russell's adultery with Peter. Both parents were to have custody of the children, who would spend their holidays equally divided between them; Russell would pay alimony. It all looked simple, but it was an agreement only in principle, and Dora continued to prevaricate until she could no longer block the decree absolute.

For John and Kate, aged ten and eight at the start of the hostilities, and fourteen and twelve when they came to an end, the entire process had been painful, embarrassing and confusing, their loyalties constantly torn as a result of being made to carry messages of reproach to and from their parents' homes. Whenever they inadvertently let slip some detail of their other life, 'reams of self justification' followed. John, anxious about many things and deeply resentful of his father, turned ever more closely to Dora, and lapsed back into baby talk. 'It was a rotten deal,' he would say much later. 'From that moment on everything went wrong.' Kate, who had always felt closer to Russell, turned violently against her mother, and concentrated on her father a childhood worship which was to bring her considerable unhappiness. In her autobiography, she compared herself to a dog the family had once owned who, 'bred more for looks than intelligence', used to pick up the scent of a rabbit, then run, not after it, but back along its original track. 'We watched the performance with lofty amusement,' she wrote, 'despising the poor dog for his stupidity and his inability to use his eyes as we did. But secretly I identified with the dog . . . He was not really stupid, only a dog, behaving as a dog behaves. That is what it was like, having Bertrand Russell for a father.'

In 1934, despite Dora's protests that Dartington was 'economically and socially snobbish' . . . 'likely to produce Fascists and Bright Young People', Russell got her to agree to transfer the children there. John, it appeared, was being appallingly teased by the other children at Beacon Hill. Not surprisingly, John and Kate, once installed in the anonymity of a school which knew nothing of the horrors of their parents' bickerings, were soon happier.

Dora and Russell have left very different verdicts on their fifteen years of marriage. Russell, who had once been so much in love with her, looked back on the experience with disgust. Dora was more generous, though when angry she would claim Russell had been responsible for Gillard's death – it was never clear whether or not he had committed suicide – and that Gillard was the only man she had ever really loved. 'I am quite unrepentant,' she wrote to Russell, on a better day; 'my only regret is that we failed together to bring the whole thing off; it would have been simply glorious if we had succeeded.' For the rest of her long life, according to her children and her friends, Dora, like Alys, never really stopped loving Russell.

How much was the failure of their marriage ultimately his? The writer Freda Utley, a long-time friend of Russell's, spoke in later years, by which time she had taken against him, of his 'terrific sexual urges' which caused him to 'assume the repulsive expression of a lustful satyr'. He was, she wrote, doomed to failure in his marriages, because he was seeking an 'impossible combination of Cleopatra, Hypatia and St Theresa, Boadicea and Joan of Arc, and was also drawn to Quakers and other Puritan types . . .'

Russell had set out on his marriage to Dora convinced that his ideas about modern relationships could be sustained by any well-intentioned couple. In the end it was he, and not Dora, who could not handle them. 'I found', he wrote later in a pious vein, 'that my capacity for forgiveness and what may be called Christian love was not equal to the demands I was making on it.' In a statement to the High Court, admittedly trying to present himself in an advantageous light, he added that his views on 'sexual subjects had . . . changed considerably', in that he was now persuaded that infidelities were undesirable 'so long as the marriage has any reality'. It had always been Dora's wish, but not his own, he said, that had led him to accept an 'unusual basis for our marriage, and experience has not shown that this was wise'.

Russell assumed that Beacon Hill School, faced with seemingly insoluble money problems, would have to close. As the depression deepened in the United States, many American parents delayed payment of their school fees. Telegraph House also suffered from an acute shortage of water, since it depended on rain to fill its cisterns; in times of drought, the start of the school term had to be postponed until the rains came.

But Dora had no intention of giving up the school. It was working better than she had ever imagined, and she felt that she had become, as she wrote to H. G. Wells, 'a sort of genius at my school job'. She was very involved in the new schools movement generally, under the chairmanship of Clifford Allen, though she and Neill felt themselves being pushed to its far left wing, as Allen turned against what he called those 'dangerous and terrible people' and the 'extremism of the Russell school of thought', saying that he had come to prefer Otto Hahn's 'dynamic outlook on life'. 'Self-consciousness about sex teaching and about the subject itself,' Allen wrote, 'whether it is the self-consciousness of the sentimentalist or the crude propagand-ist seems to me equally dangerous.' Neill increasingly saw himself and Dora as fellow pioneers, and the 'only educators', particularly when he came to believe it was the 'savage' parents and not the children who were the real problem.

The question for Dora was how to keep on attracting enough pupils without Russell's trawls in America, and how to finance the shortfall between fees and costs, at a time when the popular newspapers appeared to have grown bored with the whole subject of progressive education. In the year Russell left, Dora wrote six articles on education, but failed to sell one. Neill, whom she approached for help, advised her to pretend that Beacon Hill School was still being run officially with Russell. 'If not, all the perverted sex maniacs will make your job more difficult. In this bloody civilisation you should keep the separation dark until you have set the school on its feet.'

In the autumn of 1934, Dora left Telegraph House and reopened Beacon Hill School in a three-storey Georgian house near Brent-wood in Essex, Boyles Court. In the summer, to raise money, she turned it into a conference centre for the Progressive League, a loose federation of reform societies started by Cyril Joad. Because nudists were among their number, and few establishments in the 1930s welcomed naked guests, Beacon Hill provided an excellent setting. None the less, the school remained perpetually on the brink of financial collapse, and Dora was forced to move again, merging first with Brickwall in Kent, and then, in 1937, when she settled on Kingwell Hall, owned by a Labour supporter named William Scobell. These were probably Beacon Hill School's happiest years. The house stood in a charming patch of wild country, halfway between Bath and Bristol, with a ha-ha, paddocks and a swimming pool.

Twenty children arrived, most of them bringing their pets. John was given a capuchin monkey, which chirped like a baby when it was given a bath. In the summer, the school was again taken over by the Progressive League, bringing with them old friends like H. G. Wells and the Huxleys.

Former teachers and pupils recall these years with affection. Kate Newman, who was a dancing teacher, remembers Dora's exceptional energy and the way she seemed capable of everything, organising the plays she so enjoyed, writing to parents and campaigning for funds, even if persistent near-bankruptcy made her somewhat mean with salaries. Freed from the responsibilities of Telegraph House, where she appeared always to be in a hurry, she was more peaceful, more ready to give the children the physical affection they needed. Daphne Uribe, who went to the school at the age of nine, retains the clearest image of Dora as someone ever approachable and ever interested in the children's concerns, and feels great gratitude to her. At later schools, she found that she possessed not just the necessary educational standards but what always seemed to her far more important: a feeling that she could cope with anything. The intensity of Beacon Hill School cannot always have been easy: teachers and friends alike were aware of how bitterly Dora still felt about Russell and the divorce and how, despite a second marriage to a man much younger than herself, a somewhat thuggish member of the Communist Party named Pat Grace, she still talked endlessly of her early years with Russell. It was little comfort for her to be told by H. G. Wells that 'Russell treats other women meanly and vindictively. I know them.'

Kate and John were now at Dartington, Russell's wishes having prevailed. He had become friendly with the headmaster, Curry, and approved of his intention to run the school 'free from sentimentalism' but with high academic standards. Several times, Russell agreed to talk on topics like reason and pacifism at the Sunday evening meetings. To the headmaster, Kate and John seemed well informed, friendly and cheerful and he wrote to tell their father that he had never taken in two children who gave him less cause for anxiety, or had settled in so quickly. Admittedly, John was small for his age but 'as becomes the son of a philosopher . . . mere size is a matter of no consequence.' He believed that the two children, whom Dora now insisted on referring to as 'prisoners of Chancery', were both potential scholarship winners. Dora, the more regular visitor to Dartington, agonised Kate by turning up in slovenly dress, her long hair pulled untidily back, a cigarette hanging from her lips, sitting comfortably with her knees far apart, conveying a sense of general dottiness and lack of style. Other mothers came better turned out.

Informality, an emphasis on happiness, and an immense regard for natural curiosity were the hallmarks of the Russells' school. Was Beacon Hill a success? Dora felt that it was; Russell declared it a failure. Once freed of the tendrils of Telegraph House, he began to talk of the entire experiment as a mistake, a view he held virtually unchanged until he died, and was reluctant to discuss the school with anyone who came to see him. It was not just that Beacon Hill School had failed to usher in the new social order he dreamt of; it had destroyed some of his illusions. Cruelty, he had always believed, could be suppressed by reason and understanding: only bored children were cruel. If you took a child young enough, it would never become cruel at all. Yet Beacon Hill pupils had demonstrated the same degree of nastiness and bullying as children anywhere else, and it had been disconcerting to find that this could be curbed only by the discipline he so abhorred. It all fitted in horribly well with his growing conviction, as he saw the steady rise of nationalism throughout the world, that war and economic collapse would all too soon follow in its wake. If Russell remained physically attached to small children – photographs of him taken on the steps of Telegraph House, surrounded by beaming children and beaming himself, reveal a man who genuinely loved their company – he had in the end found the school too wearisome, the parents too casual, the administration too boring, many of the pupils too disturbed and the financial burden too heavy.

He rejected Beacon Hill because he believed that it would have to close, and he wanted a school he respected for his own children. This was Dartington, but to justify this choice meant pouring scorn on much that Beacon Hill School had stood for. Just as he now repudiated his marriage to Dora, so he later repudiated the school. Both episodes in his life had come to an end: it was another chapter closed. His silence and pessimism effectively cast a cloud over the school.

Much of his gloom was misplaced. Many of the ideals advanced by Russell and Dora in the mid-1920s proved sound and have made their way painlessly into mainstream education. Beacon Hill School was set up to combat the existing ethos that schools were meant to turn out biddable citizens, punctual and docile, never questioning the rightness or wrongness of political decisions. Both Russell and Dora considered these qualities utterly inappropriate for modern life, and believed that democracy could be made to work only if children could be helped to become questioning, responsible and happy adults. At its simplest, a good education included the arts and science, the glory of the modern age, imparted with love. Freedom was not an end in itself, but the means to attaining a 'good life'.

True, they were inspired by somewhat different credos. Russell, whose interest lay ultimately in the philosophical ideas underpinning education, placed his emphasis on the intellect, arguing that the broader the knowledge the greater the choices for finding satisfaction, and seeing educational theories in terms of the people they produced. More than Dora or Neill, Russell was drawn towards J. B. Watson's behaviourism, which appealed to him because it dealt with data which could be proved through observation. For Russell, whose forays into eugenics could strike decidedly unpleasant notes, some children were born clever and some stupid; both, however, needed information and a trained and agile mind to help them make decisions. Education was a struggle with ideas.

For Dora, intelligence came with learning, and its purpose was to create a better race of human beings, by replacing conventional 'repressive religions, laws, governments' with 'love, nurture and education'. If Russell's educational prose was crisp, hers could be startlingly flowery. 'Let there be no Achilles' heel of ignorance and repression', she wrote in *The Right to be Happy* about the children she envisaged emerging from her care: 'So equipped, so armed, so adorned, pennants flying, sails swelling, bows lifting in eager pride, they glide to the launching, they are the ark of our deliverance, the argosy of our adventure.' The adult and the child had to be seen as part of the whole natural world.

The Russells were progressive, certainly, and their views on sex in particular were shocking for the 1920s. Today, their ideas about making learning exciting, seeing it as a means for doing away with fear, and coaxing out such virtues as truthfulness and generosity, are regarded as commonplace. The differences between their two credos were not in the end great: they came to seem larger than they were because of the personal distance which came to separate them, and because Russell was so vehement in his rejection of Beacon Hill School. All along, as Neill rightly pointed out, it was really 'Dora's show'. Writing when he was in his late eighties, Neill gave his verdict on Russell. 'He dealt only with small kids . . . Their violence to each other frightened him. . . . He was a thinker, a philosopher, and although in his private sex life he was free, I fancy he distrusted too much freedom for kids.'

Russell's third marriage, to Peter Spence (who legally changed her name from Marjorie to Patricia and liked to be known as Peter), took place in Chislehurst, at the Midhurst registry office, on Saturday 18 January 1936. Russell was sixty-three; Peter twenty-five. Russell wrote, somewhat smugly, to Miriam Brudno, 'She has no child yet. I think it is a drawback to a child to be illegitimate.' Ottoline was to have been a witness, but had to refuse on grounds of ill-health. Instead she sent Peter a star brooch as a wedding present. 'I suppose you heard – or saw – that Bertie was married last Saturday to the Spence female,' Colette wrote to Elizabeth Russell. 'Do you think he will perhaps come back to me – to die?'

Russell had decided to move back into Telegraph House, once the school had gone, largely for financial reasons. His income was again precarious, with the public buying fewer books, and the Hearst organisation having reduced the number of articles they wanted from him, until finally the demand stopped altogether. Russell attributed this to having refused Hearst's invitation to stay in California during his last trip to America, in 1931.

The intense ill-feeling between himself and Dora was fuelled when he discovered that she had stripped Telegraph House of most of its furniture, and left it filthy, with lavatories overflowing and 'dust and stink everywhere'. Unable to move in, the Russells were forced to camp out in a caravan, with John, Kate, two maids and their illegitimate babies, three dogs, one of which was particularly large, one cat and a large amount of personal belongings. Because Dora owed considerable sums of money to local people, it was some time before anyone could be persuaded to come to clean the place. To the writer Gerald Brenan, Russell wrote that Peter was 'overwhelmed by bugs, fleas, cats, puppies and baby birds, not to mention sanitary authorities, builders, electricians, gardeners, babies and other minor fauna of the countryside, besides whitewash and pots of paint'. Eventually every room was fumigated, every floor scrubbed. Russell was installed in the library on the ground floor, where he sat every morning at a desk in the bay window, his spectacles on his nose, smoking a pipe, neither fidgeting nor crossing things out as he wrote, simply working steadily until eleven o'clock when a maid came with tea. He then drank three cups, warming his hands around the rim, and went back to work until lunchtime. Provided she made no sound, Kate was allowed to sit with him.

Peter was an interesting figure. Subsequent events in Russell's life have shown her to be difficult and dislikeable, but in the mid-thirties she stood up for Russell with considerable love and determination, turning Telegraph House, through immense hard work, into somewhere pleasant to live and acting uncomplainingly as his secretary and research assistant. When Russell first met her, she was doing an extra-mural course of studies in Oxford, and was closely involved in the left-wing student movement of the 1930s. She was attractive if not, by most accounts, beautiful, with copper red hair and a very white skin. She was tall, thin, even bony, and she had dimples when she smiled. When angry, she glowered. She dressed plainly, even severely, usually in tailormade trousers. Colette, possibly not the most reliable of witnesses, thought she had a 'pudding face' and an execrable taste in shoes. Peter, so called because her father is said to have wanted a boy, was a great walker and, like Dora, smoked a pipe.

Oxford friends remember her as 'rather magnificent and proud' and very fond of parties. One of her companions was Adam von Trott, whom she defended when, on his return to Germany, after spending some time in Oxford as a Rhodes scholar, rumour reached

England that he had joined the Nazi Party. The story of her loyalty got back to von Trott, who sent her a postcard saying he hoped she had not changed the colour of her red hair, and that he had not changed the colour of his.

These people were, however, about her own age. Russell's friends, twenty, thirty, or even fifty years her senior, found her withdrawn and even difficult, Virginia Woolf noting in her diary that Peter was full of 'self-conscious control' . . . 'lying on the floor in an attitude calculated to attract'. Frances Partridge recalled a dinner party in Clive Bell's house during which Peter seemed annoyed at being ignored, though when she did contribute to the conversation, she had little to say of interest. The Bloomsberries approved of her sense of style, Frances Partridge remembering a 'rather slinkily shaped bright green emerald dress, like a model, which made her look marvellous'. The Halévys compared her to a Rossetti painting, but found her more beautiful than agreeable. At their first encounter, Peter crocheted continuously but spoke hardly at all.

It cannot have been easy for her. She was not only less than half Russell's age, but she had entered a world of established, clever, confident people, most of whom had long since formed their views about politics and morality. She had also become stepmother to two children considerably nearer her age than she was to her husband's, and who had been made wary and truculent by a singularly nasty divorce case. John found her distant and somewhat aloof; but Kate, looking back on those early days, was to say that Peter brought a breath of happiness into their lives. Where Dora was unkempt, forgetful and utterly without taste or style, Peter was elegant and fastidious despite Colette's view of her shoes. Russell himself reflected this new image; normally grubby when married to Dora, with jam on his tie and his dark suits distinctly mottled, he was now spruce and tidy. Telegraph House was totally transformed; gone were the garish colours and the random collection of objects: there were new wallpapers, fresh paint and good furniture, the dining-room table was polished and laid with the Russell silver, the food excellent and beautifully presented. Kate, long embarrassed by her mother's vague ways, was charmed. Peter, who had herself felt agonisingly awkward as a girl, warmed to the uneasy schoolgirl, and taught her how to polish her nails and do her hair. If Dora was disgusted, and said so, it did nothing to lessen Kate's admiration for her stepmother.

Peter was, however, extravagant, and the bills for the redecoration of Telegraph House soon redoubled Russell's anxieties about money, already made acute by the depression in America, by Dora's constant demands for alimoney, and by the fact that he was running out not only of ideas for 'pot-boilers', but of any desire to write them. 'I am trying to revert to writing good books', he told Ottoline, 'instead of bad ones, but that means a small income.' For perhaps the first time in his life, he was finding it almost unmanageable. 'I have never in my life before been so tired,' he told Gilbert Murray, saying he could think of nothing but suicide as a way of avoiding further work. Both he and Peter seem to have had some kind of nervous breakdown, Russell averting complete exhaustion by spending eight weeks of inactivity in the Canary Islands. For two months, he told friends, he had been sitting at his desk in Telegraph House, working on the 'problem of the 27 straight lines on a cubic surface', his only 'unalloyed pleasures' being sleep and detective stories, which he took out of the local library at the rate of one a day. He found people, he wrote to Amber Blanco White, 'thinking my recent writing inferior, and I suppose I have got careless. I see ruin staring me in the face, if once people stop wanting to read me.' None of this was made easier by the attitude of his friends. Gerald Brenan wrote to tell him that he was 'a great imaginative writer of the nature of Swift and Voltaire', which was why 'I regret you should have such a desire to counsel and improve mankind: and you use only half your powers when you write homilies.'

Russell had been pleased with *Marriage and Morals*, which he felt contained some of his best writing on people and their relationships, and on his theory that knowledge is one of the great cures for fear. Written at the height of his emotional turmoil with Dora, still embroiled with various women from time to time, there is something touching about the strength with which he maintained that love was one of the most crucial things in the world, and intimacy of paramount value. Loneliness, as he wrote repeatedly during these years of packed love affairs, was the fate suffered by most of mankind: to escape it, even for a moment, was sublime.

Russell's attitude towards his pot-boilers was rather ambivalent. In conversation, he tended to dismiss them as ways of making money. But, as he wrote in *Portraits from Memory* many years later, there was more to it than that. Discussing Whitehead and his contribution to the world, Russell notes that he had 'aimed at bringing comfort to plain people'; while Russell had 'aimed at bringing discomfort to philosophers' and, perhaps more importantly, 'amusing' the plain people.

The early 1930s had been extraordinarily prolific years: a book on education, one on marriage and happiness, and one on science and society, in which he argued that science, when it came to civilisation, was not enough: wisdom was needed as well. Writing to Unwin about this book, *The Scientific Outlook*, Russell said that his intention was to 'pillory those whom the public believe to be men of science'. It made him sick to 'see the hogwash in which Eddington and Jeans *et hoc genus omne* are causing the public to wallow, and I should like to give the public a nice clean sty'. 'Even more important than knowledge', he wrote, 'is the life of the emotions. A world without delight and without affection is a world destitute of value.' Reviewers were almost always admiring of these popular books. Frank Betts, in the *New Leader*, praised him for being more provocative than any of his contemporaries; for Russell, who felt that he never achieved the popularity of Wells, it was pleasant to hear someone say 'he thinks and he knows, where Shaw and Wells only guess.' In the *Daily Telegraph*, Rebecca West remarked that an 'unbroken mood of felicity seems to have visited Mr Russell'. If, later, Russell complained that chunks of Aldous Huxley's *Brave New World* were no more than an expanded version of some views expressed in *The Scientific Outlook*, he did no more than remark on it at the time.

For some time, Russell had been contemplating a new subject, something more profound on the question of freedom. During the most acrimonious phase of his dealings with Dora he managed to start work on what rapidly turned into a 'very big and rather serious work', which he talked of making several volumes long. *Freedom versus Organisation*, a liberal-left analysis of society and politics, took eighteen months to complete, despite Peter's help as a researcher. Like *The Prospects of Industrial Civilisation*, it discussed those ideas which had seemed to change mankind, and the individuals responsible for them. 'It is not by pacifist sentiment', he concluded, foreshadowing some of his later thinking, 'but by world-wide economic organisation that mankind is to be saved from collective suicide.' C. E. M. Joad, the philosopher who always enjoyed needling him, announced that in Russell's hands history became nothing more than a 'fantasia on the themes of human greed and folly'. Shaw was more generous. He remarked that he found the title 'repulsively dry' but added that the work was that of a first-rate mind, an 'oasis in a desert of Histories of Human Humbug by people with no minds at all'. Sales, however, were poor. News of his unsavoury divorce had reached America, while the British public seemed more interested in buying copies of Wells's recently published autobiography. Russell, uncharacteristically, blamed Unwin for poor advertising, to which the normally courteous Unwin replied with irritation that the book had been advertised in eleven major and nine minor papers and magazines, in some cases three or four times.

Driven by anxiety about money, Russell was again in pressing need of a best-selling subject. There is something very touching about his endless preoccupation with his responsibilities. At Gilbert Murray's suggestion he turned to history, looking back across four centuries at the quarrels between religion and science and arguing that 'while the older religion has become putrefied . . . new religions have arisen, with all the persecuting zeal of rigorous youth and with as great a readiness to oppose science as characterised by the inquisition at the time of Galileo'. On its publication in 1935, *Religion and Science* was greeted warmly by the public, who were pleased by Russell's return to the subject, though a Jesuit priest told him off firmly for trespassing in a field about which he knew nothing. That same year he reverted to the subject of popular morality, in a collection of essays, *In Praise of Idleness*, on what to do with the leisure which people would gain in a better ordered world.

In 1938 came *Power*, a refutation of both Marx and the classical economists, regarded by Russell as the most thoughtful contribution he made to political sociology. *Power* was written at a moment when

Russell was trying to reconcile personal freedom with stable and efficient government, and it represented the drawing together of all his ethical work. His view of human nature had never been wholly pessimistic, and he had long argued that man was capable of altruism but that he was governed by an appetite for power. In *Power*, Russell examined the different historical alternatives – monarchy, oligarchy and so on – and suggested that reason alone could not determine the goals of life. Moral beliefs were essentially expressions of desire, whether personal – for a chocolate – or impersonal – for peace. Impersonal desires were concerned with the wellbeing of others as well as oneself, and were thus 'moral'. To those who argued that once the difference between good and evil has been reduced to a question of taste, all incentive to do good is bound to die, Russell replied that it was all a question of the scope of one's desires. Since people were eager to gratify their desires, if they were sufficiently broad, wholesome social policies would result. Subjectivism, therefore, led to tolerance. Later, philosophers were to pick endless holes in Russell's moral theories, but seldom find more satisfactory ones to replace them.

Not surprisingly, publishers on both sides of the Atlantic had long been interested in Russell as the subject of an autobiography. In 1936, he received a letter from the literary agent Curtis Brown, saying that Victor Gollancz was prepared to offer £1000 – a considerable sum at the time – for British rights alone. Few people knew that Russell had been playing with the idea of an autobiography for many years. As early as 1912, he had sent a memoir of his life to Ottoline, containing accounts of his childhood, the failure of his marriage to Alys and his various intellectual difficulties and successes. Though this memoir has not survived, some fragments found their way into *Forstice*. A second attempt, written while his separation from Dora was being contested, has survived, and much of it was included in the final version which saw the light in the late 1960s, though not some of the harsher details of that unhappy relationship. Between May and June 1931, he dictated a first draft to a secretary.. He explained to Unwin that though he had decided to commit his life to paper, the book was not to appear until after his death. 'Suppose I should end my days as President of Mexico. The biography would seem incomplete if it did not mention this fact.' This kind of dry wit found its way increasingly into his letters. As to a contract, Unwin assured Russell that it would be absurd to bring an agent into their long-standing relationship, for his firm would always match any offer made. A copy of the autobiography went to Crompton, with a note saying that no one was to see it until after his death. No one, that was, except Ottoline, to whom he sent another copy, and was surprised when she expressed hurt at some of his statements. He apologised, saying sadly that he always seemed to hurt those he loved. Ottoline begged him to exclude certain passages, even if the book were not to see the light for another hundred years.

With his past on his mind, it was understandable that he should react favourably to a suggestion by the Nonesuch Press that he edit a book of the many letters left by his parents. Russell never considered *The Amberley Papers* an exciting work, since by definition works of importance either attempted to improve the lot of mankind, or constituted an original contribution to philosophy. He was extremely grateful for the amount of work that Peter did on it, to the exclusion of much else, and Peter's name appeared on the cover, together with his. Peter was soon complaining to Ottoline, in humour rather than irritation, that they were living as if they were working for an examination, and that she risked 'becoming a slut like Dora'. *The Amberley Papers*, which had eventually gone to the Hogarth Press, appeared as two volumes and were well received. Russell received a letter from Elizabeth, saying that had she read the book before she married Frank, she would never have gone ahead with the wedding. 'The child's father to the man with a vengeance . . .'

Books on education, religion, science, marriage, idleness, happiness, political economy, history, and a column for the *New Statesman* started in the early 1930s: fifteen years of astonishing output. Something of his appetite, or need, for work can be seen in a letter he wrote to Unwin in the summer of 1937. He had, he told his publisher, several books in hand, nine lectures, and a new idea for a history of philosophy from Descartes to William James, intended for 'beginners in universities'. None of this, however, was enough to soothe his anxiety about money. Complaining that he had to part with a third of his income to Dora, he devoted considerable time to thinking up ways of reducing it, either by setting Peter's salary as his secretary against his earnings, or by getting some of his income paid directly to Peter. In September 1937 he decided to sell Telegraph House. It was a painful decision, for it was his last contact with the past. Even then, the money it fetched had to go into a trust until the death of Frank's second wife, the 'fat and florid' Mollie, who, Russell noted bleakly, 'is 80, but still going strong, like Johnnie Walker and (they say) by his help'.

When Frank died, Russell and Dora announced that they would not be using the title of Earl and Countess, but preferred to be known by their own names. However, it was widely assumed that sooner or later Russell would relent and take up his seat in the House of Lords, the idea provoking a certain amount of hilarity in the popular newspapers. His reservations were not only about the House of Lords, and whether he would ever find time to attend, but about the Labour Party itself, with which he had become, as he told Gilbert Murray, too dissatisfied to be a loyal party man. He approved of what he called their 'concordat with Gandhi' and most of their foreign policies, 'but not their complete inaction at home'. As he wrote to a friend, 'I do not like them, but an Englishman has to have a Party just as he has to have trousers, and of the three parties I find them the least painful. My objection to the Tories is temperamental, and my objection to the Liberals is Lloyd George. I do not think that in joining a party one necessarily abrogates the use of one's reason. I know that my trousers might be better than they are; nevertheless they seem better to me than none.'

After receiving a letter from Sidney Webb (created Baron Passfield of Passfield Corner in 1929), pressing him to join the House but warning him that it was 'deadly dull', Russell informed the party whip that he could be counted on to support the government whenever he was available to do so. His maiden speech on 24 February 1937 was brief, lasting less than twenty minutes. It was noted in the House of Lords that his dry and precise delivery contrasted strongly with 'the late Earl's courteously persuasive tones'. Nor did Russell's speech go down all that well with the Labour peers, who cheered him warmly when he spoke of the folly of the

current defence programme, but fell silent when he switched to
pacifism. Writing to friends in America about the war in Abyssinia
and the growth of fascism and nationalism in Europe, he was once
again pessimistic about the future. 'I'm afraid', he wrote to Miriam
Brudno, 'the bad times are likely to continue and get worse. The
people who direct the world's affairs are very stupid, and always do
exactly the wrong thing. No improvement is possible without international cooperation, and the world grows more and more nationalist.' And, later, 'We all live under the shadow of Hitler, with the
feeling that we may get his kind of regime here. The world is
infinitely more cruel than it was in my day.'

As the decade wore on, and Europe saw ever larger numbers of
people displaced by political violence and the Nazis' racial policies,
Russell and Peter were drawn into helping refugees and political
prisoners. There was not much they could do, but occasionally
Russell was able to act for a foreign colleague trying to leave
Germany and to find work. It was often Peter who did the lobbying;
her style was more passionate that Russell's, and effective. She wrote
urging Unwin to take up the case of a friend called Guttchen, a
German translator and interpreter – 'not a Jew but a pacifist' – while
he was at a publishers' congress in Leipzig. The congress was being
boycotted by a number of foreign firms, and Peter protested that this
would merely isolate the German publishers even more. The case
for intellectual liberty, she wrote, 'is best served by attempting to
keep in touch with them, and not by leaving them weeping and
gnashing their teeth in outer darkness'.

Helping political prisoners proved more difficult. In 1936 Arcady
Berdichevsky, the finance manager of Promexport, the largest export
organisation in the USSR, was arrested during a Stalinist round-up
and deported to a labour camp. Freda Utley was Berdichevsky's
wife, and Russell pestered his friends who had contacts in the Soviet
Union to intervene. It led to a number of revealing exchanges. The
Russells began by approaching the Webbs, whose recently published
book, *Soviet Russia – A New Civilisation*, had become required
reading for Soviet supporters in the west. They drove over to
Passfield Corner in Surrey for tea, taking Freda with them. Beatrice
Webb was in a pontificating mood, holding forth on the progressive

policies of the Soviet Union, and the delights of public ownership. Finally she was steered round to the question of Berdichevsky. When she prevaricated, Russell was unexpectedly firm. Without saying as much, he indicated that an outright refusal might mean the end of a long friendship, which, despite setbacks, had managed to survive. The Webbs produced a sheet of paper and wrote personally to Stalin.

Shaw, who had been a friend of Freda's father when they were young journalists together, proved more intractable. The Russells visited him at home, and came back pleased. Then a note arrived from Shaw saying that he had sensed that Freda was basically 'prejudiced against' the Soviet Union, so he felt he could do nothing. Could the Russells enlighten him? Was it possible that Freda was not a true believer in the communist faith? Once again, it was an outraged Peter who took up the fight. She began by writing Shaw a tactful reply, explaining that though perhaps a 'bit' prejudiced, Freda's despair about her husband was making her unduly vehement. Eventually Shaw agreed to write to the Soviet government, and a copy of a somewhat intemperate letter, referring to the 'pressure of public opinion', arrived at Telegraph House. Freda, fearing that it would merely provoke the Soviet authorities, and put her husband in greater danger, asked Shaw whether he could not soften his remarks. He refused: 'Take comfort', he wrote sententiously, 'in the fact that five years will not last forever; that imprisonment under the Soviets is not as bad as it is here in the west.' Russell was furious. Shaw, he remarked to Freda, was 'a swine'. Peter went further. 'Dear Mr Shaw,' she wrote, 'I thought when I met you that you were kind. Now I realise that it is only Mrs Shaw who is kind, and that you, as I had often been told, are frivolous and cruel. And if you really believe what you said about Soviet justice you must also be rather stupid. My husband asks me to say that he concurs in what I write.'

An 'exasperated' Shaw replied, not to Peter but directly to Freda: 'Very well, have it your own way: cook my letter to your taste and use it as you please . . . Meanwhile I still suspect that Mr Berdichevsky's exile may be less stormy than his home life.' He then sent Peter a generous note. 'I note that Bertrand "concurs". Of course he does. Would you have him wreck his home? Tyrant! Just as before,

G. Bernard Shaw.' Peter apologised for her 'abominable rudeness' and there the matter ended; except that Russell, according to Freda Utley, never forgave Shaw.

The thirties, like the years that followed immediately on the First World War, saw further breaks in Russell's friendships. Deaths accounted for some, but not all. Shaw and Russell, natural allies at moments of crisis, with shared views about man's folly and both dedicated to the spread of literacy and knowledge (some of Shaw's prefaces touch on the same themes as Russell's 'pot-boilers'), had little in common in peacetime. They were never, basically, friends, and once the world was tranquil had little desire to see each other. Wells, prickly and easily provoked, had long made clear his support of Dora. The Webbs had become, in Russell's eyes, sanctimonious, and he was no longer drawn to the company of the Fabians, although he agreed to lecture to them from time to time. A few old friends suffered from a feeling that Russell had no more time for them. Mary Sheepshanks, with whom he had discussed suffrage so long ago, was to remark that Russell, like Virginia Woolf, had the habit of dropping former friends about whom they no longer felt curious 'down an oubliette'.

Whitehead, whose last meeting with Russell had not been affable, was now permanently settled in America. Clifford Allen, once so devoted to Russell that he was prepared to put up with the cantankerousness of his Russian trip, disapproved of some of his educational theories. His wife Joan, according to their daughter Polly, disliked Russell intensely. In any case, Allen had little time left to live. In March 1939, he died in a Swiss sanatorium at the age of 49. Joan scattered his ashes over Lake Geneva. 'Poor C. A.!' Russell wrote to Colette, 'I felt absolutely nothing when he died.'

A. S. Neill, never a close friend but certainly a close correspondent, had remained more in touch with Dora. And death had taken not only Joseph Conrad but many of Russell's closest Cambridge friends, first Charles Sanger in 1930, and then Crompton Llewelyn Davies, who died of a heart attack in the middle of a dinner party in 1936. Russell's fondness for him had not wavered since Theodore's death in 1905. 'Hardly a day passes without my remembering some incident connected with him,' Russell wrote in an unpublished tribute which has a warmth sometimes lacking in his friendships. Crompton had been an 'anchor of stability in a disintegrating world', and he finished the tribute with his grandmother's words, heard so often at Pembroke Lodge: 'He was incapable of following a multitude, either for good or evil . . .'

Death was also about to close what was perhaps the single most important relationship of Russell's life: that with Ottoline Morrell. Ottoline's life, as her diaries show, was seldom happy. Tormented by self-doubt and bad health, she had spent the years since the end of her affair with Russell increasingly in pain with necrosis of the jaw, a disease in which part of the bone dies, and succumbing to greater displays of flamboyance and eccentricity as a way of dealing with loneliness. In 1928, finding life at Garsington too expensive, the Morrells bought a house in London, at 10 Gower Street, and the parties went on much as before. Thursday teas saw T. S. Eliot quarrelling with Koteliansky, the Russian émigré writer, over Anglicanism, or the Irish actress Sara Allgood singing the ballads of her childhood. The famous Garsington smell – pot-pourri, orris-root, pomanders – came to Gower Street, as did the bric-à-brac, the damask curtains, the Pekinese dogs, the drawings by Augustus John and Charles Conder's water-colours.

Just as she had always done, Ottoline continued to impress newcomers with her idiosyncratic speech, all underlined syllables and occasional trumpetings, with her distinctive scent and her clothes, 'sibilant shot-silk skirts' according to William Plomer, who met her in the last two years of her life, which set up a 'tremendous whispering campaign every time she moved'. As Ottoline grew increasingly deaf, she spent more time in bed. Her grandson, Philip Goodman, remembers how she refused to wear a hearing aid, and insisted on using an ear trumpet, which would be produced and proffered to the lips of the visitor. Milly, the parlourmaid, concocted teas of coloured jelly for the children.

Stephen Spender, who met Ottoline in the year of her death, noted that she gave the impression of falling apart, 'with hair like a curtain suddenly dropping over one eye, or a bodice bursting open'. Virginia Woolf, who seems to have felt an unwilling liking for her – she had once compared her to a 'ship with its sails rat-eaten, and its masts mouldy, and green sea-serpents on the decks', 'a weeping willow strung with pearls', an old fogey 'hawking and mousing', writing pathetic letters 'like the flight of owls on a hot day – so unsteady, top heavy, furtive, ill-judging . . .' – now noted cruelly in her diary that she had become 'so much of a ruin (without a sunset or nightingale or anything)'. But even she, watching Ottoline's last years, found her more gentle, 'shabby and humble and humorous'.

It was not only money that had driven Ottoline from Garsington. With the publication of Huxley's *Crome Yellow* and Lawrence's *Women in Love* – written by two men of whom she had been particularly fond, and very generous towards – something about the mocked house and its extraordinary gardens had gone sour for her. When Lawrence's derogatory letters appeared in the mid-1930s, Russell wrote to sympathise with her feelings of outrage, saying that Lawrence was indeed 'one of the sources of evil in the modern world'. The passion of their early love letters had long since given way to a calm intimacy. His last letter to her is dated 10 April 1938. It could have been 1914 all over again: 'I have very little hope that a great war will be avoided . . .'

Ottoline Morrell died of heart disease on 21 April, in a clinic in Tunbridge Wells; she was sixty-four. To Philip, Russell wrote, 'the news is a terrible blow and I feel stunned . . . A great part of my life, stretching back into childhood, is gone dead with her . . . I find that her gay courage, perhaps more than anything else, remains in my mind.'

Virginia Woolf wrote her obituary in *The Times*. 'As, though she listened carefully to the most intrepid doubters, she held fast to her deeply-rooted Christian mysticism, so she lived to the end, a great lady, refined, gentle, and kind to all, in spite of defying every hollow convention . . . Undeceived by appearances, undeterred by hostility, she endured, essentially gay, gallant, adventurous, and loyal to the last. A core of integrity in a world threatened by dissolution.' It was a moving tribute, if not an exact portrait; Ottoline would have been pleased. More written about, more described, more mocked than any comparable figure among her contemporaries, the final verdict, from a competitive and far sharper woman, had been kind.

Early in the war, the house in Gower Street was blasted when a bomb fell on nearby Goodge Street. Philip Morrell moved into Claridge's and lived on until 1943, playing bridge in the hotel's cellars during air raids, asking the hotel orchestra to play Mozart instead of their usual music, and becoming, according to his grandson, increasingly bad-tempered. His last dealings with Russell were acrimonious, with Morrell venting what must have been three decades of frustration and resentment. He asked Russell to write something for a memoir he was planning about Ottoline, to which a number of friends had said they would contribute, and sent him extracts from her journals to read. Russell, hard at work on a book, refused. Morrell burst out in dislike: 'What a mournful and almost incredible silence, that you should write of anything else in the world, but not a word of her.' In a postscript, he added: '. . . knowing how little you liked me in her life, I am not so foolish as to hope that I shall have any influence with you now.'

There were, of course, new friends, many of them much younger than Russell, but they were never to be as close. Shortly before they married, Russell took Peter to Spain to stay with Gerald Brenan and his wife Gamel, in a house near Malaga with two acres of walled garden and fine views over the Sierra Madre of the kind Russell liked best. Because the Brenans were short of money, Russell paid them a pound a week towards their keep;. Brenan had stayed with the Russells briefly at Telegraph House, and was nervous at the prospect of his celebrated guest, but he was instantly reassured. 'The man who descended from the bus could not have been more friendly or amiable,' he wrote, in a good portrait of Russell at the time, 'he was shorter than I had remembered, red face, looking with his large nose and jaunty step a little like Mr Punch, and covered with smiles.' The contrast with Peter, 'tall, very young and willowy . . . smooth pussycat face and a pleasant smile' as well as a 'rather determined chin', was noticeable. Russell, Brenan noted, held himself very straight, as if straining to reach higher. He was a most genial guest, working on the balcony in the mornings, quoting Dickens or Jane Austen from memory in the evenings, or reading extracts from the bible, of which he had an impressive knowledge, particularly of 'its absurd and scandalous passages'. (Leonard Woolf told Brenan that familiarity with the bible was something many atheists shared; the damaging bits were all 'part of their equipment'.)

Russell was in a good mood, writing to Miriam Brudno of his delight at 'no callers, no telephone, lovely country'. He also struck his hosts as astonishingly agile and full of energy, striding up 2000 feet of shale above the village to have tea out of a vacuum flask at the top. Apart from the punning, the jokes and the apparently inexhaustible knowledge of the English classics, Russell amazed Brenan by his 'lustfulness'. It was clear that his visitor had his eye on Gamel, openly admiring her poetry and what he called her 'lovely autumnal' personality. She, however, only 'half' liked him, considering he had wasted his talents as a mathematician on subjects of which he knew nothing, merely to gratify his senses of vanity and power. In time, she came to revise her view, and they became close friends and fond letter-writers until her death from cancer in 1968.

The closing years of the 1930s were not a good time for Russell. True, in 1937 Peter had given birth to a son, Conrad Sebastian John – the second boy to bear his Polish friend's name – but even that had been accompanied by anxiety. Obsessed since the days of his engagement to Alys with the possibility of madness in his offspring, Russell had written to the director of the asylum in which his uncle Willy had been confined after knifing a man, and where he had died three years before. The answer was not reassuring. The Honble George Gilbert William Russell, wrote the medical officer, had unquestionably been a schizophrenic, 'and in this there is a definite hereditary element . . . in my opinion the worst that can be inherited is a possible predisposition towards nervous illness, and undue strain and stress may more easily produce a breakdown than in other people.'

This chilling letter may explain Russell's excessive concern for John's and Kate's states of mind. When the children came to stay with him one Christmas, he wrote to Curry, headmaster at Darting-ton, that he found them 'listless and lifeless'. Given the 'insanity' on both sides of the family – it is not clear what evidence there was on Dora's side – the children needed close watching, particularly as he had observed that Kate was showing signs of moroseness and 'overwhelming fits of depression and languor'. So tetchy did Russell's letters become that Curry finally complained he had written to him as if he 'were a butcher who had sent you a bad piece of meat'.

For all this, Russell was delighted with his new son: the baby looked intelligent. But Peter felt guilty, fearing that the child only added to the financial burdens Russell had to bear. 'When I think of him being forced to go on struggling until he dies ... those beasts Dora and Mollie.' Ottoline, shortly before her death, agreed to become the child's godmother and sent a silver cup.

In September 1937, having sold Telegraph House to a businessman for £2500 – he was relieved about the money but sad at the loss of its magnificent views – Russell moved with Peter and Conrad to a rented house at Kidlington, outside Oxford. They had considered buying a house in Spain, but the Civil War was raging and Russell feared that the Court of Chancery would not let John and Kate join him there. The days of pot-boilers were largely over, and Russell was now eager to get back to philosophy, and be near people he could talk to. A second edition of *The Principles of Mathematics* was coming out, with a new introduction, in which Russell said he saw no reason to modify his original thesis that mathematics and logic were largely identical. He explained that his thesis had been unpopular when the book first appeared, in that mathematicians had felt logic to be little to do with them, while logicians had not been willing to master new and difficult mathematical techniques. He did, however, accept a modification to his Theory of Types, proposed by Frank Ramsay, the brilliant young Cambridge mathematician and philosopher, who had died in 1930 at the age of twenty-seven, and who had been one of the first philosophers to argue that many of the notorious paradoxes depended on the use of equivocal semantic notions, which had no place in mathematics.

Russell had put out feelers to Trinity, telling Moore that he was 'very desirous' of investigating 'the relation of language to fact', but had no encouragement. He noted that Cambridge now regarded him as an 'ossified orthodoxy'; Oxford, on the other hand, thought of him as 'revolutionary novelty' and invited him to give a series of lectures. The house at Kidlington was charming, covered in roses, with a walled garden protecting them from the road, and separate cottages for John and Kate. Russell called it Amberley House. Peter took a job as a reader with the Clarendon Press. Oxford, however, was rather less enjoyable than he had hoped. A neighbour, a biologist called Dr John Baker, taught him a game called 'Up-Jenkins', which consisted of hiding a coin between several fingers and trying to prevent the opposition from discovering where it was, but only one visitor came to call on them. 'We were not respectable,' he wrote in his autobiography; 'in this respect I have found these ancient seats of learning unique.' Writing to Logan Pearsall Smith, George Santayana observed: 'He talks of being forced to return to Brixton Prison, owing to his inability to pay his legal obligations . . .' Russell calculated that he had earnings of £300 a year and outgoings of £900.

But Oxford did make possible some kind of return to the serious work he had been hankering after, even if his main interests had for some time lain in political theory and economics. James Urmson, later Fellow and tutor at Corpus Christi, remembers Russell arriving to give his series of lectures. So many students turned up on the first day that the largest lecture room in Examination Schools overflowed. The students came, Urmson remembers, because Russell was a great man, and because they had all read *The Conquest of Happiness* and seen a message in it. What was more, he was a beguiling speaker. He had long since mastered the art of holding his audience: the voice was unmistakable, the delivery clear, coherent and consistent. There were few jokes, but there were humorous twists to his sentences, and a certain amount of emotion. Those students fortunate enough to be invited back to tea at Kidlington found Russell genial; it was only during philosophical confrontations that his tone could grow sharp. But even then, one student recalled: 'There was no side: he never talked down.'

Faced with the possibility of not finding a permanent university post in Britain, Russell had written to his publisher in America about a job at an American university. He wanted, he explained, to make money, to get down to serious work, and to leave Europe with 'its imminent risk of war'. The University of Chicago wrote to offer him an appointment as visiting professor of philosophy, lecturing in semantics for a winter term. There seemed little in England to keep him, apart from his two older children, and he had hopes of being able to persuade Dora to let them join him. The Russells sailed for New York in September 1938. He had submitted a mock obituary to the *Listener*, saying that it 'will (or will not) be published in *The Times* for June 1 1962, on the occasion of my lamented and belated death'. If not an entirely truthful portrait, it was remarkable for its foresight. The last paragraph is worth quoting in full:

> His life, for all its waywardness, had a certain anachronistic consistency, reminiscent of that of the aristocratic rebels of the early nineteenth century. His principles were curious, but, such as they were, they governed his actions. In private he showed none of the acerbity which marred his writing, but was a genial conversationalist and not devoid of human sympathy. He had many friends, but had survived almost all of them. Nevertheless, to those who remained, he appeared, in extreme old age, full of enjoyment, no doubt owing, in large measure, to his invariably good health, for politically, during his last years, he was as isolated as Milton after the Restoration. He was the last survivor of a dead epoch.

Russell was sixty-six; he had another thirty-two years to live.

Sixteen

Desiccated, divorced and decadent

By November, Russell, Peter and Conrad were installed in the Plaisance, an eight-storey residential hotel in Chicago overlooking Jackson Park. Russell wrote to friends that he would have been very happy were it not for having to leave John and Kate behind, and for the war, which he believed to be imminent, though still preventable. 'God knows whether we shall ever meet again in this world of madness,' he wrote to Gamel Brenan.

Russell already knew something of Chicago; he had been there first with Helen Dudley on his 1914 American trip, and had returned several times in the 1920s to lecture. By 1938 the university had grown vastly in size, with 12,000 students enrolled for the academic year. It was a pleasant place, set in the middle of a park, with grey limestone buildings in the English gothic style, and Russell was soon praising its mood of scholarship. He wrote, with satisfaction, to Gilbert Murray: 'This university, as far as philosophy is concerned, is about the best I have ever come across.' After the years of pot-boilers, he was delighted to be back in the company of philosophers and greatly relieved to be free of financial anxieties, the Board of Trustees having offered him $5000 for two terms. The understanding was that he would lecture every Monday on 'Problems of Philosophy', and give seminars once a week on 'Words and Facts', though he had been asked to make the title of these seminars more complicated, so they would be better 'respected'. Dutifully, he came up with 'The Correlation between Oral and Somatic Motor Habits', which was judged sufficiently obscure.

As a lecturer, Russell's 150 American students found him approachable in manner and lively in delivery. They remarked on his 'keen, almost sly sense of humour', his relaxed manner, and the way he never 'pontificated'. Peter was often seen sitting near the front of the audience. But it was the two-hour Thursday evening seminar which soon became the focus of his serious work in Chicago. He decided to use these sessions to develop the themes he had begun in Oxford with his lectures on 'Language and Fact', and which would be further explored in Harvard before being published in 1940 as *An Inquiry into Meaning and Truth*.

On the first Thursday, the seminar was allocated an ordinary room, half filled by an oval table; it became so crowded that the following week the authorities moved it to one of the larger classrooms. When this too overflowed, Russell's seminar found a regular home in the university's main auditorium. The numbers say much for his drawing powers.

One member of the seminar was Rudolf Carnap, a distinguished philosopher who had joined the faculty in 1936, and had long been grateful to Russell for having copied out by hand the principal points in *Principia Mathematica* and sent them to him, when a young and impoverished student in Germany. It also included three talented young philosophers, Dalkey, Kaplan and Copilowish – known to everyone as Copi – as well as a random assortment of university students, physicists, chemists and biologists, and a few housewives and businessmen, the seminars being open to the town as well as to the university. They were both weighty and easy-going. Every Thursday, Russell started the meeting by presenting the principal points of a chapter of his future *Inquiry*, then opened the discussion to anyone who wished to join in. Carnap later said that one of the most appealing things about the seminar was the way Russell kept the tone to that of a genuine 'inquiry', never letting it sink to a 'confrontation', despite real differences of opinion between himself and Russell. Carnap was an advocate of the logical positivist position, now gaining ground on both sides of the Atlantic, while Russell still aspired to a complete system of metaphysics, epistemology and logic.

Soon after his formal duties began, Russell decided to hold informal evening gatherings for graduate students, at which he served excellent whisky. In one corner, he held forth on philosophy; in another, Peter talked about 'relations between the sexes'. These evenings were well attended. Always gregarious with his students, Russell was equally willing to undertake any talks or lectures requested of him by the student body, and spoke all round Chicago on everything from free love to logic. He soon became a familiar figure on the campus, pushing Conrad in his pram, his teeth clenched around his pipe, his hat clamped hard on his head, his face bright red from Chicago's cold and windy weather. A handwriting 'analyst', L. E. Waterman, who had been sent a sample of Russell's neat hand, reported with surprising accuracy that he could see in it a clear thinker with a scientific cast of mind, a person of sensitivity and good will towards the world, fond of children and open skies, 'not careless with money or anything else, for carelessness is not part of his nature. He is methodical, thorough, accurate, likes to plan his work as a general maps a campaign, dislikes interruptions, hurry, changes of plans.'

After *Power* had been published in America, Russell was asked by the university to give an extra four lectures, and once again he packed every auditorium he addressed. In January, well into his second term, he agreed to a debate on 'Can democracy be defended?' with a Marxist historian from the West Indies, C. L. R. James, though on this occasion Russell was considered disappointingly less passionate and fiery than his opponent. A reporter, noting scathingly that it had been a 'tame affair', described the audience as 'socialists, parlour pinks, neighborhood mothers and their progeny'. There seemed to be a widening gap in popularity between Russell the philosopher, much admired by students, and Russell the populariser of contemporary affairs.

At first, he enjoyed Chicago, but bit by bit he began to turn against the city and its university, as he had turned so often against much of what America stood for. The next few years – by far the longest time he ever spent abroad – were marked by feelings of satisfaction, tempered by bouts of hostility. In January 1939, he wrote to Gamel Brenan, by now a regular correspondent, 'to me, love of England (not the political entity but the place) is almost as strong as love of my children, and very similar. I should find perpetual exile hardly endurable.' Chicago itself, he was soon writing, was 'beastly' and the weather 'vile'. What was worse, he had taken against the university's youthful president, Robert Hutchins, whom he criticised for being far more interested in the 'hundred best books' than in any scholarly work being undertaken by his faculty.

In March, Russell's contract came to an end. There is some suggestion that he would have wished his visiting professorship to have been extended, but no offer was forthcoming. Concluding that he neither liked, nor was much liked by, many of Chicago's teaching staff, he briefly contemplated returning to Britain, before accepting an offer from the University of California for a three-year professorship in philosophy.

The move west into the blue skies and warmth of California, after the bleak central American winter, struck him as delicious. He rented a house in Santa Barbara, settled Peter and Conrad, and took off for a lecture tour to raise more money. The journey afforded him at least one spell of happiness. Walking out along the dykes of the Mississippi river, he lay down on the grass 'and watched the majestic river, and gazed, half hynotised, at water and sky. For some ten minutes I experienced peace, a thing which very rarely happened to me.'

His new-found ease came to an abrupt end in September with the outbreak of the war he had so long been expecting. His letters to friends returned again and again to his despair for mankind, a theme that was to preoccupy him, in one form or another, until his death. He wrote to Gilbert Murray, 'having remained a pacifist while the Germans were invading France and Belgium in 1914, I do not see why I should cease to be one if they do it again . . . You feel "they ought to be stopped". I feel that, if we set to work to stop them, we shall, in the process, become exactly like them . . . Also, if we beat them, we shall produce in time someone as much worse as Hitler than the Kaiser.' Whenever he was given the chance, he said that more harm was done in life by fighting than by 'submitting to injustice' and in one of his more extreme and quixotic pronouncements he told a friend 'if the Germans succeeded in sending an invading army to England, we should do best to treat them as visitors, give them quarters, and invite the Commander-in-Chief to dine with the Prime Minister.'

In 1936, in a short and hastily written book, *Which Way to Peace?*, he had proposed absolute pacifism, of a 'commonsensical kind', if civilisation were not to be bruised forever by a second world war. Britain should devote herself to neutrality, give up all imperial presumptions, and lead the way in non-party pacifism. He had come down against the moral pacifism of Dick Sheppard's Peace Pledge Union – though not without hesitating whether or not to sign its pledge, which he did – as well as against the philosophical pacifism preached by Gandhi; instead, he had advocated a 'political pacifism', which opposed neither the rule of force in principle, nor of war as such, but objected specifically to any war likely to break out in the immediate future in Europe. Aldous Huxley, in the *Listener*, called it a 'little masterpiece'. Others, who did not subscribe to Huxley's pacifism, and had been quick to criticise the departure to America of people like Isherwood, Auden and Gerald Heard, were not so sure. Russell was neither too eminent nor, at nearly seventy, too old, not to attract the opprobrium of Cyril Connolly, who sneered in *Horizon* at the British intellectuals who were deserting 'the sinking ship of European democracy', even if Connolly's main attacks were on the 'far sighted and ambitious young men with a strong instinct for self preservation, and an eye on the main chance'.

On his arrival in America, Russell had told reporters who came to interview him that he was an 'extreme pacifist', and that even if the Allies succeeded in winning the war, they would be 'just as mad as Hitler' after they had done so. In April 1939, he congratulated President Roosevelt on his 'peace plea to Hitler and Mussolini'. 'I cannot resist', he wrote ingratiatingly, 'expressing to you my profound gratitude and admiration . . . Never before have I felt moved to express such feelings as now . . .'

Later, Russell came to be ashamed of *Which Way to Peace?* and refused to have it reprinted. As it became increasingly clear that the nazis were not being disarmed by passive resistance, he was forced to rethink his old pacifist arguments. 'I have been thinking day and night about the whole thing,' he wrote in anguish to Colette. 'At moments I think one *must* fight Hitler, but deep down I still believe that war would be worse than Hitler', returning to the old theme of the utilitarian balance sheet. As he wrote to his friend Bob Trevelyan, he was beginning to find the thought of 'Hitler and Stalin triumphant' hard to bear. Week by week, Russell came around to accepting the necessity of war. He found the process painful, remarking forlornly to Lucy Donnelly that all that was left now was to try to salvage whatever possible of civilisation. He had come to feel 'like a strayed ghost from a dead world'.

To allay what had become widespread confusion about his views on the war, Russell issued a statement on his position. 'I have never been an absolute pacifist', he reminded the public, who could well have been forgiven for being baffled, particularly if they were veterans of the First World War. He had opposed that war, he explained, because there had been no important principle at stake, and he had held out for a long time against a second war because he firmly believed it was likely to cause more misery than anything Hitler could do. He had, he now confessed, been wrong. He had underestimated Hitler's powers and inhumanity. This coming war, terrible as it would surely be, was one in which passivity would bring greater evil than fighting. His final statement rings out in characteristic Russell voice. 'If I were of military age I should now be fighting. If there were any other way in which I could take part in the war, I should be only too glad; but I have been told that so far there is nothing for me to do. The Allies do not need men, still less old men: they need machines.' No further uncertainties then, or at least not in public, and certainly none after the invasion of Poland. In private, he continued to qualify and justify his position, explaining to Bob Trevelyan that what had caused him to change his mind was that nothing as evil as Hitler had befallen the world since the fifth century, when the Roman Empire was overrun, and on that occasion too it was the Germans who had tried to reduce the world to barbarism. To Elizabeth Trevelyan, he added, 'I am still a pacifist in the sense that I think peace the most important thing in the world. But I do not think there can be any peace in the world while Hitler prospers.' If the public, and his friends, occasionally criticised him for so radical a switch in position in twenty years, they were also to observe that, as with much else in his political philosphy, the pure logician was perfectly capable of changing his mind.

During the summer, Kate and John had arrived in America to spend their holidays with their father. The plan had been for them to return home in time for the Dartington autumn term, but once war had been declared they had no choice but to stay in America, though they reacted strongly against what they saw as its frivolous attitude towards the war. Dora seems to have taken the unavoidable very well. Now aged seventeen and fifteen, both children were scholastically well ahead of their contemporaries. John was enrolled at UCLA, and Kate, after Russell had turned down one girls' school, on the grounds that it taught the 'vileness of capitalism', was coached by her father, before following John. Aldous and Maria Huxley introduced them to friends with children the same age. Among them was Peggy Kiskadden, who later recalled Russell as the most loving father, encouraging his children to join in every conversation. Thinking him a contented family man, she was surprised to hear him say bitterly, at a picnic where Peter failed to turn up: 'The world can be divided into two categories: those who do, and those who do not, have nervous breakdowns.' It was the first intimation that all was not well.

The climate was about the only thing Russell found more congenial about California. The university, he soon discovered, was ruled in a most autocratic manner by its president, Robert Sproul, who tended to fire any lecturer suspected of liberal leanings. Russell disliked him intensely, and complained that whenever Sproul visited a faculty meeting, it reminded him powerfully of the Reichstag under Hitler. He planned to get away as soon as he could. Early in 1940, after accepting an invitation to deliver the William James lectures at Harvard that autumn, he was offered a professorship at the City College of New York, and hurried to give President Sproul his notice. He then learned that his appointment had yet to be confirmed, so he asked Sproul whether he might, after all, stay on. Sproul refused.

The story of Russell and the City College of New York is a strange one. It says much both about wartime America, and about Russell's own ambiguous standing with the public and in some quarters of American academia. For years, he had been allowed to pronounce, more or less unchallenged, on the faults of American capitalism, and the stranglehold of business interests over the universities. He had complained, in the columns of syndicated newspapers and magazines, about the immorality of sending Sacco and Vanzetti to the electric chair, about the strength of American right-wing propaganda and about the 'fascism' of prominent people. His books on marriage and sex, and those on the need for freedom and tolerance towards children, had added a reputation for licentiousness. For what was the best part of twenty years, he had offended as many Americans as he had pleased. It was now the turn of all those who had felt impotent before his mockery and criticism to fight back.

On 26 February 1940, the Board of Higher Education of New York announced that Russell had been appointed professor of philosophy at the City College. The salary was $8000 a year, an improvement on Chicago. The news was greeted with outrage. A conservative afternoon paper, the *New York Sun*, published an editorial attacking the appointment. Worse was to follow. The Right Reverend William T. Manning, Protestant Episcopal Bishop of New York and a vociferous opponent of Russell's earlier lecture tours, denounced him publicly. He declared that Russell was a 'recognised propagandist against both religion and morality', and a man who 'specifically defends adultery'. The American right turned, as one, on Russell. Church groups, teachers, lecturers, priests, university presidents and perfectly ordinary Americans, many of whom had never heard Russell lecture or read a word he had written, deluged the newspapers with letters of condemnation. There was talk of moral degeneracy, repatriation, deviousness, notorious foreign atheism, the corruption of pure American youth and 'barnyard morality'. Letter-writers to the newspapers reminded one another of Russell's earlier, pernicious views, and wildly misquoted his words. The Catholic Daughters of America declared him an enemy 'not of religion or morality, but of common decency'. The Sons of Xavier and the St Joan of Arc Holy Society joined in the chant. A witchhunt broke out, with calls for Russell to be 'tarred and feathered' and driven from the country, while *The Tablet* referred to him as a 'desiccated, divorced and decadent advocate of sexual promiscuity'.

The university was in an awkward position. It was run by the city government and virtually all its students were Catholics or Jews. The invitation to Russell stemmed partly from a desire to keep up a pretence of academic freedom. The council, forced to reconsider his appointment, spent nearly four hours talking behind closed doors, while furious students and staff milled around the corridors outside and a detachment of police arrived in case a riot broke out. A resolution, brought by an opponent of Russell, was defeated by eleven votes to seven. No one, however, imagined that the matter was over. Public opinion, noted a council member smugly, was certain to 'control in the end'.

Events took a new and peculiar turn. A 'shocked' mother, prompted by the furore, went into battle. Mrs Jean Kay came from Brooklyn. Newspaper pictures show a square-faced, brown-haired woman with a determined jaw and somewhat sulky expression. Mrs Kay had a daughter called Gloria, but Gloria had not applied to enter CCNY to study philosophy. Just what prompted Mrs Kay was never clear, but on the day after Russell's appointment had been confirmed she brought a suit against the New York City municipality to rescind it. 'I don't want the minds of my children contaminated', she declared.

In her petition, she pointed out that Russell was not an American citizen, and that his immoral character made him highly unsuitable as a teacher. Her attorney, Joseph Goldstein, was a master of rhetoric. He proclaimed Russell's works 'lecherous, lustful, venerous, erotomaniac, aphrodisiac, irreverent, narrow-minded, untruthful and bereft of moral fibre', a statement so wild and so absurd that it became much quoted. Nor was Russell's philosophy up to much, added Goldstein: 'his alleged doctrines ... are just cheap, tawdry, worn-out, patched up fetishes and propositions, devised for the purpose of misleading people.' As for his morals, he was a nudist, and he 'winks at homosexualism'. In the suit, which was against the City of New York and not Russell personally, Justice John E. Geehan of the Supreme Court, an Irish Catholic sponsored by Tammany Hall, and best remembered for banning a portrait of Martin Luther

from a court mural, ruled that Russell's views would indeed under-
mine the morals of American students, and that his doctrines would
lead them straight into conflict with the law. Did CCNY really want
a 'chair of indecency'? The vehemence of these remarks made the
whole affair extraordinary.

There was, of course, more at stake than Russell's reputation.
The freedom of an institution to choose its lecturers was being
challenged, and a roar of protest rose from the liberal teachers and
defenders of civil liberties. The 1930s had seen an assault on
academic freedom throughout America, with anti-communists pushing through resolutions on loyalty oaths for teachers in twenty-one
states. The attack on Russell was another move towards repression.
Students at CCNY, when polled, declared that they were well aware
of Professor Russell's supposedly unorthodox views and held him in
such esteem that they were enrolling precisely in order to attend his
classes. One thousand signed a petition on his behalf.

As Russell's appointment turned into a *cause célèbre*, the most
distinguished intellectuals of the day, including British expatriates
living in America, rose up in his defence. His old friend Alfred
Whitehead was one of the first to speak for him; he was soon
followed by Albert Einstein, while Charlie Chaplin lent support from
Hollywood. While churchmen filled the columns of some newspapers with paeons of self-congratulation over their exposure of
Russell's moral turpitude and urged each other on, Russell's friends
and supporters filled the pages of others with articles about his
eminence as a philosopher, declaring the attacks on him a 'calamitous
setback to that freedom of thought and discussion which has been
the basis of democratic education'. The American Civil Liberties
Union, one of the first to declare on his behalf, produced a pamphlet
on the affair, written, among others, by John Dewey, challenging the
legal proceedings. Russell, wisely, said virtually nothing, replying
only when the flights of fanciful accusations reached a pitch he could
no longer ignore. Attacked for lacking the wisdom or manners to
retire from the arena in a dignified way, he announced that to do so
would be 'cowardly and selfish'. On another occasion, he was goaded
into remarking that he was clearly not nearly as interested in sex as
Bishop Manning, and that he had been hired to teach philosophy,

not morals. There was very little point in replying: no one was either interested or willing to listen. The hate mail continued to flow in, calling him a 'dirty British rat', a poor old man with a diseased mind, and much else.

Despite the letters of affection which also poured in from colleagues, friends and even complete strangers, none of this can have been easy, yet Kate recalled that her father seemed singularly unshaken by the vicious attacks which filled the papers day after day. So strong were the traditions of his family, she said, and so convinced was he that the moral ground beneath him was firm, that he remained almost phlegmatic, spending the time sitting in the garden of the house in Los Angeles, 3000 miles from the heart of the storm, reading the reports in the newspapers, listening to the radio and replying to his many letters. There were extraordinarily few references to the affair in his letters to friends in England. Part of his steadiness lay in his ability not to be unduly buffeted by personal criticism. A British Member of Parliament, W. J. Brown, on a visit to America, met Russell and found him aged and shrunken, but the 'fine precise mind and the measured articulation are as pronounced as ever'.

But the tide was flowing ever more strongly against him. In Los Angeles, a second 'shocked' woman, a Wellesley graduate called Mabel Sturgis, describing Russell as a 'man who both practises and preaches ideas of sex which savour of the jungle', tried to press a second case against him. Three judges threw out the suit, but President Sproul's office wrote to reassure her that Russell would not be staying on in California.

In due course, the members of the Board of Higher Education in New York, a collection of venerable attorneys, accountants, doctors and professors, met again. After describing Russell as a 'moral bankrupt' and an 'unwelcome alien', they voted sixteeen to five to reconsider his appointment. There were more articles, more letters, more attacks: in New York, Bishop Manning tried to put pressure on the mayor, La Guardia, who refused to take sides but is said to have crossed Russell's salary from the CCNY budget, and was later blamed by the liberals for not having come out in his favour, while a special board was convened to reopen the subject, and took on a counsel to seek a judicial review.

It was months before the matter was closed. Despite the efforts of his lawyers, and of a Bertrand Russell Academic Freedom Committee set up to co-ordinate liberal protest and raise funds for an appeal, it became obvious that even if the case were accepted by the Court of Appeal, it would not be heard before February 1941, at the very time Russell had been due to take up his professorship in New York. It was the city's final decision whether to appeal or not – and they voted against. It was left to John Dewey to rue the forces of tyranny ruling America, and to 'blush with shame for this scar on our repute for fair play', to Russell to compare himself to Socrates accused of 'atheism and corrupting the young', and to the *New York Journal* to reflect on 'this sordid . . . and thoroughly insulting campaign'. In an essay written shortly afterwards, Russell accused the opponents of academic freedom of reducing America to the level of Germany: 'New hopes, new beliefs, and new thoughts are at all times necessary to mankind, and it is not out of dead uniformity that they can be expected to rise.' He was right to be concerned. In the wake of the affair came an inquiry into subversion in schools and colleges in New York, which saw indiscriminate naming of names, parades of ex-communist witnesses, guilt by association and a call by one state senator for communist teachers to be 'shot like dogs'.

The public fury against his appointment may have vindicated many of his earlier criticisms of America, but for Russell it can have been only a Pyrrhic victory. Such comfort as it afforded him lay in the tributes of friends and from people whose respect he had not been aware of; and he had behaved with considerable dignity. It was good to have old friends like Aldous Huxley write, 'Sympathy, I'm afraid, can't do much good; but I feel I must tell you how much I feel for you . . . in the midst of the obscene outcry that has broken out.'

Russell may indeed, as he told anyone who asked him, have put the matter rapidly behind him, calling it 'ancient history'. But with John and Kate in college, and Peter and Conrad to support, his financial position was bleaker than ever before. Harvard had decided to honour an invitation for him to lecture, despite another threat of legal proceedings against him, and he was due to begin the ten-week

course in the autumn. Elsewhere in the United States open invitations to lecture were withdrawn, while most newspapers politely
declined to take his articles. Though the witchhunt calmed down,
Russell remained a favourite target of the right, who seldom let pass
the opportunity of referring to him as a 'dog', a 'bum', a 'fifth
columnist' or an 'avowed communist'.

These were not good years for Russell. He was concerned about
the effects of this public vilification on his family – the newspapers
made much of the difference in his age and Peter's, usually
subtracting a few years from hers to make the story more titillating –
and increasingly miserable about the war, and the fact that he was
in no position to make public pronouncements of the kind he had
become accustomed to making. To Gilbert Murray, with whom he
had fallen out so painfully over the First World War, he now wrote
sadly that he could do nothing for a German anti-nazi professor
known to both of them and obviously in some danger. 'However,
what I wanted to convey is that you would not find me disagreeing
with you as much as in 1914. ... We all suffer from almost
unbearable homesickness and I find myself longing for old friends. I
am glad that you are still one of them.' Little coverage had been
given to Russell's troubles in the British newspapers, partly because
of paper rationing, and Russell asked Kingsley Martin, the editor of
the *New Statesman*, to carry a short public announcement about his
current commitment to the war.

John Dewey now came to his rescue. It was a gesture of great
generosity, given the personal dislike he felt for Russell, and the fact
that he cannot have failed to have been aware of Russell's remark to
Max Eastman about him. 'I find him', Eastman recorded the British
philosopher as saying, 'such a dull writah.' On 27 May 1940, Russell
received a letter from Dewey saying that a Philadelphia millionaire,
Dr Alfred Barnes, an old friend of his, would be glad to offer him
$6000 a year to lecture to the students at his Foundation. The
appointment was to last for five years, and leave him sufficient free
time to return to his serious writing. Russell, having talked over his
proposed duties, accepted, with some relief. If he had been able to
conceal his anxiety from his family and the public, he did not always
manage so well with old friends. Apologising to Lucy Donnelly, for

having shouted at her all through dinner one night, he explained, 'Since the New York row I have been prickly, especially when I encounter the facile optimism that won't realise that, but for Barnes, it would have meant literal starvation for us all ... I used, when excited, to calm myself by reciting the three factors of $a^3 + b^3 + c^3 - 3abc$; I must revert to this practice. I find it more effective than thoughts of the Ice Age or the goodness of God.'

The offer had come at one of the rare moments of happiness for the Russell family during the wartime years in America. They had decided to escape the publicity and take for the summer a log cabin on the shore of a lake called Fallen Leaf, six thousand feet up in the Sierras. There was snow on the mountains, wild flowers in the meadows, streams, waterfalls, and the smell of pine woods. It reminded Russell of the Tyrol. The sun shone every day, and the nights were cold. Because the log cabin had room only for Conrad and his nanny, the others slept on the porch. Russell worked in a shed he had turned into his study, on finishing *An Inquiry into Meaning and Truth*, 120,000 words, which, he told Stanley Unwin, were 'intended to be serious and technical, appealing only to students of philosophy'. When the weather was very hot, he wrote naked, then swam in the lake. He was pleased with the book, complaining only that Norton, his American publisher, was jibbing at the title on the grounds that it was not 'catchy' enough. 'For my part,' he wrote to a friend, 'though I says it as shouldn't, I think it is a very good book.' He asked Unwin to send early copies to Gilbert Murray, Isaiah Berlin at New College, A. J. Ayer at Christ Church, and Professor L. S. Stebbing in Cambridge. In *Nature*, Ayer called Russell the 'Picasso of modern philosophy' but remarked on a new hesitancy of style which made it hard to read.

Russell, Peter and the older children walked for miles, finding lakes higher in the mountains, and diving into the water straight from deep snow. 'I wish we could by magic transport you here,' he wrote to Lucy Donnelly, 'you would find a place where the works of God still hold their own against those of man ... Sometimes for a little while we actually forget the war.'

*

Dr Alfred Barnes was a curious figure. Photographs show a thick-set, frowning, bull-necked man with reddish hair, in a Homburg hat. He was known to dote on his dog, but not on his wife, who doted on him. Born in 1872, the same year as Russell, into a poor Philadelphia family, with a father who was a drunk, he trained first as a doctor and chemist, while pursuing a side interest in philosophy. The invention of a chemical compound, Argyrol, which cured ulcers on the cornea and prevented blindness in babies whose mothers had gonorrhoea, was the beginning of a vast fortune which he spent on Impressionist paintings, buying Cézannes and Renoirs at a time when few Americans had heard of them and hanging them on his factory walls. In 1924, Barnes set up a Foundation in a twelve-acre park of his home city, which would house his collection of paintings – by now grown to 100 Renoirs, 50 Cézannes, 22 Picassos, 12 Matisses, and many Van Goghs and Gauguins – and a school where artists could continue with their work and lecture to students on the relationship between art and life.

During the time that Russell was in the news over the City College affair, Barnes was eager to broaden the scope of his Foundation by including lecturers who could describe the philosophical and social backgrounds from which art forms had sprung. He contacted John Dewey, who suggested Russell. Barnes saw himself as something of a radical and liked the idea of offering sanctuary to the persecuted British philosopher, with whom he felt he had much in common. He, too, he wrote to Russell, had been vilified by the public, and called a 'perverter of public morals' for praising painters like Cézanne in the early post-war years. What he now proposed was a generous deal: a salary of $6000, paid in monthly instalments, for one lecture a week during term time. Russell suggested he should base his lectures on 'philosophies of the past, and their influence on culture and social questions', with the intention of turning them eventually into a book. Barnes was delighted, and took a magnani-mous line, 'If you want to say what you damn well please, even to giving your adversaries a dose of their own medicine, we'll back you up'. To Peter, he added, 'Bertrand can put us on the intellectual-educational map in a manner I have long wished for; we can give him an opportunity to fulfil his heart's desire; and woe be to those who attempt to pull off another stunt like those of recent times in New York.'

It all looked auspicious, particularly as Barnes was eager, to the point of embarrassment, in his attentions. He offered to find them a house, 'in landscape that suffers nothing in comparison to Wiltshire', which he would then rent to them and furnish with early American antiques. Letters poured in, about the numbers of students Russell would ideally like to teach, about air tickets and whether he needed a stenographer. Barnes also raised Russell's salary to $8000 a year, saying it would save him from taking on other lectures to make money. Russell was grateful about the salary, but declined the offers of house and furniture, saying that 'choosing a house is a very personal matter, like choosing a wife. I know that in China the latter is done by proxy, but although people make mistakes, we are apt to prefer our own folly to the wisdom of others.'

He reached Philadephia at the beginning of January 1941, having enjoyed his Harvard lectures, which passed without controversy, and set about looking for a house. Before long, they had rented Little Datchet Farm, a 200-year-old stone house in the middle of country which reminded Russell of Dorset – with an orchard, a barn, fields stretching down to a river and peach trees. They were, he said, the sweetest peaches he had ever eaten. Philadephia, some twenty miles away, could be reached by train. Once again, he had time to read, remarking to Elizabeth Trevelyan that 'Karamazov is a great book, but I hate it; I think Dostoevsky evil. I dislike the doctrine that one should sin in order to experience humility.' Happiness was once more on his mind, and the difficulty of finding it in time of war. In an article for the *Reader's Digest* he drew up a set of rules for people who wished to help devise a better world. 'Never acquiesce in what you believe to be wrong,' never condone racist talk, but struggle against prejudice, laziness, credulity, 'don't be afraid of making a fuss.' Democracy, he warned, was a living force, not something to be put away in a safe. Though hard at work again on philosophy, Russell continued to see himself, as he did for the rest of his life, as a sage and mentor.

At the Foundation, Russell lectured in a gallery filled with French paintings, many of them nudes, which he found somewhat disconcerting. He wrote to Gilbert Murray that were it not for the war, he would be happy, that he had come to believe the Allies would win, and that America would come to dominate the world. He was not always quite so cheerful. 'Sometimes old days get such a grip on me that I find it hard to live in the present,' he wrote. 'And so many of the people I cared for are dead. It makes one feel like a ghost.' He was also becoming uncomfortably conscious of America's increasing illiberalism, remarking on the censorship exercised by the newspapers. He began to think more seriously about antisemitism, and to see the need to make known his strong feelings about racism in all its forms. He and Peter took the decision not to join a local swimming club when he found that Jews were not admitted.

Russell's early lectures pleased Barnes, who praised him for his manner with his students, and offered him more in the way of freedom and assistance. John Dewey, in his introduction to *The Bertrand Russell Case*, a Civil Rights Union pamphlet, remarked with some satisfaction that all was progressing well with Russell. Russell wrote to a friend in England, saying how much he was enjoying the work, learning things he had always wanted to know. 'I *can't* admire Aristotle – his *Ethics* seem to me thoroughly commonplace. Can you tell me why it is so much admired? I have been interested to learn that, in Plato's opinion, men who neglect philosophy will, in the next life, be women.' He was once again thinking about the future. 'There must first be a world-state, then an Augustan age, then slow undramatic decay,' he told Gilbert Murray. 'For a while, the yellow races may put vigour into the Hellenic-Roman tradition; ultimately something new may come from the negroes. (I should like to think St Augustine was a negro.)'

What no one had taken into account was Barnes's character. It was no coincidence that many of his early teachers had developed ulcers and fled after Barnes had begun to interfere in their classes, in a way both embarrassingly ignorant and megalomanic, or that Corbusier had been so enraged with him that he had returned an unopened letter with 'Merde' written on the envelope. Capable of intense warmth and generosity with strangers, Barnes was prone to become tyrannical, quarrelsome and vindictive with employees. He was a bully. He was also deeply paranoid and offended the art world by making what had become the finest private collection of modern paintings in America inaccessible to anyone but blacks and working-class whites to get his own back on the establishment. He took pleasure in writing 'nuts' to T. S. Eliot, when he asked whether he might visit the collection, pouring a bucket of water over one overly persistent man, and allowing in another's dog, but not its owner.

Russell did not remain long in favour. It is possible that what irked Barnes was that Russell resolutely refused to become intimate with him or his family, preferring to live a private life with Peter and the children. Whatever the reason, he soon moved to the attack. He opened the battle cautiously. The staff, he observed, were complaining that Russell was not entering fully into the spirit of 'democracy and education' which inspired the Foundation's work. Not only did he refuse to co-operate with other members of staff but after lectures he failed to mingle and hurried home instead. The spirit of the Foundation was to mingle.

It is possible that, on his own, Russell could have reached some sort of compromise with Barnes; but Peter was drawn in. Barnes complained that she seemed to have considerable difficulty in 'swallowing the impressive title of Lady Russell. It evidently gets stuck just below her larynx for she regurgitates it regularly.' When she drove Russell into his classes, furthermore, she often sat in on his lectures and, what was worse, knitted her way through them, to the annoyance and distraction of the students. Peter, he added, was 'imperious'; she had made a scene and disrupted lectures with her 'disorderly conduct'. A letter from the trustees arrived at the farmhouse forbidding her to enter the Foundation.

It would all have been comic had it not had such worrying financial implications. What happened next was absurd. Peter was not a woman to accept a rebuke lightly. She fully apologised, but was unable to refrain from ending her letter to the trustees, 'I marvel . . . that anyone should wish, in a world so full of mountains of hostility, to magnify so grandiloquently so petty a molehill.' Barnes remarked that her answer was a 'tirade composed of arrogance, rage and self pity'. The board of trustees was served by a secretary, a Miss N. E.

Mullen, whose tongue more than matched Peter's. 'Dear Madam,' she replied on 5 November, '. . . It was sweet of you to tell us . . . how . . . a superior, well-bred, learned, charitable, kind-hearted soul should not be informed by barbarians that her presence in their midst is undesirable. How to bear up under the disgrace is our most serious problem at the moment.'

Russell remained conciliatory. He continued to lecture, and Peter continued to be barred from the Foundation, though the story that now went around was that what had really offended Barnes was her failure to be sufficiently impressed by his art collection, even going so far as to say she did not much care for his choice of pictures. For a while, a truce of sorts prevailed. Russell, in any case, had his mind on the war. He had found that he could be of service to his country by lecturing on India, pleading for greater understanding between England and America at a moment when there was much anti-British feeling over British policy in India. And between October and December 1942, he gave a series of lectures at Philadelphia's Temple University and at New York's Rand School of Science, calling for full integration of the blacks into American society, and arguing that 'the war cannot be won by discriminatory methods, and it is a partial victory for Hitler when we imitate his race discrimination.'

Barnes, now on the lookout for a way of getting rid of Russell, whom he had turned against totally, used these lectures to accuse him of a breach of contract. By his 'popular lecturing' and the 'upholding of Mrs Russell's disorderly conduct', he had broken the terms of his engagement. Three days after Christmas 1942 a letter arrived giving Russell four days' notice. Russell, wondering whether he would be able to avoid bankruptcy, threatened to sue, saying that all along he had clearly stated his intention of giving public lectures, and that Barnes had never objected to the idea before. Barnes paid no attention. He issued a statement saying that, just as in the First World War, Russell was adopting the posture of a martyr. He quoted at some length criticisms made by a 'disappointed' but unnamed student. Russell, the young man claimed, spoke in a 'monotonous voice', delivered a 'sort of Cook's tour of the past', was 'dull', and could remember nothing without consulting his notes. In a pamphlet setting out his verdict on the affair, Barnes said that Russell had ridiculed Jewish rituals, established a reign of terror over his students, been 'perfunctory, even apathetic' as a lecturer, and turned his classes into a 'dreary ordeal'. The reason for his singular lack of success as a member of the Foundation, he went on, lay in the fact that he had 'no conception of democracy as a sharing or significant experience'.

Russell sued. He asked for $24,000 – the remaining three years' salary of his contract. In his autobiography, Russell mocked Barnes for complaining in court about the way he had taught the works of the men he referred to as 'Pithergawras and Empi-Dokkles', which made even the judge laugh. During the hearing, Russell sparred good-humouredly with the prosecution, who at one point accused him of 'fencing'. He was witty, provocative, and seldom missed a chance to ridicule. He was awarded $20,000.

Barnes retired from the battle to harass new employees. He had little time left to do so. In 1951, as he was driving to his summer house one afternoon, as recklessly as ever, he went straight through a stop sign. A ten-ton lorry crashed into his Packard. He died instantly.

Russell's dismissal from the Barnes Foundation was one more financial catastrophe in what had now become an almost unbroken period of anxiety and unhappiness. Though he had won the suit, the money would not be paid for some time. He gave up Little Datchet Farm, and they moved to a small cottage opposite, originally intended for the servants. For Peter, it had all become a nightmare.

Relations between the Russells had not been good for some time. The year they had spent in Chicago was possibly the last time they were happy together. In Philadelphia Peter was extremely lonely, cut off by distance and by Russell's position at the Foundation from the friends and parties she so enjoyed. She took refuge in obsessive domesticity, practising standards of perfection which consumed her days and drove successions of servants from the house. Suffering from frequent bouts of lassitude and unexplained sickness, she took to her bed, lying in a darkened room sipping rice water, then graduating to jelly, before struggling up once more to resume a frantic quest for household order. Half humorously, Russell wrote to Gilbert Murray: 'It is not growing fanaticism, but growing democracy, that causes my troubles ... My Peter's whole time is absorbed in housework, cooking and looking after Conrad; she hardly even has time to read. The eighteenth & nineteenth centuries were a brief interlude in the normal savagery of man; now the world has reverted to its usual condition. For us, who imagined ourselves democrats, but were in fact the pampered products of aristocracy, it is quite unpleasant.' Asked whether she would care to comment on the New York City College affair, Peter replied furiously: 'It would be a mistake to give me an opportunity of saying all the offensive things that patriotism and politeness induce me to bottle up. And as the only time I have at present for extra-domestic activities is in the middle of the night, forgive me if I am incoherent. I am half asleep.'

Peter's fretfulness and tricky moods finally alienated John who, in 1943, completed his degree at Harvard early and returned to England to join the navy. His interests lay in the Far East, and he was sent to the School of Oriental and African Studies in London to learn Japanese. Kate, still at Radcliffe, had become increasingly disenchanted with her stepmother and spent as little time at home as possible.

Both Russell and Peter, however, doted on Conrad, who was flourishing 'like a green bay tree'. A chronicle of the child's precocious behaviour found its way into the newspapers. Russell wrote an article for the *Sunday Referee*, saying that fifteen-month-old Conrad knew 150 words, enjoyed music, danced and sang to himself, looked at books, providing they were sensible and not what adults considered funny; he was good-tempered and well-behaved, having 'of course, never been smacked or scolded'. When he reached three, Russell described him to a friend as 'the joy of our lives – partly by his merits, partly because he doesn't know there is a war. He is very intelligent – he knows endless poems and stories by heart, and has a vast vocabulary. We love him, and he loves the cat and the cat loves her dinner.' When he turned six, in 1943, Russell wrote to Curry to ask him if he could keep a place at Dartington for him, saying that the boy was now very like John, cheerful and with an insatiable desire for knowledge, but also self-assertive and possessed of a logical mind. Schools in America were 'unbearably nationalistic' and he was afraid that Conrad, reared on liberal values, would ask embarrassing questions. Nowhere is there any mention of the insanity that had worried him so much with his older children.

Apart from Conrad, Russell had his work. To his students at the Barnes Foundation he had already given in lectures two-thirds of what was to become *A History of Western Philosophy*. His first idea had been to make it four volumes, or four separate parts of one big book: Antiquity, Catholic Philosophy from St Augustine to the Renaissance, Modern Philosophy up to Hegel and 'thence to the present day'. 'I should like the book to become a text book,' he wrote to Unwin, saying that what interested him was 'history written in the large'. He soon abandoned the idea of a separate volume on Antiquity, 'because of my ignorance of Greek' (though he devoted nearly 300 pages to it) and by September 1942 he had written 200,000 words, planning to complete the entire book of some 350,000 words within the next year. He tried to raise an advance from Norton, but he proved 'mean'. It was now due to be published in America by Simon and Schuster, who offered him $2000 immediately and $1000 six months later. In Britain, Unwin was desperately looking for enough paper to print it.

As usual, Russell was planning ahead, talking about a book on 'scientific inference'. 'This has never been formalised,' he wrote to Unwin, 'but has been left to educated common sense. People are aware of induction, but there are other principles, e. g. denial of action at a distance. I want to discover them by analysis of actual scientific procedure.' For this, he clearly needed money, and he wrote to tell Gilbert Murray that he would be happy to accept any 'honest work that would bring in a base subsistence for three people', including government propaganda. From his accounts in November 1943, it is clear that he was receiving royalties from eighteen titles in print, and had an advance on his proposed history of philosophy. Taking into account his financial arrangement with Dora – and the fact that, to make this as small as possible, he had made a deal whereby one-third of his earnings went directly to Peter as wages for being his secretary and research assistant – he calculated that he owed £731 6s 6d.

In the spring of 1943, he began pressing for a passage home. He was again brooding on the death of friends, Beatrice Webb having died recently without him seeing her again. He wrote to Colette: 'I should like to get home before any more of my old friends die.' To Gamel Brenan, he said that he felt rather like 'Rip van Winkle, and wonder if my friends of other days still remember me'. Their last months in America were spent at Princeton in a little house on the shores of a lake. Once a week, he went to Albert Einstein's house, to meet Gödel and Pauli and discuss metaphysics. He was longing to go home, but offered a priority passage for himself and Peter – he had said that he could leave at twenty-four hours' notice – he decided to wait until a berth could be found for Conrad to travel with his mother.

His final verdict on America was surprisingly mellow and without rancour. Newspapers and universities were once again clamouring for his pieces, and in an article for the *Saturday Evening Post* entitled 'Can Americans and Britons be friends?' he praised the Americans for being 'more energetic and more hopeful' than the English, and urged the two nations to mend their differences. 'It is our duty, at this time more than at any other, to forget our separate ways in the ardor of the hopes in which we are all as one.'

Peter had complained to friends of a rumour in the United States that Russell's old college had 'disowned' him. George Trevelyan, by now Master of Trinity, wrote to tell her that she was utterly mistaken, and that the hatchet had long since been buried. Better was to come. Early in 1944, Russell heard that he was to be offered a Fellowship at Trinity, to begin that autumn. 'Our warmest congratulations,' wrote Whitehead, on hearing the news, 'it is exactly what ought to have happened.'

With their separate passages home confirmed for the autumn, the Russells, with immense relief, prepared to leave America, as 'from a long tunnel'. They had been away nearly six years. 'I have much to say,' Russell wrote to Colette, 'but little to write. Socrates, at about my age, congratulated himself that in heaven there would be no one to stop him arguing. For my part, I have had enough of arguing – I want people who feel things in the same sort of way as I do.' Russell was seventy-two, and some of his pleasure in antagonism and provocation had been dulled by his skirmishes in the war years. In 1938, he had talked of spending the rest of his life in America; he was to revisit it only briefly.

Seventeen

The way to a new paradise

Russell came home on the maiden voyage of a Liberty ship, while berths were found on the *Queen Mary* for Peter and Conrad. He reached Britain shortly after them, landing at the Firth of Forth just after D-Day. Peter and Conrad were waiting for him in Sidmouth, and he travelled south to join them. Conrad had developed pneumonia, and while he recovered Russell sat on the stony beach listening to the naval guns firing off the Cherbourg peninsula. He was intensely glad to be home.

His Fellowship at Trinity was to last five years, and after finding rooms in a Cambridge boarding house for Peter and Conrad, he returned to his old college to sleep. The beauty of the place, he observed with pleasure, was undiminished. For a while, he found nothing but charm in all that surrounded him. In an article written for *Reynolds News*, he noted that the British had grown impressively in democratic feelings, national self-respect and patriotism during his time away, and that he sensed a new enthusiasm for the left among those under forty. 'All this is such a change from the unspeakable misery we endured in America,' he wrote, 'that one feels intoxicated'. When the money from the Barnes lawsuit came through, the Russells bought Grosvenor Lodge, in Babraham Road, 'small and commonplace,' he wrote to Colette, 'but the garden is nice'. Peter appeared happier than she had been for a long time and students flocked to his lectures; even the Cambridge Fellows, many previously ambiguous in their feelings towards him, were now extremely friendly. Russell resumed dining in hall, and delighted in rediscovering friends he had met forty and even fifty years before. George Trevelyan was, he decided, 'much mellowed, very friendly, and nice!' 'How Keynes has expanded since he used to come and stay at Tilford!' he commented to Lucy Donnelly. 'Last time I saw him he had an enormous paunch – but this was not the sort of expansion I had in mind!'

In these early post-war years Russell's children were a source of considerable satisfaction to him. John, by now proficient in Japanese, had been sent to the Far East. Maud Russell, his great-aunt, who had not seen the family since well before the war, found the young man charming and 'quite un-Russell-like to look at . . . and that's a thing one can't say about any other Russell'. Kate, who had recently graduated from Radcliffe *summa cum laude*, winning a $250 prize for best student of the year at Harvard or Radcliffe, had rejected a flattering offer of a professorship and decided to return to England to join Dora, who found her a job at the Ministry of Information, where she was working in the Soviet Relations Department. Conrad, as Russell wrote in a letter to Miriam Brudno, 'grows in wisdom and stature'. He was sent off to Dartington, Russell remarking to Curry that the boy had a 'prodigious' knowledge of geography.

Dartington, with its rumbustious and confident pupils, cannot have been easy for the precocious Conrad. One housemistress recalls that he was widely teased for his adult way of talking, and that he seemed remote and withdrawn. Whether or not he was aware of Dora's two children by Barry, she never knew. Harriet, now fourteen, and Roderick, twelve, badly scarred by walking into the hot ashes of a bonfire, were both pupils at Dartington and still bore the name of Russell. Through lawyers, the children were informed that he no longer wanted them to have his surname, Peter apparently having decided that they should switch to Barry to save Conrad from being confronted by unknown siblings. Dora, predictably, was furious, and John reacted to the subsequent furore by bringing up once again, and at some length, all his childhood grievances about his parents. Neither Harriet nor Roderick minded very much one way or the other, and took the name of Barry with equanimity. For Harriet at least, it was one more step in her attempt to escape from her unwanted Russell connection. 'I have spent my life', she said later, 'in trying *not* to be a Russell.'

After the financial anxieties and the public attacks in America, Russell was about to enter a period of great respectability. Honours and prizes, as well as public recognition of a kind he had not experienced before, were rapidly coming his way. The 1940s and 1950s were to be prolific and profitable: an excursion into fiction, a return to mainstream philosophy, more money than he immediately needed, and the start of a campaign to save the world from destruction, which was to occupy him for the rest of his life. 'When the time comes to die,' he wrote to a friend, 'I shall have to inform *Death* that I am too busy just now.' He felt vigorous, telling an interviewer that he was fully aware of his age, but that he did not feel it. 'In the old days,' he wrote to T. S. Eliot, 'when we were huddled together in Russell Chambers, we could hardly have expected that lapse of time would make us so respectable.'

What doubts he felt, he reserved for intimate correspondents like Gamel Brenan, to whom he wrote on Good Friday 1945:

> Yes, life is difficult. One has to eke out moments of actuality by months of memory and hope; & as one gets older it is difficult to prevent memory from overbalancing hope. I find memory a gradually increasing weight which I have to drag after me; I am only satisfactorily alive when I can occasionally slip it off. Almost every night before falling asleep I see the garden in which I passed my boyhood, which has since been destroyed; I mind its destruction quite as much as the deaths of people I have loved. But thank God I am still capable of passionate feeling about present things – in some ways, when I love now the quality of the feeling seems better than it was when I was younger because, without losing intensity, it has acquired a more impersonal setting. I have no wish to become calm . . .

During his final months in America and his first summer back in England, Russell completed what was to become his best-known book: *A History of Western Philosophy*. Based on his lectures to his students at the Barnes Foundation, it attempted to show how philosophical ideas were not just the isolated speculations of individuals but an integral part of history, being at once cause and effect of the communities and the times in which the different philosophical strands had flourished. What was intended to distinguish it from comparable books was precisely this deeper delving into history itself, and the inclusion of poets like Byron and political theorists like Rousseau to show how literature, politics and social conditions had influenced philsophical thought.

Its publication in Britain was delayed by the continuing paper rationing, and when at last it was scheduled to appear, on 19 November 1946, the initial print-run was ridiculously small. Urged by Stanley Unwin, Russell approached Sir Stafford Cripps at the Board of Trade and enough paper was eventually released to allow a first printing of 20,000 copies. Despite its length – 864 pages – and a price of twenty-one shillings, the book sold out before publication, bringing Russell an immediate £1100 in royalties, as well as the William Heinemann Foundation for Literature Prize. In America, Simon and Schuster were selling 500 copies a week, reaching 34,000 within six months. Wrangles about paper in Britain continued, however: when Russell discovered that the shortage meant that his other books were not being reprinted, he wrote furiously to Unwin: 'Quite independently of how it affects me, I think the subordination of books to cinemas and greyhound racing is utterly abominable.'

On both sides of the Atlantic, reviews spoke of what one man called the 'revelation of a mighty intellect'. The *History* was considered both profound and intensely readable, and it came at a moment when there was a great appetite for fat educational books, simply written. Ordinary people, for whom philosophy had long been a closed and bewildering subject, found statements like 'Rousseau was mad but influential, Hume was sane but had no followers', and 'Leibniz was one of the supreme intellects of all time, but as a human being he was not admirable,' reassuringly easy to follow. They felt at home with statements like 'The lunatic who believes that he is a poached egg is to be condemned solely on the ground that he is in a minority.' Serious philosophers, who questioned the authority of many of his judgements, particularly those on the medieval philosophers, with whom Russell had never felt much sympathy (except for Aquinas), complained that he was preachy and failed to put his philosophers into a real social context. They were virtually unanimous in their verdict that the chapter on Kant was the worst. And why did Carnap get just one line, Gödel one reference, and Moore and Wittgenstein nothing at all? But few could help being envious of so successful an enterprise, while admitting that when it came to the empiricists, or Byron, whose poetry Russell loved, there was something marvellous about the sweep and grandeur of the writing. In *Mind* C. D. Broad wrote a severe review which effectively voiced the misgivings of other philosophers; but few of the public were regular readers of *Mind*.

Russell's return to Trinity, after six years in America, showed him just how far he now stood from the prevailing winds in philosophy. What had happened, during the 1930s and while he had been away, was that many philosophers, inspired partly by Moore, had concluded that the ordinary beliefs of ordinary men should not be rejected as inherently wrong, and that it was a question of understanding ordinary language better, not replacing it with technical language. To Russell, this seemed the betrayal of all serious philosophical work, a failure to carry on the honoured tradition of supplying new material for successive philosophers to carry forward. A philosopher, in his eyes, had to invent a theory, containing new and wherever possible startling philosophical doctrines, couched in a special technical language. 'Everyone admits that physics and chemistry and medicine each require a language which is not that of everyday life', he was to write in *My Philosophical Development*. 'I fail to see why philosophy alone should be forbidden to make a similar approach towards precision and accuracy.'

In 1945, it became clear that his influence was on the decline, and *The Theory of Descriptions*, which many considered his major work, was in eclipse in Britain, though in the United States philosophers remained faithful and carried on in the same vein. Wittgenstein, in his *Philosophical Investigations* (which, though not published until 1953, was already being widely discussed), and Gilbert Ryle in work which was to make its way into *Concept of Mind*, were both more in fashion. Worse perhaps, Moore was greatly admired by J. L. Austin, the philosopher who did most to promote the meticulous investigation of ordinary linguistic usage. To Russell, if regarded as philosophy, the mere exploration of language for its own sake was deeply trivial. Philosophy was worth doing only if it tried to provide answers to the question of how beliefs are justified. To the end of his life, he was to remain hostile to the 'Oxford philosophy', and the idea that philosophical problems, the products of sloppy, muddled language, could be cured by linguistic analysis. About Ryle, he once said that he found his work 'always repulsive, in the sort of way a bad smell is repulsive'. He considered Peter Strawson 'completely unintelligible', and was hurt when, much later, Strawson contributed an article to *Mind* throwing doubts on Russell's particularly cherished Theory of Descriptions. He also declared that he saw no point at all in Wittgenstein's later work; and attacked Ryle's notion that what is needed is not new information but the rearranging of what we have always known 'to rectify the logical geography of the knowledge which we already possess'. His point was that linguistics, though indeed important, were over-dominant. 'The most serious of my objections', he wrote about the Oxford school, 'is that it seems to have abandoned, without necessity, the grave and important task which philosophy throughout the Ages has hitherto pursued' – that of understanding the world. 'I cannot see that the new philosophy is carrying on this tradition. It seems to concern itself, not with the world and our relation to it but only with the different ways in which silly people can say silly things. If this is all that philosophy has to offer, I cannot think that it is a worthy subject of study.'

Uneasy with these philosophers, Russell felt more sympathetic towards A. J. Ayer, author of the clearest account of logical positivism, *Language, Truth and Logic*, not simply because Ayer subscribed to the view that both mind and matter are logical constructions, resulting from sense-data and the images of our experience, but because he agreed that philosophy had little point unless it posed questions to which answers could be found. From among the modern philosophers, said Ayer, he was influenced by Russell and Wittgenstein. Despite a forty-year difference in their ages, the two men became friends. Ayer, who founded the Metalogical Society, which held meetings after dinner between philosophers and experts in the physical and biological sciences, invited Russell to take part, as a result of which he now met Karl Popper, Stuart Hampshire and Richard Wollheim, though few of them warmed to him, feeling irritated by the way he never recognized them. (Russell maintained that he had no visual memory and needed to describe them to himself before remembering them.) 'Who is that Jew at Oxford?', Russell is said to have asked one day, referring to his friend Ayer, which says something not only about his powers of recognition, but about his curiously deaf ear – or perhaps 19th century habits – when it came to linguistic sensitivity.

Russell was not, however, accustomed to philosophical scorn. Soon after his return from America, he was asked to lecture at Oxford, but far from the usual warm acclaim, he was greeted with scepticism and even aggression. Afterwards, Isaiah Berlin, who never greatly cared for Russell personally, but saw him as an eighteenth-century *philosophe* who might easily have been a friend of Diderot or Voltaire, took him to tea at the Mitre. 'Was I squashed?' Russell asked. The question, says Berlin, was phrased not with arrogance but with bafflement. 'The silence that now virtually blankets Russell's name at Oxford,' wrote G. Bergmann later, 'the failure or unwillingness to do justice to his epochal work, shocks me profoundly.'

Back at Cambridge, he fared somewhat better. He had chosen for his lecture the subject of 'non-demonstrative inference' and settled down with his students to work on probability. His intention was to deal with the question: 'How comes it that human beings, whose contacts with the world are brief, personal and limited, are nevertheless able to know as much as they do know?' It was an enormous task. Russell soon found that one would have to reject not only science, but also a great deal of knowledge of every kind, if one claimed that all that can be known is what is experienced. If much of what he said was in line with his earlier writings, the lectures contained a major difference. Whereas, in the *History*, he still maintained that 'whatever can be known, can be known by means of science,' he had now come round to the view that knowledge comes in different kinds, and that we 'know' certain principles which science can never establish because science itself depends on them.

The result of the lectures was *Human Knowledge: Its Scope and Limits*, published in 1948, when he was seventy-six. The reader, Russell warned, would be a 'traveller approaching a mountain through a haze'. He said later that its conclusions were slapdash, and that he had failed to deal with the problems encountered along the way. The lectures, and the book, which ran to over 500 pages, were the fullest statement of his thinking over half a century. Russell was disappointed in the public reaction, perhaps because *Human Knowledge* was mistakenly advertised as a book for the general reader, and not as an original work in philosophy. Though Sidney Hook, the American philosopher, spoke of it as his 'philosophical testament', others were not so kind. They complained that it was full of jargon, 'prolix and repetitive'. A. A. Milne, better known perhaps for Pooh than for philosophy, observed in the *Hibbert Journal* that the spirit of the book was 'piano' and lacking in hope. 'The motto . . . might be the legend which Dante found over the doorway to the Inferno.' The response of the professional philosophers was one of polite indifference, not least because the book was long, fragmentary and included some repetition of things Russell had already said, in *Analysis of Matter* and *An Inquiry into Meaning and Truth*.

In 1912, in his *Problems of Philosophy*, Russell had set out his famous question: 'Is there any knowledge in the world which is so certain that no reasonable man could doubt it?' Thirty-six years later, he felt bound to conclude that 'all human knowledge is uncertain, inexact and partial. To this doctrine we have not found any limitation whatever.' 'Deduction', which he had once believed capable of providing new knowledge, had turned out to be less than he had once supposed. 'Induction' – inference, from the fact that the sun has risen every day, that it will rise tomorrow – fared no better. *Human Knowledge* was Russell's conclusion that all he could do was base his philosophy on a kind of 'animal faith' which he had earlier scorned. Written in his mid-seventies, it might have been Russell's conclusions after a lifetime's work as a philosopher, but what is remarkable about it is that it is as full of problems and questions, posed and not solved, as his earlier works – a 'philosophy under construction', as Alan Wood put it. In philosophy as in all other aspects of his life, Russell still saw himself as growing. *Human Society in Ethics and Politics*, published six years later, showed how in ethics as in philosophy, his enduring concern was with questions; though the basis of his ethics remained one of 'emotion and feeling', he was forced to conclude that all he had found were some guiding principles, not objective knowledge. His great strength in ethics was that he obliged people to see that either they would have to find acceptable answers or they would have to learn to live without them. Nothing approaching certain knowledge about the world is to be obtained other than by scientific enquiry, yet even science is ultimately incapable of proving anything either right or wrong.

For all the lack of immediate success of *Human Knowledge*, Russell must have enjoyed his personal reception at Cambridge. One of his students was a young man called Vincent Buranelli, who was later to recall not only Russell's popularity – other Cambridge philosophers of the time considered themselves fortunate if they drew a handful of listeners, while Russell found no difficulty in filling an auditorium – but his charm, good humour and the youthfulness of his delivery. He could still mesmerise several hundred listeners into silence, not so much by his words, which could be very dry, as by the sweep of his personality.

As in his younger years, the mental labour that went into two books of serious philosophy did not prevent Russell from accepting other offers. With more money coming in, however, he was able to choose, in a pleasing way not open to him before. On his return to England in 1944, George Trevelyan had written to Julian Huxley about a possible job for him at the BBC. Huxley had passed the letter on to G. R. Barnes, director of talks, remarking that 'he does have a very acute mind and wide knowledge of the principles of politics, international affairs in general and the USA in particular.' If there was nothing in talks, how about propaganda? Barnes was hesitant. He was far from sure that the septuagenarian Russell would fit easily into his department. It was some time before the confusion was cleared up: Russell was not in search of a staff job, but might make a lively occasional contributor to post-war radio.

A first idea, to ask him to speak on philosophy to India, was rejected on the grounds that he had been abroad for too long and that no one was quite sure of his 'reliability and stability', a matter of understandable concern given that all programmes still went out live. A second suggestion, that he should take part in the *Brains Trust*, a popular programme where various experts answered questions sent in by the public, was accepted, and Russell agreed, for a fee of fifteen guineas and a first-class train ticket, to travel up to London for the early afternoon recording. After this, invitations followed rapidly. Two or even three times a month, Russell arrived at the BBC to talk, on the *Brains Trust* or for the Third Programme – the mandarins of which despised the *Brains Trust* as trying to introduce intellectual content into what was ostensibly a middle-brow channel. Russell served both, with a passion for exactitude and a sort of pedantry which could be off-putting to young producers, but with such politeness and tact that they seldom failed to be charmed. 'I am incredibly busy,' Russell wrote to a friend, 'as the BBC has developed a passion for me. I talk to all the countries of Europe and South America . . .' What made Russell invaluable was his ability to talk on almost any topic, from modern society to Shelley; when invited to talk on something he considered outside his competence – like contemporary education, now vanished into the past – he declined.

As a broadcaster, he soon gathered a wide following of listeners, who wrote in their dozens to praise his impeccable delivery, his curiously old-fashioned short e's, his sense of humour, and his strong views, courteously phrased. True, a few reproached him for what they considered a harsh and monotonous voice – which one man compared to that of C. E. M. Joad 'with a cold' – or complained that they found him tedious and rambling. (Russell loathed Joad, a regular contributor, and called him a 'humbug and a plagiarist'; he was particularly furious whenever he heard the ebullient popular writer with his white beard and rosy cheeks referred to as Britain's 'leading' philosopher.) But most people, like Harman Grisewood, the Controller of the Third Programme, admired Russell's lucidity, the way he talked as he wrote, in clear, comprehensible, well-rounded sentences. Grisewood recalled, 'He was simply conscious of being much more intelligent than those around him. It was a sort of Apostolic belief in superiority; he really believed that the enlightenment had come to people like himself and Moore and Lowes Dickinson and left the others in the darkness. But he wasn't vain. He didn't need to show off, like Joad did. You felt that his mind was a wonderful object, and that he knew that better than anyone, and respected it, and therefore had no need for vanity or conceit.' What Virginia Woolf had called 'that marvellous headpiece' was still intact.

Within the BBC, Russell was soon seen as the authentic voice of the liberal world, harking back to the moral values of pre-1914 Cambridge, and imbued with a belief that mankind would be better if it received a diet of highbrow talk and Beethoven. He was the perfect pundit, the cool voice of reason, intelligence and morality. His very certainties were reassuring. What was more, he was professional from the moment he started broadcasting, doing precisely what he was asked without fuss or quibble. The *News Chronicle*, early in 1945, greeted him as the first person since the death of his old friend Lowes Dickinson, who had a 'disinterested mind of the first quality using radio to lead opinion'.

Russell particularly enjoyed unscripted debates and there was nothing he welcomed more than controversy, particularly on topics he had spent much of his life exploring. He spoke out against 'racial antagonism' and urged the public to tolerate intermarriage between Jews and Gentiles, mourned the death of chivalry, rejected ghosts as 'absolute nonsense and that's all I have got to say', and called hunting 'a disgrace to the country'. When Sir William Haley became Director-General of the BBC in 1944, there was a deliberate change of policy, so that contentious views, discouraged by Reith before the war, were permitted on the air. After giving a talk on agnosticism in a series, *What I Believe* (the series featured seven Christians, one spiritualist, one Jew, and three agnostics or atheists), Russell was invited by Grisewood to join Father Frederick Copleston, the distinguished Jesuit historian of philosophy, in a debate on the existence of God. The two men met for lunch at the BBC's expense, to discuss how to approach the talk.

Distinctly nervous before this master of rhetoric and casuistry, Father Copleston was surprised to find his opponent equally ill at ease. Before long, the two men relaxed. Russell told Copleston that when he wanted to shock people, he called himself an atheist; when he did not, he referred to himself as agnostic. Copleston remembered Russell as a curiously old-fashioned figure, with an eighteenth-century vision of morality, politics and philosophy. He liked his manner and his verve, but sensed that their backgrounds and the difference in their ages (Copleston was forty-one) would effectively prevent them from becoming friends.

The debate, which took place on 28 January 1948, was characterised by its good temper. Father Copleston argued that there must be some explanation as to why the world exists. Russell, in the mannered tones of a well-brought-up Whig, said that to postulate the existence of a deity did not provide an explanation, and that the demand for an explanation for everything was itself incoherent, in that the process of explaining facts and theories by more facts and theories had to stop somewhere, and that to stop at an empirical theory was more rational than to fabricate a metaphysical one. He then launched into his familiar criticism of Christianity: his hatred of superstitious rituals and irrational taboos, his contempt for the intellectual dishonesty of Christian apologists. Socrates, declared Russell, was not as cruel as Christ. His study of the laws of physics and psychology suggested to him that an afterlife was highly improbable; if people could not be happy in this life, there would be little opportunity for them to be happy in any other. His performance was as enjoyable as it was provocative. During a pause, he told Grisewood that his first revulsion against Christian mythology had come when he was a child at Pembroke Lodge, and his aunt Agatha, kissing him goodnight and pointing to a picture hanging above his bed, had told him to think about the angels: 'I shut my eyes and tried to clutch them. There was nothing there.'

Letters, from a largely appreciative public, poured in. But it was Copleston who was considered the champion of the debate, Russell's performance being judged by some as slightly lacklustre. Haley observed that the Jesuit had been a 'find'. 'He was the first man I had heard who could stand in the same ring as Russell on these matters and not seem out of place.'

That same year Russell received another invitation from the BBC, of a most flattering kind. The organisation had decided to inaugurate a series of annual lectures to honour its first Director-General, Lord Reith, and Russell was invited to be the first speaker. He was to be paid £600 for six half-hour talks, one each week. The title agreed was 'Authority and the Individual', and it was understood that the lectures would appear as a book. This was the sort of challenge Russell most enjoyed. Apart from anything else, it was a way of finding a wider audience for his rejection of the popular idea that man's actions are moral only in so far as they are addressed to the social good, and his belief that man is called to a higher excellence and should listen to the summons.

In his diaries, Reith remarked tersely on Russell's performance: 'He went far too quickly and has a bad voice anyhow.' The public were more admiring, particularly as the weeks went by and they became involved in the wider implication of his words. They enjoyed hearing him say, 'We shall not create a good world by trying to make men tame and timid, but by encouraging them to be bold and adventurous and fearless except in inflicting injuries upon their fellow men.' Dozens wrote in to say that Russell was incapable of being dull. *The Times* praised the talks as 'another landmark in broadcasting history'. From Moscow, however, when the BBC put out the talks in Russian, came a diatribe of abuse. 'This philosophising wolf,' declared the announcer for Radio Moscow, 'whose dinner jacket conceals all but the brutal instincts of a beast . . . Hatred, murder, the eat-one-another state, seem to me the fundamental ethical principles preached by this beast in philosopher's robes.' Russell's words, which sounded like the laugh of a hyena and the howl of a wolf, were the outpourings of a demented philosopher, expounding the 'latest concept of imperialism from the angle of his own savage instincts . . .' *Authority and the Individual*, published after the broadcasts, was soon selling 500 copies a week. For the first time in many years, Russell's outlook, when it came to work, was extremely bright.

Even the British government were pleased with him, asking him to lecture to the forces and sending him, at the time of the Berlin airlift, to help persuade the people of Berlin to resist the Russian attempts to drive the Allies out. Russell declared that the destruction of Berlin was 'monstrous', that the razing of Dresden had been sickening, and warned that the treatment of Germany by the Allies was setting the stage for World War Three. All the same, the government asked him to visit Norway, to sway public opinion in favour of joining an alliance against Russia.

Russell's Scandinavian journey was nearly his last. The seaplane from Oslo to Trondheim came down into the water in stormy weather, sprang a leak and started to sink. Nineteen passengers in the non-smoking section were trapped and drowned; Russell later remarked on the irony of his insistence on a smoking seat, telling a friend who saw him off that if he was not allowed to smoke he would die. Escaping from the sinking seaplane, he swam the twenty metres to a boat, in his overcoat and clutching his briefcase, letting go of it at the last minute. He then borrowed dry clothes from the vice-consul.

The lecture was cancelled – its chairman had been one of those drowned – and Russell irritably told a reporter who asked whether, at the moment of possible death, he had been reflecting on mysticism and logic, that he had been thinking of nothing but the freezing temperature of the water. Throughout the world, there was consternation at his near-fatal accident, but to Peter he made light of the whole event. 'I was not brave,' he explained, 'only stupid . . . mainly concerned to save my attaché case. My watch goes as well as ever, and even my matches strike.'

The suggestion that Russell should lecture in Australia came from a Melbourne businessman and leading figure in the Australian Institute of International Affairs, E. C. Dyason, who, like many of his countrymen, feared that the large exodus of Australians from their native land was fast turning Australia into a cultural desert. Russell, Dyason decided, was the man to restore his country's intellectual pride. As it happened, he died before Russell arrived in Australia, but a philanthropic bequest in his will ensured that, after some initial worries, the trip proceeded as planned. Russell's fee was £600, for some sixty days of public lectures and private speeches.

By now, he was a practised hand at such tours. He informed his anxious hosts that he did not greatly care for 'functions', that he would prefer to stay in hotels rather than with Governor-Generals, that he liked to have a bathroom of his own, and that during his periods of free time he wished to visit Australia's open spaces rather than its cities. He also requested two hours' privacy each day, preferably in the mornings. Professor L. F. Giblin, a Tasmanian economist and one of Dyason's executors, noted with relief that their distinguished visitor's preferences were 'eclectic'. All was now prepared, including an agreement with a bookseller to supply him constantly with new detective stories.

Russell reached Sydney on 23 June 1950, at 7.30 in the morning. His programme for the first few days gave some idea of how hard he was expected to work. After a few hours' rest, he recorded one interview with Movietone News and a second for ABC's weekly 'Guest of Honour' slot. He went on to a press conference, where reporters observed that the radical firebrand of the early years was mellowing into a 'conservative old age', and one noted that he looked like a 'koala bear who has just thought of a funny joke'. On Monday he gave the first of his public lectures in Sydney; then two more, followed by a public tour. After this came Brisbane, Canberra, Adelaide and Perth. Everywhere he went, he drew vast crowds and was deluged with invitations to dine, write, speak and give interviews. In South Perth, a lecture hall containing 1150 people overflowed; 450 more were put to sit in a second hall, to which his talk was relayed, while a further one hundred stood. Between the formal bookings, Russell travelled to Alice Springs and to the Queensland bush.

Before his arrival, the organisers for the Australian Institute had been nervous about Russell's famously contentious views and his reception by conservative middle-class Australia. They need not have worried. He behaved soberly, keeping his views on the aboriginal question largely to himself, and took pains to be accommodating and cheerful. What little opposition there was to his trip came, predictably enough, from the Roman Catholic Archbishop of Melbourne, Daniel Mannix, who declared that Russell's presence was distracting his parishioners, and that he should be banned from Australia, as he had been from America. Since this was not true, Russell threatened to sue, and Mannix hastily cabled an apology. When he left Sydney for London at the end of August, he was exhausted but elated, not just by what he had seen, but by the extraordinary success of the tour. If he had found the people 'cordial but uninteresting', marvelling that they could ever find their way anywhere given the monotony of the landscape, he also declared the Australians to be 'pioneers', with a role to play in man's future happiness.

More difficult, certainly, were his last two trips to America, made in a spirit of increasing ambivalence concerning the country and its future. A few months after his return from Australia he was in the air again, this time to deliver a new set of lectures to American universities and foundations, intending to make money – over $10,000 on the second tour – and renew old friendships. By now there must have been something almost too familiar about the American lecture circuit, yet he dutifully talked to students and faculties about peace, science and America's relations with the west, hit out against McCarthyism, and returned again and again to his theme that scientific knowledge must be developed to further peace and increase 'human power'.

Alistair Cooke, who travelled with him by train on one leg of his tour, has left an endearing picture of Russell's American journeys. Cooke had arranged to meet him just before seven in the morning at Pennsylvania station, and arrived to see a very small elderly man in a topcoat green with age and too big for him, with a pipe in his mouth, pacing up and down before a closed news stand, waiting for it to open, 'like a caged animal impatient for feeding time'. Anecdotes, aphorisms, observations poured out during the train ride; Cooke observed that what delighted Russell most was the memory of some incident, usually of a melodramatic kind, which ended with a maxim or a shocking punch-line. During a political discussion 'he would blow hot and witheringly cold', and once he had made his point he relapsed into a 'kind of smouldering satisfaction'. His love of detective stories had long been known; to Cooke's surprise, he pulled a bunch of thrillers out of his pocket, flicked through them for about fifteen minutes each, then dropped them, one by one, on the floor.

Editors on both sides of the Atlantic pressed him once again for articles on Anglo-American relations, and Russell continued to supply them, even if he infuriated some of his readers as he became increasingly convinced that America was developing 'fanatical attitudes' about world affairs. 'Your immense power frightens us,' he wrote to Walter Graebner, European director of *Fortune*. 'We feel as if a child had run away with a new and powerful car and was careering madly about the road to the danger of all its other occupants. It is especially MacArthur and McCarthy who make us feel that way, but Taft and Hoover seem to us only a shade less ignorant'. The gist of much of what he was writing was that safety lay in educating the young to be 'citizens of the world instead of predatory warriors', members of a world federation or union, in which the rights of individual nations to act as they pleased would be abolished and a supranational federation state created. He wrote to friends, as he had so often in the past, 'America was beastly – the Republicans are as stupid as they are wicked, which is saying a good deal,' though he continued to derive considerable pleasure from many of his encounters there. His intimate correspondent since 1902, Lucy Donnelly, died in the summer of 1948, but not before Russell, who had been going through their correspondence, had told her that they had brought him 'an invigorating breath from a larger, freer world. A lifetime of gratitude I send back to you from them . . .'

If Russell now had considerably less time to write to his old friends, it was partly because, as a public figure, he was the recipient of an awesome number of letters from strangers. On some days his post-bag contained well over a hundred. People wrote to seek his opinion on everything from politics to private morality. The psychoanalyst Ernest Joyce wrote to ask him whether his 1901 'conversion' had stemmed from a personal experience of cruelty; the Bishop of Rochester, while acclaiming him as the greatest brain of his generation, wrote to say that he had blighted all his work by the 'cloven hoof of the lecher' and to ask what he felt about being responsible for the 'murder, suicide, and untold misery' caused by young people experimenting with his 'companionate marriage'.

Russell replied to them all, friends, critics and lunatics alike, in his customary courteous tone. From 8–11.30 each morning was devoted to his correspondence and to going through the newspapers. His answers were pithy, polite and witty. To children, he wrote affectionately and without guard. To one woman who thanked God for his work, he replied he was very glad she liked it 'but troubled that you thanked God for it, because that suggests that He has infringed my copyright'. To a man who invited him to send back a list of the words he most liked, he replied with twenty examples, revealing something of his taste for teasing and for the rich Byzantine sounds of some English words: 'Wind, health, golden, begrime, pilgrim, quagmire, diapason, alabaster, chrysoprase, asholala, apocalypse, ineluctable, terraqueous, inspissated, incarnadine, subliminal,

chorasmian, alembic, fulminate, ecstasy'. His letters could be trenchant, comic, and, occasionally, arch.

The most peculiar letters came from people whom he had known
as a young man and who wrote to ask for his advice. The strangest
of these was from Naomi Bentwich, the social sciences undergraduate from Cambridge whom he had known at the No-Conscription
Fellowship and who had later become friends with Moore, Ottoline
Morrell and the Huxleys. In 1919, she had gone to work for Keynes,
typing and helping him with his *Economic Journal*. She had fallen in
love with him, but after a breach in 1921 had never seen him again.
She had gone on to marry a mathematician called Jonas Birnberg,
and had given birth to two sons. In 1949, two years after Keynes's
death, his book about the early Cambridge and Bloomsbury days was
published as *Two Memoirs*. Naomi Bentwich read it and concluded
that it had been addressed secretly to her, as a reply to the many
unanswered letters she had written to him in the 1920s. She sat
down and poured out a thousand-page autobiography, and when it
was finished, she wrote to Russell, reminding him of their past
friendship and saying he was the only person still alive in whom she
could confide. Russell was fascinated. He replied that his interest
and curiosity had been stirred to the 'highest degree'. 'Keynes', he
wrote, 'was important, & I never felt I quite understood him. If you
can help me to do so, I shall be grateful.'

The two old friends met; they talked about the past, about morality
and religion. Then Naomi Bentwich recounted her story. While she
was working for Keynes in the early 1920s, he had made certain
gestures which she took to be advances. But when she wrote to tell
him that she too loved him, and was ready to join him, he replied
that it was all a complete misunderstanding. After receiving more
letters from her, Keynes had been to see her younger brother in
Trinity and warned him to tell his parents there was something
worryingly wrong about Naomi's mental state. For the next four
years she had gone on writing him long, intimate letters, combining
love with her views on religion and the state of the modern world.
His answers, when they came, were two lines long, begging her to
stop writing to him. In 1927 he had married. None of this had
prevented her from remaining convinced that he was lying, that he

secretly loved her, and that many of her views had made their way into his *Manchester Guardian* articles and into his political writings. The *Memoirs*, Naomi Bentwich told Russell, were an apology from beyond the grave.

Gentle talk of the past was one thing, hysterical musings on a total misapprehension of Keynes's behaviour quite another; Russell was repelled by her intensity. Deciding that he had had enough, he politely told her he had to go to Paris to lecture. She then wrote him a long letter, begging him to regain the 'height of vision' of his youth, and to 'discount the insidious influence on your mind of social superiority and the love-of-power . . .' Russell was no longer accustomed to personal criticism, and did not reply. She pressed him again. This time she received one of his rare brutal letters, 'I do not believe Keynes was ever much interested . . . I should advise you to get the opinion of some neutral person, preferably a psychiatrist.' On a scrap of paper among her letters and writings is Naomi's reaction to Russell's letter. 'Another member of the Bloomsbury set!' she remarks dismissively. 'Russell cannot accept the abdication of his class as the solution to the problem. He is therefore condemned to paralysis and sterility of mind. It is *he* who needs the psychiatrist, he who suavely tells lies.' (A subsequent letter to Aldous Huxley, telling the same story, drew the reply that strange as the world was, and unutterably queer its inhabitants, he found her tale 'antecedently very improbable.')

In 1949 Russell was awarded the Order of Merit, Britain's most prestigious civilian award, which had not long before gone to his old collaborator, Alfred Whitehead. George VI bestowed the order at Buckingham Palace with a mild rebuke: 'You have sometimes behaved in a way which would not do if generally adopted.' 'How a man should behave depends upon his profession,' Russell replied. 'A postman, for instance, should knock on all the doors in a street at which he has letters to deliver, but if anybody else knocked on all the doors, he would be considered a public nuisance.'

Russell was lecturing in Princeton when, the following autumn, he learned that he had also been awarded the Nobel Prize for Literature. The BBC hailed him as 'an apostle of humanity and free speech'; the *New Statesman* called him the 'wittiest and most pure of

British stylists'. He was particularly gratified to discover that he had beaten Churchill and Benedetto Croce. At New York were a larger mob of wellwishers than he had ever seen before. The crowds overflowed from the McMillan Theater in Columbia University, and two additional halls were hastily wired for the overflow, but still spectators gathered to stand three and four deep around two blocks.

His days as a public nuisance seemed to be over. In *New Hopes for a Changing World*, published soon afterwards, he appeared to have returned to the optimistic rationalism of his ancestors. Through his use of reason, man was overcoming his conflicts with nature, with other men and with himself, and even if tremendous forces were in position to tear the world apart, salvation, in the form of world government, lay not too far out of sight. Russell was in a mellow mood. 'Man,' he concluded, 'in the long ages since he descended from the trees, has passed arduously and perilously through a vast dusty desert . . . into a smiling land, but in the long night he has forgotten how to smile . . . Man now needs for his salvation only one thing: to open his heart to joy, and leave fear to gibber through the glimmering darkness of a forgotten past.'

The end of the Second World War had not been greeted by Russell with optimism. The dropping of atom bombs on Hiroshima and Nagasaki seemed to him only further proof that the twentieth century was growing ever more dangerous. His earlier concern for social and political issues was now to broaden to encompass anxiety about the future of the human race. In the 1920s and 1930s he had been a provocative but rational figure pleading for a better society; he was now to plead, in tones as lucid but with far greater urgency, for a clear understanding of what must happen if man was to survive.

A month after 'Little Boy' fell on Hiroshima, having written to a friend that he had never, not even in 1940, 'felt the outlook as gloomy as now', Russell sent an article to the *Manchester Guardian*. The wartime alliance against Germany and Japan was rapidly giving way to mistrust of the Soviet Union, and Russell became more outspoken than ever in his condemnation of all it stood for. In his article he deliberated the consequences of the Soviet Union acquiring an atom bomb, remarking that it would then 'be possible to have a really serious war'. Whatever else he felt about America, he believed that its atomic bombs could provide a brief period of supremacy, during which Truman could 'compel the world to adopt a system making great wars impossible'. He elaborated on his views before the House of Lords on 28 November, speaking for sixteen minutes, longer than on any of his rare previous appearances. He declared that the UN should set up an international atomic development authority, to which the USA should disclose its atomic secrets.

Privately, he felt very gloomy, writing to a friend that 'within 20 years England will have ceased to exist. It makes everything hectic, like the approach of closing time at a party in an hotel.' He wrote despairingly to Gamel Brenan, that he estimated an atomic war would last thirty years, and that it would take the world 500 years to recover.

> I wish I believed in a timeless Platonic world, where whatever has had a momentary existence in the stream of time survives timelessly in heaven. The moments of ecstasy in love, of sudden intellectual insight, of intoxicating glory in storms on a rocky coast . . . I should like to think of these as forever part of the universe. But that is mysticism and folly, born of fear. If we must die, let us die sober, not drunk with pleasant lies . . . I should like to end gloriously and greatly like a Shakespeare hero; it is shocking to think that as the bomb bursts I shall be wondering how to find the money for next month's bills.

The more Russell wrote and spoke, the more his hostility towards the Soviet Union grew. To a Dr Walter Marseilles of Berkeley in California, who was advocating compulsory inspection of all Soviet military installations, Russell wrote to outline his own grim scenario. 'If Russia overruns Western Europe, the destruction will be such as no subsequent reconquest can undo. Practially the whole educated population will be sent to labour camps in N.E. Siberia or on the shores of the White Sea, where most will die of hardships and the survivors will be turned into animals . . . I do not think the Russians will yield without war. I think all (including Stalin) are fatuous and ignorant.'

If Russell felt at one with the views of most British people, basking in an acceptance never before so wholehearted – as he wrote to a friend, 'Now that I yield to no one in my desire to slaughter Russians, I have become respectable' – this new fervour led to a vehemence he was later to regret. Speaking to an audience of boys at Westminster School, shortly after the Soviet Union rejected the US Baruch Plan for atomic control, he unwisely let drop a remark that it would be no bad thing if Russia were threatened with an atomic bomb, to coerce her into accepting a world authority. 'Either we must have a war against Russia before she has the atom bomb, or we will have to lie down and let them govern us.' It was a remark he was never allowed to forget. (At much the same time he was arguing that Stalin had so distorted Soviet science that Russia would never be able to develop a bomb which would actually work.)

Attacked on all sides for his unacceptable belligerence, Russell explained in a letter to *The Times* that there had been a misunderstanding, that all that he had intended to say was that the 'democracies should be *prepared* to use force . . . if Russia continues to refuse all compromise.' An article which appeared in Moscow's *The Red Star* accused Russell of being 'an open instigator of war and a preacher of pro-fascist ideas', and a 'warmonger in the scholar's gown'.

He may have been embarrassed by his apparently warlike stand, but his fears were soon justified: in August 1949, the Soviet Union exploded its first atomic bomb. World events now moved much as Russell had warned. In 1950, Truman announced the development of a hydrogen bomb. Once more voicing his earlier doubts about American policy, Russell swung round again, particularly as former friends and colleagues were being investigated by McCarthy's House UnAmerican Activities Committee. Never had his pronouncements been more ambivalent and troubled. What he felt about the two powerful protagonists at this time was summed up in an article in the *New Leader* of March 1952, where he reiterated his unchanging hostility towards Soviet imperialism, but warned that the witchhunts and erosion of civil liberties in the US was not dissimilar when it came to an invasion of people's freedom. For all its mellowness, *New Hopes for a Changing World*, published earlier that year, had contained a sad note of 'impotent perplexity'. Man, Russell seemed to be saying, could still free himself, and should indeed still continue to seek happiness, but it was highly unlikely, given the world's impulse towards self-destruction, that he would ever actually do so.

His renewed mistrust of America was not lost on his readers. The *Manchester Guardian* published a letter from a distinguished American writer, Henry Chamberlain, accusing Russell of anti-Americanism and cultural snobbery. Russell chose to reply in uncharacteristically meek terms. 'I married an American . . . and I lived in America for many years. Many of the people whom I like and admire most are Americans . . . But every nation at times gets in bad moods . . .' In an article submitted to the European *Atlantic Digest*, he was more outspoken: 'I am terrified about America,' he wrote, 'America is extraordinarily bellicose.'

On 4 November 1952, three days after the US had exploded its first H-bomb in the Pacific, the Republican candidate, Dwight Eisenhower, won a triumphant victory over his Democrat opponent, Adlai Stevenson, in the presidential elections. Russell, who had seen in Stevenson a curb on creeping McCarthyism, was appalled, and wrote that he was gloomy in the extreme about world politics, when America was dominated by such a nonentity as Eisenhower, and such wicked and foolish figures as Taft, Dulles and McCarthy. The Cold War was becoming more intense, and nine months later, the Soviet government announced it had successfully exploded its first thermonuclear device. The *Bulletin of Atomic Scientists* carried an article by Russell. 'Never since human beings first existed,' he warned, 'have they been faced with so great a danger.' In view of the new balance of power, with both states in a position to destroy the other, he had abandoned his virulent anti-Soviet position in favour of the middle ground: 'The problem for statesmanship in the present situation, as I see it, is to avoid war without surrender on our side or the expectation of surrender on the other.' The escalation of weapons now threatened everyone, and the only solution left was to place nuclear arms under a single world force. To the Parliamentary Group for World Government in the House of Commons, he proposed that neutral countries be approached to set up a commission of six people, including a bacteriologist and geneticist, to prepare a report on the likely effect on the human species of an atomic war.

*

Broadcasting for the BBC had given Russell a keen sense of the sheer number of people who could be reached by the spoken voice. Man's imminent self-destruction was too important an issue for him not to take all possible steps. The dropping of the American hydrogen bomb on Bikini, a coral reef in the Pacific, had yielded an explosive force which seemed to surprise even the scientists responsible for it. There was talk of uncontrollable radioactivity, and even a cobalt bomb, with effects more ghastly than any imagined before.

In the summer of 1954, Russell wrote to Ronald Lewin, organiser for talks at the BBC, saying that much as he disliked self-publicity and pushiness, he wondered whether he might be allowed to broadcast the last chapter of a new book, *Human Society in Ethics and Politics*, in which he had alerted people to the 'gravity' of this 'stupendous issue'? Lewin replied that he would prefer a specially written piece, looking back over the year in which the hydrogen bomb had become such an important public issue. At the last moment the BBC decided that his contribution should be one of three, each by a member of a different generation, giving their views on the bomb. Russell, not accustomed to this casual treatment, was furious. 'What I had in mind', he wrote scathingly to the talks producer, Eileen Molony, 'was an exceedingly solemn appeal to mankind to turn back from universal suicide before it was too late.' What he did not have in mind was a 'stunt'. The BBC's suggestion was 'frivolous'. 'I am sure', he concluded, 'you will have no difficulty in finding some old man who will do.'

The BBC hastily backed down. At 9.15 pm on 23 December 1954, on the Home Service, Russell gave one of the most dramatic talks ever heard on radio. His audience, it was later estimated, was somewhere between six and seven million. He was solemn, dignified and extremely alarming. No one was yet certain about the powers of these bombs, but it was now generally accepted by scientists that a war with hydrogen bombs would cause civilisation to disintegrate and possibly put an end to the human race. For a fortunate few, death would come suddenly. For the majority, there would be a 'slow torture of disease and disintegration'.

He ended his talk with words he was to use again and again, and whose sonority made them immediately memorable. 'There lies before us if we choose,' he said in those precise and Whiggish tones which made his voice so distinct, 'continual progress in happiness, knowledge and wisdom. Shall we, instead, choose death, because we cannot forget our quarrels? I appeal, as a human being to human beings: remember your humanity, and forget the rest. If you can do so, the way lies open to a new paradise; if you cannot, nothing lies before you but universal death.' It was all very stark but, in true Russell style, not without hope. It was up to mankind, he said, as in all other things, to stop the bombs. People, as he repeated all his life, are not victims unless they make themselves so. But they have to find the courage to bring about change.

The impact of his speech was extraordinary, and had not been anticipated either by the BBC or by Russell. It is hard now to remember the colossal fear first engendered by the spectre of these bombs. He touched a nerve which lay very close to the surface. The British public had long suspected the worst of nuclear weapons: here was the proof that their fears were justified. The *Manchester Guardian* immediately produced a statistic showing that Britain would survive '20 to 30 hours' after a nuclear war began. Listeners wrote to the BBC in their hundreds. They asked for the talk to be repeated, so that they could be clear about the depth of Russell's warning, and so that friends who had not heard it could understand their anxieties. The *New Statesman* called it 'the wisest utterance' of Russell's remarkable career. 'Man's Peril', as the talk had been named, gave Russell a new voice as the prophet against the nuclear age. It belongs in the great tradition of British polemical essays, as his *Free Man's Worship* had done fifty years earlier.

In 1954, Einstein was seventy-five and living in Princeton. Like Russell, he was a convinced internationalist; and as the power of the new weapons grew, he too had come to argue for a world organisation which could reduce the probability of nuclear war annihilating the human race. As a scientist, he had contributed to the work on the atom: when it seemed that the Germans were going to develop their own bomb, Einstein had argued firmly in favour of the Americans pressing ahead, but once the bomb threatened the existence of man himself, he turned fiercely against it. The two men's shared views, and a natural empathy, made them obvious allies.

On 11 February 1955, greatly encouraged by the response to his talk, Russell wrote to Einstein, saying the moment had truly come when 'eminent men of science' should draw the attention of world leaders to the impending destruction of the human race. His suggestion was that six men, all of them of the highest scientific repute and headed by Einstein himself, should sign a statement 'about the imperative necessity of avoiding war'. Einstein's answer was enthusiastic. By April, Russell had drafted a statement, outlining the perils, calling for the abolition of nuclear bombs, and urging governments to recognise their duty to find peaceful ways of settling disputes. Between them, the two men had approached distinguished scientists, but not all were willing to sign; some objected to the wording, while others had similar plans of their own. The statement was on the point of final agreement when Russell, on his way by plane from one conference in Rome to another in Paris, heard the captain announce over the intercom that Einstein was dead. Russell had not received Einstein's final signature, and it looked as though the whole plan would founder, but waiting for him at his hotel in Paris was a letter from Einstein, endorsing the manifesto.

Russell now ran into problems. How to launch the manifesto? He approached the *Observer* newspaper which agreed to help, and Caxton Hall, Westminster, was chosen as the best place. The date was set for 9 July. The final days were beset with difficulties, with the French physicist Joliot-Curie saying he now had doubts about the way it was phrased, but given that Einstein was dead, no alterations could be made above his signature. After further deliberations, the scientists agreed to go ahead: Herman Muller, Linus Pauling, Cecil Power, Percy Bridgman, Leopold Infeld and Hideki Yukawa, all Nobel Prize winners except for Infeld. To Russell's acute embarrassment, the name of Max Born, who had been a keen supporter from the first, was inadvertently left off the list.

Russell had met Professor Joseph Rotblat, the Polish physicist and vice-president of the British Atomic Scientists' Association, who had himself had the idea of bombarding uranium with neutron to produce a chain reaction, when they had both been invited to speak on television shortly after the hydrogen bomb tests on Bikini atoll. Rotblat was professor of physics at St Bartholomew's Hospital

Medical School. Seeking a judicious chairman, Russell turned to him. The offer fitted perfectly with Rotblat's preoccupations on how to persuade scientists to agree to a moratorium on nuclear physics.

On 9 July, an immense crowd gathered in Caxton Hall. Before massed rows of reporters, Russell posed the question which lay at the heart of the manifesto. 'Here, then, is the problem which we present to you, stark and dreadful, and inescapable: shall we put an end to the human race, or shall mankind renounce war?' Under the bright television lights he looked frail and gentle. He ended with the eloquent phrases taken largely from 'Man's Peril', which Linus Pauling had argued were almost too eloquent. 'Remember your humanity . . . if you can do so, the way lies open to a new paradise.' As with 'Man's Peril', these warnings, given authority by world scientists, who knew about such things, carried particular weight. The Einstein-Russell Manifesto, issued at a particularly threatening moment of the Cold War by two venerable thinkers who had survived both wars and lived in terror of a third, drew enormous publicity, and officials in Britain, Canada and the United States, as well as a few in the Soviet Union, took notice of it. That Einstein was dead, and that his warning seemed to come from beyond the grave, gave his message a certain ghoulish urgency.

The meeting at Caxton Hall ended with a call for another conference of scientists to assess the precise nature of the danger and try to find methods of involving the entire international community. Rotblat argued for a full conference, chaired by Russell, but Russell insisted that, as a non-scientist, he was unfitted for the role, and preferred the idea of a series of smaller conferences. At eighty-three, he continued to command immense respect in the scientific world, where his philosophy of science was greatly admired. The scientists now split over the usefulness of a major conference, and whether they should be taking the line that war was the main evil, or that danger lay in thermonuclear weapons and not in war itself.

One of the first personal letters to reach Russell after the meeting had come from a Cleveland industrialist, Cyrus Eaton, of the Chesapeake and Ohio Railway Company, who wrote offering to finance a meeting of scientists in his home town of Pugwash in Nova Scotia. A similar offer had been made by the shipowner, Aristotle

Onassis, who proposed Monaco as a site. (Russell refused to contemplate Onassis, saying to Rotblat: 'His money stinks'.) Cyrus Eaton's offer was also rejected, because Russell and Rotblat were in contact with President Nehru, who had suggested holding the conference in India, in January 1957, to coincide with the annual Indian science congress. But first Suez and then the Hungarian crisis made the journey impossible for some of the participants. Russell remembered Eaton's letter. He and Rotblat, somewhat suspicious of the name Pugwash, which reminded them of the popular children's cartoon strip, found Eaton's credentials impeccable. Russell wrote to him and was told that the invitation still stood, provided the meeting took place in Pugwash. Eaton would cover the costs of accommodation, food and clerical help, and travel expenses where necessary. Sixty-four invitations went out over Russell's signature. Thirty scientists accepted; the others said that they were too busy, or feared a possible political bias, or that it was not the business of scientists to meddle in world politics. A few were known to consider Russell a man of the media and not of science; or thought him too radical and liable to alienate average opinion.

On 7 July 1957, twenty-one scientists, most of them physicists, and one lawyer, from ten countries reached the lobster-fishing village of Pugwash on the Northumberland Strait. Most had flown to Montreal, where they were picked up by Eaton's private plane. Pugwash had a population of 800 people. There were no hotels, and guests stayed in Eaton's house, in the private homes of Pugwash citizens and in railway sleeping compartments, brought up by Eaton from his railway stock and parked in a siding at Pugwash station. Conference sessions took place in the one room big enough to hold them, a former schoolroom in the Masonic Temple, and meals were eaten at long tables in Eaton's white clapboard house. One day, the delegates took a boat trip. Photographs of the occasion show genial-looking men in baggy suits and ties, sitting in the sun. Russell, not feeling physically up to the long journey to Canada, did not join them, but kept in constant touch by telephone and continued to be regarded as the true inspiration of the conference.

For three days, the twenty-one scientists and one lawyer discussed the consequences of the use of nuclear weapons, their control, and the responsibilities of scientists. At four o'clock on the last afternoon, Joseph Rotblat emerged to issue a joint statement, saying they had concluded that the hazards posed by nuclear warfare were immense, and that they could lead to radiation which would affect hundreds of millions of people, and make large areas of the earth uninhabitable. The principal objective of all nations, he read out, 'must be the abolition of war and the threat of war hanging over mankind', and he warned against the intervention of the Soviet Union and the USA in local wars. 'We are convinced', he concluded, 'that mankind must abolish war or suffer catastrophe.' The significance of Pugwash, with its photographs of sleepy-looking men in spectacles rolling up their shirtsleeves in the sun, was not lost on the world. This was the first time that scientists from east and west had met to discuss the social implications of scientific discovery. Few people apart from Russell had hitherto believed that scientists could share a common purpose, which transcended nationalities but did not violate loyalties.

Neither Russell nor Rotblat had dared to plan any more such meetings, but Pugwash ended with unanimous agreement among the scientists to meet again. Eaton remained generous towards them, and offered Pugwash again as conference site, but as the years went by he began to see himself as having been responsible for the whole occasion. What began as slightly embarrassing for the scientists became – once Eaton contemplated a major role in American politics, befriending Khrushchev and sending him a present of steers – alarm that they might soon suffer by association. Pugwash continued, but broke with Eaton by the late 1950s. The meetings reached a low point during the Cuban missile crisis, when snide newspaper remarks accused the scientists of having been hijacked by the communists.

Russell remained involved for the rest of his life, mainly through lengthy conversations with Rotblat. The last conference he attended in person was in 1962, when Pugwash met in London. As the meeting closed, he received a standing ovation. Without him, believes Rotblat, such a meeting would not have taken place so soon or with such unanimity. For Russell, the major success of Pugwash lay in the partial test-ban treaty, though he was to wonder whether that was not merely a 'soother of consciences'.

*

In March 1957, despite warnings from the scientific community that radiation could have genetic effects, the United States carried out a series of nuclear tests in the Pacific. When it became clear that Britain was also planning tests, Russell wrote to the *New Scientist* calling for an end to them, and repeating that they served only to increase global insecurity. On 15 May, in the face of criticism from the Pope and Nehru, Britain exploded its first hydrogen bomb, and other tests followed. In September, the United Nations' disarmament talks ended in failure. An article appeared in *The Times* revealing that US planes, carrying primed H-bombs, were now in the skies above Britain. Feeling that he had tried every other avenue, Russell decided to appeal directly to the men who had power over the bombs – Khrushchev and Eisenhower. His open letter, addressed to 'Most Potent Sirs', appeared in November in the *New Statesman*. They alone, he wrote, possessed the 'power of good or evil exceeding anything ever possessed before by any man or group of men'. It was for them to act. To do nothing would probably result in the extermination of both sides. To Kingsley Martin, an old friend and the editor of the *New Statesman*, Russell explained,

> As regards the H-bomb question, the sensible course would be an agreement between Russia and America that no one else should have the H-bombs, as a first step towards their general abolition. If *we* abandoned H-bombs, we could support this proposal. As for the tests, each test explosion carries an uncertain number of monsters and deaths through cancer. I do not like my country to be one of those that add to this infamy.

Within weeks, to the astonishment of all concerned, a reply from Khrushchev arrived on Kingsley Martin's desk. It was published in the *New Statesman* on 21 December. Russell, said Khrushchev, was perfectly right; the arms race must be brought to an end. But what was the Soviet Union to do when the west refused to respond to his overtures? It was not enough simply to curb the deployment of nuclear weapons; their manufacture must be prohibited and their stockpiles destroyed. 'What we advocate', concluded Khrushchev, 'is that the superiority of any particular system be proved, not on the field of battle, but in peaceful competition for progress, for improved living standards of the people.'

The United States' reply came not from Eisenhower but from John Foster Dulles, secretary of state. Kingsley Martin was greatly enjoying this moment of glory, since no other western newspaper had ever carried similar contributions from world leaders. After Khrushchev's flow of rhetoric and seeming generosity of spirit, Dulles sounded strangled and pious, limiting himself to attacks on the Soviet Union and communism.

Khrushchev was evidently delighted with this ready platform for his views; he asked Martin for the right of reply. On 15 March, 9000 words appeared, rejecting Dulles's accusations, and calling for 'concrete negotiations'. It sounded plausible. Russell returned to the fray, and urged the acceptance of Khrushchev's proposals. Nothing was heard from Washington, and in his autobiography Russell attacked the 'righteously adamantine surface of Mr Dulles' mind'. The exchange was published later that year as a book.

Russell's views on the USA had become steadily tougher. In 1951, he had accepted an invitation to be a sponsor for the Congress of Cultural Freedom, but when he thought he detected in its American offshoot, of which he was a vice-president, a growing anti-liberal bias, he decided to resign, but not before he had been drawn into attacking the FBI for the 'atrocities' committed against figures like the Rosenbergs or their associate Morton Sobell, kidnapped by the FBI in Mexico and sentenced to prison on Alcatraz. The FBI, declared Russell, in one of his more intemperate and shrill moments, was turning the United States into a country not unlike 'other police states such as Nazi Germany and Stalin's Russia'. Chastised on both sides of the Atlantic for what James T. Farrell, chairman of the Congress of Cultural Freedom, called a 'major disservice to the cause of freedom and democracy', Russell hit out again, in an interview with Cedric Belfrage, a British writer who had spent some time in prison in America after being investigated by McCarthy. He made a violent attack on the FBI and praised the Soviet Union for releasing political prisoners. Having swung around so entirely, Russell apologised for ever having suggested that the west should threaten the Soviet Union with the bomb.

His views about America were becoming not only wilder but, some felt, rather foolish, as though designed to alienate a public which greatly admired him. They were a taste of what was to come. After acrimonious exchanges with members of the Congress and its American branch, Russell resigned from both, concluding that he had no further place on committees of this kind. If the American left regarded him as a desirable and solitary voice in their crusade for civil liberties, others were finding his new style offensive.

Eighteen

A complicated cocoon

Busy as these years had been, giving Russell new platforms and a new constituency at a time when most men begin to tire, they had not been domestically happy ones. Both Russell and Peter became involved with other people, even if his affairs revolved around long letters, written with the same intimacy – if not the same passion – as those of his earlier relationships. In the 1940s and 1950s, Irina Strickland – married to Derek Wragge Morley, an entomologist who fell in love with Peter – Miriam Brudno and Gamel Brenan were all regular correspondents.

Did Russell have an affair with Gamel Brenan? The tone of his letters suggests that he did; one written in 1951 declared that he loved her deeply and sincerely 'and I reckon having known you as one of the most important things in my life' – but her letters suggest the opposite. Certainly her husband Gerald did not feel threatened by their relationship, though Peter was evidently jealous of Gamel. It is far more likely that they were close friends, enjoying the kind of intimacy Russell most relished and excelled at with women, with rather more passion on his part and rather less on hers, but warm and fond for all that. 'Things are always occurring to me that I want to say to you and to no one else,' Russell wrote. 'I hate the way the months go by without our meeting, while the deserts of vast eternity draw nearer and nearer. I feel that what I miss now I may miss for ever, which I did not feel when I was younger.'

As with his work, a new urgency was creeping into his life; the years were going by and there was still so much he wished to do. On a scrap of paper, undated and with no name, but believed to be addressed to Gamel and perhaps handed to her or enclosed in a letter, is a passage of Russell at his most full-blown and sentimental: 'From the first I have loved your strange eyes, expressing a kind of gentle mockery and the wisdom of pain assimilated . . . Very soon I saw that, like me, you live in an alien world . . . I feel no longer alone, no longer dusty, for your existence sheds enchantment over this arid world.'

Gamel was a strange figure, a solitary, contemplative, fashionable woman, who reserved her emotional side for her novels and poems. She once said of Russell that, though she admired him, she could not really like him. Her replies were sometimes almost terse. The closest she got to recording her feelings about Russell on paper was in letters to her friend Alyse Gregory; they are also perceptive about him. One day, after visiting him in Cambridge in the late 1940s, she wrote that she found him older, worn thin by the storms with Peter, but somehow more distinguished. 'Sometimes I found his *vanity* so touching. He said that he always felt hostility to other people . . . The brilliance, the instinctive attack with the sharpest weapons because he expects attack. But where do such feelings come from? Something far away and long ago I'm sure – deeply hidden and deeply rooted. What maimed and halting creatures we all are. All of us with wounds . . .' Later, again to Alyse Gregory, she spoke despondently of how difficult it was to arrange to see Russell.

In January 1968, Gerald Brenan wrote to tell Russell that Gamel was dead, of a spreading cancer she had long concealed and which was, towards the end, extremely painful. 'Above all,' Russell wrote back, 'I liked the warmth and intimacy of her sympathy, which I shall miss as long as I live.' Gamel was the last of his close friendships with women.

Not long after settling in Cambridge, Peter described to a friend the kind of house she hoped to find. The wry tone of the letter, with its self-mocking asides, gives an all-too-rare picture of what she was like. It did not need to be a 'gent's residence', a cottage would do, but both Russells had a strong aversion to 'pitch pine and variegated tiles and monkey puzzles and Methodismal architecture'. I hope, she ended, this is clear 'but I doubt it, because my head isn't, being full of another cold . . . I feel uncomfortably mortal, though the doctors do say that (not having TB) I could, if I lived in a better climate and in almost complete idleness, look forward to a long lifetime of being not very well. In Cambridge the prospect is hardly to be borne, but in Wales it might be not only bearable, but, I suspect, not true at all.'

In the May after they arrived home, Russell wrote to tell Gamel that Peter was 'sunk in hysterical gloom'. By the autumn she was again ill, though how much this was caused by unhappiness it is hard to tell. Not long after Christmas she was in a nursing home in London, and Russell wrote again to Gamel, '*quite private*', that she had tried to commit suicide, after he had threatened to leave, 'and very nearly succeeded . . . I have been through a very bad time.' Peter, it seems, had grown increasingly envious of Russell's friends and popularity and was finally able to stand it no longer. When she woke to find herself still alive, she was 'very unhappy and incredibly bitter'. Russell retired to bed with exhaustion, after being questioned by the police.

Eventually, the Russells found a cottage at Ffestiniog in North Wales, with the help of Clough and Amabel Williams-Ellis, owners of Portmeirion and the Penrhyndeudraeth Hotel, where they had lived while waiting for his divorce from Dora. Here, Russell hoped 'ultimately to retire from the hubbub. I want to write a system of philosophy and an autobiography and then die.' A former village school, its one long room converted into a library and sitting room, the cottage stood on the brow of a long hill, winding up from the sea. Beyond the flagstone terrace were views over the valley of Ffestiniog, with waterfalls and rivers flowing to the sea. In the background stood Moelwyn mountain. Russell had found himself another view.

It was perhaps inevitable that he should again seek out Colette. Not long after he reached England, he met her at her sister's flat in London, having pressed her to come back from Sweden, where she was living, and offering to pay for her ticket. They had not seen each other for almost eight years. Colette had spent most of the war in Finland, before being evacuated to Sweden, where she raised money to send food to the Finns. They were soon exchanging fond letters, and Russell agreed to her suggestion that he should give a series of lectures in Sweden.

Colette returned to Sweden and filled his hotel room before his arrival with lilies of the valley, violas and golden cowslips, soaps, pine essence and bath salts, taking from her own house a Chinese jade saucer and a rock crystal 'boat of happiness', to make it seem more cheerful. She wrote to a friend in London that she had been unable to decide what to wear for this reunion, but had settled on a dress made for her in 1921, with some of Russell's mother's lace, which she had never worn. Their meeting evidently went well. In between his lectures at the university and the parliament, they wandered around the old town of Reisen, and went out to see the flowering lilac in the countryside. Peter, Russell assured Colette, knew of their meeting and 'would make little of it'.

Colette had been thinking of buying a house in England, and Russell now persuaded her to consider North Wales. She visited him at Ffestiniog, when Peter was away, and he again assured her that Peter would not mind if he were to make love to her. But when Peter rang, and a row broke out, Colette guessed that she was not alone in Russell's extra-marital affections. It reminded her of Vivienne Eliot and Katherine Mansfield so long ago. Russell, worried about the effect of a broken marriage on Conrad, wanted to wait a year before breaking with Peter, so that his youngest son could get to Eton. Colette, who was allowed to meet Conrad, remarked that he was somewhat spoilt but that his 'rombustious vitality and enthusiasm are very infectious' and that he was 'VERY delightful to look at'. Remarking on Peter's still unlined face, she added, 'My brow is like a deeply ploughed, furrowed field that you could almost grow potatoes in.'

To a Danish woman, Naille Kielland, who had sent a child to Beacon Hill in the 1930s, and later had an affair with Russell while Dora was pregnant with Harriet, Colette wrote some of her shrewder assessments of Russell's character. The two women had met and become friends, their love for Russell being a bond between them. Of all the dozens of portraits people have left of him, the most vivid are by the women he loved.

'You know, Naille,' she wrote one day, 'there are several things which bring the thought "cad" to one's mind . . . It is not, I think, his mind wh. has deteriorated: it is his character: each marriage has hastened the process: he sh. never have married ANYBODY: he knows it quite well himself: but his Weltschmerz was profound, and he grabbed every little pleasure.' Remarking on his style of abandoning people he had once loved, she explained that the reason 'each break has been completely final is simply that his entire resources of patience have been used up during each marriage; the break does not come with him until there is nothing of patience, or of anything else, left . . .'

The end of their forty-year love affair belongs here. Russell and Colette spent several holidays in Wales together, Colette writing after one particularly happy occasion, 'Cottage and garden both feel empty without you. I shall always glory in your anarchic vitality – whatever direction it may take.' After seeing him off, she had watered the tulips, put his room in order, and drunk a bottle of sherry. Did she still believe they might end their lives together? Intimate encounters were followed by long silences, while Russell battled with Peter, who again threatened suicide. Colette, still waiting for him, found a cottage in Suffolk, some forty miles from Cambridge, to house her furniture and books. One day a note arrived from Russell, suggesting a meeting, but adding curtly that there must be no scandal. Just before they were due to meet, he sent a telegram cancelling it. Colette's friends thought she was on the point of a nervous breakdown.

After the second of two brief and unsatisfactory meetings, Russell left her to visit his lawyer, Peter having found a love letter from Colette which she had insisted on reading aloud to Conrad. Colette stood at the window and watched him until he reached the corner of Tavistock Square, where he turned and waved to her. It was she who took the final step. On 20 November 1949 she asked a close friend, Phyllis Urch, to deliver a letter to him at Baldwin's Hotel. 'I see everything quite clear now', she wrote, 'and it seems a dreary end to all our years. I see now your inability to care for anybody, with the whole of you, for longer than a rather short time . . . Your life is a complicated cocoon, getting more and more involved always.

Three times I've been drawn into its centre and three times thrown aside . . . Goodnight now and goodbye. It is at least a clean break.'

Colette asked Phyllis Urch to find out Russell's true feelings before handing him the letter. Russell told her that he had loved Colette more than he had ever loved anyone, but that now the only emotion he felt was fatigue. Though he still loved the 'beauty of her face', he desired her only when he saw her. 'I shall never again live with any other woman,' he remarked mournfully, 'I don't seem to make a success of it.'

Though they were to exchange fond letters again, and Colette sent him red roses on his birthday in memory of their first meeting in 1916, they never met again. When she was in financial difficulties, Russell sent her money. According to Phyllis Urch, she never quite believed it was all over, and not long afterwards she asked her to drive up and down outside Russell's house in London, in case she caught sight of him in the garden, in which case she would have forced herself to talk to him. He was not there. It was like the early 1920s all over again when she used to take a taxi and drive past his house in Chelsea, hoping to catch sight of him at his desk. She saw him once again, at a meeting he was addressing in Westminster Hall; but by then she had become very deaf and could not hear his words. 'It is just the fact that he knows I'm always there in the world ready for him, which damps down any steps he might make towards meeting and seeing each other,' she remarked to Phyllis Urch. 'When BR really wants anything, he lets NOTHING WHATEVER stand in the way of getting it. He has always been like that.'

On top of her deafness, which in the end became total, Colette came down with osteosclerosis, but she was a woman of considerable fortitude: her letters contain no trace of self-pity, only humour and wryness. One day she had a fall, injuring, she thought, her wrist, but the next morning the whole of her left side was numb. She managed to pull herself downstairs to scramble an egg, but then found she could not stand. She dragged herself back to bed and reviewed the immediate future. It was thirteen days before she expected her next visitor; she resolved to sit them out.

A few days later, sensing that her strength was beginning to ebb, she pulled herself to the window, smashed a pane with the lid of a piece of pottery, put a scribbled call for help into an empty Bath Oliver tin, and threw it into the street below. A neighbour picked it up and called a doctor. Colette recovered, but she was paralysed down one side, from her shoulder to her toes. Russell contributed to the costs of a nursing home, but she insisted on returning home to live alone in her cottage. Four years later, a second stroke left her unable to reach for food or a drink for four days, until she was discovered by the police. She was taken, uncomplaining, to a nursing home near Bury St Edmunds. On 5 October 1975, she had a coronary thrombosis and died. Russell was the only man with whom she had wished to spend her life. Characteristically, there was no trace of bitterness in her failure to do so.

The 1940s and 1950s contained other, final, partings for Russell. None, perhaps, was as poignant as his last encounters with Alys. They had not met, or even corresponded, for thirty-eight years, when in 1949 Alys, 'feeling all passion spent', wrote to congratulate him on his forthcoming OM. He replied and early in 1950 agreed to lunch with her. Her brother Logan, whom she had looked after devotedly during the final years of his manic depression, had died three years before and Alys had gone to live in the ground floor and basement of a friend's house. After a lifetime of philanthropy, exasperating her nieces and friends with her exaggerated sense of self-denial, her jumble sales and unashamed purloining of their belongings for good causes, she had entered a milder and more attractive old age, looking distinguished rather than foolish in the dark clothes which had once served only to increase the sense of self-abnegation. Those who had once felt impatience at her manic selflessness were now charmed. She was in her eighties, with a stooping gait and a dowager's hump, and seldom left the house, preferring to sit and play patience or receive old friends.

The story of her rapprochement with Russell is most vividly told in the pages of a dark red notebook containing lists, observations, recollections and occasional diary entries. There are many references to Russell. Little, for her, had changed: it might still have been the turn of the century.

'Tho' our conversation was not intimate, it was friendly and cheerful and to me blisful [sic],' she wrote after their lunch. 'I was awfully excited and quite ill for a week afterwards ... For the first time since June 1902 I want to live & I am really tho' not completely happy until I know what he feels about the past ... In the last 39 years I felt it was self-indulgence, as well as pain to think of him & love him, and I distracted myself with activities, but I was always heart-hungry, and longing for him.' To his request for a letter he could print in the autobiography he was working on, reflecting on their marriage, Alys contributed a generous and profoundly touching offering. 'Bertie was an ideal companion, and he taught me more than I can ever repay. But I was never clever enough for him ... A final separation led to a divorce ... my life was completely changed ... I only caught sight of him at lectures or concerts occasionally, and thro' the uncurtained windows of his Chelsea house, where I used to watch him sometimes reading to his children.' The image of these two women, Alys and Colette, driving up and down outside his Chelsea house so many years before is haunting. 'Unfortunately, I was neither wise enough nor courageous enough to prevent this one disaster from shattering my capacity for happiness and my zest for life.' Privately, she wrote to Russell: 'I feel I must be honest and just say once (but once only) that I am utterly devoted to thee, and have been so for over 50 years ... But my devotion makes no claim and involves no burden on thy part, not even to answer this letter ...'

The occasional exchange of letters and visits continued. Alys's red diary recorded them all.

> March 6: I feel I shall burst with happiness & can hardly bear it.
> March 11: It is too much for poor old me ... I can't sleep and have lost my appetite ...
> March 21: I was very depressed and weepy yesterday, but cheered up today when I remembered Goethe's last love affair at 80, and his curing it by a mustard foot bath. Also ... by the suggestion (made by a friend) that Bertie shd. divorce Peter and make an 'honest countess' out of me.

Did Alys really believe that Russell, given his relationships with far younger women, might return to her? It is her only reference to the subject.

June 2: O joy, o joy, Bertie has just tel.d that he would like to dine here
tomorrow night. How can I wait till then?
July 12: I am growing calmer and less consumed by my passionate
adoration. I feel less ecstasy, less abasement, but more steady and
reliable love.

Alys had lost a stone in weight since their meeting the previous
summer, which she put down to happiness. But as she continued to
lose more weight, and began to spit blood, she feared that she would
never see him again, as he was on a long trip abroad. On 3
September, she wrote, 'Thirteen weeks since Bertie last dined here,
& I feel numb, but with sadness now, as I want to see him so
desperately.' She observed that she was calmer when he was away,
not always running to the telephone or waiting for the post.

The red notebook contains two final entries; on 1 January 1951,
'Still Bertie doesn't telephone nor come, & I feel dreadfully sad.
From 3 to 4, every day after my nap, I have a fit of the blues, I cry &
long so much to see him that I can hardly bear it.' On 12 January,
after receiving an apologetic letter from Russell to say that overwork
had prevented him from visiting her, and ending 'much love, thine
own B,' Alys wrote, 'It is the first sign of affection he has shown me,
& it makes me perfectly happy. It looks as if he really cares for me a
little.'

Alys died of cancer. The day before her death, a friend went to
see her. Frugal to the last, she was instructing visitors, 'Thee may
take my spare clothes because I won't be needing them.' When the
telephone rang, the friend rose to answer it. Alys stopped her. No,
she said, 'it might be Bertie'. It was not.

Later, Russell was to say that he had been glad to make friends
with Alys before she died, but that he had felt embarrassed in the
face of such devotion. Barbara Strachey, Alys's great niece, who
declared that the less one saw of Russell, the more one liked him,
and who objected to him as 'cruel to women, selfish and also a goat',
was there while Alys was dying. Russell scolded her for not having
called him. Alys, she told him, had stopped her from doing so.

The break with Colette came at the same time as Russell felt
increasingly estranged from Peter. Had it not been for her scenes,

her suicide attempts, and her use of Conrad as a pawn, he claimed later, he would have left her far sooner. As it was, the end came swiftly.

The Russells had been invited to Sicily, to stay in Taormina with a friend called Daphne Phelps, whom he had met in America. They believed they would be the only guests, but it turned out, to Russell's genuine pleasure and Peter's distinct irritation, that the house was full of young painters. One of them was Julian Trevelyan's wife, Mary, daughter-in-law of his old friend Bob Trevelyan. Russell, who insisted, despite the heat, on wearing a suit and high-necked shirt, bought himself a straw hat to protect his face, easily sunburnt, from turning bright red and his nose from peeling. There were picnics, long lunches on the terrace, and much laughter. He entertained the party with his funny stories, quoted at length from the more ribald passages in the New Testament, and laughed merrily at their jokes. He never made the young people feel ill-at-ease, Mary Trevelyan said later, nor did he put them down with talk of philosophers they knew nothing about. Peter, by contrast, was testy and sullen, sitting silent and glowering. Conrad, then aged thirteen, struck the other guests as a pedantic child.

One evening, Daphne Phelps proposed a picnic on nearly Isola Bella. A boat was booked and some fishermen hired to row and catch the dinner, and the party zigzagged down the twenty hairpins to the beach. Only Peter, who declared the idea of such an expedition tedious, stayed behind, keeping Conrad with her. The picnic was a success. The fishermen grilled their catch over hot stones, while the party lay about on the sand listening to Julian Trevelyan playing his oboe on a nearby hill. Everyone drank too much. Russell chased all the young women, kissing them when he caught them and declaring: 'I'm as drunk as a lord, but then I am one.'

When he had had enough, Mary Trevelyan volunteered to take him home. She left him at the door and went back to the beach. A little later, when the others arrived home, they were greeted by a furious Peter, who opened the door in a scarlet dressing gown and shouted: 'You are disgusting drunkards. Bertie is drunk. Put him to bed.' They found Russell locked in a lavatory.

When they woke the next morning, Peter had gone. She had left

Conrad behind, who had insisted on staying to see an eclipse of the sun, due in four days' time. Russell appeared rather subdued. At breakfast, turning to his neighbour, he commented, 'It's very nice to be among people who are not nasty to me all the time.' He spent the next few days looking after Conrad, who announced from time to time, 'You're a lot of disgusting wine-bibbers'.

The next time Mary Trevelyan saw Peter was soon after the divorce, in the autumn of 1952, which was finally brought about, Russell claimed, by Peter and not by him. To friends who accused her of abandoning Russell heartlessly when he was growing old, Peter explained that she would have been willing to stay had he agreed that both should be faithful, and scrupulously honest, with each other. He had refused and she had left. To Freda Utley, the wife of the imprisoned Russian whom Russell had tried to help in the 1930s, she wrote that she had just discovered, from 'independent sources', how Russell had told people that he disliked her intensely, and had done so for years. She commented that it was in his nature to loathe people but pretend to their faces that he liked them. 'By talking against each to each he has always put everyone against everyone else among his intimates, and with women it is dreadful, he collects several at a time who each believes that he loves her and hates the others. The good ones want to rescue the poor darling from his misery (as I thought I was rescuing him from Dora, who thought he loved her) and the bad ones cash in.'

No wife parted from Russell without rancour. But while Alys's break was steeped in excruciating unhappiness, and Dora felt outraged betrayal and vindictiveness, Peter's departure happened largely in silence. Later, she said they had never been happy together, that the good times had been an illusion from the start. Colette observed that the marriage had foundered because of 'a sick and feeble person (in body) going and marrying an immensely tough and vigorous one. Result: irritation on both sides'.

Russell had given Peter a percentage of the royalties from *Authority and the Individual*, *Power*, and *A History of Western Philosophy* and, after the divorce, Peter wrote anxiously to Stanley Unwin to make sure of them. The amounts involved were not negligible. In the tax year 1948–9 £2577 came her way. Later, she also received some of the Nobel Prize money. By 1952 her alienation from Russell was total. She announced that she intended to revert to her maiden name of Spence. She had been granted custody of Conrad, and such was her misery and fury that she prevented him from seeing his father until he went to university. She moved with him to Cornwall, to a mill near Morwenstow so remote that it had no water and no electricity. They had no car. Conrad later claimed that the break had come as a complete surprise to him, and that the older children, John and Kate, rallied to him. 'As for love,' Russell observed to Gamel long afterwards, 'the most unwise love of my life was in full swing when I was 63. The fruit of it, my son Conrad, won't speak to me, is a fanatical High Anglican, and has grown a beard. Philosophers and mathematicians in love are exactly like everyone else, except, perhaps, that the holiday from reason makes them passionate to excess.' Though Russell wrote to Conrad, his son never received the letters.

In all his adult years, Russell had not been alone for very long; it was not a condition he liked. Friends from the old days were dying, one by one, like Desmond MacCarthy and his cousin Mary Murray who, he insisted, had never liked him after the First World War, though Gilbert Murray wrote to reassure him that he was wrong, and that she had always put him in a special category of people 'with whom you might not agree, but who nevertheless stood high up, rather beyond criticism'. Russell wrote, sadly, to say to Elizabeth Trevelyan that she and Bob were virtually the only ones who 'still survive and are my friends – others, if they still live, have become strangers.'

The name of Edith Finch first crops up among Russell's papers in 1948, when she wrote to tell him of his old friend Lucy Donnelly's sudden death while they were on holiday together in Canada. Russell had known Edith for many years, meeting her first in Paris in the twenties, and then on visits to Bryn Mawr, where she taught. She was forty-seven in 1948, a small, pretty woman, with grey eyes specked in brown, who reminded Mary Trevelyan of a little bird, with a calm manner and infinite good sense. Her grandfather was an Episcopalian clergyman. She was quiet and extremely clever, and, like Russell, sceptical, anti-dogmatic and precise, with excellent manners. Her rather surprising past included a spell riding bareback in a circus in Paris, and the friendship of Gertrude Stein, as well as two biographies of Carey Thomas and Wilfrid Scawen Blunt.

Shortly before Christmas 1950, she arrived in London. She dined with Russell, and next day he wrote to thank her for a 'heavenly evening', signing his letter, 'All my love darling'. On April Fool's Day 1951, he was writing, 'You say that every Sunday you doubt my existence. I think today is Sunday – I think so, ergo sum. If I thought it were Monday the argument would be just as good.' By May that year, the letters were still more loving. 'My dear Heart, I love you very much indeed . . . I do not feel that your love is partly hate, as love usually is.' In October, he began to talk of a deeper love than he had ever known before, or ever expected to know. They were married on 15 December 1952; Russell was eighty, Edith fifty-one. It was to be his happiest marriage, lasting until his death in 1970, more enduring in terms of affection than any of the others and lacking all the frenzy of his earlier commitments. 'Of course I am happy,' he told reporters. 'How can one fail to enjoy life so long as the glands are in good working order? That is the only secret.' To Gamel, he added: 'I am very happy – more so than for a number of years. Both publicly and privately everything goes so well with me that I am in danger of becoming smug.' To her friend Phyllis Urch, Colette remarked that she had feared Russell was making a fool of himself with a 'pretty flapper', but that on seeing Edith's photograph in the paper 'it wouldn't surprise me if he has met his master this time.'

That year Russell entered his ninth decade. He had by now moved to Richmond in south-west London, close to Pembroke Lodge, into a large Edwardian building which he shared with his son John, who was showing all the signs of acute manic depression and the kind of insanity which Russell had spent his earlier years dreading. There was a terrible irony in his son's being visited by the very nightmare which had haunted him for so long. With them in the house were John's wife, Susan, her daughter Anne, whom John had adopted as a baby, and their two daughters, Lucy and Sarah. Russell had just completed a new book, *The Impact of Science on Society*, and was at work on something altogether different: fiction, in the shape of a series of moral satires. His health was not perfect – he was showing the first signs of having trouble eating, his throat seeming at times so full of wind that he found it hard to swallow, explaining to a friend that this affliction had been brought on by 'attempting to swallow the pronouncements of politicians' – but to viewers of a twenty-five-minute television film, made by the American NBC network to honour his eightieth birthday, he looked fit and robust. The interviewer compared him to Bishop Berkeley and Hume, and spoke of his eighteenth-century wit and the pleasure of listening to him pontificate on the horrors of the modern world.

As he told a reporter who came to see him, Russell had cut back the hours he worked each day from seven to four, and had given up swimming. He also observed that he now felt some things less strongly than he had as a young man – 'one item does not upset the balance very much' – and that he had to remind himself constantly of the importance of absorbing new ideas: 'Of all the pitfalls that lie in the path of the old, the deepest is almost certainly that labelled habit.' But he was far from abandoning his concern with the problems of modern society. 'I have lived a great deal,' he wrote, 'but am not yet sated.'

Nineteen

Elephants playing dancing mice

Shortly after his eightieth birthday, Russell wrote to tell Stanley Unwin that he had 'broken out in a new place and taken to writing *fantastic stories*'. Three were already finished, two running to 10,000 words, the third to 18,000; they were not intended to be serious or to contain a moral, 'but merely to amuse'. Would 'Horrors Manufactured Here' make a good title? Unwin sent the stories off to five of his regular readers. Four sent back unfavourable reports. 'The truth', wrote one, 'is that he is no fiction writer, not even of satirical nonsense,' and went on to complain of a 'stilted or overdecorated style' and 'a complete lack of reality'.

Unwin himself had been taken aback by the coy note of the stories, so unlike Russell's usually crisp tone, and wondered whether he was drifting into arch and sentimental frivolity. He suggested to Russell that they could better discuss the stories over lunch at the Athenaeum. Russell was characteristically persuasive; Unwin capitulated. The meal ended with a decision to add a fourth story, and to call the collection *Satan in the Suburbs*. It appeared the following year to highly mixed reviews, the *Telegraph* declaring the stories to be 'dehydrated'. A second volume, *Nightmares of Eminent Persons*, followed, which fared even worse with reviewers, despite a rather peculiar decision of Russell's to add 'a preface telling the reader when he may laugh and when he should weep'. Readers, unfortunately, felt like doing neither, while in America the reviewer for *Time* commented that 'when logicians with a sense of humor start toying with story telling, their mighty brains behave like elephants playing dancing mice.' Each nightmare was a 'cute little fantasy, as impish as it is artless'.

The poor reviews had little effect on Russell, who was enjoying himself. He had also been approached by an exiled Polish film-maker turned private publisher, Stefan Themerson, whom he would later help to acquire naturalisation papers. Themerson wrote to tell Russell that the short stories had given him the sort of pleasure he had not felt since reading *Candide*. A collection of humorous sayings, *The Good Citizen's Alphabet*, to accompany illustrations done by Themerson's wife, Franciszka – M was 'mystery, what I understand and you don't', and A, 'asinine, what *you* think', and so on – took Russell further into the realms of the absurd. Themerson, a great admirer of Russell, later depicted him in a novel urinating from the top of a mountain while discoursing on the differences between 'I do not believe p' and 'I believe not p'.

The past was evidently on Russell's mind, for he now turned to what was to be one of his more enjoyable and lasting books, a collection of reminiscences of some of his closer friends – and the occasional enemy, like D. H. Lawrence – under the title of *Portraits from Memory*. It included essays on Conrad, Whitehead, the Webbs, Bernard Shaw and H. G. Wells. Described by a reviewer as a 'mixed grill of wit and rationality', it was Russell at his best, combining odd reminiscences with excellent pen portraits.

The 1950s saw lectures issued as books, pursuits into the byways of history, and a continuous outpouring of warnings about the bomb, and man's survival, as well as an account, in 1959, of his own mental processes, *My Philosophical Development*. When Unwin proposed a new edition of *A History of Western Philosophy*, Russell suggested dropping the chapter on Bergson, who he now considered did not warrant so much space. He resisted adding to the section on recent philosophers, which he admitted being 'inadequate', partly 'owing to ignorance' and partly because he felt that they 'have little that is genuinely novel'. Dewey and James had a place; but not Sartre.

Noel Annan, celebrating Russell as the creator of modern logical analysis, poked vague fun at him as a social reformer, calling his books on society remote 'incantations and hymns on the sacred theme of freedom and reason'. He wears, declared Annan, 'an eighteenth-century full-bottomed wig, Victorian mutton-chop whiskers, and has taken off all his clothes'. Naked, perhaps, but rather pleasurably so, far from over with life, with royalties continuing to flow in – £5205 os 7d for twenty-five titles in print in 1953 – and the words still coming with apparently remarkable ease, as they had always done. Edith, writing to a friend at Bryn Mawr, reported, 'He "writes" things in his head and when he . . . dictates them, he seldom makes any correction in the text. It is as if he were reading them from some kind of mind tablet.' By now, Edith had taken over much of Russell's secretarial work. Eisenstadt, the celebrated photographer, came to take pictures of Russell, and said he would do nothing but portrait heads, because he had never before had a subject who sat 'as still as a monument'. 'The best occupation of a crocodile', replied Russell, 'is to rest.'

Edith could have not chosen a better moment to enter Russell's life. One of his reasons for moving to Richmond had been to provide a home for John, his wife Susan and their three children. Russell was appalled by John's frailties and confusions; he was also, as Kate was later to say, extremely bad at dealing with them. Matters were not helped when John took to writing short stories; Russell, engaged on his own satirical fiction, was deeply irritated. Kate was married to an American in the State Department, Charles Tait, having returned to graduate studies at Radcliffe soon after the war ended. She was becoming increasingly drawn into missionary work for the Episcopal Church – another irony, given Russell's views on religion.

It was not long before John's wife, a strikingly good-looking woman but none too stable herself, abandoned the Richmond house for a Welsh retreat, returning only to collect a fur coat she had left behind and say goodbye to the children. With John more and more away, either staying with Dora or in hospital, the task of bringing up the three little girls fell to Russell and Edith. Neither was well prepared for the challenge. Russell was too old and too busy to return to parenthood, while Edith, who had not been married before and had no children, was plainly alarmed at the prospect. The story of their attempts is a sad one, but they can hardly be blamed for the tragedies that followed; they did their best. For the children, however, those days were bleak, even though at first they welcomed the departure of an erratic mother who could turn violent, and of a father who was so forgetful as to be frightening.

Edith and Russell lived on the top two floors and the girls on the ground floor and basement, where they were supervised by a nanny called Griff. After supper, they were put into their dressing gowns and sent upstairs to say goodnight. Edith was very formal; Russell, deep in his armchair, was occasionally more approachable, lifting one of the children onto his lap and reciting Edward Lear poems. If he sometimes seemed distant, he was also fair. At Christmas each child received exactly the same, or an equal version of the same. After one party, Anne received a large cactus, Sarah a medium-sized cactus and Lucy a small one. Later, when the girls were at boarding school, he gave them generous allowances, and it became easier for him, because they spent half their holidays with Dora, during which time they saw their father, who lived in a permanently darkened room, wearing pyjamas and smoking ceaselessly. They found him fat and unnerving. Dora, who seemed to cope better with these problems, was also looking after her own son Roderick, who having refused as a pacifist to do his National Service, had been crippled in an accident down Barnsley mine, where he had volunteered to go instead. Later, both Lucy and Sarah said they had lost twenty years of childhood, missing out on parents altogether, and growing up under what Sarah called 'monoliths as grandparents'.

When the girls turned twenty-one, Edith asked them to pack up their things and take them away so that their rooms could be used for visitors; the nearest they had ever had to a real home disappeared. It was about then that Sarah had the first of a series of mental breakdowns, which were to take her in and out of hospital and sheltered housing for many years. 'Being a Russell marks one,' she said later, echoing the sentiments expressed by Harriet and Kate. 'I have always wanted to get away from it.' When she was twenty, Lucy, who was exceptionally clever, remarked to her sister that she knew she would be dead within ten years.

As soon as he could, Russell gave up the Richmond house and moved back to Wales. He kept only a small flat, first at 29 Millbank, then at 43 Hasker Street, in Chelsea, with a study full of worn academic books and row upon row of detective stories in glass-fronted cases. Driving home from Scotland after a holiday, he and Edith had visited Portmeirion and heard of a modest regency villa, Plas Penrhyn, which could be rented fairly cheaply. The house was unpretentious but large, with seven bedrooms, three bathrooms, and a series of sloping attic rooms. There was plenty of room for visitors, a study for Russell on the ground floor, with a fireplace and unusual windows on either side opening into a conservatory. Opposite the front door stood a well-tended walled garden, with roses in it. The house, like almost every house he lived in, was neither very comfortable nor very attractive. The furniture was in ginger-coloured wood, there were no good pictures, and the atmosphere was purposeful and hardworking, but a little cheerless. It was, once again, the view that captivated him: sitting on the balcony with its pretty cast-iron supports which ran the length of the house on the garden side, he could look up the valley towards Snowdonia, down to the sea, and straight ahead towards the Caernarvon hills. What pleased him most was to discover that Shelley had lived in the house directly across the valley.

Russell's was not, of course, the sole voice to be heard protesting passionately against nuclear weapons. Others, equally committed, if often less eloquent, were waiting their moment. Four events in the autumn of 1957 are said to have precipitated a British campaign of mass protest against the bomb, of a size and determination not seen since the suffragettes. These were the Labour Party conference in Brighton, at which Bevan rejected the unilateralist position; the launch of the first Russian sputnik; the Reith lectures, given by a former US ambassador to Moscow, George F. Kennan, who warned again of the dangers of nuclear confrontation between east and west, and – most crucial of all perhaps – an article by J. B. Priestley in the *New Statesman*. Writing with Russell-like urgency about 'men hag-ridden by fear' and about spectators sitting 'like rabbits waiting for the massacre', Priestley argued that Britain must cease to mumble and mutter its way along: it should lead the way to nuclear sanity. 'Alone, we defeated Hitler; and alone we can defy this nuclear madness into which the spirit of Hitler seems to have passed, to poison the world.'

Priestley could not have chosen a better moment for his rallying call. There was a restlessness in the air, a feeling that it was no longer enough to sit back and do nothing. Out of the confusion and disillusions of the left was emerging a suspicion that the old ways of governing were wrong, but no clear vision of how to improve on them. A cause, a mission, was needed.

What has since been called 'the meeting of the midwives of CND' took place in Kingsley Martin's flat towards the end of November 1957. Professor Kennan turned up, as did Russell, Priestley and his wife Jacquetta Hawkes, and Denis Healey. They talked about the nuclear threat, how best to bring pressure on Gaitskell and the Labour Party, and whether the public was in the mood for mass protest. Early in January 1958 there was a second, larger, gathering, this time in Amen Court, the house of Canon John Collins of St Paul's, an ungainly pacifist with a toothy smile and heavy spectacles. About fifty people appeared, among them Sir Julian Huxley and the Bishop of Chichester. The meeting, efficiently chaired by Kingsley Martin, elected an executive committee and agreed to set up a new movement, a loosely-knit collection of people (no need for a constitution among friends) who would raise support for a mass demonstration of hostility towards the production and deployment of nuclear weapons in Britain. It would call itself the Campaign for Nuclear Disarmament. The intention was not to waste time debating who should possess a bomb and who should not, but to work on the climate of opinion at home in such a way that the public would bring pressure on the Labour Party to adopt a unilateralist position. Britain was still seen as a leader of world opinion: it would then be in a position to influence other countries to do the same. It was not a question of pacifism, but essentially one of morality. The days of nuclear genocide and nuclear suicide had to end.

Before winding up the meeting, Martin made what was later seen to be a foolish mistake. He proposed that Russell be elected president, and Canon Collins chairman. The two men, the elderly strong-willed agnostic who would stop at nothing to make people listen, and the younger founder of Christian Action, who detested vulgar publicity, were, it soon became apparent, anathema to each other. Nor was Russell the kind of man willing merely to appear on a masthead and act only as a distant observer. Martin had unwisely assumed that, at eighty-five, he would be happy to look benignly on. He was wrong; frustrated but not beaten by his years of campaigning, Russell was acquiring a new vigour for this kind of activity.

The next step was to hold a public meeting. Before it opened, its organisers, looking around the 2000 empty seats of Central Hall Westminster, rented for the occasion, were appalled by their own audacity. They need not have feared. Five thousand people turned up, to listen to Russell saying that he doubted whether any human beings at all would exist in forty years' time, and A. J. P. Taylor asking: 'Why are we making the damn thing?' After the cheering had ended, about a thousand of the audience went on to Downing Street and shouted 'ban the bomb'. In the mêlée, several distinguished supporters were carted off to jail by nervous policemen, uncertain of the mood of the demonstrators. The excitement was extraordinary. The battle had been launched, even if the newspapers proved reluctant to give it a proper send-off. What made it so attractive was its simplicity; you did not have to belong to anything to share this moral indignation.

Tactics were now called for – what should this vast array of supporters, of all ages, classes and backgrounds, and increasing by the hour, be given to do? There were already models, in the shape of the National Council for the Abolition of Nuclear Weapons Tests, which was active in publicising the damage to health from radioactive fall-out, and the Direct Action Committee, a more radical grouping which had begun organising pickets and sit-downs at nuclear plants and bases around Britain. From America, too, came the lessons learned by those using Gandhian non-violence in pursuit of racial equality. But none of these was on the immense scale the organisers of CND were hoping for.

The Direct Action Committee was planning a march, to last the four days of the Easter weekend of 1958, from Trafalgar Square to the Atomic Weapons Research Establishment at Aldermaston. Not all CND's founders found the prospect of joining it alluring, and Priestley was seen to thump a table and declare the notion 'fatuous'. Just the same, the young CND decided to offer its forces, though how numerous they would be and who they would consist of no one had any idea.

The Easter weekend of 1958 was unusually cold, and Good Friday the wettest since the turn of the century. But at least 4000 people gathered in Trafalgar Square and, after some rousing speeches, set off on foot for Aldermaston. By Saturday it was snowing hard. A dwindling crowd staggered on, the 'sort of people who normally spend Easter listening to a Beethoven concert on the Home Service, sharing dry sherry with their neighbours and painting Picasso-like designs on to hard-boiled eggs', as Alan Brien described them in the *Daily Mail*. But on Sunday the sun came out, numbers swelled again, and wellwishers arrived along the route with picnics and bottles of wine. One farmer sent 500 hard-boiled eggs. Kenneth Tynan appeared, and Doris Lessing and Christopher Logue. They walked alongside girls in pony-tails and jeans, jiving to the 'Red Flag'. To the tune of 'Home on the Range', the marchers sang, as they straggled along in twos and threes, with Canon Collins swinging along in his cassock, and Fenner Brockway, the veteran pacifist and Russell's friend from the First World War:

> Oh give me a land that is peaceful and grand
> With concern for the whole human race,
> So we can be proud that the dread mushroom cloud
> In our future will not have a place.

Britain, *Peace News* declared, 'will not be the same again'. A few of CND's leaders had shied away from such populism: they were now to be swept along in its wake. For a while at least, *Peace News* seemed to be right. The slogan 'Ban the Bomb' was everywhere; it united people and gave them a sense of unprecedented political power. If the leaders remained a mixture of the established centre-left, and of crusaders like the inexhaustible Peggy Duff, a short, brisk woman of immense competence who became CND's secretary, the members by contrast seemed younger, distrustful of politicians, and easygoing. More often than not, they were people who had never before thought of involving themselves actively in politics. Ninety per cent of those asked why they had joined CND replied that their reason for doing so was 'moral'. At the universities, belonging to

CND was proof of political awareness, and it was said that some girl undergraduates refused to go out with young men who had declined to join.

Aldermaston was judged a success. The following year, the march was held again, only this time over 4000 supporters and several steel bands ended up in Trafalgar Square, where they were joined by 15,000 to 20,000 others who had come to listen to Russell, his nose a little beakier perhaps, his skin more tightly drawn over his forehead, but the white hair still thick and fashionably longer, and the reedlike voice still carrying. The crowd stretched under Admiralty Arch, around the National Gallery and up to St Martin-in-the-Fields. There were virtually none of the scuffles dreaded by the police, though a few teddy boys jeered and snapped off the CND lollypop signs. The next Easter, the numbers doubled again. William Hickey of the *Daily Express*, who came along to spot celebrities, counted fifteen Etonians and quite a few of the 'lunatic fringe'. 'Who are these people?' asked a bewildered René MacColl, in the same paper. 'What do they really think they're doing?' (By the following year, he had made up his mind: 'communist stooges and agents' with a 'sort of ox-like, starry-eyed air of eager martyrdom'.)

Russell was too old to march, but he did address a number of meetings, impressing all who listened to him and quelling hecklers with authority. When a young man accused him of being a 'traitor', 'subservient to atheistic Bolshevism', he replied loudly and crossly, pointing his finger like an Old Testament prophet, his thick white hair tufted on his head. 'You silly young man! Which of us, I ask you, is the greatest traitor: you, who apparently wish everybody in the world to die, or I, whose only desire is that *some* people should remain alive?' On such occasions, his voice, precise, thin, and sounding infinitely old, quavered with indignation. Russell contributed an important intellectual dimension to CND, and produced a book, *Common Sense and Nuclear Warfare*, which outlined possible ways of achieving peace. He also brought in new members, particularly from Wales.

Despite the view of many of the founders that he would not involve himself in their deliberations, he appeared at several committee meetings and gave his views, which were as clear and pungent as ever. Soon, however, his ideas about the campaign became more radical, particularly after the unilateralists scored an unexpected victory at the Labour Party Conference in 1960, only to see their gains rejected by the Parliamentary Labour Party and by Gaitskell in his famous speech when he promised to 'fight and fight and fight again to save the Party we love'. Meanwhile the Tory press reminded readers of the famous Peace Ballot of 1935, and the Oxford Union resolution on King and Country, which between them had convinced Hitler that the British were decadent, thus paving the way for the Second World War.

All his life, Russell felt that if things were to be done they should be done immediately; never more so than when he contemplated what he saw as the imminent annihilation of the world. He was anxious that he was growing too old and too frail to do anything about it. His throat was giving him trouble, a condition he and Edith insisted was due to the 'parlous state of the world'. He now lived on milk, soup, soufflés, custard, minced fish and ice cream. When, around this time, the BBC invited him to broadcast on the future of mankind, he replied with unaccustomed despondency: 'I am afraid I have nothing to say about the future of mankind that would take as long as eight minutes. I think the Great Powers of East and West will see to it that no human beings exist at the end of the present century, but it will not take eight minutes to say this.'

Ralph Schoenman came into Russell's life in July 1960. He was an American from Brooklyn, the only son of Hungarian Jews who had emigrated after the First World War, a gangling, abrasive young man of twenty-four, with a neat helmet of brown hair and a beard carefully trimmed to frame a square jaw. His eyes were a strange shade of amber; he looked a little like a Roman centurion. A graduate in philosophy and politics from Princeton, he had been a supporter of CND since 1958 and was doing post-graduate research in political theory at the London School of Economics, having raised the money for his fare to England by hitch-hiking to Alaska and working for three months on a fishing boat. Professor Ralph Milliband, his tutor at the LSE, found him 'lively, interesting, full of life and imagination and bounce'.

Others were not so sure. Among his acquaintances he was known as a bit of a bully, a heckler with rather wild ideas about bringing Britain to a standstill by cramming its jails with nuclear protesters, which he voiced in the new left clubs and the bars popular with the left-wing young in the late 1950s. Not many people actually liked him very much, or always understood what he was saying, but they enjoyed his verve and his flamboyance, and when he said 'Aldermaston and the rocket bases are Britain's Auschwitz and Buchenwald' they listened. Schoenman was to play a very strange part in Russell's life; some say a malevolent one. Russell himself left a long memorandum about this young disciple, which came to light shortly after his death. Schoenman has never said anything. He has given virtually no interviews, written no articles; he does not reply to letters. It is only from his letters at the time and from those who worked with him that his side can be put together.

On 21 July 1960, Schoenman wrote to Russell, in a 'mood of desperation'. He had been observing the tactics and gains of CND closely, and felt them to be ultimately useless. Could he come and talk to Russell in person, and put his ideas more coherently? Russell was curious; and he was usually generous towards energetic young political philosophers who wanted to see him. He wrote back with an invitation to come down to Wales. The meeting went extraordinarily well: Russell was greatly impressed by what he saw. Schoenman, he wrote later, was 'bursting with energy and teeming with ideas, and intelligent if inexperienced and a little doctrinaire about politics'. He had also been much struck by the young American's drive, and by a pleasing note of irony, so unlike the earnestness of many of the members of CND. If he had doubts, it was about Schoenman's impetuousness, but this, he felt, could quickly be channelled into the right directions by experience and discipline. Russell felt himself to be tiring, and Schoenman was not unlike the person he thought he had been at the same age. He was the man to push through the things Russell no longer felt he had the strength for; and he could travel for him, in his place.

Schoenman had come down to Plas Penrhyn with a specific proposal, and it seemed to Russell that it provided the very change of direction he had been seeking for CND. The campaign, the two men agreed, was running out of steam, precisely because it had never really become a mass movement so persuasive as to force the government to listen. The Gandhian strategy of civil disobedience might be the ingredient that was lacking. It was, in any case, the kind of tactic Russell had always contemplated. As he had written to Margaret Llewelyn Davies in 1908: 'I do not, as you know, in the least object to law breaking . . . but I have never judged it by any other test than whether it paid.' Peaceful marching had proved impotent; could civil disobedience do any better?

On his return to London, Schoenman wrote that he was already hard at work, attempting to set in motion 'the engines of subterfuge'. It was the first of many letters: every two or three days another reached Wales, setting out tactics, criticising what was happening in CND, making hostile remarks about Canon Collins. The daily log of completed tasks was mixed with filial enquiries about the Russells' wellbeing. By January, 'Lord and Lady Russell' had been replaced by 'Bertie and Edith'. Russell wrote back to say that whatever they did they must win the sympathy of the public first, and 'not appear to ordinary people to be subversive or anarchical or such as to cause serious inconvenience to average unpolitical people'.

Canon Collins, J. B. Priestley and his wife Jacquetta Hawkes, Kingsley Martin, Peggy Duff and most of the other CND luminaries did not approve of civil disobedience. They thought it messy and liable to provoke counter-productive confrontations. When Russell wrote to Collins to propose adopting it, Collins replied cautiously, urging restraint and consultation, at least until it had been proved that the Labour Party did not intend to vote for unilateralism. Russell agreed. The days that followed have been analysed so minutely by so many that it has become hard to establish precisely what took place. It seems clear, however, that Russell acted rashly, and with less than his usual courtesy, though more damage was caused by bad luck than by malicious intent. While waiting for the Labour Party to commit itself one way or the other, Russell and Schoenman went ahead and prepared a list of people who they hoped would be sympathetic to a campaign of civil disobedience. They drafted letters, sounding out whether these people might lend their name to a 'Committee of 100'.

By one of those slips of ill fortune, the letter addressed to John Connell, chairman of the Noise Abatement Society, went instead to John Connell, the right-wing journalist, and when he read the words he was astonished. Convinced that what was being proposed was subversive, he sent it straight to the *Evening Standard* for publication. The editor, long hostile to the antics of the anti-nuclear protesters, was delighted and published it the next day, adding in a leader that Russell 'offers a saddening spectacle – that of a man misusing and wasting a great talent'. 'Peers of the realm do not often advocate civil disobedience,' noted the *Manchester Guardian*. 'Few things are better calculated to alienate the British public, especially the sweet young suburban wives . . .'

There was consternation at CND headquarters, and talk of treachery, made worse by Russell's observation that now the matter was out in the open, events should move quickly. A demonstration scheduled for September in Trafalgar Square was obviously the moment to launch the new movement. There were meetings, telephone calls, confrontations of a most acrimonious kind. No one behaved very well. Collins put out statements without checking whether they were true, and Russell pushed ahead, regardless of other people's sensitivities. Reluctantly, Russell agreed to four meetings with Collins, but insisted that they be tape-recorded, which added considerably to the unpleasantness of the atmosphere. The tapes have been preserved. They are surprisingly tedious: the genteel bickerings of two aggrieved men, trying not to lose their tempers. The hours dragged on, Russell's voice the more reasonable, at times even conciliatory, Collins's rambling and long-winded. Nothing was achieved.

Various people sped down to Wales to try to convince Russell not to act precipitately, and that compromise of some kind was possible. Michael Foot was one of them; he had read Russell's books as a young man and had been charmed by his eloquence. They talked, and Foot was captivated, but nothing he said could shake Russell. The next to volunteer was Doris Lessing, who had noticed how badly the internecine squabbles were affecting CND supporters. The spectacle of two prima donnas quarrelling was turning the whole movement into a farce. She was driven down to Wales by a young woman journalist. Five hours later they arrived at Plas Penrhyn to be told by the housekeeper that Lady Russell would receive them in due course. In icy silence, she served them tea. They were then shown into Russell's study. The philosopher, Doris Lessing observed, was looking like an 'old gnome' in his armchair by the fire. He said little, beyond making a few 'spiteful remarks' and denying that the way he was behaving would split CND irrevocably. Edith was polite, but frosty. The atmosphere, Doris Lessing later recalled, was 'poisonous. I was seen as an emissary from the enemy camp.' The two visitors were shown into a bedroom together with the words, 'I'm sure that's what you like', which Doris Lessing suspected of being a jibe about the sort of people who supported the Collins faction of CND. Next morning, the housekeeper told them that neither Russell nor Edith was available. The two women drove the five hours back to London.

On 7 October, the two sides issued a statement in which they agreed to disagree, and split into two groups, with many of CND's most active members being drawn into supporting what they saw as the more relevant and aggressive tactics of Russell and the Committee of 100. Collins's supporters maintained that Russell had behaved badly, that he had become an incurable autocrat, and that he was being led astray by Schoenman and Michael Scott, a distinguished campaigner against apartheid who had long been at odds with Collins and who was a crucial figure in these events. Edith was criticised for lacking a sense of humour, which, Kingsley Martin wrote later, was precisely what had been wrong with his three other wives. Russell's supporters attacked Collins for being dishonest and vacillating, and criticised the other leaders for their élitism. As the Committee of 100 grew stronger, it drew the Direct Action Committee into its fold. Russell resigned as president of CND, and became president of the Committee of 100. He and Collins never met properly again. Later, Collins said that there were some 'Iagos knocking about' and that a death blow had been dealt to CND, just as it was growing like 'a green bay tree'.

Not everyone mourned the rupture. Apart from the bad luck and ill timing, it had basically been caused by a combination of style and personality. The well-connected founders of CND honestly believed that because they knew the right people, they were bound in the end to make good sense prevail. The younger and more radical members saw things very differently; they felt that reasonable behaviour had not achieved anything, and was never likely to do so.

Russell, breaking away from CND, moved closer to Schoenman; working hard on the new Committee released a new spurt of energy. He wrote letters, he signed petitions, he gave lectures and broadcasts, he wrote articles. Whenever he was invited anywhere, he replied that he would accept on condition that he could talk about nuclear weapons; that he did not have the time, the strength or the interest to think about anything else when the world was about to disappear. When not in London, he kept in touch by phone, or through people who went to Wales to see him, like Michael Randle, former secretary of the Direct Action Committee, and now secretary to the Committee of 100. Sitting for hours over the glasses of whisky which Russell much enjoyed, they talked tactics. Randle found Russell clear-headed, forgetting nothing, and with an undimmed sense of mischief. Edith was sometimes reluctant to agree to these visits, arguing that they excited Russell unduly, and that he then drank too much and refused to go to bed early. She looked after him with total devotion. With people she liked, she was hospitable and kind; to those she considered importunate, she would come on very 'grande dame', as Jon Tinker, a young environmentalist working for the Committe, put it.

A new note was entering Russell's voice. It was a little shrill, lacking the famous courtesy, and sometimes even offensive. After Dr Edward Teller, the inventor of the atom bomb, had written to an American newspaper minimizing the harmful effects of a nuclear war, Russell replied: 'No one knows what percentage of the human race, if any, would survive such a war as Dr Teller has made possible.' The discordant note was even more pronounced when he told a conference of young nuclear disarmers in Birmingham: 'We used to call Hitler wicked for killing off the Jews, but Kennedy and Macmillan are much more wicked than Hitler ... We cannot obey these murderers. They are wicked. They are abominable. They are the wickedest people who have ever lived in the history of man and it is our duty to do what we can against them.' It was a long way from the urbane civilities of Trinity. For the first time, there were murmurings about senility, and the possibility that this fine mind had been captured by a young Mephistopheles. Who was behind these remarks? Russell himself, or Schoenman? And what was their relationship?

Schoenman was seen to behave with respect towards Russell, though he treated his mentor as an equal. He made Russell laugh, he talked the same political language and he was highly competent, always doing precisely what he said he would do. But with others, he was becoming increasingly cocky, self-congratulatory, irascible and even violent. They found his tone self-aggrandising; and some were a little frightened of him. 'He was ultra-suspicious', remembers Michael Randle. 'He saw plots where there weren't any.' Randle voiced some of his anxieties about Schoenman's trustworthiness, and Russell wrote sharply, 'I think . . . that the Committee owes a special tolerance to Ralph Schoenman since it was he who conceived the idea of such a committee . . . We are all rebels and cannot hope to succeed if we condemn those who show even more rebellious energy than most of us do.'

The Committee of 100's first public event was a sit-down, in heavy rain, outside the Ministry of Defence, to coincide with the arrival on the Clyde of American Polaris missiles in February 1961. It was orderly and quiet, even though 5000 had turned up, and the very silence made the sense of moral outrage stronger. Before the sit-down began, a cable arrived from Augustus John. 'While under treatment following attacks of thrombosis am advised can take no part . . . very disappointed. Had looked forward to jail.' Schoenman had told all who asked him that their model was the General Strike. When Russell appeared, people clapped; they were impressed that someone of his age and stature should not just feel so strongly about the bombs, but be prepared to act on it. They felt warm and full of admiration when they watched this infinitely frail figure, with the look of what one newspaper called a 'very severe pelican', crouch down, cross his legs and settle on the pavement. His dignity stirred their consciences, just as his absolute commitment moved them. Few of those who watched him have forgotten the occasion when he said, during a television interview, 'I'm an old, old man. I have lived my life. Think of the young,' while tears trickled down his face.

Similar events followed. Writing to his old friend Rudolph Carnap, Russell explained, 'I believe that men are starved for an answer to the terror and that they will respond if their sense of helplessness can be overcome'. On 6 August 1961, Hiroshima Day, a rally was arranged in Hyde Park. The police had forbidden the use of microphones. Russell's voice, clear as it was, had little carrying power in the open air. He asked one of the organisers to bring him a microphone, saying that the Committee 100 was intended, after all, to demonstrate disobedience. When he started to speak, a policeman took it away from him. A month later, an embarrassed police sergeant on a motorcycle turned into the drive at Plas Penrhyn to deliver a summons for Edith and Russell to appear at Marlborough Street magistrates' court, where they would be charged with inciting the public to disobedience and contravening Hyde Park regulations.

Russell was delighted. A short prison sentence would be excellent publicity, and he had taken care to arm himself against a long one by having his doctors provide affidavits about his state of health. His appearance in court was not so unlike the day forty-three years before when he had stood in the dock at Bow Street and heard he was to go to Brixton for six months. Russell likened it to a Daumier etching. Cries of 'Shame, shame, an old man of eighty-eight', rose from the public gallery. The magistrate, Clyde Wilson, said drily, 'It puts me in mind of the Book of Job'. During the lunch recess, the Russells were greeted by cheering crowds, and they returned to hear that each had received a sentence of a week in jail, to be served in a prison hospital in deference to their age and standing. Schoenman was given two months. The thirty-one sentenced to prison terms sang while waiting for the Black Maria to take them to Brixton; Russell enjoyed the irony of the fact that while he had been allowed to travel by taxi in 1918, this time he was given no choice. Then came a rather unpleasant incident. A young designer named Ernest Roedker, who happened to know Russell's grand-daughters, was among those arrested. Because the prisoners were being processed in alphabetical order, Roedker was put into a cell next to Russell. The prisoners were told to undress, have a bath and put on prison clothes. As Russell took his clothes off, Roedker heard several prison warders laughing. 'We're not very well equipped down there, are we?' Appalled, he listened as comments about the size of Russell's penis continued.

Russell was delighted at his sentence. He spent the week in bed, eating a special diet of raw egg mixed with milk, Complan and iron pills, reading Madame de Staël and detective stories, arguing medicine with the doctor and theology with the chaplain. From her own bed in the prison hospital, Edith sent him notes to say that she too was perfectly content, lying comfortably reading in her own nightdress with a prison gown on top. When they were released, the crowds of wellwishers at the gates of Brixton jail had to be kept back by police. The sentencing of the Russells was declared a great victory for the Committee of 100.

From Hasker Street, where they received so many calls that they were forced to disconnect the telephone, the Russells returned to Wales, cosseted by the guards on their train and congratulated by other passengers. They found a letter waiting for them from Schoenman, who was still in Stafford prison, to which they replied, 'We miss you like anything. But your letter has been read and re-read and re-read again many times.' There was no doubting their genuine fondness for him. They praised his abilities, his devotion and the good work he had done. 'Your ears must be nearly burnt off, we talk so often of you'.

Despite the prison sentences, which were seldom severe, relations between police and supporters of the Committee of 100 had been remarkably good. September saw a new toughness on the part of the authorities. A decision seemed to have been made to quell the new movement before it gained too much ground. For their part, the protesters grew more stubborn. A meeting planned for 17 September was banned by the police, but the Committee went ahead just the same. The police gathered; there were scuffles, rough jostling and jeers. The crowd became defiant; then the police charged, using fire hoses. One thousand one hundred and forty people were arrested in London and 351 more at Holy Loch, where a simultaneous demonstration had taken place. The press coverage was enormous. The *Economist* observed that the Committee of 100 was behaving as if

Britain were a police state. At the next rally, Russell, shrunken, almost painfully old but defiant, urged the protesters on: 'I repeat,' he told a gathering in Trafalgar Square, 'and shall go on repeating: we *can* win, and we *must*.' Three days later, he was telling supporters in Cardiff, 'Never in all past history has there been so important or so terrible a crisis.'

Like CND before them, the Committee's organisers found themselves wondering where to go next. Should demonstrations be even more spectacular? And if so, how? There was talk about trying to bring military installations to a standstill. However, the police attitude was hardening; in December the Special Branch raided the houses of the Committee's leading figures and arrested them under the Official Secrets Act. At their trial at the Old Bailey, five young men, all in their early twenties – Michael Randle, a printer called Pat Pottle, an accountant, Trevor Hatton, a physicist, Terry Chandler, and Ian Dixon, who had come to the anti-war movement through watching the film of *All Quiet on the Western Front*, – and one woman, Helen Allegranza, were in the dock. The gallery was fully of noisy supporters; outside, among the pickets, was a curate with a board on which was written: 'For Christ's sake, ban the bomb'. Russell, who insisted not only on attending but on remaining on his feet throughout, explained that the purpose of setting up the Committee of 100 had been to 'try and avoid the extermination of the people in this country and of many million elsewhere'. He declared that, as president, he was as guilty as those in the dock, and possibly more so. Summing up, the attorney-general, Sir Reginald Manningham-Buller, QC, declared that never in the history of the Old Bailey had he heard such effrontery. The sentences were intended to be exemplary: the five men each received eighteen months in jail; Helen Allegranza a year. Not long after her release, she committeed suicide.

While Schoenman was still serving his sentence, the Home Office announced that he would have to leave the country, as they refused to extend his visa. Russell was furious. Michael Foot, Barbara Castle and Fenner Brockway agreed to do what they could and called on R. A. Butler at the Home Office. Schoenman, they said, was essential to Russell as a researcher, and he needed another year to complete the work he had embarked on. Reluctantly, the Home Office agreed to an extension.

In May 1962, Russell reached the age of ninety. He sat in his house in Hasker Street while the tributes poured in: telegrams from Khrushchev, Tito, Nkrumah, Nehru and U Thant; a present of tea from the Chinese government; a statue of Socrates from a young admirer. Over the next few days, postmen delivered many thousands of letters. On the afternoon of his birthday, he had tea with his grand-daughters, then went to a dinner arranged in his honour at the Café Royal by A. J. Ayer. One or two of his old friends, like E. M. Forster, were there. Two nights later there was a musical celebration at the Royal Festival Hall, at which the messages of esteem took over an hour to read out. Russell, sitting in the royal box next to Edith and the Duke and Duchess of Bedford, was called on to the stage amid a hail of presents and cheering. A renegade perhaps, a man intent on firing the British public to unacceptable heights of protest, but on this day at least, Britain's most remarkable citizen.

He had not lost his touch for the eloquent message. 'I have a very simple creed,' he declared, 'that life and joy and beauty are better than dusty death.' In an article written for the *Observer*, he noted that he had always imagined old age as a time when he could retire to a 'life of elegant culture', but instead he had found himself caught up in the follies of the world and unable to free himself. Since 1914, he declared, the world had managed to do consistently the wrong thing. 'Like Cassandra, I am doomed to prophesy evil and not be believed . . . Serenity, in the present world, can only be achieved through blindness or brutality.' Inevitably, therefore, he had become 'more and more of a rebel . . . gradually less and less able to acquiesce patiently in what is happening.'

On the day of the Festival Hall tribute, the Labour Party announced it intended to expel Russell from the Party because he had refused to withdraw his sponsorship of a Moscow peace conference which was forbidden to its members. Gaitskell and the National Executive Committee had decided that Russell and three others, Baroness Wootton, Lord Chorley and, as chance would have it, Canon Collins, were all to forfeit their cards. It was an absurd affair, and soon brought ridicule on the Party, when it turned out that they were not in a position to expel them. The NEC then accused Russell of owing six shillings in back dues, but that, too, turned out to be wrong. The Labour Party fell silent. But not Russell. When he found a suitable moment, at a debate three years later called to discuss Harold Wilson's first year in power, he solemnly took his membership card from his pocket, brandished it in the air, tore it slowly into little pieces and threw them away.

In October that year came the very confrontation between east and west which Russell had warned was inevitable. It brought the world closer to a nuclear war than ever before. It is hard to know to what extent Russell influenced the outcome, but it provided further proof of the ninety-year-old philosopher's touch when it came to world affairs, and said something about the role of international arbiter he saw as his. Russell honestly did believe he had a part to play, and that his standing on the world stage was such that its leaders would listen.

In 1958 Castro had overthrown the Batista dictatorship, cut Cuba off from the American sphere of interest and turned to the USSR for economic and political support. American hostility towards the new regime intensified after the disastrous attack on the Bay of Pigs by Florida-based Cuban exiles supported by the US. When American planes identified a series of nuclear missile bases being built on the island, it seemed likely that the US might intervene directly.

Russell had been following developments closely from Plas Penrhyn. In September 1962 he issued a statement to the press. Precipitate action by either side, he warned, was liable to lead to a world war. No one paid any attention. He persisted. In the weeks that followed he sent a telegram to U Thant, secretary-general of the United Nations, setting down his fears, and asking whether he might be permitted to address the General Assembly in person. He was politely turned down. Later, he wrote that he felt 'humanity had been brought to the edge of nuclear death'.

On 22 October, President Kennedy, learning that Russian supply ships were making their way towards Cuba, declared an American blockade of the island, and threatened to attack unless the missile bases were dismantled and the ships turned back. The Soviet vessels continued on their way. In Washington, panic mounted; politicians sent their families to their houses in the country, there was a rush on tinned food in the supermarkets, and the New York stock market fell.

After listening to Kennedy's announcement, Russell dispatched five telegrams. One went to Kennedy: 'Your action desperate . . . Ultimatum means war . . . End this madness.' The second went to Khrushchev: 'I appeal to you not to be provoked by the unjustifiable action of the United States . . .' Others went to Macmillan, Gaitskell and U Thant. Copies were sent to British newspapers. At first, the press ignored him. Meanwhile Khrushchev had let Kennedy know that he did not intend to respect the blockade, implying that, if forced to, he would go to war over the missile installations in Cuba. 'Khrushchev orders SAIL ON – OR SINK', announced the *Daily Sketch*, 'US WAITS . . . WATCHES'

At 7.30 that evening, Russell received a reply from Khrushchev. Put out by Tass, it hinted at a possible compromise. Khrushchev called on Kennedy to 'stay the execution of' the USA's 'piratical threats', and proposed a 'top-level meeting'. The only thing that would lead to war, he seemed to be saying, was American aggression: everything other than the ending of the blockade was negotiable. In Washington, Averill Harriman observed that this was the voice of a man looking for a way out. Russell replied, praising Khrushchev's attitude, and suggesting that dismantling the missile bases in Cuba might be exchanged for the dismantling of American bases in Turkey. He sent another telegram to Kennedy, urging compromise. Overnight, the press decided to take Russell seriously. Crowds of journalists flocked to North Wales, thirty-six of them camping in the drive at Plas Penrhyn. The local postmaster was overwhelmed.

By now the first Soviet ships had been stopped by the Americans and searched. When no arms were found on board, they were allowed to sail on, but others were close behind. At the last moment, Khrushchev ordered them to change direction. Everywhere, there was immense relief. It lasted a bare few hours. A different communication arrived from Moscow, containing precisely the deal Russell had suggested: a swap of Cuban for Turkish bases, and reciprocal agreements for non-aggression. It appeared that his suggestion had been listened to. He hardly had time to reflect on it, or to consider a much quoted and dismissive message from Kennedy urging him to concentrate his attention not so much on the burglars as on the burgled, before he learned that Kennedy had found the new offer completely unacceptable.

Another telegram was dispatched to Khrushchev from Plas Penrhyn, calling the USA's refusal to negotiate 'insane paranoia', and suggesting that the Soviets act magnanimously and agree to dismantle the Cuban bases, under the auspices of the United Nations and after a guarantee that the blockade would be lifted. A further telegram went off to Castro: 'Could you make a great gesture for humanity and agree to dismantle the bases? The fate of mankind rests with your decision . . .'

Later that day came the news that Khrushchev had offered to climb down. The crisis was over. Russell wrote to a friend that the solution 'made the week one of the most worthwhile of my entire life'. To Khrushchev, he wrote that he had never known a statesman 'act with the magnanimity and greatness that you have shown over Cuba'.

The timing of the various telegrams, and Khrushchev's apparent decision to make use of Russell, led many to conclude that he had played a prominent part in preventing a war. Effect seemed to follow cause very neatly. Both at the time and later, Russell said he believed that his telegrams had had some effect. 'The great ones are stranded on pinnacles of public prestige and welcome an excuse to climb down. An approach from a philosopher, a man with no power, no axe to grind, may afford them such an excuse.' After all, as his exchanges with Khrushchev in the pages of the *New Statesman* in 1957 had shown, the Soviet leader was perfectly willing to discuss things through him. And had not Khrushchev expressed his gratitude in a personal telegram? Further evidence of his influence comes from U Thant, who wrote in his memoirs that Khrushchev's conciliatory behaviour was, to some extent, due to 'Earl Russell's repeated pleadings to him, and to his congratulating him on "his courageous stand for sanity"'. Even the *Daily Mail* admitted it was conceivable that Russell had 'lent a kind of perspective to the escalating madness of Cuba at a crucial time. It may have reminded someone that civilisation is not a small thing.'

In the years since the thirteen days of the Cuban missile crisis, views have altered. It has become fashionable to deny Russell any influence at all. The Cuban episode is now seen more in an historical context, as part of a personal contest between Kennedy and Khrushchev. Both had been guilty of precipitating the crisis; both, in the event, showed restraint. Other facts also suggest that Russell played little or no part in the outcome. Most of the politicians of the day wrote their memoirs and almost all of them touch, often at length, on the Cuban crisis. Most do not even mention Russell's name; those that do refer to him merely as a figure who sent telegrams to all sides. There is no mention of Russell at all in the Soviet Intelligence Archives. Advisers to Kennedy at the time, like Pierre Salinger, say his words had no effect on anyone. His idea about swapping Turkish and Cuban bases was already being discussed by Kennedy, who was greatly embarrassed at seeing it bandied in the newspapers by Russell. Khrushchev's last-minute capitulation is usually regarded as a victory for Kennedy's nerve and for his decision to stand firm, but the fact remains that Kennedy did send his brother Robert with a secret offer to trade missiles in Cuba for missiles in Turkey, that the offer was accepted, and that the Jupiter missiles were, in due course, withdrawn from Turkey. A coincidence then; but it is still not impossible that Russell, by giving Khrushchev a face-saving way out, did act as a genuine, if modest, broker in this whole affair.

In Britain, the missile crisis provoked fresh alarm about nuclear bombs, but far from inspiring new fervour within CND and the Committee of 100, it was perceived on the contrary as evidence that sanity would ultimately prevail among world leaders. In Wales, the post office at Minffordd had never seen anything like it; telegrams and letters poured in, bringing praise from people convinced that Russell had done something to save them from a nuclear war. Not even attacks on him in the American press, which rose to new heights of vituperation – he was nothing but a tool of the far left – could diminish the air of celebration, which reached its climax in a tribute of admirers who gathered to honour him in his garden one Saturday afternoon in November.

As for the Committee of 100, it was now rapidly running down. Nothing the protesters did seemed to make the slightest difference to British policy. The Americans continued to base their Polaris submarines on the coast of Scotland, and Aldermaston to carry out its programme of weapons research. Russell announced that he intended to resign, giving as his reason his many other commitments. Later, he would say that the real reason had been that he had grown weary of 'the folly of some of the leading members', referring presumably to the more impatient of them who wanted to push ahead, even when the promised quorum of numbers was lacking. In the spring of 1963, he stepped down. The Committee turned to trying to solve the problems of housing, unemployment, women's liberation and community power, claiming, in years to come, that even if the campaign against the bombs had failed to attract sufficient working-class support, it had at least succeeded in radicalising the middle-class intelligentsia. In any event, those who had been active in CND and the Committee of 100 had been hard at it for over five years; they were exhausted. When it was announced in 1963 that a partial test-ban treaty had been signed, the sense of urgency evaporated. This was seen as evidence that the world leaders were not so bent on nuclear annihilation.

The sixth Aldermaston march, in 1963, was the last; the manufacture of weapons there was coming to an end. The event was as colourful as ever, but ended in disarray when Canon Collins was pelted with eggs and flour in Hyde Park. The newspapers, too, had grown bored. *The Times* referred to it as 'a slightly tedious annual parade', which had become a 'formless sense of protest against anything'. By the end of that year, both CND and the Committee of 100 were played out. The left was fast abandoning its commitment; its leaders were serving without complaint in a Cabinet which had no intention of turning unilateralist.

In the thirties, Russell had wanted to change society itself; now he wanted simply to get rid of weapons capable of destroying the world. CND had been an excellent idea, but it had failed. Civil disobedience had been the next logical step, but that too had failed. If he felt little sense of defeat, it was largely because he now saw some evidence that the world's leaders were at last aware of the colossal dangers involved.

Twenty

A delicious fresh breeze

Russell's tone towards America was growing ever more acrimonious. He had come to regard the United States as a police state which persecuted its dissidents and where civil liberties were steadily being eroded. His hostility was reflected in a series of articles in American magazines, and *Harper's* in particular, where he accused the United States of pursuing a 'policy of genocide' in Latin America, compared their leaders to Eichmann, and called them 'semi-literate paranoids'. Elsewhere, he warned that he could see a 'pervasive and systematic terror' sweeping the country, turning it into a ruthless promoter of dictatorships. When Kennedy was assassinated in Dallas, and his apparently solitary murderer, Lee Harvey Oswald, was then shot dead, Russell observed that something 'very nasty was being covered up'.

Agreeing to help Mark Lane, the New York lawyer who had come up with evidence challenging the official version, Russell became chairman of a 'Who Killed Kennedy?' British committee. The official version, he said, was riddled with contradictions, and when the Warren Commission, which had been set up to investigate the assassinations, produced its report, Russell declared it a 'sorrily incompetent document'. Even his supporters began to wish that he was not so prone to making extreme statements. By now, there was almost no American event or undertaking he did not attack on the grounds that the threat to world peace lay in the internal policies of the United States as well as its international belligerency.

Senator Barry Goldwater's nomination as the Republican candidate for the presidential election was greeted by Russell with an outpouring of disgust. The 'radical right,' he warned, 'the vigilante bands of fascist Minutemen', were taking over. He took an equally intemperate line towards the civil rights movement; it was a natural cause for him to champion, but now there was something unreasoning in his outbursts. 'Russell . . . likens negroes to Hitler's victims,' read a *New York Times* headline. Cables and letters of support addressed to American black leaders streamed out of Plas Penrhyn. Soon, to Russell's further fury, only the left-wing press would take his articles. Many Americans were exasperated by this barrage of abuse from an elderly English philosopher living in Wales. Writing in the *Los Angeles Times* in August 1965, Max Freedman observed that Russell was in danger of becoming a bore, an intruder and a busybody 'babbling erratic nonsense as a . . . garrulous old man'.

Nothing, however, was to inflame him more than the war in Vietnam, which he saw not as an isolated campaign but as an inevitable consequence of America's policies of global intervention. Though his revulsion against the war was shared by many, it provoked outbursts of such vitriol on his part that even his most ardent British admirers were perplexed. There was something about this vituperation – and particularly the unsubtle language in which it was expressed – so different from the voice of reason which had first captivated them, that led many to ask whether Russell was not becoming senile. They mourned the earlier eloquence, not just for its pleasing use of the English language but for its effectiveness.

By early 1964 it was clear that the Johnson administration had decided to escalate the war in Vietnam. Critics of US government policy kept Russell in touch by sending him the latest reports and casualty figures, and he put out a steady flow of articles attacking America, as well as dozens of letters to leading newspapers. At times, it seemed as though he was better informed about the progress of the war than almost anyone else in Britain; at others his claims were so extreme as to provoke total disbelief. Gradually, the war began to occupy most of his time, in the same way as the nuclear threat had done not long before. Johnson did not reply to Russell's challenging telegrams, but Ho Chi Minh of North Vietnam began to regard Russell as a possible ally. Towards the end of 1964, Russell dispatched a young secretary called Christopher Farley to Vietnam, where he was received as an important visitor; and returned with detailed information about the bombing of the North. As this was stepped up Russell issued a statement saying he believed once again that 'the human race will be exterminated', when, as seemed increasingly likely, the war spread to Russia and China. In Britain, when the prime minister, Harold Wilson, refused to criticise Johnson's policies, he was attacked as a 'craven and odious' supporter of 'American madness'.

The day came when Ho Chi Minh sent a telegram with the words 'situation now very dangerous'. As in the early days of the Committee of 100, Russell now found, at the age of ninety-three, a fresh wind of energy. Statements, recorded messages to students in America, telegrams to anyone who appeared involved in any way, issued forth again from Minffordd post office, as they had at the height of the Cold War. To a US television reporter, who went to Wales to interview him, Russell denounced the Americans as 'abominable' and said that American world domination would be very nearly as dreadful as nuclear war. Their atrocities in Vietnam, he repeated, were turning their perpetrators into war criminals, not so very unlike the nazis who had been brought to trial at Nuremberg. Their crimes were on his conscience, and he could not rest until they were brought to justice. A message to a solidarity conference of Africans, Asians and Latin Americans made his point clearly. 'Whenever there is hunger,' he said, 'wherever there is exploitative tyranny, whenever people are tortured and the masses left to rot under the weight of disease and starvation, the force which holds down the people stems from Washington.' Not long afterwards, he agreed to speak over the Vietcong National Liberation Front radio direct to American soldiers. He exhorted them to stop fighting 'any longer in this unjust war'. There was talk of his being a second Lord Haw Haw.

Much of his wrath found its way into *War Crimes in Vietnam*, a collection of articles and pamphlets accusing the United States of being solely responsible for the war in Vietnam. The *Sunday Times* called it a 'tetchy, intemperate exercise in the pornography of US-Go-Home indignation', and regretted the loss of a mind once so 'cool, clear and detached'. Even those who were sympathetic to

Russell's stand on the war remarked that he had relied over-credulously on information supplied by the North Vietnamese, thus weakening an excellent case.

The news that Russell was intending to set up a War Crimes Tribunal to try President Johnson, Dean Rusk and other American leaders for their 'brutal treatment' of the people of Vietnam over the previous twelve years, first broke in a Vietcong broadcast on 8 June 1966. The war had reached a critical point, with American casualties mounting, and it was becoming obvious that victory would never be possible unless more troops were sent in. Schoenman had been sent off to Hanoi to sound out the possibility of observers visiting North Vietnam to see what was happening. He reported that missions under Russell's auspices would be acceptable. On his return, he paid a call one evening on his LSE tutor, Professor Milliband. It was here, according to Milliband, that, sitting at the kitchen table, the idea for a tribunal was really born. A Vietnam Solidarity Campaign was now started in London, at about the same time that the United States began to bomb Hanoi and Haiphong more heavily. In the *New Statesman*, Russell compared the conflict to that between David and Goliath.

The plan, as Russell outlined it to Sartre, Danilo Dolci and other sympathisers during a three-day preliminary private conference in London in the autumn of 1966, was to convene a jury of prominent people to hear evidence from witnesses sent to investigate what was happening, American deserters and civilians brought from Vietnam. Its model was to be the Nuremberg trials. Those on the jury, said Russell, were to be 'men eminent not through their power, but through their intellectual and moral contribution to what we optimistically call "human civilisation"'. After the private meeting, there was a press conference. As Russell spoke, a whisper for silence went around the room, not an ordinary whisper but one of respect at the presence of such a frail and dedicated man. Isaac Deutscher, whom Russell had already approached to serve, stood up to declare that Russell's initiative was magnificent and courageous. Others were more sceptical. Bernard Levin, the *Times* columnist, used the occasion to attack Russell in the pages of the *New York Times*. He painted a picture of a decrepit puppet, immeasurably old and immeasurably frail, his strings pulled by Schoenman. Levin said he was saddened by one of the finest minds of all time falling into a 'state of such gullibility, lack of discrimination, twisted logic and rancorous hatred of the United States that he has turned into a full-time purveyor of political garbage indistinguishable from the routine products of the Soviet machine'. He described Russell's entry: 'A stir, a bustle, a craning of necks; he comes! He comes? Say, rather, without disrespect, *it* comes . . .'. Another reporter compared Russell to a 'pet', being led out to perform by its master.

Preparations for the tribunal took many months, and much frenetic activity on the part of Russell, Schoenman and many helpers. Jurists had to be sounded out, witnesses located, money raised, reliable and distinguished people recruited for missions to Vietnam, and a place found to hold the sessions. Deutscher had voiced his hope that the proceedings would be based on 'frankly humanitarian, democratic and socialist grounds'. Staughton Lynd, the American political historian, replying to Russell's invitation to serve, said he was bothered by the thought that one side only, the United States, would be in the dock, and hoped that the tribunal would take great care not to be accused of double standards. Among those who agreed to take part were the American civil rights campaigner, Stokely Carmichael, the author James Baldwin, a distinguished international lawyer called Lelio Basso, the French mathematician Laurent Schwartz, and a number of other professors, lawyers, writers and historians, selected to represent as many countries as possible. Simone de Beauvoir agreed to serve. Jean Paul Sartre accepted the job of executive chairman, while Vladimir Dedijer, the Yugoslav partisan, became president of the sessions. Russell was president of the entire proceedings, but because of his great age was not expected to attend. Schoenman was asked to be director-general, because it was thought this was what Russell wanted; only after Russell's death did Edith reveal that far from being pleased, he had been appalled.

The weeks leading up to the tribunal were, as many had predicted, plagued by difficulties. The intention had been to hold it in London, but this collapsed when first the home secretary, Roy Jenkins, and then the prime minister, Harold Wilson, refused visas to the North

Vietnamese witnesses on the grounds that the entire tribunal was potentially dangerous to the cause of peace. Russell paused only to attack Wilson for being 'illiberal and deceitful', liable to earn the 'justified contempt of civilisation', before asking Sartre if he could find a site in France. Sartre wrote directly to de Gaulle. De Gaulle's refusal came wrapped in flowery sentences, but said, in effect, that it was up to the state, and not a self-styled tribunal, to mete out justice. Russell turned next to the Swedish government, which posed only a few objections. The location settled, Russell contacted the men he considered most guilty, and invited them to defend themselves before the tribunal. Johnson did not reply. Nor did any of the others, though Dean Rusk told reporters that he had no intention of 'playing games with a ninety-four-year-old Briton'.

The International War Crimes Tribunal opened in Stockholm on 2 May 1967, in an amphitheatre on the first floor of the House of the People. There was considerable scepticism throughout the world about its potential for impartiality and it was feared that, if Russell's book was anything to go by, the proceedings were damned from the start. Volunteers, young girls in mini-skirts and men in jeans, scurried around the corridors with documents to photocopy, dealt with enquiries and got hold of material called for by the jury. For eight days, the tribunal heard investigators, Vietnamese civilians and American deserters describe bombings, injuries from napalm, and the destruction of schools and hospitals. A nine-year-old boy was brought forward to display his napalm wounds; films of mutilated women and children were shown. The session ended with a unanimous vote of guilty, and a short speech by Russell, read out for him in his absence, which showed that for all his recent shrillness he had lost none of his eloquence. 'Wherever men struggle against suffering we must be their voice . . . we will be judged not by our reputations but by our will to act. Against this standard we too will be judged better men.'

The public verdict on the tribunal was less hostile than people had feared. Sartre and Dedijer were considered to have conducted the hearings with fairness, refusing to let witnesses dwell on their personal feelings about the war. Swedish television provided generally sympathetic coverage. Elsewhere, attacks were stronger. Once again, reporters used the opportunity to castigate Russell. One journalist remarked that it was like the Middle Ages, when the body of a king who had died on the eve of an important battle was propped up on his horse and led out before his troops to keep their morale up. Russell was just such a corpse, a 'decrepit symbol', playing out a 'shoddy farce' with other mediocrities like himself. Schoenman was the charger he rode.

As the last session in Stockholm drew to a close, it was announced that the headquarters of the tribunal would be moving from London to Paris. The reason given officially had to do with 'concentration and efficiency', but most of those involved knew that it was largely to do with Schoenman. Dedijer made no secret that he felt Schoenman's tantrums were bringing discredit to the entire proceedings.

The story of Schoenman's behaviour over the War Crimes Tribunal is a strange one. During the months of preparation, the young American had grown increasingly bossy and argumentative. When the sessions opened, the lawyers and members of the jury were merely irritated. But in the heady days of the hearings themselves, when those involved were in a state of considerable excitement, Schoenman's interventions became erratic. As Russell's representative, he saw himself as being basically in charge. Without any warning, he gave a series of press conferences which threatened, through his ill-judged remarks, to jeopardise the impartiality of the tribunal, already under attack for bias. One evening over dinner he provoked Dedijer by questioning the tribunal's jurisdiction. A row developed. Dedijer, a respected athlete, was known to have a quick temper. He decided he could take no more, seized Schoenman by the arms, picked him up and shook him.

On another day, when the jury had met to discuss how the tribunal was going, Schoenman suddenly declared they were all persecuting him. Sartre, who had been increasingly infuriated by his ill-timed interferences, turned on him: 'Vous, Schoenman, vous n'êtes pas Lord Russell'. Sartre was not above baiting him in more personal ways. The young American's recent divorce had been particularly unpleasant, and details of his behaviour had received a certain amount of coverage in the press. Sartre, brandishing some cuttings, called out, 'And is this true, Schoenman?', at which other members of the jury joined in. Schoenman walked out, leaving Stockholm before the tribunal closed. Simone de Beauvoir was to say he was the only man she knew who grew a beard to conceal not a weak chin but a strong one.

The story has a strange sequel. In May, Russell wrote to Dedijer, 'I know of your physical attack on Ralph Schoenman ... during which you tried to strangle him and bite his head. I am further informed about your uncontrollable temper, screaming fits and threats of physical violence.' Schoenman, evidently, had been quick to tell Russell a different tale. Feeling estranged from the whole event, Russell was appalled by the travesty of his idea for a modern Nuremberg. He wrote somewhat plaintively to Isaac Deutscher, 'I should dearly like to see our difficulties resolved, as I cannot believe that they are as important as the plight of the Vietnamese. . . .' Tamara Deutscher remembers Russell complaining about the way the tribunal had been hijacked by the French, and saying that he felt they had turned him into a non-person.

It was Deutscher who, in the end, acted as peacemaker. It was perfectly true that Sartre and Dedijer, who had virtually no contact with Russell other than through Schoenman, felt that he had lost touch with the times. Deutscher now contacted the most important jurists and told them that more attention should be paid to the man who was responsible for the entire tribunal. To Professor Schwartz he wrote, 'Whatever Ralph Schoenman may have said or done ... must not be allowed to affect our attitude towards Russell.' Apologies, of a sort, were made.

The second session opened on 20 November 1967, in a trade-union building at Roskilde in Denmark, twenty miles outside Copenhagen. The hearings took place in a ceremonial hall, used on Saturday nights for dances. The jury had lost one of their most respected and temperate members: Isaac Deutscher had died during the summer. Whereas the May session had concentrated on the effects of anti-personnel bombs on the Vietnamese countryside, the jurists now examined the effects of the war on the Vietnamese people. On the third day, three American GIs rose and confessed to 'war crimes'. Russell sent a message highlighting the need to 'unite

humanity on the side of justice'. Sartre attacked the United States at
great length, for committing genocide, a topic which occupied many
hours of the final sessions, and provoked rage in American newspapers. Simone de Beauvoir wrote to a friend that this session was
'particularly thrilling'.

The Americans were accused of bombing civilians, the use of
experimental weapons, the torture and mutilation of prisoners,
forced labour, the setting up of concentration camps and saturation
bombing of 'unparalleled intensity'. As the days went by, evidence
for these crimes seemed to most of the listeners to be overwhelming.
The proceedings broke up to total condemnation of American
behaviour. When it was over, when the tribunal had been disbanded
and the reporters had gone home, efforts were made to assess what,
precisely, had been achieved. It was hard to say. No one denied that
without Russell's inspiration (or money), or even Schoenman's
tenacious energy, the tribunal would never have existed at all. The
question was whether it had been worth it.

Some points were easier to make than others. One of the attacks
on the tribunal had concerned its legality. Leo Matarasso, the most
legally experienced of the jurors, continues to insist on the legitimacy
of the proceedings. No one, he says, had ever suggested that the
tribunal was assuming legal powers to enforce anything; all it claimed
was a legal right to take evidence and draw conclusions, and this was
done in a sober and balanced way. The fact that there was no exact
precedent did not invalidate the proceedings. To those who attacked
its sessions as biased, Russell replied, with some justification, that
the Nuremberg judges could not have been said to be entirely
without bias towards the nazis in the dock, and that anyone who
doubted the seriousness of the tribunal's hearings would do well to
examine the thoroughness with which the business had been conducted. If doubt continued to persist in many people's minds, it was
over the question of one-sidedness: was it really valid, in this
particular war, to look only at the record of the Americans, and not
that of the North Vietnamese?

Public opinion was on the whole clear. On the left, especially in
France, Italy and Scandinavia, there was approval that events in
Vietnam, and particularly the conduct of the American forces, had

received a proper hearing. In Britain, the whole event was largely ignored or ridiculed, leaving it to only a few people, like Eric Hobsbawm, to observe that it had been wrongly 'treated as a characteristic piece of ultra-left propaganda'. The Soviet Union and China barely commented, though it was known that both countries felt that it was all a bit pointless. 'You are wasting your time,' a Vietnamese delegate was told on his way through Moscow, 'they are just a band of Trotskyists.' In the United States, the one country the tribunal most wanted to influence, Russell and Sartre were described in many newspapers as hysterical, and their hearings a farce. True, the young and the left wing did express admiration for Russell's passion over a war which was sending many of them to jail as draft-protesters. For them the tribunal simply provided another proof that America should withdraw, but it was one proof among many. As the war escalated, protests within America grew more vociferous and the tribunal's hearings were soon forgotten, though there were some who remembered, after the My Lai massacres were revealed, that the sessions in Stockholm and Roskilde had been about just that kind of American behaviour.

From the earliest days of the tribunal, Russell had dreamt of turning it into a permanent court, where international injustices between states could be given a hearing and judged in the eyes, if not of the law, of the public. In a small way, this happened, in the form of a tribunal set up in Rome, which lasted for thirteen sessions, where juries heard evidence of atrocities in Guatemala and the Philippines. By now, however, Russell's funds were very low. Much of the money spent on the tribunal – said to have cost many thousands of pounds – had been raised against bank loans, and these were being called in. When the full scale of the deficit became clear, Schoenman drew up a bill and sent it off to the tribunal's office in Paris. Professor Schwartz recalls that consternation followed. There had indeed been talk of a financial reckoning, but nothing had been put down on paper. He wrote to Russell, suggesting that he come to see him in person to sort the matter out. Russell agreed, but Schwartz fell ill and the meeting was postponed, after which the question was simply dropped. Later, Schwartz wondered whether the whole subject of the money had not been a put-up job by

Schoenman, getting his own back after the humiliations in Stockholm.

One other sour note came from a North Vietnamese poet, Nguyen Chi Thien, who was serving an indefinite sentence inside a Vietnamese prison for his dissident views about communism, and had tried to capture in verse something of the feelings of many ordinary people in North Vietnam about their government. He addressed his poem directly to Russell:

> You pass as quite a learned sage,
>   And yet in politics you're just a dunce,
> You loudly speak for those Vietcongs,
>   And yet about them you don't know a thing.
> Please come and visit North Vietnam . . .
>   you'll see how beasts fare better than us, men . . .

The early 1960s had seen the appearance in Russell's life not just of Schoenman but of a whole series of young people, usually young men of intellectual disposition and radical left-wing views, angry at what they saw happening around them, and perceiving in Russell's concerns a hope of change. They were prepared to work for him for nothing in exchange for the world it gave them access to. Schoenman, who was responsible for introducing many of them to Russell, was careful to guard his position as senior acolyte, but a new role was found for the others when, in the spring of 1963, Russell began to talk about setting up a foundation to further his work for peace. Plas Penrhyn and the house in Chelsea had been suitable headquarters when the causes remained small. But with the huge publicity brought by Russell's gestures during the Cuban missile crisis it seemed the moment had come to set up a proper office.

Russell began by writing to a number of world leaders for their support. Agreement to act as sponsors came from Haile Selassie, emperor of Ethiopia, and Nehru, as well as from a number of African heads of state. On 29 September 1963, two foundations were launched simultaneously, the Bertrand Russell Peace Foundation and its charitable arm, the Atlantic Peace Foundation. The directors were Russell, Edith, Schoenman and the new young secretary, Christopher Farley. Messages of support arrived from Danilo Dolci,

Albert Schweitzer and Queen Juliana of the Netherlands. Premises were found off the Haymarket, at numbers 3 and 4 Shaver's Place, and an ambitious programme – of printing presses for books, films, newspapers and even a radio station – was announced, bearing the hallmarks of Schoenman's ambitions and prodigious energy. How far any of it was Russell's idea is hard to establish, but those who were with him at this time remember how surprised he seemed when he read the accounts of what the foundation proposed to do in the press releases prepared for the launch.

The foundation clearly needed money, and Schoenman turned out to be an indefatigable if unorthodox fund-raiser. One idea was that well-known artists should be asked to donate one of their works for sale, the proceedings to go to the foundation. From all over the world, artists sent in their pictures. Picasso, who had agreed to contribute something, failed to deliver his. When contacted again, he still did nothing. Schoenman decided to handle Picasso in his own way. He went to his house in France and rang the bell. A chauffeur opened the door. 'I'm Russell's secretary, and I have come to collect the picture,' Schoenman told him. The chauffeur assured him that it would be sent. Schoenman replied that he was not leaving without it. An hour later, when Picasso and his wife, driven by the chauffeur, turned out of their drive, Schoenman was lying on the ground. Three hours later, Picasso returned home. Schoenman was still lying outside the gate. A picture was handed over.

It was intended that the new foundation should act as a research centre for Russell's interests. There were hundreds of cases of political prisoners to investigate, human rights abuses in Iraq to explore, and the whole subject of workers' control, an extension of his guild socialism, needed, he felt, further discussion. Some of the young people who volunteered were put to work answering letters. Diana Readhead, who had first read *Why I am not a Christian* as a doubting teenager and had been overwhelmed by Russell's arguments, explained that it was up to the secretaries to draft replies to the avalanche of letters which appeared with every post. If Russell was in Wales, the replies were posted to him in batches for his signature; if in London, he liked to sit over this chore in the early evenings, discussing the more controversial letters over a glass of whisky. With the young, he always seemed at ease.

Volunteers who arrived at Shaver's Place were sent off on missions around the world, as roving ambassadors bearing messages from Russell, which were read out at international gatherings. Before leaving England, they were summoned to Wales for a briefing. This, to their surprise, would often take place during a formal dinner, presided over by Edith, with candles and a maid serving. Russell appeared to enjoy these occasions immensely, reminiscing about the past when prompted by Schoenman, laughing at his visitors' jokes and plotting for the future. It was all a little like the court of a venerable potentate, particularly when he issued remarks like 'I'm very displeased with India at the moment.'

Something of the cloak-and-dagger flavour of these roving embassies comes across in an account given by the writer Jon Halliday, a founder member of the *New Left Review* and a friend of some of Russell's entourage. It was shortly before the Soviet invasion of Czechoslovakia in 1968, and there was no one else available to take a message at short notice to a youth conference in Bucharest. There was no time for a visit to Wales, so Halliday was briefed over the phone by both Russell and Schoenman. Even before he left London, he found that he was treated a little as though he *were* Russell. No plane ticket was produced, but a member of the Romanian embassy collected him and drove him straight across the tarmac to the plane. A Mercedes with a driver was waiting for him at the other end. Russell's message, as might have been predicted, was an urgent plea against invasion, and not welcomed by the Romanians. Halliday was greeted as an important visitor, and though he was denied permission to address the main conference he was allowed to talk at smaller gatherings. As Russell's mouthpiece, he was treated with deference. It all seemed a little pointless to Halliday, but it said much about the way Russell was regarded throughout Europe.

Schoenman went on many of these missions, but they were rarely harmonious when he did so. What had become a cocksure and ebullient manner in England tended to explode into immense superiority when abroad. In England, he was Russell's servant; outside the country, he was Russell himself. As such, he felt he had the right to lecture Ben-Gurion on the state of Israel, or deliver vituperative attacks on America at a world congress for peace in Helsinki, where his remarks were inappropriate to the occasion and provoked cries of protest from the audience. Schoenman was told repeatedly to sit down. When he refused, the chairman vaulted over the table and snatched the microphone from him.

Pat Pottle, one of the five Committee of 100 supporters who had been imprisoned in the 'Official Secrets' trial, had not long joined Russell's secretariat when a dispute arose on the Chinese – Indian border. Both sides said they were willing to receive emissaries from Russell, and to pay their costs. Pottle and Schoenman set off together, and were given the kind of respectful treatment guaranteed to inflate Schoenman's already considerable sense of self-import-ance. In Delhi, the two young men were greeted warmly by Nehru and asked to carry a secret message to Chou En-Lai: Nehru was prepared to withdraw from the disputed areas and discuss matters at a peace conference. From India, they called on Mrs Bandarinaike in Sri Lanka; she too received them warmly and expressed pleasure at their mission. But in China everything changed; from being free agents and fêted guests they found themselves regarded as suspect petitioners. Five aides were allocated to look after them, and they were never left alone. They were given no appointment to see Chou En-Lai, but told to wait.

Schoenman was not a patient man and his sense of humour was peculiar. At a Peace Foundation dinner in Delhi, he had been asked for his first impressions of India. 'How do you fuck in this heat?' was his reply. In Peking, growing irritable at the delay, and considering it his due to receive immediate attention, he picked up the telephone in their hotel one day and shouted down it, 'Chairman Mao is a sacred cow.' Taken by their hosts on a visit to the Forbidden City, and invited to row on the lake, Schoenman took his clothes off and swam. A visit to a prison was handled with a similar lack of tact. Finally, the two young men were summoned to see Chou En-Lai. They were given tea; it was all very formal. Then, abruptly, their Chinese hosts rose to their feet and accused them of making obnoxious remarks about China. Had it not been for the esteem in which Russell was held, they were told, they would certainly be put in prison. As for the secret note from Nehru, Chou En-Lai made it public, causing Nehru to deny that he had ever written it. Pottle and Schoenman were deported home.

It was during the year of the War Crimes Tribunal that relations with Schoenman started to go seriously wrong. His presence among the luminaries at Stockholm, albeit unsatisfactory, seemed to have left him more than usually paranoid and bellicose. His proposals for new ventures became more and more grandiose, and his manner with those around him alternated between sourness and aggression. He accused colleagues in the office of stealing things, and issued a public denunciation of President Ayub Khan of Pakistan, as a 'traitor'. Khan was a founding sponsor of the foundation. As for his behaviour towards the general public, Schoenman could be brutal: when people wrote disagreeing with Russell's nuclear position, he suggested that they visit the local store and buy rat poison or jump off a high building, thereby killing themselves, but no one else, in the process.

Having spent years telling everyone that he was only Russell's mouthpiece, he now began to say that all Russell's ideas had come from him in the first place. Because he was so canny, and so bright, he was able to merge the two voices at least enough to fool everyone except those who had known Russell for a long time. Schoenman had arrived in England calling himself a Marxist; he had since flirted with Mao; now he spoke of himself as a Trotskyite. No one was sure about him any more, except, apparently, Russell, with whom he continued to behave respectfully.

Because Russell had decided to pay no more visits to London after his appearance at the War Crimes Tribunal preliminary meetings in the autumn of 1966, anyone who wished to see him was obliged to go down to Wales. From now on, Schoenman became the screen between Russell and the world, not least because both Russell and Edith were slightly deaf and felt increasingly cut off from events. Schoenman was their intermediary. Any visitor had first to undergo his scrutiny, and those of whom he disapproved were kept away from Wales on the grounds of Russell's age and apparent ill-health. If people wished to communicate with Russell, Schoenman suggested that they talk to him first, but they would be kept waiting for considerable lengths of time at his office. His arrogance infuriated Russell's old friends, who gave up trying to see him after being rebuffed by chilly letters which bore his signature but not his voice. Those that did get through came away dispirited. Mary and Julian Trevelyan, who had so much enjoyed his company in Taormina in 1949, persevered, but when they eventually had tea with Russell and Edith, Schoenman was there, hovering, making the atmosphere awkward if not unpleasant.

Fenner Brockway, one of Russell's very few remaining friends from the First World War, found himself slowly ousted from Russell's life. This was partly, he said, because Schoenman had no time for him, and made access impossible; but when he did see Russell he found him changed. 'When we were younger, we had been friends, we shared a sense of comradeship. All that had gone. There was no real friendship left. On my part I continued to feel immense respect for him, except that he didn't seem to have any doubts any more. He became so confident in his own ideas, so determined to express his opinions.' Russell had never really liked Brockway and had certainly not become sentimental in recent years.

The question which had long exercised Russell's friends and those who had dealings with him was to what extent Schoenman actually substituted himself for Russell. Did he sign letters, written on his own initiative and never shown to Russell, in Russell's name? Because Russell's correspondence, by this time, was so large, and because he is known to have left a certain discretion to the secretaries he trusted, complaining that he had become a letter-writing factory and could no longer cope alone, he could not possibly have been aware of every letter that went out over his name. Many of them were, after all, simply trivial acknowledgements. But the evidence seems to point to a graver charge.

Before leaving for India, Schoenman asked whether he should not take with him, as gifts, some of Russell's books, signed by the author. Russell said he did not like the idea. When they unpacked their suitcases in Delhi, Pottle was surprised to see a pile of Russell's works, neatly signed by Schoenman in Russell's name. Pottle is convinced that by that time Schoenman was writing many letters and signing them 'Russell'. When Pottle was sentenced to eighteen months during the Old Bailey trial, he received two letters from Russell, one immediately after the other. Both expressed sympathy and support, but whereas the first was handwritten and clearly bore Russell's touch the second was stilted and written on a typewriter. Leo Matarasso tells the story of the appointment of not one but at least two French lawyers at the time of the tribunal, in a manner so contradictory as to be absurd if both invitations had come from the same hand. And Professor Schwartz is convinced that the request for money, after the tribunals had been wound up, came not from Russell but from Schoenman, aggrieved at the way he had been treated. When, as sometimes happened, Russell seemed bewildered at receiving a reply to a letter he was unaware of having written, Schoenman would be heard to say, with slight impatience, 'Don't you remember us discussing it together only a few weeks ago?'

A revealing story is told by Christopher Farley, who spent eight years as Russell's secretary. One day, while they were in the office, Schoenman showed him, as a joke, how he could produce a 'foolproof' version of Russell's signature. Farley, who knew Russell's hand better than anyone, was startled at the likeness. Carrying his joke perhaps a little too far, Schoenman then showed his version to Russell as well. Russell was taken aback.

The sad account of Russell's break with his publisher of fifty years, Sir Stanley Unwin, provides further proof of Schoenman's influence and the disconcerting ease with which he seemed able to step into Russell's shoes. When Schoenman was putting together a collection of articles, *Bertrand Russell: Philosopher of the Century*, for which Sir Stanley seemed slightly reluctant to pay much in the way of an advance, Schoenman arrived unannounced in the office one day, haggled unpleasantly over the terms with various senior editors, and left with a £1000 advance. From then on, relations grew strained. Sir Stanley had always acted as both Russell's publisher and his agent, and it is true that some advances might indeed have been larger had the books been offered elsewhere. But their partnership had been a long and harmonious one, and Sir Stanley had looked after Russell at times when things had been going badly.

In August 1966, Russell wrote to Sir Stanley informing him that he intended to use an agent in all their future dealings. Deborah

Rogers, a friend of one of Russell's helpers at the Peace Foundation, and then working for the agency Peter Janson-Smith, was sounded out for the part. She travelled down to Wales with Schoenman, who proved an exceptionally frightening driver, belligerent with other motorists and never once drawing breath during the entire five-hour journey. Russell and Edith were welcoming, but detached. To her, it seemed as if Russell might have been briefly taken with the novel idea of having an agent, but had rapidly lost interest in the whole subject, and was leaving it to Schoenman to pursue. Sensing that most if not all of her dealings would be with Schoenman, and that what he was after was power rather than good literature, Deborah Rogers backed off, and a new agent was suggested, Anton Felton, a former accountant. Over lunch with Deborah Rogers, Sir Stanley had been sad but courteous about the whole affair. As a final gesture, he cautioned Russell against taking on an agent better known for his experience in tax affairs than literary matters. To his intense chagrin, as Russell's next birthday approached, he received a circular letter from a secretary giving him Russell's address and informing him that it would undoubtedly give Russell great pleasure to hear from him on the day. The note instructed him to be certain that his greetings arrived as near the day as possible. The last words were underlined. The secretary received an acid reply: 'I always write to Bertrand Russell on his birthday.' It was a bitter close to what had been one of the most lasting and well-mannered literary partnerships. The letters that came from Plas Penrhyn after this were formal, and sometimes even accusatory, with no more of the old-world niceties. Some came above Russell's signature, some above Schoenman's, but on two consecutive days, two letters on the same subject arrived, with subtle differences of tone. Both bore the signature 'Russell'.

Russell was well aware what people felt about Schoenman, but as the months went by, he seemed curiously unwilling to take any steps to curb him. A visitor overheard him say to Edith, 'We must say no to Ralph some day.' When he did challenge him to explain away some rudeness or some display of ill-judged temper, Schoenman was adept at knowing how to calm Russell's fears and convince him that it was all a misunderstanding, or that it was the other people who were the villains of the piece. Even Russell's old friend Joseph

Rotblat was rebuffed; he had made the long journey down to Wales to warn Russell that he was being used by Schoenman in ways that were bringing discredit not only to his own name but to the causes he cared about so deeply. Schoenman sat in on the meeting, and Russell did not ask him to leave. Having come so far, Rotblat went ahead with his warnings. Schoenman lost his temper and left the room, slamming the door behind him. Edith took Schoenman's side. When Rotblat left, he realised that his close and enjoyable friendship with Russell was effectively over.

One by one, even Russell's young colleagues and former friends began to back away from him. They were growing uneasy about the way Schoenman appeared to be going through the resources of the foundation. Schoenman was the only person allowed to sign cheques on behalf of the foundation. One day, five active supporters, including Pat Pottle and Michael Scott, agreed that the moment had come when Schoenman would have to be checked. They drove down to Wales. Their plan had been to talk first to Edith on her own, but she insisted that Russell sit in on every discussion. The five young men described Schoenman's recent behaviour in detail. They spelt out incidents showing his arrogance and rudeness; they showed how he was spending the foundation funds; they described his dictatorial manner with world leaders, and warned that he was becoming a liability within the peace movement. Russell listened, then told them to put it down in writing. The young men went off to a nearby hotel and spent the night drafting their complaints. When they went to deliver them next day, Schoenman opened the door and took the letter from them.

Schoenman's last mission for the Peace Foundation was to Bolivia, to attend the trial of Regis Debray. Four others went with him: Tariq Ali, Robin Blackburn, Perry Anderson and a German called Lothar Menne. Schoenman staged one of his most colourful appearances by choosing to rise and berate the court on the iniquities of the Bolivian regime. Before being flung out, and repatriated to the USA, he learned that the British had decided not to allow him re-entry to Britain. He came back all the same, under an assumed name and wearing an ill-fitting yellow wig, haunting his old associates and insisting on seeing Russell. During his hour at Plas Penrhyn he managed to drop hints about the disloyalty of some of Russell's assistants, then he left. Not long afterwards, he was caught by the police in a minicab in Hyde Park, and deported. He never saw Russell again. On 10 December 1969, it was reported in the *Guardian* that Schoenman had been 'removed' from the board of the Peace Foundation.

Unknown to others, Russell had decided to commit to paper the truth, as he saw it, about Schoenman. He wrote a 7500-word memorandum, which Edith typed out; he took care to sign each page as it was finished, so that Schoenman would not later be able to claim that it was not his own work. To the finished document, he pinned a note saying that he endorsed every word 'as being mine and what I wished to say'. It was perfectly true that both he and Edith had been attached to Schoenman – there had even been talk of making him his political heir – just as it was true that it had been pleasant to have this bold American so totally engrossed in Russell's own vision of the world. But Schoenman had gone too far. There was no doubting his vitality or even his efficiency: what was at issue was his judgement.

The memorandum was a sober, lucid, detailed document. Russell praised Schoenman for his courage, quickness of mind, sense of irony, generosity and optimism. His companionship had been 'as welcome as a delicious fresh breeze on a muggy day'. Gradually, however, Russell had come to see that there was a darker side to his character. The very strength of his convictions made him blind to the importance of being truthful. For all Russell's hopes, he had failed to grow up; he had shown himself to be tactless, offensive, alienating former friends, too ready to show off and impose his own views on others. He had become flamboyant, egotistical and financially unscrupulous, a character ruined by 'impetuous egotistical folly'. Why, Russell asked rhetorically, had he put up with it for so long? Because, at least in part, of Schoenman's 'fulsome flatteries'. 'I am', wrote Russell engagingly, 'by no means immune to flattery. It is so rare as to be sweet in my ears.' And also because 'until the last few years he was the only person who could and would carry out the work that I thought should be done.' That, surely, is the real answer to what people have long chosen to regard as a mystery: Schoenman gave Russell back the power that age was fast depriving him of.

The Russell memorandum, as it became known, appeared only after his death. It is a remarkable piece of work, bearing the stamp of Russell at his most rational and clearheaded, even if he conveniently chose to ignore the question of why so many misquotations and inaccuracies had crept into his recent writings. When it was eventually published, Schoenman, contacted by reporters, remarked that Russell had clearly fallen into the hands of rogues, and that Edith was a 'woman with anachronistic political views, anti-Jewish and anti-black', who had been prone to address him as 'Jew-boy'.

In Britain, it was greeted with relief, as a sign that the old philosopher had not, after all, been duped. The few people who did feel vexed were the ones who had gone to such pains to open Russell's eyes to Schoenman's behaviour. They were guilty, said Russell, of being 'unwilling . . . to bear the consequences of plain speaking'. Their reluctance to do so, came the reedy voice from beyond the grave, 'had done great harm to me, and, what is worse, to our work'. For a man who prided himself on his accuracy and fairness, Russell, too, was capable of lapses.

On 23 December 1966, at the age of 94 years and 218 days, Russell became the oldest person ever to hold the Order of Merit. He continued to seem curiously unmarked by his great age, though his angular, stork-like features had become softer. He was a little stooped, but still held his head very straight, as if held by a stiff collar, and his movements were only a little less quick and certain. His dress remained formal, his manners Victorian. Anger at the folly of the world, he would say, kept him young. True, he could look painfully insubstantial, and his difficulty in swallowing, which had been plaguing him on and off for ten years, now grew more pronounced. Among his more analytical friends, there was a tendency to say that it was all something to do with Russell's fear of madness, with the fact that Uncle Willy, who had spent most of his life in a mental asylum, had tried to strangle someone, that his mother had died unable to swallow, and with his own memory of having, in the grips of a nightmare, tried to strangle Peter. He seldom complained, even when shingles and then pneumonia left him very weak. It became something of a family joke that during the delirium which marked the turning-point of his pneumonia he asked someone to fetch the footman.

Well into the 1960s, Russell continued to walk across the valleys and up into the mountains near Plas Penrhyn, always in the company of Edith, who seldom left his side. The mild Welsh weather, with few frosts, suited him. When he grew too frail to go far afield, he would lead visitors on to the balcony and show them the view across the valley to the house where Shelley had lived.

In January 1967 Russell announced that he intended to publish his autobiography. It had been with him for over thirty-five years, but much altered and revised, and many passages changed to tone down accounts of marriages and love affairs. It had never been his intention to bring it out in his lifetime, but a need for money for the ailing Peace Foundation led him to look back through old papers. There was too, perhaps, an element of testimonial, a settling of accounts with the past, though he worried that the project might appear 'unduly egotistical'. As he worked, secretaries at Plas Penrhyn foraged among boxes of material in search of missing items. In 1931, Russell had told Crompton Llewelyn Davies, in whose safe the first two manuscripts had been lodged, that he estimated potential royalties at between £3000 and £4000. In America, Simon and Schuster offered $30,000, Doubleday $45,000 and the Atlantic Monthly Press and Little, Brown $202,000 – which Russell took. The autobiography started as one volume, then turned into two, then became three; each consisted of passages of narrative, followed by letters, both his and those to him. It is one of the most enjoyable memoirs ever written.

When the first volume appeared, covering his childhood at Pembroke Lodge and closing with the outbreak of the First World War, Leonard Woolf commented that what was most remarkable about it was that its very flaws mirrored Russell's character: 'Mathematically Russell is a genius, and this genius, located primarily in his mind, is linked with a brilliant, fantastic, by no means integrated character.' For its frankness and its psychological revelations, it stood comparison with Pepys or Rousseau, Woolf considered. *The*

Autobiography of Bertrand Russell, 1872–1914 Volume one, rose rapidly through the bestseller lists in both America and England. Requests for interviews poured in; Russell turned down Bernard Levin on the grounds that while he might have enjoyed his hostility, he did not think him 'sufficiently serious'.

The next volume, which took readers up to the end of the Second World War, proceeded in the same smooth way, coming out to good reviews and brisk sales, though it provoked a surprisingly vehement outburst from Woolf. This second book, he said, was a 'psychological strip-teaser'. It revealed a man who was not just politically impotent, and guided by the 'most vulgar kind of prejudice', but who was essentially negative, 'anti' everything: the Americans, the Bolsheviks, the Jews and even his old friends. For Woolf, and a number of other old acquaintances, these memoirs, brilliant and readable as they were, displayed no shame in revealing traits of character – violent prejudices, a cutting tongue – which they had long felt uneasy about in Russell.

The third book, covering the anti-nuclear years, has a more stilted tone, not least because Russell was now nearing ninety-eight, and the material had yet to be assimilated. How much of a hand Edith had in its preparation no one knows, but in the last years of Russell's life she took down most of what he wrote in dictation. The dedication on the opening page bore little of Russell's crispness, but was singularly affectionate. His poem was addressed to Edith.

> . . . Now, old and near my end,
> I have known you,
> And, knowing you,
> I have found ecstasy and peace.
> I know rest,
> After so many lonely years.

There was never any mistaking the great fondness Russell and Edith had for each other. It was probably his one enduring, happy marriage. On the rare occasions when he was away from her he always left word to say where he was. In the archives of McMaster University is a fragment of paper, the words written in Russell's distinct but now quavery hand: 'Gone out for a short walk'. People who spoke to

Edith on the telephone remarked on her beautiful voice – light, very clear, with a distinctive American sound. They expected its owner to be young and beautiful, and were often surprised to find a pleasant woman in her sixties, in sensible, sober clothes, more obviously intelligent than beautiful.

In notes for a speech, Edith has left a touching tribute to Russell. He was, she wrote, compassionate, generous, loving, brave, honest, passionate and 'inexhaustibly interesting – and interested'. His laughter was a 'great gust of rollicking merriment that shook the rafters', so that other people in the room found themselves laughing even when they did not know what they were laughing at. Russell was completely without vanity, except on one subject: his flourishing white hair. 'I cover up no horrors,' she wrote, 'I have found none to cover up.' Nor were there any shadows.

Radical and liberal in almost everything, Russell was a true conservative 'in the *trivia* of manners and customs'. Both he and Edith looked forward all day to the moment when they went up to bed, when they would talk about 'things immediate or far in the past or future'. They had, she recalled, only one bitter quarrel, and that was about Chinese ideographs, a subject about which neither knew anything at all. 'We went to bed desolate . . . The morning light restored us to equilibrium.'

In the late 1960s Conrad came back into Russell's life. Russell had had only occasional glimpses of his younger son since he and Peter had parted company after the unhappy holiday in Taormina. It was Conrad, now aged thirty, who decided to make friends, though Russell took a bit of wooing, remarking to Christopher Farley, 'I don't respect his reasons for leaving me, and I don't respect those for coming back.' Unable to get over her bitterness, Peter had become a recluse; once she knew that Conrad, on his way to becoming a successful and respected historian, was seeing his father, she became more solitary, refusing even to see her son. No one is sure whether she is still alive.

Sitting in his study at Plas Penrhyn, with Edith and Conrad, Russell appeared genuinely happy, smoking his pipe and drinking whisky, complaining that his memory was going when to those around him it had never seemed better. His recall of the events and people who had crowded his life was extraordinary, and he continued to relish long discussions on the follies of the age, talking far into the night, repeating Greek tags learned as a boy or rehearsing the reasons which led him to reject Hegel almost three-quarters of a century earlier. He had lost none of his taste for aphorisms, or for challenging those around him in a half-teasing, half-baiting way. Remarks, as spare and pertinent as they had been all his life, dropped like pebbles into silences.

He took no part in the local life of the Welsh valleys, but a few new friends who lived in houses not far away were charmed by his old-world courtesy, his wit and his never-ending curiosity, not only about what was going on in the world but about their lives. When visitors arrived to stay, Russell would rise and apologise for not being able to carry their suitcases. 'He was such fun, such terrific fun', says Michael Burn, who lived nearby and was one of the few people who saw him regularly. 'He laughed so much. He loved silly shaggy dog stories and quoting "The Hunting of the Snark" and singing the "Marseillaise", with that unmistakable elfin guffaw'. Although he had spent less than a decade as a don, there was something unmistakably donnish about Russell, in his love of endless discussion. Over dinner, sitting with two glasses of milk in front of him, he would talk about everything from Spinoza and the influence of Gödel on modern mathematicians to how hard it had become to get hold of a good treacle tart.

Neither contentment nor extreme old age did much to alter either his concerns or his capacity for being morally moved. He remained as preoccupied as ever with the challenge of making the world a happier place, and reassured those who said they understood he had abandoned his lifelong agnosticism, that he was not one jot less opposed to religious orthodoxy than he had been at the age of sixteen. The great religions of the world, he would say, Buddhism, Hinduism, Christianity, Islam, and communism, seemed to him just as 'untrue and harmful' as they had always been. The world, this prophet of liberal humanism wrote, needs 'open hearts and open minds, and it is not through rigid systems, whether old or new, that these can be derived'. What people needed was not dogma but an 'attitude of scientific inquiry combined with a belief that the torture of millions is not desirable, whether inflicted by Stalin or by a Deity. . . .' Many religious leaders had indeed shown great personal courage, but what they invariably lacked was the 'intellectual courage to face the world without the comfort of such a myth. For in the final analysis, it is human responsibility which is significant in our affairs.'

At ninety-five, Russell still read the modern philosophers and discussed their contributions with Ayer. Now, he occasionally took a more sceptical and lighthearted view of the importance of philosophy. Asked by an interviewer early in 1967 what benefits he believed mankind had received from philosophers, Russell replied: 'Well, this is a very nasty question, isn't it? I don't know whether mankind has received much benefit from philosophers. They haven't, in the first place, made any discoveries . . . I suppose they've enlarged people's imagination in some ways, and given them a capacity to think about the universe as a whole,' but nothing, he added, comparable to 'what the men of science have done'.

About Russell's own achievements, and his conception of philosophy as the clarification and justification of all important beliefs, other philosophers tended to be generous. It is said that the best method for a philosopher to ensure pre-eminence lies in putting forward a major theory, which can then be disproved by successive generations of philosophers. Russell left no single theory but a number of them, for he advanced by pointing out the errors in his own work himself. As Alan Wood wrote in *The Passionate Sceptic*, 'his immortality depends on someone finding some fundamental fault in his work.' He was a philosopher of all philosophies, a man who sought objective truth everywhere – in science, mathematics, logic and religion just as much as in philosophy. On the other hand, quite apart from the advances he made in logic, and 'all the dark places which he has made plain', Russell posed questions – he once wrote that the value of philosophy lay rather in questions than their answers – and subsequent philosophers have picked them up where he left off. If he changed his mind and revised his views there were also some convictions which he never shed: that the proper method of philosophy is the analysis of the forms of propositions, the search for the true underlying form which would expose the logical connections between different kinds of empirical knowledge; and that our knowledge rests on empirical evidence. He set standards of clarity in argument. In 1919, in a letter to Virginia Woolf, Lytton Strachey compared Russell's mind to a circular saw, the teeth moving in all different directions at once, while the saw sliced straight ahead. 'I wanted certainty,' Russell reflected on his eightieth birthday, 'in the kind of way in which people want religious faith.'

There are those who argue that nearly all the serious work he did after leaving Cambridge suffers from being carried out largely in a vacuum, away from the intellectual rigour of colleagues who might have made him more critical of himself. But few deny that when he reached his tenth decade, he was the best-known of all British philosophers, a man who managed to present not only philosophy but ethics, social policies and politics so that they could be understood by people unable to comprehend the work of his peers. The lucidity of his style, and the fact that he was practically incapable of being dull, ensured the public went on buying and reading his books long after their technical contents had been challenged by professional philosophers.

In *The Philosophy of Logical Atomism*, Russell wrote,

> The process of sound philosophising consists mainly in passing from these obvious, vague, ambiguous things, that we feel quite sure of, to something precise, clear, definite . . . of which that vague thing is a sort of shadow . . . I propose, therefore, always to begin any argument that I have to make by appealing to data which will be quite ludicrously obvious. Any philosophical skill that is required will consist in the selection of those which are capable of yielding a good deal of reflection and analysis, and in the reflection and analysis themselves . . .

Was Russell wise, as he is sometimes made out to be? Those who might have conceded him wisdom concluded that he was in the end flawed by a maverick element, as powerful as the conflict between reason and passion, which surfaced when he was goaded beyond endurance by some act of folly. Then, he was capable of casting aside balance and indulging in intemperate and even childishly offensive remarks. No one, however, denied that he was consistently liberal and radical all his life, often in the forefront of change and often himself a force for change. He was a Russell in the mould of his father and grandfather, taking infinite pleasure in presenting new theories.

The generation which revived the Campaign for Nuclear Disarmament in the 1970s seldom remembered Russell's part in the early days, beyond recalling his rows with Canon Collins, but they inherited a movement which regarded civil disobedience as morally legitimate, and the historians among them appreciated that it was Russell, along with Gandhi, who made it so. In his nineties, he believed in peace at almost any cost, in the liberation from fear that people would be 'fried with their families and their neighbours and every living person they had heard of'. After the changes of mind which had marked his seventy-year crusade against war and modern weapons, he remained committed to the idea of world government, conducted by a 'balancing committee', appointed by the UN from among the uncommitted nations who would adjudicate on misunderstandings between East and West as soon as they arose.

There were some people who could not quite forgive Russell for not having died before the Schoenman years, before the Committee of 100 and the War Crimes Tribunal and the roving ambassadors who did such curious things in his name. Most, however, preferred to forget the controversial years, and to celebrate, as Michael Foot put it, 'the foremost sceptic and exponent of free thought . . . English to the core, as uniquely English as the free-thinking Whiggery in which he was reared and against whose complacencies and limitations he revolted'. They found it easy to do so when they read the closing lines of his autobiography, which seemed to return him to his pedestal as a sage commentator of his times. His life, he wrote, had contained both inner and outer failures. Communists, nazis and fascists had challenged all that he had thought good, 'and in defeating them much of what their opponents have sought to preserve is lost'. As for his work, 'I came to the conlcusion that the eternal world is trivial and that mathematics', which had once shone for him with the beauty of Dante's last Cantos of the *Paradiso*, 'is only the art of saying the same things in different words.' And he had been utterly wrong in thinking that 'love, free and courageous' could conquer the world.

He was, all the same, conscious of 'something I feel to be victory'.

Except for a missing final synthesis, he had done what he had set out to do, on that snowy March morning of 1894 in the Tiergarten in Berlin: he had written two series of books – one abstract, growing more concrete, the other concrete, growing more abstract. Russell never denied that the world was a horrible place and the universe unjust. The secret, he said, was to face the fact and not brush it aside, then you can start being happy. Nothing, he concluded in his late nineties, was absolutely certain – neither faith, nor religion, nor political dogma. His contribution was to show how an agnostic could survive without fear. All his life he had lived in pursuit of a vision: to 'allow moments of insight to give wisdom at more mundane times', and had dreamt of the day when 'hate and greed and envy die because there is nothing to nourish them. These things I believe, and the world, for all its horrors, has left me unshaken.'

Afterword

On 2 February 1970, towards six-thirty in the evening, Bertrand Russell died. He was, wrote Edith to Colette, 'gentle and kind and full of fun and entirely uncomplaining to the very end'. He was three months short of his ninety-eighth birthday.

No one had quite realised how close to the end he was. At Christmas, an occasion he always enjoyed, he appeared for lunch in a long red silk robe sent to him by a Chinese admirer, with Lord John Russell's gold watch fastened across his chest. He had a bad cold, from which he apparently recovered completely. Towards the end of January, he again fell ill, with the bronchitis which had troubled him repeatedly in recent years; but on 2 February he left his bed after lunch and sat reading and talking to Edith in their bedroom. Suddenly, he was very sick. With the help of a young man who was living in the house, Edith got him into bed and sent for the doctor. Russell was in no pain, but seemed to have trouble breathing. When the doctor did not arrive, she gave him a little oxygen; it seemed to make no difference. A few minutes later, he died. On the certificate, the doctor gave the cause of death as 'uraemia' and 'bilateral bronchial pneumonia'.

Russell had left instructions that he wished to be cremated and his ashes scattered, and that there was to be 'no funeral ceremony whatsoever'. As tributes from all over the world began to arrive, Ken Coates, the director of the Peace Foundation, who had to deal with the undertakers, issued orders that the crematorium rooms were to be closed to the public and the press, that the coffin was not to be displayed, that there was to be no music, no cortège, no flowers, and no procession, 'whether organised or spontaneous'. On 6 February, Russell's body was taken to Colwyn Bay crematorium in a plain oak coffin, on which lay a single bunch of irises and daffodils, with the words, 'In affectionate remembrance'.

The newspapers gave Russell a fine send-off. Few were so tactless as to take him to task for the wilder utterances of the last decade. They preferred to reminisce about his dedication to making the world a happier and safer place, about the campaigns he had waged with such tenacity for over seventy years and his lifelong commitment to morality and courage.

Though Alys was dead, he was survived by his three younger wives. Dora lived for another sixteen years. Peter remained a recluse. Edith stayed on at Plas Penrhyn, as unobtrusively as she had during her years as Russell's wife, dealing with enquiries which continued to come in, until she became ill and was taken into hospital in Bangor. She insisted on being in a public ward, under the name of 'Mrs Russell'. She died in her sleep on 1 January 1978. Of the other women who had greatly loved Russell, only Colette was still alive. She was one of the very few who had not felt rancour towards him. Not one of the others, particularly those cast aside in Russell's peremptory fashion, had ever found it easy to part with him, and none found happiness with anyone else. Dora's bitterness simmered on well beyond Russell's death. Most of his estate went either to Edith or to the Peace Foundation. By the terms of his will, John was to receive £300 a year, but this left a deficit, as Russell had been paying Dora £500 a year towards John's keep. Dora sued for more; and won.

Nor was Russell's personal legacy a happy one. John became increasingly disturbed, living with Dora in Cornwall, though he did attend the House of Lords until his irrational behaviour made his presence awkward. In his autobiography, Russell blamed his elder son's unhappiness on his belonging to a generation 'lost by the folly and greed of the generation to which I belong'. John died in 1987, at the age of sixty-six, in a railway station on his way home.

Russell's grand-daughter Sarah gave up a scholarship in history and wandered off to India. On her return she was diagnosed as suffering from catatonic schizophrenia, and spent long periods in a mental hospital. Her sister Lucy followed her to the east, became a Buddhist in Katmandhu, then returned to London where she, too, spent some time in hospital. She tried to commit suicide by jumping out of a window, but succeeded only in breaking her neck. In April 1975, during the American bombing of Cambodia, and apparently imitating the self-immolation of Vietnamese monks and nuns, she caught a bus to the Cornish village of St Buryan, poured paraffin over herself and set it alight. A local blacksmith, into whose yard she ran engulfed in flames and screaming, her arms held up in the air as if begging for help, was unable to save her. She was twenty-six.

Kate, by now the mother of five children, divorced Charles Tait, and in her book about her father commented bitterly on his view that puritan morals were the cause of unhappiness and their rejection its cure. '. . . Reason, progress, unselfishness, a wide historical perspective, expansiveness, generosity, enlightened self-interest. I had heard it all my life, and it filled me with despair.' Russell's life, according to his only daughter, had been dedicated to the belief that the 'coming happiness of mankind' mattered a great deal more than personal contentment – not merely his own, but that of those around him. Like Rousseau, his love for humanity was more intense than his capacity to deal with individual human beings.

Twice before in his life, Russell had come close to death. The first time had been in Peking; the second in a Norwegian fjord. On neither occasion did he experience any fear. Having longed for certainty, and failed to find it in either mathematics or religion, he was always hard on those who were unable to face life or death without the comfort of irrational beliefs: he recommended the 'stark joy' to be found in the unflinching perception of man's place in the world. 'I believe that when I die I shall rot, and nothing of my ego will survive,' he had written in 1925. '. . . But I should scorn to shrivel with terror at the thought of annihilation. Happiness is none the less true happiness because it must come to an end, nor do thought and love lose their value because they are not everlasting.' To the end, Russell, the man who ran such a fine line between passion and reason, was rational about his own mortality in a way that he was not always about the follies of man.

Bibliography
and Selected Sources

Except where otherwise specified, publication venue was London.
There are several lives and memoirs of Bertrand Russell: *The Life of Bertrand Russell*, Ronald W. Clark (1975); *Bertrand Russell, The Passionate Sceptic*, Alan Wood (1957); *Bertrand Russell, A Political Life*, Alan Ryan (1988). In 1991, the first volume of Bertrand Russell's *Selected Letters: The Private Years 1884–1914*, ed. Nicholas Griffin, was published. Volume 2 is to follow. There are also several collections of Russell's correspondence with various people: *Dear Russell–Dear Jourdain*, ed. I. Grattan-Guinness (1977); *Philosophical and Mathematical Correspondence* (to Gottlob Frege) (Oxford 1980); *Unpublished Correspondence between Russell and Wittgenstein*, B. F. McGuinness and G. H. von Wright in *Russell*, 10, 1990); *Joseph Conrad and Bertrand Russell*, *Conradiana* (vol 2. no. 1. 1966); and Russell's letters to Helen Thomas and Lucy Donnelly are the subject of a PhD thesis by Maria Forte (1988). Articles on Russell's life and work are to be found in *Russell: The Journal of the Bertrand Russell Archives* 1971–.

The many books on Russell's philosophical and mathematical work include: *The Development of Bertrand Russell's Philosophy*, Ronald Jager (1972); *Bertrand Russell*, John Watling (Edinburgh 1970); *Bertrand Russell*, Alan Dorward (1951); *Russell*, C. W. Kilmister (1984); *Modern British Philosophy*, Brian Magee (1971); *Bertrand Russell: A Collection of Critical Essays*, ed. D. F. Pears (Englewood Cliffs, N.J. 1972); *Bertrand Russell and the British Tradition in Philosophy*, D. F. Pears (1967); *English Philosophy since 1900*, G. J. Warnock (Oxford 1969); *The Spinozistic Ethics of Bertrand Russell*, Kenneth Blackwell (1985); *Bertrand Russell*, A. J. Ayer (Chicago 1972). All unpublished documents are in The Bertrand Russell Archives, Ready Division of Archives and Research Collections, McMaster University Library, unless otherwise stated.

The following are a guide to the most important sources.

One: Pembroke Lodge and the 'Deadly Nightshade'

There are several books about Russell's family, and by various of its members: *The Amberley Papers*, Bertrand and Patricia Russell (1937); *The Russells*, Christopher Trent (1966); *Lady John Russell: A Memoir*, Desmond MacCarthy and Agatha Russell (1910); *My Life and Adventures*, Frank Russell (1923); *A Victorian Childhood*, Annabel Huth Jackson (1932); *Elizabeth of the German Garden*, Leslie de Charms (1958); *'Elizabeth' The author of Elizabeth and her German Garden*, Karen Usborne (1986).

p. 7	the weather	The Amberley Papers
p. 11	in south Devon	*My Mental Development*, p. 37
p. 11	He turned to	Can war be avoided? *Fortnightly Review*, Mar. 1871
p. 12	'I know you'	*Autobiography*, vol. 1, p. 15
p. 15	Later, BR	*Autobiography*, vol. 1, p. 17
p. 16	Several people	Family papers: Margaret Lloyd
p. 16	'I grew accustomed'	*Autobiography*, vol. 1, p. 19
p. 17	'He was as usual'	*Diary*, 20 April 1878
p. 19	The boys were allowed	*Portraits from Memory*, p. 8
p. 19	Agatha never	*Autobiography*, vol. 1, p. 26
p. 21	In his own memoirs	Frank Russell, *My Life and Adventures*
p. 21	one child who did	Anne Freemantle, *The three-cornered Hat*
p. 23	'my childhood'	*Autobiography*, vol. 1, p. 38
p. 24	settled on Shelley	*My Mental Development*, p. 41
p. 24	Frank had told	*Portraits from Memory*, p. 19
p. 24	'when I got over'	*My Mental Development*, p. 40
p. 25	'led me in later'	*Autobiography*, vol. 1, p. 23
p. 27	'April 2'	Greek Exercises, vol. 1, *Collected Papers*
p. 28	'disturbance'	Greek Exercises, vol. 1, *Collected Papers*
p. 30	'on another'	*Autobiography*, vol. 1, p. 56
p. 30	on Sunday, 18 May	A Locked Diary, vol. 1, *Collected Papers*
p. 30	his writing style	ed. Josephine Piercy, *Writers at Work*, p. 11

Two: Angels and embryos

The best portraits of Oxford and Cambridge in the 1890s, and of Russell's friends at Trinity, include: *The Edwardians*, J. B. Priestley (1970); *Alfred North Whitehead*, 2 volumes, Victor Lowe (Baltimore 1985, 1990); *G. E. Moore and the Cambridge Apostles*, Paul Levy (1979); *Bloomsbury's Prophet*, Tom Regan (Philadelphia 1986); *J. McT. E. McTaggart*, G. Lowes Dickinson (Cambridge 1931); *Gilbert Murray*, Duncan Wilson (Oxford 1987); *Unfinished*

Autobiography, Gilbert Murray (1960); *Gilbert Murray*, Francis West (1984); *A Number of People*, Edward Marsh (1939); *Clever Hearts, Desmond and Molly MacCarthy*, Hugh and Mirabel Cecil (1990); *Goldsworthy Lowes Dickinson*, E. M. Forster (1934); *An Autobiography and other Essays*, G. M. Trevelyan (1949); *Men and Memories*, William Rothenstein (1931); *Persons and Places*, George Santayana (Boston 1986); *The Middle Span*, George Santayana (1947); *The Letters of George Santayana*, ed. Daniel Cory (1956); *Remembering my Good Friends*, Mary Agnes Hamilton (1944); *Memoirs of 60 Years at Eton, Cambridge and Elsewhere*, Oscar Browning (1910); *Selected Letters, vols. 1 and 2*, E. M. Forster, ed. Mary Largo and P. N. Furbank (1985); *E. M. Forster: A Life*, vols. 1 and 2, P. N. Furbank (1977–8); *Roger Fry: Letters*, ed. Denys Sutton (1972); *Lytton Strachey*, vols. 1 and 2, Michael Holroyd (1967–8); *Spinsters of this Parish: The Life and Times of F. M. Mayor and Mary Sheepshanks*, Sybil Oldfield (1984); *Gathering up the Threads*, Florence Ada Keynes (1950); *John Maynard Keynes*, Robert Skidelsky, vols. 1 and 2 (1983); *My Early Beliefs*, Maynard Keynes (1949); *John Maynard Keynes*, Charles H. Hession (1984).

p. 33	At the beginning	*Gathering up the Threads*, Florence Ada Keynes
p. 33	'boys and young'	*J. M. Keynes*, C. H. Hession
p. 33	On 20 November	*A Locked Diary*, p. 57
p. 34	'to find myself'	*Portraits from Memory*, p. 10
p. 34	'neither stared at'	*My Mental Development*, p. 41
p. 35	one of these was Charles Sanger	*Lytton Strachey*, Michael Holroyd
p. 36	A mutual friend	*A Number of People*, Edward Marsh
p. 36	There is a charming	*McTaggart*, G. Lowes Dickinson, p. 67
p. 37	something of a fop	Edith Russell, unpublished notes
p. 39	'our common bond'	*Lytton Strachey*, Michael Holroyd, vol. 1, p. 160
p. 40	'absolute candour'	*Whitehead*, V. Lowe, vol. 1, p. 115
p. 40	'less and less'	*Autobiography*, p. 64
p. 41	'the soul'	*Autobiography*, G. Lowes Dickinson, p. 68
p. 42	'I am most awfully'	*Autobiography*, Whitehead, p. 70
p. 42	'Hurrah'	Crompton Llewelyn Davies to BR, 9 March 1892
p. 42	'greatest happiness'	*Autobiography*, p. 91
p. 42	'instead of finding'	BR to Rollo, 1 May 1892
p. 44	He was at last	*My Life and Adventures*, Frank Russell, p. 105
p. 46	'Although he was'	*Listener*, 30 April 1959

p. 46	'whipped us up'	*A Number of People*, Edward Marsh, p. 56
p. 48	'I think I am'	BR to Rollo, 21 May 1893
p. 48	'artful dodges'	*Portraits from Memory*, p. 15
p. 49	having decided	*My Philosophical Development*, p. 29
p. 49	'fantastic world'	Ibid.
p. 51	Hegel, the patriotic	*History of Western Philosophy*, p. 701
p. 51	He threw his tobacco	*Autobiography*, vol. 1, p. 127
p. 52	'reverence for Christ'	BR to Alys, 2 Feb 1894
p. 52	'As I grew fonder'	Greek Exercises, vol. 1, *Collected Papers*
p. 54	'It was with'	*My Philosophical Development*, p. 28

Three: Alys

The fullest and best account of Alys's life and family appears in *Remarkable Relations*, Barbara Strachey (1980). Others in which the family appear include: *Unforgotten Years*, Logan Pearsall Smith (1938); *A Portrait of Logan Pearsall Smith*, John Russell (New York 1950); *Julia: a portrait*, Frances Partridge (1983); *A Self-Portrait*, Mary Berenson, ed. Barbara Strachey and Jayne Samuels (1983) ; *Sunset and Twilight*, Bernard Berenson Diaries, ed. Nicky Mariano (1964); *Selected Letters*, Bernard Berenson, ed. A. K. McComb (1965); *Berenson: a Biography*, Sylvia Sprigge (1960).

p. 57	'one of the most beautiful'	*The Bulletin*, 10 May 1921
p. 57	'I felt'	*Autobiography*, vol. 1, p. 76.
p. 57	'small, dark'	*People and Places*, G. Santayana, p. 440
p. 58	'The greatest day'	Journal, 12 Aug. 1893
p. 60	Alys replied	*Remarkable Relations*, Barbara Strachey, p. 130
p. 61	'world of Young Women'	Maude Stanley to BR, 11 May 1894
p. 62	'I am glad'	Hannah Pearsall Smith to Alys, 7 Mar. 1886
p. 63	'Yes, I *do*'	Logan Pearsall Smith to BR, 2 Dec. 1893
p. 63	'to acquire a habit'	BR to Alys, 17 Nov. 1893
p. 63	'I feel as though'	Journal, 20 July 1894
p. 64	'sighs, tears, groans'	*Autobiography*, p. 84
p. 65	'Intellect is'	BR to Alys, 6 Oct. 1894
p. 67	'I never mind'	Alys to BR, 14 Nov. 1894
p. 68	'I *shall* be glad'	BR to Alys, 15 Oct. 1894
p. 69	presents poured into	*A Quaker Wedding*, Sheila Turcon Russell. The Journal of the Bertrand Russell Archives. Winter 1983/4, p. 103

p. 71	'synthesis'	*Autobiography*, vol. 1, p. 125
p. 72	But the two men	BR to Bob Trevelyan, 6 Nov. 1896
p. 73	'It was announced'	Alys to Mary MacKall Gwinn, 10 Oct. 1895
p. 73	'fiery revolutionaries'	*Autobiography*, vol. 1, p. 126
p. 75	The book was widely reviewed	*German Social Democracy*, Bertrand Russell (Kenneth Blackwell, *Russell* 1976)
p. 76	'Bertie I find'	Helen Thomas to Mildred Minturn, 23 July 1897
p. 77	the author's 'mathematical'	*Science*, 24 Sept. 1897
p. 78	'associated with'	BR to Ottoline Morrell, 14 Dec. 1911
p. 78	'As for you'	Lady Russell to Alys, 11 Aug. 1896
p. 79	'He has a passion'	BR to Alys, 31 Mar. 1898
p. 79	'The Russells are'	*Diaries*, Beatrice Webb, 1 July 1901
p. 81	'the most perfect'	BR to G. E. Moore, 14 Oct. 1898

Four: Aristoteles Secundus

A great many books have been written about Beatrice Webb and the Fabians; the following touch on the Russells: *Our Partnership*, Beatrice Webb (1984); *Diaries*, 4 volumes, Beatrice Webb (1982–1985); *Letters, Beatrice and Sidney Webb* (1978); *Sidney and Beatrice Webb*, Mary Agnes Hamilton (1933); *This Little Band of Prophets*, Anne Freemantle (1966); *The Webbs and their Work*, ed. Margaret Cole (1949); *An Epic of Clare Market*, Janet Beveridge (1960); *Bernard Shaw*, 2 volumes, Michael Holroyd (1988–9); *The Genius of Shaw*, Michael Holroyd (1979); *The Life of H. G. Wells*, Norman and Jeanne Mackenzie (1987); *Experiment in Autobiography*, H. G. Wells (1934); *The Wheels of Chance*, H. G. Wells (1914); *The Haunted Mind*, Hallam Tennyson (1984); *An American Saga*, James Thomas Flexner (Boston 1984).

p. 83	'Moore and I'	BR to Alys, 16 April 1897
p. 85	'a great liberation'	*My Philosophical Beliefs*, p. 48
p. 85	'I don't know'	BR to Bradley, 30 Jan. 1914
p. 86	'La philosophie'	BR to Couturat, 18 Dec. 1899
p. 88	'rightly viewed'	The Study of Mathematics, *Collected Papers*, vol. 12, p. 86
p. 91	'Your tragedy'	BR to Murray, 26 Feb 1901
p. 91	'a sort of epoch'	Murray to BR, 2 Mar. 1901
p. 91	'the sense of solitude'	*Autobiography*, vol. 1, p. 146
p. 97	'I have been so long'	BR to Alys, 9 May 1902
p. 97	'heartiest'	Quoted Lowe, *Whitehead*, vol. 1, p. 273
p. 101	'We thus earned'	BR to Lucy Donnelly, 18 Oct. 1909

p. 103	'I used to know'	*Autobiography*, vol. 1, p. 66
p. 105	In October 1901	What shall I read? *Collected Papers*, vol. 11, p. 345
p. 105	'The house'	BR to Murray, 28 Dec. 1902
p. 106	'If only'	BR to Alys, 27 June 1902
p. 106	'Personally'	*An American Saga*, James Flexner, p. 300
p. 107	'I went out bicycling'	*Autobiography*, vol. 1, p. 147
p. 107	'And then in the bedroom'	Journal, 18 May 1903, *Collected Papers*
p. 107	'small and thin'	'Memoir of Alys Russell', Florence Halévy, unpublished
p. 108	'Bertie is grown'	*Diary*, Mary Berenson, 25 June 1902
p. 109	'I have given her'	*Diary*, Beatrice Webb, 21 July 1902
p. 110	'It is ghastly'	BR to Lucy Donnelly, 19 July 1903
p. 110	Many years later	Ann Synge to author, 3 May 1989
p. 111	'the last sacrifice'	Quoted B. Strachey, *Remarkable Relations*, p. 220
p. 111	'Dr Savage'	Journal, *Collected Papers*, 13 March 1903
p. 111	'in return'	Ibid.

Five: A secret worship of the same goals

Dozens, possibly hundreds, of books have been written about Bloomsbury. Some of those bearing on the Russells include: *Old Friends*, Clive Bell (1956); *Victorian Bloomsbury*, S. P. Rosenbaum (1987); *The Bloomsbury Group*, S. P. Rosenbaum (1975); *The Bloomsbury Group*, J. K. Johnstone (1954); *Bloomsbury: A House of Lions*, Leon Edel (1979); *The Flowers of the Forest*, David Garnett (1955); *Bloomsbury*, Quentin Bell (1968); *Sowing* and *Beginning Again*, two volumes of the autobiography of Leonard Woolf (1960 and 1964); *The Letters* and *The Diaries* of Virginia Woolf; *Virginia Woolf*, Quentin Bell, 2 volumes (1972); *Brett*, Sean Hignett (1984).

p. 112	'London is a weary'	BR to Murray, 12 Dec. 1902
p. 112	'I have been'	BR to Murray, 21 Mar. 1903
p. 112	'Two things'	BR to Lucy Donnelly, 23 May 1903
p. 114	'I am grieved'	BR to Murray, 16 Dec. 1902
p. 114	'The world'	BR to Dickinson, July 1903
p. 116	'with passion'	Quoted in *Mysticism and Logic*, p. 41
p. 117	'only great one'	Dickinson to BR, 17 Feb 1903
p. 117	'sneering and laughing'	Lucy Donnelly to Helen Thomas, 21 Dec. 1903
p. 117	'Tragedy is a pose'	*Diary*, Beatrice Webb, 18 Dec. 1903

p. 117	'The fire and inspiration'	Journal, 27 Jan. 1903
p. 119	'elusive colt'	Quoted Holroyd, *Strachey*, p. 129
p. 120	'We were intellectuals'	Quoted Edel, *Bloomsbury*
p. 121	'circumstances are'	BR to Murray, 3 Apr. 1902
p. 122	'I think your book'	Quoted Rosenbaum, *Bloomsbury's Prophet*, p. 19
p. 123	'with the tenacity'	*Beginning Again*, Leonard Woolf, p. 34
p. 127	'He is very ill'	Journal, 20 Nov. 1902
p. 128	'I feel as if'	BR to E. Trevelyan, 26 Dec. 1906
p. 128	'were chewed over'	Julian Trevelyan to author, 2 July 1987
p. 128	'One comes to feel'	BR to Lucy Donnelly, 1 July 1904
p. 128	'I enjoyed'	Forster to Alys, 30 Oct. 1906
p. 129	'kindly humour'	BR to Lucy Donnelly, 8 Feb. 1905
p. 130	'I wonder how'	Journal, *Collected Papers*, 26 July 1903
p. 131	'He was extraordinary'	Fry to Dickinson, 27 July 1905
p. 131	'Crompton's sorrow'	BR to Lucy Donnelly, 3 Aug. 1905
p. 131	'I can't hear'	Mary Sheepshanks to BR, 21 Sep. 1905

Six: A razor to chop wood

p. 133	'Oxford people'	Alys to BR, 1 Mar. 1904
p. 133	The architect . . . was asked	Grattan-Guinness, *Russell* Spring 1974, vol. 13
p. 134	'wonderful vision'	Alys to Lucy Donnelly, 30 May 1905
p. 134	'It was all'	L. Pearsall Smith to Hannah, 17 Jan. 1903
p. 135	'not quite'	*Autobiography*, vol. 1, p. 80
p. 136	'benevolent hawk'	Quoted *The Webbs and their Work*, ed. Margaret Cole, p. 121
p. 138	'I think Shaw'	BR to Lucy Donnelly, 30 July 1904
p. 138	'good instrument'	*Diary*, B. Webb, 28 Feb. 1902
p. 141	'probably the deepest'	*Daily News*, 6 Jan 1904
p. 142	'The idiocy'	BR to Elie Halévy, 19 July 1903
p. 143	according to her son	Hallam Tennyson to author, 8 June 1989
p. 145	'I detest'	BR to M. Llewelyn Davies, 4 June 1906
p. 145	'You see what faith'	M. Llewelyn Davies to BR, 4 May 1906
p. 146	'It is a howling'	BR to Ivy Pretious, 1 May 1907
p. 146	'pair of more'	G. Trevelyan to BR, 23 May 1907

p. 148   'I wonder whether'   BR to Helen Thomas, 27 Oct. 1909
p. 149   'All the brains'   BR to Lucy Donnelly, 2 Jan. 1910
p. 149   'had its funeral'   BR to O. Morrell, 5 Feb. 1916
p. 150   'flirts very charmingly'   BR to Lucy Donnelly, 1 Aug. 1904
p. 150   'My impression'   Journal, 3 Apr. 1905
p. 151   'I feel increasingly'   BR to Lucy Donnelly, 10 Nov. 1905
p. 152   'Little duties'   Alys Russell, unpublished diary, 29
                                     June 1907

Seven: Russell in love

Ottoline and Philip Morrell appear, both as themselves and as fiction, in the following: *Ottoline: the Early Memoirs of Lady Ottoline Morrell* and *Ottoline at Garsington*, ed. Robert Gathorne Hardy (1963 and 1974); *Lady Ottoline's Album* (1976); *Crome Yellow*, Aldous Huxley (1921); *Women in Love*, D. H. Lawrence (1921); *Pugs and Peacocks*, Gilbert Cannan; *Autobiography*, Enid Bagnold (1969); *Aldous Huxley*, 2 volumes, Sybil Bedford (1973).

Books on Joseph Conrad include: *Joseph Conrad*, Roger Tennant (1981); *Conrad and his World*, Norman Sherry (1972); *Joseph Conrad*, Zdzistaw Najder (Cambridge 1983); *Joseph Conrad: the Three Lives*, Frederick Karl (New York 1979).

Of the many books on Wittgenstein, the following are useful in the context of Russell: *Ludwig Wittgenstein: the duty of genius*, Ray Monk (1990); *Ludwig Wittgenstein: Letters to Russell, Keynes and Moore*, ed. von Wright and B. F. McGuinness (Oxford 1974); *Ludwig Wittgenstein: A Memoir*, Norman Malcolm (Oxford 1985); *Wittgenstein*, Anthony Kenny (1973). There is also Norbert Wiener's *I am a mathematician*.

p. 155   'I don't think'   Journal, O. Morrell, 19 Sept. 1902
p. 155   'The nine years'   *Autobiography*, vol. 1, p. 203
p. 156   'exactly timed'   *Lytton Strachey*, Holroyd, vol. 2, p. 177
p. 157   'massive projecting'   *Crome Yellow*, Aldous Huxley, p. 10
p. 159   'How can you'   BR to Ottoline, 22 Mar. 1911
p. 159   'Life is like'   BR to Ottoline, 3 Apr. 1911
p. 159   'O my heart'   BR to Ottoline, 29 May 1911
p. 159   'You are the most'   Ottoline to BR, 23 March 1911
p. 159   'remain in my memory'   *Autobiography*, vol. 1, p. 204
p. 160   'noble, great-winged'   L. Pearsall Smith to Helen Thomas, 7
                                     Dec. 1902
p. 161   'I want to'   BR to Ottoline, 29 May 1911
p. 161   'twin souls'   Ottoline to BR, 20 July 1911
p. 161   'frenzy of Bertie's meteor' Journal, O. Morrell, 26 May 1911
p. 164   'rather rampant'   Mary Pearsall Smith to Berenson, 21
                                     Dec. 1899

p. 164	'married very young'	Alys to Mary Berenson 14 June 1911
p. 164	'Caring is not'	Alys to B. Webb, 2 Sep. 1911
p. 165	'If Alys had to'	BR to Ottoline, 27 Sep. 1911
p. 166	The record Julia left	*Julia*, ed. Frances Partridge
p. 168	'See if there is'	Murray to BR, 12 Sep. 1912
p. 169	'I feel'	BR to L. Donnelly, 19 Dec. 1912
p. 170	'began as my pupil'	*The Listener*, 10 Feb. 1955
p. 173	'Have you heard'	L. Strachey to Keynes, 13 Nov. 1912
p. 174	'like great music'	BR to Ottoline, 18 Nov. 1912
p. 176	'My day passes'	Wittgenstein to BR, 15 Dec. 1913
p. 178	'keen, cold'	Wiener to his father, 1 Oct. 1913
p. 178	His landlady	*Ex-prodigy*, Wiener, p. 186

Eight: Imprisoned voices

Russell's many trips to America are covered in two volumes of *Bertrand Russell's America*, by Barry Feinberg and Ronald Kasrils. (1973 and 1984). Edith Finch wrote a biography of *Carey Thomas of Bryn Mawr* (New York 1947). The following books are also useful: *The Light of Experience* (Francis Younghusband 1927); *The Education of Henry Adams*, Henry Adams (New York 1906); and *Outlines of Philosophy*, Will Durant (1947).

p. 179	'You have released'	BR to Ottoline, 30 Mar. 1911
p. 182	' "Prisons" was wrong'	BR to Ottoline, 11 Feb. 1912
p. 183	'I have loved a ghost'	*Autobiography*, vol. 2, p. 38
p. 185	As he talked	*Portraits from Memory*, p. 82
p. 185	'I loved him'	BR to Ottoline, 11 Sep. 1913
p. 186	'As for the strange'	BR to Watts, Oct. 1961
p. 188	'Something passed'	BR to Ottoline, 21 Feb. 1912
p. 189	'Learn not to'	BR to Ottoline, 25 June 1913
p. 190	'Bertie has gone'	Journal, O. Morrell, 29 Aug. 1917
p. 191	'fat, florid'	*Persons and Places*, Santayana, p. 476
p. 193	'I cannot be certain'	BR to Mildred Minturn, 23 Dec. 1913
p. 196	'a greater natural'	*The Light of Experience*, Francis Younghusband, p. 220
p. 197	'From one point'	Lowes Dickinson to Fry, 1 Nov. 1901
p. 198	'cogency . . . certitude'	*Evening Transcript*, Boston, 10 Apr. 1914
p. 198	'against Wilson'	BR to M. Llewelyn Davies, 12 Apr. 1914
p. 200	'He seems'	BR to Barry Fox, 27 Nov. 1927
p. 200	'nobody here broods'	BR to Ottoline, 19 Mar. 1914
p. 201	'I wonder whether'	BR to L. Donnelly, 6 June 1914

Nine: Beetles and brothers

Of the many excellent books on the First World War and the pacifists, these are those most relevant to Russell: *The Abolition of War*, Keith Robbins (1976); *Bertrand Russell and the Pacifists in the First World War*, Jo Vellacott (1980); *The Hound of Conscience*, Thomas C. Kennedy (Arkansas 1981); *The Troublemakers*, A. J. P. Taylor (1957); *The Life of Edward Grubb*, James Dudley (1946).

Books on T. S. and Vivienne Eliot and their friendship with Russell include: *T. S. Eliot: a memoir*, Robert Sencourt (1971); *Eliot's Early Years*, and *Eliot's New Life*, by Lyndall Gordon (Oxford 1977 and 1988); *The Letters of T. S. Eliot*, vol. 1, ed. Valerie Eliot (1988); *Selected Essays*, T. S. Eliot (New York 1932); *T. S. Eliot*, Peter Ackroyd (1984).

Books on D. H. Lawrence include: *D. H. Lawrence's Letters to Bertrand Russell*, ed. Harry T. Moore (New York 1948); *D. H. Lawrence's Nightmare*, Paul Delany (1979); those on Katherine Mansfield, *A Secret Life*, Claire Tomalin (1987); *The Life of Katherine Mansfield*, Antony Alpers (1980); *Collected Letters of Katherine Mansfield*, ed. Vincent O'Sullivan and Margaret Scott (1984 and 1987).

p. 203	'My life before 1910'	*Autobiography*, vol. 2, p. 15
p. 204	'I am fixing some'	BR to Ottoline, 2 Aug. 1914
p. 206	'I protest against'	*Nation*, 15 August 1914
p. 206	'It is impossible'	BR to L. Donnelly, 22 Aug. 1914
p. 206	'I don't understand'	Moore to MacCarthy, 15 Nov. 1914
p. 207	'a snivelling sentimental '	BR to L. Donnelly, 14 Dec. 1914
p. 207	'Even here among'	Dora Sanger to BR, 7 Aug. 1914
p. 207	'Our job is'	Quoted *Shaw*, Holroyd, vol. 2, p. 351
p. 208	'I broke her heart'	*Autobiography*, vol. 1, p. 214
p. 209	'Just now it is dreary'	BR to Perry, 26 Feb. 1915
p. 211	'My approach'	Royden Harrison interview with BR, 19 Jan. 1967
p. 211	'Now that war'	BR to Chester Reed, 24 Nov. 1914
p. 213	'the dominating mind'	*Remembering Good Friends*, Mary Agnes Hamilton, p. 75
p. 216	'She was beautiful'	Enid Bagnold to Ronald Clark, 30 July 1974
p. 219	'I often wonder'	Eliot to BR, 11 Jan. 1916
p. 220	'I am not in love'	BR to Colette O'Niel, 1 Jan. 1918
p. 221	'much more important'	Eliot to J. H. Woods, 21 Apr. 1919
p. 223	'truths and values'	*Beginning Again*, L. Woolf, p. 20
p. 224	'double . . .'	*Autobiography*, E. Bagnold, p. 111
p. 225	'hopped about'	Lady Huxley to author, 10 Mar. 1987
p. 227	'smoking Russian'	*Autobiography*, vol. 2, p. 53

p. 228	'small . . . her sleek'	*Brett*, Hignet, p. 17
p. 230	'vivifying dose'	*Autobiography*, vol. 2, p. 23
p. 230	'see through'	BR to Ottoline, 29 May 1915
p. 231	Julian would remember	Julian Vinogradoff to author, 20 July 1987
p. 231	'It is so wrong'	Lawrence to David Garnett, 19 Apr. 1916
p. 233	'terrified of what'	Lawrence to BR, 16 Aug. 1916
p. 233	'They are static'	Lawrence to Lady Cynthia Asquith, 16 Aug. 1915
p. 235	'the bloodless'	Sidney Dark, *Daily Express*, 13 Nov. 1916
p. 238	'He has the tongue'	*Political Quarterly*, vol. 39, 1968, p. 343

Ten: A still small voice

Additional material on the First World War, and in particular on the No-Conscription Fellowship (NCF), is to be found in: *Clifford Allen: the Open Conspirator*, Arthur Marwick (1964); *Plough my own Furrow: the story of Lord Allen of Hurtwood*, Martin Gilbert (1965); *Catherine Marshall, C. K. Ogden and Mary Sargant Florence*, eds. Margaret Kamester and Jo Vellacott (1987); *The Conscientious Objector and the Community*, A. Fenner Brockway (1943); *War and the Image of Germany*, Stuart Wallace (1988); *A Mathematician's Apology* , G. H. Hardy (Cambridge 1940); *Bertrand Russell and Trinity*, G. H. Hardy (Cambridge 1970).

Constance Malleson (Colette O'Niel) wrote several volumes of autobiography: *After Ten Years* (1931); *The Coming Back* (1933); and *In the North* (1946). Portraits of her are to be found in *Half My Days and Nights*, Hubert Nicholson (1941); *Actress*, Vere Arnot (1936) and by Bennitt Gardiner in *Russell* autumn/winter 1976.

p. 241	'There is no more'	*Labour Leader*, 6 Jan. 1916
p. 242	'I have given up'	BR to L. Donnelly, 10 Feb. 1916
p. 243	'a strikingly handsome'	*Remembering Good Friends*, Hamilton, p. 116
p. 243	'intellectual, pietist'	*Diary*, Beatrice Webb, vol. 3, 8 Apr. 1916
p. 246	'poisonous and pestilential'	*Daily Express*, 28 Jan. 1916
p. 247	'Martyrdom'	Shaw to BR, 18 Apr. 1916
p. 248	Garsington became	*Ottoline at Garsington*, p. 51
p. 249	Eliot and Lytton	Naomi Bentwich to friend, 17 Apr. 1916
p. 251	'total exemption'	BR to Catherine Marshall, 11 Apr. 1916

p. 251	'We who believe'	BR to Murray, 17 Apr. 1916
p. 251	'at last perfectly'	quoted *Lytton Strachey*, Holroyd, vol. 2, p. 174
p. 254	'I think you have'	Woods to BR, 21 Mar. 1916
p. 255	'What brings us'	Hilton Young, *Cambridge Magazine,* 14 Oct. 1916
p. 256	'I find I should'	BR to Ottoline, 24 Dec. 1912
p. 257	'forlorn, indeed,'	Lowes Dickinson to Janet Ashbee, 4 Nov. 1914
p. 257	he believed that	A. C. Pigou, *Nation*, Feb. 1915
p. 259	'You and I'	General Cockerill to BR, quoted *Autobiography*, vol. 2, p. 72
p. 260	'a small man'	*After Ten Years*, Colette O'Niel, p. 104
p. 260	A Zeppelin	*Autobiography*, vol. 2, p. 26
p. 262	She likened herself	Unpublished introduction to Letters of Colette O'Niel, Phyllis Urch
p. 262	'You can fill me'	BR to Colette, 1 Oct. 1916
p. 265	Colette, delighted	Unpublished introduction to Letters, Phyllis Urch
p. 270	'your manner'	BR to Catherine Marshall, 3 May 1917 (not sent)
p. 271	'regard Bertie'	Frances Ronald to author, 22 Sept. 1987
p. 273	'There is nothing further'	Robert Graves to BR, 21 July 1917
p. 273	'To friends'	Graves to Eva Morgan, 19 July 1917
p. 274	'emotional'	*Beginning Again*, L. Woolf, p. 211
p. 277	'Everything that I do'	BR to Ottoline, 2 July 1917

Eleven: Angular thoughts

p. 279	The Foreign Office	Public Records Office, N50 33159 17 REF 141 FO 395
p. 280	As he wrote	BR to Murray 15 Feb. 1918
p. 280	'teeth chattering with fury'	Strachey to Ottoline, 3 Mar. 1918
p. 280	'concentrated venom'	BR to Ottoline, 9 Feb. 1918
p. 281	In his diary	Clifford Allen Diary, 9 Feb. 1918
p. 281	'When I read'	Mansfield to Middleton Murry, 26 Feb. 1918
p. 283	Desmond MacCarthy	John Davidson, *Everybody's Weekly*, 10 Apr. 1954
p. 286	'I long for'	BR to Ottoline, 30 Aug. 1918
p. 288	'He is very childlike'	Allen Diary, 17 Sep. 1918
p. 288	To judge by a letter	*Russell*, no. 10, Summer 1973

p. 290	'Separation is a silly'	E. Whitehead to BR, 16 Oct. 1916
p. 293	'Why do you just'	F. Russell to BR, 15 Sep. 1920
p. 294	A letter arrived	Lowes Dickinson to BR, Armistice Day 1918.
p. 294	'When the war'	*Autobiography*, vol. 2, p. 40
p. 294	'Marsh is the kind'	BR to Ottoline, 27 Aug. 1918
p. 298	'I am writing'	Scott Nearing to BR, 16 Aug. 1918
p. 298	'The mind and soul'	Lowes Dickinson to BR, 2 Nov. 1919
p. 298	'I feel I would rather'	Lowes Dickinson to Keynes, 4 Dec. 1919
p. 300	'vanished like'	Quoted in Edel, *Bloomsbury*, p. 205

Twelve: Two things in the world, or three

Dora Russell wrote three volumes of autobiography – *The Tamarisk Tree* – of which the first two, *My Quest for Liberty and Love* (1975) and *My School and the Years of War* (1980) are particularly relevant to her years with Russell.
For Russell's journey through Russia: *Through Bolshevik Russia*, Mrs Philip Snowden (1920); and *The Truth about Soviet Russia*, by Sidney and Beatrice Webb (1942).

p. 302	She was the	*Tamarisk Tree*, Dora Russell, vol. 1
p. 304	'Life is good'	Dora to Ogden, 2 Sept. 1919
p. 306	'If Colette and I'	Dora to BR, 20 Feb. 1920
p. 306	'I suppose it would'	Wittgenstein to BR, 13 Mar. 1919
p. 307	'like the devil'	Dora to BR, 28 Dec. 1919
p. 308	'mystic ardour'	*Autobiography*, vol. 2, p. 101
p. 309	'Don't be discouraged'	BR to Wittgenstein, 21 Jun. 1919
p. 309	'All the refinement'	Wittgenstein to BR, 6 May 1920
p. 309	Russell 'is a terror'	Dora to Ogden, Dec. 1919 n.d.
p. 310	'I don't know how'	BR to Colette, 16 Jan. 1920
p. 311	'I'm alone'	Colette to BR, Mar. 1920
p. 314	'I felt him'	*Through Bolshevik Russia*, Snowden, p. 43
p. 314	'Very Napoleonic'	Journal, 17 May 1920
p. 314	'drab, monotonous'	*The Practice and Theory of Bolshevism*, p. 97
p. 314	One of the delegation	*Born for Trouble*, M. Harrison, p. 210
p. 317	'I loathed'	BR to Colette, 25 June 1920
p. 318	'I have returned'	BR to Murray, 2 Aug. 1920
p. 320	'The best for me'	Wittgenstein to BR, 7 July 1920
p. 321	'Aristocracy'	Dora to BR, 29 July 1920
p. 323	'e.g. Winston'	BR to Elizabeth Russell, 16 Feb. 1921

p. 324	'ultimate source'	*Political Ideals*, 1917
p. 324	'Peking is beautiful'	BR to Colette, 8 Jan. 1920
p. 325	'We live here'	Dora to Ogden, 20 Jan. 1920
p. 325	Of her love	*Tamarisk Tree*, vol. 1, p. 121
p. 326	'amiable old'	BR to Elizabeth Russell, 16 Feb. 1920
p. 326	'Young China'	Dora to Lady Black, 21 Jan. 1921
p. 327	'soft and squashy'	Ibid., 12 Dec. 1920
p. 327	The foreign community	*Tamarisk Tree*, vol. 1, p. 116
p. 327	'They are mostly'	BR to Colette, 3 Dec. 1920
p. 328	to his children	John Dewey, 26 Oct. 1921
p. 328	'The state of the world'	BR to Colette, 16 Feb. 1921
p. 329	'doctrinaire dreamer'	*Sunday Express*, 8 May 1921
p. 330	'We are perfectly'	Dora to Lady Black, 30 May 1921
p. 330	'When I come'	BR to Colette, 27 Apr. 1921
p. 332	Above all, he urged	*The Problem of China*, p. 249

Thirteen: A watchman, telling of the night

Russell's daughter Katharine Tait has written an autobiography, *My Father Bertrand Russell* (1976), which gives an excellent picture of her childhood. *The Truth about a Publisher*, by Sir Stanley Unwin (1960), fills in details about Russell's non-academic work.

p. 334	Russell justified	BR to Rachel Brooks, 13 May 1922
p. 335	'snug and happy'	Elizabeth Russell to K. Mansfield, 7 Nov. 1921
p. 336	'The little boy'	BR to Wittgenstein, 9 May 1922
p. 336	'I have never'	*Portraits from Memory*, p. 85
p. 338	'Wittgenstein was witty'	Diary, Irina Strickland, May 1952
p. 338	'sensitive intelligence'	*Memoirs*, Gerhardi, p. 260
p. 338	'we struck out'	*Diaries*, V. Woolf, 3 Dec. 1921
p. 339	'He was too disconcerting'	*Pugs and Peacocks*, Gilbert Cannan, p. 2
p. 343	'My practice'	BR to Unwin, 16 Dec. 1926
p. 343	'cultivated old-fashioned'	BR to Josephine Piercy, 6 Aug. 1925
p. 345	'I am *most* anxious'	BR to Ogden, 7 May 1919
p. 345	so-called 'lucidity'	*Criterion*, Aug. 1927, p. 177
p. 346	'It is, in fact'	*ABC of Atoms*, p. 7
p. 349	'Never in all my'	BR to L. Donnelly, 3 June 1924
p. 349	'desert, though'	BR to Eliot, 12 June 1924
p. 350	From the point of view	*New Leader*, 22 Aug. 1924
p. 350	'strangely excited'	B. Webb, quoted Clark, p. 406
p. 351	'To the intellectual'	*Dial*, Dec. 1927
p. 354	'a strong movement'	BR to Upton Sinclair, 23 Nov. 1924

p. 354   'Hooray!'   H. G. Wells to Dora, 14 Oct. 1926
p. 357   'I have known'   Public Records Office, FO 371/102L4
                                      and FO 3166/19/10
p. 357   'The British in China'   *Nation*, 2 Mar. 1927
p. 359   'I am persuaded'   E. Russell to K. Mansfield, 28 Aug.
                                      1922

Fourteen: A benign and dancing presence

Descriptions of Beacon Hill School and the Russells' views on education appear in the following books: *Confessions and Impressions*, Ethel Mannin (1930); *Young in the Twenties*, Ethel Mannin (1971); *A Gallery of Women*, James Wedgewood Drawbell (1933); *The Modern Schools' Handbook*, ed. Trevor Blewitt; Unpublished memoir by Zora Schaupp Lasch (1980); *Summerhill*, A. S. Neill (1962); *Neill of Summerhill*, Jonathan Croall (1983). There is also a portrait of Russell by Lyndal Passerini Hopkinson in *Nothing to Forgive* (1988).

p. 360   'Children are'   BR to Helen Thomas, Oct. 1904
p. 360   John's earliest memory   John Russell to author, 29 Oct. 1987
p. 362   'The children were'   *A personal record*, Colette O'Niel, p. 311
p. 363   For Polly Allen   Polly Allen to author, 9 Sep. 1987
p. 364   'Both children'   BR to Lucy Silcox, 27 Aug. 1925
p. 364   'humiliation and despair'   *My Father Bertrand Russell*, Katharine
                                      Tait, p. 36
p. 364   'he never gave enough'   John Russell to author, 29 Oct. 1987
p. 367   The spirit behind   Michael Duane to author, 5 May 1990
p. 368   'I suppose they only'   BR to Unwin, 23 June 1032
p. 368   'to those who'   Agatha Russell to BR, August 1926
p. 370   Cruelty   *On Education*, p. 24
p. 373   Dora's idea   'What was Beacon Hill School?' Dora
                                      Russell, unpublished paper
p. 377   a woman teacher   *Weekly Illustrated*, 22 Apr. 1936
p. 379   The reactions   Polly Allen to author, 9 Sep. 1987
p. 380   science was taught   Richard Garnett to author, 4 Jan. 1990
p. 380   'There was no special'   K. Tait to author, 23 July 1987
p. 380   Barbara Hubbard   *Times Educational Supplement*, 25 July
                                      1975
p. 381   'At the moment'   BR to Unwin, 2 Sep. 1927
p. 382   'socialism run mad'   *Evening Standard*, 8 May 1929
p. 383   'I can only understand'   BR to Braithwaite, 8 May 1930
p. 385   He praised the country   *New York Times*, 25 May 1927
p. 386   The American mothers   BR to Rachel Brooks, 5 May 1930
p. 386   'He is pure German'   BR to Dora, 1 Oct. 1929

p. 387   'It was a pity'   BR to Ottoline, Mar. 1931

p. 389   'Yesterday evening'   BR to Miriam Brudno, 5 Dec. 1931

p. 389   'bleating like a sheep'   *Nothing to Forgive*, Lyndal Passerini Hopkinson, p. 56

p. 390   Fathers cannot   *The Conquest of Happiness*, p. 206

p. 390   'I feel you despise'   BR to Dora, 20 Oct. 1927

p. 390   'I somehow keep feeling'   Dora to BR, 23 Feb. 1928

p. 390   'O my darling'   Dora to BR, 23 Aug. 1928

p. 392   'I want to grow old'   BR to Dora, 29 Nov. 1931

Fifteen: A nice clean sty

Personal Record: 1920–1972, by Gerald Brenan (1974), and *Odyssey of a Liberal*, Freda Utley (Washington 1970) are useful for this chapter.

p. 395   By July   Dora to BR, 25 July 1932

p. 395   'spread your love'   *Tamarisk Tree*, Dora Russell, p. 245

p. 395   'Do try to divest'   BR to Dora, 4 Mar. 1933

p. 396   'I will never concede'   BR to Crompton Llewelyn Davies, 21 Sep. 1932

p. 398   Parents were canvassed   Jack Pritchard to author, 26 June 1990

p. 398   Russell, meanwhile,   Lady Juliette Huxley to author, 15 Mar. 1987

p. 400   'I am quite unrepentant'   Dora to BR, quoted *Tamarisk Tree*, p. 253

p. 400   'terrific sexual'   *Odyssey of a Liberal*, Utley, p. 68.

p. 401   'whether it is'   Allen to V. Trubshawe, 10 Feb. 1933

p. 401   'If not, all the'   A. S. Neill to Dora, 28 Apr. 1932

p. 402   Former teachers   Kate Newman to author, 20 June 1990

p. 402   retains the clearest   Daphne Uribe to author, 16 Jan. 1990

p. 402   'Russell treats'   H. G. Wells to Dora, 16 July 1935

p. 403   Dora felt that it was   'What was Beacon Hill School?' Dora Russell, unpublished paper

p. 404   'Let there be'   *The Right to be Happy*, p. 239

p. 405   'I suppose you'   Colette to E. Russell, 2 Feb. 1936

p. 406   'overwhelmed by'   BR to G. Brenan, 20 Aug. 1934

p. 406   She was attractive   David Astor to author, 24 Apr. 1990

p. 407   'rather slinkily'   Frances Partridge to author, 4 June 1987

p. 407   Rossetti painting   F. Halévy, unpublished memoir

p. 408   'I have never'   BR to Murray, 22 Jan. 1935

p. 409   'Even more important'   *The Scientific Outlook*, p. 278

p. 409   'unbroken mood'   *Daily Telegraph*, 2 Oct. 1931

p. 410	'fantasia'	*Fortnightly Review*, Dec. 1934
p. 412	'becoming a slut'	Peter Russell to Ottoline, 13 Mar. 1936
p. 413	'concordat with Gandhi'	BR to Murray, 8 Mar. 1931
p. 413	'I do not like'	BR to Maurice Amos, 16 June 1930
p. 414	'is best served'	Peter Russell to Miss Gardiner, 10 Mar. 1938
p. 415	'a swine'	BR to Freda Utley, 9 July 1937
p. 417	Her grandson	Philip Goodman to author, 18 Oct. 1990
p. 419	'What a mournful'	P. Morrell to BR, 20 Aug. 1938
p. 419	'The man who'	*Personal Record*, G. Brenan, p. 254
p. 420	familiarity with the	L. Woolf to G. Brenan, 23 May 1933
p. 421	'were a butcher'	Curry to BR, 15 Feb. 1938
p. 422	'He talks'	Santayana to L. Pearsall Smith, 16 Jan. 1936
p. 422	'There was no side'	J. Urmson to author, 10 Jan. 1991
p. 423	'His life'	*Unpopular Essays*, p. 223

Sixteen: Desiccated, divorced and decadent

Russell's troubles at the New York City University are extensively covered in *Bertrand Russell's America*, vol. 1, ed. Barry Feinberg and Ronald Kasrils (1973), and in a pamphlet put out by the American Civil Liberties Union, as well as in the newspapers of the day.

Books on the Second World War include *Challenge of Conscience*, Denis Hayes (1949).

p. 425	'This university'	BR to Murray, 15 Jan. 1939
p. 425	'keen, almost sly'	W. S. Rochlen to Slezak, 30 July 1974
p. 426	'not careless'	Public Records Office, 710. 107248 n.d.
p. 427	'beastly'	*Autobiography*, vol. 2, p. 217
p. 427	'if the Germans'	BR to G. Cantel, 23 May 1937
p. 428	'I cannot resist'	BR to President Roosevelt, 15 Apr. 1939
p. 429	'like a strayed ghost'	BR to L. Donnelly, 22 Dec. 1939
p. 436	'However, what I'	*Autobiography*, vol. 2, p. 246
p. 438	'If you want'	A. Barnes to BR, 24 June 1940
p. 438	'Bertrand can put'	A. Barnes to Peter, 28 Aug. 1940
p. 439	'Never acquiesce'	*Reader's Digest*, Oct. 1941
p. 440	'I *can't* admire'	BR to Lucy Silcox, 9 May 1941
p. 444	'It is not growing'	BR to Murray, 9 Apr. 1943

p. 445	'I should like'	BR to Unwin, 24 Jan. 1941
p. 446	'Rip van Winkle'	BR to Gamel Brenan, 16 Aug. 1943
p. 446	'It is our duty'	'Can Americans and Britons be friends?' 17 Apr. 1944
p. 446	'I have much to say'	BR to Colette, 16 Aug. 1943

Seventeen: The way to a new paradise

p. 448	he noted that	*Reynolds News*, 23 July 1944
p. 448	'small and commonplace'	BR to Colette, 20 Sep. 1944
p. 449	'How Keynes'	BR to L. Donnelly, 7 Oct. 1944
p. 449	'quite un-Russell'	Maud Russell to Clive Bell, 20 May 1945
p. 449	'grows in wisdom'	BR to Miriam Brudno, 11 Oct. 1945
p. 450	'I have spent my'	Harriet Ward to author, 14 July 1987
p. 450	He felt vigorous	BR to R. Hambleton, 19 Nov. 1952
p. 450	'In the old days'	BR to T. S. Eliot, 13 June 1949
p. 451	'revelation of a mighty'	*Star*, 19 Nov. 1946
p. 452	'Everyone admits'	*My Philosophical Development*, p. 241
p. 455	'prolix and repetitive'	*Times Literary Supplement*, 5 Mar. 1949
p. 456	After this	H. Grisewood to author, 26 June 1990
p. 460	'He went far too'	Reith *Diaries*, 26 Dec. 1948
p. 463	Cooke had arranged to	*Six Men*, Alistair Cooke, chapter 6
p. 464	'America was beastly'	BR to R. Crawshay-Williams, 3 Dec. 1950
p. 464	his 1901 'conversion'	E. Jones to BR, 20 Jan. 1957
p. 465	'highest degree'	BR to Naomi Bentwich, 27 Feb. 1950
p. 465	While she was working	Theodore Birnberg to author, 29 Jan. 1990
p. 468	'If Russia overruns'	BR to Marseilles, 5 May 1948
p. 469	'an open instigator'	*Red Star*, Moscow, 28 Nov. 1948
p. 470	gloomy in the extreme	BR to Julie Medlock, 17 Feb. 1953
p. 474	The offer fitted	Joseph Rotblat to author, 11 Jan. 1990
p. 477	'As regards the H-bomb'	BR to Kingsley Martin, 8 Nov. 1957
p. 478	'righteously adamantine'	*Autobiography*, vol. 3, p. 102
p. 478	'other police states'	*Manchester Guardian*, 26 Mar. 1956
p. 478	Russell hit out again	*National Guardian*, 1 May 1956

Eighteen: A complicated cocoon

| p. 480 | 'and I reckon' | BR to Gamel Brenan, 29 Jan. 1951 |
| p. 481 | though she admired | G. Brenan quoted *Russell*, summer 1985 |

p. 483	to a friend	Colette to P. Urch, 21 May 1948
p. 483	'my brow is like'	Colette to N. Kielland, 20 Oct. 1949
p. 484	After the second	Phyllis Urch to author, 20 June 1989
p. 484	'I see everything'	Colette to BR, 30 Nov. 1949
p. 485	'It is just the fact'	Colette to Urch, 25 Sep. 1952
p. 486	After a lifetime	Barbara Strachey to author, 18 Mar. 1987
p. 487	'Bertie was an ideal'	*Autobiography*, vol. 3, p. 47
p. 488	'Thee may take'	Ann Synge to author, 3 May 1989
p. 489	The Russells had been	Mary and Julian Trevelyan to author 2 July 1987
p. 490	'By talking'	Peter to F. Utley, 16 Oct. 1949
p. 490	Later, she said	Conrad Russell to author, 10 Nov. 1989
p. 490	'a sick and feeble'	Colette to N. Kielland, 7 May 1950
p. 491	'As for love'	BR to Gamel Brenan, 7 July 1957
p. 492	'I am very happy'	BR to Gamel Brenan, 9 Aug. 1953
p. 492	'pretty flapper'	Colette to P. Urch, 23 Nov. 1952
p. 493	Russell had cut	'The experience of Age', R. Hambleton, 11 Nov. 1952
p. 493	'I have lived'	BR to Gamel Brenan, 5 Mar. 1947

Nineteen: Elephants playing dancing mice

The many books written about the Campaign for Nuclear Disarmament, the Committee of 100, and Russell's part in them include: *Voices from the Crowd*, ed. David Boulton (1964); *The Disarmers*, Christopher Driver (1964); *The Bomb*, ed. Gilbert McAllister (1955); *Mud Pie: the CND Story*, Herb Greer (1964); *The Protest Makers*, Richard Taylor and Colin Pritchard (1980); *Left, Left, Left*, Peggy Duff (1971); *Faith under Fire*, John Collins (1966); *Street-Fighting Years*, Tariq Ali (1987); *Chances*, Mervyn Jones (1987); *Father Figures*, Kingsley Martin (1966); *Einstein on Peace*, ed. Otto Nathan (1963).

p. 494	'a preface telling'	BR to Unwin, 26 June 1953
p. 494	'when logicians'	*Time* magazine, 8 Aug. 1955
p. 495	'incantations'	*New Statesman*, 24 May 1952
p. 496	'The best occupation'	*Life* magazine, 14 Jan. 1952
p. 500	Not all CND's	Sheila Jones to author, 30 Apr. 1990
p. 501	'sort of people'	*Daily Mail*, 4 Apr. 1958
p. 504	'bursting with energy'	*Autobiography*, vol. 3, p. 109
p. 505	'not appear to'	BR to Schoenman, 16 Aug. 1960
p. 506	He had read	Michael Foot to author, 30 Jan. 1990
p. 507	Five hours later	Doris Lessing to author, 20 Oct. 1990

p. 507	'a green bay tree'	*Faith under Fire*, p. 318
p. 508	Sitting for hours	Michael Randle to author, 20 Nov. 1988
p. 508	'No one knows'	*New Republic*, 3 Apr. 1961
p. 509	'I think . . . that the Committee	BR to Michael Randle, 10 Apr. 1961
p. 511	'not very well equipped'	Ernest Roedker to author, 25 Jan. 1990
p. 511	'We miss you'	BR to Schoenman, 20 Oct. 1961
p. 516	'Could you make'	BR to Khrushchev, 28 Oct. 1962
p. 516	'The great ones'	*The Life and Times of BR*, BBC film, 1964
p. 516	Further evidence	*View from the UN*, p. 172
p. 517	Advisers to Kennedy	Pierre Salinger to author, 30 Sep. 1990
p. 518	'the folly'	*Autobiography*, vol. 3, p. 125

Twenty: A delicious fresh breeze

Books dealing with the Vietnam War Crimes Tribunal include: *Against the Crime of Silence*, ed. John Duffett (1968); *Sartre: A life*, Annie Cohen-Solal (1987); *Simone de Beauvoir*, Deirdre Bair (1990); *All said and done*, Simone de Beauvoir (1974).

Portraits of Russell in these years are to be found in *The Pendulum Years*, Bernard Levin (1970); *Six Men*, Alistair Cooke (1978); *Intellectuals*, Paul Johnson (1988).

p. 520	'pervasive and systematic'	'Minority of One', 1963
p. 520	'very nasty'	*Autobiography*, vol. 3, p. 165
p. 521	'babbling'	*Los Angeles Times*, 20 Aug. 1965
p. 522	Their atrocities	*Frontier*, Sep. 1965
p. 522	'tetchy, intemperate'	*Sunday Times*, 29 Jan. 1967
p. 524	'A stir, a bustle'	*New York Times*, 19 Feb. 1967
p. 524	'frankly humanitarian'	Isaac Deutscher to BR, 22 Sep. 1966
p. 524	one side only	Staughton Lynd to BR, 30 Nov. 1960
p. 526	The story of Schoenman	Leo Matarasso to author, 14 Sep. 1990
p. 527	Feeling estranged	Tamara Deutscher to author, 3 Sep. 1988
p. 531	One idea was	P. Pottle to author, 5 June 1989
p. 532	Something of the cloak	Jon Halliday to author, 24 Jan. 1990
p. 535	'When we were'	Lord Fenner Brockway to author, 3 Oct. 1987
p. 536	In August 1966	Deborah Rogers to author, 11 Feb. 1989
p. 537	Even Russell's old	Professor Rotblat to author, 11 Jan. 1990

p. 539   He wrote a 7500-word   Edith Russell's notes on Clark
                                      biography; unpublished
p. 541   Well into the 1960s   Michael Burn to author, 25 Feb. 1988
p. 541   'unduly egotistical'   BR to Unwin, 17 Apr. 1966
p. 542   'sufficiently serious'   Joy Hill to author, 3 Apr. 1990
p. 543   compassionate, generous   Edith Russell, unpublished memoir
p. 544   'that he was not one'   BR to Bette Chambers, 21 June 1968
p. 544   'open hearts'   *Why I am not a Christian*, Preface
p. 548   'allow moments'   *Autobiography*, vol. 3, p. 223

Afterword

p. 549   As tributes   Ken Coates to author, 8 Sep. 1989
p. 550   On her return   Sarah Russell to author, 16 Nov. 1989

Index